The Political Econom

Defence is the ultimate public good, and it thus falls to government to determine the appropriate amount of public revenue to commit to the defence of the realm. This will depend on history, strategic threat, international security obligations, entreaties from allies and, of course, the threat faced. *The Political Economy of Defence* is structured to identify, explain and analyse the policy, process and problems that government faces from the starting point of national security through to the ultimate objective of securing a peaceful world. Accordingly, it provides insights into how defence budgets are determined and managed, offering relevant and refreshingly practical policy perspectives on defence finance, defence and development trade-offs, sovereignty versus globalisation debates, and many other pertinent issues. It will appeal to policymakers, analysts, graduate students and academics interested in defence economics, political economy, public economics and public policy.

RON MATTHEWS is Professor of Defence Economics at Cranfield University. He advises international governments on defence offset, and teaches defence economics at universities and military colleges across the world.

The Political Economy of Defence

Edited by
RON MATTHEWS
Cranfield University, UK

CAMBRIDGE
UNIVERSITY PRESS

CAMBRIDGE
UNIVERSITY PRESS

University Printing House, Cambridge CB2 8BS, United Kingdom

One Liberty Plaza, 20th Floor, New York, NY 10006, USA

477 Williamstown Road, Port Melbourne, VIC 3207, Australia

314–321, 3rd Floor, Plot 3, Splendor Forum, Jasola District Centre,
New Delhi – 110025, India

79 Anson Road, #06–04/06, Singapore 079906

Cambridge University Press is part of the University of Cambridge.

It furthers the University's mission by disseminating knowledge in the pursuit of
education, learning, and research at the highest international levels of excellence.

www.cambridge.org
Information on this title: www.cambridge.org/9781108424929
DOI: 10.1017/9781108348058

First published 2019

Printed and bound in Great Britain by Clays Ltd, Elcograf S.p.A.

A catalogue record for this publication is available from the British Library.

Library of Congress Cataloging-in-Publication Data
Names: Matthews, Ron, editor.
Title: The political economy of defence / edited by Ron Matthews, Cranfield
University, UK.
Description: Cambridge, United Kingdom ; New York, NY : Cambridge University
Press, 2019. | Includes bibliographical references and index.
Identifiers: LCCN 2018050908 | ISBN 9781108424929 (hbk : alk. paper)
Subjects: LCSH: Defense industries – Political aspects. | National security –
Economic aspects. | Security, International – Economic aspects. | War – Economic
aspects.
Classification: LCC HD9743.A2 P565 2019 | DDC 338.4/7355–dc23
LC record available at https://lccn.loc.gov/2018050908

ISBN 978-1-108-42492-9 Hardback
ISBN 978-1-108-44101-8 Paperback

Tom, Toby and Aarish

Contents

Figures

Tables

Contributors

Irfan Ansari has a background in accounting and finance. He studied for the AMBA-accredited Masters in Defence Administration at Cranfield University, followed by a PhD in Defence Private Finance Initiatives, and he continues to research in that field as well as in defence finance generally. Irfan lectures on defence finance at Cranfield University, UK Defence Academy, on a number of courses including the MSc Defence Acquisition Management and the MBA (Defence) programmes, and also at the Baltic Defence College, Estonia.

Renaud Bellais graduated from the Institut d'Études Politiques de Lille in 1994 with a PhD in economics. He joined MBDA as institutional advisor to the CEO in 2017 after spending four years in the French defence procurement agency (DGA) and 13 years at Airbus in various positions. Bellais is an Associate Researcher in Economics at ENSTA Bretagne and a member of the CESICE research unit, Université Grenoble Alpes. He also has teaching commitments in defence economics (University Paris 2, French Army Academy), innovation economics (University Paris 1, ENSTA Bretagne) and international economics (IRIS).

Derek Braddon is Emeritus Professor of Economics at the Bristol Business School, University of the West of England, and was formerly Director of the University's Research Unit in Defence Economics from its launch in 1986 until his retirement in 2011. His academic work has been principally in the field of defence and aerospace economics, and he has published seven books along with numerous academic papers and consultancy reports in these areas.

Jurgen Brauer is Visiting Professor of Economics at the Faculty of Economics, Chulalongkorn University, Bangkok, Thailand, and Emeritus Professor of Economics at the Hull College of Business, Augusta University, Augusta (Georgia), United States. With J. Paul Dunne, he co-edits *The Economics of Peace and Security Journal*. His most recent book is Charles H. Anderton and Jurgen Brauer (eds). *Economic Aspects of Genocides, Other Mass Atrocities, and Their Preventions* (2016).

Randolf G. S. Cooper earned his PhD at the University of Cambridge. He taught on the US Army ROTC programme for a state university prior to becoming a country risk analyst working in commercial intelligence and later in the petroleum industry. His work on the political economy of defence includes a Cambridge University Press monograph exploring historic aspects of the South Asian military economy.

J. Paul Dunne is Professor of Economics in the School of Economics, University of Cape Town, a research associate of the South African Labour and Development Research Unit and Emeritus Professor of Economics at the University of the West of England. He edits the *Economics of Peace and Security Journal* with Jurgen Brauer.

Joanne L. Fallowfield is the Head of Applied Physiology at the Institute of Naval Medicine, United Kingdom. She completed her PhD in nutrition and endurance exercise at Loughborough University before undertaking a career as a university lecturer, specialising in exercise physiology and nutrition. Joanne joined the Institute of Naval Medicine in 2006 and supports the Defence Nutrition Advisory Service as a Registered Nutritionist. She sits on the Defence Lifestyles Steering Group and the Defence Musculoskeletal Health Advisory Group and is co-Chair of the Defence Health and Wellbeing Working Group, as well as Chair of the Defence Armed Forces Weight Management Implementation Task Group. She is also a member of the Royal Navy Scientific Advisory Committee.

Daniel Fiott is the Security and Defence Editor at the EU Institute for Security Studies, where he researches defence-industrial policy and defence innovation. He is widely published and teaches defence and strategic studies at the University of Kent and the Free University of Brussels. Daniel was educated at the University of Cambridge and holds a PhD from the Free University of Brussels.

Fitriani is a researcher at the Department of Politics and International Relations at the Centre of Strategic and International Studies, Jakarta, Indonesia. She obtained her PhD in Security and Defence Studies from

Cranfield University, United Kingdom. Fitriani has held visiting and research positions at the Philosophy and Political Science Faculty, Technical University of Dortmund, Germany, and the S. Rajaratnam School of International Studies, Nanyang Technological University, Singapore. Her research focus is on women in peace and security, with particular reference to women's participation in international peacekeeping operations.

Keith Hartley is a defence economist and Emeritus Professor of Economics at the University of York, where he previously served as Director of the Centre for Defence Economics and of the Institute for Research in the Social Sciences. His research interests include defence procurement policy, the economics of contracts, defence industrial policy and collaboration. He is the founding Editor of the journal *Defence and Peace Economics*. Keith has been a NATO Research Fellow and QinetiQ Visiting Fellow, as well as a consultant to the UN, European Commission and European Defence Agency. He has also been a consultant to UK Government Departments, including the Ministry of Defence, and a Special Adviser to the House of Commons Defence Committee.

Anke Hoeffler is a research officer at the Centre for the Study of African Economies at the University of Oxford. She holds a diploma in Volkswirschaftslehre from the University of Würzburg and an MSc in economics from Birkbeck College, University of London. She received her DPhil in economics from the University of Oxford in 1999. Anke's research interests are wide-ranging and often interdisciplinary. Broadly, she is interested in political economy issues in low-income countries, with a specific interest in the economics of violence. Her most recent publications include an article on the consequences of violence against children for societal development (*European Journal of Development Research*) and on the costs of violence (*Politics, Philosophy and Economics*).

David Kirkpatrick is Emeritus Professor at University College London. From 1962 to 1995 he was employed at the UK Ministry of Defence (MoD) on aeronautical research, military operational analysis and project cost forecasting, and was also responsible for investment appraisal of the MoD's air systems. During 1995–2004 he worked in the Defence Engineering Group at University College London, which was then the MoD's designated centre of excellence for research and post-graduate education in defence acquisition. He is co-author of the book *Conquering Complexity – Lessons for Defence Systems Acquisition.*

Stefan Markowski is a former permanent member of staff and presently a Visiting Fellow at the School of Business, University of New South Wales (Canberra campus), Australian Defence Force Academy, Canberra, Australia. He is also a Professor of Management at the University of Information Technology and Management in Rzeszow, Poland and Visiting Research Professor at the Centre of Migration Studies at the University of Warsaw, Poland. His research interests focus on the economics of defence, public sector procurement and, recently, international migration.

Alexander Mattelaer is the Director of the European Affairs programme at Egmont – the Royal Institute for International Relations, Assistant Professor at Vrije Universiteit Brussel and Visiting Professor at the College of Europe. His research interests include the politics of European integration, defence policy and NATO, and the ongoing redefinition of state sovereignty. He sits on the Scientific Committee of the Belgian Royal Higher Institute for Defence, and has completed a Fulbright Schuman Fellowship at Harvard University and at the National Defense University. He obtained his PhD in Political Science from Vrije Universiteit Brussel and master's degrees from the University of Bath and the University of Leuven.

Ron Matthews is a professor of Defence Economics at Cranfield University, Defence Academy of the United Kingdom. From 2007 to 2014 he also held the Chair in Defence Economics at RSIS, Nanyang Technological University, Singapore. His research specialisation examines the impact of defence offset on industrial and technological development. He has published widely in this field, including a 2014 RUSI Whitehall Report based on an MoD-commissioned research programme that evaluated the impact of offset on the UK defence industrial base. Ron is presently undertaking applied research for the UK Defence Solutions Centre exploring business frameworks beyond offset.

Diego Muro is a lecturer in International Relations at the Handa Centre for the Study of Terrorism and Political Violence at the University of St Andrews, and Senior Research Fellow at the Barcelona Centre for

International Affairs. His main research interests are terrorism, comparative politics and ethnic conflict. He is the author of *Ethnicity and Violence*, co-editor of *Politics and Memory of Democratic Transition, ETA's Terrorist Campaign* and *When does terrorism end?*. He has published articles in *Ethnic and Racial Studies, Ethnicities, Mediterranean Politics, Nations and Nationalism, South European Society and Politics, Studies in Conflict and Terrorism* and *West European Politics*.

Jean-Michel Oudot is a visiting lecturer in Defence Economics at Sciences Po, Paris, France. He holds a PhD in Economics from Paris Panthéon-Sorbonne and works as an economist for the French Ministry of Armed Forces. After four years working in international cooperation at the French Defence Procurement Agency, he spent nine years in the Financial Directorate, and now acts in the Joint Defence Staff.

Ron Smith is a professor of Applied Economics at Birkbeck University, London, and lectures on econometrics and statistics. He has been a Visiting Professor at London Business School and the University of Colorado. Ron is the author or editor of ten books, including *Military Economics*, which was shortlisted for the 2010 Duke of Westminster's Medal for Military Literature, as well as more than 200 papers mainly in applied econometrics, defence economics and political economy. He has acted as a consultant to a range of bodies including Frontier Economics and the UK National Audit Office, advised on defence projects, and is an Associate Fellow of the Royal United Services Institute. Ron was awarded the 2011 Lewis Fry Richardson award for contributions to the scientific study of militarised conflict by the European Consortium of Political Research.

Trevor Taylor is Professorial Fellow in Defence Management at the Royal United Services Institute, Whitehall, London. He is also an Emeritus Professor of Cranfield University at the Defence Academy, Shrivenham. For the past eight years he has taught and researched at the US Naval Postgraduate School. Trevor has been a two-term elected Council Member of the former Defence Manufacturers Association, the co-author of two books on the UK defence industry, the author of several studies for the UK MoD and Chairman of the British International Studies Association. He has also had a research attachment at the Royal Institute of International Affairs, Chatham House, London.

Nan Tian is a researcher in the Arms Transfer and Military Expenditure Program, where he leads the Military Expenditure Project, at the Stockholm International Peace Research Institute and Southern Africa Labour and Development Research Unit, University of Cape Town. His research interests focus on the causes and impact of military expenditure and civil conflict, along with issues relating to transparency and accountability in military budgeting, spending and procurement. He previously worked at the World Wide Fund for Nature as an economist on climate change and food security and was a lecturer at the University of Cape Town, South Africa.

Matt Uttley is Professor of Defence Studies at King's College London. Before joining King's in 2000, he held academic posts at the Centre for Defence Economics, University of York and the Department of Politics, Lancaster University. He has published widely on the historical and contemporary dimensions of UK defence policy and weapons acquisition. He is currently an Adjunct Professor at the Baltic Defence College in Estonia, Visiting Professor at the National Defence School of the Serbian Military Academy in Belgrade and Adjunct Senior Fellow at the Center for Intelligence and National Security, University of Oklahoma.

Bryan Watters OBE is a senior lecturer at Cranfield University's School of Defence and Security, where he lectures and researches on leadership, strategic management and leadership of change. He gained a PhD in leadership studies from the University of Leeds. He has a wide range of military qualifications, including psc(a) and psc(j), and is an Associate Fellow of the Baltic Defence College, Estonia. Prior to joining Cranfield in 2009, Bryan had a successful career in the British Army. His last appointments were Deputy Commanding General (Brigadier) on General Petraeus's staff in Iraq and Commander British Forces Kosovo.

Benedict Wilkinson is a senior research fellow and Interim Deputy Director of the Policy Institute at King's College London. He completed his PhD under the supervision of Professor Sir Lawrence Freedman at King's College London in 2013 before joining the Policy Institute, first as a Research Associate (2013), then advancing to the post of Research Fellow (2014) and finally Senior Research Fellow in 2015. From 2013 to 2015, Benedict also held a Lectureship in the

Defence Studies Department and taught at the Royal College of Defence Studies. Between 2010 and 2011, he worked as Head of Security and Counter-Terrorism at Royal United Services Institute, where he continues to hold an Associate Fellowship. He became an Associate Fellow of the International Centre for the Study of Radicalisation in 2013 and a Fellow of the Royal Society of Arts in 2014.

Robert Wylie joined the academic staff of the University of New South Wales (Canberra campus) in 2006. Prior to this appointment he enjoyed a varied career in the Australian Public Service, specialising in the development and implementation of Australian defence policy. As an academic, Robert has taught public sector management and project management at post-graduate level, mainly to Australian Defence Force personnel preparing for senior appointments in the Australian defence policy community. His academic research and publications are focused on defence procurement, defence industry policy and military technological innovation.

Acknowledgements

The concept of this book has gently germinated over the last three decades. This is the period I have been involved in Defence and Security at Cranfield University. My Cranfield days have been spent, firstly, at the Royal Military College of Science, and then at its successor organisation, the Defence Academy of the UK. Prior to this appointment, I had served an extended research apprenticeship undertaking fieldwork in economic, industrial and technological development, focused especially on what were then termed 'Third World' countries. The research was sponsored by development organisations, such as the UK Foreign and Commonwealth Office's Overseas Development Agency and the World Bank, allowing me to spend time at Development Institutes in Kenya, Sweden, Japan and India. Additionally, I was awarded two NATO Scholarships, affording me the opportunity to pursue defence-related research in Europe and at the Pentagon in Washington, DC. I recount these research assignments because of the deep impression they made on my understanding of the crucial role that governments and supranational organisations play in promoting defence and development capabilities. The message for me was clear: it is not so much the 'market' but rather politico-economic interventions that act as the motive force to create and sustain impulses in national security, widely defined. My subsequent Defence Economics courses at Cranfield University and RSIS, Nanyang Technological University, Singapore (2007–14), were accordingly nuanced to reflect more the 'visible' hand of government than Adam Smith's invisible hand of the market.

The destination of this academic journey is thus the present volume on *The Political Economy of Defence*. However, it is not the product of my own endeavours, but the intensely rich and rewarding intellectual contributions of peers, colleagues, industry practitioners, MoD officials and, not least, graduate students – the majority of whom were operationally seasoned tri-service military officers. I have been privileged to work with experts that read like a 'Hall of Fame' in the political and economic defence literature. It is these authors who deserve the praise if, as I hope, the book receives plaudits for offering learned insights into the political management of defence. In the practical aspects of the book's preparation and publication, I extend my appreciation to the Cambridge University Press editors, Phil Good and Toby Ginsberg, and the content manager, Grace Morris, for their guidance and support. I also owe a deep debt of gratitude to my colleague, Irfan Ansari, for his unstinting technical assistance in the formatting of innumerable manuscript drafts. Finally, a special mention to my long-suffering wife, whose patience in dealing with an absent husband provided me with the editorial space and stability of mind to ensure timely project completion.

PART 1

National Security

1 | *The Political Economy of Defence*

RON MATTHEWS

Introduction

The political economy of defence can be defined in numerous ways, but at the heart of the concept is the notion of governmental ownership and control in the defence of the state. In his seminal work *The Wealth of Nations* (1776), Adam Smith crystallised thinking on the profound role that government plays in all aspects of defence decision making, when he stated that 'in a system of natural liberty ... the first duty of a sovereign is that of protecting the society from the violence and invasion of other independent societies'.[1] Smith was clear that the provisioning of defence is the government's responsibility, not least because it is a public good:

It is produced for the community, and differs from private goods in that it is consumed by all citizens equally whereas private goods are consumed individually and exclusively by those who purchase them: once a public good such as defense is produced it does not matter whether an individual has paid taxes or not, his consumption of defense cannot be exclusive and at the expense of fellow citizens, nor can it be limited by the consumption of other citizens.[2]

Smith argued that it was incumbent on the state to ensure adequate resourcing of defence, especially as the cost of war was increasing with the invention of weapons. 'The cannon and mortar are not only much dearer, but much heavier machines than the ballista or catapulta; and require greater expense, not only to prepare them for the field but to carry them to it'.[3] In Smith's view, it was evident that defence was for the common good and it was reasonable, therefore, that the expenses of defence should be met by the whole of society, with 'all the different members contributing as nearly as possible in proportion to their respective abilities'.[4] How was this to be done, though? David

Ricardo, reflecting on the economic impact of Britain's pursuit of victory in the Napoleonic wars, claimed that government-imposed taxes were the preferable method to finance war. Taxes would ensure that the economic burden of war was imposed on the present society, and, importantly, tax adjustments would require parliamentary approval, making ministers accountable for engaging in expensive contests, unless in the national interest. Conversely, he believed that if there was ease in the creation of public debt, then the associated lack of restraint by government would increase the risk of war for frivolous reasons, or wicked ambition, or, worse, financial gain.[5] Moreover, the use of loans would be without restraint, shifting the burden of repayment onto future generations.

As the powers of the sovereign have waned, it is government that has assumed the responsibility of providing national security and protecting society from invasion. An important part of government's role in this regard was the need to secure defence industrial sovereignty. Security of supply for cannon, munitions and warships was essential for strategic rather than for politico-economic reasons, but the latter was nevertheless a linked consideration. In the eighteenth century, the international political economy comprised of 'independent' nation states that pursued trade for 'mercantilist' national benefit, harbouring no inhibitions of going to war over the bounties from colonisation. The passage of time has not dulled the appetite of nations for self-sufficiency. However, since the 1930s, defence has come to be viewed not only as a political institution but additionally as an instrument of macroeconomic management. This was symbolised by Keynes' advocacy that government should use defence as a pump-primer to revitalise a stagnating United Kingdom (UK) economy.

Today, the principal politico-strategic goal remains national security, but defence-industrial autarky has become challenging. The contextual conditions of defence have changed since the 1970s, undermining the means for securing defence-industrial sovereignty. There were firstly tectonic shifts in the geoeconomic and strategic landscape, such as the international recessionary crises of the early 1970s and 1980s, followed by the implosion of the Soviet Union, the collapse of communism, the Gulf Wars, and, finally, the 9/11 terrorist attack on New York's Twin Towers. The age of uncertainty had arrived. Moreover, in the strategic domain, the dismemberment of the erstwhile USSR, and the loss of certainty that came with the bipolar great-power stand-off, had altered the political, diplomatic and military calculus. The Cold War era had disappeared, but benign international relations remained elusive, pock-marked by numerous hot wars, insurgencies, asymmetrical conflicts, endemic violence and even genocide.

In parallel, dramatic changes were occurring in technological inno-vation. Computerisation, information technologies, space-based tele-communications and digitisation had begun to impact the commercial and military landscape. The United States was at the helm of this 'systems of systems' transformation; indeed, its economic, technolo-gical and military dominance was fundamental to winning the arms race and the associated ideological struggle against the 'bankrupt' Soviet communist system. Capitalism provided the spur for innova-tion, and in the military space this found resonance through what came to be known as the Revolution in Military Affairs (RMA). Ironically, it was a Russian, Marshall Organov, who first coined the term when describing US technological prowess in the development of revolutionary weapon systems.[6] Some observers believe that these smart, stand-off, laser-guided and often autonomous munitions represented a 'step-change' in warfare.[7] Others rejected this thesis, arguing that instead of revolutionary, discontinuous change, enhanced defence technology capability reflected more evolutionary, continuous, innovational development.[8] The debate was perhaps an intellectual distraction, because whether change was revolutionary or evolutionary the practical reality was that profound changes to weapon systems and doctrine were happening, and rapidly. The first Gulf War demonstrated the United States' military technology super-iority through the dramatic destruction of Saddam Hussein's Soviet-supplied tanks and artillery, prompting a wake-up call for Moscow and its client state, China.

Yet, the RMA came with an economic cost. The smart new weapon systems demanded intensive research and development (R&D), and this led to dramatic acceleration of procurement costs. Inflated cost structures, in turn, fuelled a decline in orders, and the subsequent loss of scale further increased unit costs, exacerbating the deterioration in market conditions. The result was 'structural disarmament', reflected via a 'Starship Enterprise' mindset, whereby affordability constraints would ultimately lead to just one galactic military system being respon-sible for the protection of Smith's 'independent society'.[9] These RMA-induced changes ensured that defence economics had firmly entered into the military's vocabulary. Affordability, the principal defence economic issue, was now forcing a rethink over defence-industrial sovereignty. Although technology multipliers associated with the RMA were an undeniable attraction to military planners, due to the benefits of precision targeting, reduced attrition of military personnel and the Cable News Network (CNN) benefits of limited collateral damage, the trade-off was a dramatic steepening in acquisition costs to the point where attainment of comprehensive defence-industrial capability was no longer financially feasible.

Notwithstanding the panoply of commercialisation initiatives designed to reduce defence costs, government remains the dominant player. It has the authority, for instance, to promote the defence and aerospace sectors as strategic industries. These sectors can then be protected and subsidised to ensure industrial vitality and sustainability. Defence is different, and its critical role in the pursuit of national security has been recognised through international norms, such as, for instance, its exclusion from the rules of the World Trade Organisation (WTO). Government and supranational interventionist policies are central to the political economy of defence. Government determines how much will be spent, and invariably influences the final decision as to the sources of military procurement. However, irrespective of whether the defence business case (based on cost effectiveness) leans towards procuring local or foreign defence systems, costly procurement programmes will always face stringent political scrutiny, with final decisions based not so much on the military capability of those systems but rather on the politics of saving jobs in marginal constituencies. In the process, the moral, ethical and even strategic justification of continued arms acquisition may also play second fiddle to the political dimension. Ministries of Defence (MoD), along with senior members of the armed forces and defence industry (the so-called iron triangle) allegedly engage in deliberate exaggeration of international threats as a means of maintaining or even increasing defence expenditures when faced with a benign strategic environment.[10]

Given the contextual backdrop of political, economic, financial and strategic uncertainty, this volume on the political economy of defence not only offers a relevant and timely contribution to knowledge, but may also offer policymakers, analysts and interested observers useful insights into the process and structure of defence. It is intended that the chapter topics will provide a 'holistic' sense of the structural linkages and influences that act to strengthen or weaken national security.

1.1 Conceptualising the Politico-Economic Defence Framework

As a means of addressing the principal contemporary politico-economic fields of policy concern, a schema has been developed, as shown in Figure 1.1. The intention is to examine the role of government in the provision of defence, cognisant of its wider social, economic and diplomatic responsibilities. National security in its various guises is the principal goal of defence and security endeavours. Yet, the achievement of 'security' depends on a complex amalgam of policy, management, resource and global environmental variables. Threats are a major driver of the level of defence spending, but in peacetime they compete with other domestic economic and political pressures. As a public good, defence imposes opportunity costs on other government spending, such as

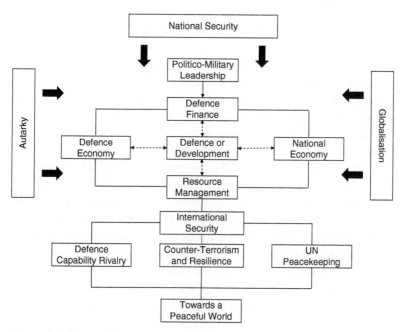

Figure 1.1: The politico-economic defence framework
Source: author

welfare, education and health spending that has a more immediate impact on public opinion, especially in relation to political polls. Thus, in a democracy, government must always be prepared to balance critical quality of life objectives with its responsibility to defend the nation state. This is a tricky trade-off, and it is understandable that politicians will respond to the short-term social needs of its citizens rather than the long-term strategic consequences of inferior military capability. In search of affordability, there is an obvious expectation that constrained defence resources will be managed efficiently, but to reduce costs there is a temptation for the defence authorities to favour lower-cost overseas and collaborative procurement options. This will inevitably impact on security of supply, the vitality of the domestic defence economy and thus sovereignty, but on the plus side globalisation will reduce costs, assist affordability and contribute in a qualified way to national security.

The structure of the book addresses themes identified in the Figure 1.1 schema, as follows:

1.1.1 National Security

National security is an awkward and ill-defined concept. It used to be interpreted solely with regard to territorial boundaries, international defence agreements and broader (defence) security interests of the state. It was grounded in military defence, and rationalised and expressed through defence policy. The contemporary interpretation of national security has changed, however. It now reflects a broader constituency of interests, including human, economic, environmental, energy, climate, as well as military security. This broader security canvas has been articulated through high-level documents, such as the UK (2015) and the US (2017) National Security Strategy documents.[11] Government has played a prominent role in ensuring that the seemingly disconnected strands of national security integrate into a coordinated and coherent strategic approach. For instance, the 'greening' of the military is consistent with the positive consequential benefits of managing climate change, including, for example, energy reduction through autonomously harvested vehicular energy, reducing the need for strategically vulnerable oil convoys in operational zones. Similarly, governments, at least Western ones, have also been actively pursuing a 'prosperity' agenda by promoting the economic benefits of defence through encouragement of their exports, technological spin-on and spin-offs, dual-use technologies, investment and skilled employment in the strategically significant industrial 'crossover' sectors of transport, aerospace, space and information systems.

1.1.2 Politico-Military Leadership

The government's agenda in protecting national security is complex, and funding is always insufficient. Focusing solely on military security, the budgetary battle commences at two levels. There will be the Service Chiefs of the army, navy and air force, and also representation from the defence-related scientific, counterterrorism and intelligence communities, pushing for higher allocations of government resources for defence as a whole. In the UK case, this is a battle that is waged against Whitehall mandarins (civil servants) and government ministers, with the Treasury holding the line in support of public finance plans as well as agreed spending limits for other Departments of State. At a second level, Service rivalry will surface, with Chiefs fighting amongst themselves to maintain or preferably increase their share of the final agreed defence budget. Decisions will be based on capability criteria, but it is likely that military culture rather than operational pragmatism and effectiveness will influence and persuade discussion, determining trade-offs between, for instance, artillery versus cruise missiles and drones versus manned fighter aircraft. Moreover, inevitably, there will be friction over how the costs of new and expensive toys like aircraft carriers, fifth-generation fighters and nuclear submarines will drain funding from the defence budget, leaving little for less glamorous, but no less important areas of military capability. The process of debating and agreeing the final Department budget and also its allocation amongst military stakeholders is akin to a leadership 'beauty contest', and is addressed by Bryan Watters in Chapter 2.

1.1.3 Defence Finance

Once budgetary decisions have been agreed, the defence 'pot' of monies has to be carefully managed to ensure value for money for the taxpayer. As funding is always taut, the pressure is intense to find cost efficiencies, even though most of the time these masquerade as cost cutting. In the United Kingdom, the policy approach since the 1980s has been to adopt best-practice commercial techniques to manage resources. As discussed by Irfan Ansari in Chapter 3, Value-for-Money (VfM) initiatives have been introduced to exploit economic (competition), efficiency (financial engineering) and effectiveness (capability) opportunities; the first two of these VfM elements relate to input cost savings, while the third has regard to output, ultimately impacting on military capability. Delegated budgets are now viewed as an essential element of defence finance for controlling excessive expenditure. However, as in the public sector more broadly, the art of restraining expenditure, in such areas as training and resource consumption, in order to hit annual budgeted targets can negatively impact on operational efficiency. Indeed, some governments now publish annual Resource Accounting and Budgeting (RAB) statements that take defence financial management to a new level. RAB merges the battle and business spaces by managing defence as though it is a business, inculcating into defence and planning staffs a more professional approach towards efficient defence management.

RAB calculates the cost and value of defence as expressed through cost operating and balance sheet statements. Military assets, such as submarines and main battle tanks, sit on the balance sheet, and are subject to (cost of use) depreciation as would assets in any commercial undertaking. The annual depreciation cost is then included in the cost statement. An additional cost of using taxpayer's capital is also estimated, based on the fact that if defence was a private business then it would need to borrow money from a bank, incurring an interest charge, or if it uses reserves lodged in a bank then there would be a loss of interest. This cost of capital is also loaded into the operating cost statement of defence. These two 'notional' costs of defence can be considerable, and when combined with other more traditional operating costs, the aggregative cost reflects the true cost of defence to society. This implies an opportunity cost of benefits foregone, meaning that the higher the level of military expenditure, the greater the diversion of scarce public resources from hospitals, universities and road networks. As defence is a public good financed by taxpayers, it is incumbent on the government and defence policymakers to ensure that resources are spent wisely and prudently. It is thus essential that there is transparency and accountability in the process. Some governments hide defence and procurement budgets from their citizens, and also engage in off-balance sheet spending. This loss of transparency erodes confidence in government's ability to manage defence, because it clouds linkages between defence policy and military expenditure, reduces transparency, breeds inefficiency and cultivates corrupt practices.

1.1.4 Defence or Development?

Ron Smith (Chapter 4) and J. Paul Dunne, Jurgen Brauer and Nan Tian (Chapter 5) revisit and update the controversial scholarship relating to the trade-off between military expenditure and economic growth. The opportunity cost of defence has spawned a huge body of empirical literature, and its significance revolves around the search to identify the elusive and appropriate balance between defence and development. Too much military expenditure can act to divert productive resources, termed 'crowding-out', from the more productive civil economy, but too little defence may leave the country vulnerable to external aggression. Government is aware of this dilemma, but the danger is that politics, power and ideology skew rational decision making. Moreover, as is often the case, empirical evidence supporting decision-makers is either absent or confusing. The traditional defence economic paradigm posits a negative relationship between military expenditure (MILEX) and economic growth; that is, rising MILEX is associated with lower growth. However, this view was turned on its head in the 1960s by the writings of Emile Benoit, a Belgian defence economist.[12] Examining India's MILEX and GDP data following the 1962–63 China-India War, Benoit observed that increased defence expenditure was, after a time lag, associated with expanded national income. This led him, heroically, to advance the view that MILEX and GDP enjoy a positive relationship; that is, that higher MILEX would lead to higher economic growth. Benoit's findings led to an explosion in academic studies seeking to establish the 'truth'; if only it was only so easy. As the debate in Chapters 4 and 5 demonstrates, this is difficult intellectual terrain, with findings influenced not only by the quality and availability of appropriate data sets, but also by the nature of the underlying assumptions.

However, there is something stronger than a suspicion that in the twenty-first century, rising defence expenditure may well lead to increased economic growth and the vitality of the broader national economy. It has become folklore that 70–80 per cent of high-value systems in modern weapons are sourced from commercial enterprise,[13] and given the close relationship between prime contractors and their predominantly commercial and innovative subcontractors, any hike in defence procurement would stimulate economic multipliers across the national economy, leading to increased activity and growth. The downside, however, is that this process would only occur in the advanced countries, possessing mature and diversified industrial bases. For the poorer states, possessing immature or nonexistent supply chains, any increase in defence spending and procurement would not sponsor domestic economic growth; rather, these countries' dependence on overseas arms suppliers would induce technology leakage, with procurement funding contributing to the growth of these already advanced states.

From the above discourse, it is clear that government has important responsibilities in its governance of adequate defence resources to protect society from external and increasingly internal threats. There are three principal areas of politico-economic concern for government: (1) establishing the correct level of defence expenditure in absolute terms, as well relative to its share of overall public spending, and as a percentage of national income (MILEX/GDP – conventionally referred to as the 'defence burden'); (2) it must also judge the appropriate balance between defence and development and local versus overseas procurement; (3) finally, it must carefully manage defence resources to ensure that taxpayers obtain the biggest 'bang for their buck'. Efficient resource management has been dubbed 'smart management'. It is nearly always concerned with searching for options and solutions to affordability and capability dilemmas.

1.1.5 Autarchy versus Globalisation

National resource management decisions are not taken in a vacuum that exclude international contexts and influences. However, according to Stefan Markowski and Robert Wylie (Chapter 6), the context defining the political economy of defence has irrevocably changed. The emergence of the modern (Westphalian) nation-state has meant that Adam Smith's 'sovereign' has been superseded by the 'state', symbolising the 'nation'. Yet, the recent globalisation phenomenon has created conceptual ambiguity in the notion of a sovereign nation-state assailed by numerous considerations, such as porous national borders, complex relationships between nationalities, citizenship and residency, sectarian violence and international treaties restraining national authority to exercise not only independent power but to assert some degree of supremacy over international entities. National sovereignty, then, is under assault from the multiplicity of influences and threats that could potentially harm it, either intentionally or unintentionally.

Defence globalisation clearly acts to erode sovereignty, but complicating the debate is the fact that over the last two decades globalisation has also emerged as a force that has confusingly been both constructive and destructive, dynamic and divisive. There are two perspectives. Firstly, governments may take a sanguine view of globalisation, especially if they are able to use defence trade as a mechanism for extracting technology transfer. The enabling policy mechanism is termed defence offset. This is where arms-purchasing countries exert market leverage on offshore vendors to release technology as a means of accelerating local civil and military industrialisation. These days, most developing country governments impose offset policies on foreign defence contractors. Yet, questions are only now being asked as to whether offset programmes are viable and deliver the anticipated development benefits, particularly since their costs of implementation are loaded into the primary defence contract and thus inflate procurement costs. This volume's editor explores the field of defence offset in Chapter 7, especially the longevity of offset and whether alternative business frameworks may emerge to replace its present dominant influence in the contemporary global defence market.

The second perspective on whether globalisation is a positive or negative force has regard to the extent to which liberalisation, as a conduit for reducing costs, impacts on national sovereignty. A small number of states have been prepared to shy away from globalisation and shoulder the economic pain of self-sufficiency, prioritising, instead, autarchy over affordability. For instance, the governments of the former and current communist military powers, Russia and China, interpret the goal of defence-industrial sovereignty and self-sufficiency as inviolable, framed by a long history of territorial insecurity and vulnerability. Russia possesses the world's lowest import dependency ratio, irrespective of the profound economic pain that its national defence programmes have exerted on the country's economic growth and social welfare. By contrast, China's continuously growing and dynamic economy is bankrolling Beijing's geostrategic ambitions. Jean-Michel

Oudot and Renaud Bellais contribute to the debate in Chapter 8 by arguing that France is also now beginning to loosen its traditionally nationalist defence posture, driven by market forces that inevitably will erode the maintenance of comprehensive domestic defence industrial capacity. As with other advanced nations, the French government is increasingly tasked with managing trade-offs between defence procurement, strategic autonomy and budgetary sovereignty, weighted by political, economic, diplomatic and strategic considerations.

Similarly, the United Kingdom, more than any other major military power, has tempered its defence-industrial self-sufficiency ambitions through its search for affordability. Numerous policies have been pursued, including economic liberalisation, commercialisation, enhanced competitive tendering, open defence trade and unfettered engagement with defence globalisation processes. The MoD's 2002 Defence Industrial Policy placed a focus on location not ownership, meaning that the economic benefits of British jobs, investment and exports took precedence over sovereignty. This has led to unprecedented levels of foreign ownership of defence capacity, with offshore defence contractors such as Leonardo (Italian), Thales (French), Airbus (German/French/Spain) and Lockheed-Martin, Boeing, General Dynamics and Raytheon (all US) accounting for major shares of local defence production. There are real dangers with this globalisation model, because foreign-owned defence multinational companies (MNCs) are motivated by profit, not UK national security. By definition, these MNCs are 'footloose', and if profit opportunities disappear, then the likelihood is that they will transfer their operations elsewhere, where there is a greater chance of making money. This will lead to a hollowing-out of the UK defence industrial base.

Further undermining defence-industrial sovereignty has been the UK government's embrace of open defence trade, elevating competition above protectionism. The MoD's objective has been to achieve cost savings through a widening of the bidding process that overcomes the rigidity of national monopoly-monopsony market structures, on the one hand, and short production runs, on the other. The obvious 'business' solution has been to procure off-the-shelf weapons systems from the United States. This avoids the heavy cost of R&D, and benefits from the economies of scale derived from comparatively long production runs of US equipment for the domestic and export markets. The United Kingdom often decides to license build US platforms as a means of keeping national production lines warm and scarce skills intact. This procurement 'halfway house' is neither indigenous nor off-the-shelf procurement, and results in considerable extra costs, but without the benefit of owning the Intellectual Property Rights (IPR) of the weapons technology.[14]

Moreover, the MoD's increasing procurement of US defence systems leads inexorably to a progressive erosion of the UK sovereign defence-industrial base. The 2005 Defence Industrial Strategy and the later 2012 Technology Through Partnership White Papers sought to partially remedy this loss of sovereignty by introducing 'selective' defence industrial self-reliance. What were deemed to be critical defence-related defence technologies, along with their IPR, would be protected. Yet, technology sharing continues unabated through regional collaborations (Eurofighter) and global consortiums (F-35). The process ought to lead to greater efficiencies, but Europe's penchant for duplicative assembly lines and the United States' dominance in financial sponsorship of IPR suggest that the supply of initiatives for participating states to enjoy 'both' cost savings and acceptable levels of sovereignty is not happening.

Yet, the trend towards international partnership, as part of the defence globalisation process, is unlikely to disappear any time soon. Thus, while the US administration advocates nationalist policies, this is not reflected in its approach to defence procurement policies. A 1999 US government-commissioned study laid bare the facts that discredit the widely held stereotype of 'Buy American' legislation safeguarding US defence-industrial sovereignty. The study states that the

DoD once depended upon, and could afford to sustain, a dedicated domestic industrial base for the development, production and provision of its equipment and services. Today, the 'U.S. defense industrial base' no longer exists in its Cold War form. Instead, DoD now is supported by a broader, less defense-intensive industrial base that is becoming increasingly international in character ... [indeed] ... most defense trading partners, including most NATO countries and selected others, have reciprocal procurement agreements with the U.S. Government that result in a waiver of the Buy American Act of 1933. The United States has such agreements with 21 countries and is in various stages of negotiations with several others, including some of the new NATO partners.[15]

Almost twenty years later, Washington now appears to recognise the implausibility of the United States gaining access to world-class weapons systems through unqualified endorsement of the Buy American Act.

Evidence to support this argument can be found by reference to the substantial foreign content integrated into competitor aircraft for the US Air Force's next-generation trainer, designated the T-X; the same applies to the F-35 Joint Strike Fighter, containing complex wiring bundles sourced from a Dutch company, vertical tailpieces from an Australian firm and huge design, development, electronics, systems and fabricated component inputs from the UK company, BAES, and its domestic supply chain.[16]

The UK government is equally committed to international defence cooperation and regional and global arms collaboration. Yet, this is somewhat less than a dynamic commitment, in that the government ensures such sharing does not erode the priority given to national defence autarchy. This has been a persistent barrier to, for instance, greater European defence-industrial cooperation and integration, irrespective of the Brussel's diplomatic chiding of EU Member States. Collaboration appears to operate in parallel with autarchy, and as Matt Uttley and Benedict Wilkinson argue in Chapter 9, Brexit, in whatever form it takes, will not resolve what they term the 'great paradox' between national sovereignty and cooperation. Yet, all observers agree that 'sharing' offers the opportunity for like-minded nation-states to mitigate the high costs of pursuing national security. This is especially reflected through the concept of alliances, operating on the assumption that participating nations are willing to sacrifice some degree of decision-making autonomy, and agree a framework of rules and obligations governing the functioning of the alliance. However, compliance with agreed financial targets in meeting member states' defence obligations constitutes a perennial point of friction. This is highlighted in Chapter 10 by Alexander Mattelaer, who refers to Washington's continued frustration at alleged 'free-riding' by European nations within the NATO alliance. There is a political context underlying these debates, as well as methodological complexity of harmonising defence budgeting cycles. The perceived inequity of burden sharing is troubling, but NATO endures, and appears to recognise that history, societal mores, international relations, as well as relative levels of GDP, all impinge on national judgments as to how much is enough with regard to defence expenditure.

While not in crisis, the international defence community is facing troubled challenges in funding the required levels of military capability in the face of remarkable increases in Russian and Chinese defence spending. Government and its delegated defence authorities are responsible for the efficient and effective management of scarce defence resources. However, full commercialisation to achieve efficiencies is infeasible. Defence remains the classic public good, rationalised on the basis that as all citizens benefit from national security, and so logically its cost must be sourced through taxation. Moreover, as defence is concerned with a nation's independence, it is inconceivable that this function is somehow given over to the private sector. Some governments have encouraged commercialisation, contractorisation and privatisation at the supply end, including training, Maintenance, Repair and Overhaul (MRO). However, other governments, including many from the developing countries, adopt the view that all aspects of defence, including the defence industry, must remain under public-sector control. Defence is too important to be operated under a commercial ethos, in which national security is relegated in favour of profit.

1.1.6 Efficient Management of Defence Resources

The concerted focus of government is to maintain national capability. As up to 40 per cent of a country's defence budget will be allocated to procurement, it is essential that appropriate procurement options are selected.[17] For major platforms, national development and production capability is now rarely an option. Instead, many advanced countries recognise the strategic, political, and most of all economic benefit of engaging in technology sharing. This topic is covered in Chapter 11 by Keith Hartley, who posits that arms collaboration has been a common feature of European procurement for decades, and embraces bilateral (Anglo-French Jaguar fighter aircraft), trilateral (German-Italian-UK Tornado fighter) and Quadrilateral (German-Italian-Spanish-UK Eurofighter) programmes. There are also more commercially integrated procurement models, such as Airbus, MBDA and even the Anglo-French partnership in the design, development and production of the United Kingdom's two Queen Elizabeth Class aircraft carriers. The US-dominated F-35 Joint Strike Fighter consortium has expanded collaborative procurement options by introducing a (nine-country) 'global' platform partnership, with workshare determined through competition rather than the much criticised *juste retour* principle, based on 'output-input' principles, a feature of Europe's multilateral arms collaboration programmes.

The first problem for defence ministries is the selection of a cost-effective acquisition pathway, whether it is national, overseas or collaborative. Trevor Taylor (Chapter 12) highlights the difficulties defence policymakers face in selecting the most cost-effective acquisition option, particularly as they are inevitably bound by extraneous political considerations. Yet, as the author makes clear this is only the start of the challenge, because what comes next is arguably the even more difficult task of managing the acquisition to time, quality and budget. It is rare, indeed, for major weapons programmes not to suffer delays or be afflicted by costly overruns. Problems often arise because the platforms represent a jump into the unknown, injecting a high level of uncertainty and risk into the venture. There is also the whole question of accurate cost forecasting, because without this capability it becomes impossible to estimate the value of intended outcomes. There is also the potential for adversarial contractual relations between the various stakeholders, especially between the government-backed sponsoring authority and the prime contractor. Moreover, at times there appears to be something inherently problematical with defence acquisition. Almost inevitably procurement costs will be significantly more than planned, necessitating the stretching of delivery schedules, reduction in acquisition volumes and pared operational capability. The defence authority frequently exacerbates the problems by seeking to exploit the remarkably long gestation periods, from concept to in-service, to demand ad hoc adaption and refinement of the system's design and technical specifications to respond to emerging strategic threats. As the government customer is by that stage locked into a contractual arrangement with the prime contractor, the benefit of competition is lost, and costs will grow, sometimes calamitously.

The decision to procure expensive weapons systems is also hampered by the absence of a credible forecast of their Whole Life Costs (WLC). As David Kirkpatrick argues in Chapter 13, the ability to undertake WLC analyses is an essential input to the proper 'concept-to-disposal' management of the project, and also to the higher-level budgeting of the complementary group of projects that contribute to sustaining a particular military capability. A defence project's WLC arises from the activities of its stakeholders, the defence authority, the armed forces operating the equipment and industrial contractors, both locally and overseas. The WLC is complex, because it seeks to place values on numerous unknown factors. It does this by identifying those components of the project's WLC that are virtually constant and others that vary according to the scale of the project, with the cost forecasts presented in different ways for different purposes. The WLC estimating process aimed at determining the cost-effectiveness of competing weapons systems is an intensely challenging task undertaken during the early acquisition phase. It is self-evident that governments will be severely handicapped when making multibillion-dollar procurement decisions if they depend solely on the up-front cost of procuring a specified volume of platforms. Thus, non-estimation of the WLC would be a grave error, given that the bulk of the procurement costs will occur during the in-service stage when MRO and midlife upgrades are required. Yet, the difficulties of making credible WLC forecasts are immense, and the inevitable errors contribute to the barriers obstructing effective project management and capability management.

Derek Braddon in Chapter 14 analyses a further salient feature of defence procurement and through-life support, that of maintaining, if not encouraging, the growth of indigenous supply chains. Most traditional supply chains comprise hundreds of Small and Medium-size Enterprises (SMEs) that have evolved over generations to service the specialist systems needs of prime contractors. Traditionally, subcontractors will focus on a narrow range of products or services, and their customers will come from a wide number of manufacturing sectors producing disparate final products, but utilising common production processes. Such technological convergence would have occurred via an evolutionary development process that may have taken centuries to complete. In the process, entrepreneurial opportunities would have been created for vertical disintegration of internalised tasks amongst major manufacturing enterprises. In turn, this would facilitate an industrial division of labour in distinctive supply chains of newly formed SMEs, reinforcing the opportunities for primes to efficiently outsource what they consider to be none core production activities. These supply chains constituent a critical component of geographically proximate industrial agglomerations, often referred to as industrial and technological clusters. A major benefit of these clusters is that they generate innovation from the close interaction between the primes and their supplier base: the former are knowledgeable of what is required to advance manufacturing capability, with the latter possessing the engineering competence to design and produce innovative technology. SMEs, supply chains and clusters have a fundamentally significant role to play in catalysing technological innovation in the strategic defence, aerospace and maritime industries. These innovational clusters are deemed essential for fostering development of high technology industries. It is no surprise, therefore, that governments of industrialising states, such as India, Malaysia, Indonesia, South Korea and China, promote policies to incentivise local and foreign primes and subcontractors to locate in institutionally predetermined cities/regions as a means of artificially accelerating the creation of dedicated manufacturing clusters. This reflects the reality that the innovative industrialised nations have supply chains, but the impoverished nations do not.

Discussion to this point has centred on the politico-economic dimensions of efficient acquisition and support of high-cost weapon systems. However, defence capability also depends on the operational effectiveness of those systems, and amongst other factors, this will crucially be influenced by the availability, skills, commitment and raw courage of military personnel. The problem today is that many of the world's armed forces are suffering dramatic declines in personnel recruitment and retention. The reasons are manifold, but include declining population growth rates and a resurgence in civilian economic growth; the latter bringing with it the opportunity for relatively higher-paid commercial jobs. One way of addressing personnel shortfalls and simultaneously achieving more inclusive armed forces is to recruit greater numbers of women, providing them with equal career opportunities, including Ground Close Combat (GCC) roles. However, central to this discourse, as Joanne L. Fallowfield highlights in Chapter 15, are the diverse and interdependent considerations that impact on women's combat effectiveness, including physical capability (injury risk and medical discharge rates), morbidity and deployability, hearing loss, lethality and survivability, medico-legal implications and, during the early years following the opening up of these roles, the costs of implementation. Optimising economic welfare of public monies is important. However, the fundamental objective of military capability from a national security perspective must always be combat effectiveness, and this is underpinned by physical capability. The US, UK and Australian governments' decisions to allow women to access GCC roles will not be costless, but it will be some time before judgements can be made as to whether the possible risks and fiscal liabilities will exceed potential benefits.

1.1.7 International Security

The world lives in an era of radical change, and a constant dynamic is superpower rivalry in the search for defence capability supremacy. This unending competitive race is driven by technological innovation and hence has a major impact on military force structures. Disruptive environmental change is a global factor, but nowhere are its consequences felt more than in the United States. Randolf G. S. Cooper in Chapter 16 advances the view that this restructuring process is influenced by the emergence of new 'balance of power' equations, such as Russian and Chinese military innovation strategies. The Russians, for instance, have leap-frogged ahead in the development of next-generation weapons technologies, including a fifth-generation Su-57 stealth fighter, capable of flying at 1,120 mph, a 'dagger' hypersonic missile that can travel at Mach 5–10 with a range of 1,200 miles and the Uran-9 remotely controlled light tank, intended for use in urban battlefields where standard tanks have proved vulnerable.[18] Arguably, the next RMA has already begun, and is centred on the development of Artificial Intelligence (AI). Vladimir Putin asserts that AI is the future, viewing it as instrumental in shaping the future battlefield and changing the character of war. There are now growing concerns over the global pursuit of AI capability, given that, reportedly, some 400 partly autonomous weapons and robotic systems are under development in twelve countries for deployment on land, air and sea.[19] As a result, the United Nations is seeking regulation of one of AI's principal research outcomes, the phenomenon of 'killer robots'; but it will prove a challenge, as global defence spending on robotics is expected to double from $90 billion in 2016 to $180 billion by 2020.[20] Robots are dual-use technologies, and China, having long recognised their importance in the development of sophisticated military systems, plans to become a world leader in AI by the fusion of civilian and military technologies.

Given this international defence capability rivalry, it is likely that in the next fifty years the US government, influenced by public opinion, will need to reach a mutually agreeable accommodation on the cost of war versus the price of peace. The cost of war can be calculated using the traditional metrics employed by defence economists, but the price of peace will entail acceptance of a new political reality – global power sharing – a price that Washington has thus far been unwilling to accept. According to Daniel Fiott in Chapter 17, technology will play a major part in the future profound transformational change, as symbolised by America's offset strategies, aimed at addressing and overcoming the powerful military competences of adversaries. Whereas the First Offset Strategy sought to overcome the Soviet Union's dominance in conventional force strength and the Second Offset Strategy developed precision-guided munitions to challenge nuclear parity with Moscow, the Third Offset Strategy is as yet operationally and doctrinally underdefined. Thus far, the Department of Defense (DoD) has been active in attempting to farm innovative technologies from the commercial sector, with a particular desire to develop and integrate technologies such as robotics, nano- and biotechnologies and advanced communication systems into military capability. As with Russia and China, the United States intends to exploit AI to maintain military superiority. An example of this search for autonomous weapons systems is the American antisubmarine vessel, *Sea Hunter,* which is able to cruise the oceans for months, scouting for enemies, with no one onboard – a sort of lethal *Marie Celeste.*[21]

Defence will always focus on the significance of frontier defence technologies, but as Diego Muro explains in Chapter 18, there is now a proliferation of supplementary technologies, such as enhanced intelligence, sensors and reconnaissance, surveillance and cyber capabilities to counter the ubiquitous terrorist threat. In recent years, European cities have borne the brunt of European jihadism. From Madrid in 2004 to Brussels in 2016, the region's capitals have suffered terrorist atrocities at the hands of homegrown and foreign terrorists, some of whom had acquired combat experience in Syria and Iraq. As much as 75 per cent of European citizens live in urban centres and existing evidence points to attacks on cities continuing in the future. The European Union's response to this security threat has been multifaceted and increasingly targets both the recruitment side of terrorism (supply) as well as the reasons why political violence is tolerated by communities of reference (demand). Cities have been at the forefront of a comprehensive strategy to integrate counterterrorist and preventive strategies at the municipal level; the main goal of these policy experiments being to prevent extremism by isolating violent radicals from their supporters and sympathisers.

National security is a complicated concept. The policy means to secure adequate defence and security capability are multidimensional, and economic and political influences intermingle in the pursuit of competing goals and priorities. Complicating still further the security equation is the proliferation of threats that have expanded from sole focus on the traditional (military) national security domains to nontraditional international security scenarios. Foreign aid, for instance, is experiencing a dilution in its focus, with government sponsors demanding that monies must now form part of a wider moral compass to cover additional 'threats' that include transnational migration and human trafficking. Similarly, the policy lens of national security is also capturing the international threats posed by natural and man-made disasters, peacemaking and peacekeeping, and the problems associated with failed states. Generally, this is the domain of the United Nations, especially its peace missions. Fitriani, in Chapter 19, points out that the United Nation's Peacekeeping (UNPKO) operations receive a relatively meagre $6.8 billion budget. It amounts to less than one per cent of US defence spending, and below half of one per cent of global military expenditure for fiscal year 2017/18. The United States, along with the other five permanent members of the UN Security Council (P5), carries the heaviest financial burden in supporting peace operations, due principally to its special responsibility for the maintenance of international peace and security. The member countries contributing the highest number of troops and police personnel enjoy lower financial contributions. This arrangement incentivises the developing countries to supply the majority of peacekeeping personnel, while the richer countries shoulder most of the UNPKO budgetary burden. This resource-sharing equation works, in a fashion, but the downside is that it polarises the rich versus poor UNPKO member groupings, and leaves the entire UNPKO operations vulnerable to the financial whims of the P5 states, especially the United States. Of course, the political dimension plays a big part in determining the resource availability and activities of the United Nations, but should this be the case in the twenty-first century? Should other emerging political actors, such as, for example, China, play a more significant role in critically important multinational security operations, given that the benefit of mitigating suffering is a global public good?

1.1.8 Searching for the End-State

In the final analysis, there are myriad threats that call for attention in a world fracturing along the fault lines of nationalism ('America First', 'Brexit') and humanitarian compassion. Organised armed conflict is a problem that mostly happens in low and middle-income countries, and there is no doubting that a strong link exists between security and development; indeed, the United Nation's 2030 Agenda for Sustainable Development specifically aims to create peaceful and inclusive societies; see Sustainable Development Goal (SDG) 16. In the spirit of Adam Smith's advocacy that society should be protected from both violence and invasion (see the first paragraph of this chapter), Anke Hoeffler argues in Chapter 20 that there is a growing need to highlight and address all forms of violence, not just military conflict. This expanded policy focus would embrace collective violence (e.g. organised crime) and interpersonal violence (e.g. homicide), not just political violent conflict. Violence, however defined, has serious welfare and development consequences. Organised crime and other violence weaken societies, constituting one of the most serious threats to peace, especially in impoverished societies. The international community as well as national governments should not only consider civil wars but all forms of violence if the overarching motivation is to create a more peaceful world.

References and notes

1. A. Smith. An Enquiry into the Nature and Causes of the Wealth of Nations. London, book V. 1776. Cited in G. Kennedy. *Defense Economics*. London: Duckworth. 1983. 5.
2. Smith. *An Enquiry*. 23.
3. Smith. *An Enquiry*. 8.
4. Smith. *An Enquiry*. 8.
5. Smith. *An Enquiry*. 9.
6. Marshall Ogarkov, Chief of the Soviet General Staff, was held to have first employed the term RMA in the 1980s. He was referring to the new revolution that was occurring in the advanced Western countries, especially the United States. According to Ogarkov, the RMA had come about because of the declining politico-military utility of nuclear weapons and the enhanced combat capabilities of emerging technologies.
7. Discontinuities in military affairs are brought about by changes in militarily relevant technologies, concepts and doctrine of operations, methods of organisation and available resources. Such revolutions occur abruptly, most typically over two to three decades, rendering obsolete the existing means for conducting war. Examples of military revolutions might include the Napoleonic Revolution (advent of universal conscription expanding the size of armies and transforming logistics and

tactics), the Dreadnought/Submarine Revolution (arrival of the world's first all big gun and turbine-driven battleship and the introduction of submarines fundamentally changed naval strategy) and the Nuclear Revolution (detonation of atomic bombs over Hiroshima and Nagasaki dramatically altering the strategic calculus of warfare).

8. There is a school of thought that rejects the notion of a 'revolution' in military affairs, based on discontinuous change, and instead argues that military change is evolutionary in character, based on a process of continuous change. For evaluation of this debate, see M. Horowitz and S. Rosen. 'Evolution or Revolution?' *Journal of Strategic Studies.* June 2005. 28(3): 437–48.

9. D. Kirkpatrick and P. Pugh. 'Towards the Starship Enterprise – Are the Current Trends in Defence Unit Cost Inexorable?' *The Journal of Cost Analysis.* 1985. 2(1): 59–80. See also N. R. Augustine. *Augustine's Laws.* London: Penguin. 1987.

10. G. Adams. *The Politics of Defense Contracting: the Iron Triangle.* Routledge. 1981. See also R. Matthews and C. Maharani. 'The Defense Iron Triangle Revisited'. R. Bitzinger (ed). *The Modern Defense Industry: Political, Economic and Technological Issues.* Praeger Security International. 2009.

11. HM Government. *National Security Strategy and Strategic Defence Review 2015: a Secure and Prosperous United Kingdom.* Cabinet Office. November 2015. https://assets.publishing.service.gov.uk/government/uplo ads/system/uploads/attachment_data/file/478933/52309_Cm_9161_NSS_ SD_Review_web_only.pdf (accessed 6 May 2018), and for the United States see The White House. *The National Security Strategy of the United States of America.* White House. December 2017, and R. Kugler. *New Directions in US National Security Strategy, Defense Plans and Diplomacy.* National Defense University Press. 2011.

12. E. Benoit. *Defense and Growth in Developing Countries.* Boston: Heath, Lexington Books. 1973; E. Benoit. 'Growth and Defense in Developing Countries'. *Economic Development and Cultural Change.* 1978. 26(2): 271–80.

13. K. Hayward. 'The Globalisation of Defence Industries'. *Survival.* December 2010. 43(2): 120.

14. See L. Page. Lions, Donkeys and Dinosaurs. Heinemann. 2006.

15. C. Clark. 'Buy America, Again. Sigh'. *Breaking Defense.* 19 April 2017. https://breakingdefense.com/2017/04/buy-america-again-sigh/ (accessed 6 May 2018).

16. Clark. 'Buy America, Again'.

17. This is the case for the United Kingdom, see Ministry of Defence. *The Defence Equipment Plan 2017.* January 2018. https://assets.publish

ing.service.gov.uk/government/uploads/system/uploads/attachment_data/f ile/677999/20180125-EP17_Final.pdf (accessed 3 May 2018). However, note that it is estimated that around $42 billion, or some 19 per cent of total EU Member State defence spending ($225 billion), was allocated to procurement in 2016, including R&D. See the International Institute for Strategic Studies. 'Chapter Four: Europe'. In The Military Balance 2018. 2018. 73.

18. T. Parfitt. 'Russia to Show off Robot Tank and Superfast Missiles'. *The Times*. 5 May 2018.

19. B. Macintyre. 'Unstoppable March of Robot Armies'. *The Times*. 5 May 2018.

20. Macintyre. 'Unstoppable March'.

21. Macintyre. 'Unstoppable March'.

2 Political versus Military Leadership: The Battle for Common Means and Ends

BRYAN WATTERS

Introduction

The UK Ministry of Defence (MoD) is a complex government department, and this complexity is compounded by its dual role as Strategic Military Headquarters. How the MoD works in order to deliver its four objectives[1] and seven military tasks[2] is of interest to those concerned with national security and associated political economic benefits. The competing national priorities for finite resources pitch government ministries against each other in a battle to secure greater Treasury support for their agendas. The MoD's budget for 2017/18 is in the region of £44.6 billion, representing 2.18 per cent of GDP.[3] This can be put into context by looking at National Health Service expenditure, which for 2017/18 has a budget in the region of £125 billion.[4] According to the government's 2016 Public Spending Statistical Analysis,[5] the MoD is the fifth-largest departmental budget after the NHS, Work and Pensions, Education and HM Revenue and Customs. It is not the aim of this chapter to argue the merits or demerits of the MoD's budget and its social or political opportunity costs, but as it consumes a significant chunk of the national treasure, that treasure should be well spent.

To understand the output required of the MoD, one must first understand what constitutes national security and how to determine the mix of military capabilities required to deliver national security's military component. This chapter will therefore explore how the MoD works or possibly does not work, and how the structure and culture of the department confound the best of intentions. The discussion begins by exploring the nature of national security and how the British government has sought to define it. National security arguably defies definition, and this adds to the problem the MoD faces as it attempts to develop ever more expensive military capabilities to meet a shifting problem with no solution. This lack of a defined requirement, while sitting comfortably within a Ministry of State, does not suit the military, which prefer a 'mission', with a clear understanding of what achieves mission success or accomplishment. This philosophical and cultural dissonance sits at the heart of the working practices of the MoD.

The very term 'military' is also simplistic, as it camouflages a further dynamic within the MoD, generated by the three single services, Royal Navy, Army and Royal Air Force. The single services, headed by their Chiefs, represent three opposing entities and as we will show their single service agendas, competing for scarce resources, drive behaviours that frustrate policy. Two apocryphal anecdotes, 'the moving of Australia' and 'who should fly the Apache helicopter', are examples of stories woven into the MoD's culture and which illustrate the damaging impact of tribalism. The chapter will conclude by offering some suggestions that might mitigate the factors confounding the delivery of the MoD's vision: 'To defend the United Kingdom and its interests, strengthen international peace and stability, and act as a force for good in the world'.

2.1 National Security: An Elusive Goal or a Wicked Problem?

In 1973, Horst Rittel and Melvin Webber developed a problem typology that aims to promote understanding of the challenge of defining and delivering national security. In their treatise 'Dilemmas in a General Theory of Planning',[6] they coined the terms 'wicked' and 'tame' problems. Wicked problems are contradictory and conflicting, with changing and interdependent components that are often difficult to recognise as they are characterised by pluralist objectives and politics that defy definition. National security is such a problem, as illustrated later in terms of the 'Irish Question'. Tame problems, by contrast, while complicated, are clearly definable and the solution is self-evident to the problem's resolution, including, for example, an engineering problem aimed at overcoming an obstacle, fixing a broken leg, balancing a chemical equation or winning a fight.

Wicked problems lack a clear definition and are characterised by differing stakeholder perspectives, and thus agreeing the formulation of the wicked problem as it pertains to national security is part of the problem. Rittel and Webber highlight what they call 'the classic systems approach beloved of the military and space programs', which they describe as a systems engineering approach. British military teach this classic systems approach as 'The Estimate': understand the problem/mission, gather information, analyse information, synthesise information, await the creative leap then work out a solution.[7] This approach relates to tame problems and does not work for wicked problems, because the problem defies planners' attempts to set up and constrain the solution space and construct the measures of performance. The problem has a 'no stopping rule', as there are no criteria for sufficient understanding, due to there being no ends to the causal chains that link the interacting open systems of the problem. Think of UK domestic terrorism as a threat component to national security. Within our liberal democracy, how does one define the solution space and the causal chains linking the context and circumstances that radicalise refugees and British citizens? This is an MoD problem, but it is also a social, educational, economic, police and historic problem. The planner, when faced with this no stopping rule, can always try to do better. The stopping point may not be for reasons inherent in the logic of the problem, but for external considerations, such as no more time, run out of money or frustration. Relevant examples of this problem might include climate change, crime, nuclear power and national security. Rittel and Webber describe ten distinguishing properties of a wicked problem, and to understand the intractable complexities and causal linkages of national security they bear reading.[8]

Wicked problems are resolved or re-resolved to the satisfaction of stakeholders; but they are not solved. In 2005, Keith Grint developed this typology and added a third problem, the 'critical problem' or crisis.[9] He also developed a heuristic that aligned problems with approaches to resolution or solution, which he described as 'manage' for a tame problem, 'lead' for a wicked problem and 'command' for a critical problem. Tame problems by definition have a solution, so the role of the leader is to find the solution and follow the steps to manage the process to solution.

Wicked problems have no solution, so the requirement of the leader is to build a broad consensus on the nature and scope of the problem and its resolution; but being careful to ensure that the impact of the problem's resolution is acceptable to stakeholders. When tackling wicked problems, the leader asks the right questions rather than provides the right answers as a means of making progress towards a resolution. A security example of a resolution dates from 15 December 1971, when the British Home Secretary, Reginald Maudling, coined the phrase 'an acceptable level of violence' when describing the situation in Northern Ireland. The problem had no foreseeable solution, so the resolution was to determine and seek a level of terrorist violence that was acceptable; one that the United Kingdom could live with. In a similar vein, Seller and Yeatmanin, in their 1931 satirical book, opine that Gladstone 'spent his declining years trying to guess the answer to the Irish Question ... [but] ... when he was getting warm, the Irish secretly changed the question'.[10] Today, both the British and Irish governments are changing the question as they face Brexit, but it remains a wicked problem.[11]

Grint argues that a critical problem be commanded. The commander coercively and resolutely directs a solution to the crisis. In the crisis, he argues that people will accept being coerced by those legitimately engaged in the crisis's resolution. Of course, if the crisis evolves from a wicked problem, then the actions of the commander while removing or mitigating the immediate danger will not solve the underlying wicked problem. If the underlying problem was tame, the commander might solve the tame problem, or at least speed up its solution. Thus, in a national security crisis the government and the MoD would act differently when confronting the everyday wicked problem of national security. Grint's heuristic is based on the fact the problems are real and apparent; they are not socially constructed by leaders, managers or commanders to suit their preferred approach to dealing with problems.[12] For instance, the global war on terror relates to a contested arena, and a persuasive interpretation of the context legitimises a particular course of action relating to the decision-makers' favoured style of engagement. As Tony Blair's government contended, Iraq had weapons of mass destruction capable of hitting the United Kingdom in forty-five minutes; it was thus a crisis, and Blair acted as commander, and from a UK perspective took unilateral decisive action.

2.2 How Defence Should Work

The MoD reforms of 2015, cogently explained in the publication *How Defence Works*, introduced a refined Defence Operating Model.[13] The former Defence Management Board (DMB), which was jointly chaired by the Chief of the Defence Staffs (CDS) and the Permanent

Under-Secretary (PUS), was the centre of power. In 2002, during a DMB study day, board chairs from FTSE 100 companies were invited to observe and comment on the DMB. The aim was to improve the DMB's working as a board. One visiting board chair asked the identity of the DMB's chair, but it was explained that rather than one chair, a co-chair system was in place; the visitor looked puzzled, and continued to press on who has ultimate responsibility. Another visiting chair asked the Board how it sacked the co-chairs if they were not performing. The DMB spokesperson looked embarrassed and said, 'we cannot sack CDS and PUS'. The visitor remarked that the term DMB was mistaken nomenclature, as it was not a board, but rather an 'orders group'. Another visiting commercial board chair asked if the DMB co-chairs had been former finance directors, a usual route to assuming a chair of a FTSE 100 company. On receiving a negative response, the visiting chair asked the Second PUS, the Finance Director, where he had done his chartered accountancy training; the response was that this is not a requirement. The visiting chair was shocked, remarking: 'you have a finance director who is not trained in finance'.[14] The 2015 MoD reforms introduced changes to this unsatisfactory system of governance.

The Defence Board is now chaired by the Minister of Defence and includes a qualified Finance Director and non-executive directors. Although still not a board in the FTSE 100 sense, it better fits the requirement. The Defence Board, Defence Council and Executive Committee constitute the subordinate governance, and the three bodies explicitly constitute the head office executive. *How Defence Works* explains that the National Security Council (including the Secretary of State for Defence) agrees the National Security Strategy (NSS), which specifies the 'ends' (security objectives), and the Strategic Defence and Security Review (SDSR) identifies the 'means' (resources/competencies) and the 'ways', utilising the 'instruments of power' (courses of action). Combined, the integrated document was presented in 2015 by the Prime Minister on behalf of the government.[15] The Cabinet Office was charged in 2017 with leading work to review national security capabilities, and at the time of writing this work is ongoing. The MoD takes the ends, the means (2.18 per cent of GDP in 2017) and the ways directed in the government's policy document, then devises the military line of operation or military strategy, representing the military component of the instruments of power (DIME: Diplomatic, Information,

Military and Economic). This is a straightforward if complicated structure that enables the output of Defence.

2.3 Tribalism, Culture and the Battle for Scarce Resources

The MoD is not about structure – it is about people. This is reflected in
Lionel Robbins's definition of economics as 'a science that studies
human behaviour as a relationship between ends and scarce means
which have alternative uses'.[16] Resource scarcity, together with the
MoD's conflicting roles and multiple cultures residing within
a Ministry of State and Strategic Military Headquarters, drive human
behaviour that acts to frustrate policy in an attempt to secure scarce
means and produce ways that achieve single service interpretations of
the end.[17]

The MoD's central tension is its dual role of Department of State led
by the Minister (ends and means) and a Military Strategic
Headquarters led by the Chief of Defence Staff (CDS), responsible for
devising the military ways for achieving the government's policy 'end'
of national security. National security may be considered as an oxy-
moron, as no nation has ever achieved national security; nations live in
a perpetual state of insecurity, and thus the 'end' (national security) is
unachievable. The government's solution is to develop a National
Security Strategy, utilising the instruments of power to manage
national insecurity. The MoD contributes to this 'good enough strategy' by developing a range of military capabilities designed as contingencies to meet an ever-changing series of military threats.

Rittel and Webber's[18] problem typology and Grint's[19] idea of critical
problems, and his heuristic, provide a useful framework for examining
why the MoD does not work. It is not that the MoD's 2015 operating
model is deeply flawed, as it is a great improvement; it is rather that the
differing cultures within the MoD, embedded in the central tension of
Ministry of State and Strategic Military headquarters, are focused on
differing agendas while seeking to justify and secure scarce resources.
The MoD may be thought of as a loose coalition of tribes subordinate
to the Minister of Defence, broadly working to the common cause of
developing military capability to fulfil the military component of
national security.[20] Each tribe has its own culture manifest in unique
artefacts, values and basic assumptions.[21] The Royal Navy, Army,
Royal Air Force and civil servants wear different uniforms, have

different designations of rank/position, address each other differently, have different published values and have very different and often unconscious ways of seeing and interpreting the context around them.

The civil service values of integrity, honesty, objectivity and impartiality highlight the divergence with those of the military tribes, because only integrity is a shared common value.[22] The military do not espouse objectivity and impartiality (fundamental to the ethos of the civil service), and arguably the military ethos requires a degree of subjectivity and partiality. The military's value system has more in common with each other than the Civil Service. For example, the Royal Navy and the Army have six similar values (commitment, courage, discipline, respect for others, integrity and loyalty), and of these, three are shared with the RAF (respect, integrity and service – otherwise interpreted as commitment). The RAF's fourth unique value is excellence. Of course, values are espoused ethical statements of rightness; they are not necessarily theories in use. While the three military tribes led by their chiefs (of the Naval Staff, of the General Staff and of the Air Staff) share some values, their artefacts and basic assumptions culturally differentiate them. The Royal Navy differentiates itself as the guardian and diplomat and key to the prosperity of Britain, the Army by stepping forward to meet every challenge, with its tasks delivered directly by soldiers through human interaction and the RAF by being the world's first independent air force and engaged today on thirteen missions, on four continents in twenty-two countries.

In the MoD, each military tribe competes to gain credence for its description of the problem and its resolution to influence the ruling political tribe and thus gain a greater share of scarce resources. If national security is viewed as a wicked problem, it requires a normative approach to resolution building through cooperation to make progress towards a resolution.[23] The political and civil servant tribes can understand this and recognise a pragmatic resolution within normative frameworks, including competing political agendas, budgetary constraints and value; for that is the approach in all Ministries of State. The military tribes appear to have a primal requirement for bipartisan continued existence and risk, seeing the problem as tame and an opportunity to achieve their zero-sum game. As Rittel and Webber[24] explain: 'the existence of a discrepancy representing a wicked problem can be explained in numerous ways. The choice of explanation determines the nature of the problem's resolution'.

The explanation of the service chiefs is generally ships (aircraft carriers), a bigger well-equipped Army and the best aircraft in the world, to be flown only by the RAF not the Navy or Army. The chiefs see the problem within the context of their worldview; it is a maritime problem for the Navy, a land problem for the Army and an air problem for the RAF. The choice of explanation determines the nature of the problem's resolution: thus the resolution is more ships, a bigger well-equipped Army or more and better planes. The job of the Defence Board is to take this military 'advice' and make sense of it within budgetary constraints and the concept of value.

The task is made harder by the MoD's cultural dissonance over duration in appointment and the rewards system. The military will generally be posted from between two and three years. The civil servants, by contrast, will be posted for much longer periods, and in some cases their entire career. The politicians are there at the whim of the prime minister. This difference drives behaviours: the civil servants are happy to take the long-term view to the wicked problem's resolution as they are there for the long term. The military generally have two years to demonstrate their potential for promotion, assessed by outperforming the competition and receiving higher grades in their annual appraisal. They cannot take the long-term view; they need to tame the wicked problem and design a solution demonstrating superior abilities and thus outperforming the competition; promotion is a scarce resource and securing it drives behaviours. The military generally have a career to the age of fifty-five; the civil servant to sixty-five, and so another factor in the approach to problem solution or resolution is that the military have less time to excel.

In addition to time as a factor driving behaviour, there is also what might be called ethos, which is either a cultural value or a basic assumption, possibly the latter. The ethos in this context is the approach to problem solving. The politicians and civil servants, recognising the problem as long-term and wicked, understand the need for a normative approach involving wide consultation while seeking a good enough resolution. The journey, managing the process, is as important as the resolution as the process will be scrutinised for compliance with mandated procedures. The forming of committees and subcommittees, supported by working groups and think tanks, that report through subcommittees back to the high-level committee is not the military way. The military do not manage process, as they are trained and inculcated with the ethos of Mission Command.[25] Simply, Mission Command requires a military officer to understand the mission (task), its purpose and how it fits within the wider context or plan two levels up. The military commander is then required to design the plan, with the resources available, to achieve the set mission. The superordinate sets the mission, explains the reason why, allocates resources and leaves the subordinate to design the solution. This philosophy is based on six principles, namely: unity of effort, decentralisation, trust, mutual understanding and timely and effective decision making. The military in the MoD struggle with decision by committee and the 'interminable' process. The need is to be told what do, why it is important, be given the resources and then get on with demonstrating their outstanding abilities by designing a brilliant solution. Time for the military is always a critical variable. The six principles of Mission Command, as will be demonstrated later, do not appear to be part of the MoD's culture and working practices.

This chapter is not arguing for the tribalism of the military to be neutered or to follow the ill-fated Canadian 1968 Forces Reorganisation Act that disbanded the Canadian Army, Navy and Air Force and unified them to create The Canadian Armed Forces, with a single culture.[26] This experiment was largely repealed in 2011 when the Canadian Army, Navy and Air Force were reinstated. What the chapter is arguing is that the MoD's role of Ministry of State appears to be compromised by its role as Strategic Military Headquarters; the cultural dissonance manifest in the tribal cultures is the problem.

2.4 Military Tribal Culture: A Positive Force?

While these military tribal cultures may create disharmony in a Ministry of State, the development of military culture is essential for dominating and winning in the battlespace. The political space is framed towards achieving the greater good, which an inevitably under-resourced but affordable military capability can achieve while responsibly acknowledging the political opportunity costs of scarce resources (money), especially acute at election time. Together with the MoD civil service, the armed forces seek to resolve the wicked problem of national security/insecurity in such a way as to be acceptable to the nation and electorate. The military cannot be categorised as natural 'Whitehall

Warriors', unlike their civil servant colleagues and political masters. The military's terrain is the sea, land and air 'battlespace', and there are no prizes for coming second in this battle. They have gained their positions and reputations solving the tame and critical problems of military conflict.

At the strategic level, the military are not comfortable with the lack of clear policy definitions and differing stakeholder perceptions.[27] The armed forces struggle to accept compromised resolutions, where they find themselves disadvantaged. The military will fight to secure solutions to tame problems by securing a larger slice of the defence budget to support the intended strategy. Ideally the military prefers a crisis (Northern Ireland, the Falkland's, Sierra Leone, Iraq, Afghanistan, Syria) in which its default style of command can coerce politicians and civil servants to see the sense in primacy of the maritime, land or air forces in delivering a solution to the crisis. This tribalism and resulting dysfunction is not new, as illustrated by two apocryphal anecdotes.

2.4.1 Relocating Australia 500 Miles West

In the 1960s, the Royal Navy was keen to acquire new aircraft carriers (CVA-01, 02, 03) to replace its aging four large World War II-era carriers. The RAF attacked the Navy's carrier plans because they were perceived to be in competition with RAF land-based aircraft programmes, specifically the BAC TSR2 strike/reconnaissance aircraft and its proposed replacement the General Dynamics F-111. The CDS (Lord Mountbatten) was briefed by the chief of the Air Staff on the capability of the TSR-2 to reach all likely targets in the Far East from inexpensive land-based airfields in Asia, Northern Australia and the Indian Ocean island of Aldabra. Mountbatten's military assistant, a Naval Officer, was not convinced by the RAF maps, and left the room to consult another map. He realised that the map projection used by the Air Force chief enabled Australia (after being conveniently but mischievously relocated 500 miles to the west of its true geographical location) to opportunely fit into the flight performance envelope of the TSR-2, thus justifying the strategy. He asked Mountbatten to slip out of the briefing, and explained the ruse. The RAF's subterfuge was then blown. The anecdote serves as an example of Air Staff duplicity in the battle for scarce resources. The battle still rages today with further stories of RAF duplicity; for example, it has been argued that the selling of the Harrier at well below its value to the US Marines was aimed at removing carrier-borne fixed-wing aircraft in favour of the RAF Tornado fleet, thus removing at a stroke the Royal Navy's fixed-wing flying capability.[28] The United Kingdom's two new carriers with as yet no aircraft and presently unknown final costs continue the battle over scarce resources. The two new Queen Elizabeth Class aircraft carriers will impose huge opportunity costs on UK defence, as the Royal Navy will likely struggle to provide manpower for the carriers, possibly at the expense of the Royal Marines,[29] and the Army and RAF are also required to deliver compensatory savings.[30]

2.4.2 Inter-Service Rivalry: Battling over the Apache Helicopter

In the mid-1990s there was a debate between the Army and the Air Force over ownership of highly capable and expensive Apache attack helicopters. The Air Force highlighted that the airframe should be attributed to the Air Forces' 'air component', as it will be employed in a 'close air support' role. The Army, however, argued that it was a 'light' attack helicopter and was thus the natural successor to the Lynx's 'armed action' capability. After much debate within the MoD, it was decided that the aircraft would go to the Army on the understanding that one of the six operational squadrons would be double ear-marked and have an amphibious capability employing RN pilots. The RAF countered by questioning the ability of the Army Air Corps (AAC) to operate the aircraft, because AAC senior non-commissioned officer aircrew would be intellectually unable to cope with an advanced aircraft (even though they qualified through a Defence Flying Training System common to all three services).[31] The story goes that this approach was outlined in an internal letter from the assistant chief of the Air Staff; unfortunately, or fortunately depending on from which perspective this is viewed, the note found its way to the assistant chief of the General Staff (his Army opposite number). Ultimately, the RAF failed to obtain ownership of the Apache, and was advised to fall back in line and stop inviting anarchy.

2.5 Can the MoD Work?

Successive structural changes have attempted to improve the operation of the MoD.[32] The refining of the structure of the MoD is an ongoing attempt to influence or limit tribal behaviours using structure to address the institutionalised agency of the services acting independently and making free choices. The use of structure to create or increase defence socialisation in order to limit tribal biases is part of the MoD's dynamic tension. *How Defence Works*[33] introduced a wide-ranging series of structural reforms to limit tribal influence by removing the service chiefs from the Defence Management Board (retitled the Defence Board) and Head Office rusticating them to the Shires. However, as guardians of their service the chiefs have access to the prime minister as a last resort.[34] Thus, the military chiefs are institutionally protected.[35]

The 2015 restructuring of the MoD[36] also created a new chief to head a new organisation called Joint Force Command.[37] The impact of the new chief and his new joint command has yet to make any quantifiable impact, as the three former chiefs retain control over their respective service careers when they are lent to Joint Force Command, thus service loyalty remains and is enforced by the single service chiefs. The 2018 Modernising Defence Programme (MDP) that builds on MoD 2015 is examining an increased role for Joint Force Command.

How Defence Works[38] written in 2015 provides detail on the structural complexities and interrelationships within the MoD, it is being updated. The 2017 National Security Capability Review[39] introduces the Modernising Defence Programme with four work streams tasked with (1) modernising the 2015 operating model, (2) introducing business efficiency, (3) a commercial and industrial approach and also (4) defence policy, outputs and capability.[40] The chiefs are rallying their troops to defend vested interests, and the tribes are going autonomously to war, as illustrated by the independent online campaign, *Save the Royal Navy.*[41] The aim is to modernise managerial defence structures and outputs, but behaviours are also to be addressed.

There has long been a perception that defence management and leadership needs to improve, and that strategic leadership in the MoD needs to be developed. As the 2001 report *Modernising Defence Training* commented, 'recognising that MoD and the Armed Forces enjoy a world-wide reputation for excellence in leadership in operations and crisis management ... the requirement for good leadership applies equally to day to day MoD business and to the corporate/ strategic management of the Department'.[42]

The 2001 Report was initiated by the 1999 Defence Training Review, itself initiated by the Cabinet Office's 1999 'Modernising Government Initiative'[43] that placed leadership and improving leadership skills as a central driver to the government's requirement to deliver change across the public sector. The implications of *Modernising Defence Training* was that the day-to-day leadership of the MoD did not enjoy the same worldwide reputation for excellence, as leadership on operations. To provide empirical evidence supporting or rebuffing this perception a survey was undertaken in 2002 of 2 Star Officers in the MoD (n = 54) to elicit their views on strategic leadership in the MoD.[44] One of the survey questions was: '*Is overall strategic Leadership of MoD good?*' The responses were recorded using a five-bar scale, with respect to: (1) no feeling; (2) strongly agree; (3) inclined to agree; (4) inclined to disagree; (5) strongly disagree. The results showed that only 2 per cent strongly agreed, and 57 per cent were inclined to disagree or strongly disagree that MoD leadership was good. The open question data from the 'inclined to disagree' and 'strongly disagree' ratings that leadership in the MoD was good were coded[45] to develop themes and explain the reasoning behind the grading. These codes, within the themes of vision, operational issues, cultural issues and communication, are shown in Table 2.1, and present a stark picture of a dysfunctional organisation.

The restructuring of the MoD in the 2015 SDSR into a new operating model[46] and the MDP[47] will continue, it is hoped, to address the 'emergent themes' outlined in Table 2.1. The cultural issues which Geet Hofstede et al.[48] eruditely described as the 'software of the mind' have been the most difficult to change; for example: territorialism, short-termism, lack of trust, internal politics and poor understanding of the real world. That, of course, was then (2002) and this is now (2018); however, the basic tensions driving behaviour, duality of role and the competition for scares resources, appears, in the author's experience, to have changed little. Perhaps the 2018 MDP will tackle the culture empirically explored in 2002. The UK Regular Armed Forces Continuous Attitude Survey Results for 2017[49] reported that 'most personnel are less satisfied with their senior leaders than two years ago', with the level of dissatisfaction reaching a high 75 per cent. This clearly represents a challenge for the MDP. The present Chief of Defence Staff, General Sir Nick Carter, will be challenged to effectively

Table 2.1: *MoD emergent themes*

Summary of emergent themes

Emergent themes	Codes	Theme construct
Vision	Perception of no clear unified vision	Vision
	Lack of inspiration from senior staff	Inspiration
Organisational issues	Organisational structure hampers leadership	Structure
	Staff lack appropriate skills	Skills
	Poor accountability	Accountability
	Central control	Control
	Breadth of responsibility too wide	Responsibility
Cultural issues	Territorialism	Territorialism
	Risk aversion	Risk
	Short-termism	Short-termism
	Focus on process over output	Process
	Over-attention to detail	Output
	Lack of trust	Attention to detail
	Internal politics	Trust
	Poor understanding of rationale for decisions	Internal politics
	Poor understanding of real world from the centre	Decisions
	Over-concern about public perception	Understanding
	Over concern about perception by peers	Public perception
	Lack of moral courage in major decisions	Perception by peers
	No time to master briefs and reflect	Moral courage
	Perception of no attention to impact of political decisions	Political decisions
Communication	Poor communication of direction and decision making	Communication
		Decision making

Source: B. S. C. Watters. 'Contemporary British Military leadership in the Early Twenty First Century'. PhD Thesis. University of Leeds. 2009. 244.

address the software of the MoD's mind, and to inculcate the principles of Mission Command, namely, unity of effort, decentralisation, trust, mutual understanding and timely and effective decision making.

2.6 Conclusion

Can the MoD work as intended? Does it need to be both a Ministry of State and Strategic Military Headquarters? If the latter's disruptive tension is removed, it would then be a Ministry of State, like other Miniseries of state, focused on the wicked problem of managing national security/insecurity. Unencumbered by a strategic military headquarters, the Ministry of State – the MoD – could concentrate on Policy (the end and the means), and Joint Force Command – the Strategic Military Headquarters – could focus on developing military strategy (the way) and commanding military forces and operations. The strategic dialogue between the MoD and the Strategic Military Headquarters would, of course, remain, as the end is always a compromise between ways and means. The tribal allegiance of the military, so disruptive in the strategic environment, would be tempered if Joint Force Command was the arbiter of career progression above unit level (commander/lieutenant colonel/wing commander). This would limit the patronage power of the service chiefs and bound the influence of the tribal system to twist the provision of military capability through patronage. The introduction of a truly Joint culture would not be easy, as reprogramming the mind would take time and be painful. The post of CDS was created in 1959 to reflect the pre-eminence of a Joint approach to military planning and operations. This pre-eminence might now be taken to the next level with CDS replaced by Commander Joint Force.

While these suggestions have logic, they do not make the assumption that the MoD is a tame problem, carrying the danger that strategic decision making is no longer the responsibility of the civilian political leadership, but military officers. The MoD's current organisational configuration ensures that civil servants and political leaders are 'in the same tent', inextricably interlinked in military planning. A cynic might argue that the military is too engaged with infighting to present a constitutional threat. However, a united military might be a different proposition.

Notes

1. These are: protect our people, project global influence, promote our prosperity and manage the Department of State. See GOV.UK. *Corporate*

Report – Ministry of Defence Single Departmental Plan. www.gov.uk/go
vernment/publications/ministry-of-defence-single-departmental-plan/minis
try-of-defence-single-departmental-plan#manage-the-department-of-state-
and-the-defence-enterprise (accessed 30 April 2018).

2. These are: defending the United Kingdom and its overseas territories,
   providing strategic intelligence, providing nuclear deterrence,
   supporting civil emergency organisations in times of crisis, defending
   our interests by projecting power strategically and through
   expeditionary interventions, providing a defence contribution to UK
   influence and providing security for stabilisation. See GOV.UK.
   Ministry of Defence – About Us. www.gov.uk/government/organisa
   tions/ministry-of-defence/about (accessed 30 April 2018).

3. HM Treasury. *Central Government Supply Estimates – Main Supply
   Estimates.* Report number: HC1127, 2017. https://assets.publishing.ser
   vice.gov.uk/government/uploads/system/uploads/attachment_data/file/6
   09174/Main-Supply-Estimates-2017–2018-web.pdf (accessed 30 April
   2018).

4. HM Treasury. *Central Government Supply Estimates – Main Supply
   Estimates.* Report number: HC1127, 2017. https://assets.publishing.ser
   vice.gov.uk/government/uploads/system/uploads/attachment_data/file/
   609174/Main-Supply-Estimates-2017–2018-web.pdf (accessed 30 April
   2018).

5. HM Treasury. *Public Expenditure Statistical Analyses 2016.* 2016. 30.
   https://assets.publishing.service.gov.uk/government/uploads/system/uplo
   ads/attachment_data/file/538793/pesa_2016_web.pdf (accessed 30 April
   2018).

6. H. W. J. Rittel and M. M. Webber. 'Dilemmas in a General Theory of
   Planning'. *Policy Sciences.* 1973. 4(2): 155–69.

7. JSCSC. *JSCSC Operational Level Planning Process Aide-memoire – V1.*
   Crown Copyright, 2017. www.sclr.stabilisationunit.gov.uk/top-ten-re
   ads/uwm-1/1238-operational-level-planning-process-aide-memoire/file
   (accessed 30 April 2018).

8. In Rittel and Webber, they propose at least ten distinguishing properties
   of a wicked problem. See Rittel and Webber. 'Dilemmas'. 161–67.

9. K. Grint. 'Problems, Problems, Problems: The Social Construction of
   Leadership'. *Human Relations.* 2005. 58(11): 1467–94.

10. W. C. Sellar and R. J. Yeatman. *1066 and All That.* New York:
    Methuen. 1955.

11. 'Leader: The return of the Irish Question'. *New Statesman.* 29
    November 2017. www.newstatesman.com/politics/brexit/2017/11/le
    ader-return-irish-question (accessed 30 April 2018).

12. K. Grint. 'Problems, Problems, Problems'. 1467–94.

13. Ministry of Defence. *How Defence Works*. Version: 4.2 1, 2015. https://assets.publishing.service.gov.uk/government/uploads/system/uploads/attachment_data/file/484941/20151208HowDefenceWorksV4_2.pdf (accessed 30 April 2018).
14. The author was present at this study day and helped arrange the attendance of FTSE 100 board chairs.
15. HM Government. *National Security Strategy and Strategic Defence and Security Review 2015 – A Secure and Prosperous United Kingdom*. Report number: Cm9161, 2015. https://assets.publishing.service.gov.uk/government/uploads/system/uploads/attachment_data/file/555607/2015_Strategic_Defence_and_Security_Review.pdf (accessed 30 April 2018).
16. R. E. Backhouse and S. G. Medema. 'Retrospectives: On the Definition of Economics'. *Journal of Economic Perspectives*. 2009. 23(1): 221–34.
17. Ends, ways and means, from Clausewitz's opus 'On War'. For the sake of this chapter we may think of this trilogy as: End(s), the goal or objective, what is to be accomplished. Ways, the actions necessary to achieve the End. Means, the resources and capabilities to facilitate the ways. See M. Howard and P. Paret, eds. *Carl Von Clausewitz – On War*. New Jersey: Princeton University Press. 1976.
18. Rittel and Webber. 'Dilemmas'. 155–69.
19. K. Grint. 'Problems, Problems, Problems'. 1467–94.
20. Tribe, a term associated with the colonial era, there is no agreed anthropological or sociological definition. See D. Senath. 'Tribe'. Cambridge Encyclopaedia of Anthropology. 2016. www.anthroencyclopedia.com/entry/tribe (accessed 30 April 2018).
21. In his book, Edgar Schein describes organisational culture as three components: Artefacts, any tangible or verbally identifiable elements in an organisation, for example, buildings, furniture, dress code and history; values, ethical statements of rightness; and lastly, basic assumptions, unconscious and taken for granted ways of seeing the world. See E. H. Schein. *Organizational Culture and Leadership*. 4th edn. San Francisco: Jossey-Bass. 2010.
22. GOV.UK. *Statutory Guidance – The Civil Service Code*. Available from www.gov.uk/government/publications/civil-service-code/the-civil-service-code (accessed 30 April 2018).
23. K. Grint. 'Problems, Problems, Problems'. 1467–94.
24. Rittel and Webber. 'Dilemmas'. 166.
25. The Reference is an Army publication; Mission Command is taught as a military approach to command, which the Army introduced into military doctrine in the 1980s as part of the Bagnall reforms, as a means of commanding within the doctrine of the Manoeuvreist Approach. It was borrowed from the German *Auftragstaktik* developed in the nineteenth

century by Helmuth von Moltke and others following Prussia's defeat in the first Franco-Prussian war (1870–71). See Army. *Land Operations*. Land Warfare Development Centre. Army Doctrine Publication. Number: AC71940. Chapter 6. https://assets.publishing.service.gov.uk/government/uploads/system/uploads/attachment_data/file/605298/Army_Field_Manual__AFM__A5_Master_ADP_Interactive_Gov_Web.pdf (accessed 30 April 2018).

26. Government of Canada. *Restoring the Historic Designations of the Royal Canadian Navy, the Canadian Army, and the Royal Canadian Air Force*. National Defence and the Canadian Armed Forces. 2013. www.forces.gc .ca/en/news/article.page?doc=restoring-the-historic-designations-of-the-ro yal-canadian-navy-the-canadian-army-and-the-royal-canadian-air-force/h nps1vdb (accessed 30 April 2018).

27. Rittel and Webber. 'Dilemmas'. 155–69.

28. Ultimately, some in the Royal Navy believe the Harrier was the victim of inter-service politics, with the RAF outmanoeuvring the Navy on the issue. See C. Wyatt. 'Struggle at the Top over Decision to Scrap UK Harriers'. *BBC*. 15 December 2010. www.bbc.co.uk/news/uk-11997084 (accessed 7 May 2018).

29. B. Farmer. 'Royal Marines to Lose 200 Men So Navy Can Crew Its Aircraft Carriers'. *The Telegraph*. 10 April 2017. www.telegraph.co.uk/news/2017/04/10/royal-marines-lose-200-men-navy-can-crew-aircraft-carriers/ (accessed 30 April 2018).

30. R. Norton-Taylor. 'Our New Aircraft Carrier Could Sink the Defence Budget Without Firing a Shot'. *The Guardian*. 7 December 2017. www .theguardian.com/commentisfree/2017/dec/07/aircraft-carrier-defence-budget-hms-queen-elizabeth-royal-navy (accessed 30 April 2018).

31. The RAF do not have non-commissioned pilots; all RAF pilots are commissioned officers.

32. Ministry of Defence. *How Defence Works*.

33. Ministry of Defence. *How Defence Works*.

34. Ministry of Defence. *How Defence Works*.

35. This chapter does not address the structure and agency debate, the issue of socialisation against autonomy in defining whether an individual acts as a free agent and the role of cultural influences. To understand the structure and agency framework further and the influence of culture, see C. Barker. *Cultural Studies: Theory and Practice*. 4th edn. London: Sage. 2012.

36. Ministry of Defence. *How Defence Works*.

37. GOV.UK. *Joint Forces Command*. www.gov.uk/government/organisa tions/joint-forces-command (accessed 18 April 2018).

38. Ministry of Defence. *How Defence Works*.

39. In 2017, the Cabinet offices were tasked to lead additional work to review national security capabilities, supporting ongoing implementation of the 2015 National Security Strategy and Strategic Defence and Security Review. See GOV.UK. *Strategic Defence and Security Review Implementation.* www.gov.uk/government/news/strategic-defence-and-security-review-impl ementation (accessed 10 May 2018).

40. In 2018, the Government directed the MoD to initiate a Modernising Defence Programme (MDP) to identify what defence needs and how defence works to deliver a better military capability as its contribution to national security and prosperity. See GOV.UK. *Modernising defence programme public consultation.* www.gov.uk/government/consulta tions/modernising-defence-programme-public-consultation (accessed 10 May 2018). The MDP has four workstreams as per:

Workstream 1 MoD Operating Model: establishing a refreshed and clearer Operating Model for Defence, to enable better and faster decision making and more efficient and effective delivery of Defence outputs.

Workstream 2 Efficiency and business modernisation: providing confidence in the MoD's ability to realise existing efficiency targets, and a set of options for future efficiency and business modernisation investments.

Workstream 3 Commercial and industrial approach: assessing how MoD can improve on commercial capability and strategic supplier management.

Workstream 4 Defence policy, outputs and military capability: analysing the global security context and its implications for Defence policy, the roles and tasks that we prioritise, and the opportunities or imperatives for modernising our workforce, military capabilities and force generation processes.

41. Save the Royal Navy. www.savetheroyalnavy.org (accessed 10 May 2018).

42. Ministry of Defence. *Modernising Defence Training: Report of the Defence Training Review.* 2001. 23.

43. UK Government. *Modernising Government.* The Stationary Office Limited. 1999. http://webarchive.nationalarchives.gov.uk/200708052 30000/http://archive.cabinetoffice.gov.uk/moderngov/download/mod gov.pdf (accessed 10 May 2018).

44. B. S. C. Watters. *Contemporary British Military Leadership in the Early Twenty First Century.* PhD Thesis. The University of Leeds, United Kingdom. 2009. 236–44.

45. A. Strauss and J. Corbin. *Basics of Qualitative Research: Techniques and Procedures for Developing Grounded Theory.* London: Sage. 1998.

46. Ministry of Defence. *How Defence Works*. 4.
47. GOV.UK. *Modernising Defence Programme Public Consultation*. www
    .gov.uk/government/consultations/modernising-defence-programme-pu
    blic-consultation (accessed 10 May 2018).
48. G. Hofstede, G. J. Hofstede and M. Minkov. *Cultures and Organisations:
    Software of the Mind*. New York: McGraw-Hill; 2010.
49. Ministry of Defence. *UK Regular Armed Forces Continuous Attitude
    Survey Results 2017*. 2017. https://assets.publishing.service.gov.uk/govern
    ment/uploads/system/uploads/attachment_data/file/636473/AFCAS_
    2017_Main_Report.pdf (accessed 10 May 2018).

3 | *Efficient and Effective Financial Management of Defence Resources*

IRFAN ANSARI

Introduction

The cost of providing defence is small, but nonetheless significant enough to drain public financial resources away from competing social and development goals. The government thus has a responsibility to prudently manage defence resources, balancing fiscal prudence with adequate military preparedness in the face of an uncertain international environment. This uncertainty makes it all the more important for governments not only to appropriately allocate scarce public financial resources to their defence departments, but also ensure their effectiveness in use. Accordingly, defence finance has emerged as a relatively new but important field of defence management. It entails the measurement, monitoring and control of defence-related financial resources.

This chapter starts by exploring the two principal accounting frameworks employed in defence finance. The MoD, like most public sector departments, requires funds in order to operate, and an examination of the different sources of finance for defence expenditures is the next area of focus. Defence budgets – the core of defence finance – will then be critically evaluated from different angles including processes and financial risks. Finally, an examination of how defence expenditure can be judged using value for money criteria, especially to taxpayers, will be undertaken. A conclusions section lists the key takeaway points from this chapter.

3.1 Defence Accounting Models

There are essentially two main approaches to reporting financial transactions in defence; the first is cash-based and the second accruals-based accounting. Cash-based accounting is the older of the two models, and records financial transactions only when cash moves between a buyer and a seller. For instance, when aircraft pilots start receiving simulator training from a defence contractor, the MoD would record the expenditures only when it makes payments for the service, not when the benefits from the training are received. The simplicity of cash accounting makes the recording of financial transactions easy: when cash is paid, expenditures are recorded even if benefits from expenditures are not being received. However, a major disadvantage of cash accounting is that when a defence contractor supplies goods and services in advance of payments, the cash system does not recognise the amounts owed as financial liabilities. Similarly, future committed expenditures such as lease payments, Private Finance Initiatives (PFIs) charges and decommissioning costs are not recognised as financial liabilities either; they will be recorded as expenses only when payments are made for them at some point in the future, even though benefits from them are received in the present. This lack of recognition of liabilities means that the MoD's financial obligations (and the public sector by extension) as well as the interests of (future) taxpayers are inaccurately represented.

In the 1990s, the UK government began to realise that cash-based accounting was to blame for the overall decline in the quality and quantity of public sector capital assets in the decades before 2000. Total gross public investment had dropped by £67 billion between 1975 and 2000.[1] Modern public services were increasingly delivered in many diverse ways, which made it essential to get better cost accounting information to help allocate scarce public funds more effectively between the competing demands. Against this backdrop, the UK public sector in 1998 adopted accruals accounting under the banner Resource Accounting and Budgeting (RAB). The MoD, like other public sector departments, adopted RAB in two steps. Firstly, from 1998 to 2001, the MoD's annual financial accounts were reported under RAB in parallel with cash-based accounts. Then, from 2002 onwards the MoD's annual financial accounts have been reported only under RAB. The purpose of the three-year transition was to allow managers and staff in the MoD to get trained and acquainted with reporting under RAB. Moreover, this transition period allowed the MoD to overcome any teething problems with the new accounting system without significantly hindering the reporting of MoD financial performance during this time. It is evident that the MoD's adoption of RAB was not just about the technical switchover from cash to accruals, but it also demanded a change in thought processes – cash-based accounting was focused only on cash movements, whereas accruals accounting takes a more holistic view of financial transactions.

In the accruals-based accounting system, the full consequences of economic activities are accounted for, not just the cash flows. The basic principle of accruals accounting is that defence expenditure is recognised when benefits from the expenditure are received. MoD's income is recorded when the MoD begins to enjoy the flow of economic benefits. Incomes and expenditures are recorded as and when they are deemed to occur, irrespective of movements in cash. Therefore, under accruals accounting, the recognition of defence expenditure is not dependent upon payment schedules negotiated with a defence contractor; instead, it is recognised based on when the benefits from expenditures are received. Therefore, as opposed to cash accounting, its successor produces accounting information that is independent of timing mismatches that may exist between receipt of benefits from expenditures and their payments. Thus, accruals accounting provides more accurate/reliable accounting information to the MoD than its predecessor.

Furthermore, since defence expenditures, using the accruals system, are recognised only when the related benefits are received, the accruals regime rightly makes a distinction between current and capital defence expenditures; an important distinction that cash accounting failed to make. Additionally, the purchase cost of a non-current asset, such as a military tank, is not fully charged in the year of purchase, but is rather spread over several years of the tank's economic life (by means of depreciation) to reflect the cost of the benefits received from the asset in each of those years. Depreciation charges incentivise the MoD to make optimal use of these assets because holding on to them is not free. Depreciation also prompts the MoD to dispose of its idle assets and use the proceeds elsewhere. However, the act of 'holding' costs is a double-edged sword – it could promote short-term financial gains against longer-term losses. For instance, in times of budgetary austerity, defence assets that have not been used for a while could be disposed of (to save depreciation charges) and may be bought later (when they are needed) at a price that may be greater than their initial purchase price.

Unlike cash accounting, financial liabilities are recognised under accruals accounting. This means that the financial position of the MoD and therefore the interests of (future) taxpayers are more accurately presented using this new accounting system. One peculiarity of accruals accounting is that there could in theory be different ways in which financial transactions of the MoD are reported. For instance, research and development costs – a major expense item in the MoD's accounts – could either be expensed or capitalised. The consequences of either approach on the defence budget and annual accounts could be significant. In order to ensure consistency over time and thereby improve comparability of accruals-based accounting information, the MoD needs to introduce rules which define how different financial transactions are reported. This the MoD has done by adopting and adapting accounting standards that are used in the private sector.

3.2 Financing Defence Expenditure

Expenditures by defence departments may be small, but usually account for a significant component of overall public sector expenditures. Global defence expenditures in 2016 amounted to about $1,686 billion or about $227 per person.[2] The ministries or departments of defence aim to deliver security for their citizens by defending them against threats. To deliver these objectives, countries need to have appropriately sized and trained armed forces as well as the necessary equipment and concepts to generate military capabilities. With personnel and assets deployed over a wide range of locations, it is not difficult to imagine that financial management in defence departments is challenging. The annual spend of the UK MoD in 2001 was about £23.5 billion.[3] Since then, defence expenditure has increased nominally to about £43.9 billion in 2017.[4] In real terms, defence expenditures increased from 2001 to 2011,[5] but since then they have been on a downward trend.[6] Yet, nominal increases have enabled the United Kingdom to achieve its NATO spending target of 2 per cent of GDP on defence in each of the last five years.[7] On a government-wide basis, annual MoD expenses amount to between 5 and 7 per cent of total annual government expenditures.[8] This indicates that in the UK a small but nonetheless significant amount of public finances is devoted to defence.

3.3 Means of Financing Defence Expenditure

3.3.1 Taxation and Borrowings

MoD expenditure (together with other public sector expenditure) is mainly government funded. Most of the public finances is sourced from taxes levied on the public and businesses. The level of taxes that a government levies has to be set according to the health of the host state's economy. When the economy is growing, raising taxes could be a prudent way to rake more money into the public purse; it could also help to dampen inflationary pressures. On the other hand, during recessionary phases, lowering taxes so that people and businesses have more spending money would be the wise approach so that the economy is pushed back towards the boom phase. Raising income via taxation in these tough times is challenging since economic output (i.e. taxed) is limited.

When taxation alone is insufficient to fund public expenditures, a deficit arises that is bridged through borrowing by selling gilts and treasury bonds to investors. These annual borrowings, accumulated over many years, comprise the public sector debt. Interest on this debt is usually lower than in the private sector because the risk of default by government is perceived to be lower. However, governments cannot borrow endlessly because the annual interest bill could squeeze the budgets of public sector departments like the MoD. For this reason, the New Labour government that came into office in 1997 introduced two self-imposed rules to control the level of state borrowing. One was that the government could only borrow money for investment. The rationale for this was that investment in the economy through the multiplier effect will eventually lead to increased economic activity and hence increased tax receipts. These will be used to pay back the loans at some point in the future. The other rule was to limit the level of public sector debt to 40 per cent of GDP[9] so that debt interest payments do not spiral out of control.

The financial crisis of 2007–08 forced the government to substantially increase borrowing to safeguard the economy. Currently, the public sector debt as a percentage of GDP has crossed the 85 per cent mark with little signs of peaking.[10] Statistically, the growth of UK public sector debt has caused annual debt interest payments over the past two decades to be similar in size to annual MoD spend, if not higher.[11] The government has been able to afford these high levels of public debt because of record low interest rates and quantitative easing since the financial crisis.[12] But towards the end of 2017, the Bank of England raised the interest rate for the first time in ten years;[13] and it has hinted that future interest rate rises could be in the pipeline.[14] These interest rate increases make servicing public debt more expensive and could further tighten the budgets of other public sector departments like the MoD. Successive governments have tried to reduce public sector debt by imposing austerity on the MoD (as well as other public departments). This means that the MoD has to generate efficiency savings, i.e. look for areas where it can cut its expenditure. This can have long-term consequences on UK defence capabilities. For instance, austerity measures over the past few years have forced the MoD to reduce headcount in the military and civilian sections as well as in capabilities, such as the Harrier.[15]

Government borrowing is a temporary measure to fix public finances. These loans will eventually have to be paid back in the future through taxation levied on current and future taxpayers. Thus, the long-term source of income for the government and, by extension, the MoD is mainly taxation. However, taxes and loans are not 'direct' sources of funding for MoD activities; rather, they are raised at the government level and disbursed to the MoD through negotiated settlements.

3.3.2 Income from Other Departments and Countries

Another source of funding for the MoD is through the income it earns from the provision of supplies and services to support other government departments, NATO, the United Nations and foreign governments. Additionally, the MoD receives rental income from its properties as well as from selling fuel.[16] The revenue from the disposal of used non-current assets like frigates is another source of income for the MoD. However, past practice has shown that money received from disposals has been minimal.[17] The MoD also receives dividends from its investments in companies. These incomes can be used to offset in-year defence expenditures. It should, however, be noted that the sum total of all these sources of income has fluctuated between £1.1 billion and £1.5 billion, representing about 2–4 per cent of the MoD's annual expenditures (over the period from 2010 to 2017).[18] The small, yet significant, size of these incomes should not come as a surprise since the MoD is not in the business of generating profits.

3.3.3 Private Finance Initiatives

PFIs began to be used in defence from the mid-1990s, and are another funding source for the MoD. The PFI is a public-private partnership

(PPP) in which the MoD enters into a long-term (10–25 years) contract to purchase services from a consortium of private companies. At the heart of a PFI is the construction/acquisition of an asset through which services are provided to the MoD. PFIs are different from privatisations in that the MoD retains a substantial role either as the main purchaser of the services or as an essential enabler of the project. Unlike contracting out, the private sector partners in PFIs not only provide the capital asset but also render the services.

As Figure 3.1 shows, PFI projects normally consist of four parties: the MoD, a Special Purpose Vehicle (SPV), subcontractors and, last but not least, financiers.[19] The MoD comes up with the specification of services (in terms of their nature, level and quality) it requires. It then builds a business case for using PFI as the preferred procurement method and invites bids from the private sector to produce outputs. The preferred bidder creates an SPV, a limited liability company, which enters into the long-term PFI contract with the MoD to deliver the outputs.

In PFI contracts, services are delivered using capital assets. In theory, these assets could be treated as assets of the SPV or the MoD, but not

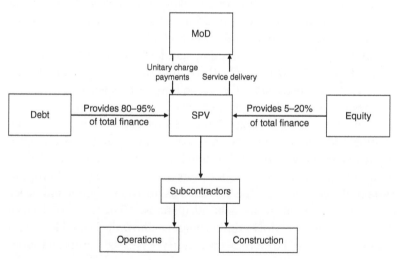

Figure 3.1: Operational defence PFIs
Source: Adapted from: PriceWaterHouseCoopers. *The value of PFI: hanging in the balance (sheet)?* [online]. PwC, 2008. Available at: http://infrastructureaustralia.g ov.au/policy-publications/publications/files/The_Value_of_PFI.pdf [Accessed 19 January 2018].

both. If PFI assets were recorded in the books of SPVs as assets, then this would increase their asset base and decrease the overall rate of return. Additionally, these assets would be subject to depreciation charges, which would increase operating costs and thus decrease annual profits. This would further dampen the rate of return for the SPVs. On the other hand, if the PFI assets were recognised as such in the MoD's books, it would increase defence spending by the amount of the depreciation charges on these assets.

For almost a decade and a half since the launch of defence PFIs, the prevailing accounting standards dictated that that about 70 per cent of defence PFI assets were to be treated as belonging to SPVs.[20] Only 30 per cent of them were recognised as assets in the MoD's accounts.[21] Therefore, for the majority of the defence PFI deals, the unitary charge payments were the only expenditures recognised by MoD accountants. For most defence PFIs, all the upfront expenditure of constructing the assets and their depreciation charges were borne by SPVs, not by the MoD. This meant that for the relatively small cost of annual fees, the MoD enhanced its military capabilities through PFIs without having to fund them and thus burden the already growing public sector debt. Additionally, future unitary charge payments over the lives of off-balance sheet defence PFIs[22] would not be recognised as liabilities of the MoD or the government. Public sector debt would therefore not be affected by such PFIs.

However, changes to accounting standards under RAB that were adopted by the MoD in 2009–10 required the use of a control-based approach[23] to determine the recognition of defence PFI assets. As a result, most of the ongoing defence PFI deals are now recognised as assets in the MoD's books;[24] their depreciation charges have now become additional annual defence expenditures, and future unitary payments are now recognised as liabilities of the MoD. Nonetheless, most PFI debt in the National Accounts (prepared under the European System of Accounts (ESA)) is classified as off-balance sheet and hence excluded from public sector debt calculations.[25] The future of defence PFIs used to finance MoD projects hinges on how the United Kingdom decides to define PFI debt once the country leaves the European Union.

3.4 The Good and Bad of Defence PFIs

The transfer of risks from the MoD to the SPV is a basic tenet of PFIs. However, because it would be too costly for the private sector to bear all the risks, the MoD transfers only some risks (such as construction cost and time overruns, service failures and financial loss) to the SPV to ensure that value for money is not compromised. Other risks, such as fluctuations in demand for service and changes in outputs, are kept within the MoD. The SPV, in turn, de-risks itself by transferring construction and service provision risks to other companies through the use of subcontractors. It transfers the finance risk to shareholders and banks. Equity finance is less attractive for defence PFIs not only because it is generally dearer than debt, but also because the long-term nature of PFI projects causes equity investors to wait a long time before reaping dividends on their investment. Hence, debt finance, in the form of project finance loans, is the principal source of private sector funding used in defence PFIs. Unlike corporate loans, where the borrowing company puts forward its assets as collateral, in project finance loans it is the unitary payments (i.e. service charges) from the MoD over the life of the PFI that act as collateral. SPVs do not have any assets of their own. Therefore, since banks bear the greatest financial risks in PFI deals, they exercise high levels of due diligence before financing the projects. This involves close scrutiny of PFI deals to ensure that SPVs have got subcontractors that will deliver the contractual outputs so that unitary charges (used to service and repay the loan) continue to be paid by the MoD.[26] Once a PFI asset is up and running and MoD payments begin to flow, the overall risk of the PFI contract reduces. This allows the SPV to refinance its loans with existing or other lenders on more favourable terms (i.e. at the lowest interest rates) and therefore boost the return for equity investors.

Operating through an SPV has several advantages – it enables a consortium of companies, instead of just one company, to bid for the contract. This helps to diversify investor risk. It also shields the operations of the SPV from financial problems of its holding companies and therefore prevents discontinuity of service provision to the MoD. Additionally, by having only a single purpose (to execute the PFI project), the SPV is unaffected by unrelated businesses. Due diligence by banks and the use of SPVs help to ensure that defence PFIs effectively deliver on the contracts. In other words, the scrutiny of PFI contracts assists in enabling risk transfer from the MoD to the private sector to be successful. However, it should be noted that if the SPV or its subcontractors fail to deliver, they may face financial penalties and suffer reputational damage, but at the cost of MoD losing capabilities being delivered through PFIs contracts. Hence, PFIs enable only the transfer of financial aspects of risks. The risk of losing capabilities remains with the MoD, and are non-transferrable.

The long duration of PFI contracts means that the MoD is locked into the SPV for an extended period of time. As it is impossible to map the MoD's future needs accurately when drafting PFI contracts, the emergence of new technologies, changes in the MoD's threat environment, as well as changes in financial pressures on the MoD may all require making changes to defence PFI deals.[27] This brings into question the flexibility of these contracts. PFIs are based on partnering relationships between the MoD (buyer) and the SPV (seller). This relationship is characterised by close collaboration between the parties for mutual gains. Here, price is not the only determinant between the buyers and sellers; the fact is that they both must look out for each other. Changes to defence PFIs can be negotiated between the parties as there is more commitment, openness and trust between them than in conventional contracting arrangements – at least this is the theory. In practice, as one NAO report highlighted, high-value changes made to operational PFIs were not always competitively tendered (even where this was possible), and that where competitive tendering was used for large changes, best value for money may not have been achieved.[28] Making minor changes to PFIs was often found to be expensive when compared with industry benchmarks, and there is also the problem of delays associated with such changes.[29] Thus, flexibility of defence PFIs is an issue. On the plus side, the inflexibility inherent in these contracts ensures that the services/capabilities provided could be future-proofed (at least for the duration of the contracts) against any defence budget cuts. This is because exit from PFIs could be possible but would require paying SPVs any outstanding unitary charges, and these could be prohibitive.

In short, it can be seen that although there are problems in using PFIs as a route to defence procurement, there are also some advantages of this method. In other words, defence PFIs are not all bad, but there is room for improvement. A fundamental reassessment of PFIs carried out by the government in 2011 not only confirmed weaknesses of defence PFIs (discussed above), but also established that management skills, innovation and risk management expertise of the private sector were plus points of this procurement route.[30] The overhauled version of PFIs, called PF2,[31] attempts to rectify some of the weaknesses of

PFIs. One is to strengthen partnering relationships between the MoD and SPVs. It will make the government a minority equity co-investor (with SPVs) in future deals so that some of the windfall profits from the private sector make their way to the government, and hence improve the value for money of defence PFIs. However, no new PF2s have been signed by the MoD to date, and none are expected to come online in the near future, as in late 2018 the UK government decided to ban PF2s altogether. It based this U-turn on their inflexibility, complexity and because they represented a source of significant fiscal risk.[32] However, in the current era of squeezed defence budgets, it is not difficult to imagine that PF2s in one form or another could return.[33]

3.5 Battling the Treasury

The limited amount of funding for the MoD and the challenges of defence inflation pressurise its policymakers into managing expenditures to realise the greatest efficiencies. A defence budget is a financial plan, expressed in monetary terms, enabling the MoD to achieve its strategic objectives and mission. It starts with planning.[34] This involves defining MoD outputs. One of the influences that shape the MoD's plans is the National Security Strategy and the SDSR. This is an exercise that is carried out every five years to identify the key threats to the United Kingdom (current and future) and the capabilities (i.e. outputs) that the MoD needs to counter. The different commands – the army, navy and air commands (i.e. the cost centres) – develop their own individual plans to achieve MoD outputs in their totality. In the process, financial figures are assigned to the different tasks carried out by these cost centres before consolidating these individual budgets to form a master plan/budget for the MoD. This defines the costs that would have to be incurred in order for the MoD to deliver the required capabilities set out by the NSS and SDSR.

The other influence (limiting factor) that defines the MoD's plans has reference to the funds made available to it by its biggest financier – the Treasury. The latter carries out spending reviews that spell out the maximum amount of money the MoD can spend annually over a number of years into the future. These upper limits for defence budgets are agreed after back-and-forth negotiations between the MoD and the Treasury. Hence, defence budgeting is a hybrid of top-down and bottom-up approaches. A top-down approach would be one where defence budgets, set by the Treasury, are imposed on the MoD. This could help to speed up the budgeting process but could also suffer from the setting of unrealistic budgets. In a bottom-up approach, the opposite happens – the MoD would prepare budgets for its cost centres and put these forward to the Treasury for funding. In this case, there is the potential for more accurate budgets to be prepared, but it could be a more time-consuming exercise than the first type. The hybrid approach, which the MoD uses, enables defence budgets to be prepared that are more acceptable to both parties, though it is a time-intensive exercise.

In the past, shortages of funds to finance the MoD's future military capabilities led to overheated defence budgets; that is, a funding gap.[35] By 2010, this gap had grown to about £38 billion, forcing the MoD to routinely delay or reduce major defence projects so as to calibrate with defence expenditures within its plans.[36] The Levene reforms in 2010 identified this as a problem and recommended that the MoD ensure that its plan for future capabilities is always funded, i.e. affordable. The planning phase of budgeting offers the MoD the opportunity to evaluate alternative courses of action (by using what-if analyses to determine the costs of different scenarios) so that it can choose the best option to achieve expected outputs. Forecasting lies at the heart of carrying out this evaluation. Statistical tools such as linear regression, time series, decision trees and probabilities could be used to develop better forecasts and hence assist the MoD in making better financial decisions about how it will deliver the required capabilities. Forecasts of future costs are inherently prone to inaccuracies, and given the nature of the security environment in which the MoD operates, it is no surprise that the MoD's budgets are seldom proved right. A cursory look at the last ten years' MoD financial accounts show that actual annual defence expenditures fell short of budgeted amounts by £1.1 to £7.9 billion in the different years.[37] The underspends are the result of actual events turning out to be different from those planned; the relative size of the positive variances hints at the magnitude of risks (that failed to materialise) built into planned costs.

3.6 Mitigating Financial Risk

The MoD faces a number of risks in its day-to-day operations. Some of these risks, called financial risks, have the potential to dent the financial performance and position of the MoD. Financial risks can be defined as the product of an event (that could financially impact the MoD) occurring and its associated probability. The financial impact could be significant and that is why the MoD attempts to manage them. One example of a financial risk the MoD is exposed to is currency risk, i.e. the risk of the exchange rate between the Pound Sterling (home currency) and the currency in which it buys equipment and services from abroad (foreign currency). The MoD spends a significant amount of money on foreign purchases, which are paid for in US Dollars and Euros.[38] When the Pound is strong relative to a foreign currency, foreign purchases are cheaper, and vice versa. In the case of the latter, a weak Pound puts added financial pressure on the already tight defence budget. The MoD attempts to manage this fluctuation in the Pound's exchange rate by entering into forward contracts with the Bank of England.[39] Forward contracts are binding contracts that lock the exchange rates at which the MoD will purchase Dollars and Euros (at certain times in the future) to make foreign payments. The upside of this arrangement is that if the Pound were to weaken against foreign currencies, forex losses for the MoD would be limited. Immediately after the Brexit vote in June 2016, the Pound-Dollar exchange rate nose-dived from $1.45 to $1.30 to the Pound[40] (this could, for instance, spike the MoD's costs on the F-35 programme by about £1 billion).[41] The forward exchange contracts (that had been entered into earlier) mitigated the loss to the MoD because it locked an exchange rate of between $1.57 and $1.51 to the pound for the next few years.[42] On the other hand, if the Pound appreciates in value, the MoD would receive fewer Euros and Dollars for each Pound compared to what it would have transacted at the market rate.

A change in the price of fuel is another financial risk that the MoD faces. The MoD purchases substantial amounts of aviation and marine fuels for use in its equipment.[43] A drop in the price of fuels is welcome; however, a rise in prices squeezes the MoD's budget. In order to manage this fuel price risk, the MoD enters into swap contracts with financial institutions. A swap contract operates like a forward contract except that in the case of the former, there are several payments between the MoD and the financial institutions over the limited life of the swap. In other words, a swap contract is a series of forward contracts that have to be settled several times over the swap's life instead of at just one date in the future as happens in the case of forward contracts. By using swaps, the MoD essentially contracts with the financial institution to pay a fixed known price for the fuels it needs irrespective of market prices. If the market price for the fuels is higher than the price of the swap, then that is a gain for the MoD and a loss for the financial institution and vice versa.

The risk of paying too much for defence contracts that are sourced from a single supplier is another financial risk in which the MoD is exposed. This risk could occur where there happens to be only a single company in the market that is able to deliver the requirements of the MoD or there are very strong reasons for maintaining a national capability.[44] Single source contracts account for about 45 per cent of the MoD's annual procurement costs.[45] Due to lack of competition, suppliers can set higher prices because they know there are no other players in the market to undercut them. There are hardly any market pressures on single source contractors to charge reasonable prices to the MoD. In order to manage this financial risk, the MoD relies on the Defence Reform Act 2014 and Regulation 11 of the Single Source Contract Regulations Act 2014. These Acts limit the profit that single source suppliers can make on defence contracts. These pieces of legislation define the profit, called the contract profit rate (CPR), that these defence contractors are allowed to make. CPR is worked out using a formula that incorporates the baseline profit rate (BPR) for the year[46] and other adjustments. The contract is then agreed between the parties based upon the CPR. During the execution of and upon completion of these contracts, defence contractors are obligated to send costing reports to the MoD. These reports show how actual costs differ from those estimated when the contract was agreed. This cost variance analysis is used by the Single Source Regulations Office (SSRO) to develop more reasonable CPRs for future contracts. This profit-limiting arrangement entails greater transparency between the MoD and defence contractors. More specifically, it requires the MoD to have access to single source suppliers' costing figures so that the former can ensure that the CPRs have been appropriately calculated.

3.7 (In)flexible Defence Budgets

A fixed defence budget remains unchanged at all levels of activity. Fixed defence budgets are appropriate to control expenditures where levels of activity remain relatively constant. However, in situations where actual activity levels fluctuate, then using a fixed defence budget will inevitably create variances.[47] An analysis of such variances will be of little benefit when the volatility in activity levels is caused by external factors outside the influence of the MoD. The latter operates in relatively unpredictable environments, especially in war situations, and thus controlling all defence expenditures using fixed budgets would be less effective, if not meaningless. In order to make defence budgeting more effective, volatile elements of defence expenditures could be controlled using flexible budgeting, where budgets are changed as activity level varies; the rest could be managed using fixed budgets.

Indeed, the MoD uses a mix of fixed and flexible budgeting systems to manage its expenditures. These are prepared using RAB, which offers a better measure than the cash regime of the true cost of providing military capabilities, thereby assisting in better resource allocation amongst competing objectives. The RAB-based MoD budget comprises two separate pots of money – the Departmental Expenditure Limit (DEL) and Annually Managed Expenditure (AME). DEL expenditures are those that can be estimated over many years with a reasonable level of accuracy. These are budgeted for several years into the future with defined yearly limits. Examples of these include expenditures on salaries and utilities. In other words, DEL defence budgets are essentially fixed budgets, though they may be revised if needed. The expenditures that cannot be forecast with a reasonable amount of accuracy over the long-term are budgeted on an annual basis. AMEs are comprised of such expenditures, which include pension liabilities and provisions for nuclear decommissioning costs. AME defence budgets are basically flexible budgets set for volatile defence expenditures. Compared with DEL budgets, the AME ones are less stringently controlled. Given that the MoD's budget is largely comprised of DEL items,[48] it means that there is a greater exercise of budgetary discipline over the defence budget.

The previous cash regime failed to distinguish between current and capital defence expenditures, and it was also biased against capital defence expenses. However, under RAB, these two types of defence expenditures are distinguished, with separate budgets for each.[49] DEL budgets are divided into capital and current elements, Capital DEL and Resource DEL, respectively. Similarly, AME budgets are also divided into two elements, Capital AME and Resource AME. The MoD is prohibited from transferring unused money from the capital pot to cover current defence expenditures. One of the reasons for this inflexibility is to ensure that capital investments in the MoD are not compromised. But this budgetary discipline could be problematic for the MoD in the event of trying to balance its books, as happened in 2011/12.[50] In that year, the MoD had breached its current defence budget by about £1 billion while it had unused capital budget for that year.[51] This dilemma was resolved by allowing the MoD to transfer £800 million from the capital budget to the current budget.

The use of a mix of fixed and flexible approaches to defence budgets could in some way enable the MoD to deliver its objectives using a limited amount of money in relatively peaceful times. A cursory glance at the MoD's annual accounts for the past several years reveals that its actual yearly expenditures have always ended up being within budgeted figures by substantial amounts. However, in less peaceful times, due to the uncertainty of possible hostilities, the MoD could breach its budgetary limits. This was the case in 2006/07 when there was an unexpected surge in the number of missiles fired in an operation very close to the MoD's financial year-end.[52] During war, when the MoD's operational environment is unpredictable, the effectiveness of defence budgeting in ensuring value for money becomes questionable.

3.8 Value for Money: The Act of Squeezing Every Penny

When an entity spends money on behalf of others, it is natural to expect the latter to demand that the money is put to good use, i.e. that value for money (VfM) is achieved. After World War II, the public sector's footprint began to expand as it took over the provision of public services from the private sector on the basis that nationalisation would be 'better' for the public.[53] Government spending rose steadily from the 1950s and peaked at 50 per cent of GDP in the late 1970s.[54] This means that almost half of the United Kingdom's output was produced by the public sector. The growing size of the public sector prompted concerns about the way government spends taxpayers' money. Since that time, VfM has become an important metric for assessing government's performance in delivering public services.[55] Today, VfM judgements are ubiquitous in the public sector. In fact, the NAO carries out about sixty VfM studies every year in an attempt to bring about lasting improvement in public services.[56] The MoD spells out that it needs to provide the armed forces with the best capabilities to protect UK security, and underscores that in doing so it seeks the best possible value for taxpayers.[57]

The government defines VfM as not paying more for a good or service than appears to be justified by its quality and availability,[58] but it is an inexact science. To reduce shades of subjectivity and thus come up with a better understanding of VfM, the Royal Institute of Public Administration, Peat, Marwick, Mitchell & Co jointly sponsored a seminar in the early development of the concept that was entitled 'Value for Money Audit', and a definition for VfM (that still holds currency) was unanimously agreed.[59] VfM was defined as a combination of three Es – economy, efficiency and effectiveness.[60] 'Economy' is about the cost of the provision of a good or service. It may be defined as producing or securing outputs using the least amount of money, and is sometimes the easiest to measure; hence it is no surprise that most VfM exercises carried out in the past focused narrowly on only reducing expenditures.[61] If economy were the only consideration, then the MoD's cheapest option would offer the best VfM.

The second dimension of VfM is 'efficiency'. This is usually defined as achieving the maximum output using the least amount of resources. It is described as 'doing things right'.[62] Using this traditional definition of 'efficiency' to measure VfM in regard to, say, the production of military tanks, means choosing the 'best' option that utilises the minimum amount of paid staff time or raw materials (i.e. the metal, rubber, paint and other materials used). But all that this traditional definition of 'efficiency' does is replicate the cost of resources (already measured in money terms using the 'economy' dimension) according to various options on a non-financial basis, i.e. measuring them, for instance, in terms of the number of staff hours, kilograms of metals and litres of paint used. This means that when measuring VfM, the traditional definition of 'efficiency' causes the resources used in the various options to be measured twice, once in money terms and again in nonmonetary terms. This double-counting provides no additional benefit in the measurement of VfM.

Instead, it would make more sense when measuring VfM to define the 'efficiency' dimension as one that measures input resources that cannot be measured in money terms, and hence are not picked up by the 'economy' dimension. In the defence world, the 'efficiency' dimension would measure the nonmonetary costs of various options under evaluation, such as changes in the morale of staff, the relationship between personnel in the MoD and defence industry and public perception of defence projects. There is an input and output side to every operation/contract. The 'economy' and 'efficiency' dimensions of VfM measure the inputs of defence operations/contracts, while 'effectiveness' measures the outputs. 'Effectiveness' is an ends-oriented concept that measures the extent to which predetermined objectives of an operation/contract are achieved. It is about achieving the right results (outputs) from the resources input. It goes without saying that in order to measure the 'effectiveness' of an output, it is necessary to establish beforehand the characteristics of the desired outcomes. In the case of a contract for, say, fighter planes, these characteristics could be expressed in terms of the number of planes required, and then their flying ranges, ammunition loads, uptime and other capabilities.

Any factors that change the 'economy' (monetary costs), 'efficiency' (nonmonetary costs) and or 'effectiveness' (objectives) of an option could change its VfM. These factors are called value for money drivers – see Figure 3.2. One driver of VfM that affects the 'economy' of options is the

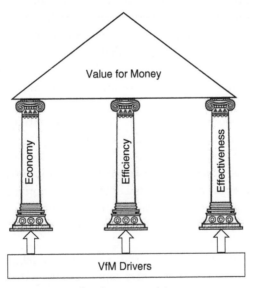

Figure 3.2: Value for money drivers
Source: author

level of price-led competition in the defence industry.[63] When there are several groups truly competing against one another for defence contracts, then market forces help to reduce waste and drive down costs. The practice of upward revisions of bids by the preferred bidder, possibly neutralising the cost advantages that competition yields, should thus be discouraged so that VfM is not compromised. Another important driver of 'economy' is risk transfer from the MoD to the defence industry or the wider private sector. Risks that are shifted to defence contractors carry a price tag; private sector companies factor such risks into the price of their contracts. Usually, the greater the amount of risk transferred, the greater the defence contract cost. Hence, striking the right balance in risk transfer is essential in achieving better MoD VfM. Similarly, technological innovation applied to reduce environmental damage caused by military equipment is an example of an 'efficiency' VfM driver. This same driver could double up as an 'effectiveness' driver if it results in more durable and capable military equipment. The secret to increasing VfM in defence requires identifying and implementing value for money drivers that boost the three Es, either individually or jointly.

In practice, when comparing the overall VfM of one option against another, it may be difficult to conclude which option offers the best value for money when the 'economy', 'efficiency' and 'effectiveness' of each of the various options are not mutually exclusive. In choosing the best option, judgement would have to be made about which, and to what extent, each of the three Es could be compromised to boost overall VfM. For instance, could a 10 per cent reduction in 'effectiveness' for a 15 per cent increase in 'economy' but no change in 'efficiency' be the option to achieve the best value for taxpayer money? This difficulty could be solved using a scoring and weighting method for each of the three Es. Working out the total weighted score for the various options would allow ranking, and hence offer a more objective way of measuring value for money.

3.9 Conclusion

One of the key 'takeaways' from this chapter is that RAB, accruals-based accounting, is better than the older, cash-based system for measuring MoD's costs, though the former is more problematical to understand. The largest source of MoD funding comes from taxes and loans over which it has no direct control. Income from work that the MoD does and controls, accounts for a much smaller source of finance.

Historically, defence PFIs have been another important source of financing for defence projects. Yet, given the recent change in PF2 policy, this source of funding for new defence projects is unavailable, at least in the near future. As discussed at the close of section 3.4, though, they may return in one form or another, primarily because acquisition of military equipment will remain pricey. Nevertheless, defence PFIs, some of which have many more years to run, continue to offer several advantages to the MoD, in spite of being expensive and inflexible. The MoD uses a mix of fixed and flexible budgets wherein it incorporates financial risk management strategies to exercise financial control over its operations. Results shows that over the past several years, it has successfully contained defence expenditures within budgetary limits, but transferring unspent budgets into future years has not always been smooth. In the final analysis, it is important that the MoD achieves VfM as measured using the three Es. It should be emphasised that objectively measuring VfM is impossible, and some degree of subjectivity will inevitably be required.

Notes

1. C. Clark, M. Elsby and S. Love. *Twenty-Five Years of Falling Investment? Trends in Capital Spending on Public Services.* The Institute of Fiscal Studies. Briefing Note number: 20. 2001. www.ifs.org.uk/bns/bn20.pdf (accessed 5 October 2017).
2. N. Tian, A. Fleurant, P. D. Wezeman and S. T. Wezeman. *Trends in World Military* Expenditure, 2016. SIPRI. www.sipri.org/sites/default/files/Trends-world-military-expenditure-2016.pdf (accessed 7 June 2017).
3. Ministry of Defence. *Consolidated Departmental Resource Accounts 2000–01.* The Stationery Office. Report number: HC 443, 2001.
4. Ministry of Defence. *Annual Report and Accounts 2016–17.* Controller of Her Majesty's Stationery Office. Report number: HC21, 2017.
5. Institute for Fiscal Studies. *Defence spending.* www.ifs.org.uk/tools_and_re sources/fiscal_facts/public_spending_survey/defence (accessed 18 January 2018).
6. N. Dempsey. *Briefing Paper: UK Defence Expenditure.* House of Commons Library. Report number: CBP 8175, 2017.
7. Dempsey. *Briefing Paper: UK Defence Expenditure.*
8. These figures have been calculated using budget statements for the period examined.
9. A measure of the indebtedness of governments.

10. HM Treasury. *Autumn Budget 2017*. Controller of Her Majesty's Stationery Office. Report number: HC 587. 2017. www.gov.uk/govern ment/uploads/system/uploads/attachment_data/file/661480/autumn_ budget_2017_web.pdf (accessed 18 January 2018).

11. This is based on figures from budget statements for the years 2001–17.

12. A. Morse. *Evaluating the Government Balance Sheet: Borrowing*. www .nao.org.uk/report/evaluating-the-government-balance-sheet-borrowing/ (accessed 18 January 2018).

13. M. Mackenzie. 'Bank of England Rate Rise: What It Means for Markets'. *Financial Times*. 2017. www.ft.com/content/fcc88c88-bfc2-11e7-9836-b 25f8adaa111 (accessed 18 January 2018).

14. T. Wallace. 'Expect "A Couple More Rate Rises" Says Bank of England Deputy Governor'. *The Telegraph*. 2017. www.telegraph.co.uk/busi ness/2017/11/03/expect-couple-rate-rises-says-bank-england-deputy-g overnor/ (accessed 18 January 2018).

15. L. Evans. 'Defence Review: See the List of Cuts in Full'. *The Guardian*. 2010. www.theguardian.com/news/datablog/2010/oct/19/defence-revi ew-cuts-list (accessed 18 January 2018).

16. MoD. *Annual Report and Accounts 2016–17*.

17. R. Evans and D. Leigh. 'Scant Return on Navy's £1.2bn Frigate Sale'. *The Guardian*. 2006. www.theguardian.com/uk/2006/jun/29/military .davidleigh (accessed 18 January 2018).

18. Based on MoD's annual accounts over the period 2010/11 to 2016/17.

19. T. Dixon, G. Pottinger and A. Jordan. 'Lessons from Private Finance Initiative in the UK: Benefits, Problems and Critical Success Factors'. *Journal of Property Investment and Finance*. 2005. 23(5): 412–23.

20. Ministry of Defence. *Annual Report and Accounts Volume Two 2008–09*. The Stationery Office. Report number: HC467-II. 2009.

21. MoD. *Annual Report and Accounts Volume Two 2008–09*.

22. Those that are off the MoD's books.

23. Put simply, according to the new accounting rule, the party that controls what the SPV must provide, for whom and at what price, and also controls any significant residual interest in the assets at the end of the PFI contract, is the party that should recognise the asset in its books.

24. MoD. *Annual Report and Accounts 2016–17*.

25. National Audit Office. *PFI and PF2*. 2018. www.nao.org.uk/wp-con tent/uploads/2018/01/PFI-and-PF2.pdf (accessed 30 January 2018).

26. It should be noted that in PFI contracts, the MoD will pay unitary charges to the SPV only when the services delivered meet the quality criteria specified by them.

27. Changes to defence PFIs have to be made through SPVs. The MoD could not independently contract a third party to implement the changes.

28. National Audit Office. *Making Changes in Operational PFI Projects.* The Stationary Office. Report number: HC 205. 2008.

29. NAO. *Making Changes in Operational PFI Projects.*

30. HM Treasury. *A New Approach to Public Private Partnerships.* 2012. www.gov.uk/government/uploads/system/uploads/attachment_data/fil e/205112/pf2_infrastructure_new_approach_to_public_private_parner ships_051212.pdf (accessed 23 January 2018).

31. The changes to PFIs will affect prospective contracts.

32. HM Treasury. *Budget 2018.* October 2018. https://assets.publishing.s ervice.gov.uk/government/uploads/system/uploads/attachment_data/fil e/752202/Budget_2018_red_web.pdf (accessed 15 February 2019).

33. Collingridge, J. *We can't live with PFI. Can we live without it?* January 2019. https://www.thetimes.co.uk/article/john-collingridge-we-cant-liv e-with-pfi-can-we-live-without-it-2dcnb7gxn (accessed 15 February 2019).

34. Planning is different from forecasting; the latter is about what is likely to happen, however, the former is about what should happen.

35. Ministry of Defence. *Defence Reform: An Independent Report into the Structure and Management of the Ministry of Defence.* The Stationery Office. 2011. 4. www.gov.uk/government/uploads/system/uploads/att achment_data/file/27408/defence_reform_report_struct_mgt_mod_27 june2011.pdf (accessed 22 January 2018).

36. National Audit Office. *Ministry of Defence, Defence Equipment and Support: Reforming Defence Acquisition.* Report number: HC 946. 2015. Available from: www.nao.org.uk/wp-content/uploads/2015/02/Re forming-defence-acquisition-summary.pdf (accessed 22 January 2018).

37. Analysis of savings using the MoD's annual accounts over the period 2007/08 to 2016/17.

38. National Audit Office. *A Short Guide to the Ministry of Defence.* 2017. Available from: www.nao.org.uk/wp-content/uploads/2017/09/A-shor t-guide-to-the-Ministry-of-Defence.pdf (accessed 22 January 2018).

39. NAO. *A short guide to the Ministry of Defence.*

40. XE. Xe Currency Charts: *GBP to USD.* 2018. www.xe.com/currency charts/?from=GBP&to=USD&view=1Y (accessed 23 January 2018).

41. A. Mostrous and D. Haynes. 'Britain Spends Billions on Flawed F-35s'. *The Times.* 17 July 2017. www.thetimes.co.uk/article/britain-spends-b illions-on-flawed-fighter-jets-qrtj95kvh (accessed 10 April 2018).

42. Ministry of Defence. *Annual Report and Accounts 2015–16.* The Stationery Office. Report number: HC 342. 2016.

43. MoD. *Annual Report and Accounts 2016–17.*

44. Ministry of Defence. *An Overview: Single Source Procurement Framework.* 2014. www.metasums.co.uk/uploads/asset_file/Overview

%20%20-%20single%20source%20procurementof%20Framework.
pdf (accessed 22 January 2018).
45. MoD. *An Overview: Single Source Procurement Framework.*
46. The BPR is annually set by the SSRO and since its introduction in 2014, it has been declining; in 2017/18 it was at 7.46 per cent. From: SSRO. *Guidance on the Baseline Profit Rate and Its Adjustment 2017/18.* 2017. www.gov.uk/government/uploads/system/uploads/attachment_data/file/599881/SSRO_Guidance_on_the_baseline_profit_rate_and_its_adjustment_2017–18.pdf (accessed 22 January 2018).
47. Differences between budgeted and actual amounts spent (or earned).
48. MoD. *Annual Report and Accounts 2016–17.*
49. National Audit Office. *Understanding Central Government Accounts.* www.nao.org.uk/wp-content/uploads/2014/04/Guide-to-understanding-departmental-accounts.pdf (accessed 23 January 2018).
50. Parliament. *Defence Committee – Ministry of Defence Supplementary Estimate 2011–12.* 2012. https://publications.parliament.uk/pa/cm2012 13/cmselect/cmdfence/99/99we02.htm (accessed 23 January 2018).
51. The MoD had not breached its total budget though.
52. Ministry of Defence. *Annual Report and Accounts 2006–07.* The Stationery Office. Report number: HC 697. 2007.
53. G. Lancaster and G. Brierly. 'A Comparative Study of the Emergence of Marketing Culture within Three Formerly Nationalised Companies'. *The International Journal of Public Sector Management.* 2001. 14(4): 341–71.
54. S. Rogers. 'Historic Government Spending by Area: Get the Data back to 1948'. *The Guardian.* 2010. www.theguardian.com/news/datablog/201 0/oct/18/historic-government-spending-area (accessed 23 January 2018).
55. Chartered Institute of Public Finance Administration. *Role and Objectives of Internal Audit in the Public Sector.* 1979.
56. National Audit Office. *Value for Money Programme.* www.nao.org.uk/about-us/our-work/value-for-money-programme/ (accessed 25 October 2016).
57. GOV.UK. *Procurement at MoD.* www.gov.uk/government/organisations/ministry-of-defence/about/procurement (accessed 25 October 2016).
58. R. Glendinning. 'The Concept of Value for Money'. *International Journal of Public Sector Management.* 1988. 1(1): 42–50.
59. Royal Institute of Public Administration. *Value for Money Audits: Proceedings of a One-Day Seminar Organised by Peat, Marwick, Mitchell & Co. in Association with the Royal Institute of Public Administration.* 1982.
60. RIPA. *Value for Money Audits.*

61. F. Akhlaghi. 'Ensuring Value for Money in FM Contract Services'. *Facilities*. 1996. 14(1/2): 26–33.
62. Akhlaghi. 'Ensuring Value for Money'.
63. HM Treasury Taskforce. *Value for Money Drivers in the Private Finance Initiative (A Report by Arthur Anderson and Enterprise LSE, Commissioned by the Treasury Taskforce)*. 2000.

PART II

Defence or Development?

4 | Military Expenditure and Growth

RON SMITH

Introduction

The vast literature on the relationship between military expenditure and the level and growth of output of a country includes qualitative case studies, historical analyses and quantitative statistical models. An early quantitative study by Benoit[1] found a positive association between the share of military expenditure in GDP, the military burden and growth. This result proved fragile, sensitive to specification and data. Subsequently, the literature has been inconclusive, some studies finding positive effects of military spending on growth, others finding negative effects. The thoughtful surveys by Ram,[2] Deger and Sen,[3] and Sandler and Hartley[4] remain very relevant. Dunne, Smith and Willenbockel[5] and Dunne and Tian[6] provide more recent surveys. Meta-analyses of this literature are provided by Alptekin and Levine[7] and also Yesilyurt and Yesilyurt.[8] Unlike other areas of economics, these meta-analyses do not reveal any publication bias, perhaps because unlike other parameters, such as price elasticity of demand, there are no strong theoretical priors for the sign or size of the effect of military expenditure on growth. This chapter will not attempt to provide another survey of this large literature, it will rather try to provide a more general framework to assess the issues and clarify the linkages.

The fact that the literature has not established a conclusive link between military expenditure and growth should not be unexpected. The effect of military expenditure on growth is likely to depend on the historical context. This will include, firstly, the institutional structure; that is, what type of government is spending the money? Is it democratic or autocratic? Secondly, why is the government spending the money? Is it to fight internal or external wars or supress dissidence by the military or others, or in response to a military industrial complex? Thirdly, where is the government spending the money? Will it be on troops at home or abroad, domestic arms production or imports? Finally, how is the government spending to be financed? Military spending is associated with a set of intervening variables in particular wars and security contexts that are associated with growth and development. But neither the relationship of military expenditure to those intervening variables nor the relationship of those variables to growth is close; many other factors intervene. As a result, the link between military expenditure and growth is not close, and the effect of military expenditure on growth is contingent on the historical context. To illustrate how context and focus matters, there is a separate literature on the peace dividend and conversion,[9] which addresses what, in formal terms, is a very similar question: what is the effect of reduced military spending on output? But the peace dividend literature approaches the question in a completely different way. It should also be noted that military expenditure is often quite a small share of output, the world average is now around 2 per cent of output, and one would not expect large effects from a small share. When military spending is a large share of output, such as during times of war, other factors are also influencing growth, including the methods used to finance military expenditure and the effect of war and financing on social structure and cohesion.

Surveying the effect of military expenditure on growth is made more difficult by the fact that there is no agreed theory of economic growth and development. Much of standard growth theory emphasises steady states, but real growth is far from steady; there are structural transformations as the agriculture, manufacturing and services sectors rise and fall; there are disruptive social and technological changes and abrupt transitions such as when Argentina, as rich as the United Kingdom in the nineteenth century, started getting poorer, or when economic reforms in China after 1979 changed its growth rate from 2 to 10 per cent.

Three types of explanation will be used to organise this chapter. At the most direct level of explanation, there are models, such as the standard neoclassical growth model, of steady state growth being determined through a production function by inputs of land, labour and capital (physical, human and social) given the available technology. Section 4.1 considers how military expenditure influences these inputs. Most of the quantitative literature has been within this framework, and Section 4.2 reviews the largely inconclusive, quantitative statistical evidence on the linkage between military expenditure and growth, and explains why one would not expect any clear result. Inputs and outputs are themselves products of deeper forces, and much historical growth is not characterised by steady states but by structural transformations. At the second level of explanation are the longer-term forces that act as proximate causes for changes in the level and composition of inputs and outputs. These include the structural changes associated with the differential growth and decline of major sectors; the geopolitical changes associated with the growth of new markets and producers; the demographic changes associated with transitions in fertility and longevity; and the historical patterns of war and conflict. These are discussed in Section 4.3. Finally there are the ultimate factors that determine growth, like the nature of social institutions within a country, including the provision of security and the structure of the state. In many respects, governance structures provide a better explanation of growth than production functions. The role of military expenditure in institutions and security is discussed in Section 4.4. Section 4.5 contains some discussion of policy issues and concluding comments. Given that most of the analysis in this chapter will be of the form 'on the one hand ... on the other hand', one should not expect any clear conclusion. This is very similar to the outcome of the survey by Ram:[10] 'There is very little evidence of an overall positive effect of defense outlays on growth in a typical case ... However, it is also difficult to say that the evidence supports the view that defense outlays have an overall negative effect on growth'.

4.1 Production Function

It is common to think of output being determined by the rate of utilisation, reflecting aggregate demand, times potential output, reflecting aggregate supply. A production function then specifies how potential output is determined by a set of inputs, the land (natural and environmental resources), labour, capital (physical, human and social) and the technology available. The amount of inputs provided is determined by incentives, which may reflect the historical conjunction and institutional structure of the society, as discussed in Section 4.4. Military expenditure is not a factor of production itself, but it may have externalities, which influence the amounts and productivity of the other inputs as well as providing security. At a social optimum, the government balances the marginal welfare benefits from the extra security provided by military expenditure against its opportunity cost: the welfare lost from resources being diverted from alternative uses. How well such behaviour describes actual government intent is a matter of dispute.

Output is usually measured by GDP. While there are major problems with the measurement of both GDP and military expenditure, we will not focus on the limitations of the data. However, it should be noted that GDP is not a measure of welfare, and one would need to take account of many other things besides GDP growth, including non-marketed activities, such as domestic labour and environmental effects, to make a welfare judgement. Jones and Klenow[11] propose a measure of welfare that combines consumption, leisure – as reflected in hours worked, mortality – as reflected in life expectancy and inequality within a coherent utility framework. One important implication of using such a measure rather than GDP is that GDP includes military expenditure while consumption does not. This can make a very large difference, since increases in military expenditure in themselves raise GDP, given that it is a component of GDP. For World War II, when over half of GDP in the United States and United Kingdom was military, it makes a lot of difference whether one is looking at the effect on GDP or civilian consumption. Other consequences of using a Jones-Klenow type of welfare measure in judging the effect of military expenditure on development is that one may need to take account of the influence of war on life expectancy, conscription on leisure and militarism on inequality.

Treating GDP as the rate of utilisation times potential output allows one to examine how military expenditure may influence the rate of utilisation; for instance, through the Keynesian demand multiplier effects of expansions in military expenditure. The rearmament for World War II in the United States reduced the high unemployment rate that followed the Great Depression of the 1930s; whereas in Germany it was infrastructure investments like building the autobahn, rather than rearmament, that ended the depression. However, it is not clear that there is any systematic pattern. Dunne and Smith[12] found that neither long time-series for the United States and the United Kingdom nor shorter time-series for eleven OECD countries suggest that military expenditure is a significant influence on the unemployment rate. The subsequent evidence for the 1990s confirmed that conclusion. The substantial cuts associated with the peace dividend following the end of the Cold War were associated with a fall in unemployment and with higher rates of growth and investment as reduced military spending allowed lower deficits and lower interest rates. But although this is an example of falling military expenditure and falling unemployment, there is no systematic pattern. The post-Cold War peace dividend raises the issue of financing, and how other elements of the government budget constraint adjust when military expenditure changes. Some have suggested that the US government has followed a policy of military Keynesianism, adjusting military expenditure to maintain full employment. But the evidence for such a policy is limited, as both the post-Cold War episode and the study by Pieroni et al.[13] illustrate.

Land and natural resources are usually excluded from neoclassical production functions, though the empirical literature that models gross output rather than value added often uses KLEM (capital, labour, energy and materials) production functions. For instance, the expansion of the frontier in North America was associated with military force, as has been access to raw materials, such as oil. While military force plays a role in the acquisition of natural resources, the direct contribution of natural resources to growth is less clear as the large literature on the 'resource curse' or 'Dutch disease' illustrates.

The labour force available for civilian production is reduced by service in the armed forces or working for the Ministry of Defence. While service in the military diverts part of the labour force from productive non-military activity, there may be offsetting effects; for instance, in the way that women were drawn into the labour force during the Second World War in the United States and United Kingdom. During their service in the military, workers may acquire useful skills that increase their human capital and productivity when they return to civilian life, though alternatively they may have been diverted from more useful study or training. The extent to which conscription builds citizenship and social capital is disputed. Asch et al.[14] have undertaken a recent survey of military manpower issues.

The most common link between military expenditure and physical capital is through investment. Smith (1980) discovered that a cross-country pattern of high military expenditure as a share of GDP is associated with a lower share of investment in GDP. This was interpreted in terms of a fairly stable share of public and private consumption in GDP, which meant that savings could be used to finance either military expenditure or investment. This negative relationship subsequently disappeared. This may be because of globalisation; the sample used in Smith[15] for fourteen large OECD countries covered 1954–73, a period of fixed exchange rates and balance of payments constraints. This ensured that domestic savings broadly equalled domestic investment. With the end of the Bretton Woods system and the introduction of flexible exchange rates and greater international capital flows, the balance of payments constraint was removed, domestic savings no longer needed to equal domestic investment, removing the negative association between investment and military expenditure shares. The effect of war on capital destruction is analysed in Auray et al.,[16] who show that the welfare losses from major wars are large.

The military is tightly coupled with the wider economy and undertakes considerable research and development (R&D). Thus, it is not surprising that technology enjoys both spin-off from the military to wider society and spin-in from commercial to military technology. Given the amount that the military spends on R&D and defence procurement of high-technology equipment, it is not surprising that many innovative technologies have military origins. Indeed, some observers have even asked whether war is necessary for economic growth, because war is a spur to technological innovation. On the other hand, it is not obvious that the technological payoff would have been any less had the same amount been spent on civilian R&D. Of course, some would argue that without the pressure of war the money would not have been spent on R&D. There are also cases where military secrecy has delayed the diffusion of important technologies.

Apart from utilisation, the focus on inputs is supply-side oriented. A demand-side stimulus could come from arms exports. Foreign aid may remove constraints on growth, e.g. of imported components for economies constrained by balance of payments. Again there are certainly examples where this has happened; however, there is little indication that it is a systematic influence. Yet, international war does have a major negative effect on trade, and this may have implications for growth.

An important route through which military expenditure can influence inputs into the production function is through the method by which it is financed. Military expenditure will have different effects depending on the source of finance. If it is financed from taxation, this may have distortionary incentive effects or cause political protests. If it is financed from money creation, this may cause inflation. If it is financed through debt issuance, this may cause crowding-out by raising long-term interest rates and depressing investment. If it is financed through cuts in other elements of government expenditure, this may involve hard choices about priorities and lead to cuts in infrastructure spending necessary for growth. If it is financed through running down foreign assets, as Britain did in both World Wars, it will damage future prosperity. The effects of any particular method of financing will depend on the associated monetary policy and the efficiency of the tax collection and public expenditure control and budgeting systems.

Gemmell et al.[17] show that the assumed method of financing is crucial for the effect of different components of public expenditure on economic growth. They found that defence had a small negative but insignificant effect on growth. In their estimates, a switch into defence involves pro rata reductions in other spending. They find positive effects on growth from spending on transport and communications and from education, which is consistent with other research. Rockoff[18] shows how the United States could fund minor wars from borrowing and taxes, but major wars used money financed with consequent inflation that had effects on growth.

Financing can be thought of either in terms of the government budget constraint, as above, or in terms of real resources that need to be diverted from consumption, investment, other government demand for goods and services, exports and imports. This diversion may be done through the fiscal system or through direct coercion. An important form of taxation, which does not show up in the military expenditure numbers, is conscription: a tax on those called up, usually young men.

4.2 Empirical Studies

While some of the empirical literature seems to suggest that there is a number that can capture the effect of military expenditure on growth, this seems unlikely given that the effect is dependent on so many contextual factors. This section considers factors in the statistical analysis that influence the measurement of the effect: specification, estimation method, type of data and sample. The choice of specification of the model that relates military expenditure to growth is central. This choice will determine the functional form, the measures of military expenditure used (share, growth rate, level and logarithm), the controls included in the growth equation and, in multivariate systems, the intermediate linkages between military expenditure and growth.

The choice of specification is made more difficult because there is no agreed theory of growth. A popular choice in the military expenditure and growth literature, though not in the wider literature on the determinants of growth, is the two-sector Feder-Ram model.[19] This allows for an unspecified externality of military expenditure on the economy and a productivity differential between the military and non-military sectors of the economy. The basic estimating equation makes the growth rate of output depend on the share of investment and the product of the share of military expenditure and the growth rate of military expenditure, though there are various extensions. Dunne, Smith and Willenbockel[20] criticise the Feder-Ram model, and it seems less widely used now.

The specification may be based on a full theoretical model or it may rest on a relatively atheoretical statistical procedure, such as those using vector autoregressions or Granger causality tests. If the estimating equation is derived from a full theoretical model, it may be easier to interpret the parameters, and one may have expectations about the appropriate signs. With time-series, the issues raised by unit roots and co-integration may be investigated. Models have typically been linear, making the growth rate a function of the share of military expenditure in GDP, but various non-linearities have been explored, particularly within the Feder-Ram framework. For instance, there may be little effect when the share of military expenditure is low but negative effects when it is high, or the effect may be different in low-income and high-income countries. Results seem sensitive to whether the data relate to OECD countries or developing countries and to which time periods have been used. For instance, Dunne and Tian[21] find that studies using post-Cold War data are more likely to have a negative effect.

Results have also been sensitive to whether time-series, cross-section or panel data have been used. If panel data is used, it makes a difference whether annual data or five- or ten-year averages are used. Using averages loses quite a large amount of information, and while it is designed to allow for cyclical effects, such effects could also be modelled explicitly through the use of dynamics. Heterogeneity is also an issue in both cross-section and panel studies. In panel studies with a large number of time-series observations one can model the hetero-geneity, dynamics and cross-section dependence in ways that are diffi-cult to do with either pure time-series or pure cross-section data. Studies differ in the extent to which there are diagnostic tests for misspecification of the estimated equations and to the extent to which robust standard errors are used if serial correlation or heteroscedasti-city is found.

The results have been sensitive to the treatment of simultaneity. This is a particular issue because of the difficult identification problem that arises from the fact that there is a two-way interaction: output influ-ences demand for military expenditure, while military expenditure influences aggregate demand and supply. Military expenditure is a component of GDP, so increases in military expenditure increase GDP directly as well as potentially influencing GDP through supply-side effects of the type discussed above. At the same time, military expenditure responds to GDP, as the large literature on the demand for military expenditure indicates. The fact that military expenditure tends to increase in line with GDP is what makes the share of military expenditure in GDP such a common measure.

To illustrate the consequence of this two-way interaction, suppose that we have a simultaneous system between the share of military expenditure in output and the growth rate, where all the other deter-minants have been partialed out. Suppose fast-growing countries spend a higher share on the military $\beta_g < 0, \beta_m > 0, \beta_m > 0$, and the higher share depresses growth $\beta_g < 0$ and denotes the variances $E(\varepsilon_g^2) = \sigma_{gg}; E(\varepsilon_g\varepsilon_m) = \sigma_{gm}$. The reduced form is:

$$m = [1 - \beta_g\beta_m]^{-1} (\beta_m\varepsilon_g + \varepsilon_m)$$
$$g = [1 - \beta_g\beta_m]^{-1} (\beta_g\varepsilon_m + \varepsilon_g)$$

Note that $\sigma_{mm} > 0$ and $[1 - \beta_g\beta_m] > 0$ so the sign of the regression coefficient of g on m, σ_{gm}/σ_{mm}, depends on

$$E(\beta_m\varepsilon_g + \varepsilon_m)(\beta_g\varepsilon_m + \varepsilon_g) = \beta_m\sigma_{gg} + \beta_g\sigma_{mm} + [1 + \beta_g\beta_m]\sigma_{gm}$$

Assuming that supply and demand shocks are independent, as is often done, $\sigma_{gm} = 0$ then with $\beta_g\langle 0, \beta_m\rangle 0$, the sign of the military expenditure coefficient in a regression of growth on military expendi-ture, will be positive if the effect of growth on the share is greater than the effect of the share on growth. Thus, on these assumptions, a positive coefficient in a regression of growth on military expenditure is not evidence of a supply-side externality.

In principle, the two effects, demand and supply, could be separately identified if there were good measures of the exogenous strategic factors, such as threats and alliances, that influence military expenditure but not GDP, and good measures of exogenous economic factors that shift GDP growth but not military expenditure. Such identifying instruments are hard to find. In particular, there is little agreement on how to model strategic threats despite considerable efforts, particularly in the demand for military expenditure literature, which have used variables like war, the military expenditures of allies and enemies, changes in strategic doctrine by NATO, such as from mutual assured destruction to flexible response and the end of the Cold War. Exogenous growth shifters are even more difficult to find. Those in the institutional growth theory literature tend to be historical, like legal systems and colonial mortality, which are of little help in the military expenditure growth literature.

As a result of the shifting economic and strategic factors one finds all four combinations of high or low shares of military expenditure with high or low growth rates. Countries with factors promoting growth potential but facing strategic threats, like South Korea and Taiwan in the 1970s and 1980s, grew rapidly despite a high share of military spending. Countries where a high share of military spending displaced investment, but where there were other factors inhibiting growth, like the Soviet Union, showed low growth and a high share of military expenditure. Countries like post-World War II Japan and Germany, where there were factors favourable to growth, and where restrictions on military expenditure meant that the resources could be devoted to investment, showed low share of military expenditure and high growth. For most of sub-Saharan Africa, shares of military expenditure are low, wars are fought with cheap conscripts and small arms, but growth is also low.

4.3 Transformations

The standard one-sector, steady state, two-input model of economic growth does not capture the qualitative transformations that are characteristic of growth. As an economy grows and develops there is a demographic transition as longevity (life expectancy) increases, and fertility (the birth rate) declines. This has consequences for the age structure of the population with implications for savings, investment and innovation, which feedback into growth.[22] Demographic structure is linked to war in that young men have typically made up the bulk of the fighting forces. Growth and development are also associated with a changing sectoral balance, as the share of primary employment in agriculture and extractive industries falls; the secondary share in manufacturing increases, then declines with deindustrialisation; and the tertiary share in services, including financial services, increases. This sectoral transformation interacts with trade, since raw materials and manufactured products are more easily traded than services. It interacts with growth, since the decline of agriculture is associated with rapidly growing productivity, from a very low base, as output tends to grow despite falling employment as people leave the land. Military expenditure does not directly influence these transformations, though war may. War sucked people off the land, and military arsenals were important examples of large-scale industrial plants.

The steady state approach also ignores declines in output, and Broadberry and Wallis[23] argue that improved long-run economic performance has occurred primarily through a decline in the rate and frequency of economic 'shrinking', episodes of negative economic growth, rather than through an increase in the rate of growth. The writers identify the main proximate factors influencing shrinking as structural change, technological change, demographic change and the incidence of warfare, but as discussed below they regard institutional change as the key ultimate factor behind the reduction in shrinking.

In another non-steady state interpretation, Kennedy[24] argues that the interaction of wealth and power is contradictory. Wealth creates power, but because economic growth enables a country to incur strategic commitments, power also destroys wealth. This is caused by the military expenditures associated with those strategic commitments undermining the economic base through imperial overstretch. While Kennedy's historical narrative may have been persuasive, his forecasting was not: he emphasised that the United States was suffering from imperial overstretch, with its economy no longer sufficient to support its strategic commitments. Yet, it was the Soviet Union, not the United States, which collapsed after the former suffered severe imperial overstretch. This was partly as a consequence of the high military expenditure, 20 per cent of output on some estimates, which undermined the Soviet Union's economy. However, this forecast failure should not detract from the force of Kennedy's central argument about the contradictory interaction of wealth and power.

4.4 Institutions, Security and Growth

Consideration of the fundamental political economy of the relationship between military expenditure and growth dates back to, at least, Adam Smith.[25] Chapters 1–3 of Book 1 of *The Wealth of Nations* argue that labour productivity resulted from the division of labour and that the division of labour was limited by the extent of the market. Growth then came from the extension of the market, through national and international trade. But trade required some security of person and property. Chapter 1 of Book V begins: 'The first duty of the sovereign, that of protecting the society from the violence and invasion of other independent societies, can be performed only by means of a military force'. It also noted the duty 'to maintain justice: to prevent the members of society from encroaching on one another's property, or seizing what is not their own'. The victims of theft lose not only their property but the incentive to produce anything that can be stolen. Thus, without security the incentive to produce or trade is removed.

Security of person and property is a precondition for production and trade, and security ultimately rests on force of some kind, and this force must be financed through spending on police and military. However, there may be little relationship between the level of military expenditure and the level of security, and rampaging armies may be the source of insecurity. The relationship between military expenditure and security depends on the nature of the threat and the efficiency with which the security services operate. In discussing the British Navigation Acts, which restricted trade, in Book IV chapter 2 Smith notes the trade-off between defence and opulence, arguing that defence is of much more importance than opulence. He ends *The Wealth of Nations* with a discussion of the danger of economic ruin posed by public debt incurred on military expenditure to defend the empire.

Broadberry and Wallis[26] also build on Adam Smith's view that growth depends on the division of labour and the extent of the market. The authors focus on the nature of the rules that are established to allow the extent of the market to grow, and in particular the transition from a system of identity rules to a system of impersonal rules.

As Smith recognised, the use of force is a major factor in allowing trade to proceed. Findlay and O'Rourke[27] of *Power and Plenty: Trade, War and the World Economy in the Second Millennium* comment:

For much of our period the pattern of trade can only be understood as being the outcome of some military or political equilibrium between contending powers. The dependence of trade on war and peace eventually became so obvious to us that it is reflected in the title of this volume.

This close connection is captured in the famous phrase from Charles Tilly,[28] 'war made the state and states made war'. But the state that war made could be either a predatory, rent-seeking, extractive institution or one that invested in building good institutions, protecting people and property, enforcing contracts and providing public goods.

In Europe, the multitude of competing states, including city-states ruled by merchants with a direct interest in prosperity, allowed innovators to move from more restrictive to more open polities, promoting productivity and trade. Countries that lost tradesmen also lost the capacity to produce the weapons of war that ensured their survival. The presence of competing polities also acted as a constraint on the state. The ability of traders to move increased the incentives for good government. In more monolithic cultures, like China, the ability to resist innovations that threatened the established order was much greater. Even a predatory state may invest in better institutions, as long as it did not discount the future too much. In such circumstances it is what Olson[29] calls a stationary bandit, which has an encompassing interest in the society: the process of investing now, and stealing less today, will encourage productivity growth, meaning more to steal tomorrow. Of course, many predatory states were and are roving bandits, which do discount the future highly, stealing as much as they can now for fear of being displaced. The military has a central role in this process, both being the means by which a predatory state maintains power and the main threat to that power; the military being the institution that is usually the most capable of displacing the current ruler. Rulers adopt various 'coup-proofing' strategies to try and prevent themselves from being displaced; these may include higher military spending to buy off the potential plotters.

Predatory states maintain power not only by the coercive use of military force but the ideological use of militarism. The trappings of nationalism, particularly the appeal to unite against a common enemy, could provide an ideological support to legitimise a predatory state.

In the process of state building, some countries saw service in the military as a way of modernisation. Not only would soldiers be turned into citizens with an attachment to the nation, but they would also be taught the national language, how to read and how to use technologies, such as learning how to drive. Again, there are other ways of educating citizens.

An important set of institutions are the fiscal and financial systems, which were intrinsically linked to war in many countries. Ferguson[30] argues that in the eighteenth and early nineteenth century, Britain's ability to tax, given government legitimacy, and borrow, given the role of the Bank of England, established in 1694, and also the national debt, gave the government not only a decisive military advantage over France, but raised the growth rate. The elements are linked: a country with an efficient tax system can borrow more easily because it has the means to repay in the future, and the borrowing can finance both military expenditure and subsidies to allies, giving it a greater probability of defeating the enemy. The enemy not only lost the war and its colonies, like Canada in the French case, but also it could not pay its debts, and default made it more difficult to borrow in future. More generally, war has implications for output, possibly positive for winners and negative for losers, though the cost of war can impose a penalty on both.

War, particularly losing a war, is a major source of institutional change breaking up pre-war power structures and destroying the power of special interest networks or elites that inhibit innovation.[31] The effect of World War II on Japan was to shift per capita income growth from 2 per cent over 1870–1939 to 7.7 per cent across 1948–73. US aid and the boost from the Korean War contributed to the rapid growth of the latter period, but transformation of the social and economic structure was central. One does not need war to make the transformation; the reforms in China around 1979 transformed its growth rate from 2 to 10 per cent. High rates of growth, such as those achieved by post-war Japan and post-reform China, following institutional reforms, depend on catch-up transfers of technology from richer countries that cannot be maintained indefinitely as they themselves get rich.

4.5 Concluding Comments

Military expenditures are determined by governments in the light of available resources and perceived threats, often as mediated by political pressures and interest groups such as the military-industrial complex. This spending is financed in a variety of different ways, with different economic effects. The money will be used to acquire forces, through the purchase of manpower and weapons, and the extent of the forces acquired will depend on the wages paid and the efficiency of the arms industry. The military capability those forces provide will depend on training, leadership, morale and logistics. This military capability will be used in an attempt to provide security to the state against domestic or foreign opposition. This may involve fighting wars with unforeseen economic and political consequences. War and the extent to which military expenditure provides security will also have impacts on the process of secular transformation, the success or failure of the dominant elite and institutions and the process of growth and development. The contingent nature of these linkages between military expenditure and the economy makes it clear why there is no simple relationship.

The economic policy issues raised by the military expenditure growth relationship concern those linkages: financing military expenditure – especially during war, post-war conversion of military to civilian activities, arms export control and industrial policy. However, partly because of the contingent nature of the relationships, there seems little indication that military expenditures can be manipulated to influence the rate of growth itself. If one wishes to influence growth, there are much more effective ways to do it than through the use of military expenditure, such as education, institutional reform and investment in infrastructure. These issues are likely to come to the fore in the near future. The end of the Cold War saw a period where there was a tendency for military expenditure to fall in many countries. With increased tension in many regions there is now a tendency for military expenditure to rise. The effects of military expenditure on growth are then likely to be a source of renewed controversy.

Notes

1. E. Benoit. *Defence and Economic Growth in Developing Countries.* Boston: D.C. Heath, 1973.
2. R. Ram. 'Defense Expenditure and Economic Growth'. In K. Hartley and T. Sandler (eds). *Handbook of Defense Economics*, vol. 1. Amsterdam: Elsevier. 1995. 251–74.

3. S. Deger and S. Sen. 'Military Expenditure and Developing Countries'. In K. Hartley and T. Sandler (eds). *Handbook of Defense Economics*, vol. 1. 275–307.

4. T. Sandler and K. Hartley. *The Economics of Defence*. Cambridge: Cambridge University Press. 1995.

5. J. P. Dunne, R. Smith and D. Willenbockel. 'Models of Military Expenditure and Growth: A Critical Review'. *Defence and Peace Economics*. 2005. 16(6): 449–61.

6. J. P. Dunne and N. Tian. 'Military Expenditure and Economic Growth: A Survey'. *Economics of Peace and Security Journal*. 2013. 8(1): 5–11; J. P. Dunne and N. Tian. 'Military Expenditure and Economic Growth 1960–2014'. *Economics of Peace and Security Journal*. 2016. 11(2): 50–56.

7. A. Alptekin and P. Levine. 'Military Expenditure and Economic Growth: A Meta-Analysis'. *European Journal of Political Economy*. 2012. 28(4): 636–50.

8. M. E. Yesilyurt and F. Yesilyurt. 'Introducing Literaturematic.com: Survey of Defence Economics'. *Defence and Peace Economics*. 2014. 25(3): 329–30; M. E. Yesilyurt and F. Yesilyurt. 'Meta-Analysis, Military Expenditures and Growth'. Working paper. Pamukkale University, Turkey.

9. M. Broska. 'Success and Failure in Defence Conversion in the "Long Decade of Disarmament"'. In K. Hartley and T. Sandler (eds). *Handbook*.

10. Ram. 'Defense Expenditure and Economic Growth'. In K. Hartley and T. Sandler (eds). *Handbook*.

11. C. I. Jones and P. J. Klenow. 'Beyond GDP? Welfare across Countries and Time'. *American Economic Review*. 2016. 106(9): 2426–57.

12. P. Dunne and R. Smith. 'Military Expenditure and Unemployment in the OECD'. *Defence and Peace Economics*. 1990. 1(1): 57–73.

13. L. Pieroni, G. d'Agostino and M. Lorusso. 'Can We Declare Military Keynesianism Dead?' *Journal of Policy Modelling*. 2008. 30(5): 675–91.

14. B. Asch, J.R. Hosek and J. T. Warner. 'New Economics of Manpower in the Post-Cold War Era in Disarmament'. In K. Hartley and T. Sandler (eds). *Handbook of Defense Economics*, vol. 2. Amsterdam: Elsevier. 2007. 1075–138.

15. R. P. Smith. 'Military Expenditure and Investment in OECD Countries'. *Journal of Comparative Economics*. 1980. 4(1): 19–32.

16. S. Auray, A. Eyquem and F. Jouneau-Sion. 'Wars and Capital Destruction'. *Journal of Economic Dynamics and Control*. 2014. 41 (April): 224–40.

17. N. Gemmell, R. Kneller and I. Sanz. 'Does the Composition of Government Expenditure Matter for Long-Run GDP Levels?' *Oxford Bulletin of Economics and Statistics*. 2016. 78(4): 522–47.
18. H. Rockoff. 'War and Inflation in the United States from the Revolution to the Persian Gulf War'. In J. Eloranta, E. Golson, A. Markevich and N. Wolf (eds). *Economic History of Warfare and State Formation. Studies in Economic History*. Singapore: Springer. 2016.
19. Ram. 'Defense Expenditure and Economic Growth'. In Hartley and T. Sandler (eds). *Handbook of Defense Economics*.
20. Dunne, Smith and Willenbockel. 'Models of Military Expenditure and Growth'.
21. Dunne and Tian. 'Military Expenditure and Economic Growth'.
22. Y. Aksoy, H. S. Basso and R. P. Smith. 'Demographic Structure and Macroeconomic Trends'. *American Economic Journal*. 2018 (forthcoming).
23. S. Broadberry and J. J. Wallis. 'Growing, Shrinking, and Long Run Economic Performance: Historical Perspectives on Economic Development'. The National Bureau of Economic Research. NBER working paper number: 23343, 2017.
24. P. Kennedy. *The Rise and Fall of the Great Powers*. Random House. 1987.
25. A. Smith. *An Enquiry into the Nature and Causes of the Wealth of Nations*. 1776.
26. Broadberry and Wallis. 'Growing, Shrinking, and Long Run Economic Performance'.
27. R. Findlay and K. H. O'Rourke. *Power and Plenty: Trade, War and the World Economy in the Second Millennium*. New Jersey: Princeton University Press. 2009. xix.
28. C. Tilly. *The Formation of National States in Western Europe*. Princeton: Princeton University Press. 1975.
29. M. Olson. 'Dictatorship, Democracy and Development'. *American Political Science Review*. 1993. 87(3): 567–76.
30. N. Ferguson. The Cash Nexus: Money and Power in the Modern World 1700–2000. Basic Books. 2001.
31. Olson. 'Dictatorship, Democracy and Development'.

5 | Towards Demilitarisation? The Military Expenditure-Development Nexus Revisited

JURGEN BRAUER, J. PAUL DUNNE AND NAN
TIAN

Introduction

For the developing economies of the world, especially, gauging the impact of military spending on the economy and society is an important issue. While most countries need (or feel they need) to have some level of armed forces to deal with threats, the resources employed do have opportunity costs. Resources steered towards the military sector can prevent monies being used for purposes that might improve the pace of economic and human development. They might also lead to (violent) conflict rather than prevent it and reflect the interests of particular interest groups rather than of the country as a whole.

Based on rather diverse theoretical approaches, an impressive body of empirical research has examined the economic effects of military spending, generally finding that it is likely to have a negative impact on the economy,[1] but a range of issues remain. Some can be dealt with and others have to be borne in mind when considering the results of any studies. The first concern is what is being measured, and how. When governments undertake military spending, they provide wages and salaries and cover other expenses for the armed forces and they procure arms for them. Unfortunately, the only reasonably reliable, or at least consistently measured, data that are available is on military spending itself, and so in reviewing the literature one has to recognise and accept that the value of arms transfers is an important component of military spending, but not separately measured. (The Stockholm International Peace Research Institute, SIPRI, maintains a database on imputed arms transfer values but actual transfer values are largely unknown.) In developing countries, especially, it is very likely that arms will be imported, particularly any advanced weapon systems, and hence will become a drain on precious foreign exchange reserves. Once arms transfers are taken into account, the opportunity cost of military spending thus is likely to be higher than simply the expenditure.

With the end of the Cold War era, considerable reductions in military expenditures occurred, although not consistently across all regions (China, India and Saudi Arabia in particular have seen large absolute increases). Globally, while in recent years the declining trend has begun to bottom out, global military spending still is lower in per capita terms, per cent of gross domestic product (GDP) and per cent of government spending than it was at the end of the Cold War era. General trends do, of course, always hide more complex patterns. Some countries have increased military spending because of local insecurity, and in some cases due to the felt need to develop a self-sufficient arms industry or to encouragement from arms-producing companies pushing for arms exports. Within developing countries, one finds substantial heterogeneity in terms of their stage and nature of development, the state of their neighbours, their military burden (military expenditure relative to GDP) and the degree of military involvement in the state. Often studies treat developing countries as versions of developed ones and use the same approach and models to analyse them, but this is not necessarily appropriate.

This chapter reviews these issues and the existing literature on the relation between military spending and development. It briefly considers theoretical perspectives, the channels through which military spending can affect the economy in developing countries, provides an up-to-date survey of the results of existing empirical studies and considers issues of concern for the evaluation of research. It provides, in essence, a fifty-year retrospective of the field. Finally, in drawing conclusions on the economic effects of military spending in developing countries, this chapter suggests that for very many countries thorough demilitarisation combined with substantial security sector reform to provide for the safety and security of their citizens should be on the policy agenda.

5.1 Data Availability and Measurement Problems

As with most empirical work, a major concern is data availability and whether the data that are available are measuring what they are intended to (construct validity), and whether this is consistently measured over time and across countries. Certainly, the published military expenditure data should be treated with care, especially when looking at developing countries. There are numerous problems with the data – definitions, coverage, accuracy and so on – which make it particularly difficult to use figures for comparison across countries or to aggregate them to larger groups.[2] There is also growing evidence that important amounts of security expenditure do not enter the accounts or budgets of developing countries.[3] This can be because of the different conventions or attempts to manipulate the figures using mechanisms such as double-bookkeeping, extra-budgetary accounts, highly aggregated budget categories, deliberate expenditure misclassification, off-budget spending, military assistance and foreign exchange manipulation. In some developing countries, the military has a much wider remit; for example, involvement in infrastructure building projects with social outcome objectives, such as building roads and hospitals, or taking part in what would normally be considered civilian police duties. Such problems are reflected in the fact that different data sources – SIPRI, ACDA, IISS and the IMF – can give markedly different numbers.[4] The problems of collecting military spending data are also seen in the copious footnotes accompanying the annual *SIPRI Yearbook* data.[5] The most extreme case was that of Argentina in 1982, where the IISS figure and that published by the IMF differed by 1,034 per cent.

Such differences are particularly important for cross-section analyses of countries, but not so much for time series data, as over time the concern lies with the *changes* in measured values rather than with the *absolute* or *relative* values of variables. So long as the definitions used and measurements taken are consistent and do not change significantly and systematically from one time period to another, one can be fairly confident of the validity of one's analysis, although there are important exceptions.[6] That said, even if definitions and measurements per se are comparable across countries, the use of foreign exchange conversion rates to put them into a common currency is not without its problems, as it will not reflect the different relative prices of the categories of military expenditure and the different compositions across countries (such problems are not unique to military expenditures but arise with all economic data used for cross-country purposes, such as the World Bank's World Development Indicators or the Penn World Tables).[7]

Regarding arms, in an ideal world we would be able to use military procurement budgets, as this reflects spending on arms transfers. However, such data are generally not available for developing countries, or are of questionable reliability. In fact, some evidence suggests that arms imports may not even be included in the military spending figures in many countries.[8] Developing countries may also differ in the way in which they treat or define military-related aid, the fungibility of aid and the way in which arms sales are financed.[9]

Even if we get a reasonable definition of military spending (an input), that does not mean we are measuring security (an outcome), and this can lead to further problems. Just what does military expenditure contribute to security? In some cases the contribution may be negative, leading to violent conflict, or be dominated by vested interests and not reflecting threats. It is also worth asking what the force structures and weapon systems made available are and whether they suit a country's security profile, or even whether developing countries need military forces at all. Costa Rica does not have an army (most violent conflicts are internal and ordinarily a matter of police forces), and Brazil in its latest official defense review stated that 'at present, Brazil has no enemies'.[10]

Another concern is what we mean by development. In applied work, normally the focus is placed on economic growth rather than development. Due to problems with defining and measuring development, economic growth is the one aspect that economists have access to readily available data. In general, having a faster-growing economy is a good thing, of course, but that does not mean it is all good, particularly for the weaker members of society. At best, growth is only a necessary condition for development and the starting point for any such analysis; there is a dearth of theoretical understanding of the links between these two terms (*see also* Chapter 4).[11]

5.2 Economic Theories

A theoretical model is important for any empirical study but, astoundingly, much of economic theory does not have an explicit role for military spending as a distinctive economic activity. This has not prevented the development of theoretical analyses, as discussed in Dunne and Coulomb.[12] The still-dominant standard neoclassical approach sees the state as a rational actor, which balances the opportunity costs and security benefits of military spending in order to maximise a well-defined national interest, as reflected in a social welfare function. Armament spending is seen as a public good and the economic effects of military expenditure will be determined by its opportunity cost, which is the trade-off between it and other spending. Early models of economic growth, which assume exogenous technical change, have since been extended to allow for the effects of changes in education and technology (human and physical capital) that produce endogenous growth. More recent works allow for the importance of institutions, although empirically still in a rather simple cross-country manner.[13]

The prototypical Keynesian approach sees a proactive state which may use military spending as one component of state spending to increase output through multiplier effects in the presence of ineffective aggregate demand. In this way, increased military spending can lead to increased capacity utilisation and increased profits, and hence to increased investment and growth. The institutionalist approach combines a Keynesian perspective with a focus on the *way* in which military spending can lead to industrial inefficiencies and to the development of a powerful interest group composed of individuals, firms and organisations that benefit from defence spending, usually referred to as the military-industrial complex (MIC). The MIC increases military expenditure through internal pressure within the state even when there is no security threat to justify such expenditure.[14]

Finally, the Marxist approach sees the role of military spending in capitalist development as important but contradictory. There are a number of strands to the approach which differ in their treatment of crisis, the extent to which they see military expenditure as necessary to capitalist development and the role of the MIC in class struggle. One offshoot of this approach has provided the only theory in which military spending is both important in itself and an integral component of the theoretical analysis, the underconsumptionist approach.[15] This sees military spending as necessary to maintain capitalism and to prevent stagnation. Monopolistic companies produce goods but control of (low) labour costs leads to inadequate consumption. Military spending may be wasteful, in the sense of not creating civilian output, but it does allow companies to sell their goods and realise profits.[16]

Most of these theoretical perspectives were developed for the analysis of developed economies and there is no inherent reason why they should be applicable to developing economies. There are general economic development theories – dependency, imperialism, growth-pole, import-substitution driven development and so on – but as for general economic theory, none have military spending playing any fundamental role in development.

5.3 Channels of Influence

In empirical work, the fact that there is no generally agreed theory of growth among economists means that there is no standard framework that military spending can fit into. Clearly, in developing countries, military spending, violent conflict (or the threat thereof) and economic capacity (education, governance, institutions, natural resources) all interact to influence growth.[17] But the theoretical work has allowed the identification of a number of channels through which military spending can affect an economy. The relative importance and sign (positive, neutral or negative) of these effects and the overall impact on growth can only be ascertained by empirical analysis.

In most empirical work the focus is on how military spending can affect an aggregate production function. The traditional inputs into the function are labour, physical capital and land (land area, arable land or, sometimes, natural resources). Institutional and social capitals are considered less often. An important problem in developing countries is creating an adequately skilled and educated labour force as the economy develops. Military spending can have both positive and negative effects in this regard. The military can train soldiers and conscripts with valuable technical and administrative skills which may be taken into post-service civilian life. This can have modernising effects, with organisational skills and modern attitudes tending to break up social rigidities. But these effects may be insignificant, or the military may attract scarce skilled labour and valuable resources away from the civilian sector and thereby place fetters on growth. Moreover, the transferability of soldiering skills to civilian economic activity may be limited and the military may be no more, or less, modern than civil institutions. Military spending might also be at the expense of civilian education and training expenditures.[18]

Military spending can have positive or negative effects on both savings and investment. If military expenditures are funded by taxation, rather than by borrowing or substitutions with other budget categories, then economy-wide savings propensities may be affected. In developing countries raising new revenue from taxation can be difficult, and thus military expenditure may be funded by an increased money supply, which may lead to inflation, potentially reducing savings. Another impact can result from military expenditure coming directly at the expense of education and health spending, requiring increased private provision and thus lowering private savings. Again, the impact of military expenditure on investment is an empirical question. On the one hand, it is hypothesised that it can crowd out private sector investment. On the other hand, it may boost demand, output and profits and lead to increased investment (other forms of government expenditure could also have the same impact). It is possible, however, that even if military expenditure was to boost investment per se, supply-side bottlenecks could prevent any significant positive effect from arising. In addition, infrastructural investment by the military can be either to the benefit of industry at large or be purely of military value, and thus remote and irrelevant to the civilian sector.[19]

In addition to considering the *level* of inputs in a production function there is also their *rate* of change, especially technological change. Imports of arms can introduce advanced product and process technology to local industry, particularly if arms offset deals mean that local production takes place through licensing, and this could have positive externalities for the rest of industry. Obviously this will depend on the prior degree of development and the existence of an advanced sector, with a well-trained and educated workforce and a supporting cast of supplier industries. But poor countries may not have at hand the needed skilled workers and technicians, and offset-based companies may use mainly expatriates, ultimately having little impact on the local economy and being unsustainable once the arms order is fulfilled. Alternatively, arms offset work could create a specialised and advanced production sector with little linkage to the rest of the country and dependent on government for support.[20]

Military spending can influence the conditions under which production takes place. It may provide control and discipline of labour, reduce internal conflict and be a modernising influence. As discussed, the military can impart discipline on conscripts, making them more suited to industrial labour when they eventually leave the forces, and can provide skills which can be of value in the civilian sector. It is, however, also possible that the military sector and its technology is capital intensive and so far removed from the rest of the economy as to impart little of value in terms of spin-offs. It may also take skilled labour away from the civil sector, and military regimes may be conservative, corrupt and inefficient and a hindrance to economic development.[21]

Military expenditure can also affect the external environment a country finds itself in. Its impact on the external balance of payments will depend upon whether or not a country imports and/or exports arms and on whether or not it receives military-related aid. In most developing countries, weapons imports will place a huge burden on the economy (through the consumption of scarce foreign exchange reserves) and will make trade deficits difficult to avoid. This may be offset by military-related aid, the exports of arms or arms import substitution, but, in general, military spending is likely to be a burden on the trade balance and hence on the balance of payments. In addition, evidence suggests that military-related debt in developing countries is substantial and that the financial burden of earlier arms imports via debt service has grown over time. In exchange for these economic costs, the military may provide genuine security from threats, encourage foreign investment and have links with foreign powers with an interest in the region that can be beneficial to trade, investment and aid. However, this must be weighed against the possibility of involvement in (violent) conflict and the damaging effects multinational investment and aid can have on weak client economies.[22] An interesting literature has developed that looks at the nature of conflicts and the extent to which they are encouraged by military expenditure. Clearly, the costs of conflict are high and can be made higher through higher military expenditure.[23] But it is not that straightforward, as military spending and arms races do not inevitably lead to conflict, and causality may be reversed in that it may well be the case that impending or actual conflict is driving the observed expenditures. In addition, some of the most damaging and bloody mass atrocities and wars have been achieved with relatively little in the way of funds or arms transfers.[24]

As a budget item, military expenditure creates the need for funding. If a rise in military expenditure cannot be financed through taxation, it will create a deficit. This may be financed in four different ways: printing money, using foreign exchange reserves, borrowing abroad and borrowing domestically. Each of these methods has some limits and implications, which are widely discussed in the literature. Although there are links among the implications of the financing methods used, as a first approximation the methods of deficit financing are associated with different macroeconomic imbalances: printing money with inflation; foreign reserve use with the onset of foreign exchange crises; foreign borrowing with an external debt crisis; domestic borrowing with interest rate rises and feedback on gross domestic private sector investment.[25] Evidence also suggests that involvement in the global arms trade is associated with corruption. Thus, multiple authors[26] find a degree of complementarity between military expenditure and corruption.

Military spending, in common with any and all forms of government expenditure, will have effects on aggregate demand and, in situations of less than full employment, will lead to increased output, with income multiplier and investment accelerator effects. Many developing countries are not natural-resource constrained but, given supply constraints in terms of physical and human capital, any possible output-generating impact of increased military expenditure may be relatively small. It is also open to debate whether military expenditure is the best form of government expenditure to foster expansionary growth.[27]

Clearly, all of these channels interact and their influence will vary depending on the countries involved. For example, relatively advanced developing countries, such as any one of the 'Asian Tigers' (Hong Kong, South Korea, Singapore and Taiwan) will have concerns over the opportunity costs of the industrial impact of any involvement in arms production and possibly the technology and foreign direct investment benefits, while the generally much poorer African economies may be more concerned with the 'conflict trap' they find themselves in (circumstances where civil wars repeat themselves).[28]

5.4 Empirical Results

In undertaking empirical work, choices need to be made, many of which will be conditioned on the theoretical perspective adopted and the data available. The results are likely to be very sensitive to the measurement and definition of the variables, to the specification of the estimated equations (especially to the other variables included), to the type of data used and to the estimation method. The resulting variety of studies does make comparisons rather difficult and explains some of the seemingly contradictory findings.

Benoit[29] started the empirical debate by finding a positive association between military expenditure and development in developing countries. There were two responses to this. One criticised Benoit's cross-sectional approach and argued that the complexities and specificities involved called instead for detailed, country-level case studies.[30] The second was to argue that Benoit's empirical work was flawed, and this led to a plethora of econometric studies. Some of the earlier contributions employed models that had both Keynesian and neoclassical features within simultaneous equation systems. This approach emphasised the importance of the interdependences among military spending, economic growth and the other variables, with the majority of the studies tending to confirm the existence of an adverse effect of military expenditure on economic development. The studies did vary in their use of data. Some dealt with cross-section averages, others with time series estimates for individual countries, while still others were more comprehensive.[31] More recently, these types of modelling approaches have become rarer as neoclassical and New Keynesian models have become more dominant.[32]

Another type of contribution used neoclassical single-equation growth models, introducing military spending (burden, per capita or absolute value) as one of the independent variables. Frederiksen and Looney[33] re-examined Benoit's data in this manner. Dividing the countries into resource-constrained and resource-unconstrained, they found that Benoit's result of a statistically significant, positive effect of military expenditure on growth held only for the resource-unconstrained group and was negative for the resource-constrained. Other studies tended to find a positive or insignificant effect of military expenditure on growth, although there were studies that found negative effects.[34] Researchers tried to deal with limitations of the earlier studies, with some using extended growth models, including Knight, Loayza and Villanueva,[35] who found that high levels of military spending detract from growth by reducing productive capital formation and distorting resource allocation. More recently, Ram[36] used a large panel of countries, and while finding no evidence of crowding out did find clear differences across groups of countries. Dunne and Tian[37] found a statistically significant negative effect of military spending on growth, and found the result to be surprisingly robust when using a range of potentially important variables (such as violent conflict and foreign aid) to stratify a large panel using post-Cold War data.

An important concern with the single-equation approach was determining causality, which led to a number of studies using Granger causality techniques. Dunne and Smith[38] critically reviewed this work and argued that the lack of theoretical underpinnings meant that it is very difficult to interpret the results of such studies in any causal manner. Also, inherent limitations of Granger causality tests often lead to unstable estimates over different time periods or countries, suggesting these methods are unreliable in testing for causal links.

More recent contributions have tried to deal with the possibility that the military spending and economic growth nexus may be nonlinear, having different effects on economic growth at different levels of military expenditure. Given the complexity of such models, the studies tend to focus on a small number of countries. Cuaresma and Reitschuler[39] estimate threshold regressions to show that there is a level-dependent effect of military spending on growth; namely, positive externality effects for low levels of military spending, but negative for high levels, while Pieroni[40] finds clear negative effects at both high and low levels of military spending.

Another concern of researchers was to allow for the opportunity cost of military spending; that is, the trade-off between military spending and other forms of expenditure. Some early studies found weak evidence of military spending crowding out spending on education and health in developing countries, but others found no evidence of trade-offs.[41]

An alternative to these types of studies was provided by the existence of large-scale, country-specific macroeconometric models and even of world models. Although developed for other purposes, these were able to look at the impact of changes in military spending on economic growth or, indeed, the impact of simulated substitution of non-military spending for military spending. Gleditsch et al.[42] provide a collection of such studies, linked into the use of a world model to illustrate the clear benefits of what, in the wake of the end of the Cold War, was popularly called the 'peace dividend'. There are few individual country studies for developing countries using relatively large macroeconometric models, for obvious reasons. Such analyses do differ from the usual studies of growth as they are no longer searching for the long-run determinants of growth but consider instead the short-run peace dividend impact, while at the same time allowing for government policy to adjust in a manner that deals with problems of economic adjustment.[43] There are also a number of studies that have considered the trade-off between military and other spending, especially health and education, as these are often the easiest in which to get consistent data.[44]

While developing countries have limited arms production capabilities, they do have some, and many have aspirations to become important arms exporters. At the same time, the trade in weapons is hugely important in providing foreign exchange for a limited number of countries (but a drain on foreign exchange and a spur for rising debt burdens for many more) and providing the possibility of developing weapons production for others through offset deals. Brauer and Dunne[45] provide a range of studies drawn from across the world on the role of arms offsets in development, finding no case where offset arrangements have yielded unambiguous net benefits for a country's economic development. A number of studies have considered the effect of military spending on debt, with Brzoska[46] finding that while indebtedness due to arms imports had not increased as much during the 1990s as it did during the 1970s, increased arms commercialisation means that countries do have to pay for weapons (they can no longer rely on military aid) and poor countries are less important as customers, possibly limiting any possibility of obtaining arms discounts. For a panel of eleven small industrialised economies, Dunne, Soydan and Perlo-Freeman[47] found military burden to have a positive effect on the share of external debt in GDP, a result that has been supported by more recent studies.[48]

Previous surveys of the military spending and economic growth literature include Chan,[49] who found a lack of consistency in the results, and Ram,[50] who reviewed twenty-nine studies, concluding that there was little evidence of a positive effect of defence outlays on growth but, also, that it was difficult to say the evidence supported outright negative effects. Dunne,[51] covering fifty-four studies, concluded that military spending had at best no effect on growth and was likely to have a negative effect, certainly that there was no evidence of positive effects. Smith[52] suggests that the large literature did not indicate any robust empirical regularity, positive or negative (although believing that a small negative effect does exist in the long run, but one that requires considerably more sophistication to find). Smaldone,[53] in a review of Africa, considers military spending relationships to be heterogeneous, elusive and complex, but feels that variations can be explained by intervening variables. They can be both positive and negative. Although usually not pronounced either way, the negative effects do tend to be wider and deeper in Africa, and most severe in countries experiencing legitimacy or security crises and economic or budgetary constraints.

Dunne and Uye[54] in a survey of 103 studies on the economic effects of military spending, and focusing on developing countries, show that negative effects of military spending on growth were reported in 39% and 35%, respectively, of cross-country and case studies. Only 20% were found to have positive effects for both types, while over 40% found unclear results. Dunne and Tian[55] updated and extended the survey, going from 103 to 168 covered studies. Almost 44% of the cross-country studies and 31% of the case studies found a negative effect of military spending on growth, with only around 20% and 25%, respectively, finding positive impacts for cross-country and case studies. Dunne and Uye[56] had suggested that the increasing use of post-Cold War data might be providing more consistency in the results, and Dunne and Tian[57] found this to be markedly the case. Almost 54% of post-Cold War cross-country studies found military spending to have a negative impact on growth compared to only 38% for the Cold War period.

Updating the survey yet again, to 196 studies, does not change the result, as we see in Table 5.1. Cross-country type studies are the more prevalent type, accounting for 58% of all studies. Of these, 46% found negative effects on growth, while 35% were unclear and only 19% found positive effects. In the case of country case studies, the most common finding remains that of unclear results (45%), while negative and positive effects were found in 29% and 26% of the studies, respectively. Considering only developing countries again shows a result that is far more suggestive of a harmful effect. Of the 118 studies that primarily focus on developing countries, almost 48% found military expenditure hindering economic growth, with only 20% finding a positive impact and 32% with unclear results. Breaking down the studies into cross-country and case studies shows a similar pattern. A majority of studies finds a negative relationship between military spending and growth, followed by unclear results, while the percentage of positive results were the lowest in both categories (see Table 5.1). Of the nine country case studies that found a positive effect between military spending and economic growth, three were on China, two on Turkey and one each on Iran, India, Mexico and Fiji. In addition, of the seventeen cross-country studies that found a positive effect, only six used primarily post-Cold War data and only four (out of forty) in the last ten years found a positive impact.

Table 5.2 divides the studies into those published between 1973 and 2006 (Panel A) and those published between 2007 and 2017 (Panel B).

Table 5.1: *Comparison of pre– and post–Cold War studies*

Type	Total No.	Per cent Positive	Per cent Negative	Per cent Unclear
Cross-country	114	19.3	45.6	35.1
Case studies	82	25.6	29.2	45.1
Total	196	21.9	38.8	39.3
Up to Cold War end				
Cross-country	60	20.0	38.3	41.7
Case studies	43	20.9	32.6	46.5
Total	103	21.3	35.0	43.7
Post-Cold War				
Cross-country	54	20.4	53.7	25.9
Case studies	39	30.7	25.6	43.6
Total	93	23.7	41.9	34.4
Developing countries				
Cross-country	84	20.2	47.6	32.1
Case studies	34	26.5	44.1	29.4
Total	118	22.0	46.6	31.4

Source: authors' compilation of studies on military expenditure and growth.

Table 5.2: *Comparison of pre- and post-2007 studies*

Panel A: 1973–2006

Type	Total No.	Per cent Positive	Per cent Negative	Per cent Unclear
Cross-country	67	20.9	38.8	40.3
Case studies	55	20.0	34.5	45.5
~~Total~~	~~122~~	~~20.5~~	~~36.9~~	~~42.6~~

Panel B: 2007–2017

Type	Total No.	Per cent Positive	Per cent Negative	Per cent Unclear
Cross-country	32	25.0	50.0	25.0
Case studies	27	37.0	18.5	44.4
Total	74	24.3	41.9	33.8

Source: authors' compilation of studies on military expenditure and growth.

Table 5.3: *Comparison of studies focusing on mostly developing and developed countries*

Panel A: Developing

Type	Total No.	Per cent Positive	Per cent Negative	Per cent Unclear
Cross-country	84	20.2	47.6	32.1
Case studies	34	26.5	44.1	29.4
Total	118	22.0	46.6	31.4

Panel B: Developed

Type	Total No.	Per cent Positive	Per cent Negative	Per cent Unclear
Cross-country	30	16.7	40.0	43.3
Case studies	48	25.0	18.8	56.3
Total	78	21.8	26.9	51.3

Source: authors' compilation of studies on military expenditure and growth.

Studies in the earlier period are more likely to be dominated by Cold War-era observations than the later ones. Panel A shows results similar to Dunne and Uye,[58] with 39% of cross-country studies showing negative effects and 40% unclear effects. The case studies show a higher proportion of unclear results, 46%. Certainly, there is little support for military spending having a positive effect on growth and this is even more apparent for the more recent post-Cold War studies. As Panel B shows, 50% of recent cross-country studies found that the military burden had a negative impact on growth, with only 25% finding positive and 25% unclear results. The proportion of case studies showing a positive relationship between military spending and growth was higher at 37%, with around 19% negative and 44% unclear.

A comparison between studies that focus mostly on developing or developed countries shows a remarkable difference in the types and results of the studies (see Table 5.3). While cross-country studies were most commonly used to assess the impact military expenditure has on economic growth in developing countries, the opposite (case studies) is true for developed countries. In addition,

Table 5.3 suggests that far more unclear results were seen in studies on developed countries (51%) versus only 31% on developing countries. Only 27% of studies on developed countries found military spending hampers economic growth, compared to 47% on developing countries. The only similarity between articles that focus on developing or developed countries is that for cross-country studies, substantially more studies (48% for developing and 40% for developed countries) find military spending to harm economic growth than boost it. However, contrary to developing country studies, the majority of case studies on developed countries find unclear results (56%), with only 27% finding a negative relationship.

5.5 Issues

The weight of empirical evidence suggests a negative effect of military spending on economic growth, particularly for the post-Cold War period and for developing countries. That said, there is still a range of issues that need to be considered in interpreting this literature critically and in further developing it.

One important issue in empirical work is the identification problem that results from the fact that we observe changing military spending and growth while both are influenced by changing security threats. If the economic determinants of growth are constant, but there are variations in the security threat, then a negative relationship between military expenditure and output will be observed. If, instead, the threat is constant but the economic variables are changing, then a positive relationship between military expenditure and output will be observed. This can be used to explain some country experiences with different combinations of growth and military expenditure. It also suggests caution in interpreting the results of empirical studies.[59]

Another concern is that of reverse causality. Military spending is treated as an exogenous variable in growth equations, but it is also possible that growth can influence military spending, leading to endogeneity. This would normally be dealt with using instrumental variables, but in this case there are no clear candidates as instruments. D'Agostino, Dunne and Pieroni[60] suggest using a security measure based upon political instability. This works well statistically and shows that any bias is likely to understate the negative effect of military spending on growth.

Additional factors influence the growth–development nexus, and these can be difficult to capture within the usual framework of analysis. Institutions are important, as is the stage of development, but not necessarily in the simple ways they are often dealt with, as cross-sectional measures of ex-colonial power, for instance. It is clearly important whether or not the country is an arms producer and hence has the potential to import-substitute or to export.[61] A number of countries, for example, Bangladesh, Ghana and Uganda, make money from using their troops in peacekeeping missions (see Chapter 19 for further discussion on this point), but it is unclear how economically important this is and the degree to which troops are hired specifically for these tasks. As mentioned, troops can be used to undertake civilian projects, like road construction, but it is unclear that the use of troops is the best or most efficient way to proceed with civilian projects. Another major variable is, obviously, violent conflict itself, which is well-established as an economic disaster for developing economies. The problem is whether the existence of arms transfers and high military spending increases or reduces the probability of conflict, and this is neither clear nor straightforward. Arms transfers and elevated defence spending could reduce the probability of conflict with neighbours, yet increase the likelihood of internal conflict.[62]

There are clear differences between developed and developing countries but this is often not reflected in studies. Evidence suggests that whether there are arms producing capabilities or not, and whether they are resource rich or not, is important.[63] Krause[64] sets out a 'ladder' of the development of arms production and trade, including the location of centres of innovation and production, patterns of arms transfers and the diffusion of military technology in a global structure in four tiers: first-tier suppliers: innovators; second-tier suppliers: producers and adapters; third-tier suppliers: reproduce and copy; and fourth-tier recipients: purchasers.

The production of arms in developing nations ranges from relatively simple to very sophisticated weaponry, but most of them are found in the last two tiers. The best of them produce good platforms, but as regards weapons, control systems and sophisticated subsystems they are highly import dependent. This would include countries such as Argentina, Brazil, Egypt, India, Indonesia, Iran, Iraq, Pakistan, Turkey and others. The notion of a ladder can be criticised as it suggests that any country wishing to produce arms starts at Stage 1 and works its way up until the highest stage is reached. Yet Singapore, for example, followed a deliberate strategy of servicing naval vessels, and Greece followed a strategy of servicing NATO aircraft, as a means of amassing knowledge and experience valuable for potential entry into more sophisticated stages of arms production later on. Also, some countries have tried to reach a stage above their capacities (e.g. Egypt, India, Israel and South Africa), while still others chose to remain at a stage below their likely capabilities (e.g. Mexico).[65] Clearly, the impact of military spending and arms transfers will have a different effect on the higher rungs of the ladder, but there is little empirical evidence on this. Some studies have introduced stages of development to deal with this issue.[66]

Another important concern is transparency. If more and better comparable data exist, policy and political decision-making are likely to be improved so that, arguably, rash regional arms races will be less likely to occur, in that it is easier to bring international pressure to bear on countries to maintain or reduce their arms and military spending. When they are unnecessary, given the regional (im)balances of power and military expenditures, there are clear benefits in reducing arms sales to poor countries. A problem lies in the 'hidden' expenditures, inaccuracies and unreliability of the data. Poor data are not always the result of governments and officials providing wrong information on purpose, but it may be that the information is not available and/or the infrastructure not in place to process it. That said, many developing economies have high levels of corruption and these often are tied to arms transfers, leading to procurement of weapon systems beyond the security needs of the country, as in South Africa.[67] This could be reduced with increased transparency and accountability of exporting countries, as could the possibilities for countries to use aid monies for arms purchases.[68] Attempts have been made for the OECD, at least, to recognise the legitimate need for some security expenditures (e.g. on peacekeeping roles) to be met from foreign aid budgets, but how this should be done is a matter of controversy.[69]

5.6 So What Can We Say?

There is some evidence that military expenditure affects national debt in adverse ways. As noted, Brzoska[70] found that indebtedness due to arms imports did not increase as much during the 1990s as it had during the 1970s. Until recently, increased commercialisation meant that countries had to pay for weapons rather than to get them as military aid, and, as a result, poor countries became less important as customers. (More recently, US arms transfers to sub-Saharan Africa, in particular, appear to shift back to military aid.) Still, Dunne, Soydan and Perlo-Freeman[71] find the military burden to have had an increasing effect on the share of external debt in GDP for a panel of eleven small industrialised economies, as do Ahmed[72] and Chiminiya, Dunne and Nikolaidou[73] for a larger sub-Saharan Africa panel.

Answering the question as to whether high military spending hinders growth is not straightforward, but, here again, there is some evidence that it does. Certainly, there can be a positive effect in the short run: a Keynesian multiplier effect similar to other forms of government spending that exploits idle capacity to ramp up economic output. That said, the literature does suggest that increasing *other* forms of government spending; that is, non-military spending, would be more beneficial. What is clear is that there is little support for Benoit's[74] initial finding that military spending has a positive effect on economic development, and that military spending levels appear to be determined mainly by strategic factors. This suggests that appropriate changes in the strategic environment for developing countries can allow a reduction in military expenditure, and this would be unlikely to affect economic growth adversely, certainly not in the long run. Whether military expenditure has a positive impact on growth will depend on the precise channels by which it affects the larger economy and on the policies taken to ease any problems of adjustment. In this way, reductions in military expenditures may be seen as an investment process with possible short-run costs but with the potential for long-run benefits. As with any investment, sound planning is required and there are risks.[75]

Individual developing countries will, of course, have the potential for cuts limited by their own particular problems, such as political problems, ongoing civil and regional wars, highly militarised security webs, military regimes, use of the military for internal repression, ethnic or religious conflicts or the involvement of foreign powers. Recent literature has started to identify nonlinearities in the relationship between military expenditure and economic growth, and also suggesting that allowance be made for the level of threat faced by countries. Arms transfers and military expenditure can readily be seen as having a positive impact when there is high threat, for instance. Indeed, ongoing disputes can mean that decreases in military expenditure may be destabilising and actually undermine any process of arms reduction, so there remains an important role for regional and global international organisations to deal with such problems. This will need new approaches to security, including the provision of effective international mediation, the promotion of non-military solutions to conflicts and the support of genuine democratisation processes (regular, unimpeded and non-interfering with voting, and with appropriate checks and balances between elections).

There are constraints in reducing military expenditures, not least because of rising costs of weapon systems. Institutional structures within developing countries can provide fierce opposition to cuts. While few developing countries have an arms industry of any magnitude, there are bureaucrats and politicians, salesmen and importers (private and state), corporate interests and workers and managers all benefiting from the global weapons trade and the maintenance of strong militaries. Their power and resistance is helped by foreign companies with their hard-selling techniques and the well-known corruption surrounding the arms trade.[76] Many developing countries have small arms and munitions production facilities but some have, or used to have, major arms-industrial sectors (e.g. Brazil, Chile, Egypt, Israel and South Africa), and the degree of influence the relevant actors possess will vary by their size and importance.

The effects of cuts in military expenditure will be contingent on the nature of government and the quality of policy responses. For example, civil society will need to be able to hold government and its officials responsible for security-related spending to ensure that such spending matches a country's security needs profile. The main effects of any reductions are likely to be as follows: (1) an initial reduction of demand in the economy, which could lead to transitory reduced output and more unemployment, although resources will also be freed up for alternative and probably more productive medium- to long-term uses; (2) demobilisation, which may lead to unemployment and may be destabilising, again, in the short run; (3) a reduction in the role of the armed forces in the non-military sector (such as policing), which may mean a reduction in any training, infrastructure and contribution to national cohesion that this may have provided; and (4) reduced imports of arms, which will free scarce foreign exchange but will also lead to a reduction in the employment of bureaucrats and of workers involved in the trade. All of these will have an effect on the corporate sector and could lead to the closure of facilities, the demise of companies and further unemployment. To overcome such problems requires an alternative use of released resources to prevent adjustment problems. Obviously, in a growing world economy and with international support the adjustments could be quick and painless (as some post-Cold War experiences have well demonstrated). Sadly, in the past, structural adjustment packages offered through the International Monetary Fund and the World Bank Group tended to *prevent* this sort of adjustment, with their required cuts in public expenditure and subsequent adverse effects on equality and unemployment often leading to political tensions and social instability. More recently, however, changes in these institutions' policies have improved things but challenges remain.[77]

5.7 Conclusion

This chapter has provided a review of research on the military expenditure–economic development nexus, covering about fifty years' worth of studies. As a starting point for a comparison of the empirical studies, a survey of the data and a discussion of methodological and theoretical issues were undertaken. There are a number of schools of thought, but without theory-based consensus regarding the effect of military spending on economic growth. Much of the empirical work has focused on Keynesian and standard neoclassical models and considers a number of channels by which military spending can affect growth. Whether or not the effect is positive, neutral or negative is widely viewed to be an empirical matter. It is important to recognise the interdependence of economies' demand and supply sides, as well as the interdependence of economies across the globe, and to consider the various political, economic and even historico-cultural determinants of military spending. The results of the empirical studies are mixed, but, on the whole, they do tend to suggest that in developing countries, at least, economic conditions are not the most important determinant of the military burden.

The empirical analyses of the economic effects of military spending, specifically including arms transfers, suggest little or no evidence for a positive effect on economic growth and that military expenditure is more likely to have a negative effect, or else no discernible, statistically significant effect at all. A range of theoretical and empirical approaches are used, with the studies that find positive effects (often statistically insignificant ones) generally adopting a single-equation estimation approach. Studies which have attempted to develop simultaneous equations models to allow for a variety of indirect effects have tended to find that military spending has a negative impact on growth. Some studies have investigated the statistical causality of military spending and economic growth but with no dominant result.

An interesting observation is that while the evidence from military expenditure to growth is weak (even if the link is negative), the opposite link is very strong: China and India, in particular, are engaged in an economic arms race of sorts because it is economic growth that, without question, generates the resources needed to feed the military.[78] Similarly, despite a constitutional requirement to keep military spending below one percentage point of GDP, Japan became a major military force due to its rapid post-World War II economic growth. It grew so fast that one percentage point of GDP translated into a huge pot of resources available for its armed forces. Conversely, natural resource-dependent countries, especially, but also petroleum export-dependent countries, have seen export revenue declines in the mid-2010s and subsequently reduced their military expenditures accordingly (see SIPRI 2017). The lesson might be that if one wants to have any hope of becoming (militarily) strong, invest in the economy. Once states are economically strong, however, there is often too much at stake to risk one's economic achievements in war. Some states may also gain security if they become too important to the world economy at large to allow them to be invaded. The best way to security may actually be through economic development.

It seems unfortunate that after fifty years or so of continual theoretical and empirical work, the scientific findings of this chapter should still be somewhat hedged. This is partly because of the problems of obtaining reliable data and, possibly, because of a hangover from Cold War debates that in some cases reflect political positions rather than the pursuit of quality research. But it also reflects the fact that military spending and arms transfers, while more important than their share of resource use might suggest, are still only a small part of any economy, and thus their effect on growth can easily be swamped by other factors. As more and higher-quality post-Cold War data become available, researchers will be able to better distinguish trends in the data and so provide further careful analyses. Clearly, given the continuing violence and slaughter in many areas of the world, more fully understanding the relation between and among arms, military expenditure and economic and human development (or harm) remains an important and urgent task, as highlighted in Chapter 20.

Overall, however, the results suggest that reducing arms and military spending need not be costly and can quite possibly contribute to, or at the very least provide the opportunity for improved economic performance in developing countries. In this regard, it is noteworthy that a number of independent nation-states, mostly islands, have no military forces of their own (often, but not always, relying on regional defence systems or bilateral defence assistance treaties) or else do have some limited militarised forces but maintain no standing army (Costa Rica, Haiti, Iceland, Mauritius, Monaco, Panama and Vanuatu). Most countries, of course, do maintain standing forces, but one wonders about their capacity to actually defend their homeland from a dedicated external attack (the cases of Argentina, the Democratic Republic of the Congo, Georgia and Ukraine readily spring to mind). Smaller countries, ranging from Lesotho to Denmark and Mongolia, and from Nepal to Tajikistan and Uruguay, would seem to be able to offer little by way of effective resistance were they to be the target of attack by large neighbouring states. Larger countries, ranging from Brazil to Indonesia and to the Philippines, would appear to be under no particular external threat. As mentioned, Brazil's latest official defence review (2012) speaks of a downright lack of enemies. Indeed, in very many countries, military forces today essentially perform patrol and policing services, and, from an economic point of view, one wonders how the efficiency of the delivery of genuine citizen security and safety might be enhanced were such services to be performed by police rather than militarised forces, and what would be the overall economic effects of re-arranging the composition of security services. Already security sector reform is a well-established topic in some academic and policy circles, and political economists may contribute to the discussion by combining concerns regarding the military, arms and war with issues of peace and security in an integrated manner rather than treating them in isolation. Movement towards demilitarisation may no longer be an outlandish thought.

That said, while some countries have made advances in lowering military outlays, there remain problems in more countries moving to lower levels of military spending. Support is likely to be required at national, regional and international levels, possibly including assistance from the developed world. In this regard, it is also worth noting that there is not necessarily an automatic improvement in development as a result of disarmament and military spending reductions. It is something that requires good governance, management and support.[79]

Notes

1. For recent surveys see J. P. Dunne and N. Tian. 'Military Expenditure and Economic Growth: A Survey'. *The Economics of Peace and Security Journal.* 2013. 8(1): 5–11; J. P. Dunne and N. Tian. 'Military Expenditure, Economic Growth, and Heterogeneity'. *Defence and Peace Economics.* 2015. 26(1): 15–31; J. P. Dunne and N. Tian. 'Military Expenditure and Economic Growth, 1960–2014'. *The Economics of Peace and Security Journal.* 2016. 11(2): 50–56.
2. R. P. Smith. 'Military Expenditure Data: Theoretical and Empirical Considerations'. *Defence and Peace Economics.* 2017. 28(4): 422–28.
3. Consider just two illustrative examples. For Venezuela see J. Colgan. 'Venezuela and Military Expenditure Data'. *Journal of Peace Research.* 2011. 48(4): 547–56. For Turkey see G. Ayman and G. Günlük-Şenesen. 'Turkey's Changing Security Perceptions and Expenditures in the 2000s: Substitutes or Complements?' *The Economics of Peace and Security Journal.* 2016. 11(1): 35–45.
4. SIPRI: Stockholm International Peace Research Institute. ACDA: Arms Control and Disarmament Agency (an agency of the US Department of State). IISS: International Institute for Strategic Studies, London. IMF: International Monetary Fund, Washington, DC. IISS republishes budget data whereas SIPRI looks into actual spending.
5. See: Stockholm International Peace Research Institute. *SIPRI Yearbook 2018: Armaments, Disarmament and International Security.* Oxford: Oxford University Press. 2018.
6. J. Brauer. 'Data, Models, Coefficients: The Case of the United States Military Expenditure'. *Conflict Management and Peace Science.* 2007. 24(1): 55–64.
7. See The World Bank. *Data Bank World Development Indicators.* 2018. http://databank.worldbank.org/data/reports.aspx?source=world-devel opment-indicators (accessed 14 March 2018); University of Groningen. 'The database – Penn World Table version 9.0'. 2017. www.rug.nl/ggdc/ productivity/pwt/ (accessed 14 March 2018); R. C. Feenstra, R. Inklaar and M. Timmer. 'The Next Generation of the Penn World Table'. *American Economic Review.* 2015. 105(10): 3150–82.

8. W. Omitoogun and E. Hutchful (eds). *Budgeting for the Military Sector in Africa: The Processes and Mechanisms of Control*. Oxford: Oxford University Press. 2006.

9. M. Brzoska. 'The Financing Factor in Military Trade'. *Defence and Peace Economics*. 1994. 5(1): 67–80.

10. Brazil: Ministerio da Defesa (2012, p. 58, para 16). Paragraph 16 reads: 'Convém organizar as Forças Armadas em torno de capacidades, não em torno de inimigos específicos. O Brasil não tem inimigos no presente'. This translates to 'The Armed Forces should be organized around capacities, not around specific enemies. Brazil has no enemies at present'. The paragraph then continues: 'Para não tê-los no futuro, é preciso preservar a paz e preparar-se para a guerra', meaning 'In order not to have them in the future, we must preserve peace and prepare for war'. While this recalls the Latin *si vis pacem, para bellum* ('If you want peace, prepare for war'), Brazil in fact established in February 2018 an Extraordinary Ministry of Public Security (Ministério Extraordinário da Segurança Pública), assigning military forces to help address the extraordinary insecurity in Rio de Janeiro and moving the defence minister, Robert Jungmann, to head up the new ministry. We return to this topic in the Conclusion. See Ministerio da Defesa. *Politica Nacional de Defesa. Estrategia Nacional de Defesa*. Brasilia: Presidenta da Republica Federative do Brasil, Ministro de Estado da Defesa, Ministro de Estado Chefe da Secretaria de Assuntos Estrategicos da Presidencia da Republica, 2012. http://defesa.gov.br/arquivos/estado_e_defesa/END-PND_Opt imized.pdf (accessed on 4 March 2018).

11. J. Brauer. 'Military Expenditures and Human Development Measures'. *Journal of Public Budgeting, Accounting and Financial Management*. 1996. 8(1): 106–24.

12. J. P. Dunne and F. Coulomb. 'Peace, War and International Security: Economic Theories'. In J. Fontanel and M. Chatterji (eds). *War, Peace, and Security*. Bingley: Emerald Group Publishing Limited. 2008. 13–36.

13. D. Acemoglu and J. A. Robinson. *Why Nations Fail: The Origins of Power, Prosperity, and Poverty*. London: Profile Books Ltd. 2012.

14. J. P. Dunne. 'Military Keynesianism: An Assessment'. In L. Junsheng, C. Bo and H. Na (eds). *Cooperation for a Peaceful & Sustainable World – Part 2*. Bingley: Emerald Group Publishing Limited. 2013. 117–30.

15. P. Baran and P. Sweezy. *Monopoly Capital*. London: Monthly Review Press. 1966.

16. J. P. Dunne. 'The Political Economy of Military Expenditure: An Introduction'. *Cambridge Journal of Economics*. 1990. 14(4): 395–404.

17. Indeed, many poor countries, even those with civil wars, spend relatively little on the military. In particular, many African countries have low military burdens, but there are other obstacles to growth. See P. Collier. *The Bottom Billion*. Oxford: Oxford University Press. 2007.

18. D. Smith and R. Smith. *The Economics of Militarism*. London: Pluto Press. 1983.

19. R. Smith. *Military Economics*. Basingstoke: Palgrave Macmillan. 2009.

20. J. Brauer and J. P. Dunne (eds). *Arms Trade and Economic Development: Theory, Policy, and Cases in Arms Trade Offsets*. London: Routledge. 2004.

21. See T. Scheetz. 'Military Expenditure and Development in Latin America'. In J. Brauer and P. Dunne (eds). *Arming the South – The Economics of Military Expenditure, Arms Production and Arms Trade in Developing Countries*. Basingstoke: Palgrave. 2002. 51–71; D. Smith and R. Smith. *The Economics of Militarism*. London: Pluto Press. 1983.

22. See Brauer and Dunne (eds). *Arming the South*; M. Brzoska. 'Research Communication: The Military Related External Debt of Third World Countries'. *Journal of Peace Research*. 1983. 20(3): 271–77.

23. J. P. Dunne. 'Armed Conflicts'. In B. Lomborg (ed). *Global Problems, Smart Solutions: Costs and Benefits*. Cambridge: Cambridge University Press. 2013. 21–53.

24. See J. Murdoch and T. Sandler. 'Civil Wars and Economic Growth: Spatial Dispersion'. *American Journal of Political Science*. 2004. 48(1): 138–51; Collier. *The Bottom Billion*; C. H. Anderton and J. Brauer (eds). *Economic Aspects of Genocides, Other Mass Atrocities, and Their Prevention*. New York: Oxford University Press. 2016.

25. See M. Brzoska. 'The Financing Factor in Military Trade'. *Defence and Peace Economics*. 1994. 5(1): 67–80; J. P. Dunne, A. Soydan and S. Perlo-Freeman. 'Military Expenditure and Debt in South America'. *Defence and Peace Economics*. 2004. 15(2): 173–87; J. P. Dunne, A. Soydan and S. Perlo-Freeman . 'Military Expenditure and Debt in Small Industrialised Economies: A Panel Analysis'. *Defence and Peace Economics*. 2004. 15(2): 125–32.

26. J. Aizenman and R. Glick. 'Military Expenditure, Threats, and Growth'. *Journal of International Trade and Economic Development*. 2006. 15(2): 129–55; Brauer and Dunne (eds). '*Arms Trade and Economic Development*'; See G. d'Agostino, J. P. Dunne and L. Pieroni. 'Corruption and Growth in Africa'. *European Journal of Political Economy*. 2016. 43: 71–88; G. d'Agostino, J. P. Dunne and L. Pieroni. 'Government Spending, Corruption, and Economic Growth'. World Development. 2016. 84: 190–205; S. Perlo-Freeman. *A Compendium of*

Arms Trade Corruption. World Peace Foundation. 2018. https://sites .tufts.edu/corruptarmsdeals/author/sperlo02/ (accessed 13 March 2018).

27. J. P. Dunne and S. Perlo-Freeman. 'The Demand for Military Spending in Developing Countries: A Dynamic Panel Analysis'. *Defence and Peace Economics*. 2003. 14(6): 461–74; J. P. Dunne and S. Perlo-Freeman. 'The Demand for Military Spending in Developing Countries'. *International Review of Applied Economics*. 2003. 17(1): 23–48.

28. Collier. *The Bottom Billion*.

29. See E. Benoit. *Defense and Growth in Developing Countries*. Boston: Heath, Lexington Books. 1973; E. Benoit. 'Growth and Defense in Developing Countries'. *Economic Development and Cultural Change*. 1978. 26(2): 271–80.

30. N. Ball. 'Defense and Development: A Critique of the Benoit Study'. *Economic Development and Cultural Change*. 1983. 31(2): 507–24.

31. J. P. Dunne. 'Economic Effects of Military Expenditure in Developing Countries: A Survey'. In N. P. Gleditsch, O. Bjerkholt, R. Smith, A. Cappelen and J. P. Dunne (eds). *The Peace Dividend*. Amsterdam: Elsevier. 1996. 439–64.

32. J. P. Dunne and M. Uye. 'Military Spending and Development'. In A. Tan (ed). *The Global Arms Trade: A Handbook*. 2010. London: Europa/Routledge. 293–305.

33. P. Frederiksen and R. E. Looney. 'Defense Expenditures and Economic Growth in Developing Countries'. *Armed Forces and Society*. 1983. 9(4): 633–45.

34. Dunne. 'Economic Effects of Military Expenditure in Developing Countries'.

35. M. Knight, N. Loayza and D. Villanueva. 'The Peace Dividend: Military Spending Cuts and Economic Growth'. *IMF Staff Papers*. 1996. 43(1): 1–37.

36. R. Ram. 'Defence Expenditure and Economic Growth: Evidence from Recent Cross-Country Panel Data'. In A. F. Ott and R. J. Cebula (eds). *The Elgar Companion to Public Economics: Empirical Public Economics*. Cheltenham: Elgar. 2006. 166–98.

37. Dunne and Tian. 'Military Expenditure, Economic Growth, and Heterogeneity'.

38. J. P. Dunne and R. Smith. 'Military Expenditure and Granger Causality: A Critical Review'. *Defence and Peace Economics*. 2010. 21(5–6): 427–41.

39. J. C. Cuaresma and G. Reitschuler. 'A Non-Linear Defence Growth Nexus? Evidence from the US Economy'. *Defence and Peace Economics*. 2004. 15(1): 71–82.

40. L. Pieroni. 'Military Expenditure and Economic Growth'. *Defence and Peace Economics*. 2009. 20(4): 327–39.

41. Dunne and Uye. 'Military Spending and Development'. In Tan (ed). *The Global Arms Trade*.
42. N. P. Gleditsch, O. Bjerkholt, R. Smith, A. Cappelen and J. P. Dunne (eds). *The Peace Dividend*. Amsterdam: Elsevier. 1996.
43. Dunne. 'Economic Effects of Military Expenditure in Developing Countries'.
44. See Scheetz. 'Military Expenditure and Development in Latin America'; Brauer. 'Military Expenditures and Human Development Measures'.
45. Brauer and Dunne (eds). *'Arms Trade and Economic Development'*.
46. M. Brzoska. 'Analysis of Recommendations for Covering Security Expenditures Within and Outside of Official Development Assistance (ODA)'. Bonn International Centre for Conversion (BICC). Research Paper No. 53. 2006.
47. Dunne, Soydan and Perlo-Freeman. 'Military Expenditure and Debt in Small Industrialised Economies'.
48. See A. D. Ahmed. 'Debt Burden, Military Spending and Growth in Sub-Saharan Africa: A Dynamic Panel Data Analysis'. *Defence and Peace Economics*. 2012. 23(5): 485–506; A. Chiminiya, J. P. Dunne and E. Nikolaidou, 'Military Spending, Conflict and External Debt in SSA'. University of Cape Town. Macroeconomics Discussion Paper 18_01, 2018.
49. S. Chan. 'Military Expenditures and Economic Performance'. In *World Military Expenditures and Arms Transfers* 1986. U.S. Arms Control and Disarmament Agency. Washington, DC: US Government Printing Office. 1987. 29–37.
50. R. Ram. 'Defense Expenditure and Economic Growth'. In K. Hartley and T. Sandler (eds). *Handbook of Defense Economics*, vol. 1. Amsterdam: Elsevier. 1995. 251–74.
51. Dunne. 'Economic Effects of Military Expenditure in Developing Countries'.
52. R. Smith. 'Defence Expenditure and Economic Growth'. In N. P. Gleditsch, G. Lindgren, N. Mouhleb, S. Smit and I. de Soysa (eds). *Making Peace Pay: A Bibliography on Disarmament and Conversion*. Claremont: Regna Books. 2000. 15–24.
53. J. P. Smaldone. 'African Military Spending: Defence versus Development?' *African Security Review*. 2006. 15(4): 18–32.
54. Dunne and Uye. 'Military Spending and Development'. In Tan (ed). *The Global Arms Trade*.
55. See Dunne and Tian. 'Military Expenditure and Economic Growth: A Survey'; Dunne and Tian. 'Military Expenditure, Economic Growth, and Heterogeneity'; J. P. Dunne and N. Tian. 'Military Expenditure and Economic Growth, 1960–2014'. *The Economics of Peace and Security Journal*. 2016. 11(2): 50–56.

56. Dunne and Uye. 'Military Spending and Development'. In Tan (ed). *The Global Arms Trade.*

57. Dunne and Tian. 'Military Expenditure and Economic Growth: A Survey'.

58. Dunne and Uye. 'Military Spending and Development'. In Tan (ed). *The Global Arms Trade.*

59. Smith. 'Defence Expenditure and Economic Growth'.

60. G. d'Agostino, J. P. Dunne and L. Pieroni. 'Military Expenditure, Endogeneity and Economic Growth'. *Defence and Peace Economics.* 2018. www.tandfonline.com/doi/full/10.1080/10242694.2017.1422314 (accessed 14 March 2018).

61. J. Brauer. 'Defense, Growth and Arms Production in Developing Nations'. In J. Brauer and M. Chatterji (eds). *Economic Issues of Disarmament: Contributions from Peace Economics and Peace Science.* New York: New York University Press and London: Macmillan Press. 1993. 229–42.

62. Collier. *The Bottom Billion.*

63. See J. Brauer. 'Arms Production in Developing Nations: The Relation to Industrial Structure, Industrial Diversification, and Human Capital Formation'. *Defence Economics.* 1991. 2(2): 165–75; J. Brauer. 'Potential and Actual Arms Production: Implications for the Arms Trade Debate'. *Defence and Peace Economics.* 2000. 11(5): 461–80.

64. K. Krause. *Arms and the State.* Cambridge: Cambridge University Press. 1999.

65. J. Brauer. 'The Arms Industry in Developing Nations: History and Post-Cold War Assessment'. In J. Brauer and J. P. Dunne. *Arming the South: The Economics of Military Expenditure, Arms Production, and Arms Trade in Developing Countries.* Houndsmill, Basingstoke: Palgrave. 2002. 101–27.

66. Dunne and Tian. 'Military Expenditure, Economic Growth, and Heterogeneity'.

67. J. P. Dunne and G. Lamb. 'Defence Industrial Participation: The South African Experience'. In J. Brauer and J. P. Dunne (eds). *Arms Trade and Economic Development: Theory, Policy, and Cases in Arms Trade Offsets.* London: Routledge. 2004. 284–98.

68. This is in fact difficult to police as aid can be fungible, meaning it can be given for one thing and used for another, and it is difficult to tell that a reallocation has taken place.

69. Brzoska. '*Analysis of Recommendations for Covering Security Expenditures*'.

70. M. Brzoska. 'The Economics of Arms Imports After the End of the Cold War'. *Defence and Peace Economics.* 2004. 15(2): 111–23.

71. Dunne, Soydan and Perlo-Freeman. 'Military Expenditure and Debt in Small Industrialised Economies'.
72. Ahmed. 'Debt Burden, Military Spending and Growth in Sub-Saharan Africa'.
73. Chiminiya, Dunne and Nikolaidou. *'Military Spending, Conflict and External Debt in SSA'.*
74. See Benoit. *Defense and Growth in Developing Countries*; Benoit. 'Growth and Defense in Developing Countries'.
75. K. Hartley. *Economic Aspects of Disarmament: Disarmament As an Investment Process.* United Nations Institute for Disarmament Research. New York: United Nations. 1993.
76. N. Ball. *Security and Economy in the Third World.* Princeton: Princeton University Press. 1988.
77. See J. P. Dunne. 'After the Slaughter: Reconstructing Mozambique and Rwanda'. *The Economics of Peace and Security Journal.* 2006. 1(2): 39–46; J. Brauer and J. P. Dunne. *Peace Economics: A Macroeconomic Primer for Violence-Afflicted States.* Washington, DC: United States Institute of Peace Press. 2012.
78. In the language of economists, the income elasticity of military expenditure is positive, meaning that increases in GDP partly spill over into increases in military spending.
79. See J. Brauer. 'Reviving or Revamping the "Disarmament-for-Development" Thesis?' *Bulletin of Peace Proposals.* 1990. 21(3): 307–19; L. J. Dumas. 'The Role of Demilitarization in Promoting Democracy and Prosperity in Africa'. In J. Brauer and P. Dunne (eds). *Arming the South – The Economics of Military Expenditure, Arms Production and Arms Trade in Developing Countries.* Basingstoke: Palgrave. 2002. 15–33.

PART III

Autarky versus Globalisation

6 | Alliances in Flux: Sovereignty and Security in a Changing World

STEFAN MARKOWSKI AND ROBERT WYLIE

Introduction

This chapter addresses two research questions, both of which stem from long-standing American demands for greater security reciprocity and more equitable military burden sharing by its numerous friends and allies. Firstly, does it make economic sense for the United States to respond to inequitable sharing of the burden of international security provision by scaling down its self-imposed role as supranational and largely benevolent military protector of its friends and allies? Secondly, if the United States does head in this direction, will its friends and allies be able to adjust by forming regional military clubs able to compensate for the withdrawal of US protection? Or will they be reduced to uninational investment in military capability and occasional participation in ad hoc military coalitions driven by specific military contingencies?

In answering these questions, we begin by reaffirming the centrality of the Westphalian nation-state in global security arrangements. We then analyse, from an economic perspective, the pattern of alliances constructed by the United States and its Westphalian state protégés post-World War II. We identify two models of US-focused international security provision: the first, plurilateral, model is represented by the North Atlantic Treaty Organisation (NATO). The bilateral, hub-and-spoke alliances that have proliferated in the East Asia-Pacific region constitute the second model. We argue that the United States elected to invest in largely autarchic capacity to project military power globally in order to counter any possible military threat to *its* national security. One consequence of this autarchic stance is that, at present, the United States has no need to rely on imports of military security services from its allies. Massive US strike and strategic manoeuvre capabilities render the marginal cost to the United States of extending its protective umbrella to shelter other countries relatively low. This combination of global military capability and autarchy has enabled the United States to behave as a Stackelberg leader vis-à-vis its various allies, i.e. its own dominant capability investments have been autonomous and it expects its allies to follow its lead.[1] However, it looks to its protégés for political support in the international arena – a form of reciprocity involving the bartering of military protection for international political legitimacy. This may involve allied participation in US-led military interventions or expressions of support for the United States in international relations with third parties. As this reciprocity has often failed to eventuate to US satisfaction, the United States has often complained of being 'exploited' by its military protégés, especially by some NATO members, which – many academic defence economists would agree – have under-invested in their own defence and free-ridden at US expense.

Whatever the merits of such complaints, we argue that the low marginal cost incurred by the United States in extending military assurances to friendly countries means that the national interests of both the US and its protégés are best served by the United States continuing to act as the pre-eminent provider of such assurances. This benefits, in particular, smaller parliamentary democracies wishing to retain a prudent measure of sovereignty in a world that favours large military powers. Our analysis suggests that efforts to form military alliances (economic clubs) by these countries are unlikely to succeed unless they are underpinned by American military power. That said, however, greater effort by US allies to develop complementary and interoperable military capabilities would make future collective defence more viable and equitable. Any such development would require the United States to reduce its current emphasis on levels and burdens of military expenditure incurred by its allies and to focus instead on enhanced reciprocity between the allies through a combination of, firstly, physical military capabilities dedicated to the collective military effort by each ally (such capabilities to be made available for shared endeavours if and when required by the alliance) and, secondly, political support for joint military activities deemed necessary to protect and advance common security interests.

6.1 The Nation-State as a Security Foundation

The 1648 Peace of Westphalia is generally accepted as the precursor for the modern notion of the state-based international order. In international law, a 'state' is a juridical entity that is recognised by its counterparts as exercising juridical 'sovereignty' over a certain (defined) geographic area; that has a permanent population governed by legitimate representatives of that population; and that is sufficiently well organised to enter into agreements and understandings with other sovereign states.[2] Under the Westphalian doctrine of international relations, such states constitute the basic building blocks of international order and are the primary agents exercising the institutional arrangements underpinning that order. The narrower concept of nation-state assumes that the state also symbolises the 'nation', broadly understood as a resident population identified by a common language, history and culture.

In the ideal Westphalian state, sovereignty means complete decision making freedom in all matters concerning governance of the designated territory and its inhabitants. In reality, obviously, no state enjoys unfettered sovereign rights. The latter are inevitably attenuated as states enter into agreements and understandings with other states, and smaller and weaker states are subject to direct interference in their affairs by other, usually larger and more powerful states. In this chapter, therefore, we interpret sovereignty as a degree of actual decision-making autonomy exercised by a particular state entity given its agreed obligations to other states under various international agreements, and the extent to which other states compromise its decision-making independence by intervening directly in its affairs.

This concept of *qualified sovereignty* also recognises the constraints imposed on nation states by internationally mobile factors of production and by, to a lesser extent, the proliferation of international institutions and regional, quasi-federal communities, such as the United Nations (UN), the European Union (EU) and NATO. Finally, nation-states have yet to exchange their qualified sovereignty for membership of Buchanan-style economic clubs.[3] This is because the formation of such clubs requires nation-states to surrender some of their independence and transfer sovereign rights to pan- and supranational bodies – along EU lines – with a view to integrating some 'national interests' and to accommodating, rather than contesting, residual national interests. The EU experience suggests that, for the foreseeable future, visions of supranational, centripetal designs will continue being curbed by the centrifugal forces of national self-interest. We conclude, therefore, that the notion of a Westphalian order based on the stylised concept of a fully sovereign and internationally recognised Westphalian state is a useful simplification of the reality of highly heterogeneous community of states with very unequal resource endowments. That said, however, the associated notion that all states are equal in international law and fully autonomous in governing their internal affairs is potentially misleading. As the Soviet interventions in Hungary in 1956 and in Czechoslovakia in 1968 suggest, and as the US-led invasion of Iraq in 2003 confirms, the notion of state sovereignty is contingent rather than absolute. The notion of contingent sovereignty recognises that larger and stronger states, e.g. global superpowers and regional hegemons, can usurp the right to determine those forms of intra-state governance that are acceptable to the 'international community' of nations, which they claim to represent; and those that, in their assessment, could and should be replaced by other, more acceptable arrangements. Similarly, the contemporary notion of a 'failed state' challenges the Westphalian notion of state sovereignty. It is the other states, most likely the global and regional hegemons, that determine which territory is deemed to be a juridical 'void' in the international legal order, and justifies external intervention to superimpose on it behavioural standards and an institutional framework more acceptable to the intervening power (e.g. the 2001 US-led intervention in Afghanistan). In sum, while we recognise the manifest limitations of the Westphalian concept of nation-state, we nevertheless retain it, like Kissinger,[4] as a useful metaphor to describe the basic decision-making unit of global governance arrangements.

We now turn to that aspect of national governance which concerns the assurance of state sovereignty to secure its survival, resilience and safety – what Adam Smith famously defined as the sovereign's first duty.[5] Smith's sovereign is a rational decision-maker capable of directing investments in national military capabilities, which could either be used defensively to protect the state concerned from predatory activities of other states, or aggressively to project power against such states in pursuit of one's own national interests, or both. Contemporary national security has obviously evolved beyond the state-on-state application of lethal power to include the use of military power to counter asymmetric threats posed by non-state actors (e.g. terrorist organisations), prevention of criminal activity, public health considerations (e.g. the prevention and containment of epidemics) and the assurance of cultural, economic, technological and environmental security. Threats faced by different states are not only interdependent and complex but also distributed very unequally among them. Further, states differ in their appetite for and tolerance of various risks: a hazard that prompts one state to invest heavily in risk mitigation may be ignored by another state. In this chapter, we try to simplify this complexity by focusing on 'traditional' military threats and associated investments in military-specific capabilities.

The formation of lethal capabilities associated with the projection of military power invariably involves the production and use of complex assets and specialist knowledge which are very costly to develop, to keep ready for use and to deploy when required. The economies of scale and scope inherent in military capability favour larger powers and/or collaborative efforts between states. In this chapter, we are particularly interested in the joint formation/production of military capability by groups of collaborating states. Economic logic suggests that, *ceteris paribus*, the capital and knowledge intensity of defence will encourage smaller and medium powers either to seek protection provided by larger powers or to collaborate and merge their security interests so to realise the potential efficiencies related to scale and scope. Such collaboration may entail the formation of federal and quasi-federal entities (such as the European Union), or permanent military alliances (military clubs), such as NATO. Put another way, the nature of war-fighting technology should encourage notionally self-reliant Westphalian states to form post-Westphalian systems in which larger federal powers provide protection for smaller states and in which pluri- and multinational military clubs enable members to benefit from economies of (power) agglomeration. In practice, reality is more complex.

Over the past century, the global order of interstate governance has been largely shaped by the United States as the economic and military superpower. During and after World War II successive US Presidents Roosevelt, Truman and Eisenhower championed post-Westphalian governance arrangements in which inter-state conflict was to be prevented and resolved through supranational bodies such as the United Nations, plurilateral military alliances such as NATO and a network of US-led (hub and spoke) bilateral alliances, predominantly in the Asia-Pacific region. In investing the resources and leadership required to make these arrangements effective, the United States assumed the role of the post-WWII champion and protector of the 'western world'. This role was initially focused on containing the Stalinist Soviet Union and countering Soviet-led communism in the Cold War. It was subsequently characterised by US-led military interventions to curb challenges to the international order, including, most recently, militant Islamism. To be able to act in this capacity and to sustain Pax Americana for over seventy years, the United States has assumed the Stackelberg-style leadership in military capability formation. It has exercised this leadership through both plurilateral NATO arrangements and via the hub-and-spoke network of bilateral alliances in Asia-Pacific.

NATO is formally organised as a military club of juridically equal member states, which have empowered the North Atlantic Council to act as their collective coordinating authority. The club's design emphasises each partner's sovereign and equal status as a Westphalian nation-state. The design is flexible in that each member state invests in its own military capability at a pace determined by its particular socioeconomic, political and strategic circumstances.[6] The design also makes contingent provision for pooling by members of their respective arsenals and for use of joint command structures while simultaneously permitting them to make their (resource) allocation decisions independently as largely autonomous agents.[7] Activities requiring formal cost sharing arrangements, for example, NATO joint commands and common infrastructural facilities, account for a very small proportion of the alliance-wide cost of defence. Instead, NATO works on the general funding principle of 'letting the costs lie where they fall'.[8] The alliance's military capability formation is essentially a 'best endeavours' arrangement, whereby each member state is essentially free to determine the size of its national force structure, its level of readiness and the scale and scope of its contribution to the joint military effort as and when such contribution is required.

In this respect, NATO is not a Buchanan-style military club producing joint club goods, investing in joint production capability and sharing the attendant benefits and costs of these joint endeavours equally between members.[9] Rather, this flexible and somewhat discordant organisational structure is more appropriately labelled an 'idiorrythmic economic club'. However, such an inchoate structure could not have countered Stalin's tanks in the early days of the Alliance. Indeed, for the entire postwar period, NATO has been a fundamentally asymmetric form of military alliance centred on the United States as the dominant, autonomous and largely self-sufficient military power: its *primus inter pares*.[10] The United States' enduring military pre-eminence has not only enabled it to act as the alliance's Stackelberg leader, but also allowed NATO to expand and accommodate new members, all the while deterring other potentially hostile state powers, particularly the USSR. Inherent in this form of joint security assurance, however, is a moral hazard in that the US-provided security umbrella has also encouraged some NATO members to free-ride at the expense of the United States and of those members of the alliance which have pulled their weight in both the formation and deployment of military capability. As observed by Sandler and Murdoch:

Throughout its (history), NATO burden sharing has been a divisive issue. All too frequently, the US has alleged that it has carried an 'unfair' and dispro-portionately large amount of the alliance burden.[11]

Thus, free-riding and underinvestment by allies are inherent in NATO's asymmetric design as long as successive US administrations are willing to sustain NATO's discordant and inequitable *modus oper-andi* and to content themselves with frequent public rebukes of free-riding allies and empty threats to redesign the club.[12]

We turn now to the second model of US-focused international security provision. In the post-World War II Pacific, early concerns about the resurgence of a defeated Japan were soon displaced by widespread apprehension about the spread of militant Asian com-munism centred on Maoist China. In response, the United States concluded essentially bilateral security arrangements with Japan and South Korea in North Asia, Taiwan and the Philippines in East Asia, Thailand and Singapore in Southeast Asia and Australia and New Zealand in the Southwest Pacific. Within this US-centred hub-and-spoke security framework, the United States used a combination of military aid, foreign military sales, technology transfer and training to encourage individual nations to develop their respective military cap-abilities. In hindsight, it is apparent that this hub-and-spoke structure did not preclude individual states free-riding on US military capability as various NATO members have done. It did, however, encourage those states to provide varying degrees of support for US deploy-ments, a form of reciprocity expressed through practical support for US-led operations ranging from Northeast Asia to the Middle East. Looking ahead, to the extent Asia-Pacific nations share the US concern about a resurgent China's strategic intentions, they have an incentive not only to keep the structure's spokes in good repair but also to consider investing in bilateral arrangements between US allies around the rim of that structure.

Two broad themes emerge from this overview of NATO-style pluri-lateral security arrangements and of Pacific-style bilateral hub-and-spoke security arrangements. The first theme is the centrality of the United States, as an essentially autarkic superpower, to both multi-lateral and bilateral security arrangements. The second theme is the moral hazard inherent in efforts by that superpower to work with other, smaller nation states to advance common security interests.

Given its economic size and commitment to military autarchy and technological leadership in nuclear weapons and strategic power pro-jection systems, the marginal cost to the United States of providing security assurance to different groups of protégé states has been rela-tively modest. The United States has had to invest in few ally-specific assets and has largely relied on effective deterrence underpinned by its nuclear military capabilities. In some cases, the protector-protégé reci-procity may involve an element of American benevolence, as a form of economic aid. By and large, though, the United States as a global economic power has benefited from, and until recently has been highly supportive of free trade in goods and services and unimpeded move-ment of factors of production. Thus, we attribute US willingness to act as a global military superpower at least partly to its vested interest in protecting those sovereign nation-states with which it trades and which participate in the rules-based Pax Americana.

The predictable moral hazard of American commitment to the global rules-based order and stability and US dominance of its various alliances has been an underinvestment in military capability formation and free-riding by many of its protégés. This is particularly likely to be the case when collective deterrence is provided as an alliance-wide public good by the dominant member state (or states): the so-called exploitation hypothesis.[13] This proposition was first advanced by Olson and Zeckhauser,[14] who pioneered the theory of military alliances. It was subsequently refined by Sandler,[15] who advanced four testable proposi-tions to establish when defence is a purely public good among allies.

The first test is when an ally provides defence as a normal good (i.e. that ally's demand for defence is positively related to the size of its GDP) *and* if military expenditure of larger allies is a perfect substitute for that of smaller allies (there being no ally-specific defence benefits) *and* defence burdens (measured by, say, the share of an ally's milex (military expenditure) in the total alliance-wide milex) are expected to be distributed unevenly between allies. Put another way, uneven distri-bution of milex implies that the larger and wealthier allies shoulder a commensurately large portion of the burden of collective security for smaller, poorer allies – the exploitation hypothesis – though it may no longer apply if a small ally, such as Israel, has a particularly strong preference for its own defence, or if it has comparative advantage in military provision.[16] Sandler's second test is the likelihood of military expenditure being used inefficiently to fund the provision of defence, set at suboptimal levels in relation to the Pareto-optimal standard. The third test relates to restrictions on the size of the alliance. If there is no restriction on the alliance size, then the addition of a new ally produces a net gain as costs are spread among a larger number of payers while benefits are not reduced for the existing allies. Alternatively, non-rivalry ensures that extending access to the pure public good costs the existing members nothing, but benefits the new club entrant. The final test relates to the extent to which an ally's demand for defence depends on its income, relative prices of defence and civil outputs, military expenditure of other allies (defence spill-ins) and the perceived threat (say, as measured by the military expenditure of potential adversaries).

These four inferences may need to be modified when an alliance's output mix is less collective and contains a larger proportion of partially and fully rival and excludable club and private goods (between states). Particularly important in this context is the scope for protégés of the dominant power to suboptimise military expenditure when that power invests in an alliance-wide capability with a high degree of publicness. Such an investment allows its protégés either to reduce their defence burden or to divert their military expenditure to country-specific objectives rather than the common defence of all allies (which we refer to as the substitution hypothesis). In these circumstances, it is appropriate to ascertain what factors are likely to impede the formation of regional military alliances that are not US-centric and not dependent on US-formed strategic capabilities, i.e. alliance models that are not 'sustained by a single *primus inter pares* ... [but] ... based on a more balanced burden sharing or *pari passu* partnership'.[17] To address this question, the next Section 6.2 deals with alternative models of military capability formation by groups of states.

6.2 Analysing Defence Capability Formation

To decide how much a state should spend on the formation of military capability, we focus on a simple representation of marginal benefits of investment in military capability and its marginal cost. Ultimately, milex has to be justified in terms of either a defensive posture, to deter or defeat hostile actions of other states, or an offensive capability to project power aggressively beyond one's own borders, or some combination of the two. Generally, it is reasonable to assume that the total benefit of milex is subject to diminishing returns, so it increases at the progressively decreasing (marginal) rate perhaps to peak at some level of spending, and may even decline at high levels of investment in military capability; the latter represented by an index of different force elements weighted for their respective states of readiness (probabilities of availability when needed).[18] In this section, we consider five models of military capability provision: a uni-national approach, a federal model, a club of nation-states, an ad hoc coalition of military powers and the global public good provision.

Figure 6.1 illustrates the uni-national case, i.e. military capability formation by a stylised, Westphalian nation-state. The horizontal axis shows the achieved level of military capability as defined, given the state's GDP, geopolitical circumstances, area to be secured and military objectives. To simplify, the total benefit of military capability forma-tion can be envisaged as the present value of the collective expected life of the resident population, which is a product of the number of people resident in a country during a particular period of time, the average life expectancy (in years) and a shadow value of a person-year, say, an annualised measure of the net national product per person. The cause of the declining segment of the total benefit curve may be explained by using North Korea as an example: here high levels of military capability are achieved at the expense of public health; and where the probability of a catastrophic military conflict with the United States triggered by North Korean demonstration of its military prowess has increased substantially, thereby conceivably shortening rather than lengthening the average *expected* life of a North Korean.[19]

The total cost of military capability formation may decrease at first, but it increases at an increasing rate as the state's military capability increases. This is because economies of scale and cumulative learning effects tend to be offset by diseconomies of scale and scope at high levels of capability, i.e. due to the compositional effects of the changing structure of capability along the total cost curve. At lower levels of capability, economies of scale and scope are likely to be strong as benefits of mass production, skill/knowledge acquisition, interoperability between capability elements and

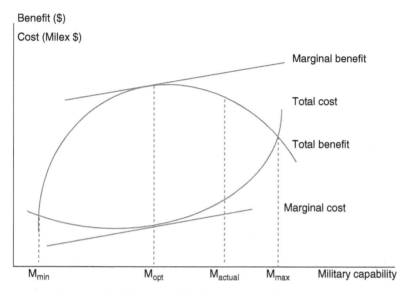

Figure 6.1: Optimal military capability by the stylised Westphalian nation-state
Source: author

commonality in materiel use and logistical support are realised. At higher levels of capability the importance of strategic components of total capability increases (e.g. command and control networks, strategic weapons systems and strategic lift capability). This is because as the technological complexity of military effort increases, lumpy investments in common and strategic capability elements have to be incurred at an increasing rate, and this is where diseconomies of agglomeration set in. Thus, the amassing of different capability elements at lower levels of aggregate capability is likely to exhibit economies of agglomeration, while at high levels of capability it is likely to display progressively stronger diseconomies of agglomeration.[20]

As a rational economic agent, the military capability manager should maximise the net national benefit of military capability formation, which occurs in the figure at the capability level M_{opt}, where the marginal benefit of capability formation equals the marginal cost, subject to the total benefit exceeding the total cost of achieved military capability. The two end points of the capability spectrum, M_{min} and M_{max}, mark the limits beyond which the cost of military capability exceeds the associated social benefit. The actual level of achieved military capability at any point in time, say M_{actual} in the figure, is very likely to differ from the optimal level M_{opt}. This is because the new capability formation requires leap-frogging into new technologies and building interfaces between different capability elements while obsolete elements may only be retired with a lag. As a result, the achieved capability is inevitably a mixture of different vintages of military technologies, often bolted together by temporary interfaces with impeded interoperability. Similarly, different elements of capability may be kept in different states of readiness as military contingencies are likely to occur with sufficient lead time to permit complementary investments to be made, if and when a particular threat becomes more likely or imminent.

Generally, a more resource-rich state will benefit from economies of size in that both the total benefit and the total cost curves are likely to shift up as the state's economy and resource base increase (e.g. as measured by the state's GDP), given its adopted military stance. However, the benefit curve may shift up relatively faster than the cost curve, creating conditions for size-related efficiencies. Also, larger powers are less likely to be threatened as their sheer size may deter potential state-on-state aggression, and they may therefore incur lower burdens of national defence.[21] Given these benefits of size, *ceteris paribus*, it should pay to federate, to take advantage of economies of (resource) agglomeration, particularly in such areas of activity as defence (e.g. a factor that contributed to the progressive federation of numerous German-speaking states into German and Austrian empires in the nineteenth century). This is the second model of military capability formation. However, the historical conditioning of national populations accounts for the difficulty that characterises most efforts to federate across national and ethnic divisions.[22] By and large, federal structures, like multinational kingdoms and empires before them, emerged as products of, and have been sustained over time by, rather unique historic circumstances, and none of the recent attempts to create federal entities *ab novo* appears to have succeeded.

The EU experiment in regional quasi-federalism is instructive in this respect. European Union members have largely succeeded in integrating regional goods, services and factor markets. European Union members have also toyed with the idea of joint EU defence, going so far as to establish the European Defence Agency (EDA), but stopping well short of creating an integrated force structure, and making at best limited progress in devising collaborative solutions to specific capability requirements.[23] Instead, the European Union has relied on US-led

NATO as a means of European defence.[24] Thus, for all practical purposes, the Westphalian nation-state remains a fundamental building block of joint security assurance within the EU. The European Union's protracted and largely unsuccessful efforts to create joint defence capability illustrate the strength of centrifugal forces inherent in efforts by groups of smaller and medium powers to try and operate as military clubs even when they are otherwise successful in forming economic clubs, such as customs unions and common markets.

Our third model is that of the Buchanan-style economic club,[25] illustrated by Figure 6.2. In this case, two or more nation-states form a permanent alliance to invest in joint military capability and sustain it over time. Let us assume, initially, that these economies are similar in size and that they share a common military objective. All members of the alliance retain their nominal sovereignty as Westphalian nation-states but surrender some of it by forming a common club management structure, say an alliance council. We further assume that the rules governing the operation of this council allow member states to invest in shared military capability and to deploy it when a particular predefined military contingency occurs. For simplicity, we draw the average and marginal cost of membership, N, as a straight line so that $AC = MC$, and each member state is assumed to have contributed to the alliance the same level of milex. Had the membership size been fixed initially and subsequently frozen, the club management would operate in a manner similar to that of the uni-national Westphalian state, shown in Figure 6.1. It would thus aim to maximise the net benefit of collective defence at the point where $MB = MC$. In Figure 6.2, this corresponds to the capability level N_{fix} at which $MB = MC$. However, the membership of a military alliance is likely to be variable rather than fixed, i.e. the club should be open to all those who wish to join, subject to their acceptance by the existing club members. In such a case the club's maximand changes from the total net benefit to the average net benefit. In Figure 6.2, this is shown as the joint capability level N_{var} at which the average benefit net of the average cost is highest.

Relative to an equivalent federal state, the military alliance set up as the Buchanan-style club underprovides defence. *Ceteris paribus*, all those potential members who would have benefited from membership at the marginal rate, MB, and incur the marginal cost of capability formation, MC, are prevented from joining the alliance by existing

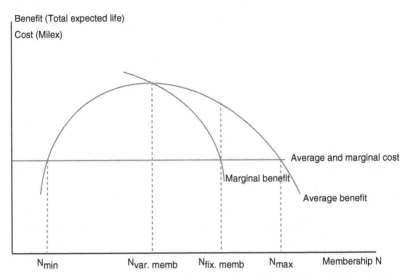

Figure 6.2: Optimal size of a Buchanan-style military club of Westphalian nation-states
Source: author

members, who prefer to maximise the average net benefit of membership, AB-AC, rather than allow the club membership to expand to N_{fix}. A simple remedy in this case is for all those keen to join an alliance, but unable to be admitted to club together, to form another military alliance or to federate. This would result in some fragmentation of military capability formation between a number of smaller alliances and federal states, but that would still be a more efficient option than the capability provision by small, unaligned nation-states.

However, as different nation-states tend to face different threats, those feeling relatively less secure are more likely to seek club membership in order to share their burden of national security provision with other states. This creates an element of adverse selection as those states that are more exposed to military threats are more likely to seek alliance membership or to federate. Yet, those that are relatively secure may object to assuming the additional risks and cost of being drawn into military conflicts through clubbing or merging with more vulnerable states. Thus, the existing club members must weigh the extent to which each potential new member adds resources to strengthen the collective military capability but also increases their exposure to additional military threats (shifting the average benefit curve down in Figure 6.2). This is the classic dilemma of whether an inclusion of another state or a group of beneficiaries results in the 'thinning' or 'thickening' of collective military capability. As in other imperfect risk-shifting markets, those states known to be relatively exposed to certain categories of military risks are less likely to be offered the benefits of club-style provision of national security unless some third party steps in and partially or wholly absorbs the additional risks and costs of providing such assurance for highly vulnerable states.

Another impediment to military club formation concerns the unequal distribution of national economic resources: at issue here is the artificiality of the assumption that all alliance member states are of equal size, with similar resource endowments. Potential member states are likely to be very diverse, and their shares of club costs and benefits commensurately differ. If the club is operated equitably between members, the larger and wealthier members and those relatively more exposed to military threats would account for a larger share of the collective burden of defence. This would be difficult to achieve when the alliance is also an Olson-Zeckhauser-style, idiorrythmic military club in which members are free to make their own commitments to capability formation and 'come to the party' with what they have when a particular contingency materialises. In these circumstances, poorer member states may free-ride at the expense of the wealthier members, particularly when the latter use their large resources to produce deterrence-based capabilities as alliance-wide public/club goods.[26] This is likely to be a disincentive for the richer and powerful states to form military clubs with smaller, resource-poor and vulnerable states.

In the Buchanan-style alliance, one type of membership contract is needed for all member states, normally underpinned by a plurilateral treaty between all members. Such a standard membership contract is likely to be incomplete in terms of describing the military contingencies demanding an allied response and prescribing the nature and scale of any such response. In the Olson-Zeckhauser alliance with heterogeneous club membership and idiorrythmic capability formation, however, each member state would need to have a member-specific contract to determine individual membership rights and obligations vis-à-vis the collective, and to reduce the scope for moral hazards associated with the provision of club-wide public goods by the larger and wealthier states. The bundle of such member-specific contracts is likely to be far more incomplete and costly to manage than the standard membership contract of the Buchanan-style alliance. This raises the problem of how such a diverse body of member states is to be effectively managed to form adequate military capabilities and sustain them over time to respond to different military contingencies. In addition, the rate and often radical nature of military innovation would necessitate frequent revisions of individual contracts to reduce contractual incompleteness in the face of growing complexity of warfighting and fast-changing military technologies. All of that would make the diverse-membership club too cumbersome to operate and very costly to manage. Not surprisingly, with the exception of NATO and ANZUS (see below) underpinned by the American provision of club-wide public goods, we are not aware of the existence of any other plurilateral military alliances.

However, nation-states have often collaborated by forming ad hoc coalitions of like-minded powers to respond to specific military contingencies. We refer to these temporary, event-focused alliances as 'coalitions of the willing': the fourth category of military capability provision. In essence, these are ad hoc arrangements in which participants may vary in size and resource endowments and are normally free to determine their contribution having regard to the size and scope of their force-in-being and its level of readiness at the time. The recent history of such ad hoc arrangements suggests that democracies can mobilise their existing military resources at short notice for a limited operational duration but have difficulty sustaining long-term engagements that require the replenishment of military resources, new investments in operation-specific military assets and continuing political support.[27] In general, ad hoc clubbing arrangements by democracies seem more likely to succeed in responding to contingencies, as opposed to preventing them. This is because such arrangements are usually facilitated by informal and highly incomplete enabling contracts, which are relatively easy to agree to enable operations to proceed. Yet, such contracts are usually vague as to what is to be specifically accomplished, how it is to be achieved and what conditions need to be satisfied to terminate the joint effort.

The last model of military capability formation involves the global provision of collective security for all member states of the United Nations as a global, non-excludable and non-rival pure public good. Arguably, this model was implicit in the formation of the United Nations as an organisation capable of both conflict deterrence (peacekeeping) and joint military intervention should preventive activities fail (peace enforcement). In practice, some joint military activities under the UN banner have taken place (the 1950–53 UN intervention in Korea was an early example, and, more recently, a host of other examples include peacekeeping operations, such as the 1999 UN mission in Kosovo). In effect, however, these have been ad hoc operations, drawing on military capabilities-in-being maintained by various participating nations. Thus, while some UN missions have endured for years (e.g. UN observers in the Middle East), the United Nations has never progressed beyond essentially ad hoc arrangements. Any other arrangement would require UN members to establish a permanent, multinational military alliance operating under UN auspices, dedicated to peacekeeping and peace enforcement, and underpinned by joint military capabilities. The attendant moral hazards and incentive to free-load render this an unlikely prospect for the foreseeable future.

6.3 Bilateral Arrangements and US-Led Alliances

The predominant form of military alliance has traditionally been between a larger military power, offering protection on a reciprocal basis, and a smaller, vulnerable power seeking external assurance of its national security. This protector-protégé relationship could be underpinned by a formal, treaty-based arrangement (e.g. the 1960 US-Japan Treaty of Mutual Cooperation and Security) or by an informal understanding between the two countries. Post-World War II, as the United States stepped into the role of the global superpower, it has effectively become a party central to several bilateral alliances: the US-centred hub-and-spoke model.

Figure 6.3 shows the strong bonding forces of the hub-and-spoke arrangement (thicker arrows) that rely on US military capability to underpin the security of each protégé state. Normally, all such arrangements are reciprocal in that the United States as the security provider may expect the protégé country to offer its military assistance in the event of a military contingency that involves the US. In practice, the degree of reciprocity may be restricted and the superpower may only call on the protégé's military capability as a measure of last resort in some global contingency (e.g. Israel has not been called to contribute its military assets to the US-led coalitions in the Middle East). In some cases, reciprocity may involve the establishment of the US military base in the

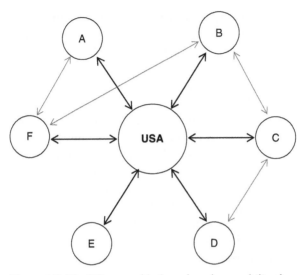

Figure 6.3: The US-centred hub-and-spoke capability formation
Source: author

protected country (e.g. the US military facilities in Okinawa) or some use of the protégé's military assets to facilitate joint training and direct logistical support in peacetime (e.g. US-Australian collaboration).

In addition to these strong bonding forces, there are also weaker bonding forces between the US protégé countries, which take advantage of the US linkage to allow additional, direct collaboration between the United States' bilateral partners. Examples of such arrangements include military cooperation between Australia and Singapore and, more recently, Australia and Japan. These are shown in Figure 6.3 as the thin arrows. In essence, these arrangements take advantage of each country's degree of interoperability with the US military to seek additional efficiencies in training, logistical support and the exchange of intelligence. Over time, and in principle, such hub-and-spoke arrangements could grow into a plurilateral military alliance along NATO lines.

Unlike the Olson-Zeckhauser plurilateral, NATO-style alliance, hub-and-spoke arrangements provide less scope for free-riding by protégé states. This is because the contract between the US and its protégé for provision of security is incomplete, being characterised by residual uncertainty regarding US willingness to take decisive action to protect a state which takes advantage of US military assurances, underinvests in its own security and/or fails to reciprocate when the United States seeks its help. Such a situation developed in the NATO model after the doctrine of Mutually Assured Destruction (MAD) was abandoned in favour of the doctrine of flexible response, which allowed the United States a degree of discretion in its response to military contingencies.[28]

The second US-centred model of joint capability formation is a plurilateral alliance between the United States as the dominant power and two or more countries. Two treaty-based examples of such an arrangement are the tripartite alliance between Australia, New Zealand and the United States (ANZUS) and the multinational North Atlantic Treaty Organisation (NATO). An example of informal plurilateral arrangements is The Technical Cooperation Program (TTCP) involving the United States, United Kingdom, Canada, Australia and New Zealand. Similar informal links exist between larger NATO powers and non-NATO countries like Australia. Formally, plurilateral arrangements such as NATO or ANZUS have been designed as conventional alliances between equal powers rather than the US-centred dominant-power model.

The credibility of US-led plurilateral alliances has largely depended on the scale and scope of US milex. In 1949, the US spending on defence represented 72 per cent of all the milex of NATO member states, and for most of NATO's existence American milex has accounted for at least 60 per cent of the alliance's total military expenditure. In particular, the United States contributed and funded the core component of NATO military capability: its strategic nuclear deterrent. This is also true of ANZUS, where US milex has dwarfed the military contributions of Australia and New Zealand. Thus, the formal institutional design of NATO and ANZUS as Buchanan-style clubs of equal members obscures the inherent inequality in the distribution of military capability between the United States and its plurilateral partners. In reality, the United States operates as NATO's dominant power and Stackelberg leader, and makes the critical and largely autonomous investment in military capability of the alliance. Other members are Stackelberg followers, which are free to determine the scale and scope of their own national military commitments given the collective deterrent and decisive power projection capacity provided by the United States. Not surprisingly, some allies may elect to underinvest in their own defence and free-ride at the expense of the leader, and the alliance as a whole, making collective burden-sharing a divisive issue.

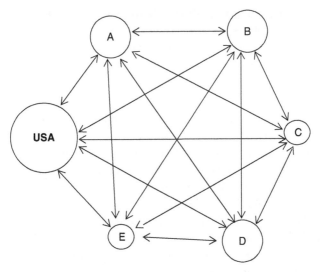

Figure 6.4: Intended stylised design of an equitable plurilateral alliance
Source: author

Figure 6.4 shows the intended design of a stylised plurilateral alliance of diverse members contributing resources to the joint capability formation equitably; that is, in proportion to their capacity to contribute (say, as a fixed ratio of milex to GDP). In many respects this is a structure reflecting the intent implicit in the 1948 design of NATO as ultimately a club of diverse members making idiorrythmic contributions to joint capability formation but willing to pull their weight rather than free-ride at the United States and other members' expense. There are denser direct linkages between member states within this stylised alliance as, in the absence of centralised resource pooling and investment, members coordinate their investment activities with one another. However, the actual model of NATO seems to resemble the hub-and-spoke model shown in Figure 6.3, with the United States operating as the largely autarchic and autonomous Stackelberg leader at the centre of the alliance and a party central to various bilateral understandings with other members.

6.4 Conclusion

Contemporary US political discourse suggests that its voters are losing their appetite for the kind of US-led and subsidised security arrangements that have characterised the post-Cold War international security environment. This is not to suggest that the United States will abandon its investment in the global rules-based order and retreat into some kind of Fortress America. But it does imply that the quality of political and military support provided by non-US members of the Western strategic community will increasingly influence US decisions about how and when it will deploy its military power to protect and advance that order.

This leads us to ask whether, in current circumstances, members of the US-led Western strategic community would have to invent NATO-style plurilateral alliances underpinned by autarchic US military power if they did not already exist. We are inclined to answer in the negative. In reaching this conclusion we recognise that the United States will continue to incur low marginal costs in extending conditional security assurances to like-minded friends and allies, and that the US is likely to gain commensurate economic and political benefit from providing such assurances. But our analysis of the moral hazard and adverse selection that characterise plurilateral alliance arrangements suggests that, for the foreseeable future, bilateral, hub-and-spoke arrangements focused on the United States are likely to generate more durable benefits with lower transaction costs for both the US and its security partners. For the parties to such hub-and-spoke arrangements to gain equitable benefits, however, the debate between the United States and its allies needs to shift away from the current preoccupation with levels of defence expenditure and the burden of defence in terms of milex share in GDP.

Instead, the debate between the United States and its allies should focus more specifically on how a nation's physical capability investment decisions contribute not only to its sovereign capacity to protect national security, but also to common security endeavours under the relevant, US-led alliance. To date, free-riding at the United States' and other allies' expense is identified and 'measured' in terms of milex underspending, relative to some benchmark defence expenditure target – commonly 2 per cent of GDP. This focus can, and frequently does, obscure underinvestment in specific, physical military capabilities by non-US alliance members.

Shifting focus to physical capability would have significant implications for military capability formation by non-US members belonging not only to plurilateral alliances such as NATO, but also of bilateral alliances like those prevalent in the Asia-Pacific. It would not, of course, preclude defence expenditure on indigenous 'make' solutions to country-specific capability requirements. But it would render such choices more transparent to both domestic taxpayers and other security partners by highlighting the relative opportunity costs and trade-offs between 'home-made' and 'imported' national security. This would help to contain moral hazards inherent in alliance-based national security provision.

Our discussion suggests that US-centred hub-and-spoke style security arrangements are likely to be less exposed to US moral hazard and less prone to free-loading by smaller participants. This is because implicit contracts underlying bilateral arrangements are relatively more complete with regard to the nature of reciprocity between the parties involved. To this extent, non-US participants in such security arrangements are more likely to invest in capabilities that are needed to complement US military capabilities, and could also make worthwhile contributions to ad hoc coalitions. Importantly, the marginal cost to the United States of helping non-US participants in hub-and-spoke style security arrangements develop interoperable forces suited to such coalition arrangements would be reduced to the extent that the countries concerned resist the temptation to free-load and make investments on their own account. But, their willingness to do so will remain a function of their assessment of how their contribution to collective security provision protects and advances their sovereign security interests – an assessment that in turn hinges on their trust in the US security umbrella.

The combination of moral hazard and free-loading that characterises NATO-style plurilateral security arrangements tends to inhibit militarily significant contributions to joint interventions by the non-US alliance members. The NATO Washington Treaty was negotiated seventy years ago in a very different security context. As a form of contract, the Treaty is highly incomplete and, as it stands, encourages not only unequal and inequitable distribution of the burden of common defence between members, but also idiorrythmic new capability formation, all of which makes for an unnecessarily fragmented collective military capability.

It is only the United States' Stackelberg leadership of NATO, and its massive autonomous investment in military capability as the global superpower, that make the alliance a credible player in the international security environment.

But US taxpayers and their representatives will always need to be convinced of the merits of both plurilateral and bilateral security arrangements. In both cases the requisite advocacy could start with recognition that, given the United States' chosen status of the global superpower, the marginal cost to the US of maintaining such arrangements is relatively low. More persuasive advocacy is likely to require America's allies to be more proactive in the formation of joint physical military capabilities. This is necessary if these allies are to convince US sceptics that they actually mean business rather than virtue-signal their willingness to spend more money on 'defence' regardless of what that money is to be spent on. If these arguments fail, then members of the Western strategic community do seem likely to be forced to make larger unilateral investments in military capability and to rely on ad hoc coalitions, but with less purposeful US leadership.

Notes

1. Named after Heinrich Freiherr von Stackelberg, who published his *Market Structure and Equilibrium* description of the dominant firm model in 1934.
2. D. Croxton. 'The Peace of Westphalia of 1648 and the Origins of Sovereignty'. *International History Review*. 1999. 21(3): 569–91.
3. For a survey of economic club literature see T. Sandler and J. T. Tschirhart. 'The Economic Theory of Clubs: An Evaluative Survey'. *Journal of Economic Literature*. 1980. 18(4): 1481–521; J. M. Buchanan. 'An Economic Theory of Clubs'. *Economica*. 1965. 32(125): 1–14.
4. H. Kissinger. *World Order: Reflections on the Character of Nations and the Course of History*. London: Penguin. 2014.
5. E. Cannan (ed). *An Inquiry into the Nature and Causes of the Wealth of Nations* Chicago: University of Chicago Press. 1976. www.econlib.org/library/Smith/smWN.html (accessed 10 January 2018).
6. Article 3 of the Washington Treaty requires 'the Parties, separately and jointly, by means of continuous and effective self-help and mutual aid, (to) maintain and develop their individual and collective capacity to resist armed attack' but it does not stipulate how this is actually to be achieved.
7. T. Sandler. 'The Economics Theory of Alliances: A Survey'. *Journal of Conflict Resolution*. 1993. 37(3): 473.
8. Until 1951, NATO required no dedicated international budgetary arrangements as the United States and the United Kingdom were paying the running costs of the organisation while national governments of other member states provided personnel at their own expense. See D. Kunertova. 'One Measure Cannot Trump It All: Lessons from NATO's Early Burden-Sharing Debates'. *European Security*. 2017. 26(4): 7. DOI: 10.1080/09662839.2017.1353495.

9. See Sandler and Tschirhart. 'The Economic Theory of Clubs'.
10. D. Driver. 'Burden Sharing and the Future of NATO: Wandering Between Two Worlds'. *Defense & Security Analysis*. 2016. 32(1): 4–18.
11. T. Sandler and J. Murdoch. 'On Sharing NATO Defense Burdens in the 1990s and Beyond'. *Fiscal Studies*. 2000. 21(3): 299.
12. See Kunertova. 'One Measure Cannot Trump It All'; Driver. 'Burden Sharing and the Future of NATO'.
13. Sandler. 'The Economics Theory of Alliances'.
14. M. Olson and R. Zeckhauser. 'An Economic Theory of Alliances'. *The Review of Economics and Statistics*. 1966. 48(3): 266–79.
15. Sandler. 'The Economics Theory of Alliances'.
16. T. Sandler and K. Hartley. 'Economics of Alliances: The Lessons for Collective Action'. *Journal of Economic Literature*. 2001. XXXIX (September): 875.
17. Driver. 'Burden Sharing and the Future of NATO'.
18. Credible military capability is also relative to what the state aims to achieve, given its location, size and military objectives. The latter may not be the directly observable dimension of capability formation as military planners are rather secretive about more nuanced aspects of military objectives.
19. Generally, a state that confines its military investment to a defensive military posture is less likely to exhibit the declining segment of the total benefit curve, and the total benefit curve may be approaching asymptotically some maximum value.
20. For example, a highly capable military power such as the United States is likely to operate at the relatively steep, increasing segment of the cost curve, incur high levels of milex and carry a relatively heavy burden of defence in part because it strives to achieve high levels of military self-sufficiency and in part because the structural complexity of its military capability increases rapidly as capability increases.
21. Perversely though, larger states may attract asymmetric aggression from terrorist groups as the demonstration effect (e.g. publicity value) of hostile acts may grow more than proportionally when a bigger state is targeted.
22. For example, while the Third Reich was partitioned by the Allies when it was defeated in World War II, federal Germany has endured. In contrast, federal experiments such as the Soviet Union and Yugoslavia have been created and held together by force and disintegrated the moment different national elements were allowed to go their separate ways. It took the highly costly secessionist war to consolidate the United States into the federal entity we know today. While some smaller powers, such as Switzerland, Canada and Australia, are examples of

conspicuous federal success, others, such as Belgium, are still threatened by disintegration, while the federal Czechoslovakia has already dissolved into the Czech and Slovak Republics.

23. S. Markowski and R. Wylie. 'The Emergence of European Defence and Defence Industry Policies'. *Security Challenges*. 2007. 3(2): 31–51.

24. J. Techau. *The Politics of 2 Percent: NATO and the Security Vacuum in Europe*. Brussels: Carnegie Europe. 2015.

25. See Buchanan. 'An Economic Theory of Clubs'; Sandler and Tschirhart. 'The Economic Theory of Clubs'.

26. Olson and Zeckhauser. 'An Economic Theory of Alliances'. *The Review of Economics and Statistics*. 1966. 48(3): 266–79.

27. Thus, the East Timor intervention in 1999–2000 illustrates a relatively successful in-and-out military operation while the 2004 US-led coalition in Iraq, initiated as a surgical intervention to remove an internationally-disapproved local dictatorship, lost its way as it evolved into a nation-building exercise and arbitration between mutually hostile ethnic and religious communities.

28. Sandler. 'The Economics Theory of Alliances'.

7 | The Rise and Demise of Government-Mandated Offset Policy

RON MATTHEWS

Introduction

The implosion of the Soviet Union and the end of the Cold War led to the collapse of global defence procurement budgets and the creation of excess defence-industrial capacity. A buyer's market ensued, whereby exporters were obliged to furnish additional benefits over and above the sale of the military product. This reciprocal investment is what is commonly, though not universally, referred to as offset.[1] Of course, vendors may refuse to play this game, but they do so in full knowledge that more obliging competitors lie in wait. If vendors do offer offset, often via transfer of the underlying production processes, then they face the danger of creating future competitive forces. This classic 'Scylla and Charybdis' dilemma is at the heart of tensions between the offshore vendor and customer offset authority, influencing vendor marketing strategies, negotiating positions and contractual relations that have evolved over the past two decades.

The immediate pressures surrounding operational management have acted to preclude longer-term analysis as to how offset policy and practice may be evolving. For instance, the viability and longevity of offset are rarely discussed in the same context, yet logically if the former is questioned then the latter will also be in doubt. It is remarkable that the future of such a controversial topic has attracted so little attention, especially given that it has been bedevilled with criticism concerning its ability to deliver the anticipated benefits. Offset is shrouded in mystery, misinformation and misunderstanding. It incites major debates: for instance, there is concern about the 'inevitable' additional cost it imposes on procurement deals; there is also the view that it lacks transparency, and hence carries major potential for corruption; and, finally, there are questions over the sustainability of the technology transfer it generates.[2]

The sustainability issue highlights tensions between country customers aiming to maximise indigenous capability opportunities
through defence offset and offshore vendors seeking compliance
with customer-mandated offset requirements, but in such a way
that their Intellectual Property Rights (IPR) and competitive advantage are protected. Foreign vendor resistance to 'giving away the
crown jewels' has led to a questioning of offset's worth to recipient
countries. Foreign vendors, therefore, face a tricky balancing act.
There is a need to win major defence contracts, but at the same
time, expectations must be managed to ensure that customers do
not become disillusioned with outcomes. As a result, offset goals are
only partially achieved across the broad swathe of customer countries. Remarkably, rising disappointment over offset's inability to
create sufficient skilled jobs, foster high value technology transfer,
promote supply chains, encourage local R&D and support exports,
has not dimmed offset's global appeal.

Indeed, offset exhibits strong dynamics. It is reportedly enjoying
compound annual growth of 3.5 per cent, with obligations expected to
increase by 36 per cent between 2012 and 2021 to reach a cumulative
total of more than \$425 billion.[3] It is reported that over 130 nations now
have official published offset requirements, and the numbers continue to
rise.[4] In 2012, Mexico launched its first offset policy, followed by
Indonesia in 2014, and a Philippines' policy is imminent. Moreover,
the impressive 143 per cent growth in Chinese arms exports across the
five-year period 2009–14, positioning it as the world's third-biggest
exporter across this period, and also the subsequent 2012–16 period, is
mainly attributable to a unique competitive package comprising offset,
extremely keen pricing structures and political noninterference.

The reason behind offset's popularity is the belief that government-
mandated offset regulations can leverage offshore vendors to release
technology and accelerate growth of indigenous industrial capability.
Whether, and to what extent, this belief is true is a moot point.
The purpose of this chapter, then, is to explore the theoretical, policy
and implementation characteristics of offset, especially whether existing approaches are fit for purpose. Government-mandated offset is the
model employed by most major arms purchasers, and if it is not
delivering the anticipated benefits, then this begs the question as to
whether the life of offset is time limited.

7.1 Offset and the Clash between Ideology and Pragmatism

Classical economic theories emphasise the importance of perfect markets and free trade. Yet, while these theoretical constructs apply to commercial sectors, the domestic defence context will feature monopoly-monopsony market structures, and, additionally, because of the sensitivity of arms exports, they will be subject to far greater institutional scrutiny, oversight and control. Furthermore, the traditional requirements of national security and sovereignty of supply set defence apart from commercial endeavour. Accordingly, protectionism is the cornerstone of the global arms trade, representing just one of myriad political, diplomatic, military and institutional barriers that vendors must navigate around to access foreign markets. A further imperfection of the modern arms market is held to be the importing countries' insatiable appetite for defence offset. Specifically, offset is held to be anticompetitive, market-distorting and welfare-reducing, with the European Commission, in particular, intervening to control and suppress member state offset regimes.

Most arms importing states prioritise direct offset, seeking technology transfer to accelerate local defence industrialisation. However, some states prefer indirect offset, requiring vendor investment to be channelled into commercial activities in support of broader economic and industrial development objectives. Governments warm to offset, because it is viewed as a 'win-win' arrangement, and hence has become *de rigueur* in major arms deals. While weapons capability is the principal qualifier for closing a sale, the attractiveness of the offset package is increasingly a critical discriminator in the marketing mix. Arms exporters are well aware of the importance of offset. Nevertheless, there is a reluctance to release high technology to secure the sale, viewing the process as sacrificing the corporate heritage of technological creativity and innovation, accumulated through generations of expensive investment. Yet, it is held that the existence of a 'buyers' market (supply exceeding demand) creates leverage for buyer governments to demand offset as an obligatory, not discretionary, component of the procurement deal. Accordingly, arms exporters fail to win orders if offset is not offered, or offered but is unattractive. Offset is an important part of the procurement package, and it is therefore essential to determine the parameters of what offset can and cannot achieve.

Offset might be described as a form of blackmail, but it is legal. It may also be viewed as 'compensation', but it is surely inappropriate to tie compensatory investment to unfettered arms procurement. Yet, it is this counterbalancing action that defines offset, with the buyer's market acting as the spigot creating and controlling the pressure. If market forces converge, then surely pressure for offset would subside. The problem with this argument is that offset was a salient feature of the global arms trade decades before the ending of the Cold War, and the collapse in arms demand. The stand-off between NATO and the Warsaw Pact created the conditions for a supplier's market, defined as limited numbers of arms exporters enjoying unlimited growth in customer nations' defence budgets and procurement spends. While the demand for offset is linked to the notion of a buyer's market, there are three other important considerations that determine the existence, and, indeed, success of offset. First and foremost is procurement scale. Large volumes drive customer leverage and, in turn, the quality of the offset package: the bigger the procurement volume, the greater the extent and degree of technology transfer the vendor is prepared to offer. The second factor influencing the nature and viability of offset is the importing country's technological absorptive capacity. This capacity embraces not only local platform manufacturers, but also the broader civil-military R&D community, including innovative supply chains and frontier engineering universities. These elements, combined with an abundance of highly skilled scientists, technicians and engineers, are principal factors determining offset success. Thirdly, the feasibility and appeal of offset will be influenced by the nature of the recipient country's offset strategy. Flexibility will be more attractive to offshore defence vendors than government-mandated prescription and penalty.

7.2 Mandatory versus Non-Mandatory Offset

Few countries are without a formal offset policy, and most of these are poor African and Asian states. Those that do have offset regimes have crafted approaches that range from ad hoc and rudimentary to formal and prescriptive. The challenge, then, is to construct a framework that adequately defines offset, covering all its 'chameleon' features. Figure 7.1 offers such a schema, distinguishing between the two principal schools of thought on offset policy: (formal) mandatory and (informal) non-mandatory offset.

The most important school of thought illustrated in Figure 7.1 is mandatory offset policy, normally designed, managed and monitored

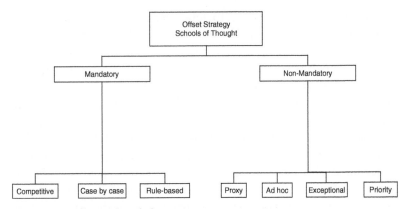

Figure 7.1: Offset policy dichotomy
Source: author

by a customer country's Offset Authority. There are three types of government-mandated policy, distinguishable by the degree of contractual flexibility. The first is characterised by a high degree of competitiveness and flexibility. Here, offset policy is broad and generalised, allowing policymakers to be judgemental about requirements. The erstwhile UK Industrial Participation (IP) policy was reflective of this particular approach. It ran from 1990 until 2012 and was held to be successful.[5] The launch and transposition of the 2009 European procurement Directive led to the abandonment of UK Industrial Participation policy. Arguably, the success of the UK model was due to its simplicity, reflected by the fact that when operational, the policy could be summarised in just one short paragraph: IP should be placed with UK companies, be defence-related, new and of equivalent technological level as the primary defence contract, arise on procurements exceeding £35,000 and not be subject to legal contractual status.[6]

Significantly, the policy was concerned with competition not compensation, and was incentivised through the encouragement provided to overseas defence contractors to search the UK defence economy for internationally competitive subcontractors. The thinking was that if IP projects could be allocated according to competitive forces rather than 'detached' institutional decision-making, then there would be no basis for an offset cost premium. Moreover, flexibility was introduced through the MoD IP Unit, firstly, leaving the specifics of IP projects to the commercial judgement of offshore vendors, subject to compliance with the 'one-paragraph' policy framework, and, secondly, through interpreting the 100 per cent offset quota as a ceiling rather than floor for negotiating offset agreements. The effect was that offset quotas were agreed on the basis of what offshore vendors could achieve rather than on arbitrary, inflexible and 'undoable' offset aspirations. Finally, as the IP agreement had no legal identity, penalties were not imposed in the event that the offset quota was not achieved. The MoD simply highlighted its long memory in such matters.

The second category of mandatory offset policies is case-by-case evaluation. Here, a policy exists but is not externally published, and thus confined to procurement staff within the MoD. The procurement body operates against an internal set of standardised guidelines that offer flexibility in their application. Offset negotiation is undertaken on a case-by-case basis, allowing offset packages to be tailor-made to align with the scale and technical specification of both the particular weapons procurement and local absorptive capability. The two best examples of countries employing internal case-by-case offset policies are Singapore and Japan. Both have long pursued policies of offset, especially licensed production. The platforms are built to foreign design specifications, and as far as possible, local subassembly and systems solutions are integrated into the final weapons configuration. Civil-military benefits are also exploited so that technology learning is not isolated to the defence economy, but permeates across the broader commercial industrial environment.

The final form of mandatory offset approach is the most dominant, the rules-based policy. It is prescriptive, normally through the publication of lengthy and complex offset policy documents. The rules-based methodology tends to be associated with states possessing limited defence-industrial capacity. Hence, greater rigour and incentivisation are required to steer offshore vendor investment towards industrial and technological gaps in the local economy. The recipient country's Offset Authority will determine strategic offset goals, including economic diversification, job creation, skill generation, R&D investment, supply chain promotion, export opportunity – often through access to OEM global supplier networks, as well as capacity widening and deepening objectives. In response, offshore vendors pursue one or a combination of options to discharge offset obligations, including: (1) deciding that it is a distraction and transferring the task to independent specialist brokers, for a fee; (2) cascading a proportion of the liability down to the vendor's supply chain; (3) proposing multiple projects within the broader offset programme to clear offset liabilities; and (4) simply defaulting, and paying the Offset Authority's penalty fee. The latter option is the least palatable, because it will sour relations between the vendor and customer country, negatively impacting on contractual eligibility scores that will influence the outcomes of future procurement bids.

The second school of offset thought is the non-mandatory approach, reflecting scenarios where formal offset policies do not apply. However, the absence of formal policy does not mean that there are no customer expectations regarding industrial cooperation. Indeed, non-mandatory models include reciprocal investment that is expected, condoned and encouraged. There is, firstly, what might be termed the 'proxy' offset model, and the best example here is that of the United States. Although Washington denies it has an offset policy, since 1933 the proxy method has been the 'Buy American' legislation. The US Department of Defense is required to Buy American first, as a general rule, under Federal Acquisition Regulation and Defense Federal Acquisition Regulation. However, the Regulation does not preclude foreign firms from competing for federal contracts, but to be eligible for Department of Defense awards, bidders must prove that 50 per cent of programme content is produced in the United States. Hence, in everything but name, 'Buy American' operates as an offset policy.[7]

Secondly, there is the European Union offset model, based on 'exceptionalism'. This approach dates back to Article 223 of the 1957 Treaty of Rome that directs: 'Any Member State may take the measures which it considers necessary for the protection of all essential interests of its security and which are connected with the production of, or trade in arms, ammunition and war material.'[8] Since that time, and including the most recent legislation, Article 346 of the 2007 Treaty of Lisbon, the European Union has tolerated the view that defence operates as an exception to open and free trade. Thus, throughout a fifty-year period, offset was allowed, though not necessarily condoned. This position dramatically changed following the 2009 publication of the European procurement Directive 2009/81/EC. Applying the 'single market' concept to defence, the European Union sought to remove what it perceived to be noncompetitive practices perpetuating Member State defence-industrial sovereignty and duplicative arms production. In the European Union's ideological pursuit of competitive and contestable markets, offset was then viewed as a barrier to Europe's evolution towards an integrated defence market.

The European Union would continue to approve direct offset, but subject to Article 346 that noncompetitive domestic production must be based on national security grounds. Indirect offset immediately became illegal, as commercial investment bore no relevance to national security. The fear of legal action by the European Court of Justice led initially to widespread abandonment of Member State offset policies. The United Kingdom, for example, fully transposed the 2009/81/EC legislation, replacing it with a voluntary and non-audited Defence and Security Industrial Engagement Policy. Yet, along with other EU Member States, the United Kingdom has continued to seek exemption from the Directive on national security grounds for major arms procurement programmes. The poorer East European and smaller Scandinavian countries have gone further, gradually re-instituting formal offset policies formulated on perceived 'compliance' with the exceptional criteria of Article 346.

The third form of non-mandatory offset has regard to the Australian model. This developed after Canberra abandoned its 1990s mandatory offset policy on the grounds that it did not work. Since that time, Australia has been without a formal offset policy, but nevertheless still requires overseas suppliers bidding on procurement contracts to 'engage' with Australian defence companies. The goal is to encourage development of Australian defence-industrial capability by securing opportunities for high-value inward technology transfer. There is no offset policy in place; no quotas, multipliers and only limited penalties, but quality investment into Australian defence industry is a *sine qua non* for the down-selection of bidders.[9]

7.3 Offset Transition Curve: From Prescription to Partnership?

Every market requires stability, and as far as possible certainty, so that businesses can invest with confidence that their assets are secure. However, offset is a dynamic and fluid process, and even the most tightly crafted policies can change. This happens on a regular basis, affecting even the world's biggest arms importers. For example, India's protracted and convoluted offset guidelines have suffered repeated amendments. Similarly, the UAE's original 1992 offset policy underwent revisions in

2010 and 2015. Repeated changes of a country's offset policy suggest it is not working as intended, either in achieving the stated policy goals (India)[10] or in the vendors' ability to discharge liabilities across the contractual timeframes (UAE).[11] Consistency in policy approach is a major problem, but so is policy implementation. A particular challenge in this regard is mutual agreement of the level and value of technology transfer. The foreign offshore vendor is obviously reluctant to 'give away' technology, but in any case, there is only so much offset that can be allocated to 'competing' players across the global customer base. Of course, the 'best' offset will be calibrated with high customer procurement volumes; but even then, it is in the interests of all stakeholders to ensure that the new capacity is sustainable, as insufficient demand inevitably leads to offset failure. Offset negotiations are often fraught, and the search for compromise is challenging.

These problems represent formidable challenges to the effectiveness of offset, and beg the question as to why countries continue to engage in this practice. On balance, offset probably does bring net benefits to 'industrialised' states, but there is a remarkable reluctance, both in the literature and by country governments, to accept that offset likely fails to work in the 'industrialising' countries. There are some success stories, but the benefits derived from offset projects are often short-lived and illusory. Huge numbers of highly skilled jobs are not created, and evidence of local R&D, supply chain and export investment opportunities is sparse. So, why does the offset star continue to shine so brightly? It is difficult to be precise, in the absence of data, but offset's allure is probably due to poor country decision-makers being seduced by the prospect of 'free' investment. The reality, though, is that offset is not costless, and the additional cost in nearly all circumstances will be borne by the customer via inflated primary defence contract prices.

So, where does this leave the impartial offset observer? There is little in the literature to support informed speculation as to the future nature and direction of defence offset. Thus, a survey was undertaken of offset managers at eight of the United Kingdom's top defence exporting companies. The sample group of companies accounted for at least 70–80 per cent of total UK defence exports. Participating companies included global multi-product prime contractors and super-subcontractors, with product structures spanning the spectrum of land, sea and air weapons systems. The biggest primes and super-subs have engaged in offset since the early 1990s, though some 60 per cent have only established stand-alone offset offices since 2010. Most of the sample firms had engaged in offset arrangements prior to this period, but the creation of dedicated offset capacity reflects the growing importance of offset in support of UK arms exports.

Offset operations at 30 per cent of survey companies are organisationally aligned with legal and compliance functions. One company situates its offset team in the commercial division, partially to maintain close links to specialists in the risk, compliance, security and legal functions. Another company that established its offset office in 2012 appointed an offset manager who 'double-hats' as the compliance officer and reports to the company lawyer. The close link between offset and compliance reflects widespread institutional concern that offset is mired in corrupt practices. The tainting of offset began with the publication of a 2010 Transparency International report that investigated the potential for corruption in offset programmes. Its findings supported the conclusion that offset is prone to corruption. Although the evidence presented to support this proposition is flimsy and inaccurate, the report's findings were widely disseminated. As a result, a view gained traction that corruption in offset was endemic.

Earlier corruption scandals embroiling UK arms exporters had led to the publication of the Woolf Report Recommendations and the Bribery Act, and these developments have considerably strengthened corporate compliance policy. Interestingly, the prevailing view amongst this study's interviewees is that defence offset is no more tainted by corruption than procurement. In fact, 100 per cent of survey responses indicate that corporate offset operations have never been compromised by actual or even alleged corrupt practices. Moreover, there is no evidence of malpractice by overseas beneficiaries of UK defence offset programmes. All offset managers confirm that foreign offset beneficiary companies are selected only after rigorous due diligence audits. If the UK arms exporters harboured suspicions over the transparency and proprietary nature of offset deals in customer countries, they state they would have no hesitation in walking away from the deal. Discussions with company representatives leave no doubt that protection of the company's brand overrides the importance of any particular defence sale.

The process of winning orders hinges on the recognition that offset acts an enabler not only in winning deals, but also in creating the opportunity to engage in long-term commercial relationships based

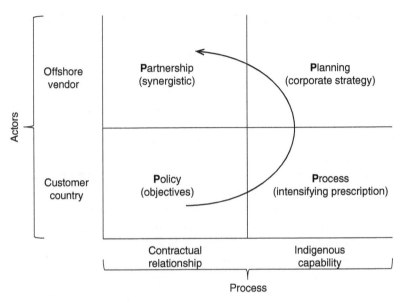

Figure 7.2: The 4P offset model
Source: author

on trust and commitment. The question is whether mandated offset is delivering the benefits promised. Based on interview responses and secondary research material, a trend has been identified that suggests the gradual demise of offset in favour of 'partnership'. This process is conceptualised in Figure 7.2, through a four-stage (4P) offset curve that proceeds through customer policy and process and corporate planning into offset arrangements that eventually morph into mutually beneficial customer-vendor partnerships.

7.4 Policy – Chasing Elusive Rainbows

The starting point in the 4P analytical framing approach is to evaluate customer offset objectives. These have remained constant over time, focused on increasing sovereign industrial and technological capability in either or both the civil and military domains. However, with the passage of time, customer governments have become more demanding in their requirements for technology access. Around 50 per cent of the offset managers surveyed state that the biggest challenge is dealing with increasingly strident offset authorities seeking excessive, over-ambitious and often unacceptable offset packages. Customers harbour irrational capability aspirations, and this creates difficulties over the sophistication of technology transfer and the associated inevitable disagreements over financial value. India is cited as a case where excessive technology demands and tortuously long delays in decision making work against constructive engagement. Also mentioned is Qatar, which is ambitiously pursuing TRL 1 technology capability, albeit that Doha probably has the finance and appetite to succeed. A further challenge is the inflexible and bureaucratic approach adopted by offset authorities. An example is given of a Scandinavian offset authority that rejected a proven and innovative project aimed at joint development of medical technology for early diagnosis of cervical cancer, because it fell outside aerospace and defence offset project parameters.

7.5   Process – 'Big Stick' Mentality

The investigative focus moves from policy objectives to the 'dynamics' of policy. In what ways are policies changing? Are they becoming more or less rigorous, flexible or bureaucratic? Is there an emerging trend that might signal future nuanced or even dramatic policy changes? The interviewees' responses to such questions suggest that offset is becoming.more, not less, prescriptive, and the rationale for this hardening of policy is likely an attempt to improve flagging performance. Predicting the outcome of enforced mandatory offset policy compliance is not easy, but made worse by the uncertainty that pervades the world's defence markets. Changes in environmental conditions drive uncertainty, including threat perceptions, fiscal positions and political expediency. Technological change can also act to undermine the longevity of weapons systems, and actual or imminent conflict may increase the 'urgency' of arms acquisition, causing user nations to bypass the strictures of national procurement and offset policy. Defence sales are in any case lumpy over time, and this will obviously have a knock-on effect with respect to the demand for offset.

The defence market has become more competitive and price sensitive, and, as a consequence, offset authorities are now increasingly emboldened to impose more prescriptive regulation. There is a hardening of offset authority positions across the plethora of regulations. Most states are demanding direct offset, but in recent years a broader array of defence, aerospace and security projects have come under the purview of direct offset. This diversification into aerospace and security has been due to the growth in counterterrorism requirements, leading one offset manager to observe that offset projects in the defence domain can be symbolised with a small 'd', and those in security with a capital 'S'. Civil offset demand is still substantial, however. For example, contrary to the legislative constraints imposed on offset by the European procurement Directive, interviewees confirm that East European states continue to demand reciprocal 'commercial' investment.

All interviewees report that offset authorities are becoming more demanding and ambitious in the search for higher-value technology transfer/work placement. It appears that customers are increasingly placing near equal weighting on product price/performance and the quality of the offset package. Turkey, for instance, requires a 40 per cent weighting for offset. More widely, it is also becoming common practice for offset to be incorporated into bid selection criteria. This prioritisation of offset applies equally to advanced states pursuing non-mandated offset models as to developing states with formal, mandated, and extremely prescriptive policies. The discernible trend towards progressive tightening of regulatory frameworks is also reflected in both falling offset thresholds and fulfilment periods; the latter now being regularly linked to arms delivery periods. Customer demand for low-value commodity countertrade has fallen away, and instead there is a growing policy emphasis on technology transfer. The mechanism for ensuring that the infusion of technology is channelled towards high value sectors is through offset multipliers. However, these are declining, and what had previously been automatic multipliers now need to be justified on the basis of higher and higher levels of technology transfer. Even more challenging is that the process of satisfying rising customer industrial ambitions via the creation of local indigenous capacity is likely to be tied to establishing local R&D, supply chain and export capabilities. Yet, while multiplier values and offset thresholds are falling, so are quotas. There seems to be a grudging recognition by offset authorities that the era of unsustainable 100 per cent quotas is over, with investment depth replacing development breadth.

Offset authorities are also adopting increasingly punitive postures. For example, South Korea no longer allows credits to be banked as a means of liquidating future liabilities. There is also a view that penalties on offset deals may sometimes be set higher than those penalising failure on the primary defence contract. One interviewee suggests that India has even introduced a negative multiplier. Moreover, offset authorities are belatedly recognising that vendors facing default on their obligations prefer simply to pay the penalty. This happens even though failure to deliver may lead to blacklisting on future projects, representing a big reputational risk to offshore vendors. A major challenge to successful discharge of obligations is finding viable offset projects, principally because there is only so much technology that can be disseminated through offset. To ensure vendors do not interpret penalties as the 'force of least resistance', offset authorities have moved to increase their severity as well as transferring any undischarged obligations to the next project. However, these punitive actions just increase the problems, adding to the pressures that caused vendors to struggle in the first place. No stakeholders, including the customer, want offset projects to fail, so it is in everyone's interest to avoid a 'race to the bottom'.

7.6 Planning – via 'Smart' Offset Strategies

Over 70 per cent of offset managers argue that growth in the numbers of global arms exporters is leading to an intensification of the buyers' market. This leaves a significant minority of managers believing that rising pressure for offset encourages exporters to bow to the inevitable and pursue 'smart' routes for establishing an in-country presence in key overseas markets. Although offset may require the release of greater technology transfer, it can also serve as an enabler for generating long-term revenue streams. Indeed, one subcontractor manager argues that offset can be a profitable line of business, especially when angled towards clearing prime contractor offset liabilities. Broader counter-trade and buy-back strategies do not figure in the business strategies of UK firms. Offset is viewed as the principal competitive strategy, but careful planning is always needed. For example, one interviewee states that offset did not feature in the respective design of two project developments begun over the last five to ten years. The reason is that offset only becomes an issue at commencement of the campaign, 'after' the development and production stages. The development of new systems may take up to twenty years, so offset is not a factor in the planning mix. Another manager echoed this view, stating that profit margins are used to fund fifteen-year product development cycles. In the process, management must decide what represents core and non-core software and systems. Offset is detached from this process, and hence the suitability of technology transfer and offshore production will always be the 'can kicked down the road'. Eventually, once the offset is negotiated, then the suitability of technology transfer will be constrained by its sophistication, and the search to secure sustainability is a customer problem. The reality is that a developing country must be prepared to continuously invest in development projects for its industry to become sustainable. In this sense, it is no different from the historical furrow ploughed by advanced country governments: over generations, it has been the taxpayers of these states that have borne the huge cumulative investment cost of expensive defence programmes in constructing the foundations of defence-industrial capability.

One interviewee argues that it is essential to formulate an integrated strategy, recognising that the primary defence contract and offset proposal are part of the same competitive package. The strategy must be proactive, aimed at exploring global markets in advance of bids as a means of winning contracts, executing offset projects and identifying local partners. The starting point is to develop an understanding of the customer's industrial landscape. Trust and close working relationships must be promoted, and openness is essential, so that all stakeholders are aware, and take ownership, of the negative as well as the positive impacts of offset. Offset affordability is the key issue, and the search for solutions must make economic sense to both parties.

At given levels of quality, UK defence manufacturers always compete on cost, and while civil and military routes to market are different, the cost pressures are similar. Therefore, in the context of offset, Indian, Indonesian and Polish markets are attractive, because they comprise relatively low-cost, labour-intensive suppliers. The process of 'Polanisation', for example, is concerned with accessing capability via the imposition of rigid requirements, including technology transfer, know-how, sourcing, multipliers and a project value formula. Yet, while this appears to contravene compliance with Article 346, it is a government, not corporate, problem. The real issue is whether overseas firms can do the work. Potential partners will be subject to a thorough prequalification process, as there is always a need to avoid financial penalties. Once trust and confidence in quality are assured, then there may be flexibility on third country exports, as these will enhance the flow of royalty payments.

The seeds for a long-term mutually beneficial relationship are being sown through the potential for partnership outside the parameters of restrictive mandated offset policy.

7.7 Partnership – Life beyond Offset?

Crystal-ball gazing into the future is a risky business. Nevertheless, speculation can prove helpful if anchored to the views of experts in the field, especially if there is consensus on the likelihood of unfolding future scenarios. Thus, it is revealing that there exists 100 per cent agreement amongst interviewees that offset will not disappear during the fifteen- to twenty-year timeframe of this investigation. This collective judgement even applies to Europe, where, irrespective of Directive 2009/81/EC, the view is that offset will continue to be demanded, albeit covertly, on mostly all defence contracts. Offset will not disappear, but it will likely gradually morph into a different identity and set of requirements, with other business frameworks emerging to offer alternative solutions to the increasingly challenging and 'confrontational' government-mandated offset model. However, the basic premise remains the same: countries demand capability and offshore vendors seek shareholder value.

Thus, the longevity of offset, or indeed any business framework, hinges on whether it delivers on corporate and customer expectations. From the corporate perspective, offset managers are divided as to whether offset does or does not deliver the required benefits. Antagonists argue that offset is a waste of resources. One offset manager put it bluntly: 'Offset is a distraction from the main purpose of making sales and profit. Invariably, it does not work, and represents a divergence of aims'.[12] Other managers echo this sentiment, stating that their companies seek to avoid offset. One major defence exporter is prepared to discuss offset with customers only after alternative arrangements, such as consultancy and commercial agreements, fail. Its corporate starting position in negotiations is to say no to offset, and, instead, seek to sell on price and quality, with the bait of a discount on price.

By contrast, there is a group of managers who hold mixed views on the impact of offset: some are ambivalent, while others are supportive. One executive argues that good offset is good business, and it is thus recognised as advancing company interests in key markets. In particular, it can increase product value by acting as a competitive discriminator in competing with the big US contractors. Under the right conditions, offset carries the potential to catalyse growth through access to new capability, but there are challenges associated with formulating and agreeing appropriate business propositions. Another manager also offers qualified support of offset, arguing that the customer must offer a minimum critical mass of capability and procurement volume. The problem is that most developing countries suffer the common malady of low volume and constrained technological absorption capacity, and, therefore, the principal challenge is to create a negotiating position that overcomes absorption and scale barriers. Pragmatism is essential, accepting that while offset poses difficulties, it can also create opportunities, provide solutions and encourage 'ownership'. For this to happen, offset authorities need to display management flexibility and maturity, but these attributes are rarely in evidence. Innovative and feasible solutions are possible, but only if staid attitudes and bureaucratic systems can be overcome.

Customer governments clearly hold a positive view on the worth of offset, otherwise demand for it would disappear. This perspective is surprising as the evidence, to date, does little to support the view that offset has had a material impact on industrial and technological development. Offset has not contributed to the accelerated industrialisation of recipient states, certainly not through the creation of large numbers of local sustainable skilled jobs, or indigenous R&D, or supply chains. Although there is some evidence that offset has maintained, though not created, skilled jobs and capacity in industrialised countries,[13] and created pockets of high value manufacturing capability in developing states,[14] this is the limit of what can legitimately be claimed.[15] There is simply no basis for arguing that offset will act as the driving force for industrial and technological transformation of civil/military capability, and certainly not in developing countries. Thus, the questions that need to be asked are why do countries still clamour for offset? Why do emerging states continue to live the dream that offset will catapult them into industrial and technological maturity? These questions are difficult to answer, but likely rest on the 'Lemming herd mentality' principle, that everyone else cannot be wrong.

Yet, the sense of disenchantment with offset has begun to spread beyond offshore vendors. Some offset authorities now appear to be questioning the benefits of offset. In October 2017, Oman terminated a contract with Raytheon after it became aware that an offset premium had been built into the procurement contract.[16] The existence of a 'cost premium' is a controversial issue, not least because the economic rationale for offset is clearly undermined in the event that the value it generates is less than the cost incurred. Several offset managers therefore suggest that the risk-free option is for customers to seek discounts through buying off-the-shelf. The problem with this approach, though, is that the offset authority's agenda is focused solely on demanding offset, even in the absence of business viability. Under such circumstances, offset is disruptive. Customers and vendors need to work together to ensure projects succeed. Smart 'optimal' solutions are required, whereby the vendor employs offset to leverage an in-country presence, while also accommodating customer requirements to build-up of local indigenous capability. This may mean that Brazil, located on the top rungs of the technological ladder, enjoys R&D investment; Malaysia, lower down the ladder, benefits from the infusion of dual-use technologies and systems integration; and for poorer states, low-skilled work is the appropriate first step on the ladder. However, the days of fish farms have long since disappeared.

Finally, returning to the purpose of this chapter, a policy question that needs to be asked, but often is not, is whether offset policy is fit for purpose. Increasingly, the answer is no. In 2014, for instance, Kuwait suspended its offset policy after criticism that overly bureaucratic processes acted as a disincentive to foreign investment.[17] There also appears to be difficulties with the UAE's offset model. It is estimated that large numbers of overseas vendors possess undischarged liabilities, with only single-digit numbers of contractors achieving their offset credit targets in 2016.[18] There are numerous operational difficulties with the UAE's implementation of its complex and demanding offset policy. India's offset policy also appears to be struggling to deliver on its objectives.[19] The revealed difficulties of offset regimes in major country markets lend weight to the judgement that industrialising states may decide to reform, downgrade or even abandon the use of offset. The term, offset, will remain part of their policy lexicon, but its meaning will become more opaque. Across Europe, a common understanding of offset has been lost since the launch of the 2009 Directive. East European states in particular are adopting differing interpretations, often reducing the transparency of reciprocal investment and raising the policy question, when is an offset an offset?

Offset was previously taken for granted, but over recent years the traditional view of the concept has been under scrutiny. The frictions and problems that have arisen between vendors and customers may lead to the evolution of business frameworks beyond offset. Stakeholder convergence is required to remedy offset's structural fault-lines, and, thus, the obvious way forward is one that is nuanced towards partnership; indeed, the process has already begun. This is not to state that offset will disappear; rather, that it will diminish in importance to become just one of a spectrum of partnership options. These will include national, regional and global defence-industrial collaboration, including partnership triages, such as the UAE (financial sponsor), Algeria (land systems buyer) and Germany's AG corporation (technical partner) in the procurement of military vehicles.[20] Moreover, as manufacturing capabilities progress, co-development procurement will increasingly become attractive, and not just with advanced states, such as South Korea, but also with industrialising countries, such as India with the Hawk fighter programme.

These alternative business frameworks to offset are categorised under what is termed 'industrialisation strategy', capturing partnering solutions that do not involve mandatory regulation. Government will also likely be more 'hands-on', engaging proactively to underpin, and even underwrite, institutional partnership arrangements. These might include government-to-government programmes, such as the UK-Saudi defence programme, but with technology transfer linked potentially to the Kingdom's Vision 2030 strategic plan, or to the promotion of SMEs, both nationally and internationally, or to 'social' investment into educational and health initiatives. Government is likely to adopt a more interventionist role in in the replacement of offset. Defence is not a free market, and government does have a role to play in the orchestration of resources. The Australian non-mandatory model is a good example of where offset has been abandoned, but offshore investment through partnership is still required.

Conclusion

The French proverb: *Plus ça change, plus c'est la même chose,* neatly encapsulates the sense of the 4P offset transition curve: a process detailing the movement from prescription to partnership, but where the underlying pressures for stakeholder convergence remain unaltered. The effectiveness of offset policy is where all stakeholders gain, but this is presently not happening. Offset is not working, and this is attested by this study's primary research findings and supported by academic studies. As a consequence, there exists modest beginnings of what looks like an emerging trend towards non-mandated partnerships between vendors and customers, and going beyond that to include governments, also. It need not have been like this, but offset has proved too confrontational. The means and ends of partnership are the same as offset, but the former is likely to be more effective based on greater flexibility, trust and the pursuit of a mutually advantageous long-term strategic vision.

References and notes

1. However, note that some countries confusingly define offset to include other forms of countertrade, such as barter and counter-purchase.
2. See R. Matthews. *The UK Offset Model: From Participation to Engagement.* Whitehall Report 1–14. RUSI. July 2014.
3. D. Kimla. *Military Offsets & In-Country Industrialisation – Market Insight.* Frost & Sullivan Report, March 2013.
4. This figure was first mentioned in in a paper by Thomas Mathew, 'Getting the Defence Offset Policy Right'. Economic Times. 5 December 2008. Many publications refer to a lower number of around eighty, referring to countries possessing full-blown countertrade and offset guidelines.
5. See Matthews. *The UK Offset Model.*
6. E-mail correspondence with Adrian Dalton, former Head of the MoD Industrial Participation Unit, 21 March 2018.
7. See C. Clark. 'Buy America, Again. Sigh'. *Breaking Defense.* 19 April 2017. https://breakingdefense.com/2017/04/buy-america-again-sigh/ (accessed 29 March 2018).
8. Hellenic Resources Institute. *Article 223 – The Treaty Establishing the European Community. Rome: 25 March 1957.* www.hri.org/docs/Rome57/Part6.html#Art223 (accessed 29 March 2018).
9. An excellent evaluation of the Australian procurement model is the paper by C. Stone. Prioritizing Defence Industry Capabilities: Lessons for Canada from Australia. Policy Paper, The School of Public Policy, University of Calgary. January 2014.
10. 'India's Policies Full of Ambiguities, Empty of Credits'. *Countertrade and Offset.* 35(21): 2017.
11. US-UAE Business Council. *The UAE Offset Program.* March 2017. http://usuaebusiness.org/wp-content/uploads/2017/03/UAE-Offset-Program-Final.pdf (accessed 29 March 2018).
12. Interview with UK company offset manager, 27 November 2017.
13. See Matthews. *The UK Offset Model.*

14. For evidence, see R. Matthews, Maharani Curie and Fitriani. 'Challenges Ahead for Indonesia's First Defence Offset Policy'. *Defence Review Asia* (April 2012), and Balakrishnan, Kogila. 'Defence Industrialisation through Offsets: A Case Study of Malaysia'. *Journal of Peace and Defence Economics*. 2009. 20(4): 341–58.

15. See Matthews. *The UK Offset Model*; and M. Chinworth and R. Matthews. 'Defence Industrialisation through Offsets: The Case of Japan'. In S. Martin (ed.), *The Economics of Offsets: Defence Procurement and Countertrade*. Harwood Academic Press (1996).

16. 'Omani MoD Shocked to Discover Offsets Cost Money – Demands Reimbursement From Raytheon'. Countertrade and Offset. 2017. 35(19).

17. 'Kuwait Suspends Offset Programme in Investment Drive'. *Oxford Business Group*. 3 November 2014. https://oxfordbusinessgroup.com/news/kuwait-suspends-offset-programme-investment-drive (accessed 12 April 2018).

18. Interview with a UK offset manager. 27 November 2017.

19. 'Minister – Make in India Policy a Failure'. Countertrade and Offset. 2018. 36(5).

20. Defence Web. 'Algerian Factory Unveils New Locally Assembled Truck for Algerian Military'. 16 March 2015. www.defenceweb.co.za/index .php?option=com_content&view=article&id=38381:algerian-factory-unveils-new-locally-assembled-truck-for-algerian-military&catid=50:L and&Itemid=105 (accessed 12 April 2018).

8 Defence Companies in the Age of Globalisation: French Defence Industry as a Case Study

JEAN-MICHEL OUDOT AND
RENAUD BELLAIS

Introduction

Private defence companies emerged in the second half of the nineteenth century, and increasingly most of them have sold a significant share of their products to international customers. After the end of the Cold War, such companies faced even more pressure to go beyond national borders to access new markets, sustain competencies and turnover in order to counterbalance insufficient domestic demand. However, what was initially a second-best solution for maintaining a domestic industrial base has progressively become a key feature of defence industries in arms-producing countries. Even in such a sensitive industry and despite strict regulations on the international flows of goods, services and know-how, the process of globalisation has been transforming the strategies and industrial organisation of defence companies. Notwithstanding these trends, the political economy literature offers little in the way of debate on this important topic, and, as a consequence, the issues are poorly understood.[1] The lack of comprehensive statistics at the international level represents constraints on analysing ongoing defence-industrial transformations despite their relevance for public policy.

To overcome such difficulties, we propose to adopt a country-based case study of France and its defence industry. Analysis will benefit from original data from the French Ministry of Armed Forces and Customs Administration, the French National Institute of Statistics (INSEE) and the OECD. Although this approach will provide only a partial perspective on the international transformation of defence industry, it will nevertheless deliver valuable politico-economic insights on the pressures and processes taking place. The aim is to understand defence companies' internationalisation strategies, albeit that most of these companies are not 'pure players' but include a civil focus in their portfolio of activities. There are a number of important policy questions to be asked. What are the specific features of such strategies in terms of turnover, sourcing and industrial footprint? What are the challenges in characterising such strategies as globalisation as defined in international economics? How do these companies articulate their defence and civilian outputs? What are the implications for state regulation? To answer these questions, this chapter is organised as follows: Section 8.1 assesses the international dynamics of defence industry by reference to the literature on international and defence economics; Section 8.2 focuses on the structure and trends in international trade from/to France; and, finally, Section 8.3 analyses the public policy implications resulting from the globalisation of defence companies.

8.1 Defence Companies and Globalisation Dynamics

Since the close of the nineteenth century, defence industries have been regarded as an essential pillar in the push towards achieving strategic autonomy. As the local defence industrial base is fundamentally important in implementing defence missions and helping fulfil sovereignty, governments often ensure that they benefit from a dedicated industrial policy. Historically, internationalisation was limited to the arms trade as a means of sustaining production and competencies when domestic orders were not sufficient,[2] as opposed to the overseas expansion of an industrial footprint (defined as globalisation). However, new trends and forces have pushed both defence companies and national industrial policies to adapt themselves to the new global context, and to be proactive in several segments of international endeavour in support of long-term objectives.

8.1.1 Globalisation of Defence Companies

For decades the internationalisation of defence companies' turnover simply represented an extension of domestic sales beyond national borders. It was similar to the features of what Berger[3] called 'the First Globalisation' (1870–1914). However, since the end of the Cold War, the globalisation process has begun to create or accelerate the emergence of transnational defence markets and corporate structures,[4] as have occurred in civil industrial markets since the 1980s. The globalisation process has led to path-breaking changes since companies reorganise productive capabilities via a global perspective, based on business criteria that go beyond national political borders. Friedman[5] uses the metaphor 'the world is flat' to describe the globalisation phenomenon post-twentieth century: even though political borders still exist, they do not represent a key parameter in corporate strategic decision-making related to productive capacities. In a globalised approach, the world represents a unique market in which companies manage their means and targets.

Recent research in the field of international economics[6] underscores the difficulties of continuing to envision industrial activities on a purely national basis, since economies are engaged in transnationalisation because of the emergence of 'trade in tasks'.[7] Today's globalisation is not a simple extension of trade; its nature is radically different, since the explosion of trade happens in parallel with deep transformations of productive activities throughout the value chains. Baldwin[8] identifies two further paradigmatic changes that have radically modified economic behaviour. In the early nineteenth century a first 'unbundling' of national economies resulted from rapidly falling transportation costs. This favoured geographic clustering of production, as companies were no longer required to co-locate production and consumption. This process also impacted on the arms industry, with transformation leading to a geographic concentration of production in few countries.[9] A second unbundling started in the 1980s: falling communication and coordination costs reduced the need to perform most manufacturing stages in one location. This favoured two radical changes that help to explain globalisation. First, through vertical disintegration companies can outsource large segments of activities and focus on the ones that deliver the highest added value. Second, the reorganisation of value chains has an international dimension through the optimisation of production often requiring offshoring of tasks to a foreign subsidiary or to external suppliers, quite often located abroad.

8.1.2 Towards a Taxonomy of Globalisation

Through vertical disintegration and overseas outsourcing of value chain activity, defence companies are engaging in transformation through globalisation.[10] Yet, this begs the question as to how we define and understand the dynamics of globalisation. It seems there are several corporate perspectives, including a purely domestic industrial position

Table 8.1: *Differentiation of (inter)national operating companies*

		Markets		
		National	International/ regional	Worldwide
Production	National	Domestic	Semi-international	International
	International/ regional	-	Multi-domestic	Multinational
	Worldwide	-	Transnational	Global

Source: Hagedoorn, Schakenraad. 'The Internationalization of the Economy'.

and a globalised footprint. Hagedoorn and Schakenraad's[11] taxonomy helps distinguish the various configurations as shown in Table 8.1.

National or domestic companies produce in one country and serve mainly the domestic market. This categorisation corresponds to most defence companies, and internationalisation forms an extension of the domestic market once it becomes saturated or not large enough to guarantee growth or sustainability. Semi-internationalisation or full internationalisation does not structurally change these companies. Even though they enlarge their market and turnover, they do not need to change productive organisation as experienced in during the First Globalisation. The internationalisation process raises export-control issues for final products and also for imported inputs if a country's defence technological and industrial base (DTIB) does not encompass all the required dimensions of value chains. The globalisation process deeply changes corporate structures when productive capacities expand beyond national borders through acquisitions or greenfield investments (e.g. fully or part-owned joint ventures with local partners). Hagedoorn and Schakenraad[12] propose four categories of such internationalisation:

– Multi-domestic and multinational companies are an important part of the globalisation of productive resources. However, they are mainly involved in either pursuing financial consolidation rather than reshuffling of industrial capabilities across borders, or in duplicating a given production unit into another country. Thus, many large defence companies correspond to this category[13] via ownership of industrial assets in different countries (e.g. Thales,

BAE Systems and General Dynamics) but stopping short of full specialisation of industrial and technological assets between home and overseas countries.

- Additionally, in the context of defence industry, this 'multinational internationalisation' is reflected through cooperative programmes. Defence companies, especially European, manage international collaborative programmes on specific projects. Examples include transnational consolidations (e.g. Airbus Helicopters or Thales Alenia Space) having international captive value chains that are restricted to countries involved in these cooperative programmes. Offset obligations can also nurture what might be termed 'half-breed' internationalisation.[14] Importing countries demand more and more local content, technology transfers or even the creation of domestic industrial capabilities. Due to offset commitments, companies increase international sourcing and industrial footprints, but on a captive basis and only as a consequence of customer requests.
- Transnational and global companies represent fully globalised entities, since this process includes not only sales but also productive and technological assets. In defence industry, MBDA represents almost the only example of such deep globalisation. It is a company that aims to organise its productive resources from a truly global perspective, and has set up centres of excellence across Europe. Hagedoorn and Schakenraad view 'global companies as the true opposites of domestic companies ... [operating] ... on a worldwide scale with respect to both their markets and their production'.[15]
- The transformation of value chains has also impacted on defence industry because many inputs are dual or purely civilian in today's defence systems.[16] Additionally, defence sectors in most leading arms-producing countries have experienced deep structural changes since the end of the Cold War, including privatisation, domestic and cross-border consolidation, with diversification into (additional) defence activities as well as civilian ones.[17]

Since companies are more and more dualistic, they are likely to participate in, and benefit from, the second unbundling, particularly in civilian activities. Nevertheless, due to their defence portfolios and globalisation dynamics, the process is likely to differ from purely civilian companies.

8.1.3   Globalisation versus Strategic Autonomy

Besides market forces, defence companies cannot implement international strategies with the manoeuvrability that purely civilian companies benefit from globalisation. They must take into consideration the rules established by arms-producing states to secure strategic autonomy. This latter requires accessing skills, assets and services essential to develop, produce and maintain defence capabilities from cradle to grave on the domestic territory.[18] This is not compatible with a free process of globalisation; that is, a reshuffle of production leading to specialisation of sites across countries. Companies must also guarantee that their supplier locations are compatible with strategic autonomy. In other words, the absence of possible barriers of trade along with measures to mitigate sourcing dependency. Also, a comprehensive policy of strategic autonomy requires an understanding of the extent and depth of defence companies' engagement with internationalisation and globalisation.[19] This requires analysing these companies' global defence-related business, including a focus on corporate strategies, not simply the economic impacts of globalisation. It is thus relevant to encompass the full portfolio of activities of these companies, and, on that basis, we will call them 'DTIB' companies.[20] This is to distinguish them from the traditional view of defence companies working mainly or even exclusively for defence needs.[21]

This chapter relies on data analysis of French companies that, directly or indirectly, contribute to the development, production, maintenance, repair and overhaul of weapons through a statistical methodology that was developed by the Directorate for Finance of the French Ministry of Armed Forces.[22] Arguments rely on economic and statistical analysis based on procurement databases. Three main sources of information have been used:

– Domestic procurement from the Ministry of Armed Forces: a database that covers all payments made to enterprises located in France,
– International procurement: information relating to collaborative programmes obtained from OCCAR and NATO (identifying the contribution of companies located in France to cooperative programmes) and data on military exports and imports, sourced from French Customs (*Direction générale des douanes et droits indirects*),

– Ad hoc surveys focused on the sourcing of French prime contractors: a confidential survey of the top seven industrial players (Airbus, Dassault Aviation, DCNS/Naval Group, MBDA, Nexter, Safran and Thales) as well as the atomic energy public agency, *Commissariat à l'énergie atomique*.

The resulting dataset covers different fields: conventional and deterrence procurement; companies working for the French Ministry of Defence and foreign customers; and large companies and SMEs. Through this process, Moura and Oudot[23] achieved an unprecedented coverage of direct and indirect defence expenditures in France. Consequently, it was possible to undertake a core assessment of the French DTIB companies, comprising 1,838 enterprises in 2011, 1,955 enterprises in 2012 and 1,738 in 2013. About 1,300 enterprises are included in this sample every year. The coverage includes DTIB companies having a defence-related turnover of between €18 and €20 billion a year on average.

In the next sections, all analyses are based on this sample. Identifying strategies of defence companies appears useful, especially when compared with civilian ones, in order to understand the dynamics at play in terms of both industrial policy and regulation.

8.2 Commonalities between Globalised DTIB and Civilian Companies

DTIB companies share many features with their purely civilian counterparts in terms of internationalisation and globalisation. International trade represents a larger and larger part of companies' turnover with a surprising share in services. Moreover, investment appears more and more globalised.

8.2.1 *Larger Weight of International Trade in both Products and Services*

Since the middle of the twentieth century, international trade has been increasing in a spectacular manner. According to the WTO, between 1950 and 2016, total trade multiplied by almost 250 times, and trade in manufactured goods by more than 490 times, as shown graphically in Figure 8.1. When compared to world GDP, which only multiplied by a factor of 11, this explosion in trade, mainly from the flows of end

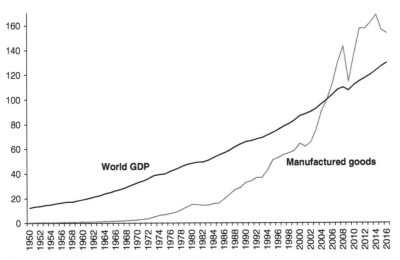

Figure 8.1: Evolution of GDP and trade in manufactured goods, 1950–2014
Source: World Trade Organisation. *World Trade Statistical Review 2017.*
WTO Press: Geneva. 2017. Table A55. World merchandise exports and
gross domestic product. 1950–2016. 144–45.

products, represents the core feature in the dynamics of international trade
from the 1950s to the mid-1990s. In 2016, world exports of goods and
services totalled $20,437 billion, representing 27.2 per cent of world
GDP.[24]

However, today's globalisation differs from previous ups and downs
in trade because the nature of flows has been transforming along two
tracks. Firstly, intermediary products take a larger share of trade,
which reflects the rise of 'trade in tasks'.[25] Secondly, services are now
an important part of international trade. For instance, world commercial services exports in 2016 reached $4,808 billion, representing
almost 24 per cent of total international flows.[26]

Although experiencing ups and downs since the beginning of the twentieth century, due to geopolitical reasons and cyclical renewals of fleets, the
arms trade has also expanded both during the Cold War, as well as in
recent years. As highlighted in Figure 8.2, while the arms trade does not
reach the highs of the 1980s, specifically $39.5 billion (1990 constant
dollars) in 1987, it has experienced a recent trend of increase to
$28.6 billion in 2015 from $17.8 billion in 2002. The volume of transfers
of major weapons across 2011–15 was 14 per cent higher than during
2006–10.[27]

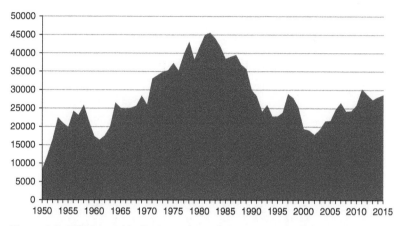

Figure 8.2: SIPRI trend indicator values of arms exports, 1950–2015 (in USD million at constant 1990 prices)
Source: SIPRI. *SIPRI Arms Transfers Database.* http://armstrade.sipri.org/arm strade/html/export_values.php (accessed 18 October 2016).

Arms exports are important for a number of reasons. On purely economic grounds, they increase the level of production and thus contribute to the sustainability of the DTIB. Economies of scale act to lower unit costs and spread fixed costs (R&D in particular) over several customers compared to autarkic production. Exports of defence systems also create additional jobs, increase the trade balance and generate hard currency.[28]

As far as the French DTIB is concerned, as detailed in Table 8.2, it exported €94 billion of military and commercial goods in 2016.[29] This is a growth of 3.2 per cent on average over the period 2011–16, three times the growth of total French exports. Exports from DTIB companies represented 21 per cent of total exports from France in 2016. These flows mainly comprise civilian exports, whereas military exports represent only 9 per cent of total exports. This reflects a highly diversified portfolio of companies contributing to the French DTIB. As both commercial and military exports increase, such trends show the competitiveness of these dual companies, and, to a certain extent, the synergies resulting from the convergence of defence-oriented and commercial industrial bases in France, contrasting with the Cold War partial segregation.

These flows of goods need to be contrasted with service exports, such as capacity-based services, R&D (e.g. adaptation of capabilities to importer requirements), training of personnel, operational maintenance,

Table 8.2: *Exports of goods by French DTIB companies, 2011–2016 (in € millions)*

	2011	2012	2013	2014	2015	2016	Average 2011–16
DTIB exports of civilian and military goods	79,961	85,204	82,337	84,898	91,800	93,681	86,314
Growth rate		7%	-3%	3%	8%	2%	3.2%
Global goods exports of France	4,28,610	4,42,014	4,36,130	4,36,398	4,55,508	4,52,978	4,41,940
Growth rate		3%	-1%	0.1%	4%		1.1%
DTIB share of global goods exports	19%	19%	19%	19%	20%	21%	20%

Source: French Customs, Direction Nationale des Statistiques du Commerce Extérieur – Ministry of defence / Observatoire Economique de la Défense estimates.

Table 8.3: *Services exports by DTIB companies, 2011–2016 (in €
millions)*

	2011	2012	2013	2014	2015	2016	Average 2011–16
DTIB services exports	8,069	9,786	9,117	9,137	10,467	10,501	9,513
Growth rate		21%	–7%	0.2%	15%	0%	5.4%
Global DTIB exports	88,030	94,991	91,454	94,035	1,02,267	1,04,182	93,551
Share of services in global exports	9%	10%	10%	10%	10%	10%	10%

Source: French Customs, Direction Nationale des Statistiques du Commerce
Extérieur; Banque de France (balance of payments) – Ministry of defence /
Observatoire Economique de la Défense estimates.

royalties and license fees, transport costs or intermediation fees.
Table 8.3 shows the performance of services exports by DTIB companies, which exported €10.5 billion of services in 2016. These exports
grew by 5.3 per cent on average over 2011–16, constituting a growth
twice as high as the increase of goods exports from DTIB companies
over the same period. Total exports of DTIB companies reached
€104 billion in 2016, with services representing about 10 per cent.

DTIB companies account for a large proportion of all exports since
the 2010s. This trend is remarkable because there are few exporting
companies in France, about 120,000, and among them, only a very
limited number of 'superstars',[30] which achieve most of the exports.
At first glance, it is surprising that defence-related companies can
achieve such large export turnover. The literature in defence economics
usually considers such companies to be inefficient and thus unable to
become competitive enough to reach the status of export superstars;
a status reserved for only highly productive and innovative companies.

8.2.2 *Expansion of French Foreign Direct Investment*

As trade in tasks becomes a feature of industrial globalisation, it is not
surprising that foreign direct investment (FDI) has enjoyed impressive
levels of growth. FDI is the cornerstone of corporate expansion abroad

through greenfield projects, subsidiaries and joint ventures. FDI is also a way to reinvest profits abroad, contributing to the value of international organisations. According to UNCTAD data,[31] FDI inflows increased to $1,746 billion in 2016, or 2.3 per cent of world GDP, from $207 billion in 1990 (value at current prices), or 0.9 per cent of world GDP.

In France, the Banque de France assesses inflows and outflows of FDI to estimate the balance of payments, both as financial assets stock (ownership of more than 10 per cent of the capital of nonresident companies) and as financial transfers (financial flows of capital or loans between parent companies). These databases are useful to understand the extent to which DTIB companies participate in such financial flows, and, indirectly, how they are transforming their industrial footprints.

As shown in Table 8.4, statistics on FDI outflows from DTIB companies reveal that these companies regularly invest abroad. Even if their transactions account only for 7 per cent of total FDI from domestic companies, they regularly invest in foreign subsidiaries, creating new ones abroad as well as acquiring foreign companies. This trend mainly results from a regional-based globalisation of the industrial footprint of defence companies.[32] At the European level, many groups are committed to cooperative bi- or multinational programmes, and they also consolidated assets through mergers and acquisitions in the 1990s and 2000s.

These investments are amplified by a significant reinvestment policy. As detailed in Tables 8.4 and 8.5, DTIB companies reinvest a share of earnings from their FDI income that is twice as large as the total of

Table 8.4: *Foreign direct investment flows from DTIB companies, 2011–2015 (in € millions)*

Flows	2011	2012	2013	2014	2015	Average 2011–14
Capital transfers	406	2,204	934	2,779	759	1,581
Reinvested earnings	399	381	333	108	nd	305
Total FDIs excl. loans and borrowing	804	2,585	1,267	2,888	nd	1,886

Source: Banque de France and Ministry of defence / Observatoire Economique de la Défense databases; from J-M. Oudot. 'Stratégies et performances des entreprises de défense à l'international'. EcoDef. March 2017. 90.

Table 8.5: *FDI stocks and earnings of DTIB companies, 2011–2014 (in €* millions)

	FDI stocks end 2014	FDI revenues Capital (dividends and reinvested earnings) + interests of intragroup loans			
		2011	2012	2013	2014
2013 DTIB	32,474	1,023	1,082	833	886
– capital	24,270	–	–	–	–
– other operations	8,205	–	–	–	–
Share of reinvested earnings in FDI revenues		39%	35%	40%	12%

Source: Banque de France and Ministry of defence / Observatoire Economique de la Défense databases; Oudot. 'Stratégies et performances des entreprises'.

companies in France (32 per cent versus 14 per cent on average over 2011–14). In recent years, international expansion represents an investment driver for DTIB companies, marking a significant change for industrial organisations that are traditionally centred on domestic manufacturing in the field of defence. This reinvestment policy tends to favour increased specialisation of sites over different countries, helping to suppress duplication and focus investment on a given domain in one site to create centres of excellence across an international landscape. The industrial consolidation that MBDA has conducted across sites in France and the UK represents a good example of such a strategy.

8.2.3 Offset Agreements and 'Trade in Tasks' for DTIB Companies

Intensifying competition in international military markets increases the market power of importing countries. The latter systematically require technology offset each time they import defence systems. Initially these offsets were aimed primarily to decrease total cost for the domestic economy (by counterbalancing financial outflows). Increasingly, since the 1990s, many countries use such agreements to seek to develop domestic industrial and technological capabilities over the long run.[33] While offset agreements are banned (save for the poorer states) in civil activities though trade treaties, they remain possible in the field of defence, and most states use this leverage as part of their industrial policies without fear of being accused of mercantilism.[34]

Offset agreements can include compensations in trade, but they focus increasingly on local production and technology transfers. Offshore companies have thus developed an industrial footprint in many countries, either through final assembly lines or through the manufacturing of intermediary products. Additionally, offset can fulfil obligations thanks to local sourcing and the integration of new partners in increasingly global value chains,[35] another way to participate in trade in tasks. Even though these requirements often constitute a *sine qua non* condition to win international contracts, such transfers are likely to eventually weaken the exporter's market share. The development of local production will reduce export markets (through import-substitution policy) and create new competitors (since new arms-producing countries want to develop or preserve their own DTIB through exports). Measuring the consequences of offset is a complex task, since it requires calculating the impact of technology transfer in the long run, which depends on the sophistication of technologies transferred and the importer's ability to master and value the same.

However, the consequence of offset can be estimated through the domestic added value of exports. To do so, one must rely on two OECD databases: *Trade in Value Added* (TiVA)[36] and *STAN Bilateral Trade Database by Industry and End-use category* (BTDIxE).[37]

8.2.3.1 Measuring Trade in Added Value

Purchased goods and services are composed of inputs from various countries in the world. The OECD-WTO TiVA Initiative measures trade between nations to assess the added value of each country's production of goods and services. The 2015 edition includes sixty-one countries belonging to the OECD, the EU-28, the G20, most countries in East and Southeast Asia and a number of countries in South America. It includes thirty-four unique sectors, including sixteen manufacturing industries and fourteen service sectors. The indicators in this database provide the following information: (1) the national and foreign value-added content of gross exports, broken down by exporting sectors; (2) services content of gross exports, broken down by export industries, types of services and the origin of added value; (3) participation in global value chains measured by the content of exports in intermediate imports (backward linkages) and the content of domestic added value of partner countries' exports (forward linkages); (4) the 'global orientation' of a given industry, i.e. the share of sectoral added value aimed at satisfying foreign final demand; (5) geographical and sectoral origins of added value in final demand, including the origin of added value in final consumption (household and government) and fixed investment (business investment); (6) bilateral trade relations determined from the flow of added value embedded in domestic final demand; and (7) inter- and intra-regional exchanges.

In addition, the OECD's BTDIxE reveals bilateral flows of international trade of goods, broken down by branch of economic activity and by end-use categories. This database provides an overview of the structure of international trade in intermediate goods to identify global production networks and supply chains. It also addresses other issues of public interest, such as trade in added value and trade in tasks. The database covers all OECD countries and thirty non-member countries, including BRIICS (Brazil, Russia, India, Indonesia, China and South Africa). Trade flows are distributed amongst forty-six sectors, including nine categories such as investment, intermediate goods and consumer spending.

These indicators gather information from worldwide customs in cooperation with the United Nations.

Some sixty-two products have been selected among 27,000 in BTDIxE. Selected systems correspond to weapons and ammunition, naval ships, armoured vehicles and aeronautics.[38] This sample constitutes only a portion of total defence exports because many defence flows are not identifiable through these databases.

Figure 8.3 presents the evolution of the domestic added value of exports over 2002–14. Both gross exports and domestic added value increased over 2002–14, but with a gradual decrease in the share of domestic added value in exports. This share declined from 61 per cent in 2002 to 57 per cent in 2014. The revealed trend derives from a growing integration of industrial activities located in France into global value chains. In addition to outsourcing parts for final goods, companies have begun to search for the most innovative and competitive suppliers

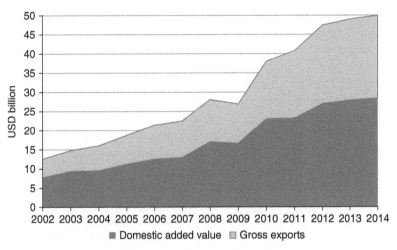

Figure 8.3: Domestic added value of exports, 2002–2014
Sources: OECD BTDIxE and TiVA (2015 editions). Ministry of Armed Forces /
Observatoire Economique de la Défense estimates based on a sample of defence
systems (weapons and ammunition, naval ships, armoured vehicles and
aeronautics).

wherever they are located. French DTIB companies have also deepened
the specialisation of their sites in different countries to maintain or
increase each site's competitiveness.

Both trends favour trade in tasks[39] that tend to compete with flows of
final goods. These trends result in an increasing share of added value
occurring at the international level, which benefits importing economies
in the long run. This hypothesis is also confirmed when aeronautics,
weighted heavily in previous statistics, is excluded from the sample.
In Figure 8.4, France is compared to the systems of other G7 countries
(United States, Canada, United Kingdom, Germany, Italy and Japan).

A long-term downward trend of the share of domestic added value in
exports of defence systems for G7 countries can be observed. This
results from the combined effects of corporate offshoring and outsourcing strategies, with significant transfers of production and added value
to emerging countries and a corresponding expansion of trade in tasks,
step-by-step. As a result of defence group globalisation, inputs from
abroad have been taking a larger share, and, consequently, the proportion of domestic added value has been decreasing in French arms
exports, despite the historical quest for strategic autonomy.

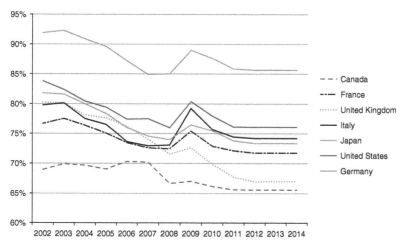

Figure 8.4: Share of national added value in military exports, 2002–2014
Sources: OECD's BTDIxE and TiVA (2015 editions). Ministry of Armed Forces / Observatoire Economique de la Défense estimates based on a sample of defence systems (weapons and ammunition, naval ships, armoured vehicles excluding aeronautics).

Additionally, based on the selected arms production sample, French companies appear less conservative or protectionist vis-à-vis integration into global value chains, compared especially to Japan, the United States and Germany. It must be kept in mind that the 2009 data in Figure 8.4 should be interpreted carefully, since the numbers would have been deeply influenced by the 2008–09 economic and financial crisis that resulted in the contraction of international trade for all G7 countries.

Overall, the defence-related companies' international strategies do not differ much from pure civilian activities. They locate an increasing share of their production abroad through a diversified package of industrial agreements. Nevertheless, they face particular regulatory constraints that help to explain specific strategies.

8.3 Specific Strategies of Defence-Related Companies

Defence industry remains strictly regulated. This is the reason why internationalisation and globalisation have different outcomes for the DTIB companies. Arms-producing countries expect to preserve a certain strategic autonomy by requiring a domestic production, which limits the globalisation of value chains. DTIB companies operate in sensitive domains. They are more likely to control their intangible assets than purely civilian companies which implement extensive outsourcing and offshoring strategies.[40]

8.3.1 Domestic Production Remains a Strong Requirement for Defence Integrators

It is important to consider not only defence integrators but also the whole supply chain, not least because defence industry relies on non-defence suppliers, which are much more globalised than defence firms, and non-domestic defence suppliers when the domestic DTIB is not able to deliver all required inputs (e.g. field-programmable gate arrays in electronics). The concept of global value chains reflects global coverage of the full range of functions and tasks that are necessary for the provision of goods or services from conception to delivery to the final consumer through the various phases of manufacturing. This restructuring of production on a regional or global scale constitutes a major feature of today's world economy.

The state carefully monitors the industrial footprint and sourcing of lead system integrators, because such decisions impact on its security of supply and strategic autonomy and also touch economic and social motives (jobs, growth and sustainability of local industrial bases). The French MoD has collected exhaustive data on the sourcing of leading defence groups based in France.[41] These data are usually confidential[42] and impossible to access from outside these companies. The collected microdata provide information on suppliers located in the domestic country and abroad. A detailed analysis of this exclusive database reveals a clear distinction between 'pure defence players' (e.g. Naval Group, Nexter, CEA) and dual civil-military groups (e.g. Airbus, Dassault Aviation, Safran, Thales).

On average, pure defence players rely to the extent of 90 per cent on domestic suppliers for their sourcing. Therefore, they guarantee a high return on investment to the state with regard to its defence procurement in the very short term. However, this ratio corresponds only to direct sourcing. Even though a more detailed assessment appears difficult to carry out for indirect sourcing, it is likely that the more distant a source of inputs from the end product (e.g. defence systems), the more international value chains become, notably because inputs are less defence specific. Additionally, integrators tend to rely on a limited number of suppliers for specialised inputs, many of them being located outside the domestic economy. For instance, the US DoD found counterfeited electronic components in American defence systems despite deeply monitoring its sourcing processes.[43] Understanding such global industrial footprints is nevertheless impossible through corporate sourcing data or existing statistical databases.

Conversely, dual or civil-military groups are more open to foreign sourcing. This trend corresponds with the internationalised or even globalised nature of their activities. Only 60 per cent of their sourcing is directed to domestic suppliers. Nevertheless, related imports are more than compensated in absolute value by the significant volume effect of their exports. This effect is measured by the ratio between sourcing in France and turnover coming from France. On average, this ratio represents 75 per cent for pure defence players. It reaches an average of 120 per cent for dual groups. Corporate diversification, both geographical and across industries, can be seen as a lever for economic development, which in return benefits the industrial base located in the home country.

The hypothesis regarding the weak mobility of the DTIB companies' industrial footprint is confirmed by collected data. However, each company pursues its own strategy of international development. These strategies differ notably through their centralised or decentralised nature vis-à-vis their home country, leading to specific economic and strategic consequences for the state.

8.3.2 Keeping Control over Strategic Assets in Offshoring Decisions

Along with sourcing, DTIB enterprises are influenced by states in their overseas deployment and more particularly for offshoring decisions. To document this aspect, INSEE conducted a global value chain survey (*Chaînes d'Activités Mondiales*) that is useful for analysing corporate actions abroad.

8.3.2.1 The Global Channels Business Survey
This CAM survey highlights the fragmentation of value chains, leading companies to outsource in France or to offshore tasks or workloads

previously undertaken internally. This survey is part of a European project coordinated by Eurostat, and called the 'International Sourcing and Global Value Chains Survey'. Data were collected in 2012 to cover the period 2009–11, for companies (legal units) exclusive of agriculture and finance, located in France with fifty employees or more in 2008. The aim of this survey was to describe outsourcing and offshoring, and Fontagné and D'Isanto[44] and Picard[45] present the overall results at the national level. The survey covers 28,612 legal units, and includes a sample of 8,093 legal units after applying stratified sampling, with a response rate of 80 per cent. Of these, 473 legal units belong to the DTIB, which represents 21 per cent of legal units identified in 2011. These 473 companies covered by the survey generate a defence turnover of €15 billion compared to €18.5 billion in 2011 for the whole DTIB. Therefore, the CAM survey includes defence companies that generate 81 per cent of the defence turnover of the French DTIB.

Between 2009 and 2011, 16 per cent of companies from the DTIB sample[46] offshored activities, and 11 per cent expected to do so. This appears less than the ratio for purely commercial companies, with a 2013 UNCTAD study estimating that in 2010, the secondary sector had 29.4 per cent of foreign value added in exports at the international level. However, offshoring and imported added value widely varies between sectors: from 5 per cent in petroleum to 45 per cent in the 'manufacturing of office, accounting and computing machinery'.[47] Concerning DTIB companies' core business,[48] offshored activities went primarily to existing foreign subsidiaries and related companies. The choice to work within a group can be interpreted as the will to find a balance between economic factors (market penetration, cost reduction) and strategic ones (control over the consequences of offshoring). On a broader perspective for French companies, an exporting company offshores on average four times more than non-exporting company.[49]

Only fourteen DTIB companies offshored all or part of their operations related to 'design, R&D, engineering and technical services' over the period 2009–11. This corresponds closely with the 'smiling curve' concept that Stan Shih, founder of Acer Group, originally developed in 1992: industrial players tend to position themselves in segments with the highest added value. When offshoring is implemented, this takes place inside the company (with one exception), confirming that they tend to create centres of excellence at an international level. Such decisions illustrate the desire to keep R&D activities internal within the company's domain, but also within national territory. If offshoring has regard to activities of 'design, R&D, engineering and technical services', the first destination was India, then Africa for competitiveness criteria (costs, skills) or as promising markets.

DTIB companies' offshoring is motivated, most often, by access to cheaper labour costs (98 per cent), reduction of other costs (80 per cent), access to new markets (79 per cent) and improvement in quality or the introduction of new products (70 per cent). Lack of skilled labour, reduced red tape, reduced exposure to exchange risks or the development of customers abroad are not considered as critical to offshoring. Between 2009 and 2011, DTIB companies chose to offshore mainly in Africa (24 per cent), India (21 per cent) and new Member States of the European Union (17 per cent). These decisions to offshore are compatible with the rising international trade in defence goods, with especially Africa,[50] as well as FDI flows in line with corporate strategic and economic expansion goals. These flows appear complementary to sustainable growth and performance for these companies.

Offshoring did not, with one exception, lead to the disappearance of subsidiaries located in France, because the process aimed at specialising production outside France in low added value tasks (mainly, labour intensive) or at looking at outsourcing specific tasks in which French production is insufficiently competitive. Additionally, these decisions led to job cuts in only 7 per cent of cases. This can be explained by the diversity and complexity of incoming and outgoing trade flows: offshoring responds in part to the requirements of export markets beyond the strategy of these companies.

8.4 Conclusion

Defence-related companies are very active in international markets, both military and civilian. Expansion of commercial markets turns out to be crucial in their business development, and this is the reason why it seems important not to analyse arms production per se, but to look at DTIB companies in their entirety in order to understand the ongoing dynamics of the industrial base in arms-producing countries. Appreciating strategies of defence-related companies requires looking beyond defence trade data and investigating the added value of these flows and also international sourcing, foreign direct investment and offshoring of French defence-related companies at large.

This chapter provides an evaluation of these dimensions thanks to access to original French data. Contrary to what one would expect, it reveals a significant orientation by the French defence industry, one of the largest DTIBs in the world, towards globalisation. This trend concerns not only the sourcing of lead system integrators but also their industrial setting, given that these companies have increased their international sales and footprint since the 1990s. As a regulator and customer, the state must take into account the economic, strategic and social consequences of such dynamics. Despite its policy to guarantee security of supply, emphasising domestic production, pressures on procurement costs and the evolution of the industrial base at large (driven by the convergence of DTIB and the civilian base), this globalisation pressure has led to a deep transformation of the sourcing of arms production even amongst the largest arms-producing military spenders. The identification of counterfeit parts in American defence capabilities evidences such a trend. The creeping globalisation of defence groups and their supply chain adds pressure to revise regulation, particularly the expectation that defence corporate strategies remain aligned with the strategic interests of the state.

Although large groups attract most attention because of their increasing globalisation, SMEs are clearly at the heart of international fragmentation of value chains. The state must thus design appropriate regulation to avoid proliferation risks and to preserve strategic autonomy though a true security of supply. Additional research should focus on providing insights into the transformation of DTIBs, but this will require statistical data that are not yet accessible. Although the lack of statistical data acts to limit such an assessment, it would be useful to conduct case studies on given programmes to analyse the value chain in its fullest extent.

References and notes

1. M. R. De Vore. 'Defying Convergence: Globalisation and Varieties of Defence-Industrial Capitalism'. *New Political Economy*. 2015. 20(4): 569–93.

2. K. Krause. *Arms and the State: Patterns of Military Production and Trade.* Cambridge, New York, Melbourne: Cambridge University Press. 1992.

3. S. Berger. *Notre Première Mondialisation: Leçons d'un échec oublié.* Paris: Le Seuil. 2003.
4. K. Hayward. 'The Globalisation of Defence Industries'. *Survival.* 2001. 43(2): 115–32.
5. T. L. Friedman. *The World Is Flat: A Brief History of the Twenty-First Century.* New York: Farrar, Straus and Giroux. 2005.
6. One can refer to Pol Antràs, David H. Autor, Richard Baldwin, Arnaud Costinot, David Dorn, Gordon H. Hanson, Andrés Rodríguez-Clare, Esteban Rossi-Hansberg.
7. See G. Grossman, E. Rossi-Hansberg. 'Trading Tasks: A Simple Theory of Offshoring'. *American Economic Review.* 2008. 98(5): 1978–97; R. Baldwin. *The Great Convergence: Information Technology and the New Globalisation.* Cambridge, MA: Belknap Press. 2016; J. B. Jensen. *Global Trade in Services: Fear, Facts, and Offshoring.* New York: Peterson Institute for International Economics. 2011.
8. R. Baldwin. Globalisation: The Great Unbundling(s). Prime Minister's Office – Economic Council of Finland. 2006.
9. Krause. *Arms and the State.*
10. See R. Bellais and S. Jackson. 'Defence Firms beyond National Borders: Internationalisation or Multi-Domestic Approach'. In R. Bellais (ed). *The Evolving Boundaries of Defence: An Assessment of Recent Shifts in Defence Activities.* Conflict Management, Peace Economics and Development. Volume 23. Bingley: Emerald. 2014. 233–51; C. Kurç, S. G. Neuman. 'Defense Industries in the 21st century: a Comparative Study'. *Defence Studies.* 2017. 17(3): 219–27.
11. J. Hagedoorn, J. Schakenraad. 'The Internationalization of the Economy: Global Strategies and Strategic Technology Alliances'. In U. Muldur, R. Petrella and M. G. Colombo (eds). *The European Community and the Globalisation of Technology and the Economy.* Commission of the European Communities. Report number EUR 15150 EN. 1994. 159–192.
12. Hagedoorn, Schakenraad. 'The Internationalization of the Economy'.
13. See D. J. Neal and T. Taylor. 'Globalisation in the Defence Industry: An Exploration of the Paradigm for US and European Defence Firms and the Implications for Being Global Players'. *Defence and Peace Economics.* 2001. 12(4): 337–60; M. Ikegami. 'The End of a "National" Defence Industry? Impacts of Globalisation on the Swedish Defence Industry'. *Scandinavian Journal of History.* 2013. 38(4): 436–57.
14. G. Ianakiev. *How Do Offset Policies Affect the International Division of Labour? The Case of the Defence Industry.* Ninth Annual Conference on Economics and Security. Bristol. 2005.
15. Hagedoorn, Schakenraad. 'The Internationalization of the Economy'.

16. P. Dowdall. 'Chains, Networks and Shifting Paradigms: the UK Defence Industry Supply System'. *Defence and Peace Economics*. 2004. 15(6): 535–50.

17. See Neal and Taylor. 'Globalisation in the Defence Industry'; R. Bellais, M. Foucault and J-M Oudot. *Economie de la défense*. Paris: La Découverte. 2014.

18. E. Gates. 'The Defence Firm of the Future'. *Defence and Peace Economics*. 2004. 15(6): 509–17.

19. M. R. De Vore. 'Arms Production in the Global Village: Options for Adapting to Defence-Industrial Globalisation'. *Security Studies*. 2013. 22(3): 532–72.

20. This concept results from both a relative decrease of military orders and a convergence with commercial markets (aeronautics, space, electronics, etc.). Thus, the DTIB includes many companies for which defence business represents only a share of turnover with dual activities serving both defence and civilian markets.

21. P. Dunne. 'The Defence Industrial Base'. In K. Hartley and T. Sandler (eds). *Handbook of Defence Economics*. Vol. 1. Amsterdam: Elsevier. 1995. 399–430.

22. S. Moura and J-M. Oudot. 'Performances of the Defence Industrial Base in France: The Role of Small and Medium Enterprises'. *Defence and Peace Economics*. 2017. 28(6): 652–68.

23. Moura and Oudot. 'Performances of the Defence Industrial Base in France'.

24. United Nations Conference on Trade and Development. *World Investment Report 2017: Investment and the Digital Economy*. Sales number E.17.II.D.3. 2017. 26. http://unctad.org/en/PublicationsLibrary/wir2017_en.pdf (accessed 29 January 2018).

25. See Grossman and Rossi-Hansberg. 'Trading Tasks'; J. B. Jensen. *Global Trade in Services: Fear, Facts, and Offshoring*. New York: Peterson Institute for International Economics. 2011; R. Baldwin. *The Great Convergence: Information Technology and the New Globalisation*. Cambridge, MA: Belknap Press. 2016.

26. World Trade Organization. *World Trade Statistical Review 2017*. Geneva: WTO. 2017.

27. A. Fleurant, S. Perlo-Freeman, P. D. Wezeman, S. T. Wezeman. *Trends in International Arms Transfers, 2015*. SIPRI. 2016. www.sipri.org/sites/default/files/SIPRIFS1602.pdf (accessed 29 January 2018).

28. C. H. Anderton. 'Economics of Arms Trade'. In K. Hartley and T. Sandler (eds). *Handbook of Defence Economics*. Vol. 1. Amsterdam: Elsevier. 1995. 524–61.

29. J.-M. Oudot, E. Montalban. 'Les entreprises de défense connaissent une croissance soutenue de leurs exportations'. *EcoDef*. 2017. 92 (May).

30. T. Mayer, G. Ottaviano. *The Happy Few: the Internationalisation of European Firms*. Brussels: Bruegel. 2007.
31. United Nations Conference on Trade and Development. *World Investment Report 2017: Investment and the Digital Economy*. Sales number E.17.II.D.3. 2017. 26. http://unctad.org/en/PublicationsLibrar y/wir2017_en.pdf (accessed 29 January 2018).
32. R. Bellais and S. Jackson. 'Defence Firms beyond National Borders: Internationalisation or Multi-Domestic Approach'. In R. Bellais (ed). *The Evolving Boundaries of Defence: An Assessment of Recent Shifts in Defence Activities*. Conflict Management, Peace Economics and Development Volume 23. Bingley: Emerald. 2014. 233–51.
33. S. Martin. *The Economics of Offsets: Defence Procurement and Countertrade*. New York: Routledge. 1996.
34. R. Bellais. 'Technologie, innovation et puissance des nations, le poids de l'armement'. In J. P. Michiels and D. Uzunidis (eds). *Mondialisation et citoyenneté*. Paris: L'Harmattan. 1999. 139–52.
35. Ianakiev. How *Do Offset Policies Affect the International Division of Labour?*
36. Organisation for Economic Co-operation and Development. 'Measuring Trade in Value Added'. In *Interconnected Economies: Benefiting from Global Value Chains*. Paris: OECD. 2013. http://stats .oecd.org/index.aspx?DataSetCode=TIVA2015_C1.
37. See OECD. *Bilateral Trade Database by Industry and End-use (BTDIxE)*. Paris. June 2017. https://stats.oecd.org/index.aspx?queryid=64755.
38. Tanks and other armoured fighting vehicles; spacecraft, satellites and spacecraft launch vehicles; ships, boats and floating structures, warships; helicopters; flight simulators and parts thereof; aircraft, spacecraft and parts thereof; air combat simulators and parts thereof; arms and ammunition; parts and accessories thereof; bombs, grenades, torpedoes, mines, missiles and similar munitions of war and parts thereof; military weapons; aero planes and other aircrafts; aircraft engines, spark-ignition reciprocating or rotary type.
39. Grossman, Rossi-Hansberg. 'Trading Tasks'.
40. S. Berger. *How We Compete: What Companies Around the World Are Doing to Make It in the Global Economy*. New York: Doubleday. 2006.
41. Airbus, Dassault Aviation, Naval Group, MBDA, Nexter, Safran and Thales.
42. The statistical service of French MoD signed non-disclosure agreements with these groups.
43. Reports since 2010. See US Government Accountability Office. *Counterfeit Parts: DOD Needs to Improve Reporting and Oversight to Reduce Supply Chain Risks*. Report number: GAO 16-236. 2016.

44. L. Fontagné, A. D'Isanto. 'Chaînes d'activité mondiales: des délocalisations d'abord vers l'Union européenne'. *INSEE Première*. June 2013. 1451.

45. T. Picard. 'La sous-traitance internationale, une pratique fréquente'. *INSEE Première*. October 2014. 1518.

46. Of the 473 companies in the DTIB covered by the CAM sample, 401 provided information on this question, 66 of them reporting having relocated part of their activities.

47. United Nations Conference on Trade and Development. *World Investment Report 2013: Global Value Chains: Investment and Trade for Development*. Sales number: E.13.II.D.5. 128. http://unctad.org/en/ PublicationsLibrary/wir2013_en.pdf (accessed 29 January 2018).

48. In the CAM survey, the core activity of companies is assimilated into the main business of the company. It may also include other activities if the company considers that they constitute a part of its core functions.

49. Fontagné, D'Isanto. 'Chaînes d'activité mondiales'.

50. J.-M. Oudot. 'L'essor des livraisons internationales des entreprises de défense'. *EcoDef*. 2017. 92 (May).

9 The Great Paradox of Defence: Political Economy and Defence Procurement in Post-Brexit United Kingdom

MATT UTTLEY AND BENEDICT WILKINSON

Introduction

At the heart of defence procurement lies a great paradox. At its simplest, the dilemma is a consequence of the tension between national 'sovereignty': an imperative to secure the supply of defence equipment and through this to realise the national security, economic and political benefits, and integration: the imperative for states to share the enormous costs of defence equipment production and procurement with other partners. The tension between these two imperatives is one of the intractable dilemmas that officials and politicians struggle with, and that academics and theorists scrutinise and explore. It is also one of the core themes that run not only through this volume, but through the wider body of literature examining the political economy of defence.[1]

For policymakers, the tensions are manifest in a series of choices and trade-offs that have serious security and economic implications. Sharing the development of a complex weapons system with allies may reduce its costs and increase interoperability, but it also presents challenges to the security of the supply chain (see Chapter 14 for supplementary observations). For academics, the tensions have spawned considerable debate over whether the notion of national security of supply in advanced weapons has become a redundant concept, and normative questions about how states can or should balance sovereignty imperatives against counter-imperatives to offset affordability constraints by meeting their defence procurement needs through forms of international cooperation and government-induced transnational industrial restructuring.[2]

These difficult choices and trade-offs harry national governments even at the best of times when budget deficits are low and economies are flourishing. But they become particularly acute when public money is tight, and wider security environments are volatile and shifting. It is in this latter position that the UK government currently finds itself, following the decision on 23 June 2016, by the majority of UK voters to leave the European Union in an 'in-out' referendum. From a defence procurement perspective, the United Kingdom and European Union now both face unresolved questions about the impact of Brexit on Britain and the EU's future defence procurement and defence industries. The United Kingdom has long preferred to emphasise sovereignty over integration in its defence procurement choices, where other EU Member States have historically advocated ever-closer European integration in defence production and supply, particularly supporting supranational initiatives with a view to creating a globally competitive and autonomous European Defence Technological and Industrial Base (EDTIB). In the Treaty on the Functioning of the European Union (hereinafter TfEU, or the Treaty), the European Union has ended up with a Treaty that supports both, on the one hand, seeking to preserve national sovereignty considerations while encouraging and driving increasingly integrated defence procurement.

In this chapter, we explore this great paradox through the prism of Brexit. In so doing, we attempt not only to provide a substantive update of our pre- and post-referendum analyses of the possible implications of Brexit for UK and EU defence procurement and industrial policies,[3] but also to draw some of the wider implications of that analysis for (and towards) a political economic theory of defence procurement.

Our analysis here falls into four sections. The first section focuses on the current state of the Brexit negotiations, highlighting the UK and EU27 negotiation 'red lines' and what they might mean for future UK-EU trade arrangements. The second section analyses the pre-Brexit 'rules of the game' in terms of the current resolution of tensions between national sovereignty and supranational integration in EU defence procurement and industrial policy. In doing so, it identifies the current frictions between the United Kingdom's commitment to EU internal market liberalisation and EU initiatives intended to develop a more integrated European defence industrial policy, which have intensified since the UK's Brexit vote. The third section explores the potential benefits and costs for the United Kingdom and remaining twenty-seven EU Member States if the outcomes of Brexit negotiations result in a scenario where the UK secures a preferential 'third country' sector agreement as part of a wider FTA. This involves the least disruption to existing pre-Brexit arrangements, and avoids the most disruptive situation whereby the United Kingdom leaves the Single European Market (SEM) and is forced to operate under WTO rules. In doing so, the section identifies the potential benefits and costs for the United Kingdom and remaining EU Member States under each scenario. In the concluding section, we draw out the wider theoretical implications of the analysis, highlighting the deep, persistent tensions – the great paradox – that underpins defence procurement.

9.1 The State of Brexit Negotiations

Some two years on from the June 2016 in-out referendum, the British government and the remaining 27 EU Member States are locked in negotiations on the nature of their post-Brexit trading relationship.[4] The British government – with relative consistency – says that the United Kingdom will leave the EU SEM and Customs Union, and that it will negotiate a bespoke free trade agreement (FTA) with Brussels that enables the most frictionless possible trade within the SEM in goods and services. Its negotiation red lines are to end the direct jurisdiction of the European Court of Justice (ECJ) and the freedom of movement of European Union citizens into the United Kingdom, together with a cessation of mandatory UK contributions to the EU budget.

In drawing up these red lines, Prime Minister Theresa May's administration has effectively closed down the 'Norway model' of third-country trading association with the European Union because it would require the United Kingdom to commit to a continuation of the ECJ's jurisdiction, free movement of people and continued British budget contributions to the EU in exchange for full SEM access. At the same time, Mrs May has also rejected a Brexit modelled on the EU-Canada Comprehensive Economic and Trade Agreement (CETA). Although this would preserve British red lines, it would significantly diminish Britain's current SEM access through new tariff and non-tariff barriers. Instead, Mrs May's government has rejected the notion of a binary choice between the Norway and Canada models by arguing that the United Kingdom will be leaving the European Union from a 'unique starting point' of full regulatory conformity with the SEM, from which bespoke trading relations can be forged in key sectors of mutual significance to the UK and EU Member States. Its objective is therefore to secure a 'middle ground' FTA that would maximise UK access to the SEM while preserving its Brexit red lines.

Conversely, Michel Barnier, the European Union's chief Brexit nego-
tiator, has responded by stating that the only option for the United
Kingdom is the binary choice that it wishes to avoid:

If the UK wanted to go further than the type of free trade agreement we have
signed with Canada, there are other models on the table. Norway and Iceland
have chosen to be in the Single Market, to accept the rules, and to contribute
financially to cohesion policy. But one thing is sure: it is not – and will not –
be possible for a third country to have the same benefits as the Norwegian
model but the limited obligations of the Canadian model.[5]

These EU red lines reflect the political concern in Brussels and
European capitals that 'if the UK is seen to get a good deal from
negotiations there is a risk of moral hazard, with other member states
questioning the link between membership in the Union and receipt of
its benefits'.[6] The European Union therefore has an incentive to 'punish' Britain in order to deter 'contagion, but also has an incentive to
portray the UK as a spoiler, since this helps reinforce solidarity between
the EU27 and distracts from genuine differences between the remaining
member states'.[7] This is reflected in Donald Tusk, the European
Council President's rejection of any notion of UK '"cherry picking"
aspects of its future relationship with the EU or being able to join
a "single market a la carte"' on a sector-by-sector approach in any post-
Brexit deal.[8]

Not surprisingly, the Brexit negotiations have ground rapidly to
a halt, and are currently at an impasse because Britain and the remaining EU27 member states have yet to resolve the dilemmas arising from
these seemingly irreconcilable red lines. For the United Kingdom, if the
EU27 prove unwilling to modify their position on SEM access then the
UK will be confronted with a stark choice between accepting the
limitations of a CETA model of third-party association, or a 'no deal'
scenario where it is forced to trade with the European Union under
World Trade Organisation (WTO) rules. Conversely, the remaining
EU27 confront a tension between 'allowing Britain to "have its cake
and eat it" ... and "cutting off its nose to spite its face" by denying
Britain access to European frameworks', which would ultimately
damage the Member States' national economies if no deal is reached.[9]

As a consequence, the exact details of the final Brexit outcome remain
a mystery, as well as its feasibility in practice, or what its implications are
for the United Kingdom and the remaining twenty-seven EU Member

States. While all this is true for numerous sectors and policy areas, the potential implications for the future of UK and EU defence procurement cooperation and defence industries are significant. This is because intra-EU armaments procurement and associated industries form a central component of the defence political economies of the EU Member States. Indeed, during the course of the Brexit process the UK government has emphasised its desire to secure a future defence relationship with the European Union 'that is deeper than any current third country partnership ... [which] ... should be unprecedented in its breadth, taking in cooperation on foreign policy, defence and security, and development, and in the degree of engagement that we envisage'.[10] It has explicitly identified the European defence industry as a sector that is 'closely integrated with leading companies having a presence across several European nations ... [where] ... open markets and customs arrangements that are as frictionless as possible are important to the continued success of this sector and to ensure that British and European Armed Forces can access the best war-fighting capability to keep us safe'.[11]

The United Kingdom's ambitions in this area suggest it is seeking to draw on its 'security surplus' – derived from its national defence budget that accounts for approximately 27 per cent of the combined defence expenditure of the EU Member States[12] – to strengthen its negotiating hand in Brexit talks. Such a security surplus is likely to involve using the promise of ongoing cooperation on defence measures to extract a bespoke deal from the European Union in the defence procurement and industrial sector, and, potentially, beyond. While the European Council has made clear its determination to secure a close partnership with the United Kingdom in areas including security, defence and foreign policy, its position remains that the depth of such a partnership will be limited if the UK is outside the Customs Union and SEM because this will 'inevitably lead to frictions in trade'.[13]

Uncertainty therefore remains about the ramifications of Brexit for the United Kingdom and the European Union in these sectors. And yet understanding the implications will be crucial, not least because defence industries are important areas of the United Kingdom's economy as well as vital parts of the country's national security infrastructure. The United Kingdom's defence industry has a turnover of £23 billion per annum, including defence exports worth £5.9 billion, which employs 142,000 predominantly highly skilled personnel.[14]

There remain crucial questions, too, about the post-Brexit future of pan-EU initiatives intended to achieve 'ever closer union' through internal market liberalisation, intra-EU armaments cooperation and aspirations to develop a European Defence Technological and Industrial Base to support the EU Common Security and Defence Policy (CSDP). These questions are not straightforward and the answers are far from resolved.

9.2 The State of Pre-Brexit EU Defence Procurement Cooperation

In essence, the pre-Brexit rules of the game in EU defence procurement and industrial policy reflect a clash between the competing logics of the primacy of national sovereignty versus the counter-imperatives for closer European integration.[15] The logic of sovereignty is enshrined in the pervasive idea that EU Member States should retain the right to autonomy in developing, producing, procuring and trading in military goods for national security reasons. It is this that is enshrined in Article 346 of the Treaty, which states that 'any Member State may take such measures as it considers necessary for the protection of the *essential interests of its security* which are connected with the production or trade in arms, munitions and war material' (italics added).[16] The intention of this is clear: it seeks to ensure that member states retain national control over security of supply in meeting their defence materiel requirements, but defence procurement expenditure and domestic defence industries are also important for national employment and economy. Member States have used Article 346 provisions to justify greater domestic defence spending to protect the industries from external competition to sustain what is seen as a manufacturing sector of national strategic and economic importance.[17] A consequence has been that while the European Union has succeeded in creating a single market for public procurement of civil goods and services, the application of Article 346 by Member States – motivated either by national security or domestic economic and industrial motives – has limited market liberalisation impact in the EU defence procurement sector.[18]

The logic of sovereignty sits in tension with the foundational EU logic of integration through 'ever closer union' and aspirations towards common defence that 'have been part of the European project since its inception'.[19] The integrationist logic holds that collective defence and the industry and armaments production to support it is a common endeavour among the EU states in the development of a credible Common Security and Defence Policy. It assumes that EU security policy should be developed within the framework of the CSDP through the pooling of defence research and development and weapons acquisition requirements among EU Member States. It also assumes that EU market liberalisation in defence procurement is essential to the development of a strategically autonomous European Defence Technological and Industrial Base. The rationale behind this logic is built on several studies that have sought to identify the 'cost of non-Europe' arising from what the European Commission describes as a 'scattergun approach' to defence procurement arising from duplication in weapons systems in production, and from existing gaps and protectionist barriers to a truly integrated and competitive EU single market in defence contracting arising from the use of Article 346 provisions by the Member States. Here, the latest European Parliament report mapping the 'cost of non-Europe' estimates these as ranging 'from some 130 billion Euro, at the high end, to at least 26 billion Euro per year, on a more cautious estimate'.[20] The report shows that 'the existence of 28 compartmentalised national markets ... hinders competition and results in a missed opportunity for economies of scale for industry and production' when compared to procurement and defence-industrial arrangements in the United States.[21] This missed opportunity for economies of scale is evident in the current level of EU duplication in procurement and production whereby EU states have in use a total of seventy-nine different weapons platforms and systems, compared to twenty-one in the United States, and have in operation thirty-six major equipment production lines, compared to eleven in the United States.[22] It is precisely this logic that has led the European Commission to attempt to reduce fragmentation and duplicative national defence programmes. In July 2009, the European Parliament and Council adopted the Defence and Security Directive (Directive 2009/81/EC) on defence procurement, which sought to liberalise EU markets and affirm the primacy of EU competition law by confining the use of Article 346 by member states to 'clearly exceptional cases' in an attempt to eradicate national protectionism on economic grounds.[23]

Faced with these two competing logics, the United Kingdom's stance is simultaneously supportive of the liberalisation of EU and transatlantic defence equipment markets and of maintaining sovereignty over key areas of procurement. Indeed, this is reflected in the United Kingdom's own procurement and defence industrial strategy. The Ministry of Defence's 2017 paper entitled 'Industry for Defence and a Prosperous Britain' reflected the United Kingdom's continued commitment to pursue 'open procurement' by fulfilling its 'defence and security requirements through open competition on the domestic and global market'.[24] This commitment to open procurement via global markets is essentially Euro-Atlanticist and reflects the primacy of the NATO alliance in its national strategy. At the same time, UK sovereignty is ensured through the principle of 'technology advantage', whereby the MoD takes action on procurement decisions to protect 'operational advantage' (the national ability to maintain and upgrade its defence technology) and 'freedom of action' (the ability to operate defence systems free from external intervention) where this is considered essential for national security.

These principles are evident in the United Kingdom's alternative weapons acquisition strategies and defence industrial policy. In addition to national programmes (e.g. the Queen Elizabeth Class aircraft carriers), its weapons acquisition strategy embraces transatlantic collaborative ventures (F-35B), the manufacture within the domestic industry of US-designed systems (e.g. the Augusta-Westland Apache AH-1 attack helicopter) and off-the-shelf import of complete weapons systems from the United States (e.g. the Boeing P-8 Maritime Patrol Aircraft). Approximately 28 per cent of total MoD equipment expenditure is allocated to European collaborative weapons programmes with other EU Member States (e.g. Typhoon aircraft) through intergovernmental agreements such as the A400M tactical and strategic airlift aircraft.[25] On the supply side, successive governments have claimed that the United Kingdom has 'one of the most open defence markets in the world'.[26] The 'British defence industry' is defined as 'all defence suppliers [to the MoD and export markets] that create value, employment, technology or intellectual assets in the UK', including 'both UK- and foreign-owned companies'.[27] Britain's 'logic of liberalisation of defence markets' has enabled major European and US defence firms to establish onshore operations, compete without discrimination for MoD contracts and export orders and develop local supply chains in the United Kingdom through forms of 'industrial engagement'.

The same approach plays out at the European level, where the United Kingdom is a vocal supporter of the liberalisation of EU defence markets, but a staunch opponent of further European Union and EDA integration initiatives that might dilute the legitimate application of Article 346. On the one hand, Britain's commitment to open procurement and market liberalisation has been reflected in its support for the Defence and Security Directive. This was evident in the British government's review of the balance of competences between the United Kingdom and the European Union in July 2012, which sought to audit 'what the EU does, how it affects the UK, where competence lies, how the EU's competences are used, and what that means for the UK's national interest'.[28] The review reaffirmed the UK government's support for efforts to open up the EU defence market to more competition and eliminate economically driven 'buy national' policies, 'while respecting member states' right to maintain certain strategic industrial capabilities for reasons of national security'.[29] It also identifies that there is scope for the Commission to take a more proactive stance within its existing competence, notably preventing 'abuses' of Article 346 by those member states using it as a pretext to discriminate against non-national bidders for non-sensitive defence contracts.[30] On the other hand, the review concluded that the European Commission has progressively claimed 'more competences in this particular area' and 'sees an even broader role for itself', and reaffirmed that the UK government 'does not support any extension of Commission competence'.[31]

These factors are significant when it comes to Brexit negotiations. On the one hand, as far as defence procurement and industrial strategy go, the UK government will prioritise gaining tariff- and barrier-free access to the increasingly integrated defence markets in the European Union, because it supports their desire for competitive markets, and because it is essential for UK-based defence firms to retain frictionless access to its European supply chains. Simultaneously, the United Kingdom will also want to retain the kind of sovereignty over defence procurement currently provided by Article 346 in its future defence trade relations with the EU Member States. Ultimately, the availability of such a position will be heavily dependent on internal factors in the European Union, and the desire of the remaining twenty-seven Member States to give the United Kingdom 'what it wants'. On the other hand, the European Union has responded to the Brexit vote by revisiting the balance of jurisdictions between the Member States and the European Commission and EDA. In 2013, prior to the United Kingdom's Brexit vote, the European Commission published the document entitled 'Towards a More Competitive and Efficient Defence and Security Sector', which outlined plans to allocate dedicated funding for defence-specific R&D programmes on behalf of the member states directly from the European Union's budget.[32] Since then, the European Commission has launched a fully fledged European Defence Fund plan worth €1.5 billion per year from the EU central budget to subsidise joint defence research and development project proposals from groupings of member states. The purpose of this initiative is to increase the strategic autonomy and self-sufficiency of the EDTIB as part of the European Union's 2016 Global Strategy. As Nick Whitney, a former EDA Chief Executive, points out, 'the rules for the subsidy regime currently being debated in the EU institutions specify that the subsidy should be available only to EU defence industries'.[33] A critical issue for the UK government and Britain's onshore defence industry is whether or how access to this initiative should or could be obtained in the post-Brexit settlement that prevails.

9.3 Scenario 1: Post-Brexit Britain in the Single European Market

Prime Minister May's objectives are for the United Kingdom to leave the EU SEM and Customs Union, and to secure a bespoke FTA with Brussels that enables the most frictionless possible trade within the SEM. If the British government is successful, then the most favourable outcome is likely to be a bespoke variant of the Norwegian model of third-country association because it would provide the United Kingdom with the highest level of post-Brexit continuity through unrestricted access to the SEM, and, in return, it would be required to adopt the same future SEM-related legislation as EU Member States.[34] Nevertheless, it would also have the effect of recalibrating the contingent choices and potential trade-offs for Britain and the remaining twenty-seven EU states as they develop new rules of the game in managing their mutual interdependence in the defence procurement and defence industrial arenas.

For the United Kingdom government, a post-Brexit relationship based on a bespoke variant of the Norwegian model is unlikely to affect the country's choices concerning foreseeable major defence procurement plans and commitments, nor the domestic legislative basis on which its defence procurement is based. In 2017, the MoD published its Defence Equipment Plan, which detailed the government's latest plans cumulatively to spend approximately £180 billion on new equipment and equipment support up to 2027.[35] A significant proportion of expenditure on major projects is already contractually committed.[36] A Brexit modelled on a bespoke variant of the Norwegian model would enable Britain to retain de facto Article 346 provisions, which would mean that it would not alter the MoD's current ability to select from domestic systems, European and US collaborative programmes, and off-the-shelf purchases when placing future orders funded from the currently uncommitted equipment budget. It is likely to incur limited disruption to existing foreign companies operating as part of Britain's onshore defence industry because it provides firms with continuing access to EU-wide markets and supply chains. Similarly, if the United Kingdom were to secure a relationship based on the EEA model, then its domestic defence procurement regime 'would very likely remain the same, and continue to evolve as the EU regime does, including continuing to be influenced by the case law of the European Courts and the requirements of the EU treaty principles'.[37] In this regard, Directive 2009/81/EC, addressing the procurement of defence- and security-related goods and services, was transposed into UK law in 2011, so this Brexit settlement would require no modification to existing domestic procurement legislation.[38]

Nevertheless, for the United Kingdom a Brexit relationship based on a variant of the SEM access provisions provided by the Norwegian model is likely to come at the cost of reduced influence over EU supranational defence procurement policy than it currently enjoys. Although the United Kingdom would be required to contribute to the common EU budget in return for access to the single market, it is likely to incur a 'democratic deficit' by losing formal influence in shaping the direction and rules governing Europe's evolving defence internal market. It is noteworthy that the European Union has been unambiguous about the status of Norway and other EEA European Free Trade Association countries:

[their] position outside the EU was chosen by them rather than imposed by the EU, so any 'democratic deficit' resulting from their obligation to adopt EU law, despite not having a voice in EU decision-making, can be seen as the 'price' they have chosen to pay for retaining full access to the Single Market, while shunning EU membership.[39]

This situation would inevitably constrain Britain's future choices and present new risks when it ceases to be an EU Member State. First, the

United Kingdom's new status 'outside the core EU political and economic circle' would result in reduced influence over the future evolution of EU defence procurement directives. Second, the European
Commission's insistence that only EU Member States will benefit
from European Defence Fund support effectively precludes third-
country participation, which suggests that UK participation would
be excluded. Even if the United Kingdom were to secure an association agreement of some kind, precedent suggests that it will be unlikely to have the same rights in the process of priority setting for the
dispersal of future EU funding because of its 'third country' status.
In effect, the United Kingdom would cede considerable influence over
the content and direction of European Commission and EDA plans
with their associated goals and aspirations to foster a more integrated
and potentially more protectionist EU-wide defence industrial policy.
Third, a chief UK government concern about defence procurement is
that the remaining twenty-seven EU states should not be seen to be
discriminating against US suppliers and that the UK freedom to buy
equipment from the United States should not be qualified. Reduced
British influence arising from its democratic deficit – coupled with the
explicit European protectionism evident in the European Defence
Fund construct – increases the potential risk of both eventualities
materialising.

On the face of it, the post-Brexit deficit in the United Kingdom's
influence and choices under an EEA Agreement scenario might be
reflected in increased options for the remaining twenty-seven EU states
to increase the tempo and extent of 'Europeanisation' of EU defence
procurement and defence markets. Paradoxically, however, with this
Brexit scenario there would be a shift in the balance of power and
influence from those EU Member States seeking more liberalisation of
EU defence markets, including Britain and Sweden, towards other
member states, notably France and Spain, which believe that the
EDTIB should shield states from non-EU competition while helping
to promote a 'buy European' policy.[40] That is to say, with reduced UK
influence, it is questionable whether other major weapons-producing
EU Member States 'would continue to push for competition and efficiency in the defence industry'.[41]

The potential barriers to European Commission attempts to intensify
intra-EU market liberalisation in a situation of reduced UK influence
are shown in statistics on the implications of initiatives to date.

The latest EDA estimates indicate that despite the pan-EU adoption of Directive 2009/81/EC, approximately 80 per cent of EU defence expenditure not assigned to international collaborative weapons projects is spent nationally, indicating that the degree of openness to suppliers from other member states has been 'relatively low'.[42] A recent study for the European Parliament on the impact of Directive 2009/81/EC demonstrated that its impact on pan-EU tendering for defence contracts has been limited.[43] Since the Directive came into force all of the major equipment contracts issued by the EU Member States have been awarded using Article 346 provisions, and where pan-EU tendering has been adopted by the Member States it has been for contracts 'dealing with services, the acquisition of equipment deemed to be of low value, and sub-systems'.[44] More recent reports suggest that the 2009 Directive has been mostly ignored by member states, and that 'most European countries have acknowledged the directive selectively, continuing to favour domestic industries'.[45] Consequently, rather than permitting the EDTIB and CSDP to advance unhindered, this form of Brexit 'might reveal deep cleavages in approach that have allowed other member states to hide behind Britain's blanket veto'.[46]

9.4 Scenario 2: The UK Operates under World Trade Organisation Arrangements

The Brexit negotiations are currently at an impasse because Britain and the remaining EU27 Member States have yet to resolve the dilemmas arising from their seemingly irreconcilable red lines. This raises the real possibility that the outcome of the negotiation process will be a 'no-deal'. If this were the case, the most likely Brexit scenario – and, in our analysis, most disruptive to the existing rules of the game that govern EU defence procurement and industrial policy – is one where the United Kingdom fails to secure an FTA and trades with the European Union under WTO rules. If the FTA negotiations fall through, the United Kingdom will at least temporarily be forced to operate outside EU rules, regulations and directives by following WTO regulations. For some, the ramifications of such a move on defence industrial policy in the United Kingdom and European Union are likely to be limited. As one analyst puts it, the European Union currently has little impact on UK defence policy, which tends to be more open to competition than is required by EU directives. Consequently, leaving the EU would have little impact on UK defence procurement. Of greater importance is wider European Defence co-operation, which the UK could still play a significant part in outside the EU given its largely intergovernmental nature.[47]

In this analysis, a Brexit based on WTO arrangements might be expected to have a limited impact on the United Kingdom's major defence procurement plans and commitments where contracts are in place, or its future ability to engage in cooperative intergovernmental defence procurement initiatives with the United States and EU members. Similarly, the major markets for UK defence exports are outside the European Union: some 4 per cent of UK defence industry turnover is accounted for by EU sales, with the remainder going to domestic sales (58 per cent) and non-EU export destinations (38 per cent).[48] This suggests that any dislocation if the United Kingdom were to operate under WTO rules would be limited in terms of national defence trade.

A key consideration is whether future UK governments will seek to increase intergovernmental defence procurement with the EU Member States to compensate for its departure from EU institutions, or whether the Brexit vote will lead to a further disassociation from European ties. The combination of President Trump's recent call for the European NATO states to shoulder a greater burden for their own defence (see Chapter 10) and growing concerns over Russia's military activities on the alliance's eastern flanks (see Chapter 17) would make this latter course difficult. Moreover, recent post-referendum events, including the United Kingdom's recent commitment to the next phase of the collaborative Anglo-French Maritime Mine Counter Measures (MMCM) project, signals that bilateral and multilateral cooperation with EU states is likely to remain a cornerstone of UK procurement.

Nevertheless, a Brexit predicated on WTO arrangements would provide the United Kingdom with new choices to mould a more independent national procurement and defence industrial policy. Britain would have choices over whether to retain or dispense with some or all of its existing defence procurement legislation currently derived from EU directives, and decisions of the European Court and EU case law would no longer be binding on the British courts.[49] This raises the potential for more variance in UK defence procurement rules and policies as governments change. It would, for example, allow UK governments to adopt defence procurement and industrial strategies that factor economic and employment implications into weapons acquisition choices, which is currently prohibited in UK procurement law derived from Directive 2009/81/EC. This option is unlikely to be pursued by the current Conservative administration, which recently reaffirmed its commitment to a 'default' principle of 'open procurement'.[50] It could accommodate the aspiration of the opposition Labour party to 'reverse this trend with a new Defence Industrial Strategy which, while accepting the importance of value for money, aims also to safeguard Britain's industrial base, secure high quality jobs throughout the supply chain, and protect our national sovereignty' if it were to be elected in a future general election.[51]

Correspondingly, a Brexit based on WTO arrangements would certainly have adverse effects for future UK government defence procurement options because of the responses of foreign defence firms with a presence in the UK to the new realities of operating outside the EU SEM. The UK-based defence industry made no secret of its antipathy towards a Brexit in the run-up to Britain's in-out referendum. The 2015 (in full) ADS survey report, entitled 'The UK aerospace, defence, security and space industry and the EU', found that 73 per cent of UK-based firms believe that EU membership is positive for their business against 1 per cent which said it was negative, and that 86 per cent of ADS members would vote for the United Kingdom to stay in the European Union against 2 per cent who would vote to leave.[52] Significant areas of concern identified by industry respondents were that a Brexit might jeopardise the opportunities for free trade with the remaining EU Member States, impede their access to EU suppliers and supply chains and undermine their ability to recruit skilled workers if the free movement of EU labour is curtailed.[53]

These concerns remain, and domestic and non-European defence firms with an established presence in the United Kingdom stand to lose out if Brexit results in a WTO arrangement in terms of reduced access to EU funds and the potential for increases in taxes and administrative burdens in trading with the remaining twenty-seven Member States. A particular concern is the future investment behaviour of the larger defence companies with operations in the United Kingdom that are headquartered in Europe, particularly Leonardo, Airbus Group and Thales UK, and investments by large US firms, notably Northrop Grumman Europe, which is based in the UK.[54] The risk for the UK government here is that a Brexit settlement based on WTO rules might lead these key industrial players to relocate within EU Member States to maintain access to the benefits of the SEM and EU-wide supply chains.[55]

For the remaining twenty-seven EU Member States, a Brexit modelled on WTO arrangements offers similar choices and constraints to a Brexit modelled on a bespoke variant of the Norwegian model of third country association. Britain's status outside the EU internal market would offer opportunities for the remaining twenty-seven EU states to pursue greater liberalisation and Europeanisation of EU defence procurement and defence markets. At the same time, the achievement of these goals might be impeded by the loss of a British voice and influence in advocating market liberalisation. A primary difference arising from a Brexit modelled on WTO arrangements is that this would inevitably fragment the closeness of the European Union's defence industrial links with Europe's most capable military powers that currently account for approximately 21 per cent of the EU defence budget.[56] A key question for EU policymakers would be over the extent to which the EDTIB initiative could progress with Britain's absence. The European Union will also lose its close ties to one of the few countries that meet the 'gold standard' by spending 2 per cent of GDP on defence. As President Trump questions the utility of NATO, this may be poor timing.

9.5 Conclusion: The Great Paradox

The British government's stated objectives in the ongoing Brexit negotiations are to leave the EU Single Market and Customs Union, and to negotiate a bespoke free trade agreement with Brussels that enables the most frictionless possible trade within the SEM in goods and services. For their part, the EU27 have an incentive to punish Britain in order to deter contagion and any further fragmentation of the Union. However, the future remains deeply uncertain. Although Prime Minister May has clearly stated a negotiating position, she may well be forced to adopt a new position if the European Union refuses to offer satisfactory terms in an FTA. In this sense, the United Kingdom's options are contingent on the choices and trade-offs of twenty-seven EU Member States. It may be that the United Kingdom is able to secure a FTA arrangement that provides bespoke third-country access to the SEM. This will be the least disruptive scenario for the United Kingdom's defence procurement and industrial strategy, but it would incur inevitable costs in terms of reduced influence and potential barriers to industrial participation. In the longer-term, however, benefits of such an FTA may be little more than a mirage; if the EU27 continues to pursue further EDTIB integration, ultimately the current scope and utility of Article 346 will be called into question. In this case, the United Kingdom, as an 'associate' member of the European Union, would be bound to follow whatever new directives were passed and would not be able to bargain for similar provisions. Correspondingly, a Brexit based on WTO arrangements provides a veneer of greater British sovereignty over defence procurement but risks the flight of key sections of the domestic industry to the European Union, and calls into question the future viability of the notion of an EDTIB.

Thus, each of the scenarios considered comes with benefits for the UK and for the EU, but each equally is likely to come at a cost. In short, British aspirations to secure an advantageous FTA which carries all the benefits of membership of the SEM without any of the trade-offs over free movement or tariffs seems to be little more than an ideal vision of the future; indeed, the future of UK defence procurement and industrial strategy, is likely to rest on the choices made, not by the UK government, but by its negotiating partners. For the EU27, the credibility of the EDTIB concept will inevitably be more diluted the more that it keeps the United Kingdom at arms-length. The issue for the EU27, therefore, remains one of resolving the tension between letting the UK 'have its cake and eat it' and 'cutting off its nose to spite its face'.

Nevertheless, the overriding conclusion that emerges is that defence procurement in the Brexit negotiations has reverted to the norm. Both scenarios see not just an interplay between the logic of sovereignty and the logic of integration, but a deep, unresolvable tension. It is this tension that necessitates and complicates the trade-offs and choices of the negotiating parties; indeed, it is this tension that also creates the great paradox: the contending logics of national sovereignty and of integration. It also suggests that the integrationist approach, though strongly advocated by the European Union, has gained less traction and less support in practice across the member states. The 'rules of the game' in EU defence procurement are skewed in favour of the logic of sovereignty, bolstered through the provisions of Article 346, and

intergovernmental cooperation rather than through supranational EU
bodies and initiatives. It is too early to say what this means for the
future of EU-wide defence procurement, though it may well indicate
that the impact of Brexit on defence procurement will be limited. More
broadly, however, it suggests that when push comes to shove, nations
will seek to protect the sovereignty of their supply chains over the
economic benefits of supranational cooperation.

References and notes

1. See, for example, J. S. Gansler. *Democracy's Arsenal: Creating a Twenty-First-Century Defense Industry*. Cambridge, MA: MIT. 2011; R. Smith. *Military Economics: The Interaction of Power and Money*. London: Palgrave. 2009.
2. See, for example, the contributions in R. Bitzinger (ed). *The Modern Defense Industry: Political, Economic, and Technological Issues*. Santa Barbara: Praeger. 2009.
3. M. Uttley and B. Wilkinson. 'A Spin of the Wheel? Defence Procurement and Defence Industries in the Brexit Debates'. *International Affairs*. 2016. 92(4): 569–86; M. Uttley and B. Wilkinson. 'Contingent Choices: the Future of United Kingdom Defence Procurement and Defence Industries in the Post-Brexit Era'. *Global Affairs*. 2017. 2(5): 491–502.
4. For an extended overview, see J. Owen, A. Stojanovic and J. Rutter. *Trade after Brexit: Options for the UK's Relationship with the EU*. London: Institute for Government. December 2017.
5. European Commission. *Single Market Scoreboard*. 2017. 4. http://ec.e uropa.eu/internal_market/scoreboard/_docs/2017/transposition/2017-scoreboard_transposition_en.pdf (accessed 2 May 2018).
6. B. Martill and M. Sus. *Known Unknowns: EU Foreign, Security, and Defence Policy after Brexit*. London: LSE!deas. 26 January 2018. 11.
7. Martill and Sus. *Known Unknowns*. 9.
8. BBC News. 'Donald Tusk: UK Brexit plans "pure illusion"'. BBC News. 23 February 2018. www.bbc.co.uk/news/uk-politics-43175201 (accessed 2 May 2018).
9. Martill and Sus. *Known Unknowns*. 9.
10. HM Government. *Foreign Policy, Defence and Development: A Future Partnership*. 2017. 18. Available from: https://assets.publishing.service .gov.uk/government/uploads/system/uploads/attachment_data/file/643 924/Foreign_policy__defence_and_development_paper.pdf (accessed 2 May 2018).
11. HM Government. *Foreign Policy, Defence and Development*. 19.

12. European Commission. Eurostat: How Much Is Spent on Defence in the EU?. *European Commission.* 17 June 2017. http://ec.europa.eu/eurostat/web/products-eurostat-news/-/EDN-20170607-1 (accessed 11 May 2018).

13. European Council. European Council (Art 50) Guidelines. 23 March 2018. 2. www.consilium.europa.eu/media/33458/23-euco-art50-guidelines.pdf (accessed 2 May 2018).

14. Parliament UK. *House of Commons Exiting the European Union Committee – Defence Sector Report.* 2017. 1. www.parliament.uk/documents/commons-committees/Exiting-the-European-Union/17-19/Sectoral%20Analyses/11-Defence-Report.pdf (accessed 2 May 2018).

15. See J. Bátora. 'European Defence Agency: A Flashpoint of Institutional Logics'. *West European Politics.* 2009. 32(6): 1093.

16. Treaty establishing the European Economic Community (TEEC). 1 January 1958.

17. J. Edwards. *The EU Defence and Security Procurement Directive: a Step Towards Affordability?* London: Chatham House. 2011. 4.

18. R. Bitzinger. 'The European Defense Industry in the 21st Century: Challenges and Responses'. In Bitzinger (ed). *The Modern Defense Industry.* 175–95.

19. See European Commission. *Defending Europe: The Case for Greater EU Cooperation on Security and Defence.* https://ec.europa.eu/commission/sites/beta-political/files/defending-europe-factsheet_en.pdf (accessed 2 May 2018).

20. European Parliamentary Research Unit (EPRU). *Mapping the Cost of Non-Europe,* 2014–19. Brussels: European Parliament. April 2015. 21.

21. Ibid.

22. V. Briani. *Armaments Duplication in Europe: a Quantitative Assessment.* Brussels: Centre for European Policy Studies. July 2013. 3.

23. For an extended analysis, see M. Blauberger and M. Weiss. 'If You Can't Beat Me, Join Me! How the Commission Pushed and Pulled Member States into Legislating Defence Procurement'. *Journal of European Public Policy.* 2013. 20(8): 1120–38; F. Castellacci. A. M. Fevolden and M. Lundmark. 'How are Defence Companies Responding to EU Defence and Security Market Liberalisation? A Comparative Study of Norway and Sweden'. *Journal of European Public Policy.* 2014. 21(8): 1218–35; C. Hoeffler. 'European Armaments Co-Operation and the Renewal of Industrial Policy Motives'. *Journal of European Public Policy.* 2012. 19(3): 435–51.

24. Ministry of Defence. *Industry for Defence and a Prosperous Britain: Refreshing Defence Industrial Policy.* December 2017. https://assets.publishing.service.gov.uk/government/uploads/system/uploads/attachment_data/file/669958/DefenceIndustrialPolicy_Web.pdf (accessed 2 May 2018).

25. European Defence Agency. *National Defence Data 2013–2014 and 2015 (est.) of the 27 EDA Member States*. June 2016. https://eda.europa.eu/docs/ default-source/documents/eda-national-defence-data-2013-2014-(2015-es t)5397973fa4d264cfa776ff000087ef0f.pdf (accessed 11 May 2018).
26. Ministry of Defence. *Defence Industrial Strategy*. The Stationery Office. Report number: Cm. 6697. 2005. 15.
27. Ministry of Defence. *Defence Industrial Policy*. Ministry of Defence. Policy paper number: 5, 2002. p. 4.
28. HM Government. *Review of the Balance of Competences between the United Kingdom and the European Union*. The Stationary Office. Report number: Cm. 8415. 2012. 6.
29. House of Commons Defence Committee. *Defence Acquisition: Government Response to the Committee's Seventh Report of Session 2012–2013*. The Stationery Office. Report number: HC 73. May 2013. https://publications.parliament.uk/pa/cm201314/cmselect/cmdfence/73/73 .pdf (accessed 2 May 2018). For an extended analysis, see House of Commons Library. *Leaving the EU*. House of Commons Library. Research Paper: 13/42. 1 July 2013. 85–90. http://researchbriefings.parlia ment.uk/ResearchBriefing/Summary/RP13-42#fullreport (accessed 2 May 2018).
30. HM Government. *Review of the Balances of Competences between the United Kingdom and European Union, The Single Market: Free Movement of Services*. London: TSO. 2014. 42.
31. Ibid.
32. European Commission. *Towards a More Competitive and Efficient Defence and Security Sector*. Commission staff working document. Brussels: European Commission. 24 July 2013. For an extended analysis, see D. Fiott. 'European Defence-Industrial Cooperation: From Keynes to Clausewitz'. *Global Affairs*. 2015. 1(2): 162.
33. N. Witney. 'The Brexit Threat to Britain's Defence Industry'. *European Council on Foreign Relations*. 1 February 2018. www.ecfr.eu/article/c ommentary_the_brexit_threat_to_britains_defence_industry (accessed on 16 April 2018).
34. European Parliament. Free Trade Agreements.
35. Ministry of Defence. *The Defence Equipment Plan 2017*. https:// assets.publishing.service.gov.uk/government/uploads/system/uploads/att achment_data/file/677999/20180125-EP17_Final.pdf (accessed 2 May 2018).
36. Approximately 72 per cent of the Equipment Plan was contractually committed in 2017/18, falling to 17 per cent at the end of the decade. See Ministry of Defence. *The Defence Equipment Plan 2017*. 10.

37. V. Moorcroft. 'Brexit: The End of Public Procurement Rules or Business as Usual?' *Bird & Bird*. 9 August 2016. www.twobirds.com/en/news/articles/2016/uk/brexit-end-of-public-procurement-rules (accessed 2 May 2018).
38. House of Commons Library. *EC Defence Equipment Directives*. UK Parliament. 2011. http://researchbriefings.parliament.uk/ResearchBriefing/Summary/SN04640 (accessed 2 May 2018).
39. European Parliament. *Free Trade Agreements between EFTA and Third Countries: An Overview*. 2016. www.europarl.europa.eu/RegData/etudes/BRIE/2016/580918/EPRS_BRI(2016)580918_EN.pdf (accessed 2 May 2018).
40. D. Fiott. 'European Defence-Industrial Cooperation'.
41. I. Bond, S. Besch, A. Gostynska-Jakubowska, R. Korteweg, C. Mortera-Martinez and S. Tilford. 'Europe after Brexit: Unleashed or Undone?' Centre for European Reform. 2016. 10. www.cer.org.uk/sites/default/files/pb_euafterBrexit_15april16.pdf (accessed 2 May 2018).
42. European Commission. Towards *a More Competitive and Efficient Defence and Security Sector – Memorandum*. European Commission. 2013. http://europa.eu/rapid/press-release_MEMO-13-722_en.htm?locale+en (accessed 2 May 2018).
43. H. Masson, K, Martin and Y. Queau. 'The Impact of the "Defence Package" Directives on European Defence'. European Parliament. 2015. www.europarl.europa.eu/RegData/etudes/STUD/2015/549044/EXPO_STU(2015)549044_EN.pdf (accessed 3 May 2018).
44. Masson, Martin and Queau. 'Impact'. 6.
45. See, for example, T. Kington. 'EU Sharply Reminds Members of Open Markets Policy'. *Defense News*. 6 March 2016. www.defensenews.com/story/defense/policy-budget/industry/2016/03/06/eu-sharply-reminds-members-open-markets-policy/81217200/ (accessed 3 May 2018).
46. Bond et al. 'Europe after Brexit'. 10.
47. F. Bungay. *Defence Policy and Procurement*. London: Trade Policy Research Centre. 2012. 18.
48. L. Béraud-Sudreau. 'The Extra-EU Defence Exports' Effects on European Armaments Cooperation'. European Parliament Directorate-General for External Policies. 2015. 18. www.europarl.europa.eu/RegData/etudes/STUD/2015/549043/EXPO_STU(2015)549043_EN.pdf (accessed 3 May 2018).
49. Moorcroft. 'Brexit: The End of Public Procurement'.
50. Ministry of Defence. *Industry for Defence and a Prosperous Britain: Refreshing Defence Industrial Policy*. December 2017. 10–11. https://assets.publishing.service.gov.uk/government/uploads/system/uploads/attachment_data/file/669958/DefenceIndustrialPolicy_Web.pdf (accessed 2 May 2018).

51. H. Pemberton. 'Britain's Defence and Security Priorities'. Bristol University. 2016. https://research-information.bristol.ac.uk/files/129207514/Submissi on_to_Labour_on_Trident_April_2016.pdf (accessed 2 May 2018).

52. ADS. *The UK Aerospace, Defence, Security and Space Industry and the EU: an Assessment of the Interaction of the UK's Aerospace, Defence, Security and Space Industry with the European Union.* Farnborough: ADS. 2015. 11.

53. ADS. *The UK Aerospace, Defence, Security and Space Industry and the EU.* 14.

54. Uttley and Wilkinson. 'A Spin of the Wheel?' 581.

55. See A. Black. 'European Defence Procurement and the Emerging EU Defence Presence'. The Federal Trust for Education and Research. 2016. 14. http://fedtrust.co.uk/wp-content/uploads/2016/06/European_ Defence_Procurement.pdf (accessed 2 May 2018).

56. Bond et al. 'Europe after Brexit'. 10.

10 Defence Burden Sharing: A Perennial Debate in International Alliance Management

ALEXANDER MATTELAER

Introduction

Ever since the days of the Peloponnesian war, states have formed alliances to pursue common military objectives. Such alliances have helped states to offset the cost of ensuring national security. Yet, they also raise difficult questions about political leadership, the division of military roles and the relative contribution of each constitutive member. One of the planning principles underlying the very first strategic concept of NATO, states that 'each nation will contribute in the most effective form, consistent with its situation, responsibilities and resources'.[1] What that exactly means, however, is the subject of constant debate that continues to the present day. When US President Donald Trump visited NATO Headquarters for the first time in 2017, the burden-sharing discussion stood front and centre on the special meeting agenda.[2] As alliance contributions can be measured using different sorts of parameters – ranging from financial metrics to strategic risk, and, ultimately, blood – such debates are difficult to resolve in any lasting way. Instead, they acquire perennial characteristics and necessitate great methodological rigour.

This chapter reviews the political economy context underlying these debates and the complexity of relating them to the defence budgeting cycle. It advances the thesis that jointly developed military plans for meeting possible contingencies constitute a more accurate mechanism for evaluating burden sharing than a mere combination of defence expenditure parameters. However, the latter continue to play an important role in predicting the future health and evolution of any given set of armed forces. This argument unfolds in three parts: Section 10.1 reviews the role played by alliances in defence resourcing. Alliances can be based on common military objectives as well as on common political values. In addition, from the point of view of defence economics, they hold the promise of lowering the overall cost of security via the effects of scale and increased efficiency. Yet any such gains must be reconciled with constraints on decision-making autonomy and may not be easy to divide equally. Section 10.2 zooms in on the burden-sharing debate within NATO as a case in point. Defence spending targets tell an important part of the story, but not the whole story: there is a real need to engage in intra-alliance negotiations about threat perceptions and related defence requirements to provide greater colour and depth on discussions of defence accounting. Section 10.3 elaborates on the methodological challenges inherent in measuring whether individual allies carry their fair share of common defence. The associated time horizon is of critical importance in this regard. Over the longer term, maintaining military readiness requires sufficient financial, material and human resources. Yet the decision by arms, as Clausewitz puts it, is what cash payment is in commerce. It is only the outbreak of war that puts defence establishments to the ultimate test. In the absence of actual conflict, defence plans therefore offer the most detailed understanding of burden sharing at any specific point in time. Yet before turning to burden-sharing discussions per se, it is imperative to review the role alliances play in the provision and resourcing of national security.

10.1 The Role of Alliances in Defence Resourcing

The most elementary function of any state is to provide physical security to its inhabitants.[3] Taking factors such as its geographical position and potential threats into account, the state maintains a three-pronged apparatus for delivering on its role as a security provider. This typically includes internal security forces for ensuring domestic security and the rule of law, intelligence agencies for tracking evolutions in the security environment and armed forces for countering external military threats that may emerge. Beyond the realm of security per se, one could also add the complementary roles of the judicial and diplomatic apparatus in providing for domestic justice and maintaining friendly international relations.

These security instruments together come at a necessary but significant expense to the taxpayer. Moreover, the question 'how much security is enough' is often mired in political controversy. This is particularly relevant to the size of a nation's armed forces; their cost usually amounting to at least a few percentage points of annual government spending, and should be balanced by the ultimate function that lies in the very irregular occurrence of war. During peacetime, large armies tend to be perceived as manifestations of wasteful public spending – the age-old 'guns versus butter' argument – whereas small armies may be easily overwhelmed by the sudden outbreak of war. Yet transforming small armies into large ones or vice versa cannot be done overnight: it requires sustained investment over a time horizon that is measured in decades. The government's responsibility is therefore to maintain a delicate equilibrium between fiscal pressure and strategic risk management; a task positioned at the heart of the challenge of forging a healthy national defence system.

Within a national context, governments allocate a share of fiscal income to defence expenditure. Any national defence budget can be analysed in different ways, but three relevant functional categories stand out.[4] Firstly, defence outlays, either in general or for each of the individual armed services, encompass a large share of personnel costs. Personnel expenditure accounts for men and women wearing the uniform at the service of the state, ready to pay the ultimate sacrifice if need be. Secondly, the defence budget can be further broken down into significant shares devoted to equipment modernisation. Equipment costs cover all hardware a military organisation requires, and via procurement as well as research, development and technology budgets, provide the financial basis for sustaining a defence industrial base. Thirdly, there are operating costs for missions and training activities that enable personnel and equipment to be combined into actual military capabilities organised at different levels of readiness.[5] The maintenance of military units at high readiness, i.e. the ability to undertake specific missions at days' notice, comes at relatively high cost. In turn, the latent ability to form and prepare units over a longer time horizon comes at a much lower cost, though expertise levels need to be retained at minimum levels to allow for mobilisation and regeneration, if required. The resulting force structure, therefore, needs to be designed as a function of the politically defined level of ambition. This dynamic also needs to consider the reality that maintaining operational readiness is expensive, yet unlike changing malleable political goals, organisation of the armed forces is relatively static. Equipment modernisation, personnel recruitment and training inevitably stretch across a long time horizon: one cannot raise capable armies overnight.

Alliances hold the promise of dramatically boosting national security, ideally at reduced cost, by joining forces amongst like-minded nations. As military threat perceptions often overlap, states facing similar challenges are likely to pursue synergies in providing for their security needs. Options for collaboration on security and military affairs may vary from low-key engagement – for instance, by exchanging military officers in training programmes – to fully fledged mutual security guarantees. Arms transfers and defence industrial cooperation ensure that a wide-ranging spectrum of parallel options exists to translate strategic cooperation amongst nations into defence-economic partnerships. A defence industrial base that groups multiple states together potentially provides for substantial efficiency gains in producing military systems, leading to a reduction of procurement costs. Essentially, alliances provide institutional frameworks for like-minded nations to pursue common military objectives together. Given that the military instrument is usually subordinated to political control, the pursuit of common military objectives tends to be grounded in a shared political outlook and a common set of political values.

In theory, states can capitalise on the benefits of scale and efficiency gains that alliances promise in both strategic and economic terms. In a military confrontation with an adversary, an alliance can draw on a common pool of financial, material and human resources that is vastly larger than that of any constitutive states on their own, and by means of efficiency gains more powerful than the simple addition of resources from all constitutive states together. This fact makes alliances of interest not only during wartime, but also in peacetime. Their deterrent effect makes conflict less likely, because it puts the onus on any individual adversary to bring about an alternative coalition of states that can rival and challenge the latent power base that an alliance has at its disposal. The benefits of scale that alliances offer can thus be measured by means of two distinct yardsticks; namely, in strategic terms (relative to any conceivable adversary) and in financial terms (relative to the absolute cost of providing for security). Moreover, efficiency gains will increase in line with the degree of mutual interdependence members of the alliance are willing to accept in organising a common defence.

In practice, however, these strategic and economic benefits carry their own cost in terms of the relative loss in autonomy of political decision making. Being a member of an alliance comes with obligations as well as advantages. As intergovernmental decision making often produces lowest-common-denominator outcomes, military logic dictates that difficult political decisions may need to be resolved through a system of automated decision making or pre-delegation of command authority. Once an attack on one member gets recognised as an attack against all, the mobilisation of military resources from across the alliance must follow as swiftly as possible to ensure military credibility and effectiveness. Consequently, allied nations reap the benefits of being part of an alliance framework every day, but at the risk of finding themselves participants in a security confrontation from which it may be difficult to disentangle. Furthermore, despite all the economies of scale, alliances still need to be resourced: cooperation is no magic wand that makes the cost of security disappear altogether. The defence-economic equivalent to this reduced autonomy of decision making is the need for binding political commitments to prevent nations from shirking the responsibilities of alliance membership – the so-called free rider problem.

Taking both advantages and constraints into account, the design of alliances needs to reflect the shared goal, and offer detailed answers to the questions of joint decision making and resourcing. Alliances can be built to fend off a very specific security challenge as well as to function as a blanket security guarantee against various threats. They can be kept under strict and non-committed intergovernmental control, or feature deep integration and quasi-automated participation in common action. Individual members may wish to retain full discretion over the resources they commit to alliance endeavours or agree to pool resources in accordance with a fixed burden-sharing mechanism. These debates may pertain to making military units available for assigned missions, contributing financial resources to common funding mechanisms, or maintaining and funding national forces that can be put under alliance command, either automatically or at least when considered appropriate. In turn, these considerations interact with national decision making on defence budgeting, resource allocation and military strategy. The greater the interdependency alliance members are willing to accept in terms of military planning, role division and integrated defence-industrial support networks, the greater the economic benefits but the higher the political cost in terms of national sovereignty. As ever, the challenge usually resides in finding an appropriate mix.

10.2 NATO Burden Sharing as a Case in Point

The North Atlantic Treaty Organisation constitutes the best-known contemporary example of a military alliance. It links the security of its North American and European members inseparably together, organised around a set of core tasks, an integrated command structure and a culture of working closely together on military affairs; the latter ranges from joint development of doctrine and technology to the conduct of missions and operations. Yet, like any alliance, its political inspirations and institutional organisation need to go hand in hand. This generates constant debate over the question: which ally should appropriate what tasks, and how much individual allies need to contribute to the common defence of the alliance as a whole, alternatively expressed in terms of military power or financial contributions. The heated debate on NATO burden sharing that has bedevilled transatlantic relations in recent years, including pressure from the Trump administration, is therefore nothing particularly new. Rather, it expresses how the old debate over balancing US commitment to European security and European contributions to US grand strategy is resurfacing once more as the strategic context undergoes massive change.[6]

The political aims underlying the NATO alliance are fundamentally unchanging, yet evolve at the surface in step with how the security environment develops. The bedrock is the 1949 Mutual Security Guarantee enshrined in Article 5 of the Washington Treaty. This states that an armed attack against one or more allies shall be considered an attack against them all, thus triggering a collective response. Historically, this phrase ensured the commitment of the United States to underwrite the security of Western Europe, subject to the condition that the Europeans contribute to their own defence, and, by extension, to US Grand Strategy.[7] A related element was the stabilisation of European geopolitical dynamics by including (West) Germany and all other (Western) European nations into a common framework led by the United States, as opposed to the Soviet Union or indeed any other contender for hegemony in Europe.[8] As the Cold War gave way to the post-Cold War period, NATO began to transform itself by taking on additional roles.[9] In addition to the primary task of collective defence, the 2010 Strategic Concept, which is still in force, codified two additional core tasks, namely, crisis management and cooperative security.

For a while, it seemed as if NATO was on track to reinvent itself not so much as a military alliance, but rather as a sprawling network of various cooperative security functions. Ever since 2014, however, Russian activities in Ukraine and elsewhere have prompted the NATO alliance to focus its activities again primarily on collective defence and the threat emanating from a revanchist neighbour in the east. Even though the process of rediscovering Article 5 is still in an early phase, it seems safe to assume that the related challenges, most notably to determine how much defence is enough and how to apportion the military requirements that result from that assessment, will occupy the centre stage in NATO discussions in the years to come.[10]

Over the past decades the NATO alliance has developed military structures and processes to give body and substance to these political ambitions. Organised as an alliance of sovereign nations, decision making takes place by consensus in the North Atlantic Council. Yet ever since the Korean War in the 1950s, the alliance has maintained a standing military command structure that can react swiftly to any contingency. Even as the NATO Command Structure (NCS) has evolved considerably in terms of its size and organisation, it continues to feature an operational command and control chain headed by a Supreme Allied Commander Europe (SACEUR) in which all nations are proportionally represented. During times of high tension, SACEUR can be endowed with a considerable degree of command authority in the event that conflict breaks out. Nations also pool their military units together into the NATO Force Structure. Throughout the Cold War period, allies pre-positioned substantial combat forces close to the border with the Eastern Bloc. During the heyday of the crisis management paradigm of the 1990s and 2000s, the NATO pool of forces provided the inventory out of which combined joint task forces could be generated and tailored to the mission at hand.[11] Yet in recent years, forward presence of the allies along the alliances' eastern flank has begun to reoccur, supported by the NATO Response Force and follow-on forces provided by other nations. Moreover, as NATO's deterrence posture relies partly on nuclear weapons, the alliance features nuclear sharing arrangements and a Nuclear Planning Group. As nuclear risks are shared, the security of individual allies is deeply interwoven and potential scenarios of intra-European nuclear proliferation are avoided. Given that consensus amongst sovereign nations is not always easy to achieve, substantial diplomatic pressure may be applied to arrive at actual decisions.

The collective force structure of the NATO Alliance is composed of national force structures that are operated, maintained and paid for by individual nations. Those national force structures are synchronised by means of various alliance planning processes. A rough division of labour in terms of military tasks and capabilities is arrived at via the NATO defence planning processes, in which the agreed level of ambition gets translated into military capability requirements that can be apportioned to member nations. This process gives substance to the 1949 principle that 'each nation should undertake the task, or tasks, for which it is best suited'.[12] As such, a variety of nations on a rotational basis provide air policing assets to the Baltic States, while the US and UK navies carry primary responsibilities for securing transatlantic sea lines of communication. Whenever an actual engagement is contemplated by the North Atlantic Council, the operations planning process enables commanders to formulate their military requirements. Force generation conferences then allow nations to make both sufficient and suitably certified forces available. As explained by Holger Pfeiffer, defence and operations planning processes thus exist in a 'chicken and egg relationship': NATO nations jointly plan and maintain their force structures over time, with a view of deploying and employing forces in joint operations when politically required.[13]

Maintaining and employing forces costs money. National defence budgets of individual nations, falling under exclusive national control, account for the lion's share (over 95 per cent) of NATO's collective resources. Yet nations have taken on a political commitment to spend 2 per cent of GDP on defence and to spend 20 per cent of their defence budgets on major equipment, including related research and development costs. These financial benchmarks provide a rough indication of the estimated cost of maintaining a combined NATO force structure capable of meeting the alliance's level of ambition. While these benchmarks were originally set in 2006, the NATO Heads of State and Government reconfirmed them in 2014 as part of the defence investment pledge made at the Wales Summit. Unsurprisingly, the burden-sharing debate is often narrowed to the question of whether individual allies meet the agreed defence spending target, which as recently as 2017 was not the case for twenty-three of them.[14] This has been a long-standing reason for complaints from the United States that allies are free-riding on the back of US defence efforts.[15]

Apart from national defence budgets, NATO features a variety of multinational funding arrangements (for instance, for resourcing

NATO production and logistics organisations), as well as common funding of the three institutional budgets at the service of NATO authorities. These include: the Civil Budget, which finances the NATO HQ in Brussels and is paid for by the foreign ministries; the Military Budget, which resources the NATO Command Structure and other military entities, with the cost being borne by defence ministries; and the NATO Security Investment Programme, which funds specific investment projects in support of alliance requirements, as determined by the member state ministries of defence. Together, these three budgets account for less than 1 per cent of the combined defence expenditures of NATO nations, but their significance is that they cover those costs that cannot be attributed to any specific nation, and thus collective funding reinforces alliance cohesion. It should be highlighted that such common costs are distributed amongst nations based on relative gross national income, albeit with one major exception. The US share of common funding arrangements accounts for circa 22 per cent, and thus it benefits from a substantial discount.

In sum, NATO provides a forum in which the United States and its closest allies can discuss what common challenges they face and formulate joint diplomatic and military responses to meet them. In doing so, they can pursue financial, material and logistical synergies whenever and wherever these can be identified. These nations can also rely on critical 'alliance enablers' such as the permanent NATO Command Structure, the NATO Airborne Early Warning system and common funding arrangements. Yet, it should be acknowledged that nations may have differences of opinion on any given problem or on how to tackle it. For this reason, decision making remains based on the consensus principle, but ensuring that decisions on operational matters and on defence resourcing constitute a sovereign choice. However, having said that, the collective defence guarantee enshrined in Article 5 ties the fate of allied nations together. In case of external aggression, nations may find they have little diplomatic leeway to walk away from the obligation to take part in a collective response. This implies that every ally is expected to take part with meaningful combat capabilities, taking its demographic size and relative economic wealth into account. But as defence resourcing decisions tend to reflect national threat perceptions – which vary with geographic and strategic culture – the debate over how much of a contribution every ally should make to the alliance is an ongoing balancing act. After all, it very much depends on how one looks at the burden-sharing problem.

10.3 Methodological Challenges in Defence Planning

Within NATO, as in other alliances, individual nations do spend money to maintain armed forces. They also enjoy the diplomatic and cost efficiency benefits that this entails. Yet this obliges them to engage in a constant debate with their alliance partners as to whether their national contribution is fair and sufficient. NATO staffs have been tracking both financial and other metrics for many years, as well as engaging individual nations in detailed defence planning discussions about their role in the posture of the alliance as a whole. Given that the problem of appropriate burden sharing has never been resolved in a satisfactory sense, we must explore in detail the methodological challenges one encounters when quantifying and qualifying any nation's defence planning efforts.

In many respects, financial parameters constitute the crudest indicator of a nation's defence effort. High levels of defence spending do not always guarantee effective combat prowess, yet it is exceptionally difficult to maintain highly capable and professional armed forces with meagre levels of financial resources. Ever since 1963, NATO staffs have been tracking different parameters quantifying the size of the defence effort linked to the supporting economic base of each ally. When evaluating these datasets over the long-term, clear patterns stand out, such as the fact that US levels of defence spending consistently exceed those of European allies (see Table 10.1). This superior spend itself reflects the larger ambitions of the United States as a global superpower, compared to the more limited aspirations of European nations in providing for collective defence, and the ability to pursue modest military goals in their wider regional neighbourhood. The financial benchmarking approach also plays well to the role of the alliance as a forum for ensuring internal transparency about defence spending among broadly like-minded democratic societies in which defence resourcing is the subject of parliamentary debate.

Financial metrics do not tell the full story, however. What allies spend on defence ultimately represents national political ambitions, threat perceptions and the perceived need for military instruments. NATO defence planners, therefore, also resort to capability and contribution metrics. The former include, for instance, the percentage of national armed forces that are deployable and sustainable and the extent to which NATO capability planning targets are effectively implemented.

Table 10.1: *Selected NATO defence expenditure data, 2017*

	Share of alliance GDP (%)	Share of alliance defence expenditure (%)	Defence expenditure as share of GDP (%)	Equipment spend as share of defence expenditure (%)
France	6.8	4.8	1.79	24.17
Germany	9.7	4.8	1.24	13.75
Italy	5.1	2.4	1.12	20.94
United Kingdom	6.9	5.8	2.12	22.03
United States	51.1	71.7	3.57	28.48

Source: Based on NATO Public Diplomacy Division. *Defence Expenditure of NATO Countries (2010–2017).* Brussels: NATO PR/CP. 2018. 16.

The latter include contributions to deployed resources on NATO operations (be it in terms of land forces, aircraft and/or vessels), as well as fulfilling the manning requirements of the NATO Command Structure. The complete overview of burden-sharing metrics therefore constitutes a colourful mosaic in which most individual allies score well on some measures but not others. It is possible for allies (such as Greece) to consistently spend over 2 per cent on defence without being able to contribute in a meaningful way to alliance operations. Conversely, it is equally possible for allies (such as Denmark) to consistently outperform most other allies based on more compressed resourcing levels.

In order to review whether national forces structures remain organisationally healthy and in keeping with alliance objectives, NATO staffs liaise with individual allies and offer recommendations on how to reach agreed defence planning targets. This qualitative dialogue on national defence efforts in relation to alliance objectives arguably paints a much more nuanced picture than what quantitative metrics can offer. As the defence budgeting process tends to move in cycles (reflecting modernisation of key weapon systems over the long-term and thus necessitating parallel waves of investment), the relative health of a force structure in terms of its operational readiness cannot be captured in metrics alone. Even well-resourced forces can be exhausted and hollowed out by operations and delayed modernisation. Another important consideration for NATO staff to take into account is that nations may well have political ambitions that are complementary but different from those of the alliance as a whole. Just like the United States, countries like the United Kingdom and France have international interests and obligations above and beyond those of the alliance. Other nations, such as Italy and Turkey, may entertain peculiar force postures due to their geographical proximity to turbulent regions in which NATO is not engaged as an alliance. It is therefore important to keep in mind that NATO defence planning attempts to streamline national defence planning, but will never replace it entirely. National defence planning efforts feed into the NATO process, but NATO membership is only one (albeit the major) planning variable from a national point of view.

Burden sharing boils down to an intergovernmental discussion that is about more than money alone; it also relates to combat power and national sacrifice. Throughout the Cold War, 'fundamentalist' (budget-focused) and 'Atlanticist' (military capability and political cohesion-focused) approaches to burden sharing alternated, prompting a constant search for objectively measurable indices such as 'division-equivalent firepower'.[16] Within a collective defence framework such discussions may feature different methodologies, each carrying its own legitimacy. Yet such debates become exponentially more complicated as collective defence gives way to wider mission roles, such as crisis management and cooperative security. As crisis management puts the emphasis on the so-called wars of choice instead of those of utter necessity, force generation on an opt-in basis becomes the political norm. Accordingly, the burden-sharing discussion becomes one about relative political priorities, in which allies may explore what is considered 'just enough' to keep the alliance intact rather than worry about the mission at hand.[17] In the absolute world of nuclear deterrence, by contrast, burden and risk sharing have quasi-existential connotations. As the alliance serves the purpose of ensuring national survival and security of all allies, it cannot come as a surprise that relative combat power – for self-defence *and* for common action – accounts for the most fundamental criterion in measuring the contribution of each ally.

In the absence of actual war, it could be argued that the division of roles and missions in NATO defence plans constitutes the most tangible way of evaluating burden sharing in the alliance. If an ally is not able or willing to contribute meaningfully to the collective defence of the alliance, then this poses a major political problem. Cast in this light, the return of the discussion on NATO's forward presence and the follow-on forces needed for defence of individual allies on the frontline brings much-needed clarity to the burden-sharing debate. After many years in which the crisis management paradigm rendered the burden-sharing discussion devoid of much strategic substance, discussions on NATO burden-sharing are again returning to their fundamentals: in what ways will allies help one another when facing the threat of aggression? Apart from military assistance that can be expected in the event of war, the alliance provides less quantifiable advantages to allies, such as transparency within the alliance and common standards and mechanisms enabling collective defence. Compared to the situation in which every nation would have to resource its national security in full independence (i.e. without relying on assistance and goodwill from allies when facing threats of aggression), every ally gains a substantial defence-economic discount. At any specific point in time, the readiness of an ally to contribute to common defence scenarios therefore offers the most fundamental burden-sharing test.

Maintaining readiness to contribute proportionally to common defence efforts requires armed forces that are capable, trained and readily available in sufficient numbers. Financial parameters continue to play an important role in enabling such a posture of military readiness. Military personnel are characterised by high salaries and capabilities, which together mean that modern weapon systems do not come cheap. Over the long-term, budgetary trends will therefore determine the overall size, capabilities and readiness of the armed forces of every ally. In that sense, financial metrics, and the direction in which these evolve over the medium-term, remain an essential foundation of the military power of the alliance *and every one of its constitutive members*. From this perspective, the alliance itself does not so much oblige its members to spend resources on defence; rather, every nation remains responsible for resourcing its own defence, and there are limits to the amount of budgetary efficiency that the alliance framework can generate. Ignoring NATO defence spending pledges does not allow nations to spend less; it, instead, confronts them with the need to contemplate national defence strategies from a position of international isolation, which typically increases the cost exponentially.

10.4 Conclusion: Measuring Security in an Era of Uncertainty

Alliances may help to drive down the cost that national security entails, but they are never easy to manage in political terms. Defence cooperation amongst nations offers important benefits of scale, but also tends to blur political and military responsibilities. In an alliance, it is always tempting to believe that the heavy lifting will be undertaken by another party, even if it is rationally clear that such an arrangement cannot possibly last. The question of how to design alliances in terms of decision making and resourcing, making explicit trade-offs between political autonomy and defence collectivism, budgetary engagements and military commitments, is therefore likely to haunt any such arrangement. Given that alliances are ultimately created to deal with the threat of war, the stakes could scarcely be higher. The responsibility that nations must provide physical security to their own citizens cannot be abdicated without a devastating loss of political legitimacy. It is in this sense that US Secretary of Defence Jim Mattis reminded European audiences that 'Americans cannot care more for your children's security than you do'.[18]

Despite stark warnings about the need for transatlantic solidarity, this case study of NATO makes clear that burden-sharing discussions require methodological rigour and nuance. Defence spending is a critical requirement for maintaining military readiness and healthy force structures over the long-term. However, financial metrics need to be complemented by other metrics, and metrics in turn need to be carefully qualified by detailed discussion about how national defence planning efforts relate to the alliance posture as a whole. Whichever way one looks at the debate, the military instrument remains subordinate to political guidance. Only when political aims and objectives are translated into military operations, whether for defence or crisis management purposes, do burden-sharing discussions materialise to their fullest extent. In the absence of actual operations, defence plans offer the closest substitute for discussions about relative combat power and associated risk. What is perhaps the most meaningful shift in the NATO debate over recent years is the one moving from (optional) crisis management to (compulsory) collective defence tasks. Burden-sharing discussions acquire much greater political salience, of course, when the challenge is potentially of an existential nature. It is, therefore, no surprise that many European nations are now starting to engage in a process of military modernisation, supported by dramatic budget hikes.[19]

The deeper challenge that alliance scholars need to confront, however, is that the resourcing of national security must unfold against a background of uncertainty about what future conflict may look like.

The experience of crisis management operations in recent decades may not offer much guidance when contemplating a return of great power rivalry. Armed forces exist to be mobilised in case of war, yet what does this mean for societal and industrial mobilisation in the twenty-first century? To what extent will competition in the information and cyber domains substitute for kinetic engagement between conventional forces? As addressed in Chapters 16 and 17, the very meaning of military prowess may be shifting in relation to available technologies and relevant societal constraints, thus defence economic parameters may need to be updated accordingly. Political discussions about what is the threat to be provided for, and about what are the instruments that need to be called upon to address that threat, must come first. In many ways, the defence accounting exercise that burden-sharing discussions entail can only take place when the referent is clear.

References and notes

1. NATO. *Strategic Concept for the Defense of the North Atlantic Area.* NATO, DC 6/1; 1949.
2. See J. Becker. 'Clearing the Air on Transatlantic Burden-Sharing, Part 1: What's Going on Here?' War on the Rocks, 25 May 2017. https://waron therocks.com/2017/05/clearing-the-air-on-transatlantic-burden-sharing-pa rt-1-whats-going-on-here/ (accessed 1 May 2018).
3. For a classical account, see D. Omand. *Securing the State.* London: Hurst & Co. 2010. 345.
4. For an introduction to defence budgeting, see M. E. O'Hanlon. *The Science of War.* Princeton: Princeton University Press. 2009. 266.
5. See T. Harrison. 'Rethinking Readiness'. *Strategic Studies Quarterly.* 2014. 8(3): 38–68.
6. A meaningful discussion about the evolution of the strategic consequence would fall outside the remit of this chapter. For an introduction to this debate, see H. Brands. *Dealing with Allies in Decline: Alliance Management and U.S. Strategy in an Era of Global Power Shifts.* Washington, DC: Center for Strategic and Budgetary Assessments. May 2017. 68.
7. For a classical account, see C. A. Cooper and B. Zycher. *Perceptions of NATO Burden-Sharing.* Santa Monica: RAND Corporation. June 1989. 43.
8. While the first NATO Secretary General Lord Ismay famously stated that NATO's purpose was 'to keep the Soviet Union out, the Americans in, and the Germans down', the contemporary relevance of this function has

proved enduring beyond the timeframe of the Cold War. See S. Rynning. 'Germany Is More Than Europe Can Handle: Or, Why NATO Remains a Pacifier'. NATO Defense College. Research Paper Number 96, September 2013. 12.

9. For discussion, see D. S. Yost. *NATO's Balancing Act*. Washington, DC: United States Institute of Peace. 2014. 404.

10. For the the first comprehensive assessment of this secular change in strategic trends, see J. R. Deni. NATO and Article 5: The Transatlantic Alliance and the Twenty-First-Century Challenges of Collective Defense. Lanham: Rowman and Littlefield. 2017. 167.

11. See A. Mattelaer. 'How Afghanistan Has Strengthened NATO'. *Survival*. 2011. 53(6): 127–40.

12. NATO. *Strategic Concept for the Defense of the North Atlantic Area*. NATO, DC 6/1; 1949.

13. H. Pfeiffer. 'Defence and Force Planning in Historical Perspective: NATO as a Case Study'. *Baltic Security & Defence Review*. 2008. 10: 103–20.

14. See NATO. *Defence Expenditure of NATO Countries (2010–2017)*. Brussels: NATO Public Diplomacy Division (Press Release 16); 15 March 2018.

15. For one particularly revealing example, see J. Goldberg. 'The Obama Doctrine'. *The Atlantic*. April 2016. www.theatlantic.com/magazine/a rchive/2016/04/the-obama-doctrine/471525/ (accessed 1 May 2018).

16. See Cooper and Zycher. *Perceptions*. 7–8, 27–28.

17. See J. Coelmont. 'End-State Afghanistan'. Egmont Institute. Egmont Paper: 29 March 2009. 17, 27.

18. See D. Lamothe and M. Birnbaum. 'Defense Secretary Mattis Issues New Ultimatum to NATO Allies on Defense Spending'. The Washington Post. 15 February 2017. www.washingtonpost.com/new s/checkpoint/wp/2017/02/15/mattis-trumps-defense-secretary-issues-ul timatum-to-nato-allies-on-defense-spending/?noredirect=on&utm_ term=.b7a95b23e822 (accessed 1 May 2018).

19. France offers an illustrative example: a series of annual budget hikes over the coming years sets the stage for substantial modernisation as well as a numerical expansion of the personnel structure of the French armed forces. See *Projet de loi de programmation militaires 2019–2025*. Paris: Ministère des armées, February 2018.

PART IV

Resource Management

11 | The Political Economy of Arms Collaboration

KEITH HARTLEY

Introduction

Collaboration reflects economic and political factors. Economic pressures reflect the rising unit costs of equipment subject to limited defence budgets. Political factors reflect preferences for retaining a national defence industrial base. Collaboration appears to provide a solution to arms procurement; but it is dominated by myths, emotion and special pleading, all of which need to be exposed and subjected to critical evaluation.

11.1 Rising Costs

Norman Augustine famously identified the long-run trend of rising unit costs for high technology items such as combat aircraft, helicopters, ships, tanks, commercial aircraft and computer software.[1] Augustine found that the unit cost of certain high technology products increased at an exponential rate with time. For example, he estimated that the unit costs of fighter aircraft rose by a factor of four every ten years. The outcome of rising unit costs is armed forces buying smaller quantities of each generation of new equipment with forecasts of a single tank army, a single ship navy and a 'Starship Enterprise' for the air force.

Table 11.1 provides evidence of rising unit costs for UK military aircraft. Between the Gladiator (1937) and the Typhoon (2003) fighter aircraft, real unit costs rose by a factor of 235; and between the Wellington (1940) and Tornado bomber aircraft (1979), real unit costs rose by a factor of 19. The introduction of jet-powered aircraft resulted in a step change in real unit costs (e.g. Spitfire to Meteor; Lancaster to Canberra). Next, within jet aircraft, further major real cost rises reflected more new technology in the form of avionics (radar;

Table 11.1: *Historical cost trends for UK combat aircraft, 1936–2017*

Fighter aircraft			Bomber aircraft		
Aircraft	Original price (£000s)	Constant 2017 prices (£000s)	Aircraft	Original price (£000s)	Constant 2017 prices (£000s)
Swordfish	6 (36)	272	Wellington	15 (40)	649
Gladiator	3 (37)	148	Stirling	41 (41)	1,572
Hurricane	4 (38)	195	Halifax	29 (42)	1,097
Spitfire	6 (39)	255	Lancaster	22 (41)	832
Typhoon	12 (43)	465	Mosquito	14 (43)	514
Meteor	28 (46)	1,037	Lincoln	26 (46)	970
Vampire	29 (46)	1,082	Canberra	54 (51)	1,616
Hunter	54 (55)	1,362	Valiant	385 (55)	9,531
Javelin	125 (57)	2,909	Vulcan	365 (54)	9,289
Lightning	199 (59)	4,397	Victor	244 (55)	6,210
Typhoon	23,160 (03)	34,785	Tornado	2,573 (79)	12,585

Sources: See DSTL. *Historical Cost Data for RAF Aircraft 1935–65.* London: Ministry of Defence using DSTL version. 2010; N. Davies, A. Eager, M. Maier and L. Penfold. *Intergenerational Equipment Cost Escalation.* Defence Economics Research Paper. 2012. London: Ministry of Defence. December 2012.
Notes:
  i. Data are for airframe unit production costs including a profit allowance where unit costs plus profits represents unit price. Other aircraft costs are excluded (e.g. engines, avionics, landing gear, radio). Also, data on costs of jigs and tools and flight testing are usually excluded.
  ii. Figures in brackets are for dates of contracts (e.g. Swordfish contract for 1936, Hurricane contract for 1938, Spitfire for 1939). Contracts chosen were early production contracts for each type. Contracts for prototypes and development work were not included.
  iii. Original price data are for the contract year shown for each aircraft (e.g. unit price of Spitfire is shown for 1939). Constant prices based on UK Retail Price Index for 1936 to 2017.
  iv. All aircraft are UK built with data from DSTL (2010). Two exceptions are the Tornado and Typhoon based on the author's estimates of their unit airframe costs.
  v. Aircraft selected represent examples of each generation: Hurricane and Spitfire represent early World War II fighter aircraft; Wellington is an early WWII bomber aircraft; Meteor/Vampire are first generation jet fighter aircraft: Hunter/Javelin are second generation; Canberra is first generation jet bomber aircraft.

computer software). Such cost increases are usually expressed as inter-generational cost escalation. They reflect arms as 'tournament goods' where the emphasis is on technical progress and the desire for superior or winning performance. Typical examples show annual real terms inter-generational cost escalation of some 4–7 per cent for fighter aircraft, 2–6 per cent for tanks and 2–4 per cent for submarines.[2] Other causes of inter-generational cost escalation include imperfect defence markets reflecting monopoly and monopsony power. There are also 'the vicious circles of cost escalation', where higher unit costs mean reduced quantities leading further to the loss of scale and learning economies, and greater increases in unit costs.[3] Arms collaboration is one response to inter-generational cost escalation. However, more generally, rising unit costs represent a challenge for policymakers requiring an appraisal of alternative procurement policies.

11.2 Procurement Options

In response to rising unit costs, governments have adopted a variety of procurement policies. Their options include abandoning a range of costly equipment (e.g. Denmark no longer has a submarine force; New Zealand abandoned its fighter aircraft force; most air forces no longer operate strategic bombers). Or, nations might accept smaller armed forces (a reduced defence capability), or imported equipment, or increased defence spending, or operating older equipment or international collaboration. There will also be efforts to 'improve efficiency' in such forms as defence management reforms, focusing on cost control, relying more on competitive tendering rather than sole-source procurement or introducing greater profit controls on noncompetitive contracts or removing 'optimism bias' in project selection. Some apparent efficiency improvements are misleading since they involve trade-offs affecting defence capabilities. Examples include achieving greater cost control on new projects at the expense of reduced quantities or delays in delivery or reduced technical performance.

Each procurement option involves different costs and benefits. Options range between the extremes of complete independence or importing arms from foreign suppliers (e.g. the United States). Intermediate procurement options include licensed production of foreign designs and international collaboration. Complete independence can be costly as nations have to fund R&D costs, and the national home market might only support relatively small production quantities, meaning a failure to achieve scale and learning economies in production. The military and economic benefits of a national defence industrial base include independence and re-supply in conflict as well as apparent economic benefits in the form of jobs, technology, spin-offs and balance of payment benefits through import-savings and possible exports. In contrast, importing arms is likely to be cheaper than national procurement, since foreign suppliers such as the United States will fund costly R&D and benefit from large-scale production orders. But arms imports involve risks to the importing nation in the form of an unwillingness to supply in conflict, exchange rate risks and the apparent loss of economic benefits in the form of jobs, technology and balance of payments effects.

The intermediate options involve different costs and benefits. Licensed production of a foreign design requires licence payments to the foreign supplier, and licensed production means the loss of scale and learning economies leading to higher unit production costs. There are some benefits in the form of independence in supply and re-supply, jobs from production, possibly some benefits from new production technology and benefits from import-saving. Similarly, international arms collaboration allows partner nations to share R&D costs and to combine production orders, enabling independence in foreign policy as well as supporting national jobs, technology and spin-offs, and contributing to balance of payment benefits through import-saving and possible exports. An illustrative example of the costs and benefits of major alternative procurement policies is shown in Table 11.2. There are variants of these options. For example, importing might involve offsets where the purchasing nations receive some work share either directly on the equipment imported or indirectly on other arms imports or civil projects (e.g. aid for tourism). Similarly, a variant of licensed production is some form of co-production where the importing nation might combine its production order with the production order of the exporting nation with the nations sharing the total production order.[4]

Table 11.2: *Procurement options: illustrative example*

Option	Total Development Cost	Unit Production Cost	Military and Economic Benefits	Military Performance
National Defence Industry	100	100	100	100
Licensed Production	10	100 (90–120)	30	80
Collaboration	50–75	90–95	50+	100
Imports	10	80	0	80

Source: author's illustrative data.

Notes:

i. Baseline comparison is with a national buy and assumes a single and common cost curve for each option (likely to be an unrealistic assumption). Numbers are illustrative examples, only providing an approximate ranking. The numbers will vary with different equipment.

ii. Military and economic benefits are aggregated and based on author's estimates. They comprise independence, re-supply and work shares. Similarly, military performance is a broad aggregate metric, reflecting speed, range and capability of various equipment, where 100 measures the extent to which the equipment meets the requirements of the national armed forces (100 means that equipment exactly meets all national requirements). It is assumed that imported equipment does not meet exactly the national requirements.

iii. Collaboration assumes a two-nation equal partnership each with equal production numbers. The deviations from equal sharing reflect collaboration inefficiencies: hence, the 50+ for benefits.

iv. Figures in brackets show the possible range of unit production costs for licensed production.

11.3 European Arms Collaboration: A Brief History

Major European arms collaborations are summarised in Table 11.3. The early projects were limited to two partner nations from France, Germany and the United Kingdom, starting in the late 1950s. Later, the number of partner nations increased, rising to seven nations for the A400M airlifter. Collaborations have been mainly aerospace projects, comprising combat aircraft, trainers, patrol aircraft, transports, helicopters and missiles. There were similar collaborations involving civil aircraft and space programmes (Airbus, Concorde, European Space Agency). Generally, arms collaborations were based on project-specific

Table 11.3: *Major European arms collaborations*

Project	Date of Agreement	Industrial Organisation (%)	Partner Nations (%)	Output
Atlantic (MPA)	1958	SECBAT: Breguet	France Germany	87
Jaguar (SA)	1966	SEPECAT: Breguet; BAC	France UK	France: 200 UK: 200 Total: 543
Anglo-French Helicopter Agreement	1968	Aerospatiale; Westland	France UK	Puma: 697 Gazelle: 1775 Lynx: 450+
Alpha Jet (T)	1969	Dassault (lead); Dornier	France Germany	France: 176 Germany: 175 Total: 480
Tornado (SA)	1969	Panavia Aircraft: BAe; MBB; Aeritalia	Germany 42.5 UK 42.5 Italy 15.0	Germany: 359 UK: 385 Italy: 100 Total: 992
Typhoon (SA)	1986	Eurofighter: Airbus; BAE Systems; Leonardo	UK: 37.5 Germany/ Spain: 43.0 Italy: 19.5	UK: 160 Germany: 143 Italy: 96 Spain: 73 Total: 623
A400M (MT)	1998	Airbus Military (now Airbus Defence and Space)	Belgium; Luxembourg; France; Germany; Spain; UK; Turkey	Belgium: 7 France: 50 Germany: 53 Spain: 27 Turkey: 10 UK: 22 Total: 174
EH101 (ASH)	1980	EHI	Italy; UK	Italy: 20 UK: 66 Total: 180+
Tiger (AH)	1992	Eurocopter (now Airbus Helicopters)	France; Germany	France: 87 Germany: 57 Total: 190
NH90 (MRH)	1992	NH Industries	France: 31.5 Germany: 31.5 Italy: 32.0 Netherlands: 5.5	France: 67 Germany: 122 Italy: 116 Netherlands: 20 Total: 529+

Table 11.3: (*cont.*)

Project	Date of Agreement	Industrial Organisation (%)	Partner Nations (%)	Output
Missiles	2001	MBDA: Airbus: 37.5 BAE: 37.5 Leonardo: 25.0	France; Germany; Italy; Spain; UK	45 missile systems; 15 programmes in 2017. Examples include ASRAAM; Brimstone; Meteor; Storm Shadow

Source: See J. Hunter (ed). *Janes All the World's Aircraft: In service 2017–2018*, 22nd edn. Surrey: Janes Information Group. 2017.

Notes:

i. AH = attack helicopter; ASH = antisubmarine helicopter; MPA = maritime patrol aircraft; MRH = multi-role helicopter; MT = military transport; SA = strike aircraft; T = trainer.

ii. Date of Agreement shows date for formation of international company. Germany includes West Germany. SECBAT was the multinational consortium for the Atlantic, namely, the Societe d'Etude et de Construction de Breguet Atlantic.

iii. Anglo-French Helicopter Agreement was a joint manufacturing and purchasing agreement between France and the UK involving plans for each nation to buy three national helicopters, namely, French Gazelle, French Puma and British Lynx. In fact, France did not buy the UK Lynx.

iv. Industrial Organisation shows main features usually for airframe collaboration. Industrial restructuring led to new organisations and different names. In addition, there are other collaborative industrial arrangements, especially for engines. Examples include Turbo-Union for Tornado engine; Eurojet for Typhoon engine; and Europrop International for A400 M. There are also procurement management arrangements such as OCCAR for A400M and NAHEMA as NATO Helicopter Management Agency for NH90 helicopter.

v. Partners shows work shares in brackets where work does not involve equal shares. For example, on Tornado, the original work shares were Germany and UK with 42.5 per cent each and Italy with a 15 per cent share. As projects develop, work shares might change to reflect changing orders.

vi. Output figures are for actual deliveries or planned orders. Figures should be regarded as broad approximations since numbers change reflecting new orders and cancellations.

vii. Missiles show MBDA as the European supplier of missiles and output is given in general terms since actual output of specific missiles is not published.

industrial consortia, except for the missile group MBDA and Airbus Helicopters, which are European-wide transnational companies.

This brief history raises three questions about arms collaborations. First, why has collaboration been dominated by aerospace projects? Costs of aerospace projects have been a factor with high and rising costs promoting collaboration. Land and sea systems remain affordable for independent national programmes, which might explain why they have not been as prevalent in arms collaborations. But rising costs will eventually provide the incentives to collaborate on these programmes. Second, why have there usually been small numbers of partner nations? Here, transaction costs are a factor with a small number of nations minimising transaction costs between partners. However, learning by doing reduces transaction costs between experienced partner nations so promoting the continuation of already established groups. Third, why have the collaborative industrial arrangements been dominated by project-specific consortia rather than the creation of transnational European companies? A preference for independence by nation-states and firms, and the opportunities for forming new industrial groupings (industrial flexibility) might be explanatory factors. Firms, for example, prefer to select partners of their choice rather than partner firms selected by governments. In contrast, consortia are often created by governments for a specific project, and lack any commercial logic and an established prime contractor.

11.4 Why Collaborate? The Benefits

Economics is a dominant explanation. The distinctive feature of European arms collaboration is that it involves nations sharing development and production in weapons acquisition. Compared with an independent national venture, collaboration leads to lower R&D and unit production costs. In a two-nation collaboration with equal sharing, R&D costs are shared and by combining production orders, scale and learning economies, will lead to lower unit production costs. These economic benefits of 'perfect collaboration' appear even greater with more nations involved in the collaborative club. Examples are shown in Table 11.4, which illustrates the cost savings from two to four nation collaborations compared with an identical independent national programme. R&D is a total fixed cost which, on a unit basis, falls with greater output: there are major cost savings in these costs as the number of partner nations increases. More partner nations lead to greater

Table 11.4: *Examples of cost savings from arms collaboration*

Number of Partner Nations: Equal Sharing	Quantity	Total R&D Costs (£ billion)	Unit Production Costs (£ million)
One Nation	100	100	10
Two Nations	200	50	9
Four Nations	400	25	8

Source: author's illustrative data.

Notes

   i. The baseline is an independent project with only one nation. Numbers are illustrative only.

  ii. Unit production costs assume a 90 per cent unit production cost curve with figures rounded. On this basis, unit production costs fall by 10 per cent for each doubling in cumulative output.

output compared with a national project, with learning economies further reducing unit production costs. With such apparent cost savings, it is not surprising that international collaboration appears to be a policy response to inter-generational cost escalation.[5]

In addition to its economic benefits, collaboration offers military, strategic and industrial benefits. It contributes to equipment standardisation and interoperability, which enhances operational effectiveness. For example, the US–European collaboration on the Multiple Launch Rocket System (MLRS) provided benefits from interoperability, with different partner nations operating the same equipment.[6] Also, by retaining a national defence industrial capability, it allows both independence in foreign policy and supply and re-supply in conflict. There are industrial benefits in the form of employment, technology and spin-offs, as well as exports and import-savings. Further industrial and political benefits include access to new technologies, opportunities for industrial restructuring and contributions to wider political and security related objectives. European nations also emphasise the protection of their national industrial interests and the promotion of European political co-operation.[7] Such benefits need to be evaluated critically. For example, nations might insist on specific national requirements which reduce the claimed standardisation benefits of collaboration. On the Tornado project, the United Kingdom was the only nation to require a fighter version of the aircraft (Tornado ADV).

Typically, European arms collaborations have been restricted to the sharing of development and production costs: there are further economic benefits where collaborations also involve the sharing of life-cycle costs. Examples include the sharing of training, repairs and maintenance, the pooling of spares and collaboration extended to mid-life updates. By definition, European collaborations have been restricted to European nations, whereas non-European nations might be the basis for lower costs. But does actual collaboration resemble the ideal model of perfect collaboration?

11.5 Collaboration Inefficiencies

A distinction can be made between European arms collaborations and collaborative programmes with other nations. The United States has a major role in collaborative programmes, although its definition of collaboration departs from the European approach. The United States often regards any form of international arms co-operation as collaboration (e.g. European co-production on the F-16 aircraft), whereas the European approach regards collaboration as the sharing of both R&D and production costs and work. Here, the focus is on European arms collaboration.

Predictably, actual European arms collaborations depart from the perfect model of economically efficient collaboration. Political markets and interest groups interfere with economic efficiency. International collaborations operate in political markets where outcomes reflect the influence of interest groups in the political-military-industrial complex. These groups, which are part of public choice models, comprise vote-maximising governments and politicians, budget maximising bureaucracies and rent-seeking producers. They are represented by government departments of defence, industry and employment, the military is represented by the armed forces and industry by the major arms companies (e.g. Airbus, BAE Systems, Leonardo).[8]

The inefficiency of actual collaborations has resulted from work-sharing rules (*juste retour*), determining operational requirements and elaborate bureaucratic arrangements. Various committees representing the procurement and industrial arrangements for collaboration have emerged with voting rules based on unanimity or majority or qualified majority decisions. Committees have led to delays and increased costs. Work-sharing rules have further increased costs as partner nations agree work shares based on political bargaining rather than work allocated by economic efficiency criteria based on competitiveness and comparative advantage. Each partner nation will demand its fair share of the high technology work on a project. For a combat aircraft, this means nations will demand their share of the high technology involved in the development of the airframe, engine and avionics and the creation of duplicate flight testing centres. All partner nations will also require a final assembly line, creating further duplication.

While these features of arms collaboration appear to be sources of inefficiency, there are problems of the counterfactual: what would have happened in the absence of collaboration? National projects are rarely perfect and efficient: they are characterised by cost overruns, delays and performance failures. Nor are national projects immune from work sharing, with work often allocated to firms in high unemployment areas. Further inefficiencies arise where national projects are undertaken by monopoly suppliers, either privately owned or state owned.

Table 11.5: *Total development costs of comparable collaborative and national programmes*

Project	National Alternative	Number of Partners	Total Development Cost as a per cent of alternative national development cost (%)
Eurofighter Typhoon	P120 Alternative UK national programme	4	196
Tornado	National development of airframe and engine	3	161
Merlin Helicopter	UK national programme	2	143

Source: National Audit Office. *Ministry of Defence: Maximising the Benefits of Defence Equipment Co-Operation.* London: TSO. 2001. Report No: HCP 300.
Notes:
i. Figures are for development costs only, showing total development costs for collaborative and similar alternative national projects at the time the programme was approved.
ii. Partner nations for Typhoon are Germany, Italy, Spain and the United Kingdom. For Tornado, partners were Germany, Italy and the United Kingdom; and for Merlin, partners were Italy and the United Kingdom.

One solution to the debate about collaboration inefficiencies is to review the available evidence. Here, there are major deficiencies due to an absence of reliable evidence and of comparable national projects. The results of a 2001 UK study are summarised in Table 11.5, which shows the estimated costs of comparable national and collaborative development programmes. Total development costs increase with the number of partner nations. For example, total development costs for the Eurofighter were estimated to be almost twice the development costs of a similar and alternative national project. However, total collaborative development costs are shared between the partner nations. Typically, for collaborative projects up to 2001, UK development costs averaged one-third of a project's total development costs.[9]

Collaborative production should also lead to cost savings from economies of scale and learning, with estimates suggesting that collaborative unit production costs should fall by 10 per cent as output doubles. However, departures from efficient production due to *juste retour* and duplicate final assembly lines suggest that the savings in unit production costs on actual collaborative programmes might be about one-half of those attained on national programmes.[10] Even with such collaborative production inefficiencies, the final unit production costs on collaborative projects could be lower than for a similar national programme if collaboration can benefit from a greater output due to orders from three or more partners.

Other examples provide more relevant evidence. For example, on the original plans for UK involvement in the US WR21 marine turbine project, the United Kingdom contributed to a US project which would have been unaffordable for the UK to have undertaken alone. On the European collaborative Common New Generation Frigate (CNGF), it was initially estimated that collaboration would save the UK up to £250 million (1995 prices) compared with a national programme. However, in 1999, the UK withdrew from the CNGF programme, selecting instead the national Type 45 destroyer project. It was estimated that the unit production cost of the national Type 45 would be 8 per cent less than the collaborative CNGF, and these savings were due to a reduced capability.[11] Finally, UK co-operation with the United States on the Joint Strike Fighter aircraft (JSF) was estimated to be considerably cheaper than a national alternative: a UK-only project would have been between 60 and 105 per cent more expensive than UK participation in the JSF. However, it was also estimated that it would be some 4 per cent cheaper to buy JSF directly from the United States compared with participating in the US joint programme.[12]

Analysis of the Eurofighter Typhoon confirms that collaboration is inefficient. Collaborative arrangements and the complexity of the technology increased total costs, with inefficient collaborative commercial and management arrangements contributing over 60 per cent of the cost increase. An official UK study confirmed that Typhoon collaborative decision-making arrangements were complex and inefficient. For example, within the UK there was no individual who was accountable and clearly in charge of the whole project. Decisions were reached through a four-level hierarchy of some fifty committees requiring consensus at every level. Predictably, decision making is slow, requiring consensus from all four partner nations: for example, it took up to seven years to agree and deliver some key upgrades.[13]

The results of the Typhoon programme reflected in cost increases, delays and reduced quantities are shown in Table 11.6. Similar data are also provided for the seven-nation A400M airlifter. Both collaborative programmes have been characterised by cost overruns, delays and reduced quantities. For Typhoon, delays of twenty-two months (some 40 per cent) were due to collaboration. Similarly, for Typhoon UK total production costs at £13.5 billion (2011 prices) were within the original

Table 11.6: *Results of collaboration*

Project	Estimated cost at approval (£ billion, 2011 prices)	Forecast to completion (£ billion, 2011 prices)	Cost increase (%)	Time delays (months)	Quantity reductions (units)
Typhoon	15.2	17.3	43	+54	72
A400M	2.2	2.7	21	+79	3

Source: National Audit Office. *Ministry of Defence: Management of the Typhoon Project*. London: TSO. 2011. Report No: HCP 755.
Notes:
i. Costs are at 2011 prices.
ii. Quantity reductions show reduced numbers compared with original plans.
   The Typhoon order was reduced from 232 to 160 aircraft, and the A400M order was reduced from 25 to 22 aircraft.

approval from 1996, but the UK purchased seventy-two fewer aircraft (30 per cent) than originally planned. In 2011, unit production costs of Typhoon were similar to comparable aircraft.[14] Overall assessment of arms collaboration will also be dependent on policymakers' valuation of retaining a national defence industrial base.

Collaboration leads to project delays. Typically, collaborative projects involving the United Kingdom were delayed by an average of twenty-eight months, with collaboration contributing some eleven months of the delay (40 per cent). Industrial arrangements and delayed approvals by partner nations were the main causes of slippages. For some projects, the UK Ministry of Defence criticised the collaborative industrial arrangements for the lack of a strong prime contractor demonstrating clear leadership: instead, the shareholder companies were more concerned about 'their own work share rather than managing the programme on an objective basis'.[15] Delays on collaborative programmes also arose from the time taken by partner nations to reach approval for future phases of the programme and the time taken to secure funding for the project (e.g. reflecting national budget constraints). Partner nations withdrawing from the programme or reducing order quantities and the time taken to agree operational requirements were further sources of delay on collaborative projects. Agreement on performance requirements for collaboration takes time and adds to transaction costs (nations have differing views on operational performance). Reaching agreement between partner nations and their national interest groups involves transaction costs as different

Table 11.7: *Employment impacts of collaboration*

Project	Numbers of UK jobs	Total number of jobs
Meteor missile	1,200	Not-available
A400M airlifter	3,400	10,000 including indirect
Typhoon	40,000	100,000+ for all partners

Source: See National Audit Office. *Ministry of Defence: Maximising the Benefits of Defence Equipment Co-Operation.* London: TSO. 2001. Report No: HCP 300; Eurofighter Typhoon. *About Us.* 2017. www.eurofighter.com/about-us (accessed 22 November 2017).
Note: Typhoon numbers are for direct and indirect.

nations are involved in bargaining, policing and monitoring complex international contracts.

Collaboration is claimed to deliver industrial benefits, including jobs and the retention of national defence industrial capabilities. Table 11.7 presents some examples of employment benefits. Initial impressions suggest impressive numbers of jobs; but appearances can be deceptive. Interpreting the numbers requires that they be based on standard definitions, distinguishing between direct and indirect jobs (indirect include supply chain jobs). Also, it has to be recognised that all economic activity creates or supports jobs. The key question is whether collaborative arms programmes make greater contributions to jobs and economic welfare than alternative uses of the resources?

Collaboration provides further industrial benefits by retaining defence industrial assets in each partner nation. For example, the Typhoon programme has retained development and production capacity in Airbus Defence and Space (France; Germany; Spain), BAE Systems (UK) and Leonardo Defence (Italy) together with firms in their supply chains. But, this capacity has been retained at a cost, where there are alternative uses of resources. Moreover, retaining *current* capacity simply transfers the capacity problem from the present to the future: how will the capacity be retained in the future and at what cost?

On management issues, various solutions have emerged to the government and industrial management of European arms collaboration. Government management structures have ranged from retaining separate national project offices with liaison arrangements, to a single national-led project office, with participants from other nations, to a dedicated international project office (e.g. NATO, OCCAR). For example, OCCAR (1996) is the European management agency for European collaborative programmes (e.g. A400M airlifter, Boxer armoured vehicle, Tiger helicopter). Industrial management structures have also varied, ranging from existing companies with international committees for coordination to a project-specific multinational industrial consortium (e.g. Eurofighter).

Some efforts have been made to increase the efficiency of European collaborative management arrangements. OCCAR aims to avoid 'reinventing the wheel' for each new collaborative programme. Also, OCCAR nations have moved away from traditional work shares based on *juste retour* to a global balance approach where national work shares are balanced over a number of programmes. OCCAR has introduced qualified majority voting and contracts awarded on the basis of competition. Elsewhere, there have been other efforts to improve management efficiency. For example, the NATO Eurofighter and Tornado Agencies were merged and the new Agency introduced modern business practices.

Nor does collaboration provide all the expected benefits from standardisation and interoperability. Partner nations often require modifications to their equipment. For example, for the Tornado project, the United Kingdom required an air defence version and was the only nation with such a requirement. Partner nations can also withdraw from a collaborative project, leading to changes in planned total orders and work shares; but there is the view that once started, collaborative projects are more difficult to cancel.

11.6 Evaluating Collaboration

Have European arms collaborations been successful? An economic evaluation requires an assessment of both the costs and benefits of collaboration to determine whether they have been worthwhile. Immediately, problems arise since there are few published studies in the partner nations to reach independent conclusions.

The United Kingdom has published the results of some official evaluations. A UK study of seventeen collaborative projects found that cost-effectiveness analysis was decisive in eleven cases. For example, cost-effectiveness analysis of the production phase of Typhoon programme concluded[16] that the next-best option – namely, a direct buy of the US Boeing F-15 aircraft – was more expensive in life-cycle costs and much less effective operationally.[17] In addition, wider industrial and political factors were included in the UK evaluations, but such wider factors were not always quantified. For example, no evidence was provided on how many jobs were created from collaboration compared with alternative public spending on hospitals, roads and schools. In contrast, other European partner nations placed greater emphasis on the wider benefits of collaboration in the form of protecting national industrial interests and promoting European political co-operation.[18] Such differences in evaluation criteria increase the problems of assessing collaborative programmes. Each partner nation has different policy objectives and places different (subjective) valuations on the benefits.

Assessing collaborative projects raises difficult methodological problems. The counterfactual issue arises of what would have happened in the absence of a collaborative project? Would each partner have undertaken an equivalent or similar national programme; or would it have imported directly from, say, the United States; and would imports involve some form of work-sharing agreement (e.g. offsets)? A foreign buy would almost certainly involve a similar but not equivalent project. Next, there are empirical problems in determining the choice of projects and the criteria for comparing collaborative and national projects. For example, the collaborative Typhoon project might be compared with similar national programmes. Comparators for combat aircraft include the Swedish Gripen, the French Rafale and the US F-15, F-16, F-18, F-22 and F-35. Ideally, these projects might be compared on the basis of their development time scales, unit prices, cost and schedule overruns, total output and export performance. Published data are not always available on all these performance indicators, and where available they might be based on different definitions. For example, development time scales measure the time from the start of the programme to its in-service date. However, start dates and in-service dates might not be based on identical definitions. In some cases, start dates might not include time spent on technology demonstrators and in-service dates might be based on aircraft at different stages of development. Some aircraft might enter service at an early stage of their development (e.g. without the required engine or avionics), while others enter service as much more fully developed aircraft (the problem of comparing like with like). Ideally, each performance indicator needs an appropriate economic model. An example for development times takes the general form:

$$DT = f \, (DC; \text{Features}; DVC; Z)$$

where DT is development time; DC is total development cost; Features represent performance features of each combat aircraft (e.g. weight and speed); DVC is a dummy variable for collaboration or a national project; and Z represents all other relevant variables.

More complications arise since projects differ in their performance capabilities and nations have different policy objectives, and place different valuations on their objectives. Further differences arise between *ex ante* and *ex post* choices. Initial choices are based on plans and expectations where outcomes might differ considerably from initial expectations, but typically assessments are based on final observed outcomes. Finally, problems arise since there is only a limited population of collaborative arms projects. This limited population comprises heterogeneous aerospace projects (combat, trainer and transport aircraft; different types of helicopters; missiles; and civil aircraft) involving different partner nations and various government and industrial organisational arrangements.[19]

A comparison of the collaborative Typhoon and similar national projects is shown in Table 11.8. This is an illustrative example only. It is predicted that the collaborative Typhoon will involve longer

Table 11.8: *Comparing collaborative and national projects*

Project	Start date	Time-scale (months)	Unit cost ($ mn, 2017 prices)	Output (numbers)	Exports (numbers)
Typhoon	6/86	206	144.0	599	127
Gripen	6/80	156	83.7	278	74
Rafale	12/82	216	75.4	356	84
F-15E	2/84	58	131.3	442	229
F-16	1/75	43	28.5	4,573	2,500+
F-18E/F	6/92	89	95.2	500+	36
F-22	10/86	230	215.6	195	0
F-35	11/96	224	139.6	3548	885

Source: See Hartley K. and Braddon D. *Collaborative Projects and the Number of Partner Nations.* Defence and Peace Economics. 2014. 25(6): 535–48; Defense-ae rospace.com. *Sticker Shock: Estimating the Real Cost of Modern Fighter Aircraft.* 2006. www.defense-aerospace.com/dae/articles/communiques/FighterCostFinalJul y06.pdf (accessed 22 November 2017).
Notes:
  i. Start date is the date when work started on the project; time scale is development time from start to entry into service; unit cost is unit production costs in 2017 prices, excluding development costs. Output and exports are in numbers and include planned numbers and licensed production numbers for exports. Planned numbers might not be realised as orders can be cancelled.
 ii. F-15 and F-18 were developed from an earlier version. The time scales and output/exports of the earlier versions are not included in the Table.
iii. US F-22 was a joint project between Lockheed Martin and Boeing so might be regarded as a joint national project.

development times, lower unit costs, greater output and greater exports. The start of development is a proxy for technical progress on each project. The US F-22 is the world's most advanced fighter aircraft, which is reflected in its unit production cost. Comparing Typhoon with the other European and US fighter aircraft shows that Typhoon took longer to develop than the Swedish Gripen, but was faster than the French Rafale. US Cold War fighters (F-15, F-16, F-18) were developed faster than their European rivals. Unit production costs are an indicator of price competitiveness, with unit costs for Typhoon higher than comparable European national projects and higher than most US projects. The more recent American aircraft (F-22, F-35) took longer to develop than the US Cold War aircraft and the collaborative Typhoon was developed faster than the US F-22 and F-35. However, such comparisons are limited since data are not available to assess the relative performance of these aircraft. Elsewhere, Typhoon output figures exceed those for most of the aircraft in the sample, and its exports exceed those for the Gripen, Rafale and F18E/F. Overall, using such available performance indicators, the evidence provides only limited support for the hypothesis that collaboration is always superior to national projects. For some performance indicators and compared with some national projects, the collaborative Typhoon was superior; but not for all indictors and not for all projects in the sample.

An alternative test is available based on pairwise comparisons of collaborative and similar national projects. Again, the results will depend on the choice of comparators and their performance indicators. An example is shown in Table 11.9 based on only two performance indicators. On the basis of six pairwise comparisons, only the collaborative Tornado is superior to the national projects. However, US projects usually have a scale advantage over European projects which needs to be recognised in comparing output and export levels. Restricting the comparisons to European national projects shows the British Hawk and French Mirage superior to their collaborative pairs. Overall, for this sample and performance indicators, there is no evidence showing that collaborative projects are always superior to national projects. This finding raises the question of why collaborate for defence equipment? The answer might be that other performance indicators provide different results, or that governments value highly other policy objectives and are willing to pay whatever the price (e.g. European co-operation; independence from United States).

There is a related question of why arms collaboration is unsuccessful. Possible explanations might be the military dimension, the number of

Table 11.9: *Pairwise comparisons: military aircraft and helicopters*

Collaborative Project	National Project
Alpha Jet (F;G: T)	*Hawk* (UK:T)
Output: 503	Output: 1,000+
Exports: 152	Exports: 800+
Jaguar (F;UK:SA)	*Mirage F1* (F;SA)
Output: 543	Output: 720+
Exports: 257	Exports: 474+
Tornado (G;I;UK: SA)	*F-111* (US:SA)
Output: 977	Output: 563
Exports: 120	Exports: 24
A400M (7 nations; MT)	*C-17 Globemaster* (US: MT)
Output: 174	Output: 279
Exports: 4	Exports: 51
NH90 (4 nations: MRH)	*Black Hawk* (US: MRH)
Output: 382+	Output: 4,000+
Exports: 167	Exports: 847+
Tiger (F;G: AH)	*Apache* (US: AH)
Output: 348	Output: 2,200
Exports: 48	Exports: 584+

Source: author's database comprising a wide array of published official reports.
Notes:
  i. See Table 6.3.
 ii. F = France; G = Germany; I = Italy; T = military trainer; SA = strike aircraft; MT = military transport; MRH = multi-role helicopter; AH = attack helicopter.
iii. Total output in numbers includes exports. All numbers, especially exports, are approximations, showing broad orders of magnitude.

partner nations and the temporary or project-specific nature of arms collaborations. These aspects of arms collaborations can easily be assessed by considering collaboration on Airbus civil aircraft projects. The Airbus group is an international collaboration with two major partner nations, namely, France and Germany (each with ownership shares of 11 per cent, with Spain as a junior partner with a 4 per cent holding and the balance owned by private shareholders). Many commentators would regard Airbus as an example of a successful European aerospace collaboration reflected in its position as a world class firm forming a duopoly with Boeing in the world market for large civil aircraft. Originally, in 1970, Airbus was a new entrant into the world civil aircraft market which was then dominated by US companies (Boeing, Convair, Douglas, Lockheed). Over time, Airbus moved from a new entrant to a duopoly with Boeing. A study comparing Airbus and Boeing concluded that the increase in the number of partner nations from one nation (Boeing) to two major partners had not affected company performance as reflected in development time scales and total sales.[20] Again, other performance indicators might not support this conclusion, nor was any allowance made for the magnitude of state funding for both Airbus and Boeing.

11.7 Conclusion: Future Prospects

Costs will continue to dominate arms procurement choices, with rising equipment costs exceeding the real terms growth of both national GDP and defence budgets. On this basis, armed forces will only be able to buy considerably smaller numbers of air, land and sea systems. Higher development costs will also mean a reduction in the numbers of new types of equipment under development. For example, over the period from 1950 to 2000, the numbers of new types of combat aircraft introduced into UK service fell from twenty in the decade 1950 to 1960 to three for 1980 to 1990.[21] The continuation of such trends will depend on technical change. As Chapters 16 and 17 demonstrate, new technology will change the concepts of war and deterrence leading to new opportunities for substitution (e.g. UAVs replacing manned combat aircraft, robots replacing soldiers). In the meantime, the pressures for arms collaboration are likely to increase. Collaboration offers cost savings, but often these are not as great as expected. How can the efficiency of arms collaboration be improved?

Improved efficiency in arms collaboration can be achieved through applying the following economic principles:

- Competitive procurement. Efficiency requires that contracts be awarded on a competitive basis with a greater use of fixed price and/or incentive price contracts. Once development contracts are awarded, competition needs to be maintained for the production phase. Without competition after the development stage, the contractor becomes a monopoly supplier with the adverse economic effects of monopoly (inefficiency, higher prices and profits) and pressures for state regulation of monopoly suppliers.

- Contract management represented by a single prime contractor, with the prime responsible for allocating subcontracts. Work shares would be based on efficiency criteria and not *juste retour*.
- Limit the number of nations to two equal partners (c.f. Airbus). More nations can join the collaboration but only as subcontractors. A similar model is used for the US F-35 Lightning II (Joint Strike Fighter). Here, Lockheed Martin is the prime contractor with Northrop Grumman and BAE Systems as major industrial partners; and the UK government as the only Level 1 partner contributing 10 per cent of the planned development cost.
- Extend collaboration to the life-cycle costs of projects, as discussed in Chapter 13. For aerospace projects, this would mean extending collaboration to aircrew training, repair, maintenance, upgrades and the sharing of bases.
- Extend collaboration to costly land and sea systems (e.g. aircraft carriers, submarines, main battle tanks).
- Be willing to broaden collaboration to nations outside of Europe.

While these principles appear attractive, they involve inevitable trade-offs. For instance, competition would allow US firms to bid for collaborative projects. This would be unacceptable for some European nations, which regard collaboration as a means of avoiding dependence on the United States. But a preference for European strategic autonomy (Fortress Europe) comes at a cost, and costs will dominate future arms procurement choices. Arms collaboration appears to offer attractive solutions to continuously rising unit equipment costs. More efficient collaboration will help, but will not remove the underlying trend of rising costs and the need for radical defence policy choices affecting all nations.

References and notes

1. N. R. Augustine. *Augustine's Laws*. London: Penguin. 1987.
2. K. Hove and Lillekvelland T. 'Investment Cost Escalation – An Overview of the Literature and Revised Estimates'. *Defence and Peace Economics*. 2016. 27(2): 208–30.

3. See Hove and Lillekvelland. 'Investment Cost Escalation'; D. Bangert, N. Davies and R. Watson, 'Managing Defence Acquisition Cost Growth'. *RUSI Journal*. 2017. 162(1): 60–67; Kirkpatrick DLI. 'The Rising Unit Cost of Defence Equipment – The Reasons and the Results'. Defence and Peace Economics. 1995. 6(4): 263–88.
4. K. Hartley. *The Economics of Arms*. Newcastle upon Tyne: Agenda Publishing. 2017.
5. Bangert, Davies and Watson. 'Managing Defence Acquisition Cost Growth'.
6. National Audit Office. *Ministry of Defence: Maximising the Benefits of Defence Equipment Co-operation*. London: TSO. 2001. 62 pgs. Report No.: HCP 300.
7. National Audit Office. *Maximising the Benefits*.
8. Hartley. *The Economics of Arms*.
9. National Audit Office. *Maximising the Benefits*.
10. National Audit Office. *Maximising the Benefits*.
11. National Audit Office. *Maximising the Benefits*.
12. National Audit Office. *Maximising the Benefits*.
13. National Audit Office. *Ministry of Defence: Management of the Typhoon Project*. London: TSO. 2011. 38 p. Report No.: HCP 755. 7–9.
14. National Audit Office. *Ministry of Defence: Management of the Typhoon Project*.
15. National Audit Office. *Ministry of Defence: Management of the Typhoon Project*. 54.
16. National Audit Office. *Maximising the Benefits*.
17. UK cost-effectiveness studies are known as COEIA, namely, Combined Operational Effectiveness and Investment Appraisal – HMT. The Green Book. London: TSO. July 2011.
18. National Audit Office. *Maximising the Benefits*.
19. K. Hartley. *The Political Economy of Aerospace Industries*. Cheltenham: Elgar. 2014.
20. K . Hartley and D. Braddon. 'Collaborative Projects and the Number of Partner Nations'. *Defence and Peace Economics*. 2014. 25(6): 535–48.
21. C. D. Coxhead. 'Pressures for Change in Military Aviation'. *Air Clues*. 1987. 41(4): 123–27.

12 Defence Procurement: Overcoming Challenges and Managing Expectations

TREVOR TAYLOR

Introduction: The Poor Image of Defence Procurement

Defence procurement has a poor image in the United Kingdom (and other countries), with major projects regularly having been late and over budget. A 1986 report from the National Audit Office (NAO) found that 'the MoD had not succeeded in overcoming the problems of cost escalation and delays'.[1] Eight years later, the NAO reported that 'for those 20 projects that feature in both the 1993 and 1994 reports the overall forecast cost variance has increased from a 6.1 per cent overrun in 1993 to a 7.2 per cent overrun in 1994'.[2] The equivalent report for 2000 found that the MoD appeared to be securing improvements in cost control, but 'it is disappointing that the average project delay is getting longer'.[3] In 2010 the Comptroller and Auditor General Amyas Morse had some encouraging words on costs and time, but argued firmly that 'central departmental decisions were taken to balance the defence budget which had the effect of driving very significant additional cost and delay into the equipment programme; this represents poor value for money for the taxpayer'.[4] After examining the NAO's work, Margaret Hodge, the Chair of the House of Commons Committee on Public Accounts, was even more scathing:

Any good progress being made on many individual defence equipment projects has again been overshadowed by the MoD's continuing failure on important major projects. Unaffordable decisions taken in the short-term, lead to inevitable waste of billions of pounds over time. In the wake of the Defence Review the MoD still has to spell out whether and how it has got its defence procurement budget under control. The MoD must demonstrate the same discipline in its defence procurement that our forces demonstrate in the field. In this one hearing, when we were able to focus on only four projects, we identified over £8 billion of taxpayers' money which has been written off or incurred simply for reasons of delay.[5]

Table 12.1: *Major reports relating to UK defence procurement improvement*

Office of the Minister for Science, *Report of the Committee on the Management and Control of Research and Development*, London, 1961 (The Gibb-Zuckerman Report).

Ministry of Technology, *Report of the Steering Group on Development Cost Estimating*, London, 1968 (The Downey Report).

Ministry of Defence, *Value for Money in Defence Procurement*, Open Government 83/01, October 1983.

G. Jordan, I. Lee and G. Cawsey, *Learning from Experience: A Report on the Arrangements for Managing Major Projects in the Procurement Executive*, December 1988.

Ministry of Defence, *The Smart Procurement Initiative*, Strategic Defence Review, London 1998.

Ministry of Defence, *Enabling Acquisition Change*, London, 2006.

Ministry of Defence, *Review of Acquisition for the Secretary of State for Defence: an independent report by Bernard Gray*, London, October 2009 (The Gray Report).

National Security Through Technology, Ministry of Defence, London, 2012.

Source: author's compilation of published official reports.

These brief comments underline that things can go wrong at the both the individual and the overall programme level. In response, multiple British administrations have sought to reform defence acquisition processes and activities on almost a constant basis since the mid-1980s,[6] as the documents listed in Table 12.1 indicate.

A similar situation has prevailed in the United States with dissatisfaction about the procurement of major equipment leading to studies, recommendations for change and the attempted introduction of some or many of them into US regulation and practice.[7] The most recent of reform efforts was associated with President Obama's Deputy Secretary of Acquisition, Technology and Logistics, Frank Kendall, who provided a sustained drive behind his multifaceted 'Better Buying Power' initiatives.[8] Shortly afterwards and separately, in May 2017, the congressionally mandated Advisory Panel on 'Streamlining and Codifying Acquisition Regulations' issued its interim report (Section 809 Panel Interim Report) while continuing its investigations.[9]

Australia is another notable case of a country which has been relatively open about examining the shortcomings in its defence acquisition practices and in seeking reform, and in introducing organisational and process changes on a regular basis.[10] Other major countries, such as Germany and France, have been less focused on defence procurement, at least in public, in part because they have been less involved with the development process; but also because they have been less transparent on defence matters as they have quietly observed the practices of others, adapting them and adopting them on a selective basis. But significant efforts to improve performance in defence acquisition are nonetheless visible in, for example, France, Germany, South Korea and India.[11]

12.1 Expectations

The proposition here is that if political figures, the media and indeed the wider public had a better understanding of the challenges and risks intrinsic to defence procurement and acquisition, they would hold a more realistic view of the uncertainties involved; and the words of Blaise Pascal, 'to understand is to forgive', would then achieve more salience.[12] Thus, this chapter seeks first to explain why defence procurement is often so problematic and why clear, simple solutions often prove to be hard to implement and/or bring unforeseen consequences. The chapter analyses in turn: the structures and pressures in the markets for major defence products, such as aircraft and warships; the nature of the 'requirements' for such systems; the complexity of the products required for defence; cost-estimating challenges; and the multidimensional, dynamic and subjective nature of value in defence projects.

However, it should be emphasised at the outset that defence procurement problems are most apparent when major projects, often involving years of technology development and integration, are under scrutiny. As Sir Kevin O'Donoghue and Andrew Tyler, the leaders of the UK's Defence Equipment & Support body, stated in 2010, the vast majority of the UK MoD's smaller and simpler contracts were delivered on time, to budget and to the specified performance.[13]

12.2 Terminology

12.2.1 Procurement

An essential starting point is to clarify terminology. Procurement is about buying things – the concepts and processes that guide the purchasing function. Defence ministries buy a huge range of goods and services, many in a non-problematic and non-contentious way, because they involve products and services for which there are large numbers of potential suppliers, that also have a large number of customers. Office furniture and cleaning services would be cases in point. On the other hand, defence ministries also buy goods such as nuclear submarines with no civilian equivalent, and where they have a very limited choice of suppliers. Purchasing normally occurs through the legal tool of a contract, though there are exceptions to this rule: items bought from the United States under the Foreign Military Sales structure involve an agreement with the US government rather than a contract. Also, it is not unknown in urgent cases for companies to be asked to work 'off-contract', with the buyer and seller agreeing that the paperwork will be settled later. Finally, not to be overlooked in the procurement function is the specification of testing processes by which verification occurs, ensuring that what has been specified in a procurement contract has actually been delivered.

12.2.2 Acquisition

Defence acquisition, on the other hand, addresses procurement, but also a very wide range of other activities. It covers how 'military requirements', i.e. the features reflecting what is to be bought, are set and presented. Clearly, details of requirement affect the technological and feasibility of projects and the number of suppliers that might be tempted to bid in any competition. It also covers how equipment is to be supported through what may be a life in excess of twenty years. As will be shown later, some defence equipment has very demanding and problematic support needs that have few equivalents in civilian life. Although the UK initiative in 1998 was initially labelled Smart Procurement, concern with the broader agenda soon appeared. The 1999 Edition of the Guide to Smart Procurement was called The Acquisition Handbook and included the simple equation that Acquisition = Requirements + Procurement + Support.[14]

12.2.3 Capability Development

Finally, there is a need to consider capability generation and sustainment, which involves the activities needed so that goods and services that have been bought can actually be used in a military operation. Readers may care to imagine that they have just taken delivery of a transport helicopter which is sitting on their lawn and then been invited to think of all the other things they would have to have in place before they could actually make good use of this kit.

To address this matter, the United Kingdom developed a framework or checklist of what needs to be generated that goes by the acronym TEPIDOIL. This covers:

- Training, of users and maintainers
- Equipment, of a satisfactory nature
- People, the right sort of which need to be available, either in the military or elsewhere, who can be trained to use and support the system
- Infrastructure, which the equipment needs, such as storage facilities, runways and training areas
- Doctrine, to spell out how the equipment will be used, including in conjunction with other related elements of the armed forces
- Organisation, in which roles (and career paths) must be defined of people who use and support the equipment
- Information, on and about the system, that must be communicable to the rest of the armed forces
- Logistics, the fuels, spare parts and varied services that the system will need for sustained operation.

The British model also includes a need to take account of the interoperability of one system with others.[15]

With some equipment, items such as training and infrastructure can involve considerable expense but may not necessarily be covered by the money allocated for the procurement project. In the United Kingdom, the Top Level Budget holder for much infrastructure is a different post (the head of the Defence Infrastructure Organisation) from the budget holder for the equipment (normally the head of the relevant Command).[16] Other elements of the TEPIDOIL structure, such as organisation and people, can have drastic implications for the culture and ways of working in the armed forces and represent one reason why armed forces are often reluctant to embrace novel but organisationally disruptive equipment.[17]

This framework opens up a central issue in defence procurement, which is how both a 'project' and 'value' are to be defined. Does the project whose time and cost is being monitored include the training and infrastructure elements? How much of the in-service, logistics elements of a piece of equipment are to be included in the scope of a project? How is an item that is expensive to buy but has low training needs to be compared with something that is cheaper to buy but with a bigger training bill? These are some of a range of procurement and 'value' questions that are raised by the TEPIDOIL framework. The chapter returns in Section 12.7 to a detailed discussion of value, but first it addresses the structure of the market for defence goods.

12.3 The Supply Base for Major Items of Defence Equipment

Defence is far from the perfect market situation in which there are numerous potential sellers and even more potential and informed buyers. There are few customers for big systems and, indeed, normally there is only one customer that counts – the launch customer, which is normally the home government where the company is based. A company's product rejected by its home government will normally struggle in the international marketplace. Figure 12.1 seeks to encapsulate some key features of the market for major defence projects. On the demand side, ministries of defence are often seeking equipment that is very complicated (see below), that can withstand future efforts by an adversary to deny its effectiveness and that may require significant development work as many of its subsystems, and even some enabling technologies, may not have reached the production stage.

There are only a small number of companies within a country that have the capacity to develop and manage major defence projects. This is largely because of the mix of very infrequent orders for some classes of system, the resultant choice of some potential suppliers to leave a sector if they lose a once-in-a-generation competition and the high entry barriers in terms of required knowledge and capital for new firms to break into defence markets for platforms and other major items.

Yet in defence, private companies are often reluctant to invest much of their own money in the development of major products for which

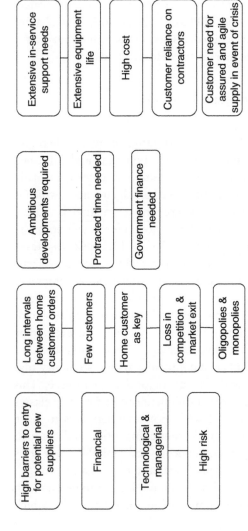

Figure 12.1: Key features of major defence markets: demand- and supply-side factors
Source: author

they do not have a firm order. This is because of the risk of reliance on a single customer's decision. There is also the complexity of what needs to be generated, implying very large monetary sums and protracted time scales that need to be justified to providers of private capital. This logic applies, albeit less strongly, to developers of subsystems, such as thermal imaging equipment, which might be fitted to a range of platforms. However, even this can have problems: the author knows of a privately developed sensor subsystem that formed one element of a bid by a separate prime contractor for an army vehicle. The platform bid was not successful and the subsystem company then sought to interest other vehicle suppliers outside the United Kingdom to take up its product, but were refused export licences by the British regulatory authorities. The subsystem developers were told that their system was better than the equivalent system in the selected platform, and the government did not want other armies having a better capability than the British Army. Government export controls are a source of government power over defence businesses' commercial options. On the other hand, the in-service costs of supporting major items of defence equipment for parts, fuel and a range of support services, including repair and obsolescence management, normally much exceeds its initial purchase price. Unless governments also buy a large amount of information from the company, they have to rely significantly on the original equipment manufacturer for much of this work. Such information is extremely valuable to companies, and they are likely to charge highly for it.

In some ways the scope of the term 'buy' is narrower in the defence world than in normal commercial life. In particular, the 'buyer' of defence items, unlike the normal civil purchaser, cannot re-sell them without the permission of the government where these items were manufactured. Given the common need also for a continuous supply of parts and information from the original supplying state, defence equipment buyers essentially gain the ability to use the equipment, so long as they do not excessively conflict with the wishes of the original supplier government.

Clearly, the relationship between a purchasing government and a major defence contractor is very different to that between the individual buyer and the shop where a washing machine was purchased or between the buyer and the washing machine manufacturer. In defence, deep and multifaceted relations are the norm.

12.4 Requirements

An initial consideration is that the word 'requirement' is something of a misnomer: it does not represent something that is absolutely necessary in the same sense that oxygen and water are requirements for human survival. Instead, it constitutes the articulation of something that the military judge will be useful in the execution of their tasks for the next twenty years or so. When the world changes drastically, there are strong implications for requirements. The Eurofighter was conceived and largely designed in the 1980s on the basis of the need to contain the threat from an offensive Warsaw Pact airpower. Speed and agility were vital if the Eurofighter was to destroy as many enemy aircraft as possible. The end of the Cold War reduced the relevance of such capabilities, and placed more value on the capability for precision ground attack. But since then, the possibility of aircraft hijacking by terrorists and the moves to a more assertive stance by Russia have restored the utility of a quick reaction and agile aircraft such as Typhoon in Europe.

Moreover, the specification of military equipment must recognise that an adversary will seek to destroy its usefulness and even existence. This is just not the case of most things we buy in civilian life: our cars are designed to deal with accidental collisions, but not with drivers on the road who are deliberately intent on using their car's destructive capability. The need of military equipment to be protected against present and future novel threats clearly adds to the development challenges and production costs.

Well into the twenty-first century it appears that the protection needs of many Western systems have been somewhat neglected, and they have become increasingly vulnerable to the growing surveillance and long-range precision strike capabilities of potential adversaries such as Russia, China and their equipment customers, including Iran. Space assets on which much of the Western civil and military capabilities rest have been rendered vulnerable by the development of antisatellite capabilities in China and Russia, and, of course, the protection of civil and military information systems against cyberattack is raising costs for all users. This prompted the development of the American Third Offset Strategy initiative, as discussed in detail in Chapter 17, calling for a step change in the rate of Western technological innovation.[18]

A third moving part regarding requirements is the potential speed and direction of technological change; this affects the capabilities that might be available to the buying state, and those to which its adversaries will have access. As a further complication, much technology that can be adapted for use in the military sphere is originating in the civil sector, not least and not only in electronics. A military requirement thus reflects future elements of uncertainty: what might be valuable and what might be technologically possible. Military requirements compel their drafters to look well into the future and to ask which sorts of adversaries will be faced, what evolving capabilities those adversaries will be able to field and what technology will offer to the home side in terms of capability, time and cost.

None of these questions have obvious or unchanging answers in a world where sudden as well as continuous change is possible. That is why governments pursuing the more ambitious capabilities struggle to heed the exhortations of those who assert that procurement would be less problematic if requirements were kept constant through the procurement processes.

Clearly, a significant aspect of a military requirement is whether it can be met by something that is already in production or whether it requires a significant development effort to generate something that has not been 'invented' to date. The language used here is deliberately selected: the lay person might expect others to have a good idea of what it will cost to 'develop' a new system, whereas few would have expected Edison to predict the money and time needed to 'invent' the electric light bulb or the telephone. In defence procurement terms, this cost consideration has traditionally been influenced by whether meeting a requirement can be achieved by the integration of components and mature technologies in new ways, or whether it will involve the need to generate real novelty at the component and sub-subsystem levels.[19] However, the increasing centrality of software development in defence systems has at least blurred the difference between 'invention' and 'development'.

Moreover, military requirements rarely prioritise reliability and maintainability to the extent that is often the case in the civilian world. The fact is that lives and battlefield success are central, and thus there is often emphasis on top-level performance rather than on sustained reliability, especially when a government thinks that it might have to deter or even defeat a peer adversary which itself has access to advanced technology. Military systems are more akin to Formula 1 racing cars than family cars: what matters for the first two is superior and reliable performance during the mission or race.

12.5 Technical Complexity of Major Projects

Any examination of why defence development projects often cost more and take longer than expected must take account of the increasing complexity of systems involved, reflecting the evolving demands of military users. Modern platforms such as ships, aircraft and vehicles do not just involve systems for their propulsion, steering and navigation. They normally also include communication systems, surveillance systems and weapons with fire control systems for their release and targeting. They may also have systems for their protection, including systems to sense if they have been detected by an adversary's radar. Manned systems need subsystems for support of the people involved. As an extreme case of complexity, a nuclear submarine can be summarised as a system with the capability to remain submerged for periods in excess of three months and able to move with minimum noise and navigate with precision. It must be able to protect itself, if necessary, and to communicate reliably but covertly with its own government. The simplest summary might say that it comprises a propulsion system, i.e. a nuclear reactor, at the rear, high explosive and even nuclear weapons at the front and a 'hotel' in the middle that can sustain the lives of its crew. That, of course, omits the sensor and communication systems. Finally, with many defence systems, space is at a premium, since the larger the system the more vulnerable it may be.

Generally, industry is asked to develop systems of increasing complexity. To illustrate, in the 1980s and 1990s, US combat aircraft delivering weapons were extensively supported by specialised surveillance systems, including the E3A AWACS air-to-air system and the JSTARS ground surveillance aircraft. The F-35, however, can be fairly described as a multisensor platform in its own right, with a capacity to inform others.

By now the reader might begin to have some sympathy for the Project Leader in the Defence Equipment & Support organisation, who is expected by the House of Commons Public Accounts Committee to arrange the generation and delivery of a complex product that does not yet exist, for a predicted price at a specified time. Complexity obviously increases when efforts are made to take account of all the non-equipment lines of development and their relationship with the hardware.

12.6 The Cost Estimating Dimension

In the acquisition perspective, which includes in-service support, major defence projects present three financial problems for governments. First, reflecting the complexity of systems sought, even the development and production costs, i.e. the 'sticker' price of major systems, have tended to increase significantly from one generation of a system type to the next (see Chapter 9); second, as noted, the actual development and production costs of major systems have often significantly exceeded their predicted levels – when these first two factors are combined, the consequence is that the one-for-one replacement of major systems becomes more and more difficult to afford unless defence budgets are increased at a greater rate than economic growth; third, the relative value and affordability of a system to a military force should always take account of its in-service running costs. In the case of a major platform, even over a period of a decade, these normally significantly exceed its initial purchase cost, and emphatically so, when the costs of the other Defence Lines of Development are taken into account. Limited attention to life-cycle costs is dangerous, as it is not unknown for states to find the money to buy a system, then lack the funds for its operation (refer to Chapter 13).

Clearly, the better the estimates of future development, production and in-service costs, the more effective government decision making is likely to be. Cost estimation is an important function, and one in which government may feel under pressure to express significant confidence, as this exchange between an MP and the head of DE&S suggests:

Q29 James Wharton: I haven't actually had the answer to my original question, which is about the MoD's capability to estimate the cost of these projects.

General Sir Kevin O'Donoghue: The answer is yes, we do have the capability. We didn't have enough of the capability. I [have recruited] over 200 professional cost-assurers and cost-estimators over the two years since the Bernard Gray Report . . . . The answer is, yes, we were quite good at it, but we didn't have enough capacity.[20]

Sir Kevin might have added that estimating is not the same as the generation of accurate predictions. Cost estimating is a recognised role in government defence as well as in the private sector, with many of its British practitioners being members of the Society for Cost

Analysis and Forecasting (SCAF).[21] It involves one or a mix of three broad techniques. The first involves parametric thinking, in which the costs of a previous system or systems, such as a multi-role combat aircraft, are assembled and examined, and then the costs of the next generation of a comparable aircraft are estimated, with allowances being made for enhanced capabilities and complexity as well as inflation and raw material cost changes. Historically, in the case of major platforms, anticipated weight has been recognised as a significant guide to eventual cost. A second and related approach is to use analogous analysis, in which the costs of a future system are estimated in the light of the past costs of a different system, but one with comparable complexity and shared key characteristics.[22] The third approach is essentially bottom-up, using what the project management world knows as 'work breakdown structures', designed to list every task that needs to be carried out to implement a project and then to calculate the cost and time associated with each task. The costs are then aggregated to yield an estimate of the project's cost. This is a challenging, yet key activity for a company that is considering bidding to undertake a project, especially if a fixed-price contract is envisaged.

Cost estimates, however, should always recognise the role and multidimensional nature of risk in a project, and thus not be confused with hard predictions; they are about what could well happen, not what will happen, and are thus normally presented within a range of possibilities. The British Ministry of Defence has long used a '10, 50, 90' percentage system of cost estimates. The 10 per cent figure gives the anticipated cost if almost everything goes well, with the percentage indicating the share of projects when this is likely to occur, i.e. only one in ten projects is expected to enjoy such a fate. The 50 per cent number gives the cost if an average number of things go wrong with half of the projects expected to be covered by this figure. The 90 per cent number addresses the expected cost if many difficult issues appear and must be addressed, and this figure is expected to cover 90 per cent of projects.

For financial planning purposes, the British Defence Ministry has been drawn to using the 50 per cent estimate, i.e. assessing affordability on the basis of an aggregation of the 50 per cent totals. This reflects the (heroic) assumption that the extra costs associated with projects that exceed their 50 per cent target will be balanced by the amounts associated with savings from the projects coming in under their 50 per cent figure. In reality, this has constituted a recipe for over-commitment, in part because the scope for cost savings is usually smaller than the scope for cost increases over the 50 per cent level. Also the '10, 50, 90' has an in-built feature that is rarely recognised to this author's knowledge: implicit in its reasoning is that it does not cover 100 per cent of projects and that around a tenth of them must be expected to exceed even their 90 per cent targets. Given that the MoD is running at least a dozen and often more major projects at any one time, it must be recognised that one or more of them will exceed their envisaged cost under the 90 per cent assessment, even if the cost and risk assessments are thorough and 'accurate'.

The above paragraphs address only the importance and challenges of cost forecasting with regard to the development and production phases, i.e. the initial procurement, rather than the in-service support costs. There is also a need to note the recognition by the US and UK governments that cost forecasters need to be organised so that they can enjoy a significant degree of independence from wider pressures. This is largely because of the impact of competition for funding in the acquisition processes. The most obvious aspect of this is the pressure on companies to submit over-optimistic bids with regard to cost, time and performance in order to win a contract in a competitive tendering process, especially when the requirement is for the development of a new system. Development projects in areas such as combat aircraft are few and far between and a company may be desperate, knowing that if it fails to succeed in a competition, it may be driven from a sector or even out of business. For instance, McDonnell-Douglas' failure in the competition for the Joint Strike Fighter in 2001 led to its purchase by Boeing. Companies also are aware that during an extended development phase, requirements are often modified, which offers the chance for price increases. Finally, contractors are also aware that the in-service phase will provide chances for further cost recovery since defence ministries normally have little choice but to use original equipment manufacturers for much support work.[23] However, as discussed in Chapter 2, from the perspective of an armed service branch or even subgroup (such as the artillery in the army), there is also significant competition within government for a project to gain investment approval and a place in the national programme. In this context, the more capability that it presents as being deliverable and at lower cost, the better the chances of success.

Trevor Taylor

These are the factors behind what is sometimes called the 'conspiracy of optimism' between the government project team and contractors: low estimates appeal to both. For these reasons, both British and US defence ministries have separated major cost forecasting functions from project teams. In the United Kingdom, the Cost Assurance and Analysis Service (CAAS) is based in the Defence Equipment and Support organisation but outside any project team. In the United States, where acquisition project teams are located within the procurement sections of the individual services, the Cost Assessment and Program Evaluation (CAPE) body is located outside the services in the Pentagon centre. Disagreements on likely costs between independent cost analysts and project teams are not unknown.

At a very basic level, perhaps politicians and even the public should not hasten to be horrified when defence development projects cost more than anticipated. While they may not have any deep understanding of the technology and engineering challenges involved, they might well have personal experience of simple domestic projects such as house extensions or a conservatory construction that end up costing much more than originally envisaged. Cost forecasting is difficult even for straightforward tasks. In many ways the acquisition of major defence projects involves a world that is nothing like the conceptual world of economics.

12.7 The Complexities of Value in Defence Acquisition

Defence choices have a high potential to disappoint some stakeholders, because for government, the concept of value in defence procurement choice is complicated, subjective and dynamic. This implies incidentally that the competitions for which the British government retains an affection are often not truly 'fair' in a legal sense, in that the assessment (evaluation) schemes provided by the government to potential bidders may not accurately capture the dimensions of value for government leaders.

'Over the last two years in particular, much attention has been devoted in the Ministry of Defence to ways of securing better value for money'; so wrote Geoffrey Pattie, the 1983 Minister of State for Defence Procurement. This was to introduce a document, entitled Value for Money in Defence Procurement, demonstrating the complexity of the subject, as it listed fifty-two relevant variables under eight separate headings. Politically it is difficult to oppose value for money decisions: who could be against value for money? But what precisely does it mean?

Figure 12.2 suggests there are four factors in which a system's value can be weighed. The first value factor is military utility and effectiveness, but this is not straightforward. How is protection achieved through armour, and how are active defences to be assessed against protection through low observability and mobility? How is the potential for a system to be quickly modified for a particular operation to be weighed against initial standard capability? How is a platform's capacity to collect information to be weighed against firepower and protection elements? How is a system that would perform well in one operational context but less well in another to be assessed against a bid that was quite good but not exceptional in both? There are a very large number of questions that can be raised in regard to this consideration.

The second dimension of value is cost, seemingly straightforward. However, what should be the weighting of initial procurement costs as against through life costs (about which there is usually significant uncertainty)? When costs are being considered, should just the equipment offers be taken into account, or should there be an effort to calculate the overall costs of generating capability with the equipment, which would involve all other Defence Lines of Development? Contentiously, but important in many countries, should the relevant cost be measured as the gross cost to the ministry of defence or should the net cost to the government be taken into account? The latter would involve trying to assess tax revenues from industry and its employees to the government associated with the various bids. Calculations show that these can exceed 35 per cent of the gross cost to the MoD if a contract is fulfilled completely within the national economy.[24]

Third, there are macroeconomic and strategic defence industrial factors to consider. The British Ministry of Defence now has the generation of national prosperity as one of its formal objectives, but even before that it was not unknown for defence contracts to be appreciated as a means of maintaining employment, particularly in vulnerable areas where alternative sources of work might be hard to generate. Defence projects may also mean the generation of technology and management expertise valuable in the wider economy, such as funding the operation of apprentice schemes in which some of those trained can become available outside defence. The strategic factors associated with defence

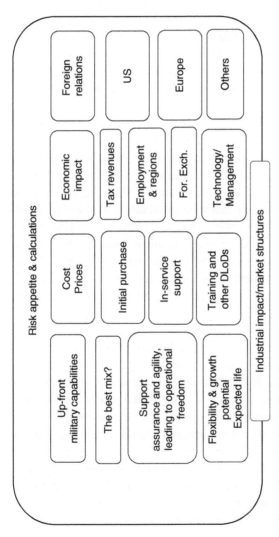

Figure 12.2: Dimensions of value in defence
Source: author

industry relate to the freedom of national military action, which capable national defence suppliers generate; they thus clearly need to be provided with an adequate drumbeat of orders if they are to remain viable. The incidence of governments seeking to develop national industrial capabilities and placing extensive 'offset' obligations on potential suppliers shows the importance of defence to the prosperity debate.

Fourth, major defence choices have international and sometimes national political implications. London's readiness to signal the building of the Type 26 warship on the Clyde and the involvement of Scottish yards with the carrier programme must be presumed to have played some part in the Scottish referendum choice to remain part of the United Kingdom in 2015. Part of the perceived price of the US military commitment to Europe during the Cold War was that European countries were expected to buy a certain amount of equipment from the United States. The F-35 has had a troubled development history, but UK government concern has been minimal because of its potential impact on the overall UK-US relationship. The British Ministry of Defence arranged multiple, piecemeal approval arrangements for the programme with the consequence that the National Audit Office reported that it was coming in under budget at a time when the US Government Accountability Office was telling a vastly different story. The programme is highly political, just as collaborative projects with European states, such as Eurofighter and the A400M, have consequences for overall relations among the governments concerned.

Affecting all these four factors are also the various elements of risk that permeate competitive bids, which at heart represent promises made by a contractor to be implemented over a future period of years. Technical risk, management and workforce risk, supply chain risk, commercial risk, foreign exchange risk, obsolescence risk and of course political risk are normal elements of offerings. All should be integrated into assessment schemes and weighted before the bids are assessed.

The above is intended to provide sufficient material to demonstrate that selecting a best value bid is certainly complicated. But also to be noted is that value is subjective, i.e. it depends on one's individual situation, priorities and risk appetite. As all students of US defence acquisition are aware, big projects are often set up to provide employment in virtually all states so that they look like 'good value' to as many members of Congress as possible. In the United Kingdom, what looks like value to the MP for Barrow may look less appealing to a taxpayer in Milton Keynes. Even within the military, in the early years of the Afghan campaign, British Special Forces felt that the Minimi light machine gun was a valuable weapon, while the Army as a whole was inclined to reject it. There are numerous people within the UK armed forces who feel that the carrier strike force is a poor way to use extensive defence resources, whereas others are strongly supportive. Value is subjective.

Finally, value is dynamic in that changing circumstances within and outside defence can change appreciation of a project. The increasing long-range anti-ship capabilities of potential UK adversaries have raised questions about the survivability, and thus value, of surface ships. The Warrior armoured vehicle, designed with operations in mind that were near or on the front line of a fight with Warsaw Pact states, proved very useful as escorts for land-based aid convoys during the Balkan conflicts. Concerns about the United Kingdom's economic prospects after Brexit, as reflected in Chapter 15, have seemingly increased government appreciation of defence projects that yield significant work in the UK. Politicians' readiness to opt for a domestic or foreign supplier may be coloured by the imminence of an election. Many value assessments can change promptly in the light of political, technological and economic developments elsewhere.

12.8 Buying Off-the-Shelf?

The complexity of value throws light on why buying from an overseas production line may not be appealing. It can leave the purchaser dependent on an external supplier for support and for the operational use of a system, and, of course, there are no macroeconomic upsides from such a programme. Modifications may be needed to meet the particular military needs of a supplier; for instance, with regard to climate or the fitting of national communications equipment. If mature systems are bought, then the sooner a potential adversary is likely to generate an offsetting capability. Moreover, proven equipment in production may be more vulnerable to obsolescence issues, and sometimes expensive upgrade commitments to maintain commonality with systems operated by the original supplier state. Currently, the United Kingdom has committed to giving up its Apache D models, intended to be in service for thirty years, and instead 'upgrade' them to the E model, at a cost of $2.3 billion,[25] in part because 'the processing chips that drive the early-model Apache systems are no longer being made'.[26] With regard to the F-35, the United States is planning a continuous upgrade programme which customers will presumably have to buy into or face support problems. No decision is without risk, and while the initial technological risks are less with buying proven systems, other risks are present and appear over time. Finally, not to be forgotten are the foreign exchange risks which brought the British Ministry of Defence a major loss of US dollar purchasing power after the Brexit referendum result.

12.9 Conclusion: The Way Forward

There is no silver bullet for effective and efficient defence. Nevertheless, there are some basic points arising from the above that can be briefly articulated.

First, defence procurement should be directed by wider defence policy, not just in terms of what systems are to be prioritised, but also regarding procurement strategies. UK policy in the 2015 Strategic Defence and Security Strategy was to be 'strong, influential, global', but the external world is unlikely to perceive it as such if it is massively dependent on external suppliers for the support and continued use of its equipment. That would not apply if the key element of the UK approach was to be 'deputy sheriff' of the United States, to use Sven Biscop's phrase.[27]

Second, the Ministry of Defence should see itself as the 'prime contractor' for the generation of defence capability, and not simply as the 'customer' of private firms.[28] Prime contractors of large firms make great efforts to understand and manage their supply chains, recognising that if their business is disrupted by problems in that supply base, their shareholders, customers and other stakeholders will hold them to account for not having managed things well. At present, the Ministry of Defence appears reluctant to recognise this except in the nuclear area.

Third, risk management must be recognised as central in defence acquisition, because any of the three core means of buying things – development and production on a national basis, international collaborative development and production, and buying off-the-shelf from an overseas supplier – have multiple elements that can go wrong, especially once the in-service support dimension is taken into account. The in-service phase also is where most of the money is spent. Risk management is about identifying potential hazards, taking steps to control their likelihood of occurring, the impact if they do occur and monitoring how these hazards evolve over time. It is also about the understanding and articulation of what risks are acceptable to the organisation, and in the case of defence, the country's appetite for different sorts of risk. A key element of risk management is that when ambitious major development projects are under consideration, spending early money on a better understanding of the technical, managerial and financial risks is widely accepted as sensible, yet did not occur in the United States with the F-35, for example.[29] As problems become clearer, the government must be ready either to modify the initial requirement, to change the acquisition numbers, to lengthen the timetable or even to cancel the project before the final targets and public expectations are set. Interestingly, this has been the UK MoD's implicit approach to the F-35, where it is dependent on the United States to deliver. De-risking, however, is not simply a matter of spending a specified percentage of estimated development cost (the UK historical target has been 15 per cent). It also requires a solid understanding of where key risks actually lie and focusing effort on them. Moreover, the rapid advances in civil-origin, but defence-relevant technologies, plus the energetic activities of potential adversaries and rivals (particularly Russia and China), are pushing Western defence ministries to move faster in their acquisition processes. This means an acceptance of taking on more risk, and being ready to write off funds in areas where good progress had been thought possible but proven elusive.

Fourth, in defence, where there is usually one key and initial customer, there must be recognition that if development and production are to be entrusted to the private sector, government and business must work cooperatively from an early stage to increase the chances of acquisition processes going well. This is best understood through a reminder that successful novel products require knowledge in four areas: how key enabling technologies have advanced and will develop; how these technologies work with each other in a functioning system; how much and how long it will take to produce the system as an engineered product, with understood reliability and safety; and what the market will bear – in other words, what the customer would like in terms of capability, performance and cost. In defence, this last element takes the form of a military requirement. Industry and government in practice both have some knowledge in these fields. In somewhat simplified terms, the UK government strives to understand and even advance some key technologies, has a little knowledge of systems integration, possesses little or no understanding of production and engineering, but has excellent awareness of what the customer ideally would like to have. These days, industry is stronger even in understanding key technologies, and at least should know about systems integration and the manufacturing stage. The reader is invited to reflect on the chances of a successful innovative product if government and industry see themselves engaged in a fundamentally adversarial position (when both sides are likely to withhold and even distort important information). This has clear implications for not only how government uses the traditional competitive tendering mechanism, but also for governance and behaviour in publicly listed companies, where short-term profit taking and reduced consciousness of the wider purpose of the business can lead to behaviour damaging to defence.

Finally, given the weight of support costs for platforms and many other major systems, there is a need to address designing for reliability and maintainability more strongly in military requirements. Lack of emphasis in this area increases the probability of the sort of significant problems that have affected the availability of the Type 45 fleet. They also make much more difficult the effective planning of support budgets for new systems, such as the Ajax fleet and of course the F-35.

Defence procurement is about making positive things happen in the future, both in terms of a system being delivered that is affordable to buy and appears useful, and then in terms of its in-service life. But it is a cliché to observe that the future is unknowable with any precision. Overall, things that go wrong in defence acquisition can be attributed either to understood and tolerated hazards coming to pass, or to unforeseen events occurring that could have been anticipated with more thorough research and effort. The public has good cause for complaint when the latter occurs, but needs to recognise that in issues as difficult and complicated as major defence procurements, sometimes the former happens.

References and notes

1. National Audit Office. *Ministry of Defence: Control and Management of the Development of Major Equipment.* HM Stationery Office. Report number: HC568. 1986. 1.

2. National Audit Office. *Ministry of Defence: Major Projects Report 1994.* HM Stationery Office. Report number: HC436. 1995.

3. National Audit Office. *Ministry of Defence: Major Projects Report 2000.* The Stationery Office. Report number: HC970. 2000. www.nao.org.uk/wp-content/uploads/2000/11/9900970.pdf (accessed 7 February 2018).

4. National Audit Office. *Ministry of Defence: Major Projects Report 2010.* The Stationery Office. Report number: HC9489-I. 2010. www.nao.org.uk/wp-content/uploads/2010/10/1011489_I.pdf (accessed 7 February 2018).

5. Parliament.UK. *MPs Report on Ministry of Defence Major Projects 2010.* 2011. www.parliament.uk/business/committees/committees-a-z/commons-select/public-accounts-committee/news/mod-major-projects/ (accessed 7 February 2018).

6. National Audit Office. *Ministry of Defence: initiatives in defence procurement.* HM Stationery Office. Report number: HC189. 1991.

7. In 2014, for example, the Congressional Research service counted 'more than 150 major studies on acquisition reform since World War II' while, in the last three fiscal years, legislators have passed 247 Defense Authorization Act provisions for re-regulating military acquisition. See, S. Reich and P. Dombrowski. 'Has a Trumpian Grand Strategy Finally Stepped into the Light?' *War on the Rocks.* 2018. https://warontherocks.com/2018/01/trumpian-grand-strategy-finally-stepped-light/ (accessed 7 February 2018); J. R. Fox, D. G. Allen, T. C. Lassman, W. S. Moody and P. L. Shiman. 'Defense Acquisition Reform 1960–2009: an Elusive Goal'. *Center for Military History*, United States Army. 2011. www.hbs.edu/faculty/Publication%20Files/11–120_e628824d-3f2d-45bc-9c07-f5b056955e50.pdf (accessed 7 February 2018).

8. Department of Defense. *Better Buying Power: Acquisition, Technology and Logistics.* http://bbp.dau.mil/ (accessed 7 February 2018).

9. Advisory Panel on Streamlining and Codifying Acquisition Regulations. *Section 809 Panel Interim Report.* Section 809 Panel. Report number May 2017. https://section809panel.org/wp-content/uploads/2017/05/Sec809Panel_Interim-Report_May2017_FINAL-for-web.pdf (accessed 7 February 2018).

10. See, Australian Government: Department of Defence. *The Strategic Reform Program 2009: Delivering Force 2030.* 2009. www.defence.gov.au/publications/reformbooklet.pdf (accessed 7 February 2018);

Australian Government: Department of Defence. *Defence: Procurement Review 2003*. 2003. www.defence.gov.au/publications/dpr180903.pdf (accessed 7 February 2018); Australian National Audit Office. *Capability Development Reform: Department of Defence*. Report number 6 of 2013–14. 2013. www.anao.gov.au/sites/g/files/net3721/f/A uditReport_2013–2014_06.pdf (accessed 7 February 2018); Parliament of Australia. Chapter 4: *Challenges for Defence Procurement*. www.aph .gov.au/Parliamentary_Business/Committees/Senate/Foreign_Affairs_De fence_and_Trade/Completed_inquiries/2010–13/procurement/report/c0 4 (accessed 7 February 2018); The Senate Foreign Affairs, Defence and Trade References Committee. *Procurement Procedures for Defence Capital Projects – Final Report*. Parliament of Australia. 2012. www.ap h.gov.au/Parliamentary_Business/Committees/Senate/Foreign_Affairs_ Defence_and_Trade/Completed_inquiries/2010–13/procurement/report/ index (accessed 7 February 2018).

11. J. Grevatt. 'India Updates Defence Procurement Processes'. *Jane's Defence Weekly*. 24 January 2018. 21.

12. B. Pascal. 'To Understand Is to Forgive'. *Goodreads*. 2018. www.good reads.com/quotes/43316-to-understand-is-to-forgive (accessed 7 February 2018).

13. Personal interviews with the two individuals.

14. Ministry of Defence. *The Acquisition Handbook: a Guide to Smart Procurement*. 2nd edn. London: HM Stationery Office. 1999.

15. Ministry of Defence. *The Acquisition Handbook: a Guide to Achieving 'Faster, Cheaper, Better and More Effectively Integrated'*. 6th edn. Smart Acquisition. 2005. 1.

16. The UK operates with four Commands: Joint Force Command, and the Army, Navy and Air Force.

17. T. C. Pierce. Warfighting and Disruptive Technologies: Disguising Innovation. London: Frank Cass. 2004.

18. See, C. Hagel. *Reagan National Defense Forum Keynote*. US Department of Defense, 2014. www.defense.gov/News/Speeches/Speec h-View/Article/606635/ (accessed 7 February 2018); C. Hagel. *The Defense Innovation Initiative*. Department of Defense, USA. 2014. www.defense.gov/Portals/1/Documents/pubs/OSD013411-14.pdf (accessed 7 February 2018); R. Martinage. *Toward a New Offset Strategy: Exploiting U.S. Long-Term Advantages to Restore U.S. Global Power Projection Capability*. Center for Strategic and Budgetary Assessments. 2014. http://csbaonline.org/uploads/docu ments/Offset-Strategy-Web.pdf (accessed 7 February 2018); J. Louth and T. Taylor. *Defence Innovation and the UK: Responding to the Risks Identified by the US Third Offset Strategy*. RUSI Occasional

Paper. 2017. https://rusi.org/sites/default/files/20170707_defence_inno vation_and_the_uk_louth.taylor.tyler_final.pdf (accessed 7 February 2018).

19. The most commonly acknowledged system for capturing the maturity of technologies is the Technology Readiness Levels framework developed originally by NASA to support the development of space exploration systems. See: T. Mai. *Technology Readiness Level*. NASA. 2017. Available from: www.nasa.gov/directorates/heo/scan/engineering/tech nology/txt_accordion1.html (accessed 7 February 2018).

20. House of Commons Committee on Public Accounts. *The Major Projects Report 2010 – Public Accounts Committee Contents*. UK Parliament. 2010. https://publications.parliament.uk/pa/cm201011/cmselect/cmpu bacc/687/10121502.htm (accessed 7 February 2018).

21. SCAF. *A Few Facts about SCAF*. 2017. www.scaf.org.uk/index.html (accessed 7 February 2018).

22. See, B. Freemouw. 'Analogous Estimating versus Parametric Estimating'. PM Learning Solutions. 2018. www.passionatepm.com/blog/analogous-estimating-vs-parametric-estimating-pmp-concept-4 (accessed 7 February 2018); E. Stellwagen. 'Forecasting 101: Forecasting by Analogy'. *Forecastpro*. 2017. www.forecastpro.com/Trends/forecasting101February 2011.html (accessed 7 February 2018); OTexts. '3.5 Forecasting by Analogy'. www.otexts.org/fpp/3/5 (accessed 7 February 2018); K. Green and J. S. Armstrong. 'Structured Analogies for Forecasting'. Scholarly Columns, University of Pennsylvania. 2007. https://repository.upenn.edu/ cgi/viewcontent.cgi?article=1166&context=marketing_papers (accessed 7 February 2018); J. P. Martino. Technological Forecasting for Decision-Making. 3rd edn. USA: McGraw-Hill. 1992.

23. This is because of companies' reluctance to release many of their key assets, i.e. intellectual property, to governments and the costs associated with the sale of corporate IPR to governments. It is also difficult to separate foreground property rights, which a government may have funded, from background rights, i.e. the knowledge that the company brought to a project, enabled it to undertake the development work from an advanced position. See, US Government Accountability Office. *DEFENSE CONTRACTING Early Attention in the Acquisition Process Needed to Enhance Competition*. 2014. www.gao.gov/assets/680/678888.pdf (accessed 7 February 2018); US Government Accountability Office. *WEAPONS ACQUISITION DOD Should Strengthen Policies for Assessing Technical Data Needs to Support Weapon Systems*. 2006. www .gao.gov/new.items/d06839.pdf (accessed 7 February 2018); C. R. Murray. 'Intellectual Property and Technical Data Rights: "It's all about the

money"'. US Army War College. 2012. www.dtic.mil/get-tr-doc/pdf?AD= ADA593245 (accessed 7 February 2018).

24. J. Louth and T. Taylor. 'The Destinations of the Defence Pound'. RUSI Briefing Paper. 2011. https://rusi.org/sites/default/files/destination_ of_the_defence_pound.pdf (accessed 7 February 2018).

25. GOV.UK. *MoD orders new fleet of cutting-edge Apache helicopters for Army.* 2016. www.gov.uk/government/news/mod-orders-new-fleet-of-cutting-edge-apache-helicopters-for-army (accessed 7 February 2018).

26. G. Jennings. 'Augusta Westland Lobbying "Is Delaying Replacement of UK's Apache Fleet"'. Jane's Defence Weekly. 18 March 2015. 15.

27. S. Biscop. 'Brexit, Strategy, and the EU: Britain Takes Leave'. Egmont. Egmont Paper: 100. 2018. 5. www.egmontinstitute.be/content/uploads/ 2018/01/ep100.pdf?type=pdf (accessed 7 February 2018).

28. J. Louth and T. Taylor. 'Beyond the Whole Force: The Concept of the Defence Extended Enterprise and its Implications for the Ministry of Defence'. RUSI Occasional Paper. 2015. https://rusi.org/sites/default/files/ 201510_op_beyond_the_whole_force.pdf (accessed 7 February 2018).

29. US Government Accountability Office. *Defense Acquisitions: Assessment of Selected Weapons Programs.* 2009. 100. www.gao.gov/new.items/d0 9326sp.pdf (accessed 7 February 2018).

13 The Whole-Life Costs of Defence Equipment

DAVID KIRKPATRICK

Introduction

It is 'a truth universally acknowledged' that any individual or organisation considering the acquisition of a new capital asset should consider not only the up-front cost of purchasing the asset, but also all of the subsequent costs associated with the operation and support of the asset. A whole-life approach to acquisition is easiest to implement if the capital asset considered uses mature technology and operates in a predictable environment. These features allow the whole-life cost (WLC) of a company car or a gas-fired power station to be forecast with sufficient accuracy to permit optimisation of the management plans for procurement, operation and support of the asset (and to optimise the design of other bespoke assets), and thus to minimise the asset's WLC.

A whole-life approach is more difficult when the capital asset uses new technology, has a long life cycle or operates in an unpredictable environment. Some of the first generation of motor cars generated large and unpredictable repair bills, and the costs of many pioneering civil engineering and information management projects, such as the UK's Humber Bridge, the Swanwick air-traffic control centre and the electrification of the Great Western Railway, have proved difficult to predict accurately.

A whole-life approach is particularly important for the MoD, which has a relatively large asset base and a correspondingly high capital/labour ratio. The MoD's planned expenditure on major projects is greater than for any other UK government department.[1] Perversely, it is particularly difficult to forecast the procurement cost and the in-service cost of a defence equipment project, because (1) such projects must incorporate the latest (untried) technology, and must operate at the limits of the equipment's capabilities in extreme environments; (2) the project's long life cycle, of several decades from concept to disposal, offers scope for project managers (under pressure from various Service, political and industrial stakeholders and from exogenous events) to make changes to the project plan affecting its specification, period in service, mode of military operations (and hence of peacetime training) and the scope of its mid-life updates and life extension programmes.

Despite the difficulties inherent in costing a defence equipment project, it is nevertheless necessary and appropriate for the MoD to forecast the WLC of the project as accurately as possible, and to use this WLC as the basis of a whole-life approach to project management. If the MoD were to ignore WLC as 'just too difficult', it would unduly favour projects which were cheap to buy but expensive to operate, maintain and repair, and it would fail to budget sufficient funds to support these projects in service.

For several decades the MoD has been trying to promote the use of WLC in project management,[2] with encouragement from the House of Commons Defence Committee, the Treasury and the National Audit Office. The MoD's procedure[3] for Combined Operational Effectiveness and Investment Appraisal (COEIA) mandated the use of WLC in the selection and management of defence equipment projects, and the Smart Acquisition reforms[4] endorsed a whole-life approach to project management. The latest MoD guidelines[5] insist that a WLC must be included in any project proposal.

The MoD annually acquires a large and varied range of goods and services to sustain its military capabilities to defend the United Kingdom and its vital interests overseas. This chapter focuses on major defence equipment projects, characterised by large budgets and long life cycles, and defines the WLC of such projects which should be used to guide project management decisions. It also presents the preferred methodology for forecasting WLC and discusses the obstacles which impede the forecasting process. If a project's WLC is assessed carelessly, or is not assessed at all, the MoD will incur higher costs which consequently raise the opportunity cost of defence to society.

13.1 The Components of Whole-Life Cost

The WLC of a defence equipment project includes the costs of all the activities which are directly associated with the project considered and which are undertaken within the MoD and its industrial contractors.

This definition excludes any share of the fixed cost of the MoD's organisation, and of any costs incurred through its support (if any) for a national defence technology and industrial base. The eleven components of a project's WLC are incurred during different phases of its life cycle (though there is some overlap in time scales). The components cover different activities and are principally dependent on different features of the project plan. The six cost components forming the procurement cost are as follows:

- **Concept:** defines the customer Services requirement and alternative technical and procurement strategy options; the cost depends on the number and complexity of alternative options.
- **Assessment:** identifies the most promising option from within multiple alternatives and defines the appropriate risk management strategies; the cost depends on the number of options to be compared and on the scale of associated risk reduction work required.
- **Demonstration:** defines the equipment design and procurement strategy of the chosen option in detail, formulates a plan for Integrated Logistic Support (ILS) and undertakes test and evaluation of prototypes if applicable; the cost depends on the number of prototypes and on the scale and complexity of trials.
- **Production investment:** procurement of special-to-type jigs, tools and production facilities; the cost depends on the planned rate and scale of production, and on any innovations in the manufacturing processes.
- **Manufacturing:** produces and delivers the required number of units; the cost depends on the scale and complexity of the equipment, and on the number of items to be produced.
- **Operational investment:** procurement of simulators, initial spares, tools and test equipment, and implementation of plans for ILS; the cost depends on the number of units deployed and on the sophistication of their design.

The cost of operational investment is largely determined by the planned deployment and operation of the equipment, and might logically be regarded as an in-service cost; however, that cost is incurred in the procurement time scale, so it is customary to class it as one of the components of procurement cost. Ideally, arrangements for ILS should include a seamless supply chain from 'factory to foxhole', but inevitably the customer Service's control of the first stages in this supply chain is limited (to the legally enforceable conditions in the industrial supplier's contract). The five cost components which are incurred later constitute the in-service cost, and are as follows:

- **Operations:** peacetime training and exercises sufficient to maintain operator skills (wartime deployment, military operations and repatriation are generally covered by special grants from the Treasury); the cost depends on the intensity of training, the quantities of fuel and ordnance used, the operating environment and the duration of operational service.
- **Support:** repair and maintenance of equipment in the field, at a depot and in major overhauls; the cost depends on the equipment's reliability and maintainability, the quantity of spares used, the logistics arrangements and the duration of operational service.
- **Post and continuing design:** design and implementation of modifications to correct problems emerging in operational service and to achieve target performance, respectively; the cost depends on the rigour of the Assessment and Demonstration phases and of the subsequent field trials.
- **Mid-life upgrade(s):** substantial redesign and implementation work to upgrade the performance of the equipment in response to changes in the threat or in relevant technologies; the cost depends on the scale of such changes and on the difficulty of integrating new subsystems.
- **Disposal by scrappage or by export sales to allied nations:** cost of disposal depends on current controls on the disposal of radioactive and other toxic materials; revenue depends on the price of recycled materials or on the market demand for the equipment considered.

In the MoD, management of all eleven phases is called acquisition (though in common English, 'acquisition' describes a transfer of ownership and is thus synonymous with procurement and purchase). In former times, the Service customer's plans for the operation and support of the equipment tended to lag behind the technical work on its design and development, so any forecast of in-service cost was vague. The current emphasis on using WLC for project management requires that the likely costs of operations and support must be considered sufficiently early in the project's life cycle to influence the equipment's design towards more economical support, and thus to minimise its WLC.

The MoD currently divides the life cycle of a defence equipment project into the six phases earlier highlighted (Concept, Assessment, Demonstration, Manufacturing, In-service and Disposal, collectively known by the acronym CADMID), but cost analysts must use a larger number of cost components because they are separately determined by different characteristics of the project considered.

The MoD's process for approving the start of a project, based on forecasts of its operational effectiveness and of its WLC, takes no account of any potential macroeconomic effects on the UK economy at national or regional level, nor of any consequent favourable or unfavourable impact on the United Kingdom's balance of trade, nor of any prospect of additional economic growth from the application of dual-use technologies developed during the project.[6] Similarly, it takes no explicit account of social and environmental issues, though these are assessed in parallel if practicable. If the project is large enough to be debated at Cabinet level, the ministers leading other government departments may introduce such macroeconomic, social and environ-mental considerations into the debate, and these inevitably attract attention from the media.

The activities within the above phases are undertaken by the MoD, its agencies and industrial contractors. The allocation of activities depends on the class of equipment considered, but generally follows the pattern shown in Table 13.1.

In all phases of a project, the MoD retains overall responsibility for decisions affecting its performance, time scale and cost. In recent years, notably with the privatisation of the Royal Dockyards and Royal Ordnance Factories and most of the Defence Evaluation and Research Agency (DERA) and with the introduction of Public Private Partnership/Private Finance Initiative (PPP/PFI) contracts (defined and evaluated in Chapter 3), industrial contractors have undertaken an increasing share of the work on UK defence equipment projects.

An enhancement of UK military capability arises not only from the entry of new equipment into service but also from the integration of additional synchronised 'lines of development', known by the acronym TEPIDOIL, as introduced in Chapter 12. The costs associated with all

Table 13.1 *Allocation of activities in defence projects*

MoD and agencies	Private contractors
Concept	
Assessment	
	Demonstration
	Production investment
	Manufacturing
Operational investment	
Operation	
Front-line support	Major overhauls
	Post and continuing design
	Mid-life upgrades
Sales to allied nations	Recycling of materials

Source: author

eight lines of development should be included within the project's WLC. In former times, some of the non-equipment lines were occasionally forgotten, or were assumed to be part of someone else's budget, and in those cases the project's WLC was incomplete; today, the acronym TEPIDOIL serves as a checklist.

Some of the project's cost components (such as Operations and Support) vary in proportion to the number of units deployed and with the duration of their active service. Other components (such as Concept, Assessment and Demonstration) are virtually fixed. Components in a third category are variable but benefit from economies of scale. A notable example of this third category is Manufacturing, where the unit cost falls as the number of items produced is increased, in accordance with the theory of the 'learning curve'. This theory has been derived from the observation that in many types of manufacturing the unit cost falls by a given percentage (often 10–15 per cent, but less if the process relies heavily on automatic machinery) whenever the scale of production is doubled, with the result that workers become accustomed to their tasks and accordingly more skilful. It is important to distinguish between the average unit WLC of the project and the (smaller) marginal unit WLC, which determines the financial impact of any alteration in the number of units procured.

Many of the eleven components of WLC are linked so that any change in the project's specification or in its management arrangements can affect several components. For example, anything affecting the unit cost of manufacture would also affect the unit cost of prototypes and of spares. Some WLC components are funded from the budgets of different Service branches, so it is important that all of the branches involved maintain close liaison to ensure that all are aware of changes to the project plan which might significantly affect its costs.

13.2 Myths About Whole-Life Costs

It is unfortunate that outside the corridors of power the WLC of defence projects is largely unknown and ignored, and that most public debate on such projects focuses on their up-front procurement costs (exceptionally, anti-nuclear campaigners have often cited their forecasts of the WLC of the UK's nuclear deterrent forces). In recent years the MoD has begun to publish its forecasts of the WLC of some major projects,[7] but so far these 'additional' costs have attracted little public attention. The relative obscurity of the WLC of most projects has allowed the genesis of several myths.

It is often claimed that the in-service cost of projects is invariably much larger than their procurement cost (generally illustrated by the picture of an iceberg with 10 per cent of its mass above the waterline and labelled procurement, and 90 per cent below the waterline, labelled support). In fact, the procurement/in-service cost ratio of a defence project varies widely depending on the scale and complexity of the project considered, the intensity of peacetime (training) operations, the equipment's fragility and the numbers of operating and support personnel involved. The ratio of planned procurement/support expenditure on different classes of UK defence equipment in 2016–17[8] varied from 0.3 for air support to 2.0 for complex weapons, and the variation would doubtless be even greater for individual projects. In the United States, the average procurement/support ratio is about 0.5;[9] however, for UK projects, with diseconomies of small scale and more dominant fixed costs, the average ratio is probably about unity. Hence, the procurement elements of the WLCs of UK defence equipment are often much more significant than the upper (visible) part of an iceberg.

It is also claimed that a project's WLC is largely determined by decisions (e.g. on its design and ILS) early in its life cycle. These decisions do indeed have a large effect, but the project's total WLC can also be significantly affected by later decisions about its period in service and about the scale of any mid-life upgrades, by operational experience of its reliability and maintainability in service, and also by variations in monetary inflation and foreign exchange rates over several decades.

More myths can arise from facile assumptions about the relationships between different components of WLC. For example, it has been observed that the development cost (broadly covering the Assessment and Demonstration phases) of a good number of new defence equipment projects, in a particular class, has been approximately proportional to the average unit production cost (UPC) of the first batch produced (see Table 13.2). This is plausible because the development of a large and complex project within that class, which has a high UPC, generally requires extensive theoretical and experimental work, and also trials involving expensive prototypes. But this rule of thumb only applies to those projects which have been preceded by a similar project of the same class and/or by a demonstrator programme. It is dangerous to apply the same rule if the new project involves any significant innovation (in, for instance, layout and propulsion), because in such cases development cost is likely to be considerably higher, as shown below.

There is no alternative to assessing the WLC of each new defence equipment project based on its own individual characteristics, though the relationships derived from preceding projects provide a helpful comparison.

Table 13.2: *Development cost variation*

Class of defence equipment	Typical number in first batch	Development cost/UPC Conventional design	Development cost/UPC Innovative design
Surface warship	5	0.4	2.5
Airframe	100	80	140
Guided weapon	1000	1600	5000

Source: Pugh PG. *Performance-based cost estimating.* London: Unpublished conference paper: 1994.

13.3 Uses of Whole-Life Costs

The WLC forecast for a defence equipment project should be used for several different purposes through the different phases of the project's life cycle, such as:

- After high-level force-mix studies have determined that a particular class of equipment should be procured to meet the customer Service's requirement, WLC forecasts should be used to decide between alternative options within that class; in practice, such decisions may be constrained by the need to avoid excessive fluctuations in annual expenditure.
- When the overall characteristics of the new project have been determined, WLC forecasts should be used to optimise its design and thus to achieve the maximum effectiveness/cost ratio, and to select the most economical procurement and support arrangements.
- At all stages of the project's life cycle, its WLC forecast for the next several years must be compared with the customer Service's planned budget, and with the likely WLC of other concurrent projects, to ensure that all the planned projects are affordable.
- During any Strategic Defence and Security Review, the project's forecast WLC can be combined with those of other current and future projects contributing to a particular military capability to identify the long-term ongoing cost of that capability.

The Concept phase considers alternative methods of meeting the customer Service's requirement for enhanced military capability. In this phase it is necessary to forecast:

- Operational effectiveness and the WLC of alternative options, including an upgrade of the customer Service's existing equipment,
- Off-the-shelf purchase of equipment in service with an allied nation (perhaps with national modifications), or
- New bespoke equipment requiring an extensive development and trials programme.

Forecasts of the WLCs of these alternative options are inevitably approximate, since none of the options are well defined at this Concept stage, and their forecast effectiveness against enemy systems in credible future scenarios is also uncertain. However, these broad-brush forecasts are generally sufficiently accurate to select the most promising option with the best available effectiveness/cost ratio. The robustness of this selection should be tested by plausible variations in the assumptions driving the performance and cost of the various options considered. In this selection process the WLC of each alternative option should be expressed as the net present value (NPV) of the annual discounted expenditure through that option's life cycle, in accordance with Treasury guidance on investment appraisal. If £(t) is the real expenditure in year t,

$$NPV = \Sigma \, £(t)/(1 + r)^t$$

where r is the current discount rate (as specified by the Treasury's guidance).[10] The selection of the most promising option should be based on comparison of the NPV of the alternatives, but in practice the selection may be constrained by limits on the MoD's budgets available in some critical years; such constraints can sometimes be overcome by a PFI, if it offers good value for money. In the early phases of a project, when forecasts of the WLC of alternative options are compared, it is more important and significant that the differences between the forecasts are robust rather than that the WLC forecast of any of the options is correct in absolute terms.

In the Assessment phase and in other later phases, forecasts of the WLC of the selected project (expressed as NPVs) are needed to guide decisions (on, for instance, design and integrated logistic support) which will maximise the project's effectiveness/cost ratio. In such studies of alternatives, it is convenient to omit from the WLC forecasts those costs which are sunk (already spent or irretrievably committed) and those costs which are fixed (such as infrastructure), and any other costs which would be unaffected by the project decisions considered. Such WLC forecasts should *always* be accompanied by caveats explaining that they are incomplete.

In all phases of the project, the customer Service must ensure that the WLC of the selected project will fit within the customer Service's planned budget. This WLC forecast must include all sunk and fixed costs, and should be expressed as the time profile of annual expenditures, with particular attention to any awkward peaks (for budget management the project's total WLC is almost irrelevant). The annual expenditures should be expressed in monetary or real (i.e. inflation adjusted) values, depending on how the planned future budget is defined. The customer Service's budgetary planning must take account of all interfaces between the WLC of the project considered and the WLCs of all current and future projects which are or will be in the Service's inventory. All such interfaces must be identified and allocated for management to one or other of the projects involved, and their associated costs must be included in the WLC of one of those projects.

Budgetary provision for future equipment projects must be made at the beginning of the Concept phase, some years before any significant expenditure on the project, when the equipment is not well defined and when the WLC forecast is inevitably imprecise. However, even at this early stage, it is generally possible to forecast with useful accuracy the annual expenditures on the project over the next several years. Fortunately, budget planners are principally concerned about the costs to be incurred over the next several years (the MoD's Equipment Plan forecasts procurement and support costs over the next decade). Beyond that period, budget planning may well be disrupted by economic or geopolitical crises, or by a new government amending the budgets which it has inherited.

In preparation for any SDSR, the time profile of the WLC of any particular project should be combined with the profiles of other concurrent projects, which together contribute to a particular military capability, to determine the ongoing annual costs of that capability. The annual costs of carrier strike capability, for example, would include the WLCs of one or more aircraft carriers, of a quota of antiaircraft and antisubmarine escorts, of supply ships to sustain operations in distant oceans, of embarked air wings with their ordnance and of organic surveillance and communications systems. The cost of a military capability should include, in principle, the costs of sustaining a national technology base and a national industrial base, if these are regarded as essential parts of the capability; in practice, such costs are a negligible fraction of the total capability costs. The ongoing costs of all desirable military capabilities can then be considered in any future SDSR, prioritising which capabilities the United Kingdom should retain. Such a review should address the security of the United Kingdom in the short, medium and long term, and accordingly needs to consider the total WLCs of all the projects contributing to the military capability considered.

13.4 Obstacles to Using WLC

It is regrettable (but understandable) that ministers and military officers, who have responsibility for a defence project for only a small fraction of its life cycle, should be most interested in its short-term cost. Their indifference to WLC represents the primary obstacle to the analysis, forecasting and application of such costs in the MoD.

When important decisions must be made early in the life cycle of a defence equipment project, the forecast of its WLC is inherently inaccurate because the project is then ill defined and its project plan may change. Such uncertainty is anathema to many military officers, engineers and accountants who are accustomed to exactitude, who are less tolerant of nebulous estimates than economists or social scientists and who may regard WLC as 'too difficult'. Such officers and officials sometimes prefer to present separately a forecast of procurement cost and a less accurate forecast of in-service cost of each alternative option; they are then inclined to take decisions based on the forecasts of procurement cost, and to use the forecasts of the options' in-service costs (along with political, diplomatic and industrial factors) as tie-breakers. In 2004, the National Audit Office concluded[11] that some project teams had difficulty in applying the MoD's preferred methodology by using WLC, and that the WLC data presented were immature and were unable to support decision making. Even in 2015, the NAO regretted that the MoD's forecasts of support costs were not well developed.[12]

Another obstacle is that responsibility for the different phases of a project is divided between several different MoD branches, with different priorities and budgets.[13] These branches are therefore inclined to focus on their own areas of responsibility rather than on the total WLC, and may be reluctant to share data. This blinkered approach was encouraged in former times by the traditional view that the point of sale was a watershed by which an asset passed from its manufacturer to a new owner, who then managed its operation and support. However, in the modern world, it is increasingly advantageous to integrate design, manufacture and support in order to minimise the total WLC of a product; aero-engine manufacturers are now paid for hours of engine availability, and take overall charge of delivery, maintenance and replacement of engines, as required, to ensure that commercial transport aircraft achieve high productivity.

13.5 Forecasting Whole-Life Costs

As part of its assessment of any new defence equipment project, the customer Service must generate a forecast of the project's WLC. The earliest WLC forecasts are inevitably approximate because only very limited information is available at that stage, and must be reviewed and improved later; as additional information becomes available, successive forecasts should be increasingly accurate. However, even approximate WLC forecasts in the early phases of a project can provide the customer Service with advance warning of potential problems with, for example, inadequate infrastructure and shortages of personnel, and can indicate whether one design or management option is better than another.

If the customer Service has a cooperative rather than an adversarial relationship with the industrial prime contractor, some components of the current Service forecast can be compared with the corresponding components of the prime contractor's own forecast to identify and resolve any major discrepancies. If the discrepancies cannot be resolved, both forecasts should be submitted to the MoD authority with responsibility for approving funds; that authority may choose to delay final approval until an independent review has assessed the credibility of both forecasts and has made its own recommendation.

The forecast of any component of the project's WLC should follow the following procedure:

(1) Formulate a list of all current data, assumptions and plans relevant to the project which might affect its WLC, e.g. technical description, procurement strategy, delivery schedules, intensity of operations and plans for ILS. It is often convenient to display data and assumptions in different fonts to ensure that all stakeholders recognise what is known and what is not. The formulation of this list, and securing the agreement of all stakeholders, can involve considerable time and debate, especially if there are important Service or industrial interests involved.

(2) Collect and analyse the known cost data on historic projects in the same class as the project considered; the analysis should put these data on a common basis by adjusting for monetary inflation, foreign exchange rates, lengths of production runs and any other circumstances which vary from one project to another.

(3) For each particular component of a project's WLC, identify the project characteristics (called cost drivers) which have a dominant effect on that cost component; for example, the manufacturing cost of an armoured fighting vehicle is driven largely by its mass.

(4) Derive a cost forecasting relationship (CFR) linking the values of that cost component in historic projects to the values of the cost drivers for those projects.

(5) Use the CFR and the known and assumed characteristics of the new project to derive a forecast of that cost component, and adjust that forecast to reflect any unique features of the new project.

(6) Use the scatter of the CFR (or a risk analysis of the new project if available) to derive upper and lower confidence limits for the forecast cost of the WLC component considered.

(7) Repeat the final three steps for all cost components and combine the results to obtain the project's total WLC.

It is important that the forecasting process should be transparent so that all the project's stakeholders are aware of the data, assumptions and plans used by the forecasters and can make alternative inputs as necessary. It is also helpful if all stakeholders are aware of the likely financial consequences of particular design and management decisions, and thus able to consider trade-offs which could increase the project's effectiveness/cost ratio. This forecasting process can be undertaken at different levels of detail according to the information then available about the project's design and performance characteristics, and about the current plans for its procurement, operation and support. For example, the manufacturing cost can be forecast at system, subsystem or work package level:

- A system forecast can be based on some of the proposed system's leading design or performance characteristics, such as the payload or speed of a vehicle. This forecast can be derived in the Concept phase as soon as the initial design has been formulated.

- Later, when the project's design has developed sufficiently to define the characteristics of its subsystems, the cost of these sub-systems can be forecast individually and then added, with a due allowance for assembly and integration, to obtain a more accurate forecast of the system cost.

- Later still, when the project plan has been formulated sufficiently to define the required work packages and the bought-in components and materials, a rigorous forecast can be assembled at that detailed level. Such forecasts cannot be made at the early stages of the project when many important decisions are made, but may contribute to later contractual negotiations.

All cost forecasts should be accompanied by confidence limits, indicating a 90 per cent probability that the actual cost will fall between the upper and lower limits; it is regrettable that even today the forecast costs of one third of the MoD's major projects lack confidence limits.[14] The gap between the upper and lower limits reflects the uncertainties within the project plan and the risks associated with successive phases of the project. It is important, when combining the forecasts and confidence limits of the individual cost components, to obtain a forecast of the total WLC. This is required for the cost forecasters to appreciate that the cost components are not independent, and that adverse events in one project phase may also affect other phases; the confidence limits on the total WLC must take account of such interactions between cost components. It may be desirable in the Concept and Assessment phases to undertake additional research and demonstration work specifically in order to increase the accuracy of the current WLC forecast, and thus to reduce the gap between the upper and lower confidence limits, even if that additional work increases the likely time and cost of those phases. Such work may also help to identify, assess and mitigate the various technical and other risks associated with the project, as well as providing greater confidence in the WLC forecast as a basis for decision making. However, it is notorious that in recent years the cost forecasts of several defence projects, in the United Kingdom and in other nations, have proved to be incorrect. The reasons are numerous, but include:

- Errors due to random variations in exogenous variables (such as weather and accidents), but these errors should be small and unbiased and so can be accommodated within departmental budgets.
- Serious errors arising when inexperienced forecasters have omitted an important cost component, have used obsolete methodology or unjustified assumptions, or have optimistically underrated the problems inherent in the special features of the project, e.g. advanced technology and/or innovative management arrangements.

- Sanguine optimism of a work-hungry contractor, which has been enthusiastically endorsed by the customer Service, seeking to make its cherished project more attractive than the others competing for limited MoD funds; on such occasions, forceful arguments from the customer Service and the industrial contractor have impelled an unrealistic forecast to be submitted for approval of funding for the project. This 'conspiracy of optimism' has inevitably yielded universal embarrassment and vociferous public criticism when the real difficulties became evident, and more realistic cost forecasts have led to drastic changes to the project plan, and even occasionally to cancellation.

To counteract such lapses, it is essential that the decision-makers responsible for approving funding for any large defence project should have access to expert and independent advice (either from an intramural unit or an extramural consultancy) on the likely WLC of the project. However, other variations in the forecast WLC can arise at any stage during a project's life cycle from the inherent divergence between the objectives of the customer Service and the MoD's bureaucrats. Military officers want the units under their command to be highly effective in any conflict, and to demonstrate high reliability and availability in peacetime exercises and inspections. These qualities are achieved by ambitious requirements and rigorous design specifications, and by the lavish provision of, for instance, support personnel and spares. On the other hand, the bureaucrats (and their political masters) are always anxious to reduce costs, wherever practicable, to overcome recurrent crises which beset the defence budget. Short-term savings can always be achieved by degrading equipment specification, deferring or curtailing some work packages, or diluting logistic support. Such measures would be unacceptable in wartime, but in peacetime any adverse effects are difficult to evaluate, and it may be expedient for politicians to ignore them. WLC forecasters can calculate (albeit approximately) the financial consequences of alternative policies, but cannot predict which will be adopted in each case. Accordingly, it is important that every WLC forecast is chaperoned by a comprehensive list of the assumptions from which it is derived.

Yet other variations in a project's WLC, between approval and disposal, can arise when the customer Service has responded constructively and reasonably to unexpected extramural changes (in the available budget, the relevant technologies, the characteristics of associated projects or of the threat) by altering its plan for the project. Such alterations might affect the time scale of procurement, technical specification and the scale of the planned fleet. Some such alterations have affected the United Kingdom's current procurement of Queen Elizabeth Class aircraft carriers. These apparent errors are not the fault of the contractor, the customer Service or the forecasters, but they are all often blamed anyway.

13.6 Special Cases with Extra Complexity

On some projects the MoD has sought to exploit the private sector's management skills and access to capital by negotiating a PFI contract by which a contractor agrees to fund and operate MoD non-core activities. For example, the MoD needs a supply of trained pilots, but it does not need to invest in and to operate flight simulators. A contractor which agrees to provide such facilities and training can, in principle, use those facilities for other civilian business, and can thus achieve economies of scale. If such a contract is in place for the Training component of TEPIDOIL, the contract's terms may specify a fixed fee per pilot, because the private contractor has assumed some of the risk. However, any forecast of this cost component must include provision for the preservation of sufficient expertise in the MoD to monitor the contractor's performance rigorously, and to recreate very promptly the training programme (if necessary within the MoD) if the contactor were to cease trading. A PFI contract is only really practicable if the service to be provided is predictable so that risks are relatively small, and if it can be defined in legally enforceable terms; anything which might involve the contractor's assets in a combat situation is unlikely to be acceptable. Public Private Partnerships present similar difficulties.

Forecasting the WLC of an off-the-shelf purchase of equipment already developed and being produced by a trusted allied nation should, in principle, be relatively straightforward. When the MoD needs to forecast the WLC of this equipment, the manufacturing cost has already been determined by the supplier's experience of producing the first batches, and the allied nation's armed forces have obtained some data on the equipment's in-service reliability and maintainability. It is necessary to establish whether or not there is any need for further trials to satisfy the United Kingdom's own release-to-service rules, and whether or not the allied government will impose an export levy to offset part of its earlier expenditure on development of the equipment. But, even after these issues are resolved during the initial negotiations, there remain additional uncertainties about whether it is necessary to make a lifetime buy of spares and/or to create a UK-based 'daughter contractor' capable of undertaking repair and maintenance work to avoid over-reliance on a distant supplier with other priorities, whether any modifications to the equipment might be required to suit UK operational doctrine and/or to ensure satisfactory interfaces with current UK equipment in service, whether the UK government is minded to agree with UK industry lobbyists that one or more foreign subsystems should be replaced by UK-sourced equivalents (which can be a very costly process) and whether there may be future fluctuations in foreign exchange rates. Ideally most of these uncertainties should be resolved during contract negotiations, but only after the initial WLC forecast has been made.

Forecasting the WLC of projects delivered and produced in collaboration between the United Kingdom and one or more allied nations presents particularly difficult challenges: firstly in forecasting the likely total WLC of the project, and secondly in agreeing the share of the cost to be paid by the MoD. Forecasters must understand the different cultures and procurement procedures (budgetary and bureaucratic) of the collaborating nations, and must appreciate any differences in their traditional practices for disaggregating costs and in their associated cost breakdown terminologies. Languages form additional barriers to dialogue, even between the United Kingdom and the United States. The forecast of the WLC of a collaborative project must make allowance for the costs of an international project management team, for the misallocation of work packages to satisfy political rather than economic considerations and for the delays arising from political or budgetary problems in one or other of the collaborating nations. Even after the several customer Services have agreed a mutually acceptable statement of their national operational requirements and the numbers to be delivered for their respective fleets, forecasters must make assumptions on whether Assessment and Demonstration will be faster because of access to a wider knowledge base and more test facilities (or slower because of chauvinistic disputes), whether nations will unreservedly accept the results of their partners' trials and demonstrations or will insist on duplicating such work (to satisfy their own criteria), whether some aspects of production investment, such as final assembly facilities, need to be created in all of the collaborating nations to sustain their prestige, and whether spares holdings and other aspects of ILS can be organised on an international basis, yielding economies of scale.

International collaboration can yield operational benefits if two or more allies are using the same equipment in a particular theatre of operations, but these benefits are difficult to evaluate and are generally neglected when the effectiveness/cost of an international collaborative project is compared with an independent national project.

At present, defence equipment projects are launched less frequently than before, a modern defence equipment project remains in service for longer periods and can be upgraded one or more times during its service life. It is advisable that a WLC forecast should make financial provision for upgrades which are characteristic in scale and frequency for the class of equipment considered (rather than making no financial provision and thus tacitly assuming that no upgrades will be required). Alternatively, a large-scale upgrade to a complex type of equipment (such as the Tornado's Mid-Life Upgrade) can be treated as a project in its own right, with its own WLC covering the design, development and installation of new subsystems and any consequent increments in the costs of operations and support through the remainder of the Tornado's service life. The WLC of a substantial mid-life upgrade is difficult to forecast because all such upgrades are different and data on previous upgrades are unhelpful. The cost of a particular mid-life upgrade depends on its scale and on the detailed design features of the equipment to be upgraded; integration of new subsystems can present a range of problematic mechanical, thermal, electrical and electronic interfaces. Potential problems at these interfaces, and how they can effectively be overcome, must be identified by detailed design work before the budget for a mid-life update can confidently be approved.

13.7 Some Challenges in Whole-Life Cost Forecasting

The forecasting process can be difficult because data on previous projects within the class of equipment considered are often scarce, incomplete, shrouded by commercial confidentiality or distorted by special circumstances. In former times, the MoD's expenditure on equipment in service was classified in terms of its inputs (for instance, labour and fuel), and the three customer Services collected in-service data in different ways and in different levels of detail, reflecting their different operating environments. In recent years, there has been greater emphasis on linking costs to specific types of equipment and to specific military activities. Simultaneously, new technology has made it easier for hard-pressed support staff to record the duration and nature of their repair and maintenance activities.

WLC forecasting is particularly difficult when the project considered is large, or has a long gestation period, or seeks to exploit some innovative technologies and/or contractual arrangements. Forecasters should make due allowance for probable delays when the project has many stakeholders with the power to interfere, when the project is (for political reasons?) relying on inexperienced contractors and when the progress of the project considered is dependent on the successful and timely completion of other concurrent projects. Many major defence projects have these characteristics.

WLC forecasting becomes virtually impossible if the project team lacks personnel with sufficient expertise, or if it cannot easily access good advice, or if some of the stakeholders are uncooperative. Officers who are expert in particular areas, such as ILS, may be fully occupied in supporting ongoing combat operations, and hence reluctant to give serious attention to forecasting costs which will be incurred many years into the future. Even before the recent cuts in personnel, the MoD had insufficient forecasters with adequate training, education and expertise, and often forecasters have been too overwhelmed by immediate crises to allocate time for professional development or to learn lessons from their predecessors' errors.

WLC forecasting is today becoming more challenging because the development cost of successive new projects has grown more rapidly than most national defence budgets, and hence defence projects are undertaken less frequently. The decline in the birth rate of new equipment projects is in sharp contrast to the continuing rapid development of most defence-related technologies. Accordingly, the data on past projects has become less relevant due to the impact of new technologies, to the adoption of diverse contractual arrangements and to the many intervening changes in the organisation and methods of the supplying industries. Furthermore, in the period between one project and its successor in a particular class, much valuable expertise in the customer Service and in the relevant industrial contractors may be lost through the retirement of key staff, making it more difficult for their less-experienced successors to anticipate problems and overcome them efficiently. Finally, the MoD's intermittent adoption of adversarial relationships with its contractors has damaged the traditionally cooperative customer/supplier relationships, which formerly encouraged information exchange (but were criticised as unduly 'cosy').

Some of the difficulties in WLC forecasting might be partially overcome by the creation of an expert and independent forecasting group responsible for the collection and analysis of data on historic and current projects. It should also review post-project evaluations of current projects to identify any flaws in the cost forecasting for those projects, and disseminate the lessons learned to other project teams (as has been attempted in the United Kingdom by the National Audit Office's annual Major Project Reports). If this specialist group also undertakes WLC forecasting for some projects (where small project teams may lack the required expertise), it *must* have sufficient personnel to allow its analytical work to be sustained.

13.8 Conclusion

The WLCs of defence equipment projects are essential inputs to the planning and management of national defence. They contribute to the selection of equipment for the armed Services, to the optimisation of the chosen equipment's design and acquisition and to the proper management of the MoD's budget. The WLC of each project must be forecast during its Concept phase, and must be regularly updated as more definitive information on the equipment becomes available.

The assembly of a whole-life cost forecast requires both the suppliers and the customer Service to give due attention to *all* the cost components of the equipment itself and to the costs of *all* associated non-equipment lines of development. Failure to consider all such costs in time to influence the equipment's design might yield equipment which would be expensive to operate and support, and which would be difficult to deploy and sustain in a remote theatre of operations.

Although the MoD has been trying for several decades to implement a whole-life approach (using WLCs) in the management of defence equipment projects, it has encountered significant obstacles. WLCs are even more difficult to forecast than procurement costs, and are inevitably less accurate; they are therefore unpopular with decision-makers unaccustomed to nebulous data. Furthermore, many of the MoD's ministers, officers and officials (in post for only a few years) instinctively give greater attention to short-term costs which could affect their reputations and career prospects, and less attention to long-term costs which are largely beyond their responsibility. These and other obstacles have hindered the adoption of a whole-life approach. Until recently the WLC data presented by the MoD was dismissed as unfit to support decision making, and even today not all of the MoD's major projects can present satisfactory WLC forecasts.

The actual WLC of a defence equipment project may turn out to be different from the forecast made when the project was originally approved, for a number of reasons. The causes of such differences include errors and omissions by forecasters, unanticipated technological or managerial problems, a conspiracy of optimism between the suppliers and the customer Service generating a spuriously low cost forecast, unexpected variations in the prices of labour, materials and other inputs and deliberate alterations in the customer Service's project plan in response to changes in the political, economic or technological environments during the project's long life cycle. Ideally, all but the last of these causes should be virtually eliminated by rigorously professional cost forecasting and risk management screening, but in practice forecasters and project managers are not infallible.

Even though the actual WLC may sometimes differ from its forecast, it is nevertheless proper that the project approval process should be based on the best WLC forecast then available, accompanied by appropriate confidence limits. Similarly, a credible and transparent WLC forecast is an essential input to project management decisions within the MoD and its contractors. Such decisions must take due account of the definitions, assumptions and caveats accompanying the WLC forecast. It can be almost as humiliating to misapply a poorly understood forecast as to tie a 'granny knot' on the north face of the Eiger. Although some unenlightened Service officers deride 'playing shops', WLC forecasting is vitally important to the success of defence equipment projects.

References and notes

1. National Audit Office. *MoD Departmental Overview 2015–16.* London: TSO. 2016.
2. ManTIS. *Defence Life Cycle Costing – Introduction and Guide.* Unpublished paper. April 1974.
3. Ministry of Defence. *Guidelines for the Conduct of COEIAs and Requirement Definition Studies.* Unpublished paper. April 1996.
4. Ministry of Defence. *The Strategic Defence Review Supporting Essay 10.* London: TSO. July 1988.
5. Ministry of Defence. *Guide to Investment Appraisal and Evaluation (JSP 507).* London: TSO. January 2014. 3.
6. Ministry of Defence. *Guide to Investment Appraisal and Evaluation.* 18.
7. National Audit Office. MoD Departmental Overview. London: TSO. July 2015. 25.
8. Ministry of Defence. *The Defence Equipment Plan* 2016. London: TSO. 27 January 2017. paras 38–69.
9. W. Cooper. 'O&S Costs Represent Largest Fraction of Life Cycle Cost, by Far'. Unpublished Boeing Co. chart. 2008.
10. HM Treasury. *Economic Appraisal in Central Government.* London: TSO. April 1991.
11. National Audit Office. *MoD Major Projects Report 2003.* London: TSO. January 2004. Appendix 7.
12. National Audit Office. *MoD Major Projects Report 2015.* London: TSO. October 2015. 10.
13. House of Commons Defence Committee. *Defence Procurement.* London: TSO. July 2014. para 57.
14. National Audit Office. *MoD Major Projects Report 2015.* 9.

14 Economic and Political Dimensions of the Defence Industry Supply Chain Revolution

DEREK BRADDON

Introduction

Over the last thirty years, the global defence sector has experienced a major transformation in almost every aspect – industrial structure, geographical location, technological focus, military strategic planning and the wider role of government in policy making in the defence arena. These events have affected, and in turn been affected, by the need for constrained defence budgets and consequent NATO burden sharing pressures, the emergence of new and expensive technologies and associated military capabilities – further stretching those limited budgets, and even the need to re-define who or what actually constitutes 'the enemy' and how best to combat this foe in the global environment.

In response to these new challenges, the defence industrial supply base has had to adjust quickly and effectively to the changing global environment, and, as a result, both prime defence contractors and national governments have driven forward major changes in their provision of defence over the period. At the heart of this business and policy revolution, and crucial to its success, lies the defence industry supply chain – the substructure of SME companies which provide the key inputs for the prime contractors. As Haywood and Peck noted:

In recent years a number of managerial trends including ... supplier rationalisation programmes and the widespread outsourcing of non-core activities have all served to increase the efficiency of supply networks. In some quarters, however, there are concerns that these measures appear to have increased supply chain vulnerability.[1]

Given the increasing strategic significance of globalisation and its impact on national defence supply chains, this chapter focuses primarily on the latest developments in this field. In particular, the chapter explores the notion of supply chain vulnerability[2] that currently confronts the world's defence industrial bases, with specific reference to the recent experiences of the United States, the United Kingdom, France, Russia and China.

14.1 Restructuring Defence Industry Supply Chains: The First Wave

Following the end of the Cold War around 1990, most major defence supply companies had no choice but to restructure their business operations to survive in a sharply declining global market. For those companies choosing to remain in the defence market, internal corporate business practices were redesigned to enhance market opportunities, and performance and greater cost savings were pursued through efficiency improvements.[3] The major defence contractors implemented significant 'core' and 'periphery' adjustments to their range of business activities, together with improved marketing strategies and, critically, major reform of the supply chain that underpins their operations.[4]

In globally competitive industrial sectors as diverse as automobiles, engineering and even food production, this corporate rationalisation process has been underway for most of the period since the 1960s, changing fundamentally the structure, conduct and performance of these key industrial sectors. During this period, circumstances had been very different for the defence industry, however, with little real global competition and governments (as essentially sole purchasers) protecting their own defence companies where possible, recognising the strategic importance of a secure defence industrial base.

The restructuring of the defence industry, consequently, began in the 1990s in the wake of the end of the Cold War years and the market downturn that accompanied it. The apparent end to the US and USSR superpower struggle for military supremacy inevitably curtailed defence budgets and ignited the search for a substantial global 'peace dividend'. Falling demand, at least in the short term, compelled major defence supply companies to respond to these new market pressures, and supply chain reform rose to the top of the agenda.[5] The pressure for change in the defence supply base gained further momentum from the coincident, technologically driven 'revolution in military affairs' which allowed governments to reconfigure military strategy to encompass 'network-enabled warfare', bringing a range of new firms and their products into the defence market.[6]

14.2   1990s Supply Chain Reform

The impact of the end of the Cold War had an immense effect on the global defence industry and its supply base. After 1990, the defence sector in the global economy had to confront a world of intense uncertainty and a much-changed, unstable and fragmented 'new world order'.[7] Perhaps the most significant change to the defence supply base after 1990 was the move by prime defence contractors away from reliance mainly on a network of national suppliers to one far more global in origin. This transformation occurred despite the limiting effects on European defence industry competition of Article 346 of the 2007 Lisbon Treaty on the Functioning of the European Union.[8]

At the same time, the traditional view of industrial supply chains as comprising a series of discrete tiers (e.g. raw materials, subassembly and final assembly), usually depicted diagrammatically in pyramid shape, was being challenged, suggesting more of a matrix arrangement than a pyramid structure with interesting implications. Evidence from a major study[9] of a leading UK aero-engine prime contractor's supply chain indicated that real world defence supply chains could be far more complex in nature than the simple pyramid version, containing significant levels of inter- and intra-tier business dependency. This research made clear the complex, interwoven nature of the defence supplier base and showed the extent to which many SME suppliers appeared in the supply chains of several prime contractors simultaneously, thereby intensifying the internal dependency, indeed, vulnerability, of the supply chain or matrix to fluctuations in the business generated by the primes. At a time of sharply declining defence expenditure, with orders falling on all sides, the 'cobweb' nature of the defence industry supply chain was seen as a major threat to corporate survival at the defence SME level.

In the more challenging market conditions after 1990, the major defence companies began to select a small range of key 'preferred' suppliers with whom they could work on a global basis. Such 'partnership sourcing' meant that the primes could drive up efficiency while reducing costs. As a result, the number of supply companies operating in the defence supply base fell significantly, while the geographic spread of supplier companies became global rather than local. As the major defence companies continued to globalise their business, new market requirements emerged, and, in turn, encouraged further supply chain restructuring. Increasingly, major defence companies were recognising that to retain their competitive edge 'the ability of key suppliers and sub-contractors to bear a greater proportion of the risks and costs associated with research and development will be critical for success and survival in the market'.[10]

Those suppliers who remained active in the defence industry after this rationalisation process had no choice but to accept the requirement to upgrade their technological capabilities and acquire highly trained and experienced staff appropriate to the specific needs of the prime contractors they supplied. Suppliers had to achieve the highest standards of quality in production and delivery on schedule to satisfy powerful clients, while securing significant cost savings over time in order to remain competitive. The economic burden of ensuring a more efficient supply base for defence was therefore passed further down the supply chain, with 'survivor' companies among the SMEs now having to bear their share of the costs of new technology. Success here requires a better understanding of the buyer-seller relationship on both sides, which, in turn, necessitates working together on the basis of 'shared aims, implicit trust, full cooperation, a joint effort to problem solve and a complete recognition of their mutual inter-dependency for survival and business success'.[11]

This new approach to buyer-supplier interaction – originally termed 'co-makership' by the Phillips Group – raises concerns about potential 'vertical collusion' in the defence supply market between prime contractors and 'preferred' suppliers. It also appears to require close linkages between the two in order to achieve cost and quality targets, which, given the 'cobweb' nature of defence industry supply chains, could actually, in practice, benefit a competitor working with the same supplier.

14.3 Threats to the Defence Supply Chain: The Second Wave

In the last few years, concern has grown within industry and government about the possible vulnerability of defence industry supply chains to external attack. In 2013, the OECD suggested that more than half of the products manufactured worldwide were intermediate (semi-finished) products used in global supply chains for the manufacture of other products, and almost three-quarters of all traded services were intermediate in nature.[12] This implies that the process of global production is highly fragmented in nature. This fragmentation can be attributed to the search for cost minimisation in the global market, the diffusion of technology and the inexorable spread of globalisation for both markets and resources. The principal characteristics of modern supply chains; namely, their interdependent and complex nature, as well as global dispersal involving different degrees of outsourcing, undoubtedly offer cost savings in the production process. Unfortunately, these features may also make modern supply chains increasingly vulnerable to attack and more difficult to protect.

Despite improvements in defence budgets in the early 2000s, as governments adjusted defence policy to respond, firstly, to the new threats from insurgent groups such as al Qaeda and, later, ISIS, and secondly, to a renewed military threat from a resurgent Russia and an increasingly militaristic China, defence expenditure again came under renewed attack after 2008. Pressure on government budgets intensified due to the 2008–10 'great recession' and from the so-called new age of austerity in government policymaking which followed. These new security and budget pressures have combined to focus attention on the increasing global vulnerability of the defence supply chain, setting in motion a 'second wave' of supply chain reform.

However, of all the pressures currently posing a threat to the defence industry supply, exposure to global cyber and other technological threats are perhaps the most serious, and likely to have the greatest impact on future supply decisions. The areas of concern here are substantial and include industrial sabotage, critical technology leakage, potential data theft, the corruption of computer systems and the supply of counterfeit parts (and their potential failure in operation), all of which can erode confidence in military effectiveness in a conflict situation.

Cyberspace lies at the heart of the contemporary business information environment and provides the critical communication link between organisations, both corporate and governmental. In a military environment that is becoming increasingly complex over time, the efficient management of leading-edge technologies operating in cyberspace will be critical for battlefield dominance. Panetta[13] noted in 2012 that the start of the next war would probably begin in cyberspace, and that the US military would urgently require a highly trained workforce of cyber professionals to develop the kind of interoperable and resilient cyberspace capabilities that could successfully counter and defeat a determined adversary in cyberspace. Effective use of cyberspace can sharpen military performance in terms of speed, agility and precision, but can also become a major vulnerability in the event the supply chain of a key military prime or subcontractor is invaded by foreign-controlled malware. As Berger noted:

The Defence Department supply chain – a critical segment of the nation's infrastructure – is particularly vulnerable to high-profile targeting: with valuable assets and limited protection, it may present itself as a hacker's paradise. As one of the largest and most operationally volatile supply chains in the world, an attack on this key resource could have potentially catastrophic effects. It may inhibit the military's ability to respond to a contingency.[14]

In the defence sector, in particular, smaller supply chain companies are most at risk; indeed, it has been estimated that some 80 per cent of cyberattacks start in the supply chain. Once active within the system, the interconnected nature of the modern matrix supply chain ensures that the virus spreads rapidly into the entire supply network. While there are recognised and established best practice measures available to deal with the cyber hacking problem, Berger noted that:

A survey conducted by the National Cyber Security Alliance revealed that approximately 59 per cent of small and medium-sized businesses in the supply chain currently lack a contingency protocol in the case of a data breach – meaning that over half of the suppliers interviewed are not equipped to report or respond to a cyber-attack.[15]

14.4 National Defence Supply Chain Issues in the New Millennium

14.4.1 *The United States*

More than twenty-five years after the end of the Cold War, the defence industrial base remains a key sector of the US economy, generating over $200bn in sales in 2015 and supporting over 1.7 million jobs across the United States; and five of the world's six largest defence prime contractors are American (Lockheed Martin, Boeing, Raytheon, General Dynamics and Northrup Grumman), with a combined defence revenue in 2016 of around $120bn.[16]

The industry has a significant regional impact within the United States, where employment effects due to defence production in the four most heavily defence-dependent states (Washington, California, Texas and Michigan) amount to over 308,000 direct jobs, with a further 380,000 jobs indirectly in the defence supply chain.[17] It has been estimated that the aerospace and defence industry across the entire United States supports over 2.8 million jobs, once direct, indirect and induced employment impacts are measured.[18] In part, this reflects the long-standing 'Buy American' approach that was so central to US defence strategy during the Cold War years and resurrected in 2018 as the 'America First' policy of President Trump.

The end of the Cold War around 1990 and the defence budget constraints imposed in the post-2008 global recession compelled US defence companies to seek lower-cost suppliers from the global market, a trend driven forward because some critical defence industry inputs were no longer accessible from domestic sources. However, the trend for US defence prime contractors to expand their geographic search for both basic and more advanced defence supply inputs has recently begun to raise concerns regarding supply chain security in defence.[19] More extensive global sourcing in the defence industry has indeed delivered significant cost savings and allowed greater access to key supplies from limited global sources. Inevitably, though, the spread of global sourcing in this industry carries with it potential dependency issues that pose substantial risks to the extended supply chain.

For example, as General Dynamics (the fourth-largest US defence contractor) noted in its 2012 Annual Report:

We manage our supplier base carefully to avoid customer problems. However, we sometimes rely on only one or two sources of supply that, if disrupted, could have an adverse effect on our ability to meet our customer commitments. Our ability to perform our obligations as a prime contractor may be adversely affected if one or more of these suppliers are unable to provide the agreed-upon supplies or perform the agreed-upon services in a timely and cost-effective manner.[20]

These concerns were again highlighted in a recent report, 'Remaking American Security', which drew attention to the growing and dangerous reliance on foreign nations for the raw materials, parts and finished products needed to defend the American people.[21] For example, the Report notes that the United States now depends on a single Chinese supplier for buta-netriol, the chemical required to manufacture the solid rocket fuel used for Hellfire air-to-ground missiles, launched from attack helicopters and unmanned drones.[22] Cytec Industries, the principal US producer of buta-netriol, discontinued production in 2004, leaving this element of America's arsenal dependent upon foreign production.

A further example of increasing US dependency on imported defence inputs was emphasised in a press briefing by Peter Navarro, the White House National Trade Council Director in 2017, commenting that:

> America's defence industrial base is now facing increasing gaps in its capabilities. There's just one company in the US that can repair propellers for Navy submarines.[23]

From the US perspective, the need to source critical defence inputs from China can only be seen as a major supply chain weakness, given that nation's rapid evolution into a manufacturing giant with significant and increasing military power. Furthermore, China presents a further supply chain risk to the United States as it is suspected of being the epicentre of state-sponsored cyber-espionage.[24]

Supply chain vulnerability from global sourcing is again highlighted by Adams, noting that:

> Foreign sourcing puts America's military readiness in the hands of potentially unreliable supplier nations and undermines the ability to develop capabilities needed to win on future battlefields ... excessive and unwise outsourcing of American manufacturing to other nations weakens America's military capability ... there is a real risk that supply chain vulnerabilities will hamper our response to future threats.[18]

The trend of increased exposure of the US national defence industrial base to potential foreign supply problems has been a growing concern. In late 2017, senior officials at the US Pentagon argued that China now posed a significant threat to the United States and global microelectronics supply chain, affecting technologies that are critical for a wide range of US military systems now and into the future.[25] Noting that China now supplies in excess of 50 per cent of all the microelectronic inputs purchased by the Department of Defense, Muldavin highlights the potential threat of a future hostile nation having the power to limit access to key military inputs in the US defence supply chain as 'not a hypothetical but a real threat'.[26] China now plans to achieve global leadership in microelectronics components by 2030, and is currently planning investment of over $150bn in this critical technology.[27] To counter the perceived threat of Chinese market dominance, the US Congress has demanded the development of a new national microelectronics strategy from the Department of Defense as well as other policy responses from the government to limit these threats to domestic defence supply chains, including:

offering tax and regulatory incentives to encourage foreign investment in production facilities in the United States; leveraging the technology of overseas allies and partners; strengthening cyber security to better protect microelectronics data; and reshaping industry standards to promote quality assurance.[28]

Such is the current concern within the United States at the perceived vulnerability of its defence supply chains that one of the first executive orders issued by the newly elected President Trump[29] addressed this issue directly. Executive Order 13806, 'Assessing and Strengthening the Manufacturing and Defence Industrial Base and Supply Chain Resiliency of the United States', issued in 2017, established a working group to make recommendations on possible legislative, regulatory and policy changes that would improve and support US defence industry.

Critically, since 2000 the US-based industrial supply chain has contracted by more than 60,000 American factories.[30] Many of these were located in the defence sector, with large numbers of key companies going out of business, and employment falling by almost 5 million manufacturing jobs.[31] In 2013, over 6 per cent of the US defence budget (approximately $20bn) was spent on overseas sourced defence inputs. Unfortunately, the Trump executive order only requests analysis of the main defence industrial base and, as Green notes, this includes:

metal makers, electronics manufacturers, tool makers, miners, refiners and many more. These companies may not be visible on the battlefield, but their products are vital to the overmatch that military leadership demands from its weapon systems ... the DoD must take an expanded view of the entire industrial base, including an understanding of the sourcing of all components used by prime contractors; this includes not only end items, but also the raw materials that enable military overmatch. Prime contractors may be easy to identify, but lower-tier suppliers are equally critical to battlefield success.[32]

This understandable desire for 'overmatch' – the DoD term explaining the capacity required by the United States to exceed the military capabilities of its enemy – may ultimately be possible if, in time, technological advances in modern manufacturing can effectively limit supply chain vulnerability to global threats for US defence manufacturers and others. For example, a recent report from Standard Chartered suggests that:

> The trend now is towards more flexible, resilient and robust supply chains to mitigate risks. This does not necessarily mean shorter chains or bringing production home. Sometimes it means sourcing strategies need to be more diversified or inventory levels of certain components need to be higher. In some cases firms may prefer to have parallel supply chains and emphasise the ability to quickly adapt production if necessary. The new communications technology trends [are] likely to help improve supply-chain resilience.[33]

14.4.2 The United Kingdom

The UK remains a significant member of the global defence supply community despite recent highly publicised criticisms by senior UK military staff and others about defence budget commitments, questioning UK capacity to withstand a serious Russian attack.[34] In recent years, the United Kingdom has maintained the second largest budget in NATO, the largest in the European Union, and ranks as the fifth largest in the world. It remains one of only five NATO members that meet the NATO guideline to spend at least 2 per cent of GDP on defence. With UK annual defence spending in 2016 amounting to approximately $48bn (£35bn),[35] and with a commitment from the UK MoD to spend an additional £178bn on defence equipment and equipment support over the next decade,[36] it remains the case that the UK provides good market opportunities for the defence supply chain, nationally and globally.

In common with other nations, however, concerns have been expressed about the viability of these defence plans, given what many commentators see as the parlous state of the current UK defence budget, and about the potential supply chain effects of defence budget contraction in the future. Perceptions of a current £20bn 'black hole' in MoD finances[37] calls into question the military commitments noted above. Dealing with this financial problem will either require additional Treasury funding, unlikely in the current national economic circumstances with the impending costs of

Brexit, or will necessitate instead a revision in the United Kingdom's global military role with implications for the supply base from the multiplier effects of reduced military expenditure.

The MoD currently spends just over 19 per cent of its annual procurement budget (or about £4bn), directly and indirectly, with some 5,400 SMEs, and plans to increase this to 25 per cent by 2020.[38] While this suggests positive market growth for the myriad of smaller UK and foreign companies supplying the MoD, the current commitment to defence provision remains subject to the outcome of a major review of UK defence procurement launched in 2017. The pressure for this procurement review stems from several sources. For example, in 2015 the independent research group, Civitas, demanded a complete review of the MoD acquisition process and argued that 'our acquisition system is no longer compatible with today's defence budget and so is in an impossible mess'.[39] Instead, and of specific relevance to the defence supply chain in the United Kingdom, Civitas recommended a shift in acquisition away from large-scale defence contractors towards prioritising defence research and development initiatives from SMEs.[40]

The UK defence industry supply chain has become increasingly import dependent in recent years, raising concerns about supply continuity and defence 'sovereignty' in the event of global political instability.[41] Noting US data showing that UK defence imports grew by 33 per cent in real terms between 2002 and 2012, Taylor has argued that:

In this Millennium and certainly since the onset of the campaign in Iraq in 2003, the UK has moved incrementally from being a country that developed and produced its own arms to being a country that relies very significantly on defence imports ... there have been a series of individual choices which together generated a fundamental change in the situation.[42]

The supply chain impact of this important trend is crucial, since, as Taylor noted:

Because of the need for a sustained supply of spares, and in some cases munitions and even labour from overseas, attaining such freedom of action, while relying on a multitude of imported systems is not straightforward and certainly not automatic.[43]

The United Kingdom's increasing propensity to import semi-manufactured goods has highlighted again the long-standing productivity gap between the UK and its main competitors. The new industrial strategy, unveiled by the government in November 2017, aims to address this gap. It focuses on five key factors determining productivity: innovation; people; infrastructure; places; and the business environment. In itself, however, the new strategy does not appear to address the supply chain issue. As Hollinger[44] noted, 'the biggest criticism of the strategy is its failure to address the productivity of small and medium-sized enterprises, where major problems lie, and ... the supply chain'. However, Hollinger also notes that a further review, focusing on SMEs in the supply chain, has been commissioned by the government, and this too will ultimately have implications for the future supply base of the UK defence industry.

14.5 The UK Defence Supply Chain and Brexit

Brexit, as discussed in Chapter 9, is an issue that will pose unique challenges to the United Kingdom and its defence arrangements (though inevitably having secondary impacts elsewhere in the European Union). Although British defence contractors have perhaps stronger business links with the United States, a significant degree of corporate interaction exists at the business level in Europe, as well as between national governments (the UK-France *entente militaire* signed in 2010 at Lancaster House being a prime example). Significant parts of the UK defence supply chain are 'European' in location, rather than domestic, and European defence contractors also operate with UK suppliers in their business chain. For example, the UK-based division of the French defence contractor, Thales, has a supply chain in which about 85 per cent of companies are located in the United Kingdom.[45] The UK part of this French company's supply chain generates some £750 million per annum, and these UK companies also benefit from the Thales Supply Chain Improvement Framework, enabling them to fulfil the UK government's SC21 supply chain programme; itself designed to create a world-class supply base for the United Kingdom in aerospace, defence, space and security.[46]

While no decision has yet been made about the United Kingdom pursuing a 'hard' or 'soft' Brexit, leaving the EU will inevitably impact on both prime and smaller defence suppliers alike. Future UK participation in European defence funding will almost certainly be hampered after EU withdrawal, and the scope for liberalising the European defence supply industrial base (which would have major opportunities for UK suppliers) will be significantly reduced. Indeed, the UK's withdrawal from the EU may, in a worst-case scenario, encourage the remaining EU governments to adopt a protectionist approach towards the European defence supply market.[47] Thomis makes the key point that:

[the] UK and Europe's defence relationship is intertwined, whether related to international strategic interests, security co-operation or commercial and industrial relationships. Brexit must not be allowed to adversely affect those common interests.[48]

There is evidence of growing concern among the UK prime defence contractors about the potential impact of Brexit, and the supply chain has become a focal point of this concern. For example, Rolls-Royce has concerns about the potential disruption to its supply chain from new border controls being introduced after Brexit. The Head of Marketing and Strategy at Rolls-Royce, Ben Story, commented recently that 'Brexit had made the company reflect more on where it would be best to manu-facture in a post-Brexit future, recognising that the company had major manufacturing facilities outside the UK in Germany, Singapore and else-where'.[49] The implications of such a locational change by a prime UK defence contractor for local suppliers would be profound. Similar concerns have been expressed right across UK industry. A recent CIPS survey of 1,118 supply chain managers in the United Kingdom and Europe found that 63 per cent were now planning to shift part of their supply chain out of Britain because of Brexit concerns, and that 40 per cent of UK firms surveyed were planning to replace European suppliers.[50] The study revealed that the Brexit impact was already having important effects on UK businesses, many of them in the defence supply sector, with 64 per cent reporting additional costs due to Brexit-related currency fluctuation, while 20 per cent were experiencing problems securing contracts that expire after Brexit, and some 14 per cent fear that part or all of their business will no longer be viable, according to the study.[51] Concerns have also been raised about the impact of Brexit on future armaments collaboration projects across Europe, and the UK government has been urged to focus attention on strengthening the United Kingdom's defence supply base in case of the need to swiftly replace foreign suppliers post-Brexit.[52]

14.6 France

For forty-three years after 1966, France maintained independence from NATO, and consequently supplied its defence requirements principally from national sources. As a result, France was able to support and develop several major defence contractors across the military spectrum including missiles (Aerospatiale), combat aircraft (Dassault), armoured vehicles (Lagardere), avionics (Sextant Avionique), naval vessels (DCN) and electronics (Thomson-CSF). The rationalisation of the defence sector during the 1990s still left France with seven major defence suppliers in 2012: EADS, Dassault, Nexter, Safran, DCNS, MBDA and Thales, with a combined revenue of some $14.5bn.[53]

France was one of the last nations to rationalise its defence sector after the end of the Cold War. Although limited defence modernisation in France began in the 1980s, it gained greater momentum in 1997 through pressures to enhance operational efficiency, with major restructuring of the Direction Generale de l'Armement (DGA), the agency responsible for national defence development and procurement. While France's defence industry is dominated by seven major companies, as listed above, the market they offer supports a vast number of SMEs. In these lower tiers of the French defence industry, however, suppliers are now chosen more on a global basis. In particular, both subassembly and component supply chains have become far more global in nature than in earlier decades. Nevertheless, the prime contractors still appear to avoid, if possible, acquiring US production inputs which are subject to ITAR (International Traffic in Arms Regulations) controls. This approach is not seen as addressing a political issue, but more attributable to concerns about the security of supply chains and avoiding the contract complexities involved in the ITAR process.[54] Relevant in this context is France's long-standing support for the creation of a European armaments policy with wider and deeper defence industrial base integration, and with significant implications for supply chains globally.

As with any other strategically critical industrial sector, the French defence industry cannot function effectively without a secure and sustainable supply chain, especially with regard to materials and technologically advanced inputs. The global shift in the supply base for the French defence industry, while perhaps less prominent than some others, nevertheless has therefore become a cause for concern. A recent report from the European Union's Joint Research Centre (JRC) highlights this point and identifies three areas where the EU defence sector may encounter potential disruption in materials supply – air missiles in space, aeronautics and electronics.[55] The JRC report explored the key raw materials required for defence applications and identified forty-seven processed and semi-finished advanced materials that are necessary for their manufacture, such as alloys, composites and compounds.[56] Some thirty-nine raw materials are needed for the production of these advanced materials.[57] The JRC study found that about half of these thirty-nine critical raw materials originate almost entirely from sources external not just to France but to the EU area as a whole, with a further 25 per cent exposed to external supply vulnerability for half of their domestic input requirement.[58] In particular, there is clear concern that China has become a major supply source for about one-third of the specified critical raw material inputs.

At the EU level, the study reveals that the EU region is:

[a] large manufacturer of alloys and special steels and should maintain its production capacities. However, the EU should improve its production capacities for speciality composite materials and their precursors in order to guarantee the integrity of the materials supply.[59]

As a result, concern about the vulnerability of some parts of the French defence industrial supply chain has stimulated the development of an EU-wide raw materials strategy,[60] which underpinned the European Defence Action Plan published by the Commission on 30 November 2016.

While France is more prepared to seek defence inputs globally, Paris has continued to propose the development of a European defence industrial base with the United Kingdom and Germany as preferred partners on major projects. A number of these multination projects has been established, such as the MU90 torpedo programme, the COBRA radar system, the TIGER helicopter and, more recently, the development of two UK aircraft carriers, all having important implications for the European defence supply base.

14.7 Russia

The revolution that has been sweeping through the defence industry supply chain in recent years has now become truly global, affecting even the major economies outside NATO, particularly in Russia and China. The defence industries of both countries are very different from those of Western nations, especially in terms of origin, structure and organisation. Their defence production is primarily located in very large, state-owned enterprises that comprise the military-industrial complex in each nation.[61]

For Russia, supply chain concerns differ in some respects from those confronting Western nations and derive from the need to drive forward the modernisation of the defence sector. This has become increasingly important as geopolitical tensions rise, and, in practice, has been underway for some time. Two key changes lie at the heart of this modernisation drive: the development of new weapons systems, and a major reform of military procurement to deliver efficiency improvements and associated cost savings. In its strategic planning to modernise the defence industry, the Russian government has had to recognise the crucial role played by the supply chain and also deal with new pressures. Until the collapse of the Soviet Union towards the end of the last century, giant Russian military factories making finished defence goods had been able to draw on inputs they required from sources across the entire Soviet Union and Warsaw Pact nations. The demise of the Soviet and East European Trading Pact states initially damaged existing supply lines and fundamentally changed the *modus operandi* of Russia's defence industrial base. More recently, the imposition of trade sanctions against Russia again threatened some parts of its military supply system, making reform an urgent priority.[62] The current dispute between Russia and the Ukraine provides a good example of the supply chain consequences of such geopolitical conflict:

Chief among these is the Ukraine crisis, which has put Russia's access to vital military components in question. Western sanctions triggered by Russian actions in Ukraine and the resulting drop in oil prices have weakened the national economy, further constraining the industry. These restrictions have forced Russia to promote joint manufacturing abroad.[63]

The dispute with Ukraine has already put Russia's military supply system under considerable pressure, blocking access to crucial weapon components. Military supply factories in Ukraine, in the past, have been long-term providers of subcomponents to the Russian defence manufacturing sector, and these suppliers were undoubtedly critical to the production of a wide range of Russian military goods, including aircraft, space systems and naval vessels. For example, key Ukrainian suppliers to Russian military enterprises included: Motor Sich (providing inputs for the MS-500 V turboshaft engine and Mi-8 helicopter); Zorya-Mashproekt (supplying inputs for the M90FR Turbine and project 22350 Frigate); Kylv Artem (supplying components for the R-27 air-to-air missile and weapons used on MiG-29 and SU-35 aircraft); Petrovsky Automation Plant (supplying inputs for gyroscope-based control and navigation systems and the VA-111 Shkval torpedo); and the Lviv Lorta Company (supplying inputs for electronic service stations and the S-300 Air Defence System).

Russia's decision to annex Crimea in 2014 and its military activities in Eastern Ukraine have effectively fractured some key parts of the Ukraine-Russia supply chain, calling into question the availability to Russia of these critical subcomponents. Action taken by global trading partners as part of the sanctions against Russia for its role in Ukraine has also created supply problems for Russia, necessitating the development of new import-substitution facilities, which in turn drive up defence costs at a time of constrained national budgets. Moreover, the economic and trade sanctions imposed on Russia in September 2014 were intended to damage the military sector in particular. Russian companies working in the defence sector were prevented from acquiring foreign military and dual-use products and technologies, and a range of EU financial services. The impact on the supply chain for Russian defence companies was considerable. As Dmitry Rogozin, deputy Prime Minister noted, 'all the chipsets and receiving modules for GLONASS [Russia's version of GPS] are produced outside of Russia'.[64] Furthermore, a NATO report from October 2015 commented that the Russian defence electronics industry would be adversely affected by restrictions on access to foreign dual-use technologies since Russia:

imports 25 to 30 per cent of its components [and] unlike the purchase of arms, Russia's efforts to modernize its defence industrial plants will likely be significantly affected by sanctions, since the domestic machine-tool industry is largely unable to produce the advanced equipment these plants require for production.[65]

The pursuit of a new import substitution policy for critical defence subcomponents brings production back under Russian control, albeit at significant cost, and thereby guarantees their availability for the Russian military and for export. While the Ukrainian crisis has given new weight to the import substitution process in the Russian defence sector, the drive towards reduced dependence on these imports has been underway for some time. For example:

Between 2007 and 2010, the share of Russian helicopters bearing Ukrainian engines dropped from 95 per cent to 70 per cent. The conflict in Ukraine forced Moscow to speed up this process. In doing so, it has been forced to tailor its military modernization to prioritize the development of certain sectors or weapon systems to both limit cost and maintain self-sufficiency.[66]

Despite this policy switch towards greater import substitution, and partly due to the pressures exerted on the economy from Western sanctions, Russia has also developed new external defence supply linkages with countries such as India and China to achieve cost reduction and market access through joint ventures in military products. China, in particular, has become a new partner for Russian military goods development in recent years with joint projects in helicopters, naval vessels, missiles, aircraft and engines. Chinese production of some key components and subcomponents (e.g. in ship engines) offer Russia an alternative supply line to that threatened by the Ukraine crisis. However, supply chain problems for Russia have also appeared in the Chinese context. Dmitry Rogozin observed in July 2016 that sanctions were even damaging technology-based trade with China.[67] Concern was also expressed by President Putin in September 2015 in the context of the Russian microelectronics industry that 'some of our foreign partners in recent years threaten the reliability of the supply of components and equipment from abroad'.[68]

14.8 China

The evolving position of China with regard to the global defence supply chain is particularly interesting. A relatively new process of domestic supply chain reform is currently underway in China. It was reported in the China Daily in October 2017[69] that China is now engaged on a major programme of supply chain reform, designed to achieve more cohesive integration of supply chains, enabling China's industrial base to develop in a more comprehensive manner. In particular, these reforms have been focused on achieving major improvements in internet and delivery services, and in logistics. Yue reports that 'Bai Ming, a researcher from the Ministry of Commerce's Chinese Academy of International Trade and Economic Cooperation, says while supply-chain businesses have been developing rapidly, this is the first time the idea of a "supply chain" was prioritized in a State-level policy guideline.'[70]

Chinese inputs already play a significant role in meeting the manufacturing supply requirements of many Western military producers; indeed, on occasions, being the only available supply source. At the same time, however, many regard China in the military context as a specific threat due to both rapidly increasing military budgets and also to their perceived major role in global cyberwarfare of various kinds. There is now increasing concern that direct Chinese involvement in global military supply chains may put those supply linkages at risk, either physically and/or technologically.

Revitalised global supply of important lower-cost inputs for military production from China will serve to further open foreign markets to their exports and, at the same time, strengthen China's own military power. However, many Western defence supply companies (and their governments) are becoming concerned about perceived Chinese involvement in their supply chains and the threat this may pose in the future.

14.9 Conclusion

The security and flexibility of supply chains have become increasingly important issues to both prime defence contractors and governments alike in recent years. For the major defence corporations, there is concern over the need to secure both lower costs and guaranteed access to the key resources and semi-manufactures they require from SMEs willing and able to share project risk as well as research and development expenditure. For governments, concern has more to do with supply chain vulnerability in an area where national security is at risk and effective defence may be compromised.

The objective of achieving a more efficient global defence supply base while ensuring it remains secure has become more challenging as research gradually reveals the true extent of supply chains that underpin the defence sector. As Hartley notes:

Recognition of supply chains makes it difficult to identify the true extent of a nation's defence industry ... A study of the supply chain for the UK Warrior armoured fighting vehicle[71] identified some 200 first-level suppliers located in various parts of Britain ... In turn, first-level suppliers used an average of 18 suppliers, second-level firms had an average of 7 suppliers, and third tier firms had an average of 2–3 suppliers. In some cases, second- and third-tier suppliers did not know that they were engaged in defence work.[72]

Strategic, technological and financial pressures have combined to transform global defence industry supply chains over the last three decades. Key suppliers before the end of the Cold War tended to be national, often local, in origin, with governments tending to source their defence equipment domestically wherever possible. Defence budget cuts both after 1990 and again following the global financial crisis around 2008 compelled the major defence companies to rationalise their operations, cutting the number of suppliers and extending supplier search globally. As we have seen, this rationalisation process also had to take account of two additional major developments: (1) a technology revolution which has transformed both military capabilities and the kinds of defence supply companies operating in the market; and (2) the recognition that new and very different enemies need to be confronted, while more traditional potential enemies are massively expanding their armed forces, and also posing a cyber-threat to the defence supply system.

Defence decision-makers, whether in industry or government, now face a difficult choice. Is it better to return to a system where most defence inputs are nationally (or perhaps regionally) sourced, enhancing supply chain security but potentially adding significantly to cost, given that some key supply sectors may no longer exist and may have to be reconstructed? Or, instead, is it strategically more sensible to accept the problems associated with globalisation of the defence industry and simply bear the costs and uncertainties associated with making secure such an extended supply chain? The answer to these important questions will necessarily shape the next phase of supply chain reform.

References and notes

1. M. Haywood and H Peck. 'Supply Chain Vulnerability within UK Aerospace Manufacturing: Development of a Vulnerability Management Toolkit'. *Supply Chain Practice*. 2004. 6(1): 72.
2. G. Svensson. 'A Conceptual Framework for the Analysis of Vulnerability in Supply Chains'. *International Journal of Physical Distribution & Logistics Management*. 2000. 30(9): 731–49.
3. D. Braddon. *Exploding the Myth? The Peace Dividend, Regions and Market Adjustment*. Amsterdam: Harwood Academic Publishers. 2000.

4. D. Braddon and P. Dowdall. 'Flexible Networks and the Restructuring of the Regional Defence Industrial Base: The Case of South West England'. *Defence and Peace Economics*. 1996. 7(1): 47–59.

5. R. Matthews and J. Treddenick (eds). *Managing the Revolution in Military Affairs*. Basingstoke: Palgrave Macmillan. 2001.

6. See, for example, T. Todorov. *New World Disorder – Reflections of a European*. Cambridge: Wiley. 2005.

7. For further discussion of Article 346, see M. Uttley and B. Wilkinson. 'A Spin of the Wheel? Defence Procurement and Defence Industries in the Brexit Debates'. *International Affairs*. 2016. 92(3): 569–86.

8. D. Braddon and P. Dowdall. 'Flexible Networks and the Restructuring of the Regional Defence Industrial Base: The Case of South West England'. *Defence and Peace Economics*. 1996. 7(1): 47–59.

9. Braddon. *Exploding the Myth?* 158.

10. Braddon. *Exploding the Myth?* 158.

11. Braddon. *Exploding the Myth?* 159.

12. OECD. *Interconnected Economies: Benefiting from Global Value Chains*. Synthesis Report. 2013.

13. E. Bumiller and T. Shanker. 'Panetta Warns of Dire Threat of Cyberattack on US'. *New York Times*. 11 October 2012. www.nytimes.com/2012/10/12/world/panetta-warns-of-dire-threat-of-cyberattack.html (accessed 25 April 2018).

14. B. Berger. 'WannaCry Exposes Defence Supply Chain Vulnerabilities'. *National Defense*. 19 June 2017. www.nationaldefensemagazine.org/articles/2017/6/19/wannacry-exposes-defense-supply-chain-vulnerabilities (accessed 31 January 2018).

15. B. Berger. 'WannaCry'.

16. Federal Register. *Executive Order 13806: Assessing and Strengthening the Manufacturing and Defence Industrial Base and Supply Chain Resiliency of the United States*. 2017. www.federalregister.gov/documents/2017/07/26/2017–15860/assessing-and-strengthening-the-manufacturing-and-defense-industrial-base-and-supply-chain (accessed 31 January 2018).

17. Federal Register. *Executive Order 13806*.

18. Federal Register. *Executive Order 13806*.

19. M. Stone and A. Rascoe. 'Trump Orders Review to Strengthen U.S. Defense Industry'. *Reuters*. 21 July 2017. www.reuters.com (accessed 25 April 2018).

20. J. Harper. 'China Threatens Microelectronics Supply Chain, DoD Official says'. *National Defense*. 19 December 2017. www.nationaldefensemagazine.org/articles/2017/12/19/china-threatens-microelectronics-supply-chain-dod-official-says (accessed 25 April 2018).

21. J. Adams. *ReMaking American Security; Supply Chain Vulnerabilities & National Security Risks Across the U.S. Defence Industrial Base.* Alliance for American Manufacturing. 2013.

22. Adams. *ReMaking American Security.*

23. Stone and Rascoe. 'Trump Orders Review'.

24. Alliance for American Manufacturing. 'Report Says U.S. Military Dangerously Dependent on Foreign Suppliers'. May 2013. www.amer icanmanufacturing.org/blog/entry/report-says-u.s.-military-danger ously-dependent-on-foreign-suppliers (accessed 25 April 2018).

25. Harper. 'China Threatens Microelectronics Supply Chain'.

26. Harper. 'China Threatens Microelectronics Supply Chain'.

27. Harper. 'China Threatens Microelectronics Supply Chain'.

28. Harper. 'China Threatens Microelectronics Supply Chain'.

29. Federal Register. *Executive Order 13806.*

30. J. Green. 'Pentagon Must Target Weak Points, Improve Resiliency in the Defence Supply Chain'. *Defence News.* 1 November 2017. www.defense news.com/industry/2017/11/01/pentagon-must-target-weak-points-impro ve-resiliency-in-the-defense-supply-chain-commentary/ (accessed 25 April 2018).

31. Green. 'Pentagon Must Target Weak Points'.

32. Green. 'Pentagon Must Target Weak Points'.

33. M. Jha, S. Amerasinghe and J. Calverley. 'Special Report – Global Supply Chains: New Directions'. Standard Chartered Global Research. 2015. www.sc.com/BeyondBorders/wp-content/uploads/2015/05/2015–05-28-BeyondBorders-Report-Global-supply-chains-New-directions.pdf (accessed 31 January 2018).

34. D. Haynes. '£20bn Hole in Budget Delays Defence Review'. *The Times.* 2018. www.thetimes.co.uk/article/20bn-hole-in-budget-delays-defenc e-review-8cnwxl72z (accessed 1 February 2018).

35. N. Tian, A. Fleurant, P. D. Wezeman and S. T. Wezeman, 'Trends in World Military Expenditure, 2016'. Stockholm International Peace Research Institute (SIPRI) Fact Sheet. 2017. www.sipri.org/sites/default/files/Trend s-world-military-expenditure-2016.pdf (accessed 31 January 2018).

36. GOV.UK. Cabinet Office. *Strategic Defence and Security Review: £178bn of Equipment Spending.* 2015. www.gov.uk/government/new s/strategic-defence-and-security-review-178bn-of-equipment-spending (accessed 1 February 2018).

37. Tian, Fleurant, Wezeman and Wezeman, 'Trends'.

38. B. Jenkin. 'Defence Acquisition for the Twenty-First Century'. CIVITAS. 2015. www.civitas.org.uk/pdf/DefenceAcquisition (accessed 1 February 2018).

39. GOV.UK. Cabinet Office. *Strategic Defence and Security Review.*

40. GOV.UK. Cabinet Office. *Strategic Defence and Security Review*.
41. F. Churchill. 'Inquiry Launched into UK Defence Procurement'. Supply Management. 2016. www.cips.org/supply-management/news/2016/sep tember/inquiry-launched-into-uks-defence-procurement/ (accessed 1 February 2018).
42. T. Taylor. *Publications – Defence Acquisition and Procurement*. Defence Committee. Reference number: ACQ0022, 2017. http://data .parliament.uk/writtenevidence/committeeevidence.svc/evidencedocu ment/defence-committee/defence-acquisition-and-procurement/writ ten/44710.pdf (accessed 1 February 2018).
43. Taylor. *Publications – Defence Acquisition and Procurement*.
44. P. Hollinger. 'Four Key Challenges Raised by the UK's New Industrial Strategy'. *Financial Times*. 2017. www.ft.com/content/f2857abc-d398-11e7-a303-9060cb1e5f44 (accessed 1 February 2018).
45. Thales Group. 'Our UK Supply Chain'. 2018. www.thalesgroup.com/en/our-uk-supply-chain (accessed 1 February 2018).
46. Thales Group. 'Our UK Supply Chain'.
47. See, for example, O. D. France, B. Giegerich, A. Marrone, J. P. Maulny and T. Taylor. *The Impact of Brexit on the European Armament Industry*. Armament Industry European Research Group. Report number: 19. 2017. www.iris-france.org/wp-content/uploads/2017/08/Ares-19-Brexit-25-August-2017-IRIS.pdf (accessed 1 February 2018).
48. A. Thomis. 'Opinion: Post-Brexit Europe and Guarding Against Continental Drift'. *Jane's Defence Weekly*. 12 April 2017.
49. B. Story cited in: S. Rai and A. J. Koilparambil. 'Brexit: Rolls Royce Warns Border Checks Will Disrupt Global Supply Chain'. *The Independent*. 2017. www.independent.co.uk/news/business/news/brex it-latest-ws-rolls-royce-uk-border-checks-eu-customs-union-global-sup ply-chain-europe-a8056781.html (accessed 1 February 2018).
50. Chartered Institute of Procurement and Supply (CIPS). *EU Businesses Say Goodbye to UK Suppliers as Brexit Bites into Key Relationships*. CIPS, 2017. www.cips.org/en-gb/news/news/eu-businesses-say-good bye-to-uk-suppliers-as-brexit-bites-into-key-relationships/ (accessed 1 February 2018).
51. P. Tran. 'Brexit Consequences Raise Doubts over Future Defense Industrial Collaboration'. Defence News. 2017. www.defensenews.co m/global/europe/2017/09/01/brexit-consequences-raise-doubts-over-fu ture-defense-industrial-collaboration/ (accessed 1 February 2018).
52. See, for example, National Manufacturing Competitiveness Levels. 'ADS Looks to Chancellor to Boost Supply Chains'. 2017. www.nmcl .co.uk/2017/11/16/ads-looks-to-chancellor-to-boost-supply-chains/ (accessed 1 February 2018).

53. Reuters. 'Factbox: France's Military and Defense Contractors'. 2013. www.reuters.com/article/us-france-defence-factbox/factbox-frances-mi litary-and-defense-contractors-idUSBRE93R01X20130428 (accessed 1 February 2018).

54. Export.gov. *French Defense Business Overview*. 2016. www.export.g ov/article?id=French-Defense-Business-Overview (accessed 1 February 2018).

55. For further discussion, see European Commission. *EU Science Hub – The European Commission's Science and Knowledge Service: Raw Materials*. 2016. https://ec.europa.eu/jrc/en/research-topic/raw-materi als (accessed 1 February 2018).

56. European Commission. *EU Science Hub*.

57. European Commission. *EU Science Hub*.

58. European Commission. *EU Science Hub*.

59. European Commission. *EU Science Hub*.

60. European Commission. *EU Science Hub*.

61. See W. Frieman. 'China's Defence Industries'. *The Pacific Review*. 1993. 6(1): 51–62; R. A. Bitzinger. 'Reforming China's Defense Industry'. *Journal of Strategic Studies*. 2016. 39(5–6): 762–89.

62. O. Fritz, E. Christen, F. Sinabell and J. Hinz. *Russia's and the EU's Sanctions: Economic and Trade Effects, Compliance and the Way Forward*. European Union. Report number: EP/EXPO/B/INTA/2017/ 11. 2017. www.europarl.europa.eu/RegData/etudes/STUD/2017/6038 47/EXPO_STU(2017)603847_EN.pdf (accessed 1 February 2018).

63. Stratfor Worldview. 'The Hidden Challenges of Modernizing Russia's Military'. https://worldview.stratfor.com/article/hidden-challenges-mo dernizing-russias-military (accessed 1 February 2018).

64. A. Borshchevskaya. 'The Case for Keeping Sanctions against Russia's Defense Sector'. *Forbes*. 2016. www.forbes.com/sites/annaborshchevs kaya/2016/08/12/the-case-for-keeping-sanctions-against-russias-defens e-sector/#64736cd2e226 (accessed 1 February 2018).

65. Borshchevskaya. 'The Case for Keeping Sanctions'.

66. Stratfor. 'Ukraine Turmoil Is Creating Big Problems for Putin's Military Modernization Plan'. *Business Insider*. 2015. www.businessinsider.com/ ukraine-turmoil-is-creating-big-problems-for-putins-military-moderniza tion-plan-2015–5?pundits_only=0&get_all_comments=1&no_reply_filt er=1&IR=T (accessed 1 February 2018).

67. Borshchevskaya. 'The Case for Keeping Sanctions'.

68. Borshchevskaya. 'The Case for Keeping Sanctions'.

69. Z. Yue. 'Supply Chain in Focus with New Approach'. *China Daily*. 2017. www.chinadaily.com.cn/china/2017–10/27/content_33763006 .htm (accessed 1 February 2018).

70. Yue. 'Supply Chain in Focus'.
71. K. Hartley, N. Hooper, M. Sweeney, R. Matthews, D. Braddon, P. Dowdall and J. Bradley. Armoured Fighting Vehicle Supply Chain Analysis, Study of the Value of Defence Industry to the UK Economy. Centre for Defence Economics, University of York. Unpublished report. 1997.
72. K. Hartley. *The Economics of Arms*. Newcastle upon Tyne: Agenda Publishing. 2017. 30.

15 | The Cost of Women in Ground Close Combat Roles

JOANNE L. FALLOWFIELD

Introduction

A real-term decline in defence budgets over recent years[1] has required all nations to think carefully about their requirements for national security – and their financial liabilities to deliver this security. The 'value' of defence to a nation state comprises both tangible and intangible assets. The military hardware, real estate and the knowledge, skills and competencies of Service and civilian defence personnel represent tangible assets whose value can be estimated in monetary terms. In contrast, a 'defence deterrent' to potential aggressors and the public's perception of their intrinsic security and safety are less readily expressed in such terms, but equally contribute to the value of defence. As the costs of defence equipment and resources to deliver security and safety escalate, with new threats driving new technologies, governments and defence ministries have had to make difficult decisions.[2] These decisions must address both military capabilities and the policies and practices defining how these capabilities will be delivered – and under what circumstances.

In the United Kingdom, the Secretary of State for Defence has changed the government's policy stance with respect to women undertaking Ground Close Combat (GCC) roles. As well as benefits, this policy decision will have economic implications in which the inherent risks and financial costs must be considered relative to maximising 'economic welfare' for the UK. Economic welfare refers to the prosperity and quality of living standards provided by an economy. Thus, if a government changes spending in one policy area, then this will impact on others as a consequence of the finite nature of public resources. This, in turn, could alter the quality of living for parts of society, and indeed could exert differential effects across the different economic strata of society. As such, it would be appropriate to consider the economic dimension of any change in Defence policy as part of wider government spending policies.

Allocative efficiency considers both the efficiency of production (i.e. the costs) and the efficiency of outcome distribution (i.e. the benefits).[3] Specifically, goods or services can continue to be produced and/or provided as long as the marginal cost of production/provision does not exceed the marginal benefit delivered to consumers. With its antecedents in welfare economics, state allocative efficiency has implications for the opportunity cost of the investment of public resources. Maximising economic welfare from public monies is important, especially during this time of continued national austerity. Indeed, the opportunity costs of allocating public money in different ways across Defence should therefore be evaluated from a consideration of the marginal cost of a policy decision weighed against the marginal benefit; that is, the policy decision that led to the opening up of GCC roles to women, from an economic perspective, should be justified on the basis that marginal benefits for the nation are greater than marginal costs. The scale of the difference, in terms of how much greater the marginal benefit is over the marginal cost, should then inform the opportunity cost analysis of that policy decision. Such an analysis would therefore need to demonstrate that supporting women in GCC roles, as opposed to investing public monies elsewhere, provides for greater allocative efficiency than other potential government investment and spending options.

Women have long made significant contributions to the UK Armed Forces. Women's Services were permanently established following the Second World War in recognition of the important roles they had played in that conflict.[4] However, there was a step change in women's duties during the 1990s, when the women's Services were fully integrated with those of their male counterparts. Up until the Secretary of State's change in policy with respect to women undertaking GCC roles, they had performed frontline duties on ships and submarines, as combat pilots and aircrew, as well as contributing to a number of combat support roles in the army. The majority of Armed Forces roles have therefore been opened up to women who had attained the required academic, professional and physical standards on completion of military training. However, women have previously been excluded from roles that are primarily intended and designed with the purpose of requiring individuals on the ground, to close with and kill the enemy.[5]

These roles included the Infantry, Royal Armoured Corps, Household Cavalry, Royal Marines (RM) and the Royal Air Force (RAF) Regiment.[6] A commonality of these arms is a requirement to work as small, four-person fire teams, who engage with enemy forces at close range (i.e. GCC roles).[7] As such, physical capability and team cohesion are essential for success and survival.

The MoD has been exempt from the Sex Discrimination (1975)[8] and Equality (2010)[9] Acts with respect to women in GCC roles, but this exemption reflected concerns of mixed-gender team dynamics and combat effectiveness rather than physicality per se.[10] Nevertheless, previous government policy reviews have concluded that women should continue to be excluded from these roles.[11] This approach was supported by EU legislation, but a requirement under this legislation was that the position must be reviewed every eight years.[12] That said, the Secretary of State for Defence brought forward the most recent review,[13] where levers for change included a desire for positive gender messaging in the military, external perceptions of discrimination, recent evidence from other nations' experiences[14] as well as maximising talent to the Armed Forces and possibly realising economies of scale benefits in recruitment.[15] The 2014 review aimed to reassess the potential contribution of women to GCC roles, evaluate policy change risks and benefits and provide recommendations for future policy.[16]

In the light of the UK government's decision to change its policy stance, whereby the MoD must seek optimal allocative efficiency of its scarce resources, this chapter examines the economic issues of opening up Armed Forces' GCC roles to women, and specifically the associated potential costs to the UK government. The principal tenets informing this economic discourse for women in GCC roles, which have previously informed government reviews on the subject,[17] are focused on considerations of combat effectiveness, physical capability – such as injury risk and medical discharge rates – morbidity and deployability, heat illness, hearing loss, lethality and survivability, medico-legal implications and – during the early years following the opening up of GCC roles – the costs of implementation. The full economic impact of the decision to open up GCC roles is unlikely to be known until many years into the future, but awareness of possible risks and fiscal liabilities should be of importance to military planners in the short term.

15.1 Combat Effectiveness

Combat effectiveness is defined as:

The ability of a ground close combat team to carry out its assigned mission, role or function. The cohesion of a [GCC] team is a vital factor in its combat effectiveness.[18]

Combat effectiveness is multifaceted, comprising professional military judgement, as well as psychological and physiological dimensions. The 2014 review considered twenty-one combat effectiveness factors.[19] Team cohesion was considered fundamental to combat effectiveness, as it is built on mutual confidence and trust. These characteristics, in turn, reflect individual knowledge, technical expertise and military capability, borne out of time spent working together.[20] When the impact of these factors is controlled, mixed-gender groups do not demonstrate poorer team cohesion.[21]

Indeed, in high-stress environments, education, training and the influence of the organisation's culture are fundamental to team cohesion,[22] where these factors can be determined and readily managed by the organisation in preparing personnel for challenging occupational roles. Moreover, an individual's trust in other team members, along with the impact of direct management and top management are vital for team cohesion and team performance;[23] an observation which emphasises the importance of leadership and the overarching command. Moreover, Gillespie et al.[24] concluded that after observing personnel engaged in tasks involving life-or-death decisions, interdisciplinary diversity with mutual professional respect and effective communication contributed to high-level team performance. Thus, in terms of close quarter team working, gender has not been shown to negatively impact on cohesion, communication, decision quality, time on task and, ultimately, task outcome.[25]

However, team cohesion and team performance may be adversely affected if other factors, such as levels of morbidity are significantly higher, and survivability and lethality significantly lower in women compared to men.[26] Physical capability and physical robustness are fundamental to all these combat effectiveness factors. Indeed, failure to preserve the physical abilities underpinning combat effectiveness could result in death or injury to Armed Forces personnel or the general public, compromising the outcome of an operation and potentially causing significant damage to Crown property.[27] As such, if these attributes were significantly lower in women when undertaking GCC roles, this would represent additional costs compared with when GCC roles were undertaken exclusively by men, and hence would present a less attractive economic argument for a government policy change.

15.2 Physical Capability, Injury Risk and Medical Discharge Rates

Female anatomy and physiology represent real physical capability disadvantages relative to men.[28] Women have lower body mass, lower muscle mass, higher fat mass, shorter stature and narrower bones than men.[29] Functionally, women have different muscle structure, smaller hearts and lower aerobic work capacity.[30] Consequently, women perform poorer than men on military tests of strength, power and aerobic performance,[31] and would be generally required to work harder than their male counterparts in completing standard military tasks. Women of a similar body mass to men (where body mass is advantageous for military tasks such as load carriage)[32] are physiologically unlikely to have similar muscle mass; women generally have a higher body fat percentage and lower fat-free (muscle and bone) mass. For example, in a sample of British Army recruits undertaking Phase-1 military training, Blacker et al.[33] report that males had a mean (± standard deviation) body mass of 68.0 ± 7.9 kg and a percentage body fat of 11 ± 4 %, while females had a body mass of 62.4 ± 6.9 kg and a percentage body fat of 24 ± 4 %.

Anatomical and physiological differences between male and female military personnel have important implications for aerobic fitness, strength, load carriage capability and injury risk in GCC roles.[34] The physical fitness capabilities required to undertake a role are defined by the Physical Employment Standards (PES) of an occupational role.[35] The PES must be evidence-based and legally defensible, and represent both the minimum acceptable performance standard and best practice methods for the execution of the required occupational tasks. Failure to determine appropriate PES for female GCC personnel, through applying an internationally recognised auditable approach,[36] could leave the

MoD financially liable. This liability might arise from not fully minimising the risk of injury to 'as low as reasonably possible' (or ALARP). Alternatively, the MoD could be liable for compensation claims of circa £30,000–£50,000 per claimant if either direct[37] or indirect[38] discrimination were to be proven. Hence, a 'do nothing' policy option for the government in the twenty-first century is no longer viable. The MoD could incur financial risk either in allowing women into GCC roles if the potential for harm was not fully explored, and mitigated where possible, or equally if women continued to be barred from entry to GCC roles without just cause.

Robust PES mitigates injury risk,[39] where the most common cause of medical discharge from the Services is musculoskeletal injury (MSKI).[40] Poor aerobic fitness,[41] low body mass,[42] weaker bone strength[43] and female gender[44] are risk factors for MSKI. For comparison, the medical discharge rates for 2013/14[45] were higher for (GCC) Royal Marines personnel (12.4/1000) compared with (non-GCC) Royal Navy personnel (8.7/1000). The all-Services medical discharge rate for females was 60 per cent higher than for males (females: 14.4/ 1000; males: 9.1/1000).[46] Thus, following this line of argument, the medical discharge rates of females undertaking GCC roles could be at least 60 per cent higher than for males (circa 18/1000).

Women have a two-fold higher risk of MSKI during initial military training compared with men.[47] Women undertaking RAF Phase-1 (11 weeks) recruit training were at a higher risk of stress fracture compared with men, where increased risk was associated with poorer aerobic fitness, height and smoking habit.[48] Moreover, the risk of MSKI has been estimated to be six times higher in male Infantry recruits (i.e. GCC trainees) compared with male Army Standard Entrants (i.e. non-GCC trainees), who undertake a shorter and less physically arduous course.[49] Injuries to the lower limbs were the most prevalent reported injury site, where the most frequently reported injury cause was high impact activity.[50] However, 'overuse' injuries (i.e. any type of muscle or joint injury that is caused by repetitive strain and/or trauma over time) were the most commonly reported cause for medical discharge and the termination of a trainee's military career.[51] Thus, women in military training would incur proportionately higher medical care costs (i.e. costs for diagnosis, treatment, rehabilitation and recovery back into mainstream training), relative to the number of females successfully completing training and passing into service, and this would likely be a greater risk burden once GCC roles were opened up to women. This injury risk could potentially be mitigated without compromising training effectiveness through training in single sex platoons,[52] and reducing marching stride length.[53] Such mitigation will be essential as, on completion of military training, women in-service have a higher rate of medical downgrading (i.e. a medical category assigned to injured/ill personnel and used to temporarily remove an individual from situations that could exacerbate their condition) across all Service Arms (i.e. Army, RAF and the Royal Navy) compared with men, particularly in the first four years of service.[54]

The burden of MSKI on the MoD can be detailed in terms of loss-of-days in training and/or work due to temporary downgrade, reduced productivity (in training or in work) due to placement on light duties, increased strain on the medical chain to provide diagnosis, treatment and rehabilitation, the significantly increased risk of future re-injury – and the potential risk of subsequent medical discharge, and eventual loss from the service in cases of personnel deemed 'unfit to attend'.[55] Thus, MSKI presents an ongoing challenge to the organisational effectiveness of the UK Armed Forces, impacting upon operational capability and deployability. But the true financial burden has been difficult to determine. The cost to the British Army for MSKI-related medical discharges from both military training and the Field Army was estimated to be of the order of £1.02 billion over fifteen years from 2016 to 2031.[56] However, it is important to emphasise that this estimate excludes medical care costs (as detailed previously), which represent a significant financial burden for Defence.

In the Royal Marines, as a case example, MSKI during recruit training has long been recognised as a significant burden,[57] where 16 per cent of the annual recruit intake sustains an injury.[58] The median recovery time for all injuries in this specific military population is 17.8 weeks,[59] where recruit rehabilitation costs are circa £1,600/week.[60] Thus, the economic liability to the MoD of Royal Marines recruit rehabilitation is >£4.5 million/annum (i.e. [annual recruit injury incidence] x [median recovery time] x [rehabilitation costs per week]), with an additional £5.7 million/annum costs for lost training days (calculated from the costs of the additional 'time in training' arising from MSKI over and above the programmed thirty-two weeks for the Royal Marines Recruit Syllabus).[61]

These costings are generally viewed as conservative estimates, given that considerable 'unknowns' exist with respect to the actual costs for MSKI. The categories of financial liabilities arising from MSKI in the UK Armed Forces can be considered under six headings. First, there are the personnel costs. These include the sunk costs associated with recruitment and the issuing of kit, lost training days and the staffing of Employability Boards to manage the career implications of injury and reduced functionality of Service personnel. Second, costs will obviously be incurred in the diagnosis, treatment and management of injuries, which are borne by Defence Primary Healthcare.[62] Third, there will also be the capitation costs of those injured and potentially not able to work, including salaries and pension contributions. Fourth, costs will be incurred by the MoD if there are personal liability or common law claims arising from the injury, which impact upon quality of life and/or future employability of Service personnel. The fifth category to consider relates to the intangible costs of MSKI; these relate to entities that have no physical presence, and as such are difficult to define with any precision. There will be the physical and psychological impact of an injury on the individual, but there will also be second-order effects on those who work with the individual and who may be required to carry an extra work burden due to their absence. This could result in increased work-based stress and higher occupational strain, which in turn could, in itself, have further mental and physical health consequences for those individuals. The sixth category of costs to the MoD arising from MSKI relate to direct and indirect reputational costs. News stories can be rapidly disseminated in today's multimedia world, such as the case where compensation was paid to three female RAF recruits for injuries incurred during military training,[63] and such stories adversely impact on the national and international reputation of the UK's Armed Forces. Many of these costs arising from MSKI have presently not been determined, such that the estimate of £1.02 billion over fifteen years[64] relates, in the main, to capitation costs.

15.3 Morbidity and Deployability

During recent operations, female morbidity for non-GCC roles was 15–20 per cent higher than that of their male counterparts.[65] Frontline GCC roles are associated with high-energy demands, periods of sustained energy deficit and associated loss in body mass.[66] These physical demands could have a disproportionately greater impact upon female skeletal and reproductive health,[67] such that female morbidity in GCC roles would be higher than that of males.[68] Data are presently not available to specifically evaluate this potential risk. However, this chapter has presented evidence that women are at a greater MSKI risk than men during military training,[69] and are at a higher risk of being medically discharged.[70] Thus, it could be intuitively hypothesised that the morbidity of trained women GCC personnel would be higher and the deployability would be lower than men, representing an additional circa 15–20 per cent financial burden to the MoD.

15.4 Heat Illness

Heat illness continues to pose a threat to the health and wellbeing of UK Armed Forces personnel,[71] despite the significant drawdown of personnel on operational deployments to hot-dry and hot-wet global locations. Stacey et al.[72] also suggest that the current data available on heat illness incidence, evident across all sectors of the Armed Forces from training through to operational commitments, in regulars and reservists, is likely an underestimate of the true figure. Early studies investigating the number of heat illness episodes across the three Services in the United Kingdom[73] were subject to huge errors due to under-reporting. Data collated between 2002 and 2014 would have been elevated due to the significant UK presence in the hot-dry environments of Iraq and Afghanistan, as part of Operations TELIC and HERRICK, respectively. Data describing gender differences in heat illness incidence for UK Armed Forces personnel has not been determined. Nevertheless, heat illness per se will degrade all areas of operational effectiveness through increasing morbidity rates, and also occasionally mortality rates,[74] and it is important to determine if there is a gender difference in the likely risk.

Heat illness can be manifest in all environments, where risk factors include poor physical fitness, dehydration, obesity, sleep deprivation (i.e. poor quantity and/or poor quality), lack of adequate (heat) acclimatisation, impaired or poor sweat gland function, previous history of heat illness episodes, medications (e.g. antidepressants or diuretics), sweat gland dysfunction, as well as illnesses such as upper respiratory tract infection or gastrointestinal disorders.[75] Men and women differ in terms of their respective physiological responses to environmental heat exposure, as well as in terms of their responses to internal heat generated during exercise (work) performance.[76] Invariably, women perform worse than their male counterparts. This has been attributed to women having a higher body surface area to body mass ratio, a higher subcutaneous fat content and lower physical fitness.[77] Even when these differences are controlled for, the sweating response of women is smaller than that of men,[78] such that at a population level women appear to be less heat tolerant than men.[79] However, more importantly from a GCC perspective, due to their lower physical capability and hence higher relative work intensity, women working at the same rate as their male colleagues would be at a higher risk of heat illness.[80] However, due to the paucity of good quality epidemiological data in this area, it is not possible to even attempt to attribute a financial cost to this risk.

15.5 Hearing Loss

The MoD is currently carrying significant financial risk with respect to personnel affected by noise-induced hearing loss (NIHL).[81] Recent NIHL compensation claims have settled at circa £300,000, largely for loss of income and pension.[82] Audiometric standards provide age and gender-related normative values, where males generally have a greater degree of hearing loss, and females demonstrate a greater degree of hearing sensitivity. Men have a higher level of 'uncomfortable' loudness compared with age-matched women, who tend to be more sensitive to loud noises when emotionally exhausted following acute stress challenges.[83] The inference is that women in GCC roles could be more susceptible to NIHL than men, further adding to the likely financial risk to Defence.

15.6 Lethality and Survivability

Load carriage is an essential physical capability for GCC roles due to the occupational requirements to lift and move equipment, weapons, ammunition and rations. Absolute loads carried during infantry training range between 14–35 kg, but in-service can be >50 kg during operational patrols of up to 12 hours/day.[84] Patrolling activity on recent operations has tended to comprise of slow walking. Soldiers have also been required to traverse ditches, climb compound walls, sprint over open ground, fire weapons and evacuate casualties.[85] High external loads will impact upon physical performance (mobility, agility), health (survivability, thermal burden) and military capability (lethality).[86] The proportionately greater physical strain for women to complete the same load carriage-patrolling tasks[87] could result in greater levels of fatigue and reduced shooting accuracy.[88] Load carriage per se requires muscular strength to maintain postural stability; muscle fatigue during prolonged load carriage is associated with decreased postural stability,[89] which would increase injury risk.

In the event of a soldier becoming traumatically injured during combat, pre-injury muscle mass is a determining factor of recovery and rehabilitation.[90] As such, personnel with lower muscle mass pre-injury may have a less favourable prognosis during the immediate post-trauma recovery phase. This would again adversely impact on women to a greater extent than men, where women tend to have a lower muscle mass.[91] Thus, the lower body mass and muscular strength of women could reduce lethality, negatively impact on survivability, and may be associated with less favourable outcomes from traumatic combat injury compared with men. While these issues might be mitigated through appropriate selection and physical training, such risks could increase the financial burden on the MoD,[92] and the adverse impact on the individual.

15.7 Medico-Legal Implications

If the MoD fails to exercise its duty of care in terms of adequately and appropriately evaluating the risks to its employees, and mitigating those risks as far as is reasonably possible, it will be subject to personal injury claims. Returning to the case example of the three female former RAF recruits; they successfully sued the MoD in 2013 for £100,000 compensation for spinal and pelvic injuries sustained during initial military training.[93] In this instance, the claimants argued that marching in mixed-gender flights caused over-striding due to a requirement to keep pace with taller male recruits in the same cohort. This over-striding, in turn, led to training injuries that ultimately ended these former recruits' military careers.

The Armed Forces paid out compensation in excess of £108.9 million in 2012/13, an increase of £21 million on 2011/12.[94] This figure could further escalate when GCC roles are opened to women without appropriate education and training safeguards in place.[95] Indeed, while direct evidence of the risks is not available, indirect evidence of likely risks is known. The MoD would therefore be in breach of its statutory duty if not fully mindful of these risks with respect to GCC policy decisions. A research programme has been initiated as an output from the 2014 review,[96] and this research will inform the mitigation of risk for women in GCC roles. However, it should be considered whether the opportunity cost of the necessary action required to mitigate the risk of harm to women is in the public interest, and indeed is proportionate in terms of cost, time and associated military resources.[97]

15.8 Reputational Costs

The tangible costs discussed above would need to be balanced with the intangible costs to the MoD's internal and external reputation, where it has been deemed to not be in the public interest for the exclusion of women in GCC roles to continue. The negativity bias and asymmetrical nature of news reporting, whereby negative news is more intensely reported and saleable than positive news, represents considerable potential for hidden costs to be incurred through under-mining public confidence in the UK Armed Forces. Public confidence in the Armed Forces is fundamental to their perception of providing intrinsic security and safety, and hence the value that the public will place on UK Defence. The estimated costs associated with continuing to exclude women from GCC roles in terms of impacting on the reputation, profile and status of UK Armed Forces would need to be assessed in terms of wider national and international cost implications.

15.9 Implementation Costs

While there are presently many unknowns, infrastructure costs for implementation across the three Services have been estimated to be circa £20 million over ten years.[98] Establishing physical pre-conditioning programmes, as part of a MSKI mitigation strategy, will require circa £1 million per year.[99] A further circa £20 million has been allocated to the PES research programme to inform all GCC roles, optimisation of physical training and nutrition, as well as the systema-tic collation and analysis of morbidity health surveillance data from GCC men and women following implementation.[100]

These costs should be offset against the potential numbers of women joining GCC units. Taking into consideration the required physical fitness standards, it has been estimated that circa 80 women per year would achieve the entry standards across all Service GCC Arms.[101] However, women passing out as GCC trained ranks would be far fewer.

15.10 Conclusion

In terms of the economic debate on women entering GCC roles in the UK Armed Forces, and based on the data presented in this chapter, MoD up-front costs over the next ten years have been estimated to be at least circa £50 million to support an additional 800 personnel starting training. Costs for working days lost and the medical rehabilitation of training and occupationally related injuries, where a higher incidence and possibly more severe injuries would be anticipated in females, should also be considered but are presently unknown. Moreover, a contingency should be set aside to cover any legal liability claims with respect to discrimination, injury or hearing upheld against the MoD, especially during the transition period where lessons must be identified *and* learned in real time.

Tangible frontline benefits of increased manning are likely to be small, such that greater economic welfare might be realised from public monies by maintaining the previous policy stance of excluding women from GCC roles. However, wider intangible benefits might be realised from this policy change through maximising talent, fairness in gender messaging and enhanced national and international reputation of the UK Armed Forces. Indeed, declining numbers of deployable personnel in all three Services continues to be a cause for concern for military planners. This will have important implications for international relations, if the United Kingdom is perceived as a nation state that cannot fulfil its commitments and obligations in promoting and maintaining international security. As such, the government must take steps to redress this decline, where the merit of all options should be systematically considered.

The legal costs and compensation that might be payable in the future if women were continued to be excluded needs to be calculated, as do the benefits associated with reducing the risks of reputational damage and the impact this may have on recruitment, and indeed the costs of a reduced talent pool to support future recruitment. Thus, the marginal cost of (at least) £50 million might feasibly be outweighed by the probable marginal benefits. As long as the benefits outweigh the costs, the government's policy decision to open up GCC roles to women would enhance allocative efficiency. However, whether economic welfare has been maximised will only be evident in generations to come.

References and notes

1. K. Hartley. *The Economics of European Defence*. #11 Comment Paper. Armament Industry European Research Group. 2016. www.iris-france.org/wp-content/uploads/2016/12/ARESGroup-Economics_of_European-Defence-déc2016.pdf (accessed 24 December 2017).
2. K. Hartley. *The Economics of European Defence*.
3. M. Drummond. 'Output Measurement for Resource-Allocation Decisions in Health Care'. In A. McGuire, P. Fenn and K. Mayhew (eds). *Providing Health Care. The Economics of Alternative Systems of Finance and Delivery*. Oxford: Oxford University Press. 1991.
4. Ministry of Defence. *Women in the Armed Forces*. Briefing Paper for the Directorate of Service Personnel Policy Service Conditions. May 2002. http://webarchive.nationalarchives.gov.uk/20121026065214/www.mod.uk/NR/rdonlyres/10B34976-75F9-47E0-B376-AED4B09FB3B3/0/women_af_summary.pdf (accessed 24 December 2017).
5. Ministry of Defence. *Women in Ground Close Combat (GCC) Review Paper, 01 December 2014*. Corporate Report, 2015. www.gov.uk/government/uploads/system/uploads/attachment_data/file/389575/20141218_WGCC_Findings_Paper_Final.pdf (accessed 24 December 2017).
6. Ministry of Defence. *Women in Ground Close Combat (GCC) Review Paper*.
7. Ministry of Defence. *Women in Ground Close Combat (GCC) Review Paper*.
8. HM Government. *Sex Discrimination Act*. 1975. www.legislation.gov.uk/ukpga/1975/65 (accessed 24 December 2017).
9. HM Government. *Equality Act*. 2010. www.legislation.gov.uk/ukpga/2010/15/contents (accessed 24 December 2017).
10. L. Brooke-Holland. *Women in Combat: A Bibliography*. Standard Note: SN06886. International Affairs and Defence Section, House of Commons Library. 2014. http://researchbriefings.files.parliament.uk/documents/SN06886/SN06886.pdf (accessed 24 December 2017).
11. See Ministry of Defence. *Report on the Review of the Exclusion of Women from Ground Close-Combat Roles*. 2010. www.gov.uk/gov

ernment/uploads/system/uploads/attachment_data/file/27403/Repor
t_review_excl_woman_combat_pr.pdf (accessed 24 December 2017);
Ministry of Defence. *Women in the Armed Forces.*

12. G. Thorn. 'Council Directive on the Implementation of the Principle of
Equal Treatment for Men and Women as Regards Access to Employment,
Vocational Training and Promotion, and Working Conditions'. *Official
Journal of the European Communities.* No. L39/40, 76/207/EEC, 9
February 1976. http://eur-lex.europa.eu/legal-content/EN/TXT/PDF/?ur
i=CELEX:31976L0207&from=EN (accessed 24 December 2017).

13. E. MacAskill. 'Women Set to Get Green Light for Combat Roles in the
British Army'. *The Guardian.* 2014. www.theguardian.com/uk-news/2
014/may/08/women-set-for-combat-roles-in-british-army (accessed 24
December 2017).

14. P. Cawkill, A. Rogers, S. Knight, L. Spear. *Women in Ground Close
Combat Roles: The Experiences of Other Nations and a Review of the
Academic Literature.* DSTL/CR37770 V3-0. 29 September 2009. www
.gov.uk/government/uploads/system/uploads/attachment_data/file/274
06/women_combat_experiences_literature.pdf (accessed 24 December
2017).

15. See Ministry of Defence. *Women in Ground Close Combat (GCC)
Review Paper*; L. Brooke-Holland. *Women in Combat: A
Bibliography.*

16. Ministry of Defence. *Women in Ground Close Combat (GCC) Review
Paper.*

17. See Ministry of Defence. *Women in the Armed Forces*; Ministry of
Defence. *Report on the Review of the Exclusion of Women from
Ground Close-Combat Roles.* 2010. www.gov.uk/government/uploa
ds/system/uploads/attachment_data/file/27403/Report_review_excl_
woman_combat_pr.pdf (accessed 24 December 2017); Ministry of
Defence. *Women in Ground Close Combat (GCC) Review Paper.*

18. Ministry of Defence. *Women in Ground Close Combat (GCC) Review
Paper.*

19. Ministry of Defence. *Women in Ground Close Combat (GCC) Review
Paper.*

20. Berkshire Consultancy Ltd. *Qualitative Report for the Study of
Women in Combat.* UK Government. 2009. www.gov.uk/govern
ment/uploads/system/uploads/attachment_data/file/27405/study_wo
man_combat_quali_data.pdf (accessed 24 December 2017).

21. Berkshire Consultancy Ltd. *Study of Women in Combat – Investigation of
Quantitative Data.* UK Government. 2010. www.gov.uk/government/u
ploads/system/uploads/attachment_data/file/27404/study_woman_com
bat_quant_data.pdf (accessed 24 December 2017).

22. B. M. Gillespie, W. Chaboyer, M. Wallis. 'The Impact of Organisational and Individual Factors on Team Communication in Surgery: A Qualitative Study'. *International Journal of Nursing Studies*. 2010. 47(6): 732–41.

23. M. Mach, S. Dolan, S. Tzafrir. 'The Differential Effect of Team Members' Trust on Team Performance: The Mediation Role of Team Cohesion'. *Journal of Occupational and Organizational Psychology*. 2010. 83(3): 771–94.

24. Gillespie, Chaboyer, Wallis. 'The Impact of Organisational and Individual Factors'.

25. D. J. Canary, K. S. Hause. 'Is There Any Reason to Research Sex Differences in Communication?' *Communication Quarterly*. 2009. 41(2): 129–44; S. G. Rogelberg, S. M. Rumery. 'Gender Diversity, Team Decision Quality, Time on Task and Interpersonal Cohesion'. *Small Group Research*. 1996. 27(1): 79–90.

26. Ministry of Defence. *Women in Ground Close Combat (GCC) Review Paper*.

27. A. J. Allsopp. *Occupational Fitness in the RN – Focus on Royal Marines and Women in Ground Close Combat*. Brief to the Minister of the Armed Forces. Institute of Naval Medicine, Alverstoke, Hampshire. 2018.

28. Y. Epstein, C. Fleischmann, R. Yanovich, Y. Heled. 'Physiological and Medical Aspects That Put Women Soldiers at Increased Risk for Overuse Injuries'. *Journal of Strength and Conditioning Research*. 2015. 29(Suppl 11): S107–10.

29. L. Wentz, P-Y. Liu, E. Haymes, J. Ilich. 'Females Have a Greater Incidence of Stress Fractures Than Males in Both Military and Athletic Populations: A Systemic Review'. *Military Medicine*. 2011. 176(4): 420–30.

30. See Epstein, Fleischmann, Yanovich, Heled. 'Physiological and Medical Aspects'; Wentz, Liu, Haymes, Ilich. 'Females Have a Greater Incidence of Stress Fractures Than Males'.

31. M. Rayson, D. Holliman. *Physical Selection Standards for the British Army. Phase 4 Predictors of Task Performance in Trained Soldiers*. Defence and Evaluation Research Agency. Report No: DRA/CHS/PHYS/CR95/017. 1995.

32. J. J. Knapik, K. L. Reynolds, E. Harman. 'Soldier Load Carriage: Historical, Physiological, Biomechanical, and Medical Aspects'. *Military Medicine*. 2004. 169(1): 45–56.

33. S. D. Blacker, D. M. Wilkinson, M. P. Rayson. 'Gender Differences in the Physical Demands of British Army Recruit Training'. *Military Medicine*. 2009. 174(8): 811–16.

34. See Epstein, Fleischmann, Yanovich, Heled. 'Physiological and Medical Aspects'; Wentz, Liu, Haymes, Ilich. 'Females Have a Greater Incidence of Stress Fractures Than Males'.

35. M. J. Tipton, G. S. Milligan, T. J. Reilly. 'Physiological Employment Standards I. Occupational Fitness Standards: Objectively Subjective?' *European Journal of Applied Physiology*. 2013. 113(10): 2435–46.

36. Tipton, Milligan, Reilly. 'Physiological Employment Standards I'.

37. *Allcock* v. *Chief Constable*. 1997. Hampshire Constabulary. Case number: IT/3101524/97. www.xperthr.co.uk/law-reports/failure-to-s et-a-gender-neutral-job-test/66511/ (accessed 24 December 2017).

38. *Jo-Anne Dougan* v. *the Chief Constable of the Royal Ulster Constabulary*. 2012. Case number: 03244/97SD. Cited in: Secretary of State for the Home Department. *Independent Review of Police Officer and Staff Remuneration and Conditions. Final Report – Volume 1*. The Stationery Office. Report number Cm8325-I. 2012. http://webarchive.nationalarc hives.gov.uk/20130312170833/http:/review.police.uk/publications/part-2-report/report-vol-1?view=Binary (accessed 22 June 2015); R. Verkaik. 'Woman Inspector "Humiliated" by Failing Riot Test Wins up to £30k'. *Mail on-line*. 2011. www.dailymail.co.uk/news/article-2002610/Woman-inspector-humiliated-failing-riot-test-wins-30k.html (accessed 4 December 2017); S. Blacker, D. M. Wilkinson, M. Rayson, V. Richmond. 'The Gender-Neutral Timed Obstacle Course: A Valid Test of Police Fitness'. *Occupational Medicine*. 2014. 64: 391–92.

39. Tipton, Milligan, Reilly. 'Physiological Employment Standards I'.

40. See I. M. Gemmell. 'Injuries among Female Army Recruits: A Conflict of Legislation'. *Journal of the Royal Society of Medicine*. 2002. 95(1): 23–27; Ministry of Defence. *Annual Medical Discharges in the UK Regular Armed Forces 2009/10 – 2013/14*. Defence Statistics (Health). 2015. www.gov.uk/government/uploads/system/uploads/attachment_ data/file/328699/medical_discharges_1_apr_09_31_mar_14_.pdf (accessed 24 December 2017).

41. S. D. Blacker, D. M. Wilkinson, J. L. J. Bilzon, M. P. Rayson. 'Risk Factors for Training Injuries among British Army Recruits'. *Military Medicine*. 2008. 173(3): 278–86.

42. T. Davey, S. K. Delves, S. A. Lanham-New, A. J. Allsopp, J. L. Fallowfield. 'Body Composition of Royal Marine Recruits During 32 Weeks of Military Training'. *Proceedings of the Nutrition Society*. 2011. 70 (OCE4): E150. doi:10.1017/S0029665111002011 (accessed 25 January 2018).

43. T. Davey, S. A. Lanham-New, A. M. Shaw, R. Cobley, A. J. Allsopp, M. O. R. Hajjawi, T. R. Arnett, P. Taylor, C. Cooper, J. L. Fallowfield. 'Fundamental Differences in Axial and Appendicular Bone Density in

Stress Fractured and Uninjured Royal Marine Recruits – A Matched Case–Control Study'. *Bone.* 2014. 73(2015): 120–26.

44. Blacker, Wilkinson, Bilzon, Rayson. 'Risk Factors for Training Injuries'.
45. Ministry of Defence. *Annual Medical Discharges in the UK Regular Armed Forces 2009/10 – 2013/14.*
46. Ministry of Defence. *Annual Medical Discharges in the UK Regular Armed Forces 2009/10 – 2013/14.*
47. Ministry of Defence. *Interim Report of the Health Risks to Women in Ground Close Combat Roles.* Report number: WGCC/Interim-Report/10/2016. 2016. www.gov.uk/government/uploads/system/uploads/atta chment_data/file/536381/20160706_ADR006101_Report_Women_i n_Combat_WEB-FINAL.PDF (accessed 24 December 2017); J. L. Fallowfield, R. G. Leiper, A. M. Shaw, D. Whittamore, S. A. Lanham-New, A. J. Allsopp, S. Kluzek, N. K. Arden, M. T. Sanchez-Santos. 'Risk of Injury in Royal Air Force Training: Does Gender Really Matter?' *Military Medicine.* https://doi.org/10.1093/milmed/usy177 (accessed 13 January 2019).
48. Fallowfield et al. '*Risk of Injury in Royal Air Force Training*'.
49. Ministry of Defence. *Interim Report of the Health Risks to Women.*
50. R. D. H. Heagerty, J. Sharma, J. Clayton. 'Musculoskeletal Injuries in British Army Recruits: A Retrospective Study of Incidence and Training Outcome in Different Infantry Regiments'. *International Journal of Sports and Exercise Medicine.* 2017. 3(5): 1–9. doi: 10.23937/2469-5718/1510071 (accessed 25 January 2018).
51. Heagerty, Sharma, Clayton. 'Musculoskeletal Injuries'.
52. V. L. Richmond, J. M. Carter, D. M. Wilkinson, F. E. Horner, M. P. Rayson, A. Wright, J. L. J. Bilzon. 'Comparison of the Physical Demands of Single-Sex Training for Male and Female Recruits in the British Army'. *Military Medicine.* 2017. 177(6): 709–15.
53. R. P. Pope. 'Prevention of Pelvic Stress Fractures in Female Army Recruits'. *Military Medicine.* 1999. 164(5): 370–73.
54. Ministry of Defence. *Interim Report of the Health Risks to Women.*
55. Heagerty, Sharma, Clayton. 'Musculoskeletal Injuries'.
56. Heagerty, Sharma, Clayton. 'Musculoskeletal Injuries'.
57. G. W. Evans. 'Stress Fractures at Commando Training Centre Royal Marines, Lympstone–A Retrospective Survey (September 1979–October 1981)'. *Journal of the Royal Naval Medical Service.* 1982. 68(2): 77–81; R. Ross, A. J. Allsopp. 'Stress Fractures in Royal Marines Recruits'. *Military Medicine.* 2002. 167(7): 560–65.
58. K. Munnoch. *The Psychological Impact of Physical Injury on Recovery in Royal Marines' Recruit Training.* Southampton: University of Southampton. 2008.

59. Commando Training Centre Royal Marines. Internal CTCRM Audit of Hunter Company for 2010. Medical Centre. 2011.

60. Email dated 24 November 2009, Major D. Phillips to Dr D. Roiz-De-Sa. Subject: CTCRM insole study/costs of Hunter Coy.

61. Berkshire Consultancy Ltd. *Qualitative Report for the Study of Women in Combat*. UK Government. 2009. www.gov.uk/govern ment/uploads/system/uploads/attachment_data/file/27405/study_wo man_combat_quali_data.pdf (accessed 24 December 2017); Email dated 24 November 2009, Major D. Phillips to Dr D. Roiz-De-Sa.

62. Heagerty, Sharma, Clayton. 'Musculoskeletal Injuries'.

63. M. Nichol. 'Female RAF Recruits Get £100,000 Compensation Each … Because They Were Made to March Like Men'. *MailOnline*. 23 November 2013. www.dailymail.co.uk/news/article-2512412/Female-R AF-recruits-100-000-compensation–march-like-men.html (accessed 24 December 2017); BBC News. 'Female RAF Recruits Paid Compensation for Marching Injuries'. *BBC*. 2013. www.bbc.co.uk/news/uk-25078544 (accessed 24 December 2017).

64. Heagerty, Sharma, Clayton. 'Musculoskeletal Injuries'.

65. Ministry of Defence. *Women in Ground Close Combat (GCC) Review Paper*.

66. J. L. Fallowfield et al. 'Energy Expenditure, Nutritional Status, Body Composition and Physical Fitness of Royal Marines During a Six-Month Operational Deployment in Afghanistan'. *British Journal of Nutrition*. 2014. 112(5): 821–29.

67. Epstein, Fleischmann, Yanovich, Heled. 'Physiological and Medical Aspects'.

68. Ministry of Defence. *Women in Ground Close Combat (GCC) Review Paper*.

69. See Epstein, Fleischmann, Yanovich, Heled. 'Physiological and Medical Aspects'; Wentz, Liu, Haymes, Ilich. 'Females Have a Greater Incidence of Stress Fractures Than Males'; S. D. Blacker, D. M. Wilkinson, J. L. J. Bilzon, M. P. Rayson. 'Risk Factors for Training Injuries'; J. L. Fallowfield et al. 'Risk of Injury in Royal Air Force Training'.

70. Ministry of Defence. *Annual Medical Discharges in the UK Regular Armed Forces 2009/10 – 2013/14*.

71. M. J. Stacey, S. Brett, D. Woods, S. Jackson, D. Ross. 'Case Ascertainment of Heat Illness in the British Army: Evidence of Under-Reporting from Analysis of Medical and Command Notifications, 2009–2013'. *Journal of the Royal Army Medical Corps*. 2016. 162: 428–33. doi:10.1136/ jramc-2014-000384 (accessed 25 January 2018).

72. Stacey et al. 'Case Ascertainment of Heat Illness in the British Army'.

73. J. G. Dickinson. 'Heat Illness in the Services'. *Journal of the Royal Army Medical Corps*. 1994. 140: 7–12.

74. Stacey et al. 'Case Ascertainment of Heat Illness in the British Army'.

75. E. E. Coris, A. M. Ramirez, D. J. Van Durme. 'Heat Illness in Athletes; the Dangerous Combination of Heat, Humidity and Exercise'. *Sports Medicine*. 2004. 34(1): 9–16.

76. H. Kaciuba-Uscilko, R. Grucza. 'Gender Differences in Thermoregulation'. *Current Opinion in Clinical Nutrition and Metabolic Care*. 2001. 4(6): 533–36.

77. G. Havenith. 'Temperature Regulation, Heat Balance and Climatic Stress'. In W. Kirch, B. Menne and R. Bertollini (eds). *Extreme Weather Events and Public Health Responses*. 2005. Berlin: Springer-Verlag. 2005. 69–80.

78. Kaciuba-Uscilko, Grucza. 'Gender Differences in Thermoregulation'.

79. Havenith. 'Temperature Regulation, Heat Balance and Climatic Stress'. In Kirch, Menne and Bertollini (eds). *Extreme Weather Events*.

80. Havenith. 'Temperature Regulation, Heat Balance and Climatic Stress'. In Kirch, Menne and Bertollini (eds). *Extreme Weather Events*.

81. Ministry of Defence. *Number of Currently Serving Armed Forces Personnel Who Have Impaired or Poor Hearing*. Report number 19-12-2013-081103-002. 2014. www.gov.uk/government/uploads/system/uplo ads/attachment_data/file/276357/FOI-hearing-loss-PUBLIC_1390997818.pdf (accessed 24 December 2017).

82. See Ministry of Defence. Review of the Armed Forces Compensation Scheme. The Stationery Office. Report number: Cm 7798. 2010; Ministry of Defence. *Joint Service Publication (JSP) 765: MOD Compensation Schemes Statement of Policy. Part 1: Directive*. Report number: Version 4. 2016. www.gov.uk/government/uploads/ system/uploads/attachment_data/file/390236/JSP765__Pt1_AFCS_an d_WPS.pdf (accessed 24 December 2017).

83. D. Hasson, T. Theorell, J. Bergquist, B. Canlon. 'Acute Stress Induces Hyperacusis in Women with Higher Levels of Emotional Exhaustion'. *PLoS One* . 2013. 8(1). doi: 10.1371/journal.pone.0052945 (accessed 25 January 2018).

84. Fallowfield et al. 'Energy Expenditure, Nutritional Status, Body Composition'.

85. Fallowfield et al. 'Energy Expenditure, Nutritional Status, Body Composition'.

86. J. Drain, R. Orr, R. Attwells, D. Billing. *Load Carriage Capacity of the Dismounted Combatant – A Commander's Guide*. Human Protection and Performance Division, Defence Science and Technology Organisation. Report number: DSTO-TR-2765. 2012. www.dsto.def

ence.gov.au/sites/default/files/publications/documents/DSTO-TR-276 5.pdf (accessed 24 December 2017).

87. Richmond et al. 'Comparison of the Physical Demands of Single-Sex Training'.

88. N. Nibbeling, R. R. Qudeians, E. M. Ubink, H. A. Dannen. 'The Effects of Anxiety and Exercise-Induced Fatigue on Shooting Accuracy and Cognitive Performance in Infantry Soldiers'. *Ergonomics*. 2014. 57(9): 1366–79.

89. H. Rice, J. Fallowfield, A. Allsopp, S. Dixon. 'Influence of a 12.8-km Military Load Carriage Activity on Lower Limb Gait Mechanics and Muscle Activity'. *Ergonomics*. 2017. 60(5): 649–56.

90. J. L. Fallowfield, C. Bentley, Maj M. Foster, N. E. Hill, Lt Col D. Woods, A. Shaw, S. J. Brett, S. A. Lanham-New, S. E. Britland, G. Frost, K. Murphy, Surg Capt M. Midwinter, Col D. R. Wilson, A. J. Allsopp. *Surgeon General's Casualty Nutrition Study Report – 7: Food and Energy Intake, Body Composition and Physical Status of Injured Personnel from Op HERRICK (UHB / Headley Court Data Set)*. Institute of Naval Medicine. Report number 2014.009. 2014.

91. Blacker, Wilkinson, Rayson. 'Gender Differences'.

92. Ministry of Defence. *Review of the Armed Forces Compensation Scheme*.

93. Associated Press. 'Three Female RAF Recruits Awarded £100,000 Payouts for Marching Injuries'. *The Guardian*. 2013. www.theguar dian.com/uk-news/2013/nov/24/female-raf-recruits-compensation-m arching-injuries (accessed 24 December 2017).

94. S. Robehmed. 'MoD Pays out £100,000 to Female RAF Recruits Injured from Marching in Step with the Men'. *The Independent*. 2013. www.independent.co.uk/news/uk/home-news/mod-pays-out-1 00000-to-female-raf-recruits-injured-from-marching-in-step-with-th e-men-8960468.html (accessed 24 December 2017).

95. Ministry of Defence. *Interim Report of the Health Risks to Women*.

96. Ministry of Defence. *Women in Ground Close Combat (GCC) Review Paper*.

97. Ministry of Defence. *Women in Ground Close Combat (GCC) Review Paper*.

98. Ministry of Defence. *Women in Ground Close Combat (GCC) Review Paper*.

99. Ministry of Defence. *Women in Ground Close Combat (GCC) Review Paper*.

100. Ministry of Defence. *Women in Ground Close Combat (GCC) Review Paper*.

101. Rayson, Holliman. *Physical Selection Standards*.

International Security

16 Battlegrounds Yet Unknown: America's Future Military Force Structure?

RANDOLF G. S. COOPER

Introduction

The abbreviated title of this chapter, *Battlegrounds Yet Unknown*, may suggest various things to those tasked with envisioning potential scenarios for the deployment of America's military forces. Technologically focused individuals might suppose such a piece on force structure to be built around descriptions of marvellous military hardware; the latest wonder weapons and innovative concepts for integrating those pieces of kit effectively within organisational structures. But technology is no guarantee of victory, as witnessed in Vietnam and more recently Afghanistan. Other readers may think that *Battlegrounds Yet Unknown* alludes to a series of predictions about where America's next war will be staged and what force structure will be required for confrontation. And while there is a modicum of 'trend analysis' embodied in the concluding portion of this chapter, that is not the main thrust of the work either.

In contrast, this chapter assumes that military technology is constantly evolving, and that history shows that it is problematic to try and predict the next battleground, as unforeseen wars have plagued civilisation for thousands of years. During the past two and half centuries, US military force structure has been influenced by various factors running the gamut from past performance in combat, to the evolution of new doctrine, modes of warfare and – yes, in some cases – new technology. In most instances, though, we see old and new technology mixed within larger force structures, a technological 'buffet' catering to user needs in a manner that mitigates the risk of over-concentrating on one form of technology or another.

At the planning and budgetary stage, force structure change tends to occur over time, and the process is not associated with radical overnight transition. The Congressional Budget Office observed of the DoD that 'in general, adding or eliminating major combat units appears to take DoD about three to five years'.[1] Yet when speed is required, as in the case of having to immediately augment force structure, modify support provisions or return to finish the job via redeployment, there are means by which the US government can expedite the situation. Ultimately, as a mature democracy in which civil-military relations are balanced by an economically responsible governance system, there are budgetary mechanisms to help America cope with the phenomenon of 'impossible to predict' future battles.

This chapter pivots on an assertion that the transparent as well as resilient nature of US civil-military relations not only strengthens the political economy of America's military force structure, it represents a key national security mechanism in itself. If we consider the People's Republic of China and the Russian Federation as contemporary military superpowers, transparency in the United States' public debate remains a striking hallmark of the evolutionary process that produces the country's force structure. Perhaps more importantly, from the standpoint of studying the cross-strengthening of the political and military models that underpin a nation state's survivability, is the way in which the US democratic system functions to regulate force structure. America may not always prevail militarily on future battlegrounds, and one must admit that fiscal responsibility does take the occasional beating over the ever-present issue of deficit spending. Nevertheless, the nation not only endures but prospers with a governance system that can trace the roots of its political approach to defence spending back to its eighteenth-century Continental Congress.

If we were drawing a vehicular analogy, with the military serving as a vehicle for the further expression of national security policy, America's political system yields the mechanism for both acceleration and braking. Publicly elected political figures in the House of Representatives and the Senate vote on pieces of proposed legislation directly impacting force structure. When that legislation takes the form of a bill, it will find its way to the desk of the President of the United States, who serves as both the nation's democratically elected civilian head of government and the Commander-in-Chief of its military forces. The much-lauded system of checks and balances is far from harmonious, but it has proven to be remarkably robust over the past two and half centuries in comparison with America's contemporary superpower rivals.

16.1 Drivers of Force Structure Modification

Over the years, the US armed forces have been subjected to several major approaches concerning their restructuring or 'future structure'. The majority of these 'drivers' relate to concerns over defence preparedness (aka military readiness), changes to the national security environment and economic considerations. In turn, each of these drivers has regard to a series of basic questions, which look something like this: does the military have enough personnel and the right tools to do the job? Are there new enemies or threats, and can we deal with them? Do we need to spend more or less, and what structure will that result in?

It should be noted that drivers of force change and actual transformative change within force structures rarely occur as isolated events. In examining what we may term 'rationalisation for change' documents, it is quite common to see direct linkages made between the three areas of concern noted above. Moreover, it has been said that 'it is easier to do just about anything – enhance readiness, modernize weaponry, or increase sustainability levels – than it is to constitute a new force structure (or perhaps more importantly, to replace a posture once it is gone)'.[2]

As a technologically oriented global power, the United States has experienced multiple cases in which technological progression was directly incorporated into existing force structures. This can be seen in the incorporation of nuclear-powered aircraft carriers in Carrier Strike Groups and the deployment of Unmanned Aerial Vehicles or drones in the Air Force Unmanned Air System Squadrons.[3] In addition to technological factors, other major drivers of proposed structural modification include military failure as well as success, with Vietnam (1964–73) and Desert Storm (1991) serving broadly as respective exemplars of the limitation of conventional force in the former and the promise of an RMA in the case of the latter.

Generalisations, however, remain precarious. The battlefields of Vietnam, often studied in the context of the misapplication of conventional troop deployment, also witnessed innovative modifications to force structure. In retrospect, Vietnam can be seen to have built progressively upon the helicopter's baptism by fire in the Korean War, where it was used by the Marines for casualty evacuation, resupply, transport and ultimately limited combat operations in 1951.[4] Vietnam provided the ideal testing ground for the structural recommendations of the US Army's Tactical Mobility Requirements Board (commissioned in 1962 and known widely as the Howze Board).[5] The recognition of the new structure's entry into service came just prior to the Battle of Ia Drang Valley in 1965 as the 11th Air Assault Division (Test) was renamed the 1st Cavalry Division (Airmobile).[6] The structural accommodation of the helicopter from first appearance in 1945 to its coming of age in 1965 underscores the point that force structure decisions, even those relating to technology, take time to reach full expression.

Vietnam also spawned monumental decisions to tackle the way personnel were fed into the nation's force structure. This was reflected in President Nixon's dramatic move in November 1969 to sign Executive Order 11497 Amending the Selective Service Regulations to Prescribe Random Selection. This move to a so-called draft lottery progressed with his signing of a new law in 1971 to end the draft and put selective service on stand-by, thereby setting the stage for the abolition of conscription in 1973.[7] The all-volunteer force remains as a fundamental building block in US current force structure. Yet an argument can be made that an all-volunteer force carries a separate cultural price in that America's warriors seem more detached from society. The issue of sustainable recruiting may yet influence events on future battlefields if there is a full-blown superpower confrontation.[8]

During the 1970s and 1980s, military thinkers in the Soviet Union began to ponder how a 'military technical revolution' could influence the evolution of military doctrine. America, not to be outdone, and certainly leading in technological innovation, embraced the RMA. This move seemed to be underscored by US technological leadership of Operation Desert Storm (January 1991–February 1991), a deployment in which many of the other thirty-four coalition members were able to send little more than token 'boots on the ground'. But in the years following the action there were several calls to pause and reflect upon the experience of Desert Storm and what it meant in the context of technology, strategy and force structure. In 1995, the Strategic Studies Institute of the US Army War College published a paper provocatively stating that RMA thinking within the defence establishment was the domain of a few, and it was in the national interest to open a debate on a wider basis.[9] While the publication acknowledged that information age technology 'would be combined with appropriate doctrine and training to allow a small but very advanced US military to protect national interests with unprecedented efficiency', the authors of the paper remained concerned.[10] This was not an unreasonable Luddite fear; rather, it was an acknowledgment that Desert Storm was but one operation and that as a putative 'war' it had been terminated without the capture of Baghdad. There was concern that the attempted seizure of the capital had the potential to degenerate into prolonged urban warfare. In what was arguably a prescient moment in comparison to the course of later events in Iraq (2003–11), the paper called for a more balanced dialogue. That request does not appear to have been a backlash against new age technocrats, but rather the rational voice of risk assessment; it spoke to the strength of a wider integrated force structure.

Two years later, in a report focusing on force structure for the twenty-first century published by the Association of the United States Army's Institute of Land Warfare, there was a direct challenge to those who thought Operation Desert Storm exemplified an RMA.[11] The Report took a cautious approach in acknowledging the need to continue further development of precision weapons associated with annihilating enemy command and logistics centres, as the 'critical nodes in an opposing force'. But at the same time, it stipulated the force must also be structured to conduct the traditional operations associated with the army. It disputed the assertion that a proportionately smaller high-technology force could bring about a more cost-effective victory alone by surgically destroying the 'critical nodes' of an opposing military force. It stated that theories of 'nodal' destruction failed to make any difference in Vietnam. It then went further and directly challenged the accuracy of anyone who claimed that nodal theory could be applied to the events in Iraq in 1991, stating that ultimately it took conventional forces to accomplish the job.[12]

Despite the clash of opinions over the RMA's changing emphasis on the role of high technology in relationship to doctrine, there had been a collective acknowledgement that the Cold War was over. That meant a need for new thinking about the size of structures for deployment and the method by which firepower could meet a doctrinal shift away from two generations of thinking about conventional warfare.[13] One of the key studies in swinging thought towards smaller self-contained combat units, the so called modular approach to brigade combat teams (BCTs), was the 1994 publication of a seventy-two page 'pamphlet' entitled *Force XXI: A Concept for the Evolution of Full-Dimensional Operations for the Strategic Army of the Early Twenty-First Century*. This work recognised a new force structure was needed in view of the

Soviet Union's demise. In exploring post-Cold War options for force structure, it ventured into the RMA debate by noting: 'We must also recognise that success on past battlefields has resulted not so much from technological advances but from innovative ways of considering and combining available and sometimes new technologies as they apply to warfighting.'[14] In the context of this chapter, however, it lends credence to the view that evolving US force structures often consciously integrate old and new technology in what appears as a stepping-stone approach.

It was this type of measured progression that took place at theatre level during Operation Iraqi Freedom. The new Stryker medium-weight eight-wheeled armoured vehicle became the focal point of what was called the Stryker brigade.[15] This was an explicitly modular brigade formation that represented a cornerstone in the Army's twenty-first century transformation process:

The first Stryker brigade entered combat on December 3, 2003. As this convoy crossed into Iraq, the magnitude of the change became clear: The heavy equipment transport systems needed to carry Abrams tanks or Bradley fighting vehicles were unnecessary for the Stryker formations.[16]

It was not that this family of wheeled armoured vehicles was new, as the Stryker's international design lineage stretched well back into the 1970s.[17] Rather it was the latest high-technology edition of a proven design deployed in a new way that pointed towards structural as well as doctrinal evolution.[18]

America's future force planning calls for 'transitioning' military assets on hand to cover emerging needs until larger decisions can be taken on, for instance, strategy, structure and budget objectives. When it came to deploying BCTs in Iraq, there was a wider technological mix than just Strykers. As noted previously, the acceptance of combat force structures with old hardware, or what might be termed 'transitional assets', is commonplace. This helps explain the lengthy presence of Vietnam era M113-A3[19] armoured personnel carriers in support roles within the Army's Armoured Brigade Combat Teams. Their continued coexistence within US force structure meant serving beyond Operation Iraqi Freedom in support of vehicles such as the Stryker.[20] In corresponding fashion, the US Air Force may take pride in its fifth-generation aircraft, the F-35 multi-role stealth fighter. Yet, the USAF still retains and uses B-52 bombers manufactured in the 1960s. They have been kept fit for service through a continuing series of updates and plans calling for them to remain in operation through 2040.[21] This distribution of old and new hardware in evolving structures introduces a minor element of risk mitigation. The flaws, shortcomings and workarounds for older systems generally tend to be well known. Rather than over-concentrate the risk of new technology in highly specialised structures, the old plus new hardware distribution factor spans the evolutionary timelines of force restructuring. This combined approach has frustrated more radical thinkers, but it lends itself to greater performance predictability in force deployment.

16.2 Budgetary Battleground

William Nolte, serving in the capacity of Deputy Assistant Director of Central Intelligence for Analysis and Production, once noted:

> The point remains: while resource restriction can clearly reach a tipping point that destroys capability, public institutions – including security instruments – can sometimes benefit from austerity that promotes innovation and even competition, simulating some of the characteristics that the market provides private sector institutions.[22]

In most cases of legislated change to America's defence force structure, the DoD puts forth its force-related budgetary requests to Congress, which usually either approves them or sends them back to the DoD.[23] When they are sent back, it is usually with requests for budgetary reduction, which in turn impacts structure directly, or indirectly, by impacting operational support services. Over the years, hawks and doves were found in both major political parties and a working equilibrium was not uncommon. But a change in the legislative balance of power can function in a more partisan fashion to influence force structure. If Congress sought to take a more high-profile role in altering America's military force structure, it has several options that it could exercise to directly increase or decrease its force structure:

- Legal Codification of force structure. This is exemplified in Section 5063 of US Code Title 10, which actually specifies: 'The Marine Corps, within the Department of the Navy, shall be so organized as to include not less than three combat divisions and three air wings',[24]
- Setting the final or 'end strength'[25] of the armed services. Congress is required to set the total number of military personnel for each

branch of the US military. It does not, however, have to meet the personnel figures requested by the DoD, and Congress can have a direct and more immediate impact on the force structure. The DoD would be obliged to try to achieve congressionally mandated 'new end strengths' in the same fiscal year, while it is reckoned that it takes three to five years for the DoD to add or eliminate major combat units when left to its own devices,[26]

- The Congress can act to prohibit the DoD from employing any funding to alter force structure in a manner that is at odds with what the Congress approves. This was the case when the Air Force sought to 'divest' itself of A-10 close air support aircraft in order to save funds for an advanced multi-role aircraft programme. Following an investigation by the US Government Accountability Office, Congress moved to halt the Air Force's planned retirement of the A-10.[27]

The previously mentioned element of transparency in US civil-military relations, as manifest in the government's public disclosure of information, is a tremendous asset in assessing the relationship between government spending and defence force structure. This is especially true in analysing the impact of America's early twenty-first century wars, such as the War on Terror, as well as the wars in Afghanistan and Iraq. Take, for example, the paper entitled *Approaches for Scaling Back the Defense Department's Budget Plans*, which was issued in March 2013. It was a thought-provoking piece that had its origins in the Budget Control Act of 2011, which was congressional legislation that aimed to limit annual funding for defence and non-defence agencies between 2013 and 2021. 'It imposed caps on annual appropriations for defence from 2013 through 2021; it also established procedures that led to automatic spending reductions, which took effect at the beginning of March 2013.'[28]

That restraint was deemed to be wise by the Congressional Budget Office (CBO) in view of what was termed 'a period of generally increasing real resources' for the Department of Defense, from 2001 to 2010 when funding for the DoD's basic budget rose by more than forty per cent after adjustments for inflation.[29] This was a critical time in the context of national as well as international security. By 2013, the military establishment realised that the incremental or 'step-like' approach of the legislation was helpful in not immediately calling for huge matching compensatory savings. But that same year, as the DoD faced a congressionally mandated eleven per cent cut in funding, the reality of living with a prolonged period of regularised reductions began to bite. The CBO took a reasonably pragmatic view in stating that to lessen costs, policymakers could (a) reduce the number of military units, (b) reduce funding to equip and operate those units or (c) both. The choices were further delineated by means of four options, each of which specifically cited the impact in relation to military force structure:

Option 1: Preserve force structure; cut acquisition and operations.
Option 2: Cut acquisition and operations; phase in reductions in force structure.
Option 3: Achieve savings primarily by reducing force structure.
Option 4: Reduce force structure under a modified set of budget caps.[30]

The CBO could not offer advice, but it did provide an insightful analytical synopsis. If the decision was taken to reduce the number of units in the field while maintaining the funding levels per unit, it could impair the military's capacity to respond to multiple conflicts simultaneously, or to engage in prolonged conflicts necessitating extended overseas deployments for weary personnel. The CBO also pointed out that reducing the funding for equipping and operating the military units – the 'hardware option', if you will – would permit the maintenance of force size. But it did have a significant potential downside in delaying the purchase of new weaponry and limiting the amount of training, both of which could impact US military superiority and the ability to conduct peacetime operations.[31]

Certain elements of the armed services did not react well to the threat of 'sequestration', a term referring to the cancellation of budgetary resources after they had been appropriated. Under the terms of the Budget Control Act (BCA), if legislators provide defence funding within the BCA's limits on the funding for national defence, no sequestration would occur for the DoD's basic budget or Overseas Contingency Operations (OCO) funding. But in order to compensate, if legislators appropriated more in any year for national defence than the Budget Control Act permits (excluding OCO or emergency funding), then sequestration would take effect in an amount equal to the overage – meaning the difference between the appropriated amounts and the BCA's limit in that year. In such a scenario, sequestered funding for Overseas Contingency Operations would also then contribute to reducing the overage.[32] The military newspaper *Stars and Stripes* characterised the reduction in military spending as 'part of a larger deficit-reduction plan ... designed to be so unpalatable to both parties that they'd come up with alternative spending trims to avoid hurting the military'.[33]

What the Budget Control Act could not foresee, however, were changes to America's security environment and the nation's political trajectory as reflected in the election of President Donald J. Trump. Historic timing then seemed to take on a sense of serendipitous prophecy. Trump, who had run on a slogan of 'Make America Great Again', experienced a rapidly shifting first year in office. The Islamic State of Iraq and Levant (ISIL) was dealt serious territorial blows in Mosul and Raqqa. But Islamic State Khorasan (ISK),[34] Afghanistan's officially recognised affiliate of the so-called Islamic State, took on new life. The most immediate result of ISK proliferation was augmentation of the US Air Force structure with the dispatch of additional F-16s along with a corresponding increase in B-52 missions.[35] This change in security status compounded a fractured and unstable Afghan political scene, and led to American military and political leaders, on a bipartisan basis, rapidly reassessing the Obama administration's plans to end US troop commitments in what had become America's longest war. While a decision to augment troop deployments was in keeping with the overall objectives of the War on Terror, formerly known as the Global War on Terror (GWOT), there were developments in Korea that brought a sense of Cold War deja vu. Rapid improvements in North Korean nuclear weapons technology and intercontinental delivery systems called for the United States to take immediate steps to strengthen its antimissile systems and lend coverage to long-term allies such as South Korea and Japan.

The DoD budget for 2018 was drawn up well in advance of President Trump's November 2017 request that additional funding[36] be allocated for higher troop levels in Afghanistan and enhanced missile defences to counter the new level of threat posed by North Korea.[37] This unforeseen spending, along with President Trump's existing plans to strengthen the armed forces, meant there would be a growth of twelve per cent over the Obama Administration's plan to trim defence costs in the years ranging from 2018 to 2027. Among the factors leading to the Trump administration's increases were an approximate increase of ten per cent in the number of personnel serving in the military, a commitment to an ultimate goal of a three hundred and fifty-five ship Navy by the year 2027 (representing an increase of thirty per cent),[38] as well as funding allocated to new weapons and research for future weapons.[39]

President Trump's increased defence spending put further strain on attempts to limit the 2018 to 2021 'near horizon' spending goals governed by the previously cited BCA of 2011. Although the president's immediate requests concerning Afghanistan and North Korea were exempt from the calculations, as Overseas Contingency Operations funding, research by the CBO revealed that 2018 to 2021 defence costs would exceed BCA caps by $295 billion.[40] In the face of a potential intercontinental threat from North Korea and the unknown impact of what some observers saw as ambiguity in President Trump's foreign policy, there was no immediate outcry over failure to meet BCA goals. The President had come to office on a platform advocating military strength and most legislators realised that this stance implied additional costs.

The complicating factor in constructing defence spending models aligned to the BCA caps revolved around President Trump's newness to office. It is customary for the CBO to base its projected defence costs on what is termed a 'Future Years Defense Program', or FYDP, which is drawn up each year along with the DoD budget request. The FYDP 'describes changes in force structure, outlines schedules for anticipated major purchases of weapons, and provides estimates of costs for the ensuing five years'.[41] However, these five-year plans are not usually available the year a new president takes office. Exceptions are associated with the transition of power and changes to the political machinery accompanying a new administration. So, what does this mean in the context of budgetary battlefields yet unknown? It suggests that there would have to be considerable effort made to ensure both Democrats and Republicans are thinking along similar lines when it comes to the costs related to national security, the cost of defence spending and the impact on the budget in relation to the national deficit. All was not without hope as there was precedent for seeking exceptions to the BCA's goals. The spending cap limits imposed by the BCA of 2011 were previously adjusted as exemplified by the American Taxpayer Relief Act of 2012, the Bipartisan Budget Act of 2013 and the Bipartisan Budget Act of 2015.[42] This underscores the assertion that there is tremendous elasticity in the American system, but to work effectively the system must rely on a significant amount of consensus building.

16.3 Horizon Scanning 2025–2050

In 1999, *Joint Force Quarterly* published an article by Roxborough and Eyre, entitled 'Which Way to the Future?'[43] In contemplating the direction of warfare, the authors acknowledge that inherited or 'legacy' images of the last war tend to influence future force prediction. They posited that single-minded 'war planning scenario' advocates, meaning those who cling to the belief that their chosen scenario foretells the future, tend to dismiss opponents as unwilling to change rapidly enough to prepare for future wars.[44] The article warned that the actualisation or fulfilment of scenarios need not occur singly, and that in effect 'multiple futures are possible and likely to occur simultaneously'. Focus was then drawn down to four takes on future wars that were prevalent on the cusp of the twenty-first century. Although the article predates this chapter by a generation, cyberwar was identified as one of the four likely elements of the future.

Roxborough and Eyre were ahead of their time in advocating a more open-minded approach to restructuring the forces they saw as responsible for delivering traditional combat capability. They went so far as to question whether the traditional branches of the armed services (Army, Navy, Marine Corps and Air Force) were the ideal components of future force structure. They speculated that 'it might be sensible to form a dedicated organization for each future scenario'. However, as strikingly radical and forward thinking as they were on the traditional armed services, it is equally surprising to see how their more conservative take on cyberwar is reflected in contemporary thought a generation later:

> The cyberwar corps will be small, relatively inexpensive, and staffed by a mix of military personnel and civilians who will be indistinguishable from one another. The prized qualities of its personnel will be intellect and imagination. Together with computer engineers, the cyberwar corps will consist of anthropologists, political scientists, and psychologists. Many will operate from think tanks rather than traditional organizations and serve on an ad hoc basis for specific operations.[45]

The article developed a number of other themes and made valid observations on military culture at odds with progressive thinking on force restructuring. It also considered critical aspects of command and control in cyberwar and warned that more thought had to be given to how one proposes to 'exercise command and control over civilian infowarriors sitting at computer terminals'.[46] But one of Roxborough and Eyre's more insightful conclusions may help us understand why little progress was made on the evolution of a cyber force structure. They warned of an almost 'unconscious drift in doctrine and force structure as the services seek missions that will preserve their institutional integrity' within an overall movement to a more modernised battlefield still dominated by bombs and bullets.[47] This in turn would increase the need for the Army, Navy, Marine Corps and Air Force to defend their respective identities and budget allocations within a larger game of self-justification. This led Roxborough and Eyre to conclude that 'competition of this sort might be healthy, but it also runs the risk of leading to a force structure driven by efforts to preserve service autonomy'.[48]

In the event of a major military confrontation with a rival superpower, cyberwarfare operations are a certainty. As distasteful or unlikely as it may be to think that conflict could erupt with another superpower, force structure planning must take such scenarios into account. In horizon scanning, for the years ranging from 2025 to 2050, this chapter urges a much more radical approach to cyberwarfare thinking. This is advocated in full knowledge that changes in force structure take years to evolve and that the previously detailed 'transitioning' of military assets is part of the status quo. Earlier in this chapter, when remarking on the speed of change in Brigade Combat Teams, the comment was made that this 'combined approach has frustrated more radical thinkers'.[49] But let us now indulge that element of frustration and look at the slowness of change. It is against that backdrop that this chapter concludes with a bold proposal in order to open minds to what may be needed for *Battlegrounds Yet Unknown*. First, let us examine the pace of predictable thinking that signifies a continuum of the stereotypical cyberwarfare structure presented by Roxborough and Eyre in 1999.

America's first major step towards a cyberwarfare force structure came in the form of the establishment of a US Cyber Command (USCYBERCOM) as a Subordinate Unified Combatant Command within the United States Strategic Command. US Cyber Command represents a different form of force structure. It was actually created within the National Security Agency's (NSA) headquarters at Fort Meade in 2009,[50] with a tremendous level of dependency upon the NSA's operational capability.[51] Controversy arose almost immediately about this relationship, and there were vocal advocates for an amicable divorce. Others, such as Senator John McCain, who chaired the Senate Armed Services Committee, pointed out that the NSA was traditionally headed by military personnel, and urged continuation of the combined relationship. This was in keeping with the NSA's profile as a DoD intelligence agency. In speaking with the *Washington Post*, an unidentified source provided a rationalisation which implies that there was no option other than a continuation of the cooperative structure. The source allegedly said:

Cyber Command's mission, their primary focus, is to degrade or destroy ... NSA's is exploit [to gather intelligence] only. So without having one person as the leader for both, the bureaucratic walls will go up and you'll find NSA not cooperating with Cyber Command to give them the information they'll need to be successful.[52]

The comment might be construed as a sad reflection on inter-service rivalry, but it is also fair to suggest that it may have been a creative transitional accommodation to shore up a known weakness.

It took until 2011 for the DoD to publicly issue a *Strategy for Operating in Cyberspace*. Some might question whether there is ever a need to publicly disclose military strategy, but the transparent nature of US defence funding and force structure demand the forthright display of basic organisational features. While the timing of the public disclosure was not readily apparent, it is fair to suggest that America did need to publicly flex some cyber muscle in view of the successful Stuxnet attack on Iran's nuclear programme. Regardless of who was responsible for planting the 'weaponised malware' known as Stuxnet in Tehran's control systems software, thereby setting back the schedule for uranium enrichment, the worm's discovery in 2010 meant America would be on any shortlist of suspects for potential retaliation.[53]

According to the *Strategy for Operating in Cyberspace*, US Cyber Command was intended to offset cyberspace risk by increased training, information assurance, greater situational awareness and creating secure and resilient network environments; by engaging in smart partnerships and working closely with Combatant Commands, Services, and Agencies to rapidly deliver and deploy 'innovative capabilities where they are needed the most'.[54] USCYBERCOM was given responsibility for synchronising and coordinating service components within each branch of the military, including (but not limited to) US Army Cyber Command,

US Fleet Cyber Command/US 10th Fleet, the 24th Air Force, US Marine Corps Forces Cyber Command and US Coast Guard Cyber Command.[55] As questions persisted about the structure and force integration model, there were those that warned there was no need to reinvent the wheel:

We have a requirement to determine how cyber-space impacts national security policy, grand strategy, and conflict theory; force development including personnel recruiting, development, and retention; all aspects of resourcing from joint capabilities development to programming, budgeting, execution, and defense acquisition; military support to entities outside of DOD; and force structure across the Active and Reserve components. In these and other endeavors, we should fight the temptation to invent new and unique ways of doing business.[56]

Note in particular above, the preservation of the status quo in fighting the temptation to change. It is not just a fight to preserve structure, but also to preserve budgets and resourcing.[57] This siloed approach remains potentially divisive to combined operations during war as the four main branches of service may have 'a tendency to view cyber operations through the lens of how it impacts the basic function of their branch'.[58] Also of interest is the degree to which this thinking from 2014 confirmed Roxborough and Eyre's 1999 observation about established forces driven by efforts to preserve their respective domains (e.g. individual budget allocation).

Some opponents of a shift towards a separate cyberwarfare branch of service based their stance on the 'multi-layered aspects of cyberspace in which all services have equities'.[59] High-ranking opposition to a fifth branch of service was posed by Chief of Naval Operations Admiral John Richardson and Marine Corps Commandant General Robert Neller, both arguing on behalf of an integrated approach.[60] Admittedly, it is a very radical idea in the minds of traditionalists, who see the Army, Air Force, Navy and Marine Corps as holding greater legitimacy to contribute directly to the 'mailed fist' of traditional combat-oriented force structures. But could part of their reluctance to consider this 'outlandish' proposal for a separate cyberwarfare branch of service be based on the historic continuum of the cyberwarrior stereotype articulated more than a generation ago? Might they have thought it would diminish their own service's warrior profile if they were to be seen on an equal footing with the cyberwarriors that Roxborough and Eyre described as a 'mix of military personnel and civilians who will be indistinguishable from one another'?[61]

Perhaps those critics did not have sufficient time to reflect upon the progress made by America's superpower rivals and what their next generation doctrine may look like. It is somewhat surprising that Russia's successful integrated combat application of cyberwarfare in the 2008 Russo-Georgian War was not used more widely to spur innovate free-form thinking about force structure. The 2008 conflict was said to have set a precedent as 'the first case in history of a coordinated cyberspace domain attack synchronized with major combat actions in the other warfighting domains (consisting of Land, Air, Sea, and Space)'.[62] Given that it was integral to an evolving Russian doctrine, in which cyberwarfare's legitimacy was proven, it is interesting to note that the US Army's 2025–40 concept for cyberspace and electronic warfare operations remained so committed to the previously discussed transitionary model of evolution.[63]

On the one hand, the Army's approach could be said to have represented a bold attempt to look into the future in noting that 'the enhanced development of autonomous technologies portends a future where machines make decisions for themselves on the battlefield using advanced algorithms and artificial intelligence'.[64] On the other hand, it remained wedded to an older tactical era of mechanised infantry in ensuring 'a commander's access to cross-domain combined arms capabilities for both mounted and dismounted operations'.[65] Therein lies an anomaly in how cyber warfighting was viewed. For although the US Army had established the Army Cyber Institute as well as the US Army Cyber Center of Excellence in 2014, and followed it up with an Army Leaders Cyberspace Operations course in 2015, in 2018 it was looking towards battlegrounds yet unknown over 2025–40 and stating 'cyberspace operations are not presented as a warfighting function, cyberspace operations are cross-cutting and integral to all joint functions and Army warfighting functions'.[66]

16.4 Conclusion

Using this concluding portion of the chapter as a 'think piece' to generate alternative thoughts about force structure, let us consider the alternative to what we have inherited since 1999 as the historic model of cyberwarrior force structure. For exploratory purposes, we should be considering warrior culture and warrior values as integral to the construction of cyberwarrior identity. As a cyber-dependent superpower, the extent of cyber saturation in the everyday lives of American citizens is extensive. What if we changed our stereotype of the cyberwarrior and our model of cyberwar? What if America determined that the future of cyberwarfare lay in the military use of computers to kill, maim and destroy as many enemy soldiers and civilians as possible? Is it too shocking to consider computer-assisted killing of enemy civilians when it is precisely that type of thinking that will help spur creation of America's defence against an enemy's efforts to do just that?

We must remember that as theoretically new and sophisticated as cyberwar may sound in the opening quarter of the twenty-first century, it is the ideal weapon to use on America's technology-dependent civilian population. Making civilians the focus of attacks represents a much older and arguably regressive view of 'total war', defined here as unrestricted warfare targeting the civilian population. To date, the laws of armed conflict have not applied to cyberwar as they were established for physical combat, focused on destruction and injury.[67] But assumed behavioural norms in warfare can change over time, and the cultural certainty of wargames does not always reflect the lessons of history. By 2016, American intelligence services had already established that at least thirty foreign nations were working to develop offensive cyber capabilities.[68] Retribution and revenge factors that play directly into the hands of potential enemies and advocates of cyber-oriented frontline thinking are justified in asking what price American civilians on the home front might pay for events on foreign battlefields.

If we changed our way of thinking about cyberwar and acknowledged the possibility of a separate cyberwar branch of service ranking alongside the Army, Navy, Air Force and Marine Corps, how could it be made to fit the traditional pattern of a transitional force structure? A RAND Corporation study in 2015 demonstrated that there may have been as many as 100,000 men and women in the Army National Guard and US Army Reserve with 'some degree of cyber competence, including thousands with deep or mid-level cyber expertise'.[69] Veterans drawn from the reserves hold the advantage of already having been indoctrinated with warrior values and proven their willingness to embrace America's military culture. In the event of a national emergency demanding immediate mobilisation, their military records form a reference point in a critical vetting process. Existing conventional

force research conducted for the Congressional Budget Office concluded that of the major branches of service, the US Army had the
most effective model of Active and Reserve force integration.[70] This
integrated Army force structure model could be used as the nucleus
upon which points of interface could be grafted; meaning that such
personnel seconded to USCYBERCOM, from various branches of
service, could be reassigned to an enlarged and enhanced cyberwar
branch of service built on the active and reserve force model.[71]

Is there a potential 'tipping point' in the future when force structure
assets become force structure liabilities? As demonstrated in this chapter, America's force structure is constantly undergoing evolutionary
change. Also apparent is the fact that force restructuring can often take
years to work its way through regular channels, and will continue to
integrate a mixture of old, updated and new technology, in preparation
for *Battlegrounds Yet Unknown*. That mixture will serve to diversify or
distribute some aspects of risk associated with technological dependency. But if major transformative changes must be enacted on short
notice, be they technologically or organisationally oriented, America
can rely on the inherent strength of its political system to lend a hand in
expediting the funding needed. In view of the new levels of cyberwarfare risk, America may have to develop correspondingly new force
structures and conceivably new forms of civil-military relationships
to ensure global superpower competitiveness.

References and notes

1. Congressional Budget Office. *The U.S. Military's Force Structure: A Primer.*
   Congress of the United States. Publication number: 51535. 2016. 13.
2. K. N. Lewis. *Historical U.S. Force Structure Trends: A Primer.* RAND
   Corporation. Report number: P-7582. 1989. 1.
3. See J. Schank, G. Smith, B. Alkire, M. V. Arena, J. Birkler, J. Chiesa, E.
   Keating, L. Schmidt. *Modernizing The U.S. Aircraft Carrier Fleet:
   Accelerating CVN 21 Productions Versus Mid-Life Refuelling.* RAND
   Corporation. 2005; Congressional Budget Office. *The U.S. Military's
   Force Structure.*
4. K. J. Dougherty. 'The Evolution of Air Assault'. *Joint Force Quarterly.*
   1999. 22(August): 51–58.
5. J. A. Stockfisch. *The 1962 Howze Board and Army Combat
   Developments.* RAND. 1994.

6. T. Graves. *Transforming the Force: The 11th Air Assault Division (Test) From 1963 to 1965*. Strategic Studies Institute and U.S. Army War College Press. 2017.
7. B. Rostker. *The Evolution of the All-Volunteer Force*. RAND Corporation. Research Brief. 2006. 1–4.
8. See M. Thompson. 'An Army Apart: The Widening Military-Civilian Gap'. *Time Magazine*. 2011. http://nation.time.com/2011/11/10/an-army-apart-the-widening-military-civilian-gap/ (accessed 29 January 2018); K. W. Eikenberry and D. M. Kennedy. 'Americans and Their Military, Drifting Apart'. *New York Times*. 2013. www.nytimes.com/2013/05/27/opinion/americans-and-their-military-drifting-apart.html (accessed 29 January 2018).
9. S. Metz and J. Kievit. *Strategy and the Revolution in Military Affairs, From Theory to Policy*. Strategic Studies Institute and U.S. Army War College. 1995.
10. Metz and Kievit. *Strategy and the Revolution*.
11. Association of the United States Army's Institute of Land Warfare. *Force Structure and Force XXI*. Defense Report number: DR 97–8. 1997. 1–2.
12. Association of the United States Army's Institute of Land Warfare. *Force Structure and Force XXI*.
13. Headquarters Department of the Army. *FM 100–5 Operations*. 1993. vi. www.fs.fed.us/fire/doctrine/genesis_and_evolution/source_materials/FM-100–5_operations.pdf (accessed 29 January 2018).
14. United States Army Training and Doctrine Command (TRADOC). *Force XXI: A Concept for the Evolution of Full-Dimensional Operations for the Strategic Army of the Early Twenty-First Century*. TRADOC Pamphlet number: 525–5. 1994. 5.
15. M. J. Reardon and J. A. Charlston. *From Transformation to Combat: The First Stryker Brigade at War*. Center of Military History, United States Army. Report number: CMH Pub 70–106-1. 2007.
16. S. E. Johnson, J. E. Peters, K. E. Kitchens, A. Martin, J. R. Fischbach. *A Review of the Army's Modular Force Structure*. RAND Corporation. Santa Monica California. 2012. 10. www.rand.org/content/dam/rand/pubs/technical_reports/2012/RAND_TR927-2.pdf (accessed 27 April 2018).
17. The Stryker is derived from the Canadian LAV III, a variation of the Grizzly, a wheeled armoured vehicle that can trace its earliest design lineage back to the Swiss manufacturer MOWAG Motorwagenfabrik AG in the 1950s.
18. Reardon and Charlston. *From Transformation to Combat*.
19. The M113, developed by the Food Machinery Corporation, first entered service with the US Army in 1960.

20. Congressional Budget Office. *The U.S. Military's Force Structure: A Primer*. 23–26.
21. Congressional Budget Office. *The U.S. Military's Force Structure: A Primer*. 91.
22. W. Nolte 'Operation Iraqi Freedom and the Challenge to Intelligence: Keeping Pace with the Revolution in Military Affairs'. *Studies in Intelligence*. 2004. 48(1): 2.
23. Congressional Budget Office. *The U.S. Military's Force Structure: A Primer*. 12.
24. Office of the Law Revision Council. *Chapter 507- Composition of the Department of the Navy*. http://uscode.house.gov/view.xhtml?path=/prelim@title10/subtitleC/part1/chapter507&edition=prelim (accessed 29 January 2018).
25. The term 'end strength' is defined as the number of uniformed military personnel as of the final day of the fiscal year in *CBO Approaches for Scaling Back*. 13.
26. Congressional Budget Office. *The U.S. Military's Force Structure: A Primer*. 12–13.
27. United States Government Accountability Office. *FORCE STRUCTURE: Better Information Needed to Support Air Force A-10 and Future Divestment Decisions*. Report number: GAO-16–816. 2016. 1–69.
28. Congressional Budget Office. *Approaches for Scaling Back the Defense Department's Budget Plans*. Congress of the United States. Publication number: 4412. 2013. p. 7.
29. Congressional Budget Office. *Approaches for Scaling Back*. 1–2.
30. Congressional Budget Office. *Approaches for Scaling Back*. 34–39.
31. Congressional Budget Office. *Approaches for Scaling Back*. 4, 16, 32–33.
32. Congressional Budget Office. *Analysis of the Long-Term Costs of the Administration's Goals for the Military*. Congress of the United States. Publication number: 53350. 2017. 10.
33. L. Shane III. 'Despite White House Report, DOD Won't Plan for Sequestration Cuts'. *Stars and Stripes*. 2012. www.stripes.com/news/despite-white-house-report-dod-won-t-plan-for-sequestration-cuts-1.189671 (accessed 29 January 2018).
34. Islamic State Khorasan (ISK) is known by various names including Islamic State of Iraq and Levant – Khorasan Province and/or ISIL-KP.
35. Special Inspector General for Afghanistan Reconstruction. *Quarterly Report to the Unites States Congress*. Report number: Oct 30 2017. 98–99.
36. The request was for $1.2 billion designated as Overseas Contingency Operations funding for Afghanistan, and $4 billion in 'emergency

funding' for the North Korean missile threat. See Congressional Budget Office. *Analysis of the Long-Term Costs*. 11.

37. Congressional Budget Office. *Analysis of the Long-Term Costs*. 11.
38. The size of the naval building programme is not in dispute, but the projected delivery timeline is subject to question with congressional sources saying 2035 is a more realistic date. See Congressional Budget Office. *Costs of Building a 355-Ship Navy*. www.cbo.gov/system/files/115th-congress-2017-2018/reports/52632-355shipnavy.pdf (accessed 29 January 2018).
39. Obama's 2018 plan called for 2.074 million military personnel, while Trump's 2018 figure was 2.130 million. See Congressional Budget Office. *Analysis of the Long-Term Costs*. 1.
40. Congressional Budget Office. *Analysis of the Long-Term Costs*. 2.
41. Congressional Budget Office. *Analysis of the Long-Term Costs*. 2.
42. Congressional Budget Office. *Analysis of the Long-Term Costs*. 11.
43. I. Roxborough and D. Eyre. 'Which Way to the Future?' *Joint Force Quarterly*. 1999. 22(August): 28–34.
44. Roxborough and Eyre. 'Which Way to the Future?' 28.
45. Roxborough and Eyre. 'Which Way to the Future?' 31.
46. Roxborough and Eyre. 'Which Way to the Future?' 34.
47. Roxborough and Eyre. 'Which Way to the Future?' 33.
48. Roxborough and Eyre. 'Which Way to the Future?' 33.
49. Reardon and Charlston. *From Transformation to Combat*. 11–12.
50. The creation date of US Cyber Command is popularly listed as 2009, but it appears as 2010 in C. A. Theohary and A. I. Harrington. *Cyber Operations in DOD Policy and Plans: Issues for Congress. Cyber Operations in DOD Policy and Plans: Issues for Congress*. Congressional Research Service. Report number: R43848. 2015.
51. Theohary and Harrington. *Cyber Operations in DOD Policy and Plans*.
52. E. Nakashima. 'Obama to Be Urged to Split Cyberwar Command from NSA'. *The Washington Post*. 2016. www.washingtonpost.com/world/national-security/obama-to-be-urged-to-split-cyberwar-command-from-the-nsa/2016/09/12/0ad09a22-788f-11e6-ac8e-cf8e0dd91dc7_story.html?utm_term=.2daea9e58999 (accessed 29 January 2018).
53. T. M. Chen. *Cyberterrorism After Stuxnet*. Strategic Studies Institute and U.S. Army War College Press. 2014.
54. Department of Defense. *Department of Defense Strategy for Operating in Cyberspace*. 2011. 5. https://csrc.nist.gov/CSRC/media/Projects/ISPAB/documents/DOD-Strategy-for-Operating-in-Cyberspace.pdf (accessed 23 April 2018).
55. Department of Defence. *Department of Defense Strategy for Operating in Cyberspace*.

56. B. T. Williams. 'The Joint Force Commanders Guide to Cyberspace Operations'. *Joint Force Quarterly*. 2014. 73(April): 19.
57. The FY2015 requested cybersecurity budget for the Department of Defense was approximately $5.1 billion. See Theohary and Harrington. *Cyber Operations in DOD Policy and Plans*. 13.
58. T. Ricks. 'We Need a Cyber Corps as a 5th Service'. *Foreign Policy*. 18 March 2015. http://foreignpolicy.com/2015/03/18/we-need-a-cyber-co rps-as-a-5th-service/ (accessed 22 April 2018).
59. Theohary and Harrington. *Cyber Operations in DOD Policy and Plans*. 28.
60. H. H. Seck. 'Service Chiefs Reject Proposal to Develop New Military Cyber Force'. Military.com. 2018. www.military.com/daily-news/2016 /02/22/service-chiefs-reject-proposal-develop-new-military-cyber-force .html (accessed 22 April 2018).
61. Roxborough and Eyre. 'Which Way to the Future?' 31.
62. D. Hollis. 'Cyberwar Case Study: Georgia 2008'. *Small Wars Journal*. 2011. 7(1): 2.
63. United States Army Training and Doctrine Command (TRADOC). *The U.S. Army Concept for Cyberspace and Electronic Warfare Operations 2025-2040*. TRADOC Pamphlet number: 525-8-6. 1994. 1–34.
64. TRADOC. *The U.S. Army Concept for Cyberspace*. 10.
65. TRADOC. *The U.S. Army Concept for Cyberspace*. 7.
66. TRADOC. *The U.S. Army Concept for Cyberspace*. 8.
67. M. C. Libicki. *It Takes More than Offensive Capability to Have an Effective Cyberdeterrence Posture*. RAND Corporation. Testimony number: CT-465. 2017. 6.
68. J. R. Clapper, M. Lettre and M. S. Rogers. *Joint Statement for the Record to the Senate Armed Services Committee: Foreign Cyber Threats to the United States*. www.armed-services.senate.gov/imo/media/doc/Clapper-Lettre-Ro gers_01-05-16.pdf (accessed 29 January 2018).
69. I. R. Porche III and B. D. Wisniewski. *Reservists and the National Guard Offer Untapped Resources for Cybersecurity*. www.rand.org/blog/201 7/04/reservists-and-the-national-guard-offer-untapped-resources.html (accessed 29 January 2018).
70. Congressional Budget Office. *The U.S. Military's Force Structure: A Primer*. 38–39.
71. The Congressional Research Service reported that the Cyber Mission Forces recruitment target for FY2016 was 6,200 individuals and that the preferred composition ratio was 80 per cent military and 20 per cent military, with the force being divided into 133 tactical teams to be distributed in support of all Combat Commands. See Theohary and Harrington. *Cyber Operations in DOD Policy and Plans*. 14.

17 Innovating and Offsetting? The Political Economy of US Defence Innovation

DANIEL FIOTT

Introduction

In 2014, the United States DoD announced that it would embark on a new defence innovation initiative termed the 'Third Offset Strategy'. For the purposes of this chapter, 'offset' does not refer to defence procurement and awarding of defence contracts to national firms. Instead, offset specifically relates here to the need for a state to become more technologically advanced than its nearest rivals in the military domain – it means offsetting military power. The driving military-strategic logic of the strategy is to overcome the perceived military-technological rise of states such as China, Russia, Iran, North Korea and non-state actors such as Daesh. In essence, the DoD understands that if the United States is to retain the mantle of the world's superpower, it needs to ensure that it sits closer to the edge of the technology frontier than its actual and potential adversaries. Washington seeks to avoid military-technological parity at all costs. Only by harnessing the potential power of technologies such as autonomous systems, robotics, nano and biotechnologies, artificial intelligence, big data and cyber can the United States continue to be militarily unrivalled – or so the argument goes. The United States has been here before, of course, as two offset strategies precede the current effort. Whereas the First Offset Strategy sought to overcome the Soviet Union's dominance in conventional force strength in Europe and the Second Offset Strategy developed precision-guided munitions to challenge nuclear parity with Moscow, the Third Offset Strategy is as yet operationally and doctrinally undefined.

While the DoD, American defence research institutes and numerous US think tanks have attempted to breathe conceptual life into the Third Offset Strategy, there is as yet no settled understanding of what the latest offset strategy should look like. This chapter, however, uses a broad definition to describe the strategy. Indeed, for our purposes the strategy can be broadly defined as a set of policies and funding mechanisms designed to harness new technological innovations and operational concepts to offset growing technological parity with the United States' adversaries, and to maintain Washington's ability to project conventional power. Even with this definition, however, understanding the precise nature of the Third Offset Strategy has become a harder task since the election of a new US administration. Under the Obama presidency, successive Secretaries of Defence, first Chuck Hagel and then Ash Carter, and their deputy, Robert Work, pushed the debate on a new offset strategy forward. During Work's time at the DoD, the Department managed to establish a Strategic Capabilities Office and an offset body in Silicon Valley called the Defense Innovation Unit Experimental (DIUx) to harvest commercial technologies for the US military. The DoD even dedicated $18 billion to the third offset over its five-year Future Years Defense Program under Carter.

Under the Trump administration, however, the concept of the Third Offset Strategy, or that label at any rate, appears to have fallen out of favour.[1] In fact, the US National Security Strategy (NSS) published in December 2017 does not refer to the Third Offset Strategy once. This is not to say that innovation more broadly is not important to US defence. The NSS clearly states that 'losing our innovation and technological edge would have far-reaching negative implications for American prosperity and power'.[2] The NSS even calls for the creation of a National Security Innovation Base that cannot be separated into commercial and defence sectors. It goes on to state, in a familiar tone to the Third Offset Strategy, that 'to retain military overmatch the United States must restore [its] ability to produce innovative capabilities'.[3] The NSS' counterpart, the National Defense Strategy (NDS), even goes as far as to state that 'maintaining the Department's technological advantage will require changes to industry culture, investment sources and protection across the National Security Innovation Base'.[4]

Rhetoric and labels aside, the importance of the United States' military-technological position is still of importance to the Trump administration; it has, in fact, been a perennial challenge and issue of the US military and government for many years. While it is true that the national security budget request for fiscal year 2019 dedicates most of the $686 billion to more troops, the nuclear arsenal, naval vessels and combat aircraft, there is still room for sizeable investments in defence innovation (approximately

$92 billion).[5] Notwithstanding the complexity of calculating R&D funding in the United States, there is in fact recent evidence to suggest that during President Obama's tenure, US investment in R&D increased in relative terms. Despite decreases in advanced technology development from 2005 to 2013, from 2013 to 2017 the budget for advanced technology development increased by about 19 per cent.[6] The place of investments in advanced R&D in the United States cannot be discounted, regardless of the president or the party in power.

Even if the label 'Third Offset Strategy' has fallen out of favour in Washington's corridors of power, there is still a need to understand in more detail the chief political and economic factors that drive forward defence innovation efforts in the United States. This chapter therefore focuses on and is structured in accordance with two broad aspects of these efforts: (1) the economic rationale behind defence innovation, especially as it relates to emerging technologies and the civilian industrial base; and (2) the politico-military rationale, especially as it relates to the composition of US armed forces and the operational concepts that underlie US military strategy. Overall, the chapter aims at providing an updated analysis of how far the United States has come in developing its latest defence innovation strategy over the past few years and what challenges in defence-industrial development and military doctrine persist. Although the chapter principally focuses on the efforts taken by the United States in the domain of defence innovation, it does so in a comparative manner that also touches on the defence innovation strategies of actors such as the European countries, China and Russia.

17.1 The Political Economy of Offset Strategies

One of the principal politico-military dynamics underpinning the Third Offset Strategy is what is sometimes referred to as an 'arms race' of competing states seeking to maintain or enhance their relative military-technological power.[7] Not only are major states, such as the United States and China, increasingly investing in parity-busting technologies, but a number of middle-ranking powers, such as Iran and North Korea, are also increasing their technological prowess.[8] Despite these broader strategic concerns, one must also look at the political economy of the Third Offset Strategy and its variants to uncover the domestic dynamics that impinge upon the technological development of the

US military. Doing so is vital to understanding how successful the United States is applying emerging and disruptive technologies to its fighting force and military doctrine.

17.2 Expanding the Defence-Industrial Base?

A first major aspect of the United States' latest defence innovation initiative relates to the increasing importance of the commercial sector in relation to the traditional defence-industrial base. As the 2017 National Security Strategy states:

> The landscape of innovation does not divide neatly into sectors. Technologies that are part of most weapon systems often originate in diverse businesses as well as in universities and colleges.[9]

In fact, the idea that a Third Offset Strategy can bring the commercial and defence sectors closer together is not novel. For example, during the 1990s it was argued that developing dual-use synergies between the civilian and military bases could meet the twin ambition of capitalising on commercial technologies and breaking the monopoly of large defence firms in the US market.[10] By bringing in commercial firms, the then US government believed that it could diversify suppliers and inject a much-needed dose of competition into the defence sector.[11] It is, therefore, no surprise to learn that one of the obvious places for the DoD to turn to after initiating the Third Offset Strategy was Silicon Valley and other technology hubs in California and Boston. Yet, a major challenge in enhancing civilian and defence base integration is effectively managing the diverse and unique needs of each industrial sector.

The commercial sector is driven by profits, the quest for innovation and the protection of intellectual property rights (IPRs), and public image and reputation. The defence sector is also driven by profits and innovation, but there is a different ethos behind IPRs and the public reputation function. At least on the issue of IPRs and reputation, the commercial and defence sectors divert quite radically. It is not a given that commercial firms will want to share IPRs with the defence establishment. Indeed, while any 'dual-use system of innovation may leave space for an IPR regime that stimulates defence-commercial collaboration ... designing a regime that allows commercial firms to secure IPRs in a context where military establishments are loathe to share IPRs is extremely challenging'.[12] The US government is trying to unleash the full force of its industrial and technological creativity and innovation for the purposes of national defence, but it has enormous challenges in this regard because the commercial and defence sectors operate under almost completely different sets of logic (although in some technology areas the two sectors are closer than others). This is not a challenge that the United States faces alone, however.

Over many years and decades, countries such as China, Israel, Japan and South Korea have been looking at ways to better integrate their civilian and defence industrial bases. In particular, China's own steps began in about the late 1980s and it has been relatively easier for the Chinese government to channel R&D funding into both the commercial and defence sectors. While it is true that China's state capitalist model perhaps presently lacks the innovation potential of the United States, the Chinese government has gone to great lengths to mandate a solid partnership between commercial and defence firms on science and technology.[13] As Cheung asserts, 'the establishment of a vibrant dual-use economy provides a valuable opportunity for the defense economy to gain access to advanced technologies, knowledge, techniques and practices that narrow the gap with the top tier of advanced defense industrial powers'.[14] The integration of civilian and defence sectors with Chinese characteristics has led to the rapid development of capabilities such as the Shenyang J-31 stealth fighter, the Dong Feng 21 'carrier killer' missiles, electromagnetic railguns, the DF-17 hypersonic missile and more. While these technologies are at various stages of development, it is clear that China is also investing in its own offset strategy. Indeed, not only has China recently announced the creation of its own Military Science Research Steering Committee (the so-called 'Chinese DARPA'), but Xi Jinping recently called for the country to revitalise its military through technology.[15]

17.3 Offsetting Manpower with Technology?

Beyond the management of civilian and defence industrial bases is the challenge of dealing with the escalating costs of maintaining high troop levels. As militaries are increasingly professionalised, it should be expected that governments allocate resources not only to salaries and pensions, but also to social care and housing for troops. This is an acute issue in the United States given the size of its military. Indeed, it was estimated that between 2000 and 2014 the United States experienced a 46 per cent increase in military personnel costs.[16] Based on this logic, technology can potentially be seen as a way to not only reduce overall troop numbers, but to ensure the health and vitality of service members to a point where overall social and medical costs are reduced to a sustainable level.

If one of the driving rationales behind defence innovation strategies is the need to manage costs related to maintaining active troops, then it is worth looking at quantitative data to ascertain the extent to which the United States has attempted to balance its personnel numbers and associated costs with technological advances. The data in Figure 17.1 have been produced using a variety of sources and it attempts to show the relationship between US troop levels, the personnel costs associated with these levels and investment in Research, Development, Test and Evaluation (RDT&E). The right-hand axis reveals total combined active armed services for the US military, including the Army, Navy, Air Force and Marines (but not the US Coast Guard). The left-hand axis reveals estimated spending allocations on personnel costs and RDT&E from 1996 to 2018.[17] The time range has been selected to include the presidencies of Bill Clinton, George W. Bush, Barack Obama and the beginning of Donald Trump's tenure. It should first be recognised, of course, that the fluctuations in active service members, personnel costs and innovation investment also correspond to the United States' strategic engagement in the world and not just to a need to offset personnel costs with technologies.

Across-the-board increases in troop numbers, personnel costs and RDT&E from 2000 to 2003 are a response to the 9/11 terrorist attacks on US soil and the preparations for the Iraq War which began on 19 March 2003. The so-called surge in Iraq that began in 2007 also explains the increase in troop numbers and personnel costs from 2007 to 2010 – even if RDT&E costs plateaued over this period. The surge in Afghanistan which began in 2009 also spiked personnel costs and active service members from 2009 to 2010, but one will note the decline in defence innovation spending from 2010 to 2013. It is perhaps no coincidence that RDT&E spending in the US starts to increase in 2014 at the same time as the Obama administration showcases the Third Offset Strategy. However, establishing a causal link between RDT&E and personnel cost spending is not easy. The only firm conclusion one can make based on the data presented in this chapter is that personnel

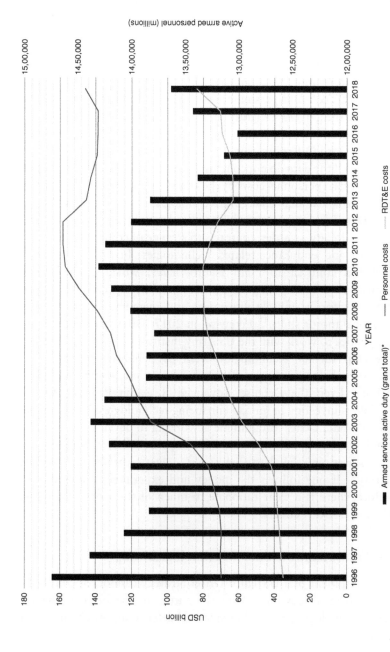

Figure 17.1: Troops, spending and technology, 1996–2018

Source: US Department of Defense. *DoD Personnel, Workforce Reports & Publications.* Defense Manpower Data Center. www.dmdc.osd.mil/appj/dwp/dwp_reports.jsp (accessed 18 April 2018).

costs represent a much larger share of defence spending than RDT&E; indeed, such a spending balance hardly lends itself to enhancing the United States' technological superiority over actual or potential adversaries. In fact, over the 1996 to 2018 period, there is no evidence to suggest that RDT&E spending ever offsets personnel cost spending. Interestingly, the data provided in Figure 17.1 do, however, show a strong correlation between RDT&E and personnel cost spending between 1996 and 2002. From 2002 to 2012, the spending gap between RDT&E and personnel costs widens and it is only in 2014 that we see the gap close slightly. Again, this is the period in which the US DoD began investing time, intellectual energy and money in developing the Third Offset Strategy.

Yet, even if the data do not conclusively show that RDT&E spending is used to offset personnel costs by the US government, there is plenty of evidence to show that emerging technologies are being used by the US DoD to deal with personnel cost-related issues. For example, DIUx has already awarded contracts to a range of companies working on health and endurance-related technologies. In 2016, the DIUx awarded a contract to Halo Neuroscience, which is developing a headset that is currently being tested by US Special Operations Forces to improve muscle movement and memory, endurance and fine tactical motor skills.[18] Likewise, in 2017, DIUx contracted Qool Therapeutics to work with the US Army Institute of Surgical Research to develop further technologies, such as nebulised frozen saline designed to help speed up recovery from cardiac, spinal and brain injuries.[19] Even the Defense Advanced Research Projects Agency (DARPA) is investing in human enhancing technologies. For example, DARPA's 'Safe Genes' programme is working to develop gene editing technologies designed to protect US troops from harmful pathogens and diseases in the battlefield (e.g. genetic protection against malaria).[20] If one follows the money and experimental endeavours, therefore, there is a clear rationale to much of the work underlying DIUx and DARPA efforts.

17.4 Transatlantic Military-Technological Gap

The development of a US Third Offset Strategy cannot, of course, be divorced from discussions about the nature of the NATO alliance. Indeed, the widening of the United States' defence supply chain cannot be confined to the territory of the United States, as in many cases, as discussed in Chapter 7, the DoD may even look to places such as Europe and/or Asia for cutting-edge technologies that can be harnessed for the benefit of the US military. Indeed, Udis and Maskus suggested some time ago that 'it is clear that American prime contractors ... have become increasingly aware of the significant technical capabilities of smaller firms in Western Europe and elsewhere'.[21] By engaging in technology-sharing practices, the US defence industrial base may be able to improve its overall ability to innovate by extending to Europe. As Robert Work remarked at the outset of the strategy, 'all of us [NATO member states] together need to decide if this innovation effort is a priority or not ... we have to get allied participation'.[22] Key European allies, such as France and the United Kingdom, have risen to these calls with their own offset strategies.

For example, despite the fact that the United Kingdom is dwarfed by the United States in terms of defence innovation spending, the UK government has been relatively vocal about the importance of the Third Offset Strategy. The strategy was specifically mentioned in the 2015 SDSR, and on 12 August 2016 the MoD announced that it would embark on its own Innovation Initiative.[23] One of the key strands of the initiative seeks to mimic the DIUx with the creation of an Innovation and Research Insights Unit (IRIS) tasked with identifying new disruptive technologies and their implications for UK defence. Another strand of the UK's Innovation Initiative is a special innovation fund worth some £800 million ($1.2 billion) over a ten-year period from 2015. The fund is supposed to invest in emerging technologies, especially those being developed by SMEs. Additionally, in December 2015, the then Secretary of State for Defence, Michael Fallon, stated that the United Kingdom would also create a £1.2 billion (US$1.6 billion) innovation fund 'to keep ahead of [the UK's] adversaries: in cyber, robotics, autonomous systems, and space'.[24] Despite these efforts, however, a major question for European allies within NATO is whether the resources required to embark on a serious defence innovation initiative can be made available.[25]

Without broader European buy-in to the US defence innovation efforts, questions could arise about the military-technological gap between NATO allies. Such a gap already exists, of course, but the question is whether NATO allies can agree on the politico-military rationale for investing in certain technologies over others.

Some NATO allies in Europe can perhaps agree to the need for technologies designed to overcome the anti-access/area denial (A2/AD) threat posed by Russia, but others might justifiably ask how increased investment in defence innovation will help deal with security problems such as home-grown terrorism and/or refugee flows. NATO has been here before, of course. During the 1990s, with the development of the RMA, the United States was concerned that European allies would not be able to match, or indeed see the need for, technological investments in areas such as common, control, communications, computers, intelligence, surveillance and reconnaissance (C4ISR). While many European countries did eventually start to invest in C4ISR capabilities, there were questions about how committed the Europeans were to the RMA and whether they could incorporate advanced technologies into their military planning quick enough to meet operational demands.[26]

In this context, it should also be recognised that members of the European Union are also developing their own common strategy on defence innovation. In particular, EU institutions and Member States are devoting much more time and energy into defence research, even if, as yet, no coherent overall strategy for the use of military technologies by the EU and its Member States has emerged. As the European Defence Agency has stated, the EU needs to remain:

a strategic player on the world stage, in particular sustaining technical credibility in innovative technologies. This will allow the EU to maintain political relevance and military interoperability with the US, which has been pressing ahead with innovation in its Third Offset Strategy.[27]

The 2017 establishment of the European Defence Fund has already led to European investments in defence research programmes, such as adaptable camouflage, unmanned maritime systems and battlefield situational awareness.[28] The €25 million invested in defence research by the European Union in 2017 is, of course, a comparatively tiny amount of money when compared to what the United States invests, although future plans include a €500 million per year investment in defence R&D by the EU. However, the larger issue at stake here is whether EU efforts on defence innovation will address the same types of politico-military threats and assumptions underlying the Third Offset Strategy, and what consequence this will have for NATO over the longer term.

17.5 Operational Implications of Offset Strategies

The issue of strategic coherence within NATO could be amplified in light of the latest US National Security Strategy. One of the initial criticisms of the Third Offset Strategy was that it lacked clarity over the identification of the United States' main adversary. In fact, ideas at the time pointed to China and Russia, but also middle-ranking powers such as Iran and North Korea, plus even non-state actors such as Daesh. The intent behind not identifying one principal adversary, departing from the course taken during the first and second offset strategies that specifically targeted the Soviet Union, may of course reflect the multifaceted nature of threats facing the United States, but also the previous administration's desire to nurture cooperative ties with China. On the face of things, while the Trump administration seems to have shelved the title of the Third Offset Strategy, it has rhetorically named China as its major adversary in the NSS[29] and Nuclear Posture Review.[30] On this basis, one may ask whether this would mean that US military-technological strategy should now largely be geared towards possible conflict with Beijing. Beyond this rhetoric, however, the 2017 NSS and NDS still do not point to a single adversary, which means that scientists and military planners must plan for a full spectrum of conflicts and adversaries when thinking about what military technologies to advance and develop. As the NSS and NDS note, in addition to North Korea and Iran, 'China and Russia challenge American power, influence, and interests [in their attempts] to erode American security and prosperity.'[31] This is no great advance on the concept underlying the Third Offset Strategy.

17.6 Overmatch and A2/AD

As they relate to defence innovation, however, the operational-doctrinal assumptions that flow from the Trump administration's security and defence strategies are interesting. One of the more significant reversals of policy since the Obama administration relates to the relationship between technology and force. As the current US government states, past governments 'incorrectly believed that technology could compensate for [their] reduced capacity for the ability to field enough forces to prevail militarily'.[32] In respect of this observation, the Trump administration has placed greater stock in increasing the overall personnel size of the US military, the modernisation of US nuclear weapons and infrastructure, promotion of space as a priority domain, development of cyberspace capabilities and the enhancement of US intelligence capabilities. These priorities have given rise to a number of ideas about how the US military should prioritise capabilities in the Trump era. Studies have focused on the need for the United States to maintain and extend superiority on a geopolitical basis.[33] In particular, the threat from A2/AD capabilities, which are creating less permissive operational theatres and communication lines, has been widely touted as one area where the United States needs to invest money and procurement decisions. This is why one of the major policy prescriptions in the US NDS is to develop greater advanced autonomous systems (particularly in the fields of artificial intelligence, machine learning and advanced manufacturing) and to develop the concept of 'dynamic force employment'.[34]

Both China and Russia pose an A2/AD challenge for the US military, and for the NATO alliance as a whole. In particular, Russia's 'A2/AD bastions' are geared to frustrating NATO access to allies, such as the way Kaliningrad threatens NATO's ability to reinforce its Baltic allies by air and sea, via the adjacent, thin land corridor at Suwalki that connects Poland to Lithuania.[35] Aside from the nuclear aspects of Russia's A2/AD bastions, the Russian Federation has also taken important steps into the autonomous systems and robotics domains, albeit in a different fashion to the US military. Instead of looking for disruptive technologies through intense research and development, the Russian model of innovation looks to make incremental advances in areas such as autonomous systems and robotics, and to then gradually introduce such technologies into their conventional force structures and capabilities. In particular, Russian forces have integrated robotics systems in their fire-fighting and mine clearing activities, but increasingly the Russian Federation is also making great strides in automated turret systems placed on manned armoured personnel carriers, armoured cars, support vehicles and even used as secondary weapons on large weapons systems such as self-propelled artillery pieces.[36] When aggregated, Russia's advances in nuclear force prepositioning, hybrid and robotics/automation change the strategic calculus for the United States and its NATO allies.

China has also made great strides in its A2/AD capabilities. Firstly, it is clear that Beijing is developing conventional forces, such as modern aircraft, carriers and missiles to ensure strategic overmatch in relation to the United States and the Asia-Pacific region. Yet, China's ambitions are not just restricted to conventional forces as the country is also developing technologies such as guided missiles and hypersonic, electromagnetic and directed energy weaponry. In particular, the Chinese are reportedly dedicating much of their high-end R&D efforts to developing hypersonic cruise missiles.[37] Such weapons would be much harder to repel with existing antimissile systems, and they are designed to travel fast enough to be able to penetrate targets such as aircraft carriers in a more effective manner. It should be noted that hypersonic speeds are usually defined as exceeding five times the speed of sound, or Mach 5 (3,836 miles per hour).[38] As stated earlier, China's ability to mandate cooperation between the commercial and defence industrial bases is contributing to leapfrog advances in key advanced weapons systems. The strategic calculus for US force planning in the Asia-Pacific and beyond has to rapidly evolve to take stock of China's own revolution in military technology.

17.7 Multi-Domain Battle and Technology

However, when taking into consideration recent Russian and Chinese developments in defence innovation, US military technology strategy appears to be shifting away from a predominantly technology-first policy. Indeed, while many of the United States' recent strategic assumptions in the NSS and NDS point to the continuation of the Third Offset Strategy (albeit by other names), the US military has perhaps tried to seize back the discussion on overmatch from the more industrially minded elements within the DoD.[39] Under the rubric of the Third Offset Strategy, for example, the problem of not having automatic access to maritime areas close to China and in the Asia-Pacific was seemingly remedied by inventing so-called Upward Falling Payloads (or armed unmanned systems buried in the ocean in a stealthy manner in special storage capsules). Such innovations do, of course, push the envelope in terms of individual technology and capability ideas, but they do not necessarily address the larger issue of what broader operational concepts should apply for such overmatch-style military capabilities. Here, the US military has over the course of the past year or so flipped the rubric of their overmatch thinking on its head: instead of thinking of technology first and doctrine later, it has devoted much more time to thinking about operational and tactical needs first, and then what technologies could be adapted for their strategic purposes.

This conceptual development is best seen in relation to the work conducted by defence planners and analysts in the United States, especially with regard to the work on the so-called Multi-Domain Battle concept. While some analysts suggest that there is nothing new about the Multi-Domain Battle concept,[40] the US military is attempting to identify ways in which the Joint Force will be able to operate simultaneously across space, cyber, air, land and maritime domains. The need for such a concept derives not only from changes in the military capabilities of adversaries, but from the evolving hybrid operational environment as well. Under Multi-Domain Battle the United States seeks to augment its forward presence, to integrate capabilities and to ensure greater resilience in the field.[41] More specifically, there are concerns that the future of warfare will increasingly be characterised by an ability to combine conventional and non-conventional forces and technologies, densely populated urban areas of action and information warfare as well as the control of political narratives. Yet, even if the idea of Multi-Domain Battle is designed to give greater coherence to the US military's overmatch strategy, technology must necessarily play a role in making conceptual propositions a reality. For many in the US military, technology domains such as unmanned systems, electromagnetic weapons, information warfare, hypersonic payloads, nanoexplosives, artificial intelligence, additive manufacturing and robotics are essential but they will not be effective without a coherent military doctrine. The continued dilemma for the US military, despite the conceptual work on the Third Offset Strategy, is effectively melding emerging technologies with a coherent overall military doctrine.

An added challenge for the United States is that adversaries such as China are also simultaneously developing military doctrine to plan for the wars of the future. Not only has China released its own national development plan for artificial intelligence technologies (in July 2017), but Kania[42] has argued that Beijing is developing a military doctrine designed to overmatch US military-technological prowess. It is doing this through the development of new paradigms in warfare, based on the idea of 'singularity' on the battlefield. Whereas the United States continues to expend intellectual energy on developing concepts centred around human-machine interaction, the Chinese believe that because human cognition can no longer keep pace with the speed of decision making and tempo of combat in future warfare, it may be wise to take humans 'out of the loop' altogether in order to secure a military advantage.[43] Technology areas such as artificial intelligence are increasingly seen by China's leadership as a core aspect of national and military power.[44] China's approach is evolving from an obsolete doctrine centred on guerrilla warfare tactics (based on the principle of a 'People's War') to one which is geared towards developing military capabilities that can inflict decisive damage on adversaries based upon identification of weaknesses in their capabilities and decision-making processes.[45] Thus, for the United States the issue is not just maintaining a technology overmatch over rivals such as China but also ensuring a doctrinal overmatch too.

17.8 Conclusion

This chapter has focused on the United States' latest efforts to enhance its military-technological overmatch compared to stated adversaries such as China and Russia. Defence innovation has been a perennial concern for Washington, but the changing global military balance of power now means that powers such as China are also increasingly looking at ways to overmatch US military power. This suggests that the United States is presently locked into a strategic race with powers such as China to be the first to: (1) effectively farm commercial technologies that are of benefit to military capability development; (2) develop military technologies and capabilities that enhance its overall military power; and (3) design military doctrine at the broader strategic and tactical levels that can coherently use new military technologies for military effect. To better understand this triple military-technological global race, this chapter has focused on the economic and politico-military rationales that are guiding the latest US defence innovation initiative. The chapter has adopted a comparative approach that predominately looks at US efforts in relation to military-technological developments in China, Russia and Europe.

Overall, the chapter has shown how China has taken great strides forward in developing its own defence innovation initiative. Beijing is spending more on advanced defence R&D, it is rapidly developing advanced technologies such as stealth fighters and hypersonic weapons and it is evolving the military doctrine guiding the Chinese military. China's drive to field advanced technologies derives from a desire to be able to capitalise on identified weaknesses in the militaries of adversaries. Beijing also appears to conceptually approach technology domains such as artificial intelligence differently from the United States, especially when it comes to thinking about human-machine collaboration. Lastly, whereas a great challenge for the United States is to effectively combine the innovative energies of both its defence and commercial sectors, China's model of state capitalism may confer on Beijing an ability to mandate cooperation between its civil and defence industrial bases. While this model of state capitalism raises questions about how innovative the Chinese market can be, it marks a radically different strategy for managing national innovation when compared to the United States.

The United States faces a number of hurdles if its latest defence innovation initiative is to be a success. First, Washington faces the perennial challenge of managing manpower and technology costs. We have seen how an increasingly large proportion of the US defence budget is dedicated to recruiting troops and ensuring that they have adequate social and health care, housing and pensions. In theory at least, the introduction of emerging and disruptive technologies can be seen as a way of offsetting manpower costs by using technology to replace personnel for certain tasks, or to ensure that technological developments in, say, biotech and health can improve the resilience of troops in the field. This chapter has shown how in the recent past the United States has been unsuccessful at using technology to offset manpower costs. In fact, for varied and numerous political reasons the US government invests in both personnel and technology, but the overarching challenge of keeping defence spending within the United States' broader resource constraints remains. The initial indications are that President Trump's administration wants to focus the bulk of US budgetary resources on personnel and conventional/nuclear capabilities. What this refocus in spending means for the future of defence innovation in the United States remains unclear at this time.

Second, the US military continues to face the challenge of developing military doctrine that effectively utilises recent advances in military technology. The development of concepts such as Multi-Domain Battle represents important advances in US thinking, but the drive towards doctrinal innovation is hampered by a lack of clarity over what rivals the United States should focus on when developing capabilities, and how best to respond to the ever evolving military doctrines of adversaries, such as China and Russia. Innovation in doctrine (rather than technology) is fraught with political considerations that emanate from within the DoD itself and across the United States' military services. The seeming shift from technology-centric thinking within the DoD to more operationally minded considerations may suggest that the United States has reached a more mature stage in thinking about defence innovation, but it may also perhaps symbolise a drive by military planners to wrestle back control of US defence innovation efforts from industry and the political class. Furthermore, while in theory having multiple adversaries should not pose a problem as far as military capability development is concerned, the development of full spectrum capabilities is not free from politics. Naturally, as noted in Chapter 2, each branch of the US military is keen to promote capabilities that ensure its own primacy and relevance.

Overall, therefore, the United States has taken important strides forward in developing its latest defence innovation initiative. A number of technology programmes launched under the Obama Administration are starting to bear fruit, and the US military has placed a great amount of stock in developing doctrine to keep up with technological advances. While the defence innovation initiative is mainly a national affair for the United States, this latest wave of innovation sees China, Russia and European countries focus ever more on developing military technologies. For the NATO alliance in particular, a collective defence innovation strategy is still absent and the European Union has only just started funding defence R&D. These broader political considerations will no doubt continue to inform what any Third Offset Strategy may look like in the future. In fact, what is perhaps clearest of all from a study of the US defence innovation initiative is that whereas in the past the first and second offset strategies were confined to particular moments in history, the United States, its partners and adversaries may be entering into an unending military technology race due to the scale and pace of technological developments and military rivalries.

References and notes

1. See P. McLeary. 'The Pentagon's Third Offset May be Dead, But No One Knows What Comes Next'. *Foreign Policy*. 2017. http://foreignpolicy .com/2017/12/18/the-pentagons-third-offset-may-be-dead-but-no-one-k nows-what-comes-next/ (accessed 18 December 2017); T. R. Johnson. 'Will the Department of Defense Invest in People or Technology?' *The*

Atlantic. 2016. www.theatlantic.com/politics/archive/2016/11/trump-m ilitary-third-offset-strategy/508964/ (accessed 26 February 2018).

2. US Government. *National Security Strategy of the United States of America.* 2017. www.whitehouse.gov/wp-content/uploads/2017/12/N SS-Final-12–18-2017–0905.pdf (accessed 26 February 2018).

3. US Government. *National Security Strategy.*

4. US Government. *National Defense Strategy of the United States of America.* www.defense.gov/Portals/1/Documents/pubs/2018-National-Defense-Strategy-Summary.pdf (accessed 26 February 2018).

5. J. Gould and T. Copp. 'Pentagon Unveils $686 billion Military Budget for FY19'. *Defense News.* 2018. www.defensenews.com/breaking-news/20 18/02/12/pentagon-unveils-686-billion-military-budget-for-2019/ (accessed 26 February 2018).

6. J. F. Sargent. *Defense Science and Technology Funding.* US Congressional Research Service. 2018. https://fas.org/sgp/crs/natsec/R45110.pdf (accessed 26 February 2018).

7. V. Koubi. 'Military Technology Races'. *International Organization.* 1999. 53(3): 537–65. doi: 10.1162/002081899550986 (accessed 26 February 2018).

8. R. Martinage. *Toward a New Offset Strategy: Exploiting U.S. Long-Term Advantages to Restore U.S. Global Power Projection Capability.* Center for Strategic and Budgetary Assessments. 2014. http://csbaon line.org/research/publications/toward-a-new-offset-strategy-exploit ing-u-s-long-term-advantages-to-restore (accessed 26 February 2018).

9. US Government. *National Security Strategy.*

10. J. Reppy. 'Dual-Use Technology: Back to the Future?' In A. R. Markusen and S. S. Costigan (eds). *Arming the Future: A Defence Industry for the 21st Century.* New York: Council on Foreign Relations. 1999.

11. Reppy. 'Dual-Use Technology'. In Markusen and Costigan (eds). *Arming the Future.*

12. See R. Bellais and D. Fiott. 'The European Defense Market: Disruptive Innovation and Market Destablization'. *The Economics of Peace and Security Journal.* 2017. 12(1): 28–35; R. Bellais and R. Guichard. 'Defense Innovation, Technology Transfers and Public Policy'. *Defence and Peace Economics.* 2006. 17(3): 273–86.

13. T. M. Cheung. *Fortifying China: The Struggle to Build a Modern Defense Economy.* Ithaca: Cornell University Press. 2009.

14. Cheung. *Fortifying China.*

15. A. Ni. 'China Reveals New Military Technology Agency'. *The Diplomat.* 2017. https://thediplomat.com/2017/07/china-reveals-new-military-tech nology-agency/ (accessed 26 February 2018).

16. Congressional Budget Office. *Growth in DoD's Budget from 2000 to 2014*. 2014. www.cbo.gov/publication/49764 (accessed 26 February 2018).

17. A note on the data is required. Figures for armed services active duty totals are derived from the Defense Manpower Data Center, US Department of Defense, which reports on active service duty totals in September of each year. The data for personnel costs and RDT&E have been collected from the annual report on national defence budget estimates (the so-called green book), which is produced by the comptroller of the office of the under-secretary of defense. While the data included in the green book refer only to budget authority estimates provided by Congress in each year, the data – when subsequently revised by adjusting totals found in subsequent green book reports – are a good indication of the legally binding obligations of the US government for immediate and future spending on defence.

18. DIUx. *Halo Neuroscience*. 2016. www.diux.mil/portfolio (accessed 17 April 2018).

19. DIUx. *Qool Therapeutics*. 2017. www.diux.mil/portfolio (accessed 17 April 2018).

20. R. Wegrzyn. *Safe Genes*. Defense Advanced Research Projects Agency. 2018. www.darpa.mil/program/safe-genes (accessed 16 April 2018).

21. B. Udis and K. E. Maskus. 'US Offset Policy'. In S. Martin (ed). *The Economics of Offsets: Defence Procurement and Countertrade*. Oxon/London: Routledge. 1996.

22. R. Work. 'The Third Offset Strategy and America's Allies and Partners'. Speech made at RUSI, London. 2015. www.defense.gov/News/Speeches/Speech-View/Article/617128/royal-united-services-institute-rusi (accessed 26 February 2018).

23. HM Government. *National Security Strategy and Strategic Defence and Security Review 2015: A Secure and Prosperous United Kingdom*. Report number: Cm9161. 2015. www.gov.uk/government/uploads/system/uploads/attachment_data/file/555607/2015_Strategic_Defence_and_Security_Review.pdf (accessed 26 February 2018).

24. M. Fallon. 'Stronger Defence in a More Dangerous World'. Speech by Michael Fallon, Secretary of State for Defence. 11 December 2015. www.gov.uk/government/speeches/stronger-defence-in-a-more-dangerous-world (accessed 16 April 2018).

25. D. Fiott. 'A Revolution Too Far? US Defence Innovation, Europe and NATO's Military-Technological Gap'. *Journal of Strategic Studies*. 2017. 40(3): 417–37.

26. E. C. Sloan. *The Revolution in Military Affairs: Implications for Canada and NATO*. Montreal: McGill–Queen's University Press. 2002.

27. European Defence Agency. *Towards Enhanced European Future Military Capabilities: European Defence Agency Role in Research & Technology*. www.eda.europa.eu/docs/default-source/eda-publica tions/eda-r-t-2016-a4–v09 (accessed 12 April 2018).

28. D. Fiott. *EU Defence Research in Development*. European Union Institute for Security Studies. Issue Alert 43. 2016. www.iss.europa.eu/ content/eu-defence-research-development (accessed 26 February 2018).

29. US Government. *National Security Strategy*.

30. US Department of Defense. *Nuclear Posture Review*. 2018. https://media .defense.gov/2018/Feb/02/2001872886/-1/-1/1/2018-NUCLEAR-POST URE-REVIEW-FINAL-REPORT.PDF (accessed 26 February 2018).

31. US Government. *National Security Strategy*.

32. US Government. *National Security Strategy*.

33. US Department of Defense. *Summary of the National Defense Strategy of the United States of America: Sharpening the American Military's Competitive Edge*. 2018. www.defense.gov/Portals/1/Documents/pubs/ 2018-National-Defense-Strategy-Summary.pdf (accessed 12 April 2018).

34. US Government. *National Defense Strategy*.

35. S. Frühling and G. Lasconjarias. 'NATO, A2/AD and the Kaliningrad Challenge'. *Survival*. 2016. 58(2): 96–116. doi: 10.1080/00396338. 2016.1161906 (accessed 26 February 2018).

36. L. W. Grau and C. K. Bartles. *The Russian Way of War: Force Structure, Tactics and Modernization of the Russian Ground Forces*. US Army Press. 2016. www.armyupress.army.mil/Portals/7/Hot%20Spots/Docu ments/Russia/2017-07-The-Russian-Way-of-War-Grau-Bartles.pdf (accessed 26 February 2018).

37. M. S. Chase. 'PLA Rocket Force Modernization and China's Military Reforms'. *RAND Corporation*. Report number: CT-489. 2018. www .rand.org/pubs/testimonies/CT489.html (accessed 26 February 2018).

38. US-China Economic and Security Review Commission. *2017 Report to Congress*. 2017. www.uscc.gov/sites/default/files/Annual_Report/Chapter s/Chapter%204%2C%20Section%202%20-%20China%27s%20Pursu it%20of%20Advanced%20Weapons.pdf (accessed 26 February 2018).

39. D. Morgan. 'The New National Security Innovation Base: Charting the Course for Technology in War'. *Modern War Institute*. 2018. https:// mwi.usma.edu/new-national-security-innovation-base-charting-cours e-technology-war/ (accessed 26 February 2018).

40. S. Shmuel. 'Multi-Domain Battle: Airland Battle, Once More, With Feeling'. *War on the Rocks*. 2017. https://warontherocks.com/2017/06/ multi-domain-battle-airland-battle-once-more-with-feeling/ (accessed 26 February 2018).

41. R. B. Brown and D. G. Perkins. 'Multi-Domain Battle: Tonight, Tomorrow, and the Future Fight'. *War on the Rocks.* 2017. https://wa rontherocks.com/2017/08/multi-domain-battle-tonight-tomorrow-an d-the-future-fight/ (accessed 26 February 2018).

42. E. B. Kania. 'Battlefield Singularity: Artificial Intelligence, Military Revolution and China's Future Military Power'. Center for New American Security. 2017. https://s3.amazonaws.com/files.cnas.org/doc uments/Battlefield-Singularity-November-2017.pdf?mtime=20171129 235804 (accessed 26 February 2018).

43. Kania. 'Battlefield Singularity'.

44. Kania. 'Battlefield Singularity'.

45. A. C-C. Huang. 'Transformation and Refinement of Chinese Military Doctrine: Reflection and Critique on the PLA's View'. In J. C. Mulvenon and A. N. D. Yang (eds). *Seeking Truth from Facts: A Retrospective on Chinese Military Studies in the Post-Mao Era.* Santa Monica: RAND Corporation. 2001. 131–40.

18 | The Political Economy of Terrorism

DIEGO MURO

Introduction

Over the past decade, radicalisation towards violent extremism has become a matter of great concern for the European Union.[1] The attacks in Madrid (2004), London (2005), Stockholm (2010), Paris (2015), Copenhagen (2015), Brussels (2016), Nice (2016), Berlin (2016) and Barcelona (2017) have demonstrated the harm that violent extremism can cause to the social cohesion of European societies. In addition to the division between communities, the terrorist attacks have brought deaths, injuries, emotional stress and economic costs to European Union Member States, not to mention a loss of public confidence in the authorities. These attacks fuelled public fears about both home-grown and international terrorism and pressured EU leaders to update and intensify their efforts to counter and prevent Islamist-inspired violent radicalisation.[2] Since the Madrid attacks, the EU has developed administrative tools (e.g. the European Arrest Warrant), but also new institutions such as Europol, Eurojust and the European Counter Terrorism Centre, which have increased the collaboration between law enforcement agencies. These administrative measures and counterterrorist institutions have increased the operational capability of Europe as a whole and have facilitated the sharing of data and lessons learned, as well as threat analyses, cross-border investigations, arrests and prosecution cooperation.

European counterterrorism has also proved to be path-dependent, for better or worse. By path dependence is meant that where Europe is going, or is able to go, depends on where it has been. As is well known, many European states have had their own experiences with domestic and international terrorism over the years. The old continent has had its fair share of political violence since World War II, as practically all EU Member States have directly experienced political violence against

398

non-combatants at some point in their recent history. In at least two cases, Spain and the United Kingdom, terrorist groups were able to sustain long-term campaigns of ethno-nationalist political violence against two consolidated democracies, partly due to substantial levels of public support. As a result, the counterterrorist policies of both Spain and the UK were dependent on the past knowledge and experience of countering the terrorist campaigns of ETA and the IRA. Other European countries have also begun to update their counterterrorist policies and adapt their legal-institutional framework to counter the 'fourth wave' of religious terrorism.[3]

The goal of this chapter is to apply the political economy metaphor to examine the European Union's measures to contain and defeat terrorism, a tactic which is defined by Bruce Hoffman as 'violence or the threat of violence used and directed in pursuit of, or in service of, a political aim'.[4] The EU is particularly concerned about home-grown terrorists and an estimated 7,000 European foreign fighters who have travelled to combat zones in the Middle East and North Africa (MENA) region to join Islamic State (often abbreviated as IS, ISIS, ISIL, or Daesh), which is a Salafi jihadist group that follows an ultraconservative branch of Sunni Islam. Some of these 'European mujahideen' may return to the continent in the next few years as a result of the containment and defeat of Islamic State in the territories of Syria and Iraq. European security agencies worry that these combatants will return to their home countries or venture into neighbouring Member States to launch attacks. There is also concern about whether some of these fighters and their spouses can be reintegrated into European society, as well as about what to do with the children born in ISIS territory, who may soon be stateless because of the lack of proper documentation on marriages and births. In addition, the demise of Islamic State has provided a window of opportunity for Al Qaeda and its affiliates to revive and present a likely threat once again. All in all, then, there is credible information that the next stage of violent jihad will be fought on European soil.

The remainder of this chapter is organised as per the following structure. Section 18.1 considers the 'political economy of terrorism' by depicting the public policies that aim to integrate both counterterrorist (supply-side) and prevention efforts (demand-side) into a coherent response. According to this approach, an effective response to terrorism needs to involve the arrest and prosecution of those actively involved in acts of violence against civilians but also the development of an effective counter-recruitment strategy that deals with the driving forces of terrorism, also known as root causes, and prevents rank and file replenishment. Societies affected by terrorism need to engage with the social, political, religious, economic and ethnic 'grievances' motivating terrorists, and do something about them. Section 18.2 discusses the EU's counterterrorist response to the ongoing threat of Salafi jihadism, particularly since 2014 when Islamic State started to claim responsibility for a number of high-profile attacks outside Iraq and Syria. The European ambition is to integrate both 'hard' counterterrorist measures and 'soft' preventive measures designed to stop vulnerable individuals from becoming radicalised, joining extremist groups and carrying out acts of violence. The integration of supply-side and demand-side approaches is far from perfect, but it is providing fruitful responses in the fight against Salafi jihadism, perhaps even a blueprint that could be implemented in a variety of contexts experiencing the threat from both home-grown terrorists as well as returnees from combat zones. Section 18.3 pays special attention to the so-called radicalisation agenda and the prevention of violent extremism, which includes measures such as the dissemination of counternarratives to bring about attitudinal and behavioural change. The goal of prevention strategies is to delegitimise the use of violent means for political purposes and isolate violent radicals from their supporters and sympathisers. Terrorist cells often hide in neighbourhoods where relative deprivation and criminality are rife and where their criminal activities go undetected. Ultimately, the goal of preventive strategies is to make it difficult for European jihadists to continue disguising themselves within communities of immigrants and diasporas. Section 18.4 discusses whether counterterrorism and prevention efforts can be successfully integrated into a single strategy, for example at city level. As many as 75 per cent of European citizens live in urban centres and evidence indicates that attacks on cities may continue in the future. Thus, cities have been at the forefront of a comprehensive strategy to integrate counterterrorist and preventive strategies at the municipal level in order to stop terrorist attacks against civilians. Cities are obvious settings in which to implement the motto 'think globally and act locally'. Finally, Section 18.5 provides a set of concluding remarks and directions for future research.

18.1 A Political Economy Approach

In order to understand terrorism, predict the behaviour of clandestine groups using indiscriminate violence and even their responses to state counterterrorism, it is necessary to have some plausible theory about terrorist behaviour. A political economy approach would suggest that terrorism can be studied like an industry or company which has scarce resources and wants to maximise the expected value of its utility. This is not to say that terrorism is a marketplace where the intersection of supply and demand curves define the point of equilibrium for a quantity of terrorism that is produced and consumed. There is, of course, no physical space for trading where buyers and sellers regularly gather for the purchase and sale of a good called 'terrorism', as no-one wishes to be on the receiving end of indiscriminate violence. Instead, what is suggested here is, quite simply, that terrorist groups can be analysed as agents with a set of preferences that pursue certain objectives and function according to a normal cost-benefit logic. From this rationalist point of view, terrorist organisations have a set of tactical and strategic goals and have decided to use unlawful violence, intimidation or fear to further those goals. Like any organisation with limited means, terrorist groups will aim to devote the minimum amount of resources possible (explosives, operatives, political capital) and obtain maximum effect (maximise the expected value of their utility). Thus, the agency of terrorist groups is influenced and constrained by the political and economic realities that affect other actors, and their decision making is analogous to the calculations of other organisations. Ultimately, the point of using a political economy approach to study terrorism is not to condone the use of illegitimate violence (even less to justify its indiscriminate nature), but to use social science tools to fathom what often appears to be an incomprehensible phenomenon, such as the use or threat of use of violence to obtain a political objective through intimidation or fear directed at a large audience.[5]

The advantage of adopting this political economy approach is that analysts can distinguish between the 'supply' and 'demand' of terrorism to successfully explain the quantity and cost of this violent tactic. Correspondingly, the 'supply' of terrorists would be composed of those people who are willing to perform violent acts, the compensation for which may be either monetary or nonmonetary. It is important to note that terrorist groups devote considerable time to recruiting the most skilful and devoted individuals possible and do their best to weed out uncontrollable, unpredictable or psychopathological individuals.[6] According to Martha Crenshaw's famous dictum: the 'outstanding common characteristic of terrorists is their normality'.[7] By contrast, the 'demand' for terrorism captures the extent to which supporters and sympathisers share the view that any means (violent ones included) are licit in order to bring about the desired sociopolitical change. In short, the political economy of terrorism would see political violence as the result of support for terrorism (demand) as well as the presence of individuals willing to use violent methods (supply).

The idea of using political economy to study political violence and terrorism is not novel. Walter Enders and Todd Sandler applied economic models and statistical analyses to examine political violence in their outstanding book, *The Political Economy of Terrorism.*[8] In earlier works they also made extensive use of rational actor models and game-theoretic analysis to account for domestic and transnational terrorism as well as to capture the interplay between terrorists and targeted governments.[9] In one example, Walter Enders argued that 'terrorist groups have a finite set of resources, including financial assets, weapons and buildings, personnel, and entrepreneurial abilities' and that the choices made by a group will be influenced by 'the prices of the various terrorist and non-terrorist activities'.[10] The 'full price' of any terrorist attack, he argued, includes the value of resources used to plan and execute the attack, and the cost of casualties to group members. Since the resources of these rational terrorist groups are 'finite' there is an incentive to 'save' some resources for future attacks, which might enhance their overall effectiveness (or utility). As with any political economy approach that studies the relationships between individuals and society and between markets and the state, the antiterrorist policy is seen as a variable that influences the prices, resource supplies and payoffs facing the terrorist firm. More specifically, Enders uses a game-theoretic framework to investigate how terrorist choices are constrained by governmental policies and government choices are similarly constrained by terrorist actions.

This chapter argues that both demand and supply factors need to be tackled in order to contain terrorism. A counter-recruitment strategy that focuses on arresting or killing individual terrorists is unlikely to succeed unless it also deals with the mechanisms that produce new waves of recruits. Similarly, a strategy of counter-radicalisation that solely focuses on terrorist sympathisers while neglecting the operational aspect of terrorist militants can only lead to disappointing results. Therefore, advanced democracies are required to fight a 'long war' against violent extremism through a combined approach of both counter-recruitment and counter-radicalisation. The next section examines how European efforts have combined supply- and demand-side approaches to counter the current security threat.

18.2 European Counterterrorism

The counterterrorist effort within and across Europe has traditionally focused on the supply side of terrorism, which encompasses individuals who are willing to perform violent acts. Although there is great consensus over the importance of high-grade intelligence in countering terrorism, there are also scholars who are critical of the militarisation of state reactions to terrorist challenges. The key argument is that an over-reliance on military means produces counter-productive effects such as lower effectiveness of counterterrorist efforts, not to mention the reproduction and future trajectory of violent conflict.[11] With regards to terrorists, the authorities have often focused on learning who they are, where they come from, what weapons they use, their networks of friends and so on and so forth. Understanding who joins the ranks of jihad and who wants to reshape the Muslim world by building a caliphate is of great interest to European countries, given their close proximity to the Middle East where jihadist activity is most intense and weak governance provides a window of opportunity for the politicisation of grievances.[12] Thus, the mission of police forces and intelligence agencies across the European Union is to focus on those who are willing to perform violent acts in order to counter, and whenever possible prevent, those attacks. We clearly see, hear, and read considerably more about the supply than the demand side of terrorism, which continues to affect a disproportionate amount of OECD democracies.[13]

The European counterterrorist legal and institutional framework was further developed in the aftermath of 9/11 and, in particular, the attacks on Madrid (2004) and London (2005). The term 'radicalisation' was brought into policy discussion after these coordinated suicide bombing attacks, which targeted civilians using the public transport system, resulting in 191 and 52 casualties, respectively. Several of the attackers in both incidents were home-grown terrorists who had either been born or socialised in the country and had adopted a new identity in which the struggles of their Muslim homelands played a powerful role in fomenting anger against the West. For the authorities, it soon became a priority to have a clearer picture of how young men from Muslim immigrant backgrounds radicalised in the West and were swept up by a seductive outlaw culture of violent jihad. Needless to say, the interest in radicalisation was not to understand how individuals adopted radical ideas but why they came to 'radicalise to violence', and not to just any type of violence, but to a specific type of political violence, namely illegitimate violence directed against civilians and non-combatants, also known as terrorism. According to the European Commission's Expert Group on Violent Radicalisation, its working definition of violent radicalisation was 'socialisation to extremism which manifests itself in terrorism'.[14] As rightly pointed out by Alex Schmid, what is generally meant by radicalisation is the 'individual or group process of growing commitment to engage in acts of political terrorism'.[15]

In addition to the EU Action Plan for Combating Radicalisation and Recruitment to Terrorism (approved in 2005 and revised subsequently), several other initiatives have demonstrated the EU's interest in funding pilot programmes related to the prevention of radicalisation and fortifying the 'Prevent' pillar, which had been rather underdeveloped in comparison with the other three counterterrorism strategy pillars (Protect, Pursue and Respond). All things considered, the European Union's institutional adaptation is a response to the current threat of jihadist terrorism, which is qualitatively different from the previous 'waves' of terrorism.[16] As a matter of fact, ongoing research on foreign fighters, returnees and lone wolves has provided us with some patterns worth summarising.

Evidence-based policymaking is now central to the collaboration of researchers and practitioners and recent findings suggest a number of areas where European conventional wisdom has been challenged. Firstly, the 'crime-terror nexus' has become an essential concept for comprehending the current wave of jihadism. The relationship between criminal gangs and radicalised individuals is stronger than expected and involves both issues of funding and recruitment. In contrast with previous cases of terrorism, some of the perpetrators of the Paris (2015) and Berlin (2016) attacks, such as Salah Abdeslam and Anis Amr, were known to the police and the intelligence services. Three members of the terrorist cell that carried out the attacks on the city of Barcelona and the town of Cambrils in 2017 also had criminal records, although they were completely integrated into the local community.[17] Whereas Al Qaeda militants were highly ideological, reports indicate that ISIS-inspired terrorists may be less so. As suggested by research carried out by Peter Neumann, several European terrorists were petty criminals that radicalised very quickly and saw joining ISIS as an opportunity to cleanse themselves of prior sins.[18] Having a criminal record and a predisposition to gang-like culture has become a facilitator for recruitment to small and flexible cells.

Secondly, there is an association between radicalised diasporas and demographics. Whereas first-generation migrants are unlikely to become terrorists, the probabilities seem to increase with second-generation migrants, possibly due to perceptions of inadequate social integration and low social mobility. As argued by Marc Sageman in *Leaderless Jihad*,[19] a significant number of home-grown terrorists who were inspired by Al Qaeda were part of the Muslim diaspora and predominantly came from poor to middle-class families. Since they could not afford to travel to Pakistan or Afghanistan to train with like-minded jihadists, they used chat rooms and other internet forums to communicate with their peers, which made them harder to detect by security agencies. The policy response to online radicalisation has been to build all-inclusive databases of individual suspects to identify patterns, profiles, and, ultimately, understand 'what makes terrorists tick'. While the sharing of information at European level can only bring benefits, the expectation that a quantitative analysis of existing cases will provide a clear profile is clearly misplaced. The European experience of terrorism and counterterrorism since the 1960s proves that human behaviour rarely resembles social science models. The number of 'push' and 'pull' factors working at the individual level is very large and often intersects with key factors such as demography, sociocultural integration and links to criminal milieus.[20]

Thirdly, both agents and spaces of radicalisation have mutated in the last decade. The online aspect of radicalisation has grown in importance, as has the role played by exclusive cliques of friends. Whereas a decade ago, the mosque and the radical preacher played a central role, the prison and the local neighbourhood have gained relevance. In addition, the internet, and especially the dark web, has also been prioritised by intelligence units who struggle to understand and trace how terrorists communicate, organise and plot on the dark web.[21] The three patterns identified above, to name a few, do not have predictive power but they indicate the importance of both offline and online elements of radicalisation.

In spite of these significant advances, it is impossible to forecast with precision what makes some people join extremist groups and when the socialisation to extremism will manifest itself in terrorism. Ongoing research into the causes of militancy has underlined the complexity of the motives of recruits and volunteers, as well as the differences between the various contexts. Factors contributing to violent radicalisation processes can be familial, social, gender-based, socioeconomic, psychological, religious, ideological, historical, cultural, political and linked to propaganda, social media and the internet. The events and conditions leading a person from radical ideas to violent action are also numerous, and the mechanisms so complex that they need to be broken down to be understood. To put it differently, indiscriminate murder is too complex a subject to synthesise into a simple model, and any attempt to understand terrorism needs to assume a multilevel understanding of radicalisation that covers individuals, groups and the mass public, and tries to specify the interactions between them. Furthermore, though there are common factors at the global and regional levels that facilitate radicalisation, it is clear that radicalisation is very context dependent. Regrettably, the European endeavour of identifying the causes of radicalisation is so far inconclusive, suggesting that efforts to counter violent extremism could be complemented by a strategy of prevention.

18.3 Prevention of Violent Extremism

The goal of this section is to deal with the 'demand' side of terrorism or belief that the use or threat of use of political violence is both a necessary and legitimate tool to obtain a political or social objective through intimidation of a large audience beyond that of the immediate victim. Demand for terrorism is driven by issues and grievances (real or perceived), but also by 'radical milieus' that provide social legitimation for unconventional means.[22] The process of political radicalisation by which individuals come to adopt extreme beliefs and behaviours occurs in a social context of group identification and reaction to a perceived threat and potential victimisation.[23] This element of radical socialisation is a necessary but not sufficient condition to account for why individuals embark on violent lives in different contexts and economic conditions.[24] For example, understanding the strength of the idea of the 'caliphate' as Muslim power striving for unity is as important as understanding perceptions of relative deprivation and the need for groups to use terrorism, the 'weapon of the weak', in a strategic manner against a much stronger opponent.

Within the European context, efforts to deal with the demand side of domestic and transnational terrorism have been driven by an 'agenda of radicalisation'. Violent radicalisation has gradually moved to the top of the EU counterterrorism agenda, but regrettably it has been accompanied by a relatively embryonic understanding of the processes that contribute to adoption of radical ideas and/or behaviour. As argued earlier, the term 'radicalisation' was brought into policy discussion after the coordinated suicide bombing attacks in Madrid (2004) and London (2005), and, in spite of its lack of precision, it continued to be used in the aftermath of attacks in Europe, such as Stockholm (2010), Paris (2015) and Brussels (2016). Regrettably, about the only thing radicalisation experts agree on is that radicalisation is a process.

Within the European Union, the demand-side approach has mainly focused on the prevention of radicalisation, and, to a lesser extent, on the possibility of producing counternarratives. Efforts have focused on developing programmes in schools, prisons and neighbourhoods that could prevent the adoption of radical ideas and methods. The so-called war of ideas has received less attention, and the historical experience is particularly important here. With regard to the campaigns of both ETA and the IRA, it was only when states made an effort to understand the underlying ideas and mobilising narratives of these underground groups that they were able to fine-tune the counterterrorist effort in areas such as security sector reform and penitentiary policy.[25] In the current context, European elites need to think long and hard about the integration of ethnic and religious minorities and the provision of equal social mobility opportunities that allow individuals to improve their own socioeconomic conditions (e.g. in the *banlieues*, or underprivileged suburbs of big cities).

The demand side of terrorism also requires a targeted approach that directly tackles hotbeds of radicalisation. Government-led campaigns that are broadcasted indiscriminately in the mass media are ineffective, partly because the state is not a credible agent in the eyes of radicalised audiences, but also because radicalisation is context-dependent and immune to a one-size-fits-all policy. Too often, government campaigns are a caricature and conflate holding radical beliefs and religious practice with socialisation to violent extremism (hence the term 'religious radicalisation'). However, the rules that govern the world of ideas and the world of actions could not be more different. The idea that communities inevitably proceed from having 'moderate' views to an increasingly violent or extremist involvement could not be further from reality. Individuals often support violent groups for non-religious reasons, though it cannot be denied that religious interpretations play a role in legitimising nonviolent means. Hence, there is an urgent need to incorporate credible actors (local leaders, activists, teachers, doctors) who can provide targeted and persuasive responses from the bottom up (as opposed to top-down government approaches). In the United Kingdom, a variety of civil society groups supported the Prevent programme in countering radicalisation, though there has also been criticism that the antiradicalisation scheme created an atmosphere of suspicion and stigmatisation of Muslims. There is clearly much to learn, but the state response needs a societal response to regain prestige and counter radicalisation.

Police agencies are advised to focus on the 'signs' of radicalisation, such as growing a beard, traveling to far-off conflict zones, becoming discreet or stopping using a telephone (which might suggest that an attack is imminent). Given the enormous difficulty of preventing an attack, the reaction of security agencies has been to demand increasing coordination across the European Union. Police and intelligence agencies have argued that they have insufficient resources to counter a complex phenomenon that does not only affect the security realm. However, it may be possible to combine both counterterrorism and preventive strategies, as some European cities are trying. As violent extremists continue to target urban centres and their host societies, the European experience of countering terrorism and preventing radicalisation may prove useful to a variety of governments worldwide.

18.4 Can Counterterrorism and Prevention Efforts Be Integrated?

From Madrid in 2004 to Barcelona in 2017, European capitals have become the main targets of European jihadism in recent years.

As a result, evidence-based policies and best practices on how to tackle terrorism at local, regional and state level are being flagged up to tackle the transnational security challenges faced by European urban centres. Although incipient, there is a clear movement by European cities towards combining counterterrorist and preventive strategies into an integrated local strategy. The European push for this development is coming from a variety of cities (e.g. Aarhus, Mechelen, Granada) as well as the EU network of experts known as the Radicalisation Awareness Network Centre of Excellence (RAN CoE), an epistemic community of practitioners from around Europe working on the prevention of radicalisation. While the number of best practices and positive examples is clearly limited, there are sustained efforts to come up with action plans that may be applied to a variety of local contexts. The theoretical basis for these city blueprints is that radicalisation is a complex issue and that counter-radicalisation needs to be equally comprehensive. This approach assumes that it is necessary to develop a better understanding of the local causes and processes that may lead to innovative, ethical solutions to counter violent actions taken by radicalised male or female individuals at city level. These may include policies for preventing violent extremism, such as counter-communications disseminated online (e.g. YouTube, special forums, Twitter) or offline (e.g. in the classroom or in one-to-one interventions). It is also clear that preventing violent radicalisation is also about winning hearts and minds and countering extremist propaganda while preserving the fundamental rights of citizens.

The main characteristics of city initiatives that try to combine supply and demand approaches of terrorism in a coherent strategy at local level can be summarised in four points. First, effective local initiatives are multi-stakeholder. Mechanisms of coordination within the city facilitate discussion and concerted action between agents devoted to security, education, health and social services, but also communities and civil society at large. The basis for the prevention of radicalisation is that cities need to provide inclusive spaces where local actors (both public and private) can interact, discuss openly and work collectively towards devising effective measures to counter violent extremism. Prevention strategies at the local level need the participation of multiple agencies (e.g. government, judiciary, social services, schools, local police) as well as the collaboration of civil society organisations and citizenry at large, who need to be empowered to influence decision making.

Second, effective local initiatives require both vertical and horizontal coordination. In other words, resilient cities can be built if a variety of stakeholders are involved in prevention strategies and there is both vertical coordination (between different levels of the state administration) and horizontal coordination (between local stakeholders). According to local activists, one of the priorities is to avoid the concerns raised by the Prevent strategy, one of the four strands of the UK government's counterterrorism strategy known as Contest, including the lack of a precise definition of extremism, the potential for religious discrimination and acceptance of the false premise with regard to an 'escalator' model in which there is a progression from holding conservative religious ideals to violent extremism. In addition, the UK government's counterextremism strategy has also been criticised for stigmatising Muslim society and for securitising diaspora communities and immigration.

Third, local initiatives overcome the false dilemma between 'hard' and 'soft' approaches. Cities and towns are creating institutionalised mechanisms to facilitate the participation and coordination of local actors and stakeholders and to promote a shift from 'hard' police-based approaches and strategies to multiactor strategies that incorporate 'soft' approaches; the latter ultimately designed to win the hearts and minds of radicalising or radicalised individuals by employing noncoercive methods. As argued above, an emphasis on the local level does not exclude participation of higher levels of the state administration. This would allow the development of tailored initiatives that engage with a wide series of local actors, and hence reduce the weight put on the security forces and intelligence agencies. Needless to say, preventing and countering radicalisation must engage the whole of society and requires a multidisciplinary approach that overcomes the false dilemma between 'soft' and 'hard' approaches. A balanced and comprehensive approach towards countering violent extremism must feature the two. Civil society and the security community must inevitably come together in fighting this common threat.

Fourth, local initiatives are based on the principle of subsidiarity, which argues that social and political issues should be dealt with at the most immediate (or local) level that is consistent with their resolution. Research and practice in the area of counter-radicalisation have increasingly shown that subsidiarity should drive the focus of prevention policies. At the international level, it is worth highlighting the UN-sponsored project on the prevention of radicalisation in major cities which aims to create a global network of mayors, municipal-level policymakers and practitioners united in building social cohesion and community resilience to counter violent extremism in all its forms.

18.5 Conclusion

Around 75 per cent of the EU population lives in cities, and there is a clear need to make these urban environments safer to protect the prosperity, political stability and well-being that European citizens enjoy. As jihadist terrorist cells continue to target medium-sized and large cities, there is an increasing need for local actors and civil society organisations to remain vigilant. After all, most of the individuals who established these terrorist cells lived in cities and moved with ease within their host societies (and between urban centres). Very often, they were members of the communities they inhabited or they mixed with the local population and blended into deprived neighbourhoods and communities. Furthermore, criminal dynamics at a local level became catalysts for radicalisation and had a direct impact on the acquisition of radical attitudes and behaviours by individuals who then perpetrated urban violence against innocent civilians.

An effective response to both ISIS and Al Qaeda requires an understanding of why individuals become militants as well as an appreciation of why sympathisers and supporters of terrorist organisations share the view that political violence is necessary. Counterterrorism mainly focuses on arresting terrorist individuals (supply side) but a comprehensive strategy of counter-recruitment needs to tackle the reasons why the radical message resonates (demand side). In short, individuals radicalise towards violent extremism because of personal processes (micro level) but also for organisational reasons (meso level) as well as societal and systemic reasons (macro level). European Union members are best equipped to tackle the current threat of Salafi jihadists by adopting a multilevel approach that deals with both demand and supply factors.

The political economy approach suggested above has policy implications at the international and domestic levels. This chapter did not use a game-theoretic framework to capture the interactions between rational agents (such as terrorist groups) that are trying to act according to how they think their counterparts (targeted governments) will act and react. Instead, the chapter argues that terrorism can be studied as an industry or company, where organisations with scarce resources want to achieve their preferred outcomes. According to this political economy approach, the 'supply' of terrorists would be composed of those people who are willing to perform violent acts, the compensation for which may be either monetary or nonmonetary, whereas the 'demand' for terrorism would capture the extent to which supporters share the view that in order to bring about sociopolitical change any means are licit. In a nutshell, the political economy of terrorism would see political violence as the result of support for terrorism (demand) as well as the presence of rational individuals willing to use violent methods (supply).

With regard to foreign policy, the territorial defeat of ISIS is fundamental to European security. The European Union is not facing an 'existential' threat but a 'serious' security issue with domestic and international ramifications. Policing is mostly concerned with foreign fighters, returnees and lone-wolf actors but international conflicts in the MENA region are an intrinsic part of this security challenge. The group known as ISIS has taken advantage of areas with limited state governance, such as Libya, Syria and Iraq, and uses these territories to conceive, plan and direct attacks. The territorial control of ISIS has direct consequences for the security of Europe, as foreign volunteers continue to be trained in military camps, and it is expected that some of these foreign fighters will eventually return to Europe. And while the self-proclaimed Islamic State has dominated the headlines and preoccupied national security officials for the past years, Al Qaeda has been quietly rebuilding a global movement of more than two dozen franchises.

At the domestic level, the integration of counterterrorist and preventive strategies can be carried out by cities – the main targets of the new jihadism – in cooperation with other levels of state administration. Measures to increase security originate at the national level but are often deployed at lower administrative levels, such as cities. Urban centres are on the front line of the fight against radicalisation because they often suffer violent extremism in their streets and neighbourhoods. It is in European cities where transnational extremist threats take shape in the form of hate speech, recruitment networks, radical cells and terrorist attacks, and it is also in European cities where prevention mechanisms need to be devised. In short, cities are the obvious settings in which to implement the motto 'think globally and act locally'.

References and notes

1. Parts of this article are drawn from Diego Muro, 'The Political Economy of Terrorism in Europe: The Integration of Supply and Demand Side Approaches at City Level'. *The Georgetown Security Studies Review.* Special Issue: What the New Administration Needs to Know About Terrorism and Counterterrorism. 2017. 61–69. Reprinted by permission of GSSR (http://georgetownsecuritystudiesreview.org/).
2. R. Coolsaet (ed). *Jihadi Terrorism and the Radicalisation Challenge: European and American Experiences.* 2nd edn. Farnham: Ashgate Publishing Ltd. 2011.
3. D. C. Rapoport. 'The Four Waves of Modern Terrorism'. In A. K. Cronin and J. M. Ludes (eds). *Attacking Terrorism: Elements of a Grand Strategy.* Washington, DC: Georgetown University Press. 2004. 46–73.
4. B. Hoffman. *Inside Terrorism.* New York: Columbia University Press. 2017. 2.
5. W. Enders and T. Sandler 'Terrorism: Theory and Applications'. In K. Hartley and T. Sandler. *Handbook of Defense Economics.* Vol. 1. Amsterdam: Elsevier. 1995. 215.
6. C. R. McCauley and M. E. Segal. 'Social Psychology of Terrorist Groups'. In C. Hendrick (ed). *Review of Personality and Social Psychology, Vol. 9. Group Processes and Intergroup Relations.* Thousand Oaks, CA: Sage Publications. 1987. 231–56.
7. M. Crenshaw. 'The Causes of Terrorism'. *Comparative Politics.* 1981. 13(4): 379–99.
8. W. Enders and T. Sandler. *The Political Economy of Terrorism.* Cambridge: Cambridge University Press. 2006.
9. See Enders and Sandler. 'Terrorism'. In Hartley and Sandler (eds). *Handbook.* Vol. 1. 214–49; T. Sandler and D. G. Arce. 'Terrorism: A Game-Theoretic Approach'. In T. Sandler and K. Hartley (eds). *Handbook of Defense Economics Vol. 2 – Defense in a Globalized World.* Amsterdam: Elsevier. 2007. 776–813.
10. Enders. 'Terrorism: An Empirical Analysis'. In Sandler and Hartley (eds). *Handbook.* Vol. 2 . 833.
11. See R. English (ed). Illusions of Terrorism and Counter-Terrorism. Oxford: Oxford University Press & British Academy. 2015.

K. McConaghy. *Terrorism and the State. Intra-State Dynamics and the Response to Non-State Political Violence.* London: Palgrave. 2017.

12. G. Wood. 'What Isis Really Wants'. *The Atlantic.* 2015. www .theatlantic.com/magazine/archive/2015/03/what-isis-really-wants/384980 / (accessed 27 March 2018).

13. See E. Chenoweth. 'Terrorism and Democracy'. *Annual Review of Political Science.* 2013. 16: 355–78; Q. Li. 'Does Democracy Promote or Reduce Transnational Terrorist Incidents?' *Journal of Conflict Resolution.* 2005. 49(2): 278–97; P. Wilkinson. *Terrorism and Liberal State.* London: Macmillan. 1986; P. Wilkinson. *Terrorism Versus Democracy: The Liberal State Response.* London: Frank Cass. 2001.

14. European Commission's Expert Group on Violent Radicalisation. *Radicalisation Processes Leading to Acts of Terrorism.* 7. www .rikcoolsaet.be/files/art_ip_wz/Expert%20Group%20Report%20Violent %20Radicalisation%20FINAL.pdf (accessed 27 March 2018).

15. A. P. Schmid. *Radicalisation, De-Radicalisation, Counter-Radicalisation: A Conceptual Discussion and Literature Review.* International Centre for Counter-Terrorism – The Hague. Research Paper. 2013. 1. www.icct.nl/ download/file/ICCT-Schmid-Radicalisation-De-Radicalisation-Counter-Radicalisation-March-2013.pdf (accessed 27 March 2018).

16. Rapoport. 'The Four Waves'. In Cronin and Ludes (eds). *Attacking Terrorism.* 46–73.

17. F. Reinares and C. García-Calvo. '"Spaniards, You Are Going to Suffer": The Inside Story of the August 2017 Attacks in Barcelona and Cambrils'. *Combating Terrorism Center.* 2018. https://ctc.usma.edu/s paniards-going-suffer-inside-story-august-2017-attacks-barcelona-cam brils/ (accessed 27 March 2018).

18. P. Neumann. *Radicalised: New Jihadists and the Threat to the West.* London & New York: I.B.Tauris. 2016.

19. M. Sageman. *Leaderless Jihad. Terror Networks in the Twenty-First Century.* University of Pennsylvania Press. 2008.

20. O. Roy. *Jihad and Death: The Global Appeal of Islamic State.* Oxford: Oxford University Press. 2017.

21. G. Ramsay. *Jihadi Culture on the World Wide Web.* New York: Bloomsbury. 2013.

22. See R. Pantucci. *'We Love Death as You Love Life': Britain's Suburban Terrorists.* London: Hurst and Company. 2015; S. Malthaner and P. Waldmann. 'The Radical Milieu: Conceptualizing the Supportive Social Environment of Terrorist Groups'. *Studies in Conflict & Terrorism.* 2014. 37(12): 979–98.

23. C. McCauley and S. Moskalenko. 'Mechanisms of Political Radicalisation: Pathways Toward Terrorism'. *Terrorism and Political Violence*. 2008. 20(3): 415–33.

24. D. Gambetta and S. Hertog. *Engineers of Jihad: The Curious Connection between Violent Extremism and Education*. Princeton: Princeton University Press. 2016.

25. See L. Richardson. *What Terrorists Want: Understanding the Enemy, Containing the Threat*. New York: Random House Trade Paperback. 2007. 200–40; R. English. *Terrorism: How to Respond*. Oxford: Oxford University Press. 2009. 56–117.

19 | *The Political Economy of Peace Operations*

FITRIANI

Introduction

The $6.8 billion United Nations Peace Operations (UNPKO) budget for 2017–18 is less than 1 per cent of US defence spending, and below half of 1 per cent of global military expenditure.[1] This relatively small UNP budget, finances over 100,000 blue helmet personnel deployed on thirteen of the fifteen current UN missions.[2] However, the monies are spread thinly. A 2015 High-level Independent Panel on UN Peace Operations (HIPPO) Report revealed that the UNP lacks specialised equipment, intelligence, logistics and other assorted military capabilities required to engage in an ever-widening array of military stabilisation, humanitarian and relief operations.[3] Arguably, peace is an international public good, because it benefits all who belong to the world community, without exclusion or exception, and the 'consumption' of peace does not reduce its availability to others. However, peace production – or in this regard peace maintenance – is an 'impure' public good, in the sense that countries participating in UN peacekeeping expect some sort of economic gain.

Naturally, contributing countries (CCs) seek the highest returns from their investment in peacekeeping, and these may come in many forms; for example, regional stability, a better commercial environment, market access and enhanced international standing. However, for some countries there is a 'free-riding' problem associated with UNPKO financing, given that they receive little or no benefit from peace operations located far from their territory, and are thus less inclined to offer financial contributions additional to those assessed non-voluntarily. Moreover, while there are member states that choose to show support through sending uniformed officers to UNP missions, critics, such as Gaibulloev et al. (2015) argue that these CCs are actually self-serving, in that they receive reimbursement from the United Nations, allowing some to make net gains by deploying inexpensive and poorly trained troops and police.[4] Increasingly, the trend is for relatively poorer countries, such as Ethiopia, Bangladesh and India, to deploy the highest number of troops, while relatively rich countries, like Japan and Canada, contribute more to the UNPKO budget based on the size of their economies. This division of labour results in several CCs shouldering a disproportionate share of the UNPKO cost, potentially creating financial fatigue and reducing their interest in supporting peacekeeping missions.

There is also the downside that such resource sharing polarises the rich versus poor UNPKO member groupings, leaving the entire operations vulnerable to the financial whims of the five permanent member states, especially the United States, due principally to its special responsibility for the maintenance of international peace and security. In a sense, UNPKO vulnerability is already being tested as, alarmingly, the budget has begun to suffer deep cuts. Its 2017–18 budget is 7.5 per cent, or $600 million lower, compared to the previous financial year.[5] The causes are not hard to find. Firstly, the 2007–08 global austerity gripped nearly all UN member states, and, secondly, the UNPKO's biggest donor, the United States, had begun to reduce its UN regular budget and peacekeeping contributions, as President Trump moved to fulfil his election pledges on the new agenda of nationalism and isolationism.

Financial contributions to UNPKO can rouse heated political debate. An inadequate budget will lead to ineffective outcomes, with peacekeepers deployed on missions without adequate support. Also, intense global economic competition has reduced margins and increased countries' unwillingness to 'donate' hefty sums, while suspecting others of free-riding in the collective pursuit of global security and stability. Yet, every member state is legally obliged to pay their share toward UN peace operations. The five permanent members (P5) – China, France, the United Kingdom, the United States and Russia – of the UN Security Council (UNSC) carry the heaviest financial burden in supporting peace operations. There has been a stand-alone budget for peace operations since 1994, and the P5 states have shouldered a higher financial contribution in the maintenance of international order. Liberalist arguments underscore this arrangement by noting that the 'great powers' have the capability beyond other member states to preserve peace. However, realist observers would argue that the P5 have a vested interest in preserving their positions as great powers, thus addressing major security challenges that might undermine the status quo. The P5 countries hold a decision-making veto, and this is important because the Council decides the deployment, maintenance or expansion of UNPKO, and this, of course, impacts on the peacekeeping budget.

Given these introductory observations, this chapter will examine the political economy of UN peace operations, from budgetary allocation to disbursement, as well as the political debate that lies beneath the day-to-day financing of peacekeepers. In an attempt to provide a broad evaluation of the political economy of UNPKO, the chapter will firstly provide a historical overview of peace operations, including the underpinning principles supporting decisions to deploy troops or police, or shoulder a higher cost of peacekeeping. The chapter will then discuss the impact of shifts in the global political economy of UNPKO, before offering a conclusion on whether the current financing arrangements support mission effectiveness or whether they lead to the unintended effect of undermining the peacekeeping process.

19.1 Genesis of UN Peace Missions

Maintenance of world peace is in the interest of all nations, but only a small number have the financial capacity to engage. The first international peace mission was undertaken in the late nineteenth century by the great European powers (Austria-Hungary, France, Germany, Great Britain, Italy and Russia) in an effort to stabilise Crete.[6] The thrust of the mission was to prevent escalation of conflict between the Ottoman Empire that ruled the island and its Greek majority population that sought independence. The European great powers later also sent joint forces to China to deal with the Boxer rebellion in 1900, and to the Albanian conflict to limit Serbian access in 1913. The history of peace maintenance suggests that great power alliances between strong states possessing the resources to intervene were invariably forged on issues of self-interest. Yet, the success of the great European powers' peace operations did not prevent wars amongst the great powers themselves. The devastating impact of World War I, a horrific global conflict that led to approximately 40 million deaths, inspired the creation of the League of Nations. It was created as part of the 1920 Paris Peace Agreement, with the goal of promoting international cooperation and achieving international peace and security. Under the League, peace operations were undertaken in a more structured manner, rather than through the previous ad hoc efforts.

Peace operations were now provisioned by the new League of Nations, comprising sixty-three member nations, though not the United States. The League's most renowned peace operation was the mission to German Saarland in support of the early 1930s plebiscite to reunite with Germany or unite with France. Dubbed as the 'International Force in Saar', the 3,300 men provided jointly by Britain, Italy, Sweden and the Netherlands[7] adopted two peacekeeping principles, namely, obtaining the consent of the host country and limiting the use of force, save for self-defence. The League, however, was too focused on its peace operations in Europe, and failed in its responsibility to provide collective security in the invasions of Manchuria (1931) and Abyssinia (1935). As a consequence, international trust in the League of Nations slowly reduced as the perception grew that it was only committed to maintaining the status quo of Europe's great powers.

The League's demise was complete when it failed to stop World War II (1939–45), because it was unable to prevent the rise of Nazism in Germany and fascism in both the West (Italy) and the East (Japan). As with the League of Nations, created after the previous large-scale war, the end of World War II witnessed the birth of a new international organisation, driven also by the need to prevent future catastrophic loss of life and material devastation. This new organisation was called the United Nations, and was again tasked to maintain global peace and order. The UN had learnt from history that to obtain global authority it would need to have great power members (including the United States), as well as a system that would guarantee that the organisation could never act without the consent of *all* the great powers. This system lay in the UN Security Council including five permanent members that would act as the world's 'policemen' to safeguard international politics.[8] However, despite the dominant role of the P5, UN peacekeeping operations were established as a mechanism through which all member states could help countries devastated by conflict.

In the early days of the UN, the concept of peacekeeping, as endorsed by the UN Military Staff Committee, was that military force should be supplied from the P5 and placed at the disposal of the Security Council, with planned strength able to stop any threat to the peace of all member states.[9] Yet, with the Cold War occurring immediately after World War II, this approach never materialised as tensions increased between the P5. Yet, even with these P5 difficulties, the UN still managed to organise military observer missions to monitor borders in disputed areas. Activities included oversight of peace agreements and transitional government arrangements between the colonial powers and the newly independent states, covering Greece (1947–51), Indonesia from the Netherlands (1947–51), and the two other missions that continue today, Palestine (1948-) and Kashmir (1949-).[10] The first war in which UN forces were involved was Korea (1950–53), due to the absence of the Soviet Union in the Security Council, and the dominant role the United States played at that time in the UN command structure; this forming the basis for the concept 'coalition of the willing', and thereafter the second UN Secretary-General, Dag Hammarskjold, created a new model (explained in the next section) for UN peace operations in the 1950s.[11] The Hammarskjold initiative continues today, albeit in amended form.

19.2 Peacekeeping Principles

The purpose and role of peacekeeping is not clearly stated in the Charter of the United Nations, but emerged from the vision and narrative of UN Secretary-General Hammarskjold, who believed that the organisation's rationale was as a protector of the interests and integrity of the 'less powerful nations'.[12] The creation of the 'blue helmets', or UN peacekeeping forces, happened in the 1956 Suez Crisis, when British-French forces intervened to secure the Suez Canal, and at the same time the Israelis advanced into Sinai. Hammarskjold with the Canadian Foreign Minister, Lester Pearson, formulated the concept of preventive diplomacy, through the means of armed and impartial UN peacekeeping forces; their role being to stabilise fragile situations and facilitate political dialogue for peace. The Secretary-General then assembled the first United Nations Emergency Force (UNEF I), consisting of 6,000 troops.[13] Within weeks, UNEF I deployed to pressure the withdrawal of Suez intervention forces, and subsequently to patrol the armistice line between Egypt and Israel. In the mission, the UNEF I troops wore their national uniforms with blue-painted helmet liners, later becoming blue berets and blue field caps, with badges having UN insignia.[14] This gave birth to the term 'blue helmets' in reference to UN peacekeeping forces.

In the UNEF I deployment and operations, Secretary-General Hammarskjold followed several core principles; these being consent amongst the conflicting parties, no enforcement actions and only a limited military function of temporary duration that would not influence the politico-military power balance between the conflicting parties.[15] These principles are reflected in the Charter of the United Nations, Chapter VI: The Pacific Settlement of Disputes. The articles in Chapter VI that support traditional peacekeeping roles include:

Article 33

1. The parties to any dispute, the continuance of which is likely to endanger the maintenance of international peace and security, shall, first of all, seek a solution by negotiation, enquiry, mediation, conciliation, arbitration, judicial settlement, resort to regional agencies or arrangements, or other peaceful means of their own choice.
2. The Security Council shall, when it deems necessary, *call upon the parties to settle their dispute* by such means.

Article 36

1. The Security Council may, at any stage of a dispute of the nature referred to in Article 33 or of a situation of like nature, *recommend appropriate procedures or methods of adjustment.*

Article 37

1. Should the parties to a dispute of the nature referred to in Article 33 fail to settle it by the means indicated in that Article, they shall refer it to the Security Council.
2. If the Security Council deems that the continuance of the dispute is in fact likely to endanger the maintenance of international peace and security, *it shall decide whether to take action* under Article 36 or to recommend such terms of settlement as it may consider appropriate.[16]

Chapter IV of the Charter of the United Nations is the foundation of traditional peacekeeping. Traditional peacekeeping is a term that holds to the principle of obtaining consent from warring factions and avoidance of the use of force, with a relatively clear objective.[17] This type of peacekeeping operation was undertaken largely, but not exclusively, in the Cold War era. To maintain impartiality in the face of a bipolarised world, the UN peacekeeping operations were restrained by tensions between the Eastern Bloc (championed by the Soviet Union) and the Western Bloc (by the United States). Hence, the main goal of UN peacekeeping at that time, according to the UN Under-Secretary for Political Affairs, Sir Brian Urquant, 'was to prevent regional conflict from triggering an East-West nuclear confrontation'.[18] Due to such limitations, there were only fourteen UN peacekeeping operations initiated during the Cold War period, and these were mostly concerned with the decolonisation process, allowing old great powers to withdraw, while preparing for the establishment of new sovereign states.[19]

Not all UN peacekeeping operations in the Cold War can be categorised as traditional. Erwin Schmidl argues, for instance, that UN operations in West New Guinea (UNTEA) and Cyprus (UNFICYP) are 'wider' peacekeeping.[20] In other words, the West New Guinea operation provided interim administration to assist transition from the Netherlands to Indonesia, and is thus considered different from the regular force missions that use specialised government skills in their execution. Also, the UN Mission to Cyprus required a wider peacekeeping approach due to the multiple roles required when the mission began in 1964; the need being to prevent a recurrence of fighting between the Greek Cypriots and Turkish Cypriots through monitoring, transitional administration and the restoration of law and order.[21] UNFICYP only became a traditional peacekeeping operation when Turkish troops invaded Northern Cyprus in 1974, allowing the UN forces to conduct their 'classic' role of maintaining the ceasefire agreement. The UN mission in Cyprus provides an example of the fluidity of peacekeeping operations when facing military realities in the field. Bellamy and Williams consider UNFICYP to be traditional peacekeeping (rather than the wider type), because stabilisation of the crisis was achieved through limited use of force, thus securing cessation of hostilities.[22] From what was predicted to be a temporary mission when it started in 1964, UNFICYP has remained in place to patrol the ceasefire line until today.

The longevity of several UN missions, including traditional peacekeeping operations in Lebanon (UNIFIL) and in the Golan Heights (UNDOF), raises questions regarding the efficacy of traditional peacekeeping operations. The presence of peacekeeping forces instead of leading to peace may create a 'comfortable' stalemate encouraging belligerents to become disinterested in a permanent conflict resolution. This scenario resonates with Christopher Bellamy's interpretation of conflict as cyclical, where post-conflict and pre-conflict cannot be clearly distinguished. This makes the presence of peacekeeper boots on the ground necessary to maintain peaceful stability and deter possible reoccurrence of conflict.[23] The best way for UN peacekeeping forces to end their mission is to ensure that the root causes of the previous conflict have been successfully dealt with, to create the necessary government infrastructure and to train the local population's security forces so they can be ready to maintain peace and order. However, these aims can only be achieved when the peacekeepers themselves are well trained and equipped. The problem is that the UN expects all CCs to invest in pre-training of peacekeepers, but the UNP will only reimburse the costs of deployment much later, and some countries may lack the capacity to bear this financial burden.

19.3 Deploying for Peace

Over the course of seven decades, the UN has conducted seventy-one peacekeeping operations (with fifteen still ongoing as of October 2017).[24] There was an increase in CCs engaged in UN peacekeeping operations during the post-Cold War period, from 46 in 1990 to 125 in 2017.[25] There is also a shifting dynamic in the sourcing of troops and police from small and relatively wealthy countries, to countries with large populations and less wealth.[26] In the early 1990s, France and Britain were amongst the top three troop contributors for UNPKO, but two decades later in the early 2010s they had been replaced by Bangladesh and India, as shown in Table 19.1.[27] There are two factors explaining this trend: firstly, large population countries have a greater human resource pool compared to smaller countries, and hence are able to send more peacekeepers. Secondly, rich but relatively less populated countries are unable to provide greater numbers of peacekeepers due to human resource constraints, exacerbated by engagement in global operations, such as NATO's engagement in Afghanistan and Iraq.

At the start of UN peacekeeping operations, smaller but richer countries provided a high number of peacekeepers, but when the higher-population countries joined the UN forces, the smaller countries' contribution declined in percentage terms. Gowan and Gleason highlight Europe's falling contributions to UN troop deployments, from 33 per cent (2008) to 8 per cent (2011).[28] An exception is France, which in 1990 deployed 525 peacekeepers on UN peacekeeping

Table 19.1: *Top ten UN peacekeeping country contributors, 1991–2015* *(per cent of total peacekeepers)*

1991–1995	%	1996–2000	%	2001–2005	%	2005–2010	%	2011–2015	%
France	9.9	India	6.5	Pakistan	12.0	Pakistan	12.0	Bangladesh	8.9
Pakistan	7.0	Bangladesh	5.9	Bangladesh	11.9	Bangladesh	11.5	Pakistan	8.4
UK	6.0	Poland	4.9	India	7.0	India	10.2	India	7.9
India	4.6	Ghana	4.7	Nigeria	6.4	Nigeria	4.7	Ethiopia	6.9
Canada	4.5	Jordan	4.0	Ghana	5.1	Nepal	4.4	Rwanda	4.9
Bangladesh	4.0	Pakistan	3.8	Jordan	4.4	Jordan	4.0	Nepal	4.6
Nepal	3.2	Austria	3.7	Kenya	3.6	Ghana	3.6	Nigeria	4.4
Jordan	3.1	Finland	3.6	Nepal	3.5	Uruguay	3.0	Egypt	3.1
Ghana	2.9	US	3.5	Uruguay	3.2	Egypt	2.7	Ghana	3.0
Poland	2.8	Ireland	3.4	Ukraine	2.4	Ethiopia	2.7	Jordan	2.8

Sources: Adapted from B. Heldt. Trends from 1948 to 2005: How to View the Relation between the United Nations and Non-UN Entities. In Daniel DCF, Taft P. and Wiharta S. (eds). *Peace Operations: Trends, Progress, and Prospects.* Washington, DC: Georgetown University Press. 2008. 25; Additional statistics from United Nations Peacekeeping. Troop and police contributors. https://peacekeeping .un.org/en/troop-and-police-contributors (accessed 3 May 2018).

operations, increasing to 934 in 2015 (annual growth rate of 3.92 per cent), but despite this rise, France's contribution was still substantially lower compared to India, which deployed only 40 in 1990, increasing to 7,798 in 2015 (annual growth rate of 42.12 per cent).[29] If these increases are compared to the UN peacekeeping forces' annual growth from 1990 to 2015, at 16.89 per cent, then the growth of French peacekeeping forces also lagged well behind the UN average growth.[30]

A study by Donald Daniel et al. (2008) analysed the location of CCs, their types of government, wealth, levels of development and stability, size of their ground forces and the implications of the current mix of CCs to UN peacekeeping operational efficiency.[31] The regions where most UN peacekeeping personnel are sourced are Africa and Europe, followed by America and Asia-Pacific. However, the regions with the highest proportion of CCs are South Asia (83 per cent of countries in the region) and Europe (77 per cent).[32] Across 2008 to 2011, increased contributions from especially Egypt and Ethiopia have meant that the African region has raised its military personnel support to UN peacekeeping operations from 29 to 38 per cent, becoming a more important contributor than Europe.[33] When combined, troops from South Asia and Africa constitute around 75 per cent of UN uniformed peacekeepers.[34] Hence, in recent times the UN relies heavily on force contributions from just two regions, Africa and Europe. Most of the CCs are democratic (48 per cent), somewhat less are autocratic[35] or non-democratic (28 and 11 per cent, respectively); the majority of CCs have stable government (52 per cent), and the biggest proportion are middle-income countries (38 per cent), with high- and low-income countries following suit (25 and 24 per cent, respectively).[36] Unsurprisingly, the CCs' active ground force numbers have a direct correlation with their troop contributions. Countries with large active ground forces (100,000 or more personnel) contributed on average 3,500 troops, while those having medium-sized forces (99, 000–25,000 personnel) contributed 1,000 troops, and small-sized forces (below 25,000 personnel) contributed around 600 troops.[37]

In general, CCs that have the greatest impact on peacekeeping operations are democratic and politically stable, and have medium-income and large active ground forces. Therefore, on operational efficiency grounds, if the UN wishes to expand its peacekeeping forces, it should target countries with these qualities. The UN could also use the emerging middle-income countries having large active ground forces, such as China, Brazil, Egypt, Sri Lanka and Indonesia, to contribute more to UN peacekeeping.[38] Dependent on the geographical location of the CCs, there are different regional sentiments expressed towards UN peacekeeping operations. UN peacekeeping has better support from South Asia and European countries, compared to regions like the Middle East. This is not to say that the UN should seek personnel for peacekeeping operations only from countries and regions where recruitment has been successful, but rather it should develop alternative strategies to gain support from those countries and regions with low or zero UN peacekeeping participation.

19.4 Motivations behind 'Blue Beret' Contributing Countries

Why do countries contribute troops to UN peacekeeping operations? Article 43 of the UN Charter provides the justification for the organisation to request member state support for UN peacekeeping operation needs. Article 43 reads:

All Members of the United Nations, in order to contribute to the maintenance of international peace and security, undertake to make available to the Security Council, on its call and in accordance with a special agreement or agreements, armed forces, assistance, and facilities, including the rights of passage, necessary for the purpose of maintaining international peace and security.[39]

As such, it is the willingness and interest of member states that dictate how many troops they are willing to contribute to UN peacekeeping missions. The liberalist school of international relations proposes democratic peace theory as the reason why UN member states contribute to peacekeeping missions.[40] The theory posits that democratic countries respect an individual's unalienable rights everywhere, and thus can join international peacekeeping efforts because they trust the activity, and support the proliferation of democracy and respect for human rights.[41] However, scholars supporting the public good theory would argue that self-interested countries contribute to UN peacekeeping because the creation of peace as a public good may benefit those countries privately.[42] For example, peace in a specific area may benefit the CCs by creating stability on trade routes, decreasing the numbers of refugees, creating friendly governments and obtaining economic contracts for post-conflict rebuilding. It is perhaps no coincidence that China's involvement in UNP deployments to Africa occurred at the same time as its huge aid and investment programmes in the continent had begun to take-off.[43]

Aside from the willingness and interest of the CCs to engage in peacekeeping activities, the reasons when and why peacekeepers can be deployed are also influenced by, firstly, the host country that receives the multinational troops, and, secondly, by the UN that has the authority to decide the composition of its peacekeeping troops to ensure political neutrality and non-aligned contingents.[44] Hence, a member state's contribution depends on its interest, the approval of the host country and the UN Security Council's decision as to whether a CC can act impartially in handling the conflict a particular UNP mission is seeking to solve. With these three prerequisites in mind, CCs deployment becomes a matter of identifying the target destination, as member states would not send their security personnel into areas where they are not needed. In September 2017, the regions where the majority of UN peacekeeping operations were located comprised Africa (eight missions), followed by the Middle East (three missions), with just three missions in Europe and Asia, and one mission in the Americas.

A further question concerns the process of CC deployment on UN missions. In 2013, Perry and Smith identified the patterns of CCs preferences in sending their troops on certain missions and the types of contingents deployed.[45] Firstly, geopolitical proximity is one of the deliberations determining country deployment. After 2007, Europe's contribution to UN peacekeeping operations was largely made up of forces from Spain, Italy and Ireland, and sent to UN missions in Lebanon (UNIFIL). South American CCs, by contrast, preferred to send their troops to the UN mission in Haiti, due again to proximity reasons.[46] Secondly, the existence of a long-term policy and commitment by CCs will determine the consistency of their contributions in the provision of UN peacekeepers; for example, the UK policy stance in the 1990s, through its participation in the UN Protection Force in Bosnia (UNPROFOR), propelled it into becoming one of the United Nation's top CCs at the time.[47] Countries that do not have a steering policy have relatively unstable contributions to UN peacekeeping missions, as internal political and security dynamics influence contributions; for example, witness Malawi's increased troop contributions since 2011, while Namibia's contributions ceased in 2007.[48] Thirdly, member states interested in gaining a bigger stake in the UN tend to contribute more to UN peacekeeping operations. This applies to those countries seeking membership of the UN Security Council, including Brazil, Germany, India and Japan (the G4 countries), which increased their UN peacekeeping contribution three-fold between 2004 and 2007.[49] Unlike the permanent members of UNSC that provide steady but relatively low contributions (around 1,000 peacekeepers from the P5 combined), the G4 countries sense that high troop contributions are proportional to the capability required to support the maintenance of international peace.[50] This, arguably, is because higher force contributions in UNPKO increase the CCs' legitimacy to a seat in UNSC.

The above discussion begs the question as to what are the underlying push factors that make countries willing to contribute to UNPKO. Scholars, including Alex Bellamy, Paul Williams and Andrzej Sitkowski, have probed the motives behind countries sending military and/or police forces to support UN missions.[51] They argue there are four rationales behind member states contributing to peacekeeping operations. Firstly, states may participate in UN peacekeeping to achieve political objectives, such as prestige or authority. A member state's role in UN peacekeeping, if undertaken successfully, will command more respect in the international fora than most other engagements.[52] Secondly, there may be economic motives, especially for countries having lower ability to financially compensate their security forces in comparison with UN peacekeeping remuneration. The UN monthly standard reimbursement rate for each peacekeeper deployed since July 2016 has increased to $1,365 from $1,028 in 2002; however, that amount is transferred to the CCs' government, which in turn distributes the compensation according to national rank and salary scale.[53] Therefore, the national Treasury could benefit from the surplus. Thirdly, there will likely be institutional professionalism motives, whereby the UNP missions offer invaluable training and overseas experience for national security forces.[54] This is especially the case for CCs in post-conflict situations where the need for military personnel is lower, so UNP is useful to reduce redundancy. Fourthly, CCs may possibly pursue altruistic motives to act as 'good international citizens', including, perhaps, the moral obligation to repay the 'debt' incurred when benefitting from earlier UNP support. For example, in the 1990s Rwanda was the host of a UN Assistance Mission (UNAMIR), and later in the 2010s it deployed 90 per cent of the peacekeepers in Sudan and Darfur, all of whom had previous experience in dealing with genocide.[55]

19.5 The Costs of Peace

Between 1948 until 2017, as many as seventy-two UN peace operations were deployed.[56] In the beginning, when there were only a few peace operations, UNPKO were still funded through the UN regular budget with additional voluntary contributions. The contribution to the UN's regular budget was assessed on the principle of 'capacity to pay', and accordingly the wealthier countries would bear a higher financial cost compared to the poorer countries. This was done through providing a discount, or a reduction of the nonvoluntary assessment, for poorer countries' assessed financial contribution, at the same time as offsetting the cost to wealthier member states that are obliged to pay a premium. In the Cold War era, peacekeeping expenditure was relatively low due to decision-making deadlocks at the Security Council, and the United States and Soviet Union regularly vetoed each other, thus putting the brake on deployment of peace missions. Between 1948 and 1974 there were only twelve mostly small UNPKO missions, except for the UN Operation in Congo, ONUC (1960–64). The unanticipated ONUC expenses put a strain on the UN regular budget that could not be covered by voluntary contributions from member states.

The concern with voluntary contributions is that although peace is a public good and UNPKO non-excludable and non-rival benefits are enjoyed by all countries, this system fostered free-riding behaviour. The United Nation's first financial crisis was created by the inadequacy of ONUC financing, and compelled member states to seek a better financing solution for peace operations. In 1973, the UN General Assembly adopted Resolution 3101 setting the rule for nonvoluntary assessment of all member states. As there is no such thing as a free lunch, the UN Security Council members holding veto rights were required to pay an additional 22 per cent on top of the nonvoluntary assessment scale, referred to as a premium.[57] There are three other member categories beside the P5 that are required to pay a premium to maintain their status quo, and these are the developed countries, developing countries and least developed countries. All UN members are obliged to pay nonvoluntary financial contributions to UNPKO, but they can also provide additional voluntary contributions beyond their assessed share of peacekeeping cost.

As illustrated in Figure 19.1, the cost for UN peace missions rose after the Cold War. This increased peacekeeping spending may reflect the peace dividend, or the increased availability of public money, as defence spending declined. There was also an increase of intrastate wars, requiring the UN to initiate a range of conflict-prevention and peacebuilding policies, which faced less UNSC deadlock, and, as a consequence, UNPKO numbers increased by over 400 per cent.[58] The amplified number of UNPKO necessarily impacted on peacekeeping expenditure. Prior to 1989, UNPKO expenditure was consistently lower than $300 million, but in 1993 the cost spiked to over $3 billion following the commencement of fifteen missions during the previous three years.[59] The cost of peacekeeping that was relatively miniscule in the 1940s to 1980s had grown to become a significant burden for member states after the 1990s. This was especially felt by those assessed to pay a higher percentage. Although the 1973 nonvoluntary financial contribution assessment may have been fairer than voluntary contributions, some of the P5 and developed countries felt that the UNPKO

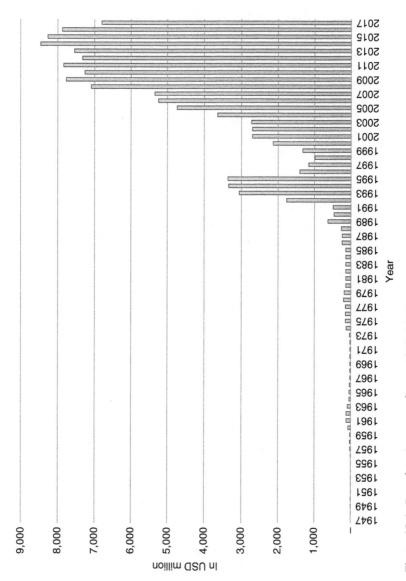

Figure 19.1: Peacekeeping expenditure, 1947–2017
Source: Michael Renner and Global Policy Forum. *Peacekeeping Operations Expenditures: 1947–2005.* www.globalpolicy.org/images/pdfs/Z/pk_tables/expend.pdf and UN General Assembly. *Approved Resources for Peacekeeping Operations. 2006–2017.*

burden sharing was tilted too heavily towards them, not least because the developing countries and least developed countries received discounts on their required assessment. The developed countries pay equivalent to their assessment rate, and the P5 shoulder a premium of 22 per cent on top of their assessment rate. Therefore, in the 1990s, the P5 funded 63.15 per cent of the peacekeeping budget, developed countries 34.78 per cent, developing countries 2.02 per cent and the least developed countries only 0.05 per cent.[60]

The United States, in particular, paid a contributor ceiling rate of 30 per cent of the total budget.[61] This amount was roughly equal to the total assessment of all European Union nations combined. Due to its high financial contribution, the United States has the ability to pressure for lower UN operating costs by delaying payment. In the 1980s and 1990s, US payment arrears brought financial difficulties for the UN, leading to a series of reforms in the following decade. The reforms included an expansion of the financial burden-sharing calculation from four to ten categories (A-J) to lessen pressure on the P5 states. After heated debates, the UN General Assembly adopted the new assessment A/58/157 in July 2003, bundling the principle of 'capacity to pay' with other criteria, as follows:

a. Comparison of average per capita Gross National Income (GNI) during the past three-year period, using a US dollar conversion rate.
b. Demographic composition of the population, acknowledging that member states with a higher children and dependent ratio should be rated lower on the GNI scale.
c. Specific economic conditions, such as the poverty rate, income distribution, amount of foreign currency reserves and debt service commitment.[62]

The 2003 nonvoluntary contribution assessment system is perceived to bring a sense of fairness, as it provides a relief of payment or 'discount' for member states having relatively low GNI per capita, but still adds a premium on the P5 members' contribution assessment. The discount ranges from 7.5 to 90 per cent depending on member states' economic conditions. Countries in every category of assessment will enjoy discounts every period based on their GNI performance, except for Category A, which refers to the five permanent members of the UNSC. The following Table 19.2 contains a breakdown of the UNPKO expenditure burden assessment for the years 2016–18.

Table 19.2: *Category levels for burden assessment of UN Peace Operations, 2016–2018*

Category	Criteria	Arrangement	Countries
A	Permanent members of the UNSC	Pay premium	China, France, Russia, UK, US
B	All members, except Category A and those covered below	0% discount	Andorra, Australia, Austria, Bahamas, Bahrain, Belgium, Canada, Cyprus, Denmark, Estonia, Finland, Germany, Greece, Iceland, Ireland, Israel, Italy, Japan, Liechtenstein, Luxembourg, Malta, Monaco, Netherlands, New Zealand, Norway, Oman, Portugal, Republic of Korea (South), San Marino, Slovenia, Spain, Sweden, Switzerland (Saudi Arabia transition to B)
C	Countries listed in the annex to UN General Assembly Resolution A/RES/55/235	7.5% discount	Brunei Darussalam, Kuwait, Qatar, Singapore, United Arab Emirates
D	Member states with per capita GNI less than two times the average for all member states (except categories A, C and J)	20% discount	Czech Republic
E	Member states with per capita GNI less than 1.8 times the average for all member states (except categories A, C and J)	40% discount	Slovakia
F	Member states with per capita GNI less than 1.6 times the average for all member states (except categories A, C and J)	60% discount	Barbados, Latvia, Trinidad and Tobago
G	Member states with per capita GNI less than 1.4 times the average for all member states (except categories A, C and J)	70% discount	Antigua and Barbuda, Chile, Croatia, Hungary, Libya, Lithuania, Poland, Saint Kitts and Nevis (Argentina, Uruguay transition of G)
H	Member states with per capita GNI less than 1.2 times the average for all member states (except categories A, C and J)	70–80% discount	Brazil, Nauru, Seychelles, Turkey, Venezuela

| I | Member states with per capita GNI less than the average for all member states (except categories A, C and J) | 80% discount | Albania, Algeria, Armenia, Azerbaijan, Belarus, Belize, Bolivia, Bosnia and Herzegovina, Botswana, Cabo Verde, Cameroon, Colombia, Congo, Costa Rica, Côte d'Ivoire, Cuba, Democratic Republic of Korea (North), Dominica, Dominican Republic, Ecuador, Egypt, El Salvador, Fiji, Gabon, Georgia, Ghana, Grenada, Guatemala, Guyana, Honduras, India, Indonesia, Iran, Iraq, Jamaica, Jordan, Kazakhstan, Kenya, Kyrgyzstan, Lebanon, Malaysia, Maldives, Marshall Island, Mauritius, Mexico, Micronesia, Mongolia, Montenegro, Morocco, Namibia, Nicaragua, Nigeria, Pakistan, Palau, Panama, Papua New Guinea, Paraguay, Peru, Philippines, Moldova, Saint Lucia, Saint Vincent and the Grenadines, Samoa, Serbia, South Africa, Sri Lanka, Suriname, Swaziland, Syria, Tajikistan, Thailand, Macedonia, Tonga, Tunisia, Turkmenistan, Ukraine, Uzbekistan, Viet Nam, Zimbabwe |
| J | Least developed countries (except categories A and C) | 90% discount | Afghanistan, Angola, Bangladesh, Benin, Bhutan, Burkina Faso, Burundi, Cambodia, Central African Republic, Chad, Comoros, Democratic Republic of the Congo, Djibouti, Equatorial Guinea, Eritrea, Ethiopia, Gambia, Guinea, Guinea-Bissau, Haiti, Kiribati, Lao, Lesotho, Liberia, Madagascar, Malawi, Mali, Mauritania, Mozambique, Myanmar, Nepal, Niger, Rwanda, Sao Tome and Principle, Senegal, Sierra Leone, Solomon Islands, Somalia, South Sudan, Sudan, Timor-Leste, Togo, Tuvalu, Uganda, United Republic of Tanzania, Vanuatu, Yemen, Zambia |

Source: UN General Assembly. Resolution adopted by the General Assembly *55/235*. Scale of assessments for the apportionment of the expenses, A/RES/55/235, 30 January 2001 of the United Nations peacekeeping operations and UN General Assembly. Implementation of General Assembly Resolutions *55/235* and *55/236*. Annex: Effective rates of assessment for peacekeeping operations, 1 July 2016 to 31 December 2018, A/70/331/Add.1, 28 December 2015.

Although the 2003 financial burden-sharing assessment is more detailed than the previous scales of assessment, it still has shortcomings. From the burden-sharing perspective, Schaefer noted that the 2003 assessment scale is unfair for the United States because it requires it to contribute more than the 185 countries in the categories B to J combined, and more than all of the four other permanent members of the UNSC.[63] From the economic perspective, Sheehan criticised the inaccurate assessment of GNI per capita on several counts. Firstly, it may not effectively reflect member states' capacity to pay as countries have different ways of measuring GNI. Secondly, countries with increasingly high GNI but also large populations could be positioned in lower categories. Finally, the structure of the distribution of member states within a certain category is sensitive to economic changes, if the base period of assessment is set too far back.[64] For example, the category levels of contribution for the period of 2016–18 are based on the average per capita GNI of 2008–13. The assessment therefore provided a lower assessment to member states, such as Latvia and Trinidad and Tobago, that were affected by the global financial crisis that took place in 2007–08, but which then managed to improve their financial position in 2016. Meanwhile, member states that experienced a commodity prices boom in 2011, such as Argentina and Brazil, could be assessed at a higher contribution rate, which may not necessarily reflect a much lower level of commodity prices in 2016.

Aside from the complex technicalities of assessing member states' nonvoluntary financial contribution, another contentious issue central to the political economy of peacekeeping is the great divide between advanced countries that fund the UNPKO and the poorer states that provide the 'boots on the ground'. The debate arises because of the stakeholders' differing agendas: the countries that financially provide for UNPKO would like to keep costs down, while troop-contributing countries, conversely, seek their deployment risk, personnel training costs and equipment rent fairly rewarded. Deploying well-trained troops supported by quality equipment is critical for mission success; however, critics argue that the despatch of police and military personnel by the developing and least developing countries is driven by the profit obtained from reimbursement rather than the intangible benefits of participating in UN peace operations. Gaibulloev et al. and Sandler, for example, highlight the fact that there are countries which enjoy a net gain from deploying relatively inexpensive and poorly trained police and soldiers on UNP operations.[65] A 'profit/loss assessment' can be made that approximates the financial gain or loss of member states from participation in UNPKO through both financial and troop contributions.

Table 19.3 illustrates that member states providing relatively small financial contributions are able to 'profit' from deployment of peace-keepers. For example, in 2017 the approximate profit obtained by Ethiopia, Bangladesh and Rwanda was more than the 'loss' experienced by the Netherlands. This is only an estimate because it does not factor in the real cost of CC deployment of peacekeepers, consisting of a monthly salary (possibly subsidised by the CC's government as the UN reimbursement rate is lower than the salary paid) and the costs of pre-departure training and replacement of deployed personnel. Nevertheless, the profit/loss assessment is useful to illustrate the different roles of the funders and peacemakers of UN peace operations.

19.6 Shifting Global Politico-Economic Pressures on UNP

The comparison between the UN peacekeeping budget (noting what it achieves) against world military expenditure, as illustrated in Table 19.4 and Figure 19.2, suggests that UNPKO punch above their weight. Yet, while the UNPKO budget is dramatically smaller than global military expenditure, member states are nevertheless reluctant to pay their non-voluntary assessed contributions. The reason for this is twofold. Firstly, the 2008 global financial crisis squeezed the public finances of the P5 and developed countries, such that they are looking for opportunities to cut expenditure, anywhere. Secondly, since 1990, the forces of globalisation have intensified economic competition amongst member states.[66] This has also compelled countries to cut budgets and elect leaders who promote narrow nationalism, instead of global collaboration and burden sharing. These parallel cost reduction pressures reduce member countries' contributions to global causes, including international peace operations.

Since 2014, the UNPKO budget has been in decline. The approved budget of 2014 was $8,467 million, but the General Assembly meeting in 2017 only agreed a total budget of $6,804 million.[67] This reflects a decline of roughly 7 per cent per year. The budget reduction is not only due to the closing of one mission in Côte d'Ivoire and a change of mandate from a Haiti mission of stabilisation to a mission for justice support, but also because there was pressure from member states, especially the United States and Japan, that provide the highest

Table 19.3: *UNP profit/loss statement of selected member states, 2017*

Member State	Financial contribution assessment rates 2017 (%)	Nonvoluntary financial contribution for 2017–18 (US$ thousands)	Total peacekeeper deployment Dec 2017 (Nos)	Approximate reimbursement obtained from peacekeeper deployment 2017 (US$ millions)	Approximate 'profit/loss' 2017 (US$ thousands)
Permanent members: UN Security Council					
United States	28.5	1,936,820	55	901	(1,934)
China	10.3	697,345	2,644	43,309	(654)
France	6.3	427,774	816	13,366	(414)
United Kingdom	5.8	392,907	679	11,122	(382)
Russian Federation	4.0	271,857	80	1,310	(270)
Selected country contributors					
Japan	9.7	658,553	2	33	(659)
Germany	6.4	434,659	717	11,744	(423)
Italy	3.7	254,985	1,079	17,674	(237)
Canada	2.9	198,722	43	704	(198)
Spain	2.4	166,203	645	10,565	(156)
Australia	2.3	158,992	31	508	(158)
Republic of Korea	2.0	138,718	627	10,270	(128)
Netherlands	1.5	100,824	324	5,307	(95)
Brazil	0.8	52,017	248	4,062	(48)
Argentina	0.3	18,205	331	5,422	(12)
India	0.1	10,028	6,697	109,697	100

Indonesia	0.1	6,858	2,688	44,029	37
South Africa	0.0	4,953	1,199	19,639	15
Pakistan	0.0	1,265	6,238	102,178	101
Bangladesh	0.0	68	7,246	118,689	119
Ethiopia	0.0	68	8,420	137,920	138
Tanzania	0.0	68	2,673	43,784	44
Nepal	0.0	40,819	5,492	89,959	90
Burkina Faso	0.0	27,213	2,148	35,184	35
Rwanda	0.0	13,606	6,498	106,437	106

Source: Financial contribution assessment rates 2017 are from UN General Assembly, *Effective Rates of Assessment for Peacekeeping Operations, 1 January 2016 to 31 December 2018*, UNGA 2015, document number A/70/331/Add.1, https://undocs.org/en/A/70/331/Add.1. Nonvoluntary financial contribution for 2017–18 is obtained by calculating member states' rates of nonvoluntary financial assessment against the total peacekeeping budget of US$6,803,236,100 for 2017–18 (see, UN General Assembly, *Approved resources for peacekeeping operations for the period from 1 July 2017 to 30 June 2018*, document number A/C.5/71/24, UNGA 2017, https://digitallibrary.un.org/record/1291034/files/A_C-5_71_24-EN.pdf). Approximate reimbursement obtained from peacekeepers deployment 2017 is calculated by taking member states' total number of peacekeepers deployed in one month (using Dec 2017 as a sample) times twelve months in a year, times monthly rate of reimbursement of $1,365 (see, UN General Assembly, *Resolution adopted by the General Assembly on 30 June 2014 No 68/281. Rates of reimbursement to troop-contributing countries*, document number A/RES/68/281, UNGA 2014, http://www.un.org/en/ga/search/view_doc.asp?symbol=A/RES/68/281). Approximate 'profit/loss' is calculated by deducting approximate reimbursement obtained from the deployment of peacekeepers by nonvoluntary financial contribution 2017–18.

Note: Financial contribution assessment rates 2017 are from Effective rates of assessment for peacekeeping operations, 1 January 2016 to 31 December 2018 A/70/331/Add.1. Nonvoluntary financial contribution for 2017–18 is obtained by calculating member states' rates of nonvoluntary financial assessment against the total peacekeeping budget of $6,803,236,100 for 2017–18 (see UN General Assembly document number A/C.5/71/24). Approximate reimbursement obtained from peacekeepers deployment 2017 is calculated by taking member states' total number of peacekeepers deployed in one month (using Dec 2017 as a sample) times twelve months in a year, times monthly rate of reimbursement of $1,365 (see UN General Assembly Resolution 68/281 year 2014). Approximate 'profit/loss' is calculated by deducting approximate reimbursement obtained from deployment of peacekeepers by nonvoluntary financial contribution 2017–18.

Table 19.4: *Comparative analysis of the*
UN peace operations budget and global
military expenditure, 2006–2017

Year	UNP Budget ($ m)	GME ($ m)	Ratio UNP Budget/ GME (%)
2006	5,246	1,401,590.45	0.37
2007	5,348	1,456,709.30	0.37
2008	7,093	1,538,589.60	0.46
2009	7,770	1,648,215.55	0.47
2010	7,264	1,679,487.18	0.43
2011	7,842	1,684,541.47	0.47
2012	7,327	1,673,014.44	0.44
2013	7,543	1,644,444.56	0.46
2014	8,467	1,641,949.37	0.52
2015	8,270	1,666,455.11	0.50
2016	7,874	1,668,275.67	0.47
2017	6,803	1,685,904.85	0.40

Source: UN General Assembly – Approved
Resources for Peacekeeping Operations,
2006–16 and SIPRI Military Expenditure
Database. 2006–16.

nonvoluntary financial contribution, to reduce the UNP budget.[68] Although the 2003 assessment reduced the premium (the additional amount member states need to pay on top of their regular assessment) from previously 30 per cent to 22 per cent, the United States still demands a lower burden share. It is understandable, because even after reducing the premium ceiling, the United States still pays a relatively high voluntary assessment compared to other member states. For the period 2016–18, the United States was assessed to pay 28.5 per cent of the total annual peacekeeping budget, which for the July 2017–June 2018 budget amounted to around $1.9 million.[69] President Donald Trump considers this sum to be too high, and is seeking ways to cap the US contribution at 25 per cent,[70] with the difference borne by the other 192 member states.

Similarly, Japan, as the third biggest financial contributor to the UNPKO, is demanding that the peace operations budget should be more

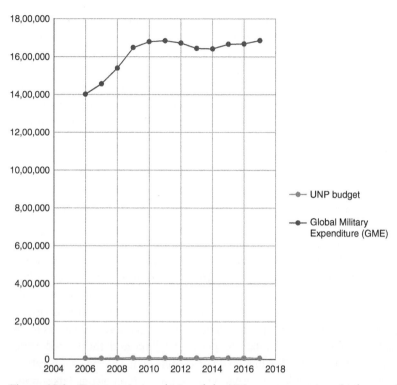

Figure 19.2: Comparative analysis of the UN peace operations budget and global military expenditure

Source: Comparative analysis of the UN peace operations budget and global military expenditure (GME) UN General Assembly, *Approved Resources for Peacekeeping Operations, 2006–2017*, (United Nations Digital Library System, 2018), https://digitallibrary.un.org/search?ln=en&as=1&m1=p&p1=approved +resources+for+peacekeeping+operations&f1=title&op1=a&m2=a&p2=& f2=&op2=a&m3=a&p3=&f3=&rm=&ln=en&fti=0&sf=year&so=d&r g=100&sc=0&c=United+Nations+Digital+Library+System&of=hb and SIPRI, *Military Expenditure Database, 2006–17*, (SIPRI, 2018), https://www.sipri.or g/sites/default/files/SIPRI-Milex-data-1949–2017.xlsx

efficient and effective. The Permanent Mission of Japan to the United Nations, Counsellor Katsuhiko Imada, requested enhanced transparency through better presentation of peacekeeping budgets.[71] In spite of Japan's long-standing national financial difficulties, the country has dutifully paid its assessed financial contributions and additionally paid voluntary contribution to support UN missions in Kosovo and East Timor.[72] However, Japan has been firm in its demand to 'rationalise' the peacekeeping budget, and expects serious discussion on issues of support and scalability, budgetary redeployment and programmatic activities, as relate to UNP financing. For 2016–18, Japan's assessed financial contribution was 9.68 per cent of the total UNP budget, and in value terms for the July 2017–June 2018 UNP budget, Japan's nonvoluntary financial contribution was around $660,000, ranking it as the third biggest contributor to UNPKO.[73]

Since 2016, China took over from Japan as the second biggest contributor to UNPKO financing. Over the three year period of 2016–18, the country was assessed to provide around 10.25 per cent of the total peacekeeping budget, which for the July 2017–June 2018 UNP budget amounted to around $700,000.[74] Aside from financing peace operations, China had also deployed over 2,500 peacekeepers in December 2017, positioning it as the twelfth biggest troop contributing country globally.[75] This is dramatic progress considering that in the 1950s China opposed the United Nations because it believed the latter was acting as the US global gendarmerie in China-Taiwan relations, and had refused to pay its financial contribution until relations between China and the United States improved in 1970s.[76] After finally accepting that UN peace operations play a stabilising role in international security, China pledged its support in 1982 and started to pay its financial arrears. If China is able to maintain its contribution in peacekeeping, the country will likely increase its global influence and leadership, overtaking an internally focused United States under President Trump.

19.7 Payment Arrears and UNPKO Effectiveness

A final issue pertaining to the political economy of UN peace operations is the nonpayment of arrears, placing peacekeeping in a financial crisis. There are diverse reasons for member states' late payments, ranging from genuine inability to pay due to internal crises or war, to deliberate procrastination as a means of demonstrating disagreement with UN 'politically' motivated decisions or unease over perceived inequitable financial burden sharing. Ideally, states should pay their assessment within thirty days of billing, but they can exercise discretion by delaying payment.[77] Member states can only postpone payment obligations for two preceding years, and then Article 19 of the UN

Charter kicks in and the offending country loses its votes in the UN General Assembly (unless the payment delays are beyond the control of the member). Otherwise, countries can pay a minimum of the total sum to maintain voting rights. Payment delays are not uncommon. For instance, it was under President Reagan's leadership that the United States began delaying its contribution payments, which compelled the UN DPKO to reform its burden-sharing percentage in 2003. Moreover, as per February 2018, Venezuela and Libya are amongst eight countries that have suffered restrictions on UN General Assembly voting. Venezuela could not fulfil its $25 million minimum payment due to domestic economic and political crises, and Libya was also in default over its $6.5 million minimum payment due to domestic economic and political disputes.[78] If the United States proceeds with President Trump's plan to limit financial contributions by a 25 per cent cap, then it will also be in default with arrears of around $240 million annually.[79]

Payment arrears impact on troop-contributing countries the hardest, as any budget deficit may delay financial reimbursement of the costs for troops, equipment and materials. This is particularly difficult for developing countries' that may lack sufficient funding to maintain the continuation of deployment, obviously undermining UNPKO effectiveness. Based on the data available, outstanding contribution payments to UNP amounted to approximately $1.85 billion in 2009, with the UN owing $431 million to countries deploying troops, trained police units and equipment on peacekeeping missions.[80] For example, the UNPROFOR mission in Croatia and Bosnia was concluded in 1995, but in 2001 the United Nations still owed $4.5 million in back payments to Kenya.[81] There is also the danger that countries suffering from a lack of reimbursed funds may have insufficient money to pay compensation for death and disability amongst contingent forces.

Troop-contributing countries that are experiencing delays in reimbursement are disincentivised to pay their nonvoluntary financial assessments on time and in full. These countries may also be reluctant to deploy their best equipment because of uncertainty over rental fee payments, providing UNPKO with only second-best and aged equipment that could affect mission capability. The financial pain felt by the UN caused by arrears not only impacts on the troop-contributing countries, but also may delay payments to manufacturers and suppliers of goods and services. Ultimately, they will not provide the goods and

services that are crucial for the successful running of UNPKO operations. Lack of adequate funding will also force UNP to cut the numbers
of support staff and to procure goods and services of low quality, in
aggregate reducing the effectiveness of UNPKO missions.

19.8 Conclusion: Maintaining the Relevance of UN Peace Operations

UNPKO, with their basic principles of obtaining host country consent
and limited use of force, are the preferred instrument for securing the
global public good of peace and stability. However, the problem is that
'globalisation' has decreased the willingness of countries to contribute
to the collective pursuit of peace without obtaining benefits. Countries
only voluntarily contribute when mission objectives are aligned with
their best interests. These interests may be intangible, such as enhanced
international status, and global and regional stability; this being con-
ducive for increasing trade, lowering refugee flows and the opportunity
to secure economic contracts for post-conflict rebuilding. There are
also tangible benefits from CCs' participation in UNP missions; for
instance, the possibility of earning a financial surplus from deploying
national troops and police forces, as well as equipment rental reimbursement. Research has shown that the CCs which have the greatest
impact on peacekeeping operations are likely to be the politically stable
democratic countries, with medium national income and large active
ground forces. However, it does not mean that UNP should limit CCs
to those that qualify under these conditions, but caution should be
exercised concerning CCs seeking only to exploit beneficial returns
from deployment of their security personnel.

   Ideally, there should be an independent mechanism in place to
monitor a CC's involvement in UNPKO. Similarly, it may be beneficial
to have independent and neutral observers monitor UN personnel with
respect to their effectiveness and impact, either intentionally or unintentionally, on the stability of the host country. However, the possibility of establishing a UNPKO monitoring and evaluation unit is still
a subject of controversy, as it is the less developed countries that tend to
deploy personnel, while the relatively wealthier countries prefer to set
mandates and fund missions. Such a unit will also increase the peacekeeping costs borne by member states, which may not sit well at the
current time when the UNPKO budget is experiencing cuts. While

voluntary financial contributions no longer cover UNPKO expenses, a system of nonvoluntary assessment was established in the 1990s, and later reformed in 2003, to fund peace missions using a 'capacity to pay' principle. Yet, the fairness of the UNP nonvoluntary assessment scale continues to attract criticism, especially from the P5 and developed countries, believing that they that continue to bear a disproportionally higher share of peacekeeping expenditure.

The United States, in particular, has objected to funding more than 25 per cent of overall UNPKO expenditure, and chastised the other 192 member countries for free-riding on its contribution. Based on the nonvoluntary assessment scale that uses metrics linked to the value of a country's economy, the US contribution for 2016–18 was over 28 per cent of total UNPKO nonvoluntary funding. If the United States ultimately defaults on a portion of this payment, and other member states are not able, or willing, to share the differential burden, it is hoped that countries with strong economic power would be disposed to step up to the plate and assume the responsibility. However, US avoidance of its international responsibility sets a bad precedent that may be followed by other UN member states. As China is a growing economic power and engaged in international trade that relies heavily on global peace and stability, it can be surmised that Beijing may be tempted to take the helm of UNPKO. These divergent trends represent dangerous geo-political headwinds, and UNPKO member states need to be proactive in evolving policies that support and protect the norms and principles behind recent developments to create a more robust multidimensional peacekeeping mandate. The world needs to approach with caution any possible vacuum in UNPKO leadership in the event of reduced US involvement. Without the backing from major powers, this important international organisation may lose its relevancy and meet the same fate as the League of Nations.

References and notes

1. The financial year of the UN peacekeeping operation budget is from July to June, instead of the commonly practiced January to December. See UN General Assembly. *Approved Resources for Peacekeeping Operations for the Period from 1 July 2017 to 30 June 2018*. A/C.5/ 71/24. 30 June 2017; SIPRI Military Expenditure Database. 2017.

2. MINURSO, United Nations Mission for the Referendum in Western Sahara; MINUSCA, United Nations Multidimensional Integrated Stabilization Mission in the Central African Republic; MINUSMA, United Nations Multidimensional Integrated Stabilization Mission in Mali; MINUSTAH, United Nations Stabilization Mission in Haiti; MONUSCO, United Nations Organization Stabilization Mission in the Democratic Republic of the Congo; UNAMID, African Union-United Nations Hybrid Operation in Darfur; UNDOF, United Nations Disengagement Observer Force; UNFICYP, United Nations Peacekeeping Force in Cyprus; UNIFIL, United Nations Interim Force in Lebanon; UNISFA, United Nations Interim Security Force for Abyei; UNLB, United Nations Logistics Base at Brindisi, Italy; UNMIK, United Nations Interim Administration Mission in Kosovo; UNMIL, United Nations Mission in Liberia; UNMISS, United Nations Mission in South Sudan; UNOCI, United Nations Operation in Côte d'Ivoire; UNSOS, United Nations Support Office in Somalia. The budget also funds the African Union Mission in Somalia (AMISOM), and provides support and logistics to all peace operations through two global service centres in Brindisi (Italy), Valencia (Spain) and a regional service centre in Entebbe (Uganda). The UN Truce Supervision Organization (UNTSO) and the UN Military Observer Group in India and Pakistan (UNMOGIP) are two UN missions that are financed by the UN regular budget.

3. UN Department of Political Affairs. *Uniting our Strengths for Peace: Politics, Partnerships and People, Report of the High-Level Independent Panel on United Nations Peace Operations*. A/70/95-S/2015/446. 17 June 2015.

4. K. Gaibulloev, J. George, T. Sandler and H. Shimizu. 'Personnel Contributions to UN and non-UN Peacekeeping Missions: A Public Goods Approach'. *Journal of Peace Research*. 2015. 52(6): 727–42.

5. UN General Assembly. *Approved Resources for Peacekeeping Operations for the Period from 1 July 2017*.

6. A. Bellamy and P. Williams. *Understanding Peacekeeping*. 2nd edn. Cambridge: Polity Press. 2010. 72–74.

7. E. Schmidl. *Peace Operations Between War and Peace*. London: Frank Cass. 2001. 9.

8. R. Thakur. *The United Nations, Peace and Security*. Cambridge: Cambridge University Press. 2006. 33.

9. *United Nations Armed Forces*. UN Archives. New York: DAG-1/2.3. Box 42, file 399. In Schmidl. *Peace Operations*. 9–10.

10. E. Aksu. *The United Nations, Intra-State Peacekeeping and Normative Change*. Manchester: Manchester University Press. 2003. 76–77.

11. C. Bildt. 'Dag Hammarskjöld and United Nations Peacekeeping'. *UN Chronicle*. 2011. 48(2): 5–7.
12. Bildt. 'Dag Hammarskjöld'. 5.
13. See *A Brief History of UNEF*. Ms, c. 1958, UN Archives. New York: DAG-1/2.2.5.5.1, Box 9; N. Pelcovits. The Long Armistice: UN Peacekeeping and the Arab-Israeli Conflict, 1948–1960. Boulder: Westview. 1993. 123–27.
14. Schmidl. *Peace Operations*. 10.
15. *Second Report of the Secretary-General on the Feasibility of UN Emergency Force*. 6 November 1965 (A/3302).
16. United Nations. Chapter VI: *Pacific Settlement of Disputes*. Repertoire of the Practice of the Security Council. www.un.org/en/sc/repertoire/se ttlements.shtml (accessed 3 May 2018).
17. W. Durch. 'Introduction'. In W. Durch (ed). *The Evolution of UN Peacekeeping*. Basingstoke: Macmillan. 1994. 1–15.
18. Lee Michael Katz, 'World Peacekeeping: Do Nation-States Have a "Responsibility to Protect?"' In *Issues in Peace and Conflict Studies: Selections from CQ Researcher*. California: Sage Publications. 2011. 16.
19. Bellamy and Williams. *Understanding Peacekeeping*. 85.
20. Schmidl. *Peace Operations*. 11.
21. Schmidl. *Peace Operations*. 11; T. Findlay. *The Use of Force in UN Peace Operations*. Oxford: Oxford University Press and SIPRI. 2002. 80–93.
22. Bellamy and Williams. *Understanding Peacekeeping*. 183–85.
23. C. Bellamy. 'If You Can't Stand the Heat . . . New Concepts of Conflict Intensity'. *RUSI Journal*. 1998. 143(1): 25–31.
24. List of the latest and past UN peacekeeping operations can be seen here www.un.org/en/peacekeeping/operations/current.shtml and www .un.org/en/peacekeeping/operations/past.shtml (accessed 3 May 2018).
25. UN PKO. *Summary of UN Peacekeeping Forces by Country*. November 1990. https://peacekeeping.un.org/sites/default/files/nov-19 90.pdf (accessed 3 May 2018); United Nations. *Summary of Troop Contributing Countries by Ranking*. December 2017. https://peacekeep ing.un.org/sites/default/files/summary_of_troop_contributing_coun tries_by_ranking.pdf (accessed 3 May 2018).
26. B. Heldt. 'Trends from 1948 to 2005: How to View the Relation between the United Nations and Non-UN Entities'. In D. C. F. Daniel, P. Taft and S. Wiharta (eds). *Peace Operations: Trends, Progress, and Prospects*. Washington, DC: Georgetown University Press. 2008. 23–25.
27. Heldt. 'Trends from 1948 to 2005'. In Daniel, Taft and Wiharta (eds). *Peace Operations*. 25.

28. R. Gowan and M. Gleason. *UN Peacekeeping: The Next Five Years.* New York: New York University Center on International Cooperation. 2012. 14.
29. Calculated from UN Peacekeeping statistics, see United Nations Peacekeeping. *Troop and Police Contributors.* https://peacekeeping .un.org/en/troop-and-police-contributors (accessed 3 May 2018).
30. UN peacekeeping forces annual growth is calculated from UN Peacekeeping statistics, see United Nations Peacekeeping. *Troop and Police Contributors.*
31. D. Daniel, K. Heuel and B. Margo. 'Distinguishing among Military Contributors'. In D. C. F. Daniel, P. Taft and S. Wiharta (eds). *Peace Operations: Trends, Progress, and Prospects.* Washington, DC: Georgetown University Press. 2008. 27–46.
32. Daniel, Heuel and Margo. 'Distinguishing'. In Daniel, Taft and Wiharta (eds). *Peace Operations.* 32.
33. Gowan and Gleason. *UN Peacekeeping.* 2.
34. Gowan and Gleason. *UN Peacekeeping.* 2.
35. A type of governance that is pseudo-democracy or having partly democracy and partly autocratic elements, where the elites maintain power despite the existence of democratic procedures. See D. C. Jordan. Drug Politics: Dirty Money and Democracies. Norman: University of Oklahoma Press. 1999. 21.
36. Daniel, Heuel and Margo. 'Distinguishing'. In Daniel, Taft and Wiharta (eds). *Peace Operations.* 35.
37. Daniel, Heuel and Margo. 'Distinguishing'. In Daniel, Taft and Wiharta (eds). *Peace Operations.* 30, 39.
38. The World Bank. *The World Bank in Middle Income Countries.* 2018. www.worldbank.org/en/country/mic (accessed 3 May 2018); IISS. The Military Balance 2013. 2013. 286–415.
39. Charter of the United Nations. 'Chapter VII: Action with Respect to Threats to the Peace, Breaches of the Peace, and Acts of Aggression'. www.un.org/en/sections/un-charter/chapter-vii/ (accessed 3 May 2018).
40. A. Bellamy and P. Williams (eds). *Providing for Peacekeepers: The Politics, Challenges and Future of United Nations Peacekeeping Contributions.* Oxford: Oxford University Press. 2013. 11.
41. See Bellamy and Williams (eds). *Providing for Peacekeepers.* 12; J. M. Owen. 'How Liberalism Produces Democratic Peace'. *International Security.* 1994. 19(2): 123–24.
42. T. Sandler. 'The Impurity of Defense: An Application to the Economics of Alliances'. *Kyklos.* 1977. Vol. 33: 443–60.

43. F. P. Van der Putten. China's Evolving Role in Peacekeeping and African Security: The Deployment of Chinese Troops for UN Force Protection in Mali. The Hague: Clingendael Institute. 2015.

44. UN General Assembly, 13th Session – Annexes. Document A/3943. para 160. 28.

45. C. Perry and A. C. Smith. *Trends in Uniformed Contributions to UN Peacekeeping: A New Dataset,* 1991–2012. New York: International Peace Institute. June 2013.

46. Perry and Smith. *Trends.* 5.

47. D. Curan and P. Williams. 'Peacekeeping Contributor Profile: The United Kingdom'. *Providing for Peacekeeping.* August 2016. www .providingforpeacekeeping.org/2014/04/03/contributor-profile-the-uni ted-kingdom/ (accessed 3 May 2018).

48. Perry and Smith. *Trends.* 9.

49. Perry and Smith. *Trends.* 9.

50. Perry and Smith. *Trends.* 9; H. Agam. 'Equitable Geographic Representation in the Twenty-First Century'. In Thakur Ramesh (ed). *What Is Equitable Geographic Representation in the Twenty-First Century.* Seminar Report. New York: United Nations University. 1999. 40–46.

51. A. Sitkowski. *UN Peacekeeping: Myth and Reality.* Westport: Preager. 2006. 29.

52. A. Sotomayor. 'Why Some States Participate in UN Peace Missions While Others Do Not? An Analysis of Civil-Military Relations and Its Effects on Latin America's Contributions to Peacekeeping Operations'. *Security Studies.* 2010. 19(1): 160–95.

53. See United Nations Peacekeeping. *Deployment and Reimbursement.* https://peacekeeping.un.org/en/deployment-and-reimbursement (accessed 3 may 2018); A. J. Bellamy and P. D. Williams. Providing Peacekeepers: The Politics, Challenges, and Future of United Nations Peacekeeping Contributions. Oxford: Oxford University Press. 2013. 218; K. Krishnasamy. '"Recognition" for Third World peacekeepers: India and Pakistan, International Peacekeeping'. *International Peacekeeping.* 2001. 8(4): 56–76.

54. Contributing countries such as Uganda and Burundi obtained training given by US-owned security company Northrop Grumman prior to UN mission deployment to Darfur. See E. Dickinson. 'For Tiny Burundi, Big Returns in Sending Peacekeepers to Somalia'. *Christian Science Monitor.* December 2011; Daniel, Heuel and Margo. 'Distinguishing among Military Contributors'. In Daniel, Taft and Wiharta (eds). *Peace Operations.* 39.

55. See Bellamy and Williams (eds). *Providing for Peacekeepers.* 20.

56. UN Department of Peacekeeping Operations. *List of Peacekeeping Operations 1948–2013*. https://peacekeeping.un.org/sites/default/files/peacekeeping/en/operationslist.pdf (accessed 3 May 2018).

57. T. Sandler. 'International Peacekeeping Operations Burden Sharing and Effectiveness'. *Journal of Conflict Resolution*. 2017. 61(9): 1880.

58. A. Mack. 'Peace on Earth? Increasingly, Yes'. *Washington Post*. 28 December 2005. www.washingtonpost.com/wp-dyn/content/article/2005/12/27/AR2005122700732.html (accessed 3 May 2018).

59. M. Renner and Global Policy Forum. *Peacekeeping Operations Expenditures: 1947–2005*. www.globalpolicy.org/images/pdfs/Z/pk_tables/expend.pdf (accessed 3 May 2018).

60. N. Sheeham. *The Economics of UN Peacekeeping*. Oxon: Routledge. 2011. 95.

61. B. Crossette. 'Spending for U.N. Peacekeeping Is Given Hard Look in Congress'. *The New York Times*. 6 March 1992. www.nytimes.com/1992/03/06/world/spending-for-un-peacekeeping-is-given-hard-look-in-congress.html (accessed 3 May 2018).

62. Sheeham. *The Economics of UN Peacekeeping*. 99.

63. B. D. Schaefer. 'Diplomatic Effort to Reduce America's Peacekeeping Dues Must Start Now'. *The Heritage Foundation Issue Brief*. No. 4781. 1 November 2017. 2.

64. Sheeham. *The Economics of UN Peacekeeping*. 100–14.

65. K. Gaibulloev, J. George, T. Sandler and H. Shimizu. 'Personnel Contributions to UN and non-UN Peacekeeping Missions: A Public Goods Approach'. *Journal of Peace Research*. 2015. 52(6): 727–42; Sandler. 'International Peacekeeping Operations'. 1881.

66. OECD. *Measuring Globalisation: OECD Economic Globalisation Indicators 2010*. September 2010. www.oecd.org/sti/sci-tech/measuring globalisationoecdeconomicglobalisationindicators2010.htm (accessed 3 May 2018); *KOF Swiss Economic Institute. KOF Globalisation Index*. www.kof.ethz.ch/en/forecasts-and-indicators/indicators/kof-globalisation-index.html (accessed 3 May 2018).

67. UN General Assembly. *Approved Resources for Peacekeeping Operations for the Period from 1 July 2014 to 30 June 2015*. A/C.5/69/17. 14 January 2015; UN General Assembly. *Approved Resources for Peacekeeping Operations from 1 July 2017*.

68. Schaefer. 'Diplomatic Effort'. 2; United Nations. *Fifth Committee Seventieth Session, 36th Meeting (AM): Fifth Committee Considers Budget Performance, Proposals, Support Account of Peacekeeping Operations*. 2016. www.un.org/press/en/2016/gaab4198.doc.htm (accessed 3 May 2018).

69. Calculated from UN General Assembly, *Approved resources for peacekeeping operations for the period from 1 July 2017 to 30 June 2018. A/C.5/71/24.* 30 June 2017; UN General Assembly, *Implementation of General Assembly Resolutions 55/235 and 55/236, Annex: Effective rates of assessment for peacekeeping operations, 1 July 2016 to 31 December 2018. A/70/331/Add.1.* 28 December 2015.
70. Schaefer. 'Diplomatic Effort'. 1.
71. United Nations. *Fifth Committee Seventieth Session, 36th Meeting (AM): Fifth Committee Considers Budget Performance, Proposals, Support Account of Peacekeeping Operations.* 2016. www.un.org/pre ss/en/2016/gaab4198.doc.htm (accessed 3 May 2018).
72. United Nations. *Secretary-General Salutes Japan's Contributions to Multilateralism; Urges Greater Involvement in Peacekeeping, Regional Initiatives* . 10 November 1999. www.un.org/press/en/1999/ 19991110.sgsm7209.doc.html (accessed 3 May 2018).
73. Calculated from UN General Assembly. *Approved Resources for Peacekeeping Operations for the Period from 1 July 2017*; UN General Assembly. *Implementation of General Assembly Resolutions 55/235 and 55/236, Annex: Effective Rates of Assessment for Peacekeeping Operations, 1 July 2016 to 31 December 2018. A/70/ 331/Add.1.* 28 December 2015.
74. Calculated from UN General Assembly. *Approved Resources for Peacekeeping Operations for the Period from 1 July 2017*; UN General Assembly. *Implementation of General Assembly Resolutions 55/235 and 55/236.*
75. United Nations. *Summary of Troop Contributing Countries by Ranking.* December 2017. https://peacekeeping.un.org/sites/default/files/summary_ of_troop_contributing_countries_by_ranking.pdf (accessed 3 May 2018).
76. Y. Matsuda. 'China's UN Peacekeeping Operations Policy: Analysis of the Factors behind the Policy Shift toward Active Engagement'. *International Circumstances in the Asia Pacific Series (China).* Japan Digital Library. March 2016. www2.jiia.or.jp/en/pdf/digital_library/ch ina/160331_Yasuhiro_Matsuda.pdf (accessed 3 May 2018); C. Y. Shih. *China's Just World: The Morality of Chinese Foreign Policy.* Boulder: Lynne Rienner. 1993. 191.
77. H. Shimizu. 'An Economic Analysis of the UN Peacekeeping Assessment System'. *Defence and Peace Economics.* 2005. 16(1): 1–18.
78. Voice of America. 'Venezuela and Libya Lose UN Vote for 3rd Time in 3 Years'. *Voice of America.* 13 February 2018. www.voanews.com/a/vene zuela-libya-lose-un-vote-for-third-time-in-three-years-/4252786.html (accessed 3 May 2018); United Nations General Assembly. *Countries in Arrears in the Payment of Their Financial Contributions Under the Terms*

of Article 19 of the UN Charter. www.un.org/en/ga/about/art19.shtml/ sections/about-website/zh/index.html (accessed 3 May 2018).

79. Calculated from 3.5 per cent out of UNP 2017/2018 budget of $6,803,236,100.
80. Sheeham. *The Economics of UN Peacekeeping.* 136–37.
81. Sheeham. *The Economics of UN Peacekeeping.* 136–37.

PART VI

End Game

20 | *Towards a Peaceful World*

ANKE HOEFFLER

Introduction

Organised armed conflict is a problem that occurs predominantly in low- and middle-income countries. Thus, there is a strong link between security and development, and the United Nation's 2030 Agenda for Sustainable Development specifically aims to create peaceful and inclusive societies (Sustainable Development Goal 16). This chapter uses global data to describe patterns of violence and discusses the possible policy instruments for violence reduction. The development community has focused on political violent conflict, excluding almost all other forms of collective violence (e.g. organised crime) and interpersonal violence (e.g. homicide). However, all of these other forms of violence have serious welfare and development consequences, and governments/ supranational authorities need to recognise that violence reduction strategies should target all forms of violence. The empirical evidence suggests that the reduction in the availability of arms and regulations on illicit drugs and alcohol as well changes in norms can reduce violence.

20.1 The Aspiration

Organised armed conflicts are overwhelmingly a problem faced by developing countries; most violent conflicts take place in low and middle-income countries. However, when the Millennium Development Goals (MDGs) were set out in 2000, there was no mention of violence. Fast forward to 2015, and violence had belatedly come to be accepted as a major impediment to societal development. The UN's 2030 Agenda for sustainable development now explicitly states that member states should 'promote peaceful and inclusive societies for sustainable development' (SDG 16). More specifically, the targets must include the reduction of 'all

453

forms of violence and related death rates everywhere' (SDG 16.1), ending 'all forms of violence against ... children' (SDG 16.2) and the significant reduction of 'illicit financial and arms flows ... and combat-[ing] all forms of organized crime' (SDG 16.4). Furthermore, the agenda aims to 'eliminate all forms of violence against all women and girls in the public and private spheres' (SDG 5.2). Here, two issues should be highlighted. First, unlike the MDGs, the 2030 Agenda sets goals and targets for all countries, not only for developing countries. Second, the understanding of violence is a broad one. The aspiration of 'peaceful and inclusive societies' does not only mean an absence of war, but also a reduction of 'all forms of violence', where violence against women, children and the fight against organised crime should receive specific attention.

The aim of this chapter, therefore, is to discuss how the aspirations set out in the SDGs can become a reality. How can we shape our world so that more people live in peace and security? In order to answer this question, there is a need to examine the magnitude of the problem before discussing some effective violence reduction strategies. The focus throughout is on violence as a development problem, not on the human rights issues or public health dimensions. Many readers may be sceptical as to the ambitious nature of the SDGs. Violence is part of human nature and it appears unlikely, even for an optimist, that violence can ever be completely eradicated. Note that there is only one zero target, namely ending all violence against children. The other SDGs suggest 'significant' reductions in violence. Some countries have already achieved significant reductions, thus it appears possible to address this apparently intractable challenge. Other worldwide targets were also seen by many as too ambitious, but as the eradication campaigns for diseases show, great progress can be achieved. Smallpox and rinderpest are now eradicated worldwide, while Guinea worm and polio are only endemic in very few areas. The fight against measles is also well progressed, saving the lives of hundreds of thousands of children every year. Of course there is no simple vaccine against violence, but there are a number of programmes and policy measures that can tackle the problem of violence. Like in public health initiatives, knowledge of the drivers of violence can help us design measures to prevent its occurrence and spread, and isolate cases to prevent the spread. As the examples from public health show, medical progress has made a significant impact on morbidity and mortality. The flipside is that the social causes of illness, disability and death become relatively more important in improving human welfare. Reducing and preventing violence is thus an important current and future policy issue facing governments and the international community.

20.2 The Problem

In order to assess the magnitude of the problem this section offers an overview of prevalence rates of different forms of violence. Before presenting this overview, violence has to be defined; broadly, violence is *force which is used to cause harm*.[1] A comparison of the different forms of violence does not only require a theoretical definition, but also measures of violence. It is therefore easiest to use the definition of violence as stated by one of the big data providers, such as the World Health Organisation (WHO), which defines violence as follows:

The intentional use of physical force or power, threatened or actual, against oneself, another person, or against a group or community, that either results in or has a high likelihood of resulting in injury, death, psychological harm, maldevelopment or deprivation.[2]

The WHO provides statistics on the causes of death and these include three broad categories of violence: (1) self-directed; (2) collective; and (3) interpersonal violence. Self-directed violence and focus on the harm that is directed at others is excluded from this analysis. *Collective violence* includes violence perpetrated by organised groups, including, for example, states, rebel organisations and terrorists. The WHO also includes deaths from legal interventions in the category of collective violence; these are, for example, deaths caused by police forces while making arrests. *Interpersonal violence* is perpetrated by an individual. Although violence can take many forms (physical, sexual, psychological, abuse and neglect), the focus in the WHO data, and most other databases, is on physical harm. Although considerable resources and expertise go into collecting data on internationally comparable statistics concerning violence, the numbers should be treated with great caution. Violence is often not observed by others, only the victim and the perpetrator are aware. The best data are available for deadly violence; these will be discussed first, before moving on to presenting some data on nonfatal violence.

20.3 Deadly Violence

The data efforts by the Uppsala Conflict Data Project (UCDP) in collaboration with the Peace Research Institute in Oslo (PRIO) provide detailed data on collective violence. The definition of organised violence depends on a number of issues, and the number of battle deaths is a key indicator.[3] Only organised violence that resulted in more than twenty-five battle deaths is included in the database. If one of the parties is the government of a state, involving armed conflicts between and within states, these conflicts are referred to as *state-based armed conflicts*. Most of the state-based armed conflicts are internal, i.e. fought within states.

If the armed conflict is between non-state actors, such as, for example, between Islamic State (IS) and the Taleban in Afghanistan, then this is referred to as *non-state armed conflicts*. When only one party is organised, and kills unarmed civilians, this is termed *one-sided violence*. The organised party can either be the government or a non-state actor. Examples include the killing of civilians by the South Sudanese government or by rebel groups such as the Lord's Resistance Army (LRA) in northern Uganda. Figure 20.1 provides an overview of the fatalities.

There are a number of characteristics of the fatality data that are worth pointing out. Since 2000, the number of fatalities from state-based armed

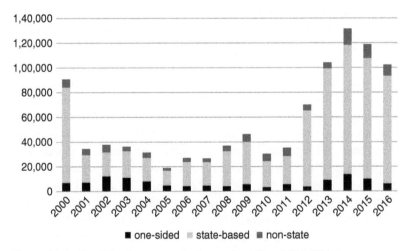

Figure 20.1: Fatalities from organised armed conflict, 2002–2016
Source: Uppsala Conflict Data Project, Dataset Download Center, yearly datasets. https://ucdp.uu.se/downloads/

conflicts was relatively higher than from non-state based conflicts and one-sided violence. Since 2011, the number of fatalities resulting from state-based armed conflicts shows an upward trend. This is mainly due to the Syrian civil war, but also due to the wars in Afghanistan, Iraq, Ukraine, Pakistan, Somalia, South Sudan and Yemen. For 2015, the total number of fatalities was about 97,900; and many will think that this is a relatively low number. It is important to keep in mind, however, that the social science researchers carry out a verified body count and only consider fatalities that were the result of direct violence, i.e. deaths due to hunger and disease that are a consequence of armed conflict are not part of these statistics.

The WHO uses these UCDP/PRIO estimates and adjusts the fatalities by applying a factor to account for additional nonviolent deaths in state-based armed conflicts. For some conflicts, additional survey material is used, and for 2015 the WHO estimates that about 156,000 died as a result of collective violence.[4]

Public health studies of specific conflicts – for example, the civil wars in the Democratic Republic of the Congo and Iraq – have produced fatality estimates that are multiples of the count data generated by social scientists.[5] These public health estimates are based on survey evidence which is then used to extrapolate the total number of fatalities. This short discussion indicates that the UCDP/PRIO data should be understood as conservative approximations of the fatalities resulting from organised violence.

For interpersonal violence, there are two main sources that provide comparable data across countries: the WHO and the UN Office on Drugs and Crime (UNODC). The UN data focus on intentional homicides, defined as 'unlawful death purposefully inflicted on a person by another person'.[6] In most countries homicides are chiefly murder and manslaughter, but the definition also includes unlawful deaths from terrorism and extrajudicial killings, where governmental authorities kill without the sanction of any judicial proceeding or legal process. There are many problems with the homicide data, e.g. murder and manslaughter are defined differently across countries and time, high-income countries provide better quality data, some countries do not include deaths from terrorism in the homicide statistics and extrajudicial killings can only be approximated. However, keeping these weaknesses in mind, the UNODC reported about 376,000 homicides for 2010. The WHO estimates for the same year are about 464,000, almost 90,000 more deaths. This may be partly due to the difference in definitions;[7] for example, extrajudicial killings and terrorism victims are treated differently. Furthermore, the criminal and justice agencies that report to the UNODC are likely to under-report homicides. Infanticide, for instance, is still prevalent in some societies, and the health professionals at the WHO make adjustments to death statistics to account for neglect or violence. Another source of discrepancy could be extrajudicial killings, where states are likely to under-report. One example is Mexico, where a comparison between police records and death certificates suggests that in the state of Veracruz only 64 per cent of all homicides were reported to the police.[8] The WHO data have the advantage that they are reported by age and sex. Using these higher numbers a breakdown of worldwide homicides is depicted in Figure 20.2.

Child homicides are relatively rare (about 7 per cent of total homicides), as are female victims (about 16 per cent). A large percentage of women are killed by a former or current intimate partner (IP), about 43 per cent of women are killed by their husband, partner or boyfriend.[9] The overwhelming majority of homicide victims are men. About 77 per cent of all victims are men, with only a small proportion killed by their intimate partner. Worldwide, adolescents and young

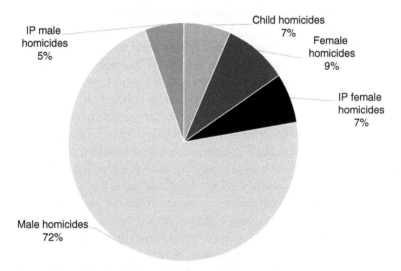

Figure 20.2: Homicide by age and sex, 2015
Source: World Health Organisation, Global Health Observatory Data. https://www.who.int/gho/mortality_burden_disease/en/

adult men are at the highest risk of becoming a victim of homicide. In the Americas, the main cause of death amongst 14–29 year old males are not traffic accidents, suicide or disease, it is violence.[10]

Notwithstanding the difference in fatality estimates, many more people are killed by interpersonal than collective violence. Many so-called peaceful countries, i.e. those without organised armed conflicts, are very violent. For example, in 2015, Brazil recorded about 55,600 homicide victims, while about 45,200 were killed in the Syrian civil war.[11]

20.4 Nonfatal Violence

Organised armed conflict kills people, but many are also injured and maimed.[12] However, it is very difficult to provide an assessment of how many are *war wounded* because research is mainly focused on counting the numbers of *war deaths*. As the discussion above indicated, even counting deaths is very difficult. There is no global data set that provides high-quality estimates on the injuries and disabilities caused by armed conflict. Due to technological and medical advances, many of the injured now survive; in other words, armed conflict may now result in fewer war dead, but in more war wounded than in the past.[13] It may therefore be particularly important to provide estimates of the numbers wounded in armed conflict. Although there are some detailed statistics on war wounded for some conflicts, they are mainly available for high-income countries, and there is too little comparable information on the numbers of war wounded in low- and middle-income countries for making any attempt to present even rough estimates on the numbers injured in wars. This is a serious omission.

Despite the issues raised in the previous section, homicide data are generally seen as the most reliable and internationally comparable violent crime statistics, because they are based on evidence: dead bodies. But violence so severe that it ends a human life is relatively rare; many more people experience far less severe violence. The evidence for experiences of nonlethal violence is often less strong and statistics are not as reliable. Take the example of assault, where assault is broadly defined as *bodily harm caused by another*. According to the UNODC, about 4 million people suffer an assault every year.[14] Or at least, these people were assaulted, reported this to their national police and the national police reported this to the UNODC. It is likely that many victims do not report assault to the police, either because they fear further violence or because they do not trust their police force to handle the complaint sympathetically, fairly and competently. Ideally, victimisation surveys should be used to find out how many people have suffered an assault. Although some countries produce these surveys, there are currently too few to provide an internationally comparable dataset. However, comparing the available victimisation surveys it is obvious that reported data provide a gross underestimation of assaults.

The problem of under-reporting is likely to be even greater for sexual violence, which is explicitly excluded in the assault statistics and reported separately. Sexual violence includes the categories *rape* and *sexual assault*. Rape is defined as sexual penetration without valid consent. *Sexual assault* covers any unwanted sexual act that does not amount to rape. Examples include unwanted groping and fondling, sexual harassment and drug facilitated sexual assault.[15] Many victims of sexual assault feel ashamed and embarrassed, and, additionally, in many societies, reporting of sexual violence is very difficult. One internationally comparable data source provides some information on the prevalence of (sexual) violence against women: The Demographic and Health Surveys (DHS), consisting of over 300 surveys in ninety countries so far. Some of the surveys ask women about their experiences of violence, and these interviews are carried out in private. Although women can be the victims of gender-based violence in the community and at work, the surveys suggest that most of the violence happens in the home. About 13 per cent of partnered women state in confidential interviews that they had experienced some form of intimate partner violence (IPV) during the past year.[16] Prevalence rates vary considerably across regions. While only 4 per cent of women aged fifteen and older in high-income countries had reported IPV during the past year, about 28 per cent of women in Sub-Saharan countries had done so.

Men can also be victims of domestic violence and survey evidence from some countries suggest that female-on-male violence is also common, although physical injuries tend to be less severe and do not instil as much fear as male-on-female violence. Nonetheless, female-on-male violence occurs frequently and most often among teenage couples or when they are in their early twenties.[17] However, there are no comparable data on male victimisation for a large sample of countries.

As set out in the SDGs and the United Nations Convention on the Rights of the Child, improving children's lives to protect them and safeguard their development and well-being is a global aspiration. Sadly, the reality is very different; worldwide, many children are maltreated. Maltreatment of children includes neglect, physical, sexual and emotional abuse and happens at home, in school, in care institutions, prisons, at work and in the community. Most of the violence happens in the home[18] in the form of physical punishment. This clearly constitutes violence because force is intentionally used to cause harm.[19] The acceptability of such physical punishment varies across societies, but in many societies this is still an acceptable part of educating children. However, every society has norms where certain behaviours are considered abusive. Some representative evidence on corporal punishment in the home comes from the UN's Multiple Indicator Cluster Surveys. In these surveys the primary caregivers were asked about their child disciplinary practices at home.[20] Primary caregivers were asked whether they or any other member in the household had used specific disciplining methods during the past month, ranging from nonviolent discipline (e.g. taking away privileges), psychological aggression (e.g. shouting), physical punishment (e.g. spanking) to severe physical punishment (e.g. beating repeatedly with a belt, stick or similar). Given that attitudes vary, a conservative definition of violence against children is the use of the last category only (severe physical punishment). The self-reported evidence from primary caregivers suggests that the global prevalence rate is a staggering 17.5 per cent.[21] In absolute numbers this means that about 311 million children are subjected to this form of violence every month.[22] The data also indicate that primary caregivers in low-income countries use more violence to discipline their children than care givers in high-income countries.

To summarise, the prevalence of violence is higher in lower-income countries. This is the case for collective as well as interpersonal violence. The overwhelming majority of homicide victims are men, but there is also evidence of considerable violence against women and children. This violence happens mainly in the domestic sphere.

20.5 Towards Solutions

The previous sections established that violence, and interpersonal violence in particular, is highly prevalent. This violence does not only cause pain and suffering to individuals, but has also adverse consequences for societal development.[23] A number of studies examining violence over time suggest that prevalence rates for different forms of violence, such as civil war and homicide, have decreased,[24] generating hope that the world could become even more peaceful. This section highlights some of the empirical evidence of violence reduction strategies.[25]

The international community intervenes in a number of different ways: diplomacy, sanctions, development aid, military assistance, peacekeepers and through the design of rules on arms transfers and security operations.[26] The impact of diplomatic interventions and sanctions is difficult to assess, primarily because it is difficult to define what constitutes success. In this context, success could mean negotiations between the parties, reduction in hostilities, a ceasefire or peace for a number of years. The literature on the effect of aid on conflict suggests that aid does not appear to have a conflict-reducing impact; in some circumstances, aid may even increase the likelihood and duration of conflict. There is some evidence that this is the case for food aid,[27] but over time food aid has been decreasing and now only makes up about 2 per cent of total aid. It is thus unlikely to be a considerable factor in determining levels of violence.

20.6 United Nations Peacekeeping Operations

As discussed in the previous chapter, coordinated attempts to secure peace have been pursued through UNPKOs. Such operations are set up when the UN Security Council determines that this is an appropriate intervention and has adopted a resolution. Since 1948 there have been seventy-one UN operations worldwide. Since the Cold War the number of operations has considerably increased; the regional focus shifting towards sub-Saharan Africa and the remit of the operations has widened. So called 'traditional peacekeeping' operations in which the United Nations deploys a relatively small interposition force between warring parties, mostly in interstate conflicts, are now rare, with peacekeeping currently characterised by expanded mandates and greater levels of coercion. Even though peacekeepers are deployed to keep the peace, there have been highly publicised cases where peacekeepers were ineffective, violated human rights and were involved in corruption and sexual exploitation.[28] Are these cases typical or are UNPKOs effective, i.e. do they keep the peace? A considerable number of studies have investigated this question using duration analysis and have found either a positive impact of peacekeepers or no impact.[29] One of the important questions is whether peacekeepers are deployed to the less difficult situations; this would bias the statistical results in favour of success. However, UNPKOs appear to be more often deployed to severe security situations.[30] Recent work suggests that UNPKOs prevent minor armed conflicts from scaling up,[31] and that operations help to secure the peace after negotiated settlements.[32] Since UNPKOs contribute to making the world more peaceful, strengthening existing operations and deploying new ones would be an effective use of public money. The current UNPKO budget is about $6.8 bn, but to put this in perspective it is less than half of one per cent of global military expenditure. Increasing UNPKO spending would put a minimal financial burden on each contributing state.[33]

20.7 Arms Trade Regulation

An effective channel to reduce current levels of violence is to restrict the availability of arms. The small literature on arms embargos[34] provides evidence that restricting arms flows reduces levels of organised violence. In principle, it should be feasible to regulate the trade in conventional arms, because it is highly concentrated. During the period of 2012–16, the United States and Russia alone accounted for 56 per cent of all arms exports, followed by China, France, Germany and the United Kingdom.[35] For some time the United States and the European Union have had controls on arms exports, but a coordinated international effort to prevent the use of weapons for acts of genocide, crimes against humanity, war crimes or terrorism has only recently led to the UN Arms Trade Treaty (ATT). The ATT is perceived as having the potential to create a more peaceful world, but so far it is not clear whether it has changed behaviour. Although 130 states have signed since 2013, some important arms exporters (e.g. China and Russia) are not part of the ATT, and many of the signatories have not fulfilled their reporting obligations.[36] Monitoring and reporting is crucial because, contrary to popular belief, there is no amorphous black market where arms are bought for illegal purposes.[37] Mainly, arms end up being misused when they are illegally transferred from a legitimate importing country to another state. For example, Ukrainian arms exports to Kenya were shipped on to South Sudan, where they were used in the civil war.[38] Monitoring the ATT is therefore crucial to preventing illegal use of arms, and sufficient resources have to be made available for end user checks.

20.8 National Regulation of Firearms and Other Weapons

Guns greatly increase the capacity to kill and firearms account for over 40 per cent of all homicides worldwide.[39] The regulation of firearms is thus a promising avenue to reduce violence. Much of the evidence in the literature comes from the United States, where in 2016 about 73 per cent of all homicides were committed by using a gun, or in absolute numbers there were just over 11,000 victims.[40] This is more than double the number of American service personnel killed in hostile action in Afghanistan and Iraq over the past fifteen years.[41] A large number of studies examine the impact of gun ownership in the United States.[42] While causality is difficult to establish, there is considerable evidence to support the hypothesis that higher levels of gun ownership cause higher levels of homicides.[43] For example, cities in the United States and in Europe have similar crime rates, but the higher number of associated deaths indicates that Americans are better armed. Thus, when guns are more easily available they are used more often, and due to their relative ease of use and their lethal force they tend to cause more fatal and nonfatal injuries than physical force or other weapons.[44]

In contrast to the United States, the United Kingdom has very strict rules on private ownership of guns, and as a result, gun crime is low by international comparison. Only 7 per cent of all homicides are committed with a gun (44 out of 640 homicides).[45] The low rate of gun ownership also has an impact on policing. In the UK, police officers are not routinely armed with guns, and only in serious cases are specially trained firearms officers dispatched. During 2015, UK police officers only discharged their firearms six times.[46] Compare this to the United States, where police routinely carry firearms and no discharge statistics even exist; but reliable estimates suggest that in 2015, police officers killed over 1,100 people.[47]

Although some other countries have considerably tightened gun laws, these legal reforms have had variable outcomes. Australia introduced a strict gun law and two waves of firearm buyback schemes (1996/97 and 2003), which resulted in the handing-in of over one million guns.[48] However, the downward trend in the number of deaths due to firearms had begun before 1996, and it is unclear how much the change in legislation and the buyback scheme contributed to this reduction.[49] In Brazil, the government passed a Disarmament Statute in 2003, representing a comprehensive approach to gun control. In addition, a voluntary disarmament programme took place, leading to about 500,000 firearms being handed in. The introduction of this statute appears to have halted the increasing trend in the number of homicides, but Brazil remains a violent society, where during the past decade the homicide rate has been around 22 per 100,000.[50]

Sharp objects, such as knives, were used in 24 per cent of homicide cases worldwide,[51] and some countries (e.g. the United Kingdom) have made the carrying of knives a criminal offence in order to reduce knife violence. In other societies, restrictions on harmful substances are important. For example, in Bangladesh legal changes to the sale of acid led to a considerable reduction in acid attacks.[52]

20.9 Alcohol Regulation

Alcohol makes individuals more likely to perpetrate violence and to be victimised. Although a large number of studies demonstrate a correlation between alcohol consumption and violence, the question of causality is difficult to disentangle. Some of this violence would have been perpetrated in any case, irrespective of the use of alcohol. Violent individuals tend to have low self-control or suffer from personality disorders. These personal characteristics also make them more likely to abuse alcohol. Certain environmental factors, such as economic deprivation and social marginalisation, could also simultaneously drive violence as well as alcohol consumption.

However, evidence obtained from diverse studies, e.g. victimisation surveys, statistical analysis over time and space and evaluating policy experiments, all support the argument that alcohol consumption increases violence. Drinking patterns also appear to be important. In some countries, meals are regularly eaten with beverages that contain relatively low alcohol content (beer and wine). In some countries, the drinking culture is different, where people drink less frequently, but when they do drink they are more likely to be intoxicated. Often, they consume drinks that are high in alcohol content (spirits), and this is associated with more violent behaviour.[53] Alcohol consumption is also linked to IPV,[54] and treatment for alcoholism decreases this form of violence.[55]

One policy experiment that illustrates the effect of restrictions was the anti-alcohol campaign in the Soviet Union under Mikhail Gorbachev from 1985 to 1987. This resulted in an estimated reduction in alcohol consumption by about 25 per cent and a fall in the homicide rate by about one third; the homicide rate increased to previous levels once the campaign ended.[56]

If policymakers want to tackle alcohol consumption they have to increase prices[57] and limit the availability of alcohol,[58] in particular spirits. The exact formulation and enforcement of policies will depend on regional and national circumstances. In general, these strategies are not popular, but although the public support education and information campaigns, these are generally ineffective.[59] In democracies, policymakers have to make difficult choices by balancing the desire of the public to consume alcohol with public policy aims, such as reducing mortality and morbidity from alcohol consumption, including assaults and homicides.

20.10 Illicit Drugs

Illicit drugs generate crime and undermine peace and security. The main reason why illicit drugs are so closely associated with violence is not that they tend to make the consumers of drugs more prone to violence, but because prohibition of drugs for non-medicinal purposes generates black markets. Criminal organisations and local gangs use violence to control this illicit market, and the National Gang Center estimates that in the United States about 13 per cent of all homicides are gang related (averaged over 2007–11). Most of these gangs are primarily financed by drug sales. Moreover, drugs increase interpersonal violence outside gangs. Many drug addicts can only finance their addiction through theft, fraud, burglary, robbery and prostitution.

A further unintended consequence is that just like the control of the end user market, criminals organise trans-national shipments, or narco-trafficking, from the producer country to the destination country. This is a particular problem in Central American countries, where homicide rates are well above the global average. Given the strong relationship between violence on the one hand, and drug production, trading and consumption on the other, the question is how existing drug policies should be altered to reduce violence. Current efforts focus on the supply side, i.e. drug seizures, forceful destruction of crops and alternative development strategies for poppy and cocoa producing farmers. There are also a number of options to decrease the demand for drugs. One strategy is to criminalise the use of drugs and incarcerate users, while other strategies address demand through public education, drug rehabilitation programmes and substitution programmes, such as state-controlled consumption of methadone for heroin addicts. Programmes in a number of European countries, e.g. Switzerland, Germany and the United Kingdom, have resulted in a reduction of hepatitis and HIV rates and acquisitive crime. Thus, these programmes are likely to reduce some drug-related violence in the user countries. However, there is also a growing movement to deregulate the market for drugs. This is not per se aimed at reducing either the supply or the demand of drugs, but aims to reduce the mark-up that results from prohibition. Further research and a careful evaluation of existing deregulation efforts may be useful in determining how violence can be reduced through developing new global strategies for narcotic drugs.[60]

20.11 Institutional Change for Violence Reduction

Political, social and economic interactions are governed by formal rules (constitutions, laws, property rights) as well as informal rules (sanctions, taboos, customs, traditions, codes of conduct).[61] Legal reform can include antidiscrimination laws, to establish the rights of women, children, homosexuals and transgender persons, minority ethnic and religious groups. There are many examples where legal change has confirmed and encouraged social change, e.g. Sweden was the first country to outlaw the physical punishment of children in 1979, and rates of physical discipline are very low.[62] However, if legal reform runs counter to societal beliefs and norms, the reforms will have little effect.[63] Take the example of female genital mutilation: all of the twenty-six African countries in which this custom is practised have outlawed it, but introducing bans has not significantly reduced the number of girls subjected to this harmful tradition.[64] Informal rules on the acceptability of maltreatment can be influenced in a number of different ways. 'Infotainment', such as broadcasting episodes featuring domestic violence in soap operas, can encourage debate and uncover violence that is hidden.[65] Other strategies include more targeted interventions, such as 'dating violence' programmes, in which female and male teenagers learn about healthy relationships[66] and parenting programmes that encourage violence-free discipline techniques.[67]

20.12 Concluding Comments

Based on conservative data collection efforts, violence kills about half a million people every year and many more experience nonlethal violence.[68] The majority are not killed in organised armed conflicts but are victims of homicide. Violence causes enormous human suffering by inflicting death, pain, suffering, trauma and fear. In addition to harming individuals, violence is also detrimental to societal development. Human welfare can be greatly increased through violence prevention and reduction. Recently, the world has experienced more organised armed conflict and the numbers of fatalities have risen. Restricting the flow of arms to these conflict zones is one important strategy and further efforts should be made to (1) persuade arms exporters to sign the Arms Trade Treaty and (2) to substantially increase the monitoring of arms transfers.

Over the past twenty-five years the trend for several forms of interpersonal violence has experienced a downward movement. This is due to a number of factors, some of which are country specific. However, in general, demographic changes, with smaller concentrations of young people, are one reason for the decline. Another is that modern technology makes surveillance easier, and burglar alarms, CCTV cameras and electronic tracking devices assist in the prosecution of perpetrators and act as deterrence.[69] Furthermore, according to Stephen Pinker, the 'rights revolution' has made aggression and violence less acceptable over recent decades.[70] A number of rights movements, i.e. the civil rights movement, the feminist movement and the gay rights movement, largely argued for peaceful change, spread the idea of equality and lobbied for public policy changes.

Although there is a large literature discussing the drivers of violence and how it can be reduced, causality and the size of the impact are often difficult to establish. Randomised controlled experiments provide excellent insights into the causality and impact of interventions, but it is often neither ethical nor practical to use such experiments when assessing violence reduction strategies. Social scientists have to collaborate across the disciplines to develop improved evaluation methods.

Globally, the data show a clear pattern: violence is more prevalent in poorer countries. Economic development is thus an important strategy in violence reduction, but it is often violence that hinders this development. However, there is emerging evidence that even in low-income settings interventions can reduce levels of violence. Most of the interventions for violence reduction have so far been developed in high-income countries and there are concerns that these cannot be transferred to different contexts. On the other hand, recent research on reducing violence against children suggests that cultural transferability is perhaps less of an issue than often assumed.[71] More research on transferring existing interventions, adapting them and designing new strategies may provide very effective solutions.

References and notes

1. For more discussion see A. Hoeffler. 'What Are the Costs of Violence?' *Politics, Philosophy & Economics*. 2017. 16(4): 422–45.
2. E. G. Krug, L. L. Dahlberg, J. A. Mercy, A. B. Zwi and R. Lozano (eds). *World Report on Violence and Health*. World Health Organization. 2002. http://apps.who.int/iris/bitstream/10665/42495/1/9241545615_eng.pdf (accessed 12 February 2018).
3. M. Allansson, E. Melander, L. Themnér. 'Organized Violence, 1989–2016'. *Journal of Peace Research*. 2017. 54(4): 574–87.
4. World Health Organization. *WHO Methods and Data Sources for Country-Level Causes of Death 2000-2015*. Global Health Estimates Technical Paper: WHO/HIS/IER/GHE/2016.3. 2017. 38–39. www.who.int/healthinfo/global_burden_disease/GlobalCOD_method_2000_2015.pdf (accessed 12 February 2018).
5. M. Spagat, A. Mack, T. Cooper, J. Kreutz. 'Estimating War Deaths: An Arena of Contestation'. *Journal of Conflict Resolution*. 2009. 53(6): 934–50.
6. United Nations Office on Drugs and Crime. *Global Study on Homicide 2013 – Trends, Contexts, Data*. Sales number: 14.IV.1. 2014. www.unodc.org/documents/data-and-analysis/statistics/GSH2013/2014_GLOBAL_HOMICIDE_BOOK_web.pdf (accessed 12 February 2018).
7. For more discussion on homicide statistics see C. Andersson, L. Kazemian. 'Reliability and Validity of Cross-National Homicide Data: A Comparison of UN and WHO Data'. *International Journal of Comparative and Applied Criminal Justice*. September 2017. 10: 1–6; S. Kanis, S. F. Messner, M. P. Eisner, W. Heitmeyer. 'A Cautionary Note about the Use of Estimated Homicide Data for Cross-National Research'. *Homicide Studies*. November 2017. 21(4): 312–24.
8. Institute for Economics and Peace. *Mexico Peace Index 2016 – Mapping the Evolution of Peace and Its Drivers*. IEP Report: 38. 2016. http://economicsandpeace.org/wp-content/uploads/2016/04/Mexico-Peace-Index-2016_English.pdf (accessed 12 February 2018).

9. H. Stöckl, K. Devries, A. Rotstein, N. Abrahams, J. Campbell, C. Watts, C. G. Moreno. 'The Global Prevalence of Intimate Partner Homicide: A Systematic Review'. *The Lancet*. 2013. 382(9895): 859–65.

10. World Health Organization. *Top 10 Causes of Death – Situations and Trends*. 2018. www.who.int/gho/mortality_burden_disease/causes_ death/top_10/en/ (accessed 12 February 2018).

11. UNODC Statistics. *Crime and Criminal Justice*. https://data.unodc.org/ (accessed 31 January 2018).

12. H. A. Ghobarah, P. Huth, B. Russett. 'Civil Wars Kill and Maim People – Long after the Shooting Stops'. *American Political Science Review*. 2003. 97(2): 189–202.

13. T. M. Fazal. 'Dead Wrong? Battle Deaths, Military Medicine, and Exaggerated Reports of War's Demise'. *International Security*. July 2014. 39(1): 95–125.

14. UNODC Statistics. *Crime and Criminal Justice*.

15. Penetration refers to the penetration of the vulva, anus or mouth with any body part or object. Invalid consent includes cases of intimidation, force, fraud, coercion, threat, deception, use of drugs or alcohol, abuse of power or a position of vulnerability or the giving or receiving of benefits. The rape definition includes *statutory rape*, where sexual penetration takes place with a person below the age of consent. In these cases it is immaterial whether the underage person consented or not. Definition: UNDOC (2015) International Classification of Crime for Statistical Purposes (ICCS) Version 1.1.

16. K. M. Devries, J. Y. Mak, C. García-Moreno, M. Petzold, J. C. Child, G. Falder, S. Lim, L. J. Bacchus, R. E. Engell, L. Rosenfeld, C. Pallitto. 'The Global Prevalence of Intimate Partner Violence against Women'. *Science*. 2013. 340(6140): 1527–28. Estimate based on past year violence and only nationally representative surveys but includes any sexual and physical violence.

17. M. A. Straus. 'Thirty Years of Denying the Evidence on Gender Symmetry in Partner Violence: Implications for Prevention and Treatment'. *Partner Abuse*. 2010. 1(3): 332–62. See also Institute of Development Studies (IDS), Ghana Statistical Services (GSS) and Associates. *Domestic Violence in Ghana: Incidence, Attitudes, Determinants and Consequences*. https:// opendocs.ids.ac.uk/opendocs/bitstream/handle/123456789/12168/DVR eport.pdf?sequence=1&isAllowed=y (accessed 12 February 2018).

18. P. S. Pinheiro. *World Report on Violence Against Children*. United Nations. 2006. www.unicef.org/lac/full_tex(3).pdf (accessed 12 February 2018). See also A. Hoeffler. 'Violence Against Children: A Critical Issue for Development'. *The European Journal for Development Research*. 2017. 29(5): 945–63; M. Stoltenborgh, M. J. Bakermans-Kranenburg, L. R. Alink

and M. H. IJzendoorn. 'The Prevalence of Child Maltreatment across the Globe: Review of a Series of Meta-Analyses'. *Child Abuse Review*. 2015. 24 (1): 37–50.

19. For more discussion see Hoeffler. 'Violence Against Children'; Stoltenborgh et al. 'The Prevalence of Child Maltreatment'; and Ending Violence in Childhood: Overview. *Global Report 2017. Know Violence in Childhood*. New Delhi, India.

20. The discipline tactics were assessed according to the Parent-Child Conflict Tactics Scale. See M. A. Straus, S. L. Hamby, D. Finkelhor, D. W. Moore and D. Runyan. 'Identification of Child Maltreatment with the Parent-Child Conflict Tactics Scales: Development and Psychometric Data for a National Sample of American Parents'. *Child Abuse & Neglect*. 1998. 22(4): 249–70.

21. Hoeffler. 'Violence Against Children'.

22. In their comparison of meta-analyses Stoltenborgh et al. (2015) suggest a global prevalence rate of 22.6 per cent for physical abuse, however they do not distinguish between severe and less severe physical punishment.

23. The World Bank. *World Development Report – Governance and the Law*. 2017. www.worldbank.org/en/publication/wdr2017 (accessed 12 February 2018).

24. For a comprehensive discussion and further literature see S. Pinker. *The Better Angels of Our Nature: The Decline of Violence in History and Its Causes*. London: Penguin. 2011.

25. This builds on the discussion presented in J. Fearon, A. Hoeffler. *Benefits and Costs of the Conflict and Violence Targets for the Post-2015 Development Agenda*. Copenhagen Consensus Center. 2014. www.copenhagenconsensus.com/sites/default/files/conflict_assess ment_-_hoeffler_and_fearon_0.pdf (accessed 12 February 2018).

26. A. Hoeffler. 'Can International Interventions Secure the Peace?' *International Area Studies Review*. 2014. 17(1): 75–94.

27. N. Nunn, N. Qian. 'US Food Aid and Civil Conflict'. *American Economic Review*. 2014. 104(6): 1630–66.

28. More information on the standards of UNPKOs and how to hold perpetrators to account, see Code Blue. *Updates, Statements and Press Releases*. www.codebluecampaign.com/welcome (accessed 12 February 2018).

29. Fortna finds that peacekeeping stabilises the peace. See V. P. Fortna. 'Does Peacekeeping Keep Peace? International Intervention and the Duration of Peace after Civil War'. *International Studies Quarterly*. 2004. 48(2): 269–92; V. P. Fortna. *Does Peacekeeping Work? Shaping Belligerents' Choices after Civil War*. Princeton: Princeton

University Press. 2008. These recent studies find no effect: Peter Rudloff and Michael G. Findley, 'The Downstream Effects of Combatant Fragmentation on Civil War Recurrence'. *Journal of Peace Research.* 2016. 53(1): 19–32; B. F. Walter. 'Why Bad Governance Leads to Repeat Civil War'. *Journal of Conflict Resolution.* 2015. 59(7): 1242–72.

30. L. Hultman. 'UN Peace Operations and Protection of Civilians: Cheap Talk or Norm Implementation?' *Journal of Peace Research.* 2013. 50 (1): 59–73.

31. H. Hegre, L. Hultman, H. M. Nygård. 'Evaluating the Conflict-Reducing Effect of UN Peacekeeping Operations'. The Peace Research Institute Oslo. 2015. http://cega.berkeley.edu/assets/miscellaneous_files/122_-_Hegre_Hultman_Nygard_-_PKO_prediction_2015_-_ABC A.pdf (accessed 12 February 2018).

32. R. Caplan, A. Hoeffler. 'Why Peace Endures: An Analysis of Post-Conflict Stabilisation'. *European Journal of International Security.* 2017. 2(2): 133–52.

33. For more information on the UNPKOs budget and operations, see United Nations Peacekeeping. *How We Are Funded.* https://peacekeep ing.un.org/en/how-we-are-funded (accessed 12 February 2018).

34. L. Hultman, D. Peksen, 'Successful or Counterproductive Coercion? The Effect of International Sanctions on Conflict Intensity'. *Journal of Conflict Resolution.* 2017. 61(6): 1315–39; M. Brzoska. 'Measuring the Effectiveness of Arms Embargoes'. *Peace Economics Peace Science and Public Policy.* 2008. 14(2): 2; D. Fruchart, P. Holtom, S. Wezeman, D. Strandow, P. Wallensteen. 'United Nations Arms Embargoes – Their Impact on Arms Flows and Target Behaviour'. SIPRI and Uppsala University. 2007. www.sipri.org/sites/default/files/SIPRI07UNAE.pdf (accessed 12 February 2018).

35. K. Blanchfield, P. D. Wezeman and S. T. Wezeman. 'The State of Major Arms Transfers in 8 Graphics'. SIPRI. 2017. www.sipri.org/commentary/blog/2017/state-major-arms-transfers-8-graphics (accessed 12 February 2018).

36. Information on the ATT: Control Arms Secretariat. 2017. ATT Monitor 2017. New York. 11 September 2017 and personal communication with Nicholas Marsh.

37. M. Bourne. 'Small Arms and Light Weapons Spread and Conflict'. In O. Green and N. Marsh (eds). *Small Arms, Crime and Conflict: Global Governance and the Threat of Armed Violence.* London: Routledge. 2012: 29–42.

38. P. Holtom. 'Ukrainian Arms Supplies to Sub-Saharan Africa'. SIPRI Background Paper. 2011. www.sipri.org/sites/default/files/files/misc/SI PRIBP1102.pdf (accessed 12 February 2018).

39. United Nations Office on Drugs and Crime. *Global Study on Homicide 2013*.

40. Federal Bureau of Investigation. *2016 Crime in the United States*. https ://ucr.fbi.gov/crime-in-the-u.s/2016/crime-in-the-u.s.-2016/tables/expa nded-homicide-data-table-4.xls (accessed 12 February 2018).

41. Between 7 October 2001 and 16 April 2018, 5,421 American military personnel were killed in hostile action in Overseas Contingency Operations. Source: www.defense.gov/casualty.pdf (accessed 17 April 2018).

42. For example, see P. J. Cook, K. A. Goss. *The Gun Debate: What Everyone Needs to Know*. New York: Oxford University Press. 2014; R. J. Spitzer. *The Politics of Gun Control*. 5th edn. Abingdon: Routledge. 2012.

43. See for example D. Webster, C. K. Crifasi, J. S. Vernick. 'Effects of the Repeal of Missouri's Handgun Purchaser Licensing Law on Homicides'. *Journal of Urban Health*. 2014. 91(2): 293–302.

44. F. E. Zimring, G. Hawkins. *Crime Is Not the Problem: Lethal Violence in America*. Oxford University Press. 1999.

45. Citizens Report. *Murders in the UK – Location, Rate and Victim Profile of Murderer, Homicide and Fatal Violence*. 2013. www.citizensrepor tuk.org/reports/murders-fatal-violence-uk.html (accessed 12 February 2018).

46. J. Stone. 'Police in Britain Fired Their Guns Just Seven Times in the Last Year'. *The Independent*. www.independent.co.uk/news/uk/politics/uk-police-shooting-statistics-discharge-firearms-figures-freddie-gray-bato n-killings-homicide-a7160391.html (accessed 12 February 2018).

47. The Guardian. 'The Counted – People Killed by Police in the US, Recorded by the Guardian – with Your Help'. *The Guardian*. www.th eguardian.com/us-news/series/counted-us-police-killings (accessed 12 February 2018).

48. For more details on the Australian gun buy back scheme see P. Alpers. 'The Big Melt: How One Democracy Changed after Scrapping a Third of Its Firearms'. In D. W. Webster and J. S. Vernick (eds). *Reducing Gun Violence in America: Informing Policy with Evidence and Analysis*. Baltimore: The John Hopkins University Press. 2013. 205–11.

49. For more details on the Australian gun buy back scheme see Alpers. '*The Big Melt*'. In Webster and Vernick (eds). *Reducing Gun Violence*.

50. A. R. Bandeira. 'Brazil: Gun Control and Homicide Reduction'. In Webster and Vernick (eds). *Reducing Gun Violence*; J. Murray, D. R. C. Cerqueira and T. Kahn. 'Crime and Violence in Brazil: Systematic Review of Time Trends, Prevalence Rates and Risk Factors'. *Aggression and Violent Behavior*. 2013. 18(5): 471–83.

51. United Nations Office on Drugs and Crime. *Global Study on Homicide 2013*.

52. See Acid Survivors Foundation. *You Are Here: Home*. www.acidsurvi vors.org/ (accessed 12 February 2018); T. Wahed, A. Bhuiya. 'Battered Bodies & Shattered Minds: Violence Against Women in Bangladesh'. *Indian Journal of Medical Research*. 2007. 126(4): 341.

53. E. K. Bye, I. Rossow. 'The Impact of Drinking Pattern on Alcohol-Related Violence among Adolescents: An International Comparative Analysis'. *Drug and Alcohol Review*. 2010. 29(2):131–37.

54. For example, see K. E. Leonard. 'Alcohol and Intimate Partner Violence: When Can We Say That Heavy Drinking Is a Contributing Cause of Violence?' *Addiction*. 2005. 100(4): 422–25; I. B. Zablotska, R. H. Gray, M. A. Koenig, D. Serwadda, F. Nalugoda, G. Kigozi, N. Sewankambo, T. Lutalo, F. W. Mangen, M. Wawer. 'Alcohol Use, Intimate Partner Violence, Sexual Coercion and HIV among Women Aged 15–24 in Rakai, Uganda'. *AIDS and Behavior*. 2009. 13(2): 225–33.

55. R. Caetano, C. McGrath, S. Ramisetty-Mikler, C. A. Field. 'Drinking, Alcohol Problems and the Five-Year Recurrence and Incidence of Male to Female and Female to Male Partner Violence'. *Alcoholism: Clinical and Experimental Research*. 2005. 29(1): 98–106.

56. A. Nemtsov. *A Contemporary History of Alcohol in Russia*. Södertörns högskola. 2011; W. A. Pridemore. 'Vodka and Violence: Alcohol Consumption and Homicide Rates in Russia'. *American Journal of Public Health*. 2002. 92(12): 1921–30.

57. A. C. Wagenaar, A. L. Tobler, K. A. Komro. 'Effects of Alcohol Tax and Price Policies on Morbidity and Mortality: A Systematic Review'. *American Journal of Public Health*. 2010. 100(11): 2270–78.

58. S. Duailibi, W. Ponicki, J. Grube, I. Pinsky, R. Laranjeira, M. Raw. 'The Effect of Restricting Opening Hours on Alcohol-Related Violence'. *American Journal of Public Health*. 2007. 97(12): 2276–80.

59. T. Babor. *Alcohol: No Ordinary Commodity: Research and Public Policy*. 2nd edn. Oxford: Oxford University Press. 2010.

60. United Nations Office on Drugs and Crime. *World Drug Report 2017*. UNODC. 2017. www.unodc.org/wdr2017/index.html; Count the Costs of the War on Drugs. 'The Alternative Drug Report, 2nd ed'. www.countthe costs.org/alternative-world-drug-report (accessed 12 February 2018).

61. D. C. North. 'Institutions'. *Journal of Economic Perspectives*. 1991. 5 (1): 97–112.

62. E. M. Douglas, M. A. Straus. 'Assault and Injury of Dating Partners by University Students in 19 Countries and Its Relation to Corporal

Punishment Experienced as a Child'. *European Journal of Criminology.* 2006. 3(3): 293–318.

63. J. P. Platteau and Z. Wahhaj. 'Strategic Interactions Between Modern Law and Custom'. In V. A. Ginsburgh and D. Throsby (eds). *Handbook of the Economics of Art and Culture, Volume 2.* Oxford: Elsevier. 2014. 633–78.

64. United Nations Children's Fund. *Female Genital Mutilation/Cutting: A Statistical Overview and Exploration of the Dynamics of Change.* 2013. www.unicef.org/media/files/UNICEF_FGM_report_July_2013_ Hi_res.pdf (accessed 12 February 2018).

65. A popular UK radio soap featured a domestic violence story and this resulted in a 20 per cent increase in calls to the National Domestic Abuse Helpline. See P. Kerley and C. Bates. 'The Archers: What Effect Has the Rob and Helen Story Had?' *BBC.* 2016. www.bbc.co.uk/news/maga zine-35961057 (accessed 12 February 2018).

66. V. A. Foshee, K. E. Bauman, S. T. Ennett, C. Suchindran, T. Benefield, G. F. Linder. 'Assessing the Effects of the Dating Violence Prevention Program "Safe Dates" Using Random Coefficient Regression Modeling'. *Prevention Science.* 2005. 6(3): 245; A. J. Gage, J G. Honoré, J. Deleon. 'Short-Term Effects of a Violence-Prevention Curriculum on Knowledge of Dating Violence among High School Students in Port-au-Prince, Haiti'. *Journal of Communication in Healthcare.* 2016. 9(3): 178–89.

67. For example, see M. R. Sanders. 'Development, Evaluation, and Multinational Dissemination of the Triple P-Positive Parenting Program'. *Annual Review of Clinical Psychology.* 2012. 8: 345–79; A. R. Piquero, D. P. Farrington, B. C. Welsh, R. Tremblay, W. G. Jennings. 'Effects of Early Family/Parent Training Programs on Antisocial Behavior and Delinquency'. *Journal of Experimental Criminology.* June 2009. 5(2): 83–120.

68. The most recent year for which almost complete homicide counts exist is 2012. UNDOC (2013) suggests that there were about 437,000 homicide victims, and according to UCDP just under 70,000 people were killed in organized group based violence during 2012.

69. E. P. Baumer, K. T. Wolff. 'The Breadth and Causes of Contemporary Cross-National Homicide Trends'. *Crime and Justice.* 2014. 43(1): 231–87; T. Gash. *Criminal: The Truth about Why People do Bad Things.* London: Penguin. 2016.

70. S. Pinker. *The Better Angels of Our Nature.*

71. W. Knerr, F. Gardner, L. Cluver. 'Improving Positive Parenting Skills and Reducing Harsh and Abusive Parenting in Low- and Middle-Income Countries: A Systematic Review'. *Prevention Science.* 2013. 14(4): 352–63.

21 | *Drawing Threads, Weaving Patterns*

RON MATTHEWS

Introduction

This book addresses the political economy of defence. The previous and possibly only other book devoted explicitly to this topic was a 1991 edited volume by Andrew L. Ross. In the nearly thirty years since this publication, the world has moved on. Defence has become fused with security, expanding the number of threats requiring government attention. Many of these emerging threats have wider economic, social and political dimensions over and beyond military security. In parallel, it is no longer feasible to scope twenty-first century defence as a state-centric political and economic endeavour, based on sovereignty and security of supply. Rather, national defence is interwoven within a broader international security canvass that is defined, influenced and shaped by defence globalisation. Notwithstanding these dramatic changes to the politico-economic defence ecosystem induced by innovation and globalisation pressures, defence emphatically remains a public good. This offers a political economy legitimacy to the study of modern defence, but intellectually it needs to accommodate the policy compromises forged between Adam Smith's liberalist free market principles and Keynesian macroeconomic 'interventionist' policies. The present volume is an attempt to address the above gaps in our understanding of the how defence is 'managed'. Simply put, the approach has been to re-examine the notion of national security, and in the process identify, explain and analyse the multiplicity of threats, along with the menu of policy responses that governments have at hand to ensure their satisfactory resolution. Thus, the starting point for discussion is national security.

21.1 National Security

The political economy dilemma for governments and their defence agencies is how to secure required capability targets when resources

476

are neither available nor affordable, especially when there are competing demands for resources from other segments of society. If a government can successful manage the economy, there will be economic growth that will generate increased national income, expand tax revenue and allow it to more generously finance defence and other departments of state. A strong and dynamic economy has the financial capacity to accommodate the need to sponsor advanced defence capability. By contrast, a weak and faltering economy is associated with rising public deficits, and is often the spring-board for austerity, defence cuts and weakening military capability. Moreover, meshed into the economic growth and military expenditure relationship is the idea that even with growth, greater and greater invest-ment into defence will likely lead to a 'crowding out' of scarce defence resources from more productive commercial activity. This balance between defence and development is a core feature of the contemporary political economy policy framework for developmental states such as Japan, Singapore and China. Elsewhere across the world, governments may not be aware of or inclined to debate the longer-term strategic implications of this intellectual polemic, but they will be conscious that higher defence spending carries a social opportunity cost of reduced spending on hospitals, welfare and education. Governments of advanced countries entertain poli-cies that influence the supply side through enhanced integration of civil-military enterprise, value chains and local R&D infrastructure, but such options are not so easily open to the poorer nations suffering from impo-verished industrial and technological infrastructure. While the advanced democratic states are constrained by the imperative of ensuring an appro-priate balance between defence 'and' development, this is not an issue for autocratic states, such as North Korea and Russia, where political concerns for their citizens' quality of life carry a lower priority than enhancement of military capability.

21.2 International Security

In the modern era, national security has been impacted by the defence globalisation phenomenon, which has shaped institutional thinking on defence and security. The change process has not just been about the projection of 'national' security beyond territorial borders, to address the profusion of non-traditional security threats, but also traditional military engagements overseas in Syria, Afghanistan and Iraq. However, this all comes with a cost, and the contemporary strategic scenario can be described in terms of the rising number of threats against declining defence resource provision. Grudgingly, European nations are finally acting to increase defence spending in response to threatening Russian militarism and President Trump's recent berating of European leaders that NATO burden sharing is falling disproportionately on America's taxpayers. Western nations are also alive to the emerging Chinese threat in Asia-Pacific. Washington is devoting greater amounts of national income to advancing its military capability to respond to what it sees as a Chinese assault on its 'national' interests; for instance, international trading routes in the South China Sea. The world, therefore, is once again entering a period of international distrust and military tension. Of some concern is that it comes at a time, echoing events in the 1930s, when nationalism and protectionism are on the rise. 'America first' and 'Brexit' crystallise the fears over internationalisation, but the fissures in international solidarity are not isolated to the United States and the United Kingdom; they also afflict European states concerned by uncontrolled migration, the impact of growing autocracy (such as in Turkey), regional and religious disputes (Saudi Arabia and Iran) and substantial falls in foreign aid linked to widespread austerity and nationalist preferences. Government may not always be the instigator of such crises, but it will be expected to act to resolve them, and defence and security resources will likely play an important role in this process.

Defence and security has moved from a national to an international public good, but the core *problématique* of affordability remains, transcending the political and economic divide, and permeating discussion in almost every chapter of this book. The national merges into the international, whether it relates to international acquisition, global supply chains, globalisation of defence industry, multinational defence corporations, transnational arms collaboration, defence alliances, burden sharing, counterterrorism, asymmetrical and non-traditional threats and broader international security, including disaster management, conflict prevention, humanitarian relief and international peacemaking and peacekeeping initiatives. Globalisation is symbolic of the problem as well as representative of the solution to affordability. National security remains important for providing the rationale for protecting the contracting vestiges of sovereignty, but in the process must increasingly highlight the importance of transparency, accountability, good governance and value-for-money objectives. Defence more than nearly any other public good also demands cost effectiveness, because in the final analysis survival of independent states depends on an appropriate and acceptable balance between affordability and combat capability. Aspects of the defence estate, the logistical tail, defence-industrial actors, both prime and subprime, training and so on, can be commercialised, contractorised and outsourced, but the armed forces and their military equipment remain under public sector control.

Governments in the future, as in the past, must determine how much money will be allocated to defence, how much of the budget will be spent on the different branches of the armed forces, including R&D, intelligence and counterterrorism, and how best to protect overseas national security interests. This necessarily includes the ethical and moral responsibilities of, for instance, international peacekeeping, drug control, disaster relief; indeed, all those non-traditional security areas where armed forces can, and often do, play a crucial role. Every level of defence decision making will involve choices, trade-offs and opportunity costs in balancing the needs and interests of different stakeholder communities focused on the policy divides between defence and development, national and international responsibilities, sovereignty and globalisation and present and future populations, with respect to the debt incurred via military expenditure.

21.3 Future Research

Notwithstanding the claim by Andrew Ross in the book's preface that the 'political economy of defense research has reached the takeoff stage', the reality is that the subject continues to lay dormant in the scholarly shadow of defence economics. While defence economists acknowledge the role of government, the discourse is implicit, inevitably threaded within a collection of 'resource allocation' topics. The purpose of this book is to 'out' the central role of government by emphasising two pervasive thematics in the political economy of defence. Firstly, the book attempts to evaluate government's challenging role in funding and managing defence. Defence is an expensive business, and it is incumbent on government and its defence agencies to manage resources wisely to ensure value for money for the taxpayers. Invariably, government gets it wrong, whether it is through dubious threat analysis, inappropriate acquisition, insoluble funding and capability gaps or weak political and military leadership. Defence also possesses unique challenges that distinguish the sector not just from commercial endeavour but also other elements of the public sector. There is, therefore, a need for more focused and informed scholarly research that lays bare the inherent problems associated with the public ownership of defence.

Secondly, the ubiquitous defence globalisation process that is now embracing even the United States and France provides an opportunity to address domestic labour and financial constraints, 'failed' market structures, scale limitations and other national resource allocation challenges. These new developments and challenges give rise to the need for an expanded disciplinary dialogue highlighting the internationalisation of emerging political and economic perspectives in relation to twenty-first century defence. Accordingly, the present volume has attempted to expand and deepen the scope of enquiry by exploring the relationship between the national and international defence contexts. Further research is needed to provide an integrated perspective on fast-moving political economy issues which touch the defence domain. It suggests that a dedicated scholarly focus on the international political economy of defence would be a worthwhile exercise.

21.4 Concluding Statement

This book comprises a compilation of the research and thoughts from some of the world's leading defence economists, political scientists, military historians and governmental and industry practitioners, reflecting an eclectic and interdisciplinary array of informed perspectives. The authors have risen to the challenge of designing, developing and drafting chapters that go beyond the traditional two-dimensional 'boundary-constrained' politics and economics framework. The chapter contributions bring into play topics that transcend the theoretical and policy thresholds of defence in a widening interpretation of national security. Thus, in drawing this book's discussion to a close, there is a growing recognition that defence in its different forms can contribute to stability, development, leadership, trust and the broader eradication of violence. Government has a higher, separate and decisive role to play in managing defence so that it can lever a constructive rather than destructive military presence, making a positive contribution to the achievement of national and international security, and edging the world closer towards the universally desired peaceful end-state.

Index

481